Mr. Keen, Tracer of Lost Persons

ALSO BY JIM COX
AND FROM McFARLAND

*Rails Across Dixie: A History of Passenger Trains
in the American South* (2011)

American Radio Networks: A History (2009)

Sold on Radio: Advertisers in the Golden Age of Broadcasting (2008)

*This Day in Network Radio:
A Daily Calendar of Births, Deaths, Debuts, Cancellations
and Other Events in Broadcasting History* (2008)

The Great Radio Sitcoms (2007)

*Radio Speakers: Narrators, News Junkies, Sports Jockeys, Tattletales,
Tipsters, Toastmasters and Coffee Klatch Couples Who Verbalized
the Jargon of the Aural Ether from the 1920s to the 1980s
— A Biographical Dictionary* (2007; paperback 2011)

*The Daytime Serials of Television,
1946–1960* (2006; paperback 2010)

*Music Radio: The Great Performers and Programs of the
1920s through Early 1960s* (2005; paperback 2011)

*Frank and Anne Hummert's Radio Factory: The Programs and
Personalities of Broadcasting's Most Prolific Producers* (2003)

*Radio Crime Fighters: More Than 300 Programs
from the Golden Age* (2002; paperback 2010)

Say Goodnight, Gracie: The Last Years of Network Radio (2002)

*The Great Radio Audience Participation Shows: Seventeen
Programs from the 1940s and 1950s* (2001; paperback 2009)

The Great Radio Soap Operas (1999; paperback 2008)

Mr. Keen, Tracer of Lost Persons

A Complete History and Episode Log of Radio's Most Durable Detective

JIM COX

McFarland & Company, Inc., Publishers
Jefferson, North Carolina, and London

The present work is a reprint of the illustrated case bound edition of Mr. Keen, Tracer of Lost Persons: A Complete History and Episode Log of Radio's Most Durable Detective, *first published in 2004 by McFarland.*

LIBRARY OF CONGRESS CATALOGUING-IN-PUBLICATION DATA

Cox, Jim, 1939–
Mr. Keen, tracer of lost persons : a complete history and episode log of radio's most durable detective / Jim Cox.
p.   cm.
Includes bibliographical references and index.

ISBN 978-0-7864-4494-6
softcover : 50# alkaline paper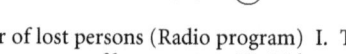

1 Mr. Keen, tracer of lost persons (Radio program) I. Title:
Mister Keen, tracer of lost persons. II. Title.
PN1991.77.M7C68   2011   791.44'72 — dc22   2004001530

BRITISH LIBRARY CATALOGUING DATA ARE AVAILABLE

© 2004 Jim Cox. All rights reserved

No part of this book may be reproduced or transmitted in any form or by any means, electronic or mechanical, including photocopying or recording, or by any information storage and retrieval system, without permission in writing from the publisher.

Cover photograph: Philip Clarke as Mr. Keen and
Jim Kelly as Mike Clancy (CBS/Photofest)

Manufactured in the United States of America

*McFarland & Company, Inc., Publishers
Box 611, Jefferson, North Carolina 28640
www.mcfarlandpub.com*

For radiophiles everywhere —
may the "Saints preserve us!"

Acknowledgments

In times past I've observed that no author works alone. This is certainly true of me and of many others I know who document their thoughts in some permanent form as they record history. Once again I'm grateful to a host of individuals whose personal contributions and sacrifices allowed this work to be realized. At the top of the list are Stewart Wright, who devoted several tedious days to laboring by my side as together we gathered voluminous data in the Hummert and Klee script files; and a perseverant Claire Connelly, whose ability to trace the most obscure details on old radio personalities utterly astounds me. A raft of other individuals selflessly shared of themselves, their expertise, their time and recollections, their photographs and recordings from personal *Mr. Keen* collections.

Here are the names of several who made worthy contributions: George Ansbro, Howard Blue, Carol Bowers (and the archival staff at the American Heritage Center), Ted Davenport, Paul Feavel, Martin Grams, Jr., Al Hubin, Paul F. Klee, Ted Kneebone, Patti Wever Knoll, Margaret Klee Lichtenberg, Howard Mandelbaum, Ted Meland, Gary Mercer, Elizabeth Minney, Charles Niren, Robert Sabon, Jim Snyder, Derek Tague and Ingrid Meighan Waldron.

I'm indebted to a host of kindred spirits—vintage radio and nostalgia journal editors—who encourage me to preserve old time radio history. Among their number are: Jim Adams, Bob Burchett, Sue Chadwick, Jack French, Jay Hickerson, Ken Krug, Patrick Lucanio, Robert Newman, Chuck Schaden, Carol Tiffany and Marilyn Wilt. In addition, there are many other vintage radio hobbyists, too many to name here, who support every effort we authors make to sustain the past for present and future generations. I am in their debt for the unheralded, enduring encouragement they provide to each of us.

My family has supported me through an arduous task, one that seemed never ending at times. To them I express my deep appreciation, for this is a commitment on their part as well as mine.

Contents

Acknowledgments	vii
Preface	1
Chronology: A Mr. Keen *Radio Almanac*	5
1 — The Aural Sleuth: Murder and Mayhem on the Air	7
2 — Origins of a Supersleuth	14
3 — Lost and Found	22
4 — The Tracer as Chaser	35
5 — Funny Business	51
6 — Hired Guns	57
7 — Sold on Radio	73
Radio Episode Guide	77
Notes	345
Bibliography	349
Index	351

Preface

In my adolescent days Jimmy Witter and I were inseparable boyhood pals. As far back as I can remember we attended the same school together and were routinely assigned the same teachers. Neither of us ever seemed burdened by the weightier matters of education — we usually saw something humorous at every turn. One of our common goals was to provide amusement to our classmates — or anybody else we might corral as an audience. We took our cues from copying the professionals available to us. That was almost altogether limited to radio in our day.

Radio was readily accessible and it was absolutely free. (Technically, it wasn't free, of course — you had to have access to a set and somebody had to pay for the electricity or batteries to operate it.) As a result, we often parodied what we heard on the air, and shared a lot of laughs over it. Playing on my chum's name, in fact, I often repeated announcer George Ansbro's daily introduction to *Young Widder Brown*, solemnly stating before the class (or whoever I could get to listen): "Now it's time for Young Jimmy Witter!" He'd come on "stage" and entertain — he'd tell a few jokes and maybe sing and dance a little jig. He was clearly the talented half of our performing duo. I remember that he brought down the house at a ninth grade variety show I directed when he warbled and boogied "The Dark Town Strutter's Ball," complete with live band accompaniment.

Back in elementary school, however, the two of us became enthralled with an aural detective series that neither of us ever wanted to miss. It became a "game," in fact (as it probably did, I realized later, with millions of others who tuned in), to try to discern the identity of the guilty party before *Mr. Keen, Tracer of Lost Persons* revealed the answer just prior to signing off every Thursday night.

We had fun with the series, even on the days it wasn't broadcast. I would write radio plays that the seventh graders produced for the other classes. *Mr. Keen* was a frequent topic. As early as the fourth grade I recall scads of drawings that Jimmy and I scrawled in class (as our minds went out to play), so many inspired by our radio heroes. I'd often draw *Mr. Keen*, and repetitiously create virtually the same scene over and over.

I'd take a sheet of white paper and bring my concept of a CBS sound stage to life, complete with open curtains, a control booth window to one side, a sound effects man to the rear, and several actors and an announcer standing around two or three floor microphones. It didn't matter that the studio in New York City might not have appeared like that at all. This was the "theater of the mind," and I could draw it any way I imagined. In my illustrations there would inevitably be one actor standing on a ladder to the side of the stage (why a ladder, I don't know). He'd be pointing a revolver at another actor. A third would be exclaiming—his words enclosed by a comic-strip balloon—"Saints preserve us, Mr. Keen! He's got a gun!" (It *had* to have been that Irishman Mike Clancy, the guy that asked the "Boss" all those obtuse questions, if only to raise the audience's level of awe for the hero.)

My diagrams were done for laughs and provoked many of them, no matter how many times I scribbled that farce and no matter who saw it. (Once in a while it was a teacher; I wonder what *she* thought.) "Saints preserve us" was accepted into the American vernacular back then. Nearly everybody recognized it instantly, and the source from which it sprang.

Mr. Keen, Tracer of Lost Persons was, without doubt, my preferred show during those prepubescent days. It possessed a magnetism that drew me to the radio for every installment. I could hardly get enough of it. I might forgo another radio series from time to time, but *Mr. Keen*—never.

As I tuned in, often in the dark, I imagined that the very individual the kindly old investigator sought was then in hiding in one of three places: under my bed, outside my window or on the stairway that led from my bedroom to our attic. At times I could scarcely move, certain that the slightest tremor on my part would cause the culprit to reach out for me as his next victim. As the show ended weekly, I lit out of my room in a flash, seeking whoever else was in the house, convinced that impending doom was about to overtake me! That's how caught up in the program I could get at eight, nine and ten years of age. My mother often advised, "You just really shouldn't be listening to that stuff any more." But I brushed her well-meant warning aside and did the same thing the next week. I was like an addict, and *Mr. Keen* was my fix.

It never crossed my mind that my favorite crime show wouldn't last forever. As I grew older I took it for granted, even skipping the series for long periods of time, secure in the knowledge that it would be there when I returned. Therefore I was shocked (and immediately went into a kind of mourning) when I suddenly realized that *Mr. Keen, Tracer of Lost Persons* couldn't be found on my dial anymore. I was really in need of a fix then, and there was no source to supply it.

In the late 1960s I discovered that a few tapes of old radio shows were being released by a handful of enterprising individuals dedicated to helping folks ride a wave of nostalgia. The first reel-to-reel recording I ordered featured four episodes of *Mr. Keen, Tracer of Lost Persons*. It rekindled a passion in me that had lain dormant since the great dramas left the airwaves years before. I began to amass a library of old-time radio shows on tape (as did many others, I was to later learn).

This book is an attempt to scratch an itch that has persisted within me for decades. It is a long overdue tribute to the Tracer of Lost Persons. In preparing it, the greatest surprise of my endeavors was the locating of more than 1600 *Mr. Keen* scripts—an incredible number, considering there were but 1690 broadcasts altogether. I devoted two weeks to photocopying pertinent data from those documents. I also found a few second-generation family members whose kin had performed on many of the *Keen* dramas. They added legitimacy to the project.

The journey was not altogether a bed of roses, for it was often fraught with delay and disappointment. At times I came perilously close to giving up. For about eight months I was hindered by problems obtaining copyright clearance. Then I experienced a total computer crash — losing almost everything, retaining less than 20 percent in hard copy of a nearly completed manuscript. Several professionals whose livelihoods involve recovering such data had no luck at all. I started over, backing up everything every day. It was onerous.

Mr. Keen, Tracer of Lost Persons was the most resilient private detective to cross the ether, either in radio or television. Nobody on TV ever came close to his durable accomplishment. The nearest aural competitors to *Keen*'s stunning 1690 nationwide broadcasts — and this assumes those rivals never experienced any preemptions, which is hardly likely — are *Nick Carter, Master Detective* (726 performances), *The Adventures of Sherlock Holmes* (657) and *The Adventures of the Falcon* (473).

Many readers may be surprised to learn that *Mr. Keen, Tracer of Lost Persons*, whom they recall as a forceful, unwavering crimefighter with little time to relax between missions, was something else altogether in a previous incarnation. Initially Keen was a charming, at times giddy, grandfatherly figure who dispensed advice while tracking individuals who had gone missing. Keen then was a far cry from the dogged manhunter he would evolve into in succeeding years. It was like two very different shows. Only those familiar with the early years (from 1937 through roughly 1944) realized that there ever was an earlier *Mr. Keen, Tracer of Lost Persons*, one who actually sought lost people rather than tracking down criminals and murderers. Many who heard only the final decade or last dozen years will hardly believe that such a near 180-degree transformation occurred.

A concerted effort has been made in chapters 3 and 4 to properly define each *Keen* era and to distinguish between them. The advice-giving, feel-good, happy-ending narratives of the early epoch could hardly have fared well among the majority of postwar listeners, who seemed to prefer faster-paced action. At the time, radio was doing all it could to stave off the encroachment of television so, those leisurely, happy-go-lucky stories of the 1930s and early 1940s could not possibly have passed muster as the 1950s approached. Following the shift to pursuing murderers full time, the tracer attracted many new fans. For a while, at least, the show was well received by the home audience, until the tube became more plentiful and, more importantly, affordable to the average American family.

When the series left the air for the very last time in late 1955, it had reached remarkable proportions. No airwave sleuth had ever persisted for nearly two decades. In a half-century since then, none has come close to *Mr. Keen*'s formidable airtime success. Without stretching the truth, an era ended with his sudden departure.

Let us enthusiastically relive those days of melodramatic narratives in which the kindly old investigator searched for misplaced individuals and unscrupulous killers. *It's time now for Mr. Keen, Tracer of Lost Persons.*

Chronology:
A *Mr. Keen* Radio Almanac

This guide, a timeline of the on-the-air appearances of *Mr. Keen, Tracer of Lost Persons*, is supplied to assist the reader in quickly glimpsing the full breadth of the broadcast series and to provide a handy reference tool for checking pertinent data while proceeding through the text. It is a compendium of some of the facts discussed in more detail in the individual chapters and the elements presented in the Radio Episode Guide.

Tuesday, October 12, 1937   7:15–7:30 p.m., NBC Blue, Tuesday, Wednesday and Thursday nights, through Thursday, October 22, 1942, for American Home Products
   Mr. Keen— Bennett Kilpack
   Mike Clancy— Jim Kelly
   Announcers— Ben Grauer (1937–1940), James Fleming (1940–1943)
   Director— Martha Atwell

Wednesday, October 28, 1942   7:45–8:00 p.m., CBS, Wednesday, Thursday and Friday nights, through Friday, November 26, 1943, for American Home Products
   Announcers— Ken Roberts (1943), Larry Elliott (1943–1951)

Thursday, December 2, 1943   7:30–8:00 p.m., CBS, weekly, through Thursday, June 26, 1947, for American Home Products (preemptions: April 12, 1945; April 26, 1945)
   Director— Richard Leonard (1943–1955 except weeknights in 1954–1955)

Thursday, August 28, 1947   8:30–8:55 p.m., CBS, weekly, through Thursday, June 17, 1948, for American Home Products

Thursday, June 24, 1948   8:30–9:00 p.m., CBS, weekly, through Thursday, July 12, 1951, for American Home Products
   Mr. Keen— Bennett Kilpack (through October 26, 1950), Philip Clarke

Friday, July 20, 1951   9:30–10:00 p.m., NBC, weekly, through Friday, August 31, 1951, for multiple sponsors
 Announcer — Jack Costello

Thursday, September 6, 1951   8:30–9:00 p.m., NBC, weekly, through Thursday, April 24, 1952, for multiple sponsors

Thursday, May 1, 1952   9:30–10:00 p.m., CBS, weekly, through Thursday, May 29, 1952, for multiple sponsors
 Announcer — Harry Kramer (1952–1955 except weeknights)

Thursday, June 5, 1952   8:00–8:30 p.m., CBS, weekly, through Thursday, September 25, 1952, for multiple sponsors

Friday, October 3, 1952   8:00–8:30 p.m., CBS, weekly, through Friday, June 25, 1954, for multiple sponsors

Monday, June 21, 1954   10:00–10:15 p.m., CBS, weeknights, through Friday, January 14, 1955, sustained (preemption: November 2, 1954)
 Announcers — Stuart Metz, George Bryan (Fridays) (1954–1955)
 Director — Edward Slattery (1954–1955)

Friday, July 2, 1954   8:00–8:25 p.m., CBS, weekly, through Friday, October 1, 1954, sustained
 Announcer — Harry Kramer (continuing weekly duty)
 Director — Richard Leonard (continuing weekly duty)

Tuesday, February 22, 1955   8:30–9:00 p.m., CBS, weekly, through Tuesday, April 19, 1955, sustained

Monday, April 25, 1955   8:00–8:25 p.m., CBS, weekly, through Monday, September 26, 1955, sustained

1

The Aural Sleuth: Murder and Mayhem on the Air

During radio's golden age—between the late 1920s and early 1960s—private investigators (PIs) achieved far more than simply providing American ears with gratifying amusement. Such heroes also contributed to the nation's moral fiber, passing on precepts upon which a culture's ethics are founded. As one observer put it, "The essence of those [programs'] messages lay in the fact that within each drama the villain never won and the hero never lost. Whether ... a program openly declared that 'crime does not pay,' this was the message expounded in all broadcasts."[1] Any who attempted to gain private property outside the socially accepted channels—whether it was life, currency or possessions—were reformed, imprisoned or executed "so that the society of the propertied might be secure and enduring."[2]

Such radio dramatizations, and their central characters, "championed the simple pattern of Good over Evil, Truth over Lie, and Civilization over Anarchy." Programs were "secular allegories of the middle-class; ... their heroes were agents of bourgeois America, there to tell criminals and citizens alike ... that good was always victorious."[3]

The aural sleuth stemmed from a tradition whose gestation may be traced back more than two centuries. Out of the broad category of mystery or crime fiction, disparate patterns emerged. Among them was the detective story, and from it the private investigator surfaced as one of the mystery genre's foremost figures.

American poet-editor-critic-author Edgar Allan Poe (1809–1849) is commonly mentioned as the chief architect of the detective story—primarily through a series of tales he published in 1841, 1842 and 1844 that focused on a fictional hero named C. Auguste Dupin. Yet documented evidence indicates that others predate the venerated Poe in the realm of detective fiction. Allen J. Hubin, a devout student of crime fiction and an author and former mystery fanzine publisher, suggests that William Godwin's 1794 story *Things as They Are; or, The Adventures of Caleb Williams* should be accepted as "the first novel of crime and detection."[4]

As technology advanced, the mystery yarn stretched beyond the confines of the printed page, infiltrating both film and broadcasting. In regard to the latter, *Empire Builders* is sometimes cited as the first thriller drama on the ether, premiering over the NBC Blue chain in 1928.[5] That sequence set a precedent for dramatic adventure, expelling any notions of limited horizons that may have held sway earlier.

The precise origins of the radio detective, on the other hand, may be attributed to a series that featured a wily terrorist of the twentieth century, *Fu Manchu*. This despot unleashed his wicked venom on earth's denizens for the first time near the close of the 1920s. The diabolical schemer was to be held in check, however, by Scotland Yard's Sir Dennis Nayland Smith. Detective Smith invariably thwarted the little man's insidious plotting, offering a constructive role model to counterbalance the malevolence. *Fu Manchu* (aka *The Shadow of Fu Manchu*) debuted in serialized form in 1929 as part of an ongoing *Collier Hour* on the NBC Blue network. It was re-launched as a separate series over CBS on September 26, 1932, and continued in varied formats through 1940.

Radio historiographers Christopher Sterling and John Kittross maintain that aural crimefighting took a new twist via NBC on October 20, 1930, with the radio introduction of Sherlock Holmes.[6] For the first time, listeners encountered an independent investigator who wasn't linked directly to any law enforcement agency. Augmented by a devoted assistant, Dr. John H. Watson, Holmes valiantly unraveled some stupendously puzzling cases (at least puzzling to the common man). Dubbed "the most universally recognized fictional character in history,"[7] Holmes on the ether was patterned after an 1887 supersleuth concocted by novelist Arthur Conan Doyle. Although intermittently beset by gaps in broadcast continuity, Holmes performed his startling intellectual feats on radio across 26 years. One wag fittingly opined that he was "the most revived major character of the airwaves."[8]

Since those humble beginnings, the detective drama has become one of the most gripping and celebrated forms of creative expression in American popular culture. The genre achieved wide-ranging success in literature, film, on radio and — several decades later — on television. In terms of entertainment, the aural sleuth — reaching far greater audiences than cinema ever could — allowed listeners the opportunity to mix the intellectual detecting process with the emotional intensity of fantasy. Novelist and fanzine columnist William DeAndrea, making discerning observations about a genre widely respected by mystery aficionados, infers, "It's nice to be able to enter a world where justice is always striven for and usually attained.... The intellectual appeal of the mystery lies in its heuristic elements. There is always a problem to be solved, and the protagonists are going to try to solve it." He further attests: "The real message of the detective story is that even in the worst of circumstances, a man or woman can make things right using courage, tenacity, and brainpower."[9]

The private eye is an enduring hero, author John Conquest maintains. Writing extensively in the discipline, Conquest sets the hero in a fitting perspective:

> The underlying message of the PI ... is, that law and injustice are two entirely different things. When the law fails the individual, whether through corruption, indifference, incompetence or inability, the PI is a Galahad for hire, confronting a violent, cruel and unjust world with an uncompromising code of honor. He, or she, cannot be bought off or bullied off. For the classical detective a crime was, and indeed still is, a problem to be solved, after which justice would automatically be done and the proper order of things restored.[10]

Modern crime fiction buff Al Hubin, who recorded extensive data in a series of published bibliographies, offers a simple definition of the private eye: "[He/she] seeks clients, accepts pay for services, and is not a member of an official law enforcement agency; thus both the likes of Sherlock Holmes and Mike Hammer are included, as are investigators working for private firms—such as insurance companies—and lawyer-sleuths."[11]

For years the genre delivered some of the most consistently intriguing characters on the air every week. Possessing socially enviable traits, and engaging in laudable endeavors, they were often personable and debonair. Some of them sketched current predicaments for their listeners in rich, colorful detail. A handful were widely acclaimed for providing consistently distinctive performances virtually every time out.

One of radio history's most astute and admired observers, John Dunning, cites *The Shadow* as "perhaps radio's most famous fictitious crimefighter." The revered author terms the series "a synonym for 'old-time radio' ... [and] the epitome of radio crime drama." Sterling and Kittross label *The Shadow* (who, when not incognito, was "wealthy young man about town" Lamont Cranston) "the classic crime drama."[12] Writer Gerald Nachman refers to the series as "a total aural experience," and dubs it "the ultimate radio show."[13] Linking comedians *Fibber McGee & Molly* and *The Lone Ranger*'s epic western narrative with *The Shadow*, Dunning suggests that that triumvirate excelled as the most memorable of the medium.[14]

The infamous "private insurance investigator with the action-packed expense account," [*Yours Truly*] *Johnny Dollar*, became an icon of the vintage radio hero-worshipers. In a series duly marked by both quality and longevity, *Dollar* still reigns virtually unchallenged among celebrated audio sleuths. Without doubt, that show was a radio watershed: It held the dubious honor of featuring the very last aural-only detective on the ether. A 13-year veteran who swam upstream against an ebbing tide, *Johnny Dollar* pressed for nearly two years beyond the medium's well documented "day radio drama died," when, on November 25, 1960, almost all other dramatic fare simultaneously departed the airwaves.

In the opinion of a coterie of critics (one calling him "the most striking detective on the air," another branding him the "archetype" of the breed[15]), Sam Spade was the epitome of the case-hardened, cynical radio private eye. His charismatic appeal, repeatedly flaunted in absorbing exploits, earned him a strong following among listeners. John Dunning avers: "The show was loved in its time and still is.... [It] had a style and class that the others all envied.... The wit and charm of the show has weathered decades, and *The Adventures of Sam Spade* remains today the pinnacle of radio private eye broadcasts."[16]

Among PIs, a few of their number — a very few, percentage-wise — were of the tender gender. While their series rarely lasted for long, some of those heroines proved just as tenacious as their masculine colleagues. They included Ann Scotland, Candy Matson, Kitty Keene, Carolyn Day and a few others.

Women were just as important to the success of a handful of married-couple detective series (including *The Abbott Mysteries*, *The Adventures of the Thin Man* and *Mr. and Mrs. North*) as were the male leads. On numerous occasions the distaff members contributed angles that genuinely enhanced what might have become otherwise drab yarns.

There were many more aural sleuths who offered comparable quality, most of them cherished by their admiring fans. The dynamic guardians of integrity became colossal members of an airwave coterie, some remaining on the air for many years. In a published analysis of 308 American crimefighting dramas carried over network radio between the late 1920s and the early 1960s, 58 of the series (19 percent) featured private eyes as their central characters— each one functioning independently of public law enforcement officials, even though they may have teamed up with those "official" detectives from time to time. Beyond these, another 84 (27 percent) radio programs offered amateur or part-time sleuths whose livelihoods were derived largely from unrelated professions, if indeed they were gainfully employed at all.

The full-time, career-oriented PIs, combined with those of the avocational strain, offered radio audiences at least 142 separate opportunities to tune in to series with private detectives at their core. (Another 92 programs focused on professional law enforcement, including city, state and federal agents; 66 series could be classified as presenting juvenile- or adventure-oriented perspectives; and another eight fit unspecified crimefighting categories.[17]) By sheer numbers alone, the aural sleuth saturated the ether during radio's golden age, providing ample opportunities to hear several private eye narratives daily.

Not only did airing the PI dramas translate into some rather large and faithful audiences, it also made a strong positive impact on the networks' bottom lines. A factor that simply cannot be denied is that such fare was comparatively inexpensive to produce, yet regularly drew substantial numbers of listeners to the national chains. For example, star-studded series like *The Jack Benny Program* and *The Bing Crosby Show*—featuring large casts, live orchestras and guest celebrities— were budgeted at $40,000 per week in 1950. A PI drama at the same time, however, normally could be produced for between $4,000 and $7,000 a week.[18]

Admittedly, the PIs seldom earned the incredibly lofty numbers that the Nielsen or Hooper ratings systems logged for the renowned music and comedy series. Yet those detective dramas delivered more listeners per advertising dollar than the more prestigious shows. According to the trade publication *Variety*, in 1950 the average evening mystery program attracted 267 households per advertising dollar, whereas musical-variety programs drew only 215 households, while general dramas pulled in just 187. Comedy-variety shows garnered 163 households, and concert music features settled for a mere 123.[19]

Talent-wise, with few exceptions (Joan Blondell, Jeff Chandler, Glenn Ford, Van Heflin, Edmund O'Brien, Dick Powell, Basil Rathbone and Frank Sinatra come to mind), high-paid stars with legendary status weren't essential to the efficacy of PI dramas. All that was needed was "a clear and distinctive voice and an ability to read fluidly and to inject emotion into the performance," one pundit noted.[20]

There was a myriad of talented radio thespians, experienced, eager and available, from which advertising agencies and producers could select their heroes and support players. The actors usually received little, if any, notoriety, and small recompense for their sterling efforts. But the networks airing the shows and the agencies producing them, enjoyed an entirely different level of reward. The PI and similar mystery dramas netted much of the prime revenues that the chains and agencies received. Without any doubt, *they* were rolling in dough!

Charles Hull Wolfe directed the radio and television testing bureau of Batten, Barton, Durstine & Osborne, an advertising agency in the 1940s. Near the close of that decade he released some discerning figures that compared 16 diverse types of sponsored series airing in 1946 on the national radio hookups.[21] Wolfe made the following discoveries:

Variety series starring "name" comedians (Fred Allen, Jack Benny, Bob Hope,

Red Skelton, et al.) achieved the highest ratings (audience size) among the 16 types reviewed, each show averaging 20.5 points; variety topped by "name" vocalists (Bing Crosby, Dinah Shore, et al.) were runners-up, at 13.4 points. Mystery-detective-horror dramas, including PIs, ranked sixth, at 11.3 points. (One source claims that, in 1945, 10 million listeners concentrated on 31 broadcast mystery shows of varied persuasions.[22])

Talent costs typically ranged between $15,250 (for name comedians) and $2,211 (for women's daytime serials, in sixteenth place). At $4,347, mystery-detective-horror dramas ranked twelfth in cost.

In the all-important, often defining cost-per-ratings-point comparison (reflecting what advertisers ultimately paid for their listeners), classical music concerts were the most expensively produced genre, at $3,156.43 per point. Mystery-detective-horror programs placed fifteenth, or next-to-last (which again was women's daytime serials), costing a mere $397.21 per point to produce.

Translated, the research reveals that the typical PI drama drew fairly sizable audiences at low talent fees, delivering more listeners per advertising dollar than all but one programming category. Other studies have disclosed similar results. The bargain basement rates of detective dramas obviously gave the sponsors more bang for their bucks than nearly any other commercial network fare.

Broadcast PI narratives were often predictable and even repetitious. Even so, the attention of their fans seldom waned. Fred MacDonald observes that, at the start of a new tale, "The hero was usually found peacefully and calmly uninvolved. With the introduction of other characters, he inexorably found himself enmeshed in trouble and was physically and intellectually challenged." He accepted the new reality and eventually solved the dilemma, ending the adventure "with a sense of self-confidence and achievement."[23]

Writer R. Austin Freeman simplified the detective story into a four-step pattern that is repeatedly displayed in such mystery series: a crime is committed; clues are gathered; the crime is solved; and the solution is validated.[24]

Providing a sobering reflection on the popularity and endurance of the private eye, David Geherin cites five qualities that appear to characterize the breed.

First, and underlying all the others, is the fact the PI is predictable and candid in the challenges he encountered. "Though he can never perhaps fully restore justice and order to a corrupt society, his actions proclaim the value of honorable behavior in a world which too often rewards dishonorable activities."[25]

Second, diversity is synonymous with the PI. He may be married or single, black or white, man or woman, young or old, Democrat or Republican, Christian or atheist, straight or gay, physically challenged or not, rich or poor, employee or employer, rural or urban, or possess a myriad of supplementary dimensions. The range distinguishes PIs from law officers, undercover agents and technical heroes, for the PI doesn't have to meet the stringent physical, political and moral standards that are often required of public servants.

Third, PIs have typically developed a dialect all their own, separating themselves from the common vernacular. Their narrative style, often emphatically colloquial and fortified by quips and dark humor, underscores the toughness of their profession. Their detailed summaries are punctuated by both first and third person descriptions.

Fourth, the PI readily adapts to shifts among societal and economic castes. "His investigations bring him into contact with characters that include bank presidents and dope pushers, housewives and hookers, saints and sinners." Forming his own opinions about those around him, the PI is personified as "an implacable foe of those people and organizations that regard the rule of law as something that does not apply to them," whatever the social standing or environment.

Fifth, a PI is often seen as energetic, forceful and productive in ever-evolving circumstances. Encountering greed, revenge and jealousy, some of their number also bumps into "real life" concerns like juvenile delinquency and substance, domestic and preadolescent abuse. Invariably, PIs face the conflicts that beset contemporary civilization head-on, and deal with them adroitly.

The astute and provocative critic John Conquest claims that, for private investigators, "trouble is their business." Conquest offers a sixth attribute that distinguishes these heroes:

The PI is dependably authentic. "The personal views and moral judgments of private eyes ... are of the essence, for, morally, they are free agents, answerable to nobody but themselves"—perhaps even beyond their clients, law enforcement and state licensing boards. This dynamic is in opposition to that of police detectives, for example, whose personal opinions and ethical conclusions may be "interesting" but "always irrelevant."[26]

MacDonald offers a cogent perspective on the world of radio during its golden age, asserting: "Detective heroes in the popular arts must be viewed as social and cultural symbols, that more than pure entertainment, such characterizations are important reaffirmations of the moral values at the base of American civilization."[27] That authority underscores a strong belief that the aural icons "embodied the essence of those morals and values upon which the society was founded."[28]

MacDonald classifies the programs that personified those unwavering heroes, segmenting them into a trio of well-defined categories: the realistic, glamorous and neo-realistic detectives.

In the earliest days of the fictional dramas, the *realistic detective* could be discerned by a determined fondness for pursuing conventional, traditional styles of crime solving. These could invariably be recognized by habitual and predictable patterns. Logical tactics were highlighted. Clues appeared in narratives; the protagonist and listeners were encouraged to doggedly follow them and thereby crack each case.

It all resulted in a solitary goal, MacDonald surmises: "The emphasis upon solving the mystery in an organized, dispassionate manner suggested ... that ... the forces for Good within society were forever at work eradicating irrational criminality."[29] Everything else, including the central figure's persona and outlook, mattered not; the singular intent was to ferret out the guilty and thus preserve order in a world beset by chaos. There were "no unsolvable mysteries," MacDonald underscores. "Once the most baffling radio crime was submitted to a rational analysis by human intellect ... its solution was assured."[30]

Ellery Queen, Sherlock Holmes, the *Eno Crime Club* "Manhunter" Spencer Dean and cohort Danny Cassidy were private investigators that pursued this technique, along with a barrage of professional law enforcement agents (in dramas like *Gangbusters*, *Counterspy*, *Mr. District Attorney* and *The FBI in Peace and War*).

Once the foregoing type had been firmly established, a second category appeared, which MacDonald labeled the *glamorous detective*. In this classification the leading character's behavior dominated the action. Frequently adventurous, the figure—usually male—was often paired with an aide who could be anything from a near equal to a virtual neophyte adding little more than the opportunity for verbal exchange. Although a vigilant pursuit of criminals was still essential, the traits of the investigator eclipsed those quests. These heroes exuded much more than mere intellect; audiences were favorably impressed by their vibrant charisma and animated repartee. Any or all of these conditions abounded: "Trivial conversations between the hero and the people he encountered, loquacious descriptions, comedic relationships between the hero and his partner, and even sexual tensions between male and female characters."[31]

The private investigator was in his element in this classification, including a wide range of career and avocational gumshoes like Lamont Cranston (aka *The Shadow*), Mr. and Mrs. North, Richard Diamond, Sam Spade, Johnny Dollar, Mr. Keen, Michael Shayne, Michael Waring (aka *The Falcon*) and plenty of others.

By the late 1940s, listeners were introduced to a more earthy style of crimefighter, one MacDonald tags as the *neo-realistic detective*. He claims such individuals helped "expose imperfections within the American system" in series that turned into "positive cultural achievements with intimate ties to progressive realities."[32]

The protagonists were characteristically "disillusioned, embittered men" who grudgingly performed their duties, typically addressing clients, culprits, law officers and spectators in an "abusive tone."

Declares MacDonald: "They also articulated a general disdain for most of the positive symbols of civilization and social order."[33] Their dramas emphasized lawbreaking activity as an indicator of hidden social illnesses. He typifies their central figures as "brutalized" detectives in a "depressingly grim environment." Minus love interests and flirting secretaries, they gained reputations as an unappealingly tough, hard-boiled lot.

The group included Pat Novak, Johnny Madero and Jeff Regan among PIs, and lots of cops (Sergeant Joe Friday of *Dragnet*, Captain Frank Kennelly and staff of the *Twenty-First Precinct*, Lieutenant Ben Guthrie and cohorts of *The Line-Up*, Danny Clover of *Broadway Is My Beat*, et al.).

The various aural sleuth series introduced satisfying suspense to American ears daily or weekly through fictionalized drama that — along with the intrigue — offered some of radio's most compelling heroes. These private eyes of the air, whose inception coincided with a stepped-up war against crime in the real world, brought to the nation's living rooms some of the most popular cultural idols of that epoch.

Nowhere in the pages of history can one find greater champions of justice. Their style of amusement was an art, and it struck a note with vast audiences for ages, holding them virtually spellbound by their radios. After all, in the theater of the mind, possibly no other form could have been as uniquely germane.

2

Origins of a Supersleuth

It began as a fantasy in one medium. It ended in another, roughly half a century later. By then it had attained a remarkable and unchallenged record as the longest-running continuous private eye drama ever to cross the ether. Its unprecedented feat remains unsurpassed as the close of yet another half-century approaches.

In a span of 18 years—from autumn 1937 to autumn 1955—"the famous old investigator" Mr. Keen, Tracer of Lost Persons tracked down missing citizens, as well as those responsible for the adversities that overtook many of them. Fans were reminded on every program that their supersleuth was "one of the most famous characters of American fiction in one of radio's most thrilling dramas."

At its inception, this engaging narrative aired in serialized quarter-hour installments three nights a week. Later, when it became a weekly 25- or 30-minute feature, the drama offered self-contained plots unfolding within each episode. In its final year on the air, the action expanded into yet another sequential arrangement, consisting of a five-part dramatic tale relayed in quarter-hour segments on weeknights. In each arrangement the kindly old investigator checked his files and brought to waiting ears "one of his most widely celebrated missing persons cases." It was the stuff that entranced aficionados of the theater of the mind and kept them glued to their radios.

The individuals most responsible for introducing Mr. Keen to a wide radio audience were Frank and Anne Hummert. They are the same husband-and-wife duo whose sudden, impressive and prolific expansion into daytime melodrama had securely established them as the moguls of matinee several years before *Mr. Keen's* arrival.

Their personal lives also read like a soap opera.

The bespectacled Edward Frank Hummert was tall, thin and wiry. His professional experience included advertising copywriting and newspaper reporting. Anne Schumacher Ashenhurst Hummert, on the other hand, was a diminutive woman about two decades Frank's junior, who also had newspaper experience in her brief professional background. Married young, she became a mother within a year and divorced a short time later, relinquishing custodial rights to an at-times shiftless, alcoholic ex-spouse. Career-oriented, she took a job as Frank Hummert's editorial assistant at Blackett-Sample-Hummert, a prestigious Chicago advertising firm. Her creative gifts surfaced quickly, bringing her to the forefront as a decision-maker, and pushing her up the corporate ladder. Within a brief span she married Hummert.

In the half-dozen years from 1932 to 1938 — overlapping the premier of *Mr. Keen, Tracer of Lost Persons*— Mr. and Mrs. Frank Hummert gained wide acclaim within the advertising industry. For one thing, Frank Hummert earned a reputation as the single highest-paid personage in American marketing. His spouse was distinguished as the dominant feminine wage earner in that sphere. By 1938 the couple left Chicago, headed for New York. There the radio networks and many of the country's leading advertising agencies maintained headquarters. There they would also find an unlimited supply of theater and broadcast professionals.

Soon the couple moved to an exclusive Greenwich, Connecticut, estate. Separating themselves from their former ad agency in 1943, they established and oversaw a burgeoning radio production empire, Air Features Incorporated. Perhaps surprisingly to most old-time radio fans, among all the medium's series developers, the Hummerts had no equals. Their input in crafting daytime programming was so pervasive that they literally established an agenda for U.S. network radio during the sunshine hours.

By the early 1940s the pair controlled four-and-a-half hours of national weekday broadcast schedules, and were responsible for airing 18 quarter-hour serials five times a week. That was a total of 90 original episodes every week — with none of those ever repeated. In private life, meanwhile, the twosome operated in a vacuum. Becoming social recluses, they shunned the public eye and acquired numerous eccentricities that built a legendary reputation for quirkiness in the broadcast industry. Their strange behavior characterized them for life, in fact, but if they cared at all it never showed. The fascinating details of their personal and professional lives are recounted in the volume *Frank and Anne Hummert's Radio Factory* by this author.

In addition to the washboard weepers that branded their careers, during the late afternoon, early evening and after dark hours, the Hummerts provided the big national chains with impressive numbers of mystery, music and juvenile-oriented adventure features. Given a little time, they would field at least 125 separate programs altogether. Although they refrained from appearing on the air themselves, and seldom submitted to interviews, their names were readily established among radio broadcast patrons.

In addition, during the first half-dozen years of their swift rise to prominence, the couple realized an awesome escalation of their own personal net worth. Their take-home pay topped, by some accounts, a combined $300,000 annually. While they presided over fully half of the radio serials on the ether during that epoch, by 1938 they were airing 36 separate series concurrently and purchasing $12 million of commercial radio time per year, an eighth of all network hours sold. Their programming workshop reportedly churned out 6.5 million broadcast words yearly. And at their peak, Hummert productions annually received in excess of 50 million pieces of fan mail, according to published reports.

How did one couple simultaneously produce all those shows? There's a very simple explanation: The answer lies not only in their abilities and drive, but in their savvy business acumen that led them to minimize costs and significantly increase their bottom line.

The couple auditioned actors for the leads in their dramatic series, carefully making selections from among the many competitors available in radio thespian pools. Handpicked program directors — who were among their most trusted minions — were charged with hiring the actors who filled the numerous support roles. The directors communicated with a production's staff while at times passing along cryptic messages from on high. Simultaneously, they were held accountable for enforcing widely publicized policies that were sacrosanct in the Hummert organizational regime.

Furthermore, the founding pair developed an ingenious plan for scripting their shows, leaning heavily on assembly-line techniques. For their daytime dishpan dramas, they dictated plot outlines, characterization and action. Then they assigned a corps of wordsmiths to flesh out the dialogue. Critics claimed those scribes turned out some of the most banal discourses that ever crossed the airwaves. Convoluted plots frequently involved romantic triangles and incorporated amnesia and other maladies of the mind, body and heart. Despite such predictably depressing exchanges, for decades millions of homemakers tuned in faithfully, while the sponsors—who were most likely soap and health commodity manufacturers—watched with glee as their coffers swelled.

For their nighttime productions, the Hummerts routinely summoned and assigned — sometimes on a rotating basis, other times for sustained periods— a handful of conventional scribes from among their stable of apposite authors. The creative juices of those subordinates spilled into quarter- and half-hour action thrillers. Story lines (outlines of proposed plots and characterization) were submitted to the producers for approval before scripts could be written. If a hack was any good, he or she could become a primary contributor to a specific feature for lengthy periods of time.

Lawrence M. Klee may have possessed the most fertile pen among the Hummert coteries of nighttime thriller-writers. For years he conceived the dialogue and exploits for *Mr. Keen, Tracer of Lost Persons*.

Today no fewer than 618 of his *Keen* scripts exist. During that lengthy run, he also wrote many of the Hummerts' other enduring dramas, including chapters of *Backstage Wife, Chaplain Jim U.S.A., Front Page Farrell, Hearthstone of the Death Squad, Mr. Chameleon, Real Stories of Real Life, The Romance of Helen Trent, Valiant Lady* and *Young Widder Brown*. In addition, Klee provided scripts for the narratives of several other producers, both in radio and television. While functioning as a freelance writer, Klee's employment was generally steady and relatively assured throughout radio's golden days.

The Hummerts based some of their broadcast series on pulp fiction, motion picture and stage productions. Early in their audio careers, for instance, they adapted *David Harum* from Edward Noyes Westcott's best-selling novel by that name that was released in 1899. Before they carried it forward, the tale also had been turned into a 1934 box office smash featuring renowned homespun entertainer Will Rogers.

After their experiment in turning *David Harum* into a radio serial proved successful, the Hummerts soon offered listeners *Our Gal Sunday*. That narrative was taken directly from a turn-of-the-century Broadway production simply titled *Sunday*, which had starred Ethel Barrymore.

Another of their durable melodramas, *Stella Dallas*, was based upon Olive Higgins Prouty's turn-of-the-century novel of the same name. In a couple of celluloid versions, Belle Bennett (1925) and Barbara Stanwyck (1937) portrayed the heroine before the Hummerts introduced that indomitable figure to radio audiences.

With those successes adapted from literature and other sources, is it any wonder that the creative duo turned to pulp fiction as they pondered the launch of a private detective series? In June 1906 Robert William Chambers (1865–1933) saw a manuscript he had simply titled *The Tracer of Lost Persons* published. How could he possibly have known that some three decades later it would become the most durable detective drama ever presented in a medium that didn't even exist at the time he conceived it?[1] (Ironically, for all of its broadcast years, *Mr. Keen*'s announcers would state that "*Mr. Keen, Tracer of Lost Persons* is based on the novel *Mr. Keen*," an obvious misnomer.)

Robert W. Chambers was nearly as prolific as the famous investigator he created. The son of a prestigious New York attorney, Chambers was born into wealth and social standing, and enjoyed a distinguished heritage dating from colonial America. His earliest U. S. ancestor was the illustrious Roger Williams, the founder of Rhode Island. Chambers was educated at the Brooklyn Polytechnic Institute. After he demonstrated a talent for drawing, he entered New York's Art Students' League, where he studied painting. Chambers continued his artistic pursuits (for seven more years) in Paris at the Julien Academy and Ecole des Beaux Arts.

Returning to the states in 1893, Chambers became an illustrator for several popular journals, including *Life, Truth* and *Vogue*. But when his first book was released only a year later, his interest in painting waned. From then on he devoted his professional attention to writing. In two decades Chambers turned out 45 volumes. Many more novels, short stories and magazine articles were produced over his lifetime. As a result, similar to the fictional Mr. Keen, the native New Yorker attained affluence and status in his own right.

For several years he maintained a downtown office whose address he kept secret even from his family, where—for eight hours daily—he created fictional works.[2] Among his eccentricities, Chambers once confessed that, on more than one occasion, having written as many as 30,000 words that needed some adjustment before he could reasonably proceed, rather than "fix it," he'd throw away the manuscript and begin again. Away from the typewriter, he developed a love for the outdoors, becoming something of an ecologist, reportedly planting 20,000 trees in his lifetime.

Authors Today and Yesterday noted that the creator of *The Tracer of Lost Persons* claimed, "I write the sort of stories which at the moment it amuses me to write; I trust to luck that it may also amuse the public." Chambers is better recalled for his horror and fantasy fables. Yet, a publication of that era observed, "Mr. Chambers already ranks among the foremost writers of romantic fiction ... [and] discovers an individuality and originality which sufficiently differentiate him from any others of his school."[3]

Chambers' Mr. Keen, however, was a far cry from the one whom radio audiences would follow and fondly recall in successive decades—certainly so by the time the aural series reached its zenith. While the Keen in print operated a New York private detective agency and attempted to locate specific individuals, *that* kindly old tracer was limited to romantic matchmaking and little more. He certainly never stumbled upon the mysterious, life-threatening intrigue that filled the imaginations of millions of radio listeners in the drama's later heyday.

Without doubt, his forte was in finding just the right partner — invariably feminine in Chambers' stories—for the masculine clientele who could afford his firm's upscale services, and who (for one reason or other) found it impossible to locate an acceptable marriage partner on their own. In essence, Keen and Company's business was a forerunner of the professional dating outfits and web site matchmaking services that would surface decades later.

Chambers portrays Keen as an erudite,

elderly, exceedingly affluent bachelor. Keen was accustomed to the finer things in life. His pleasant steel-gray eyes often expressed a "singularly agreeable smile."[4] In one encounter, Keen likened himself to "an old man, alone, with nobody to fear for."[5] A client certified his confidence in Mr. Keen, believing "whatever the Tracer attempted could not result in failure."[6]

While Frank and Anne Hummert never let it slip that Mr. Keen was born with a first name, R. W. Chambers was quick to mention one — and did so repetitiously. On Keen's business card, *Westrel* preceded the tracer's surname. The card read:

KEEN & CO.
Tracer of Lost Persons
Keen & Co. are prepared to locate the whereabouts of anybody on earth.
No charges will be made unless the person searched for is found.
Blanks on Application.
Westrel Keen, Manager.[7]

Nobody, but nobody, ever heard the name *Westrel* on the air. The familiar appellations were invariably limited to a formalized "Mr. Keen" or — in the case of partner Mike Clancy — simply "Boss." Narrators proclaimed him an assiduous "kindly old investigator" or "kindly old tracer," and occasionally replaced "kindly" with "eminent," "famous" and similar sobriquets that celebrated the character's reputed triumphs. But never was he Westrel. The mystery of his forgotten moniker seemed to add to the inscrutable aura that enveloped this furtive, mythical creature.

Running a global syndicate dedicated to finding the perfect girl for wealthy young men who couldn't (or wouldn't) do so on their own, the original Keen once expressed his mission to a patron: "You have no conception of our business, no realization of its scope — its network of information bureaus all over the civilized world, its myriad sources of information, the immensity of its delicate machinery, the endless data and the infinitesimal details we have at our command ... no idea of the number of people of every sort and condition who are in our employ, of the ceaseless yet inoffensive surveillance we maintain."[8]

He informed the man that his firm was "obliged to know about people who call on us." On receipt of an inquiry from that prospective client, Keen informed him: "I immediately set every wheel in motion; in other words, I had you under observation from the day I received your letter to this very moment."[9] Is hardly the character remembered from radio days!

The firm was so busy that appointments had to be scheduled at least a week in advance. But on the air, a disillusioned or grieving customer could walk into Keen's inner office at any moment — and some even hid in the tracer's automobile or broke into his apartment in order to coerce him into helping them.

In pulp fiction, Keen & Company's physical facilities bore an ironic similarity to the well-documented assembly-line production domain that Frank and Anne Hummert constructed a quarter-century later. Keen's office — and that of the Hummerts — included a myriad of "young women garbed in black, with white cuffs and collars, all rattling away steadily at typewriters."[10] Not surprisingly, comparable images abounded in *Legend of a Lady*, a thinly veiled fictional biography of Anne Hummert, which was authored by one of her most prolific dialoguers, Robert Hardy Andrews.[11] Hummert is clearly depicted there as a black-dressed, white-collared advertising agency staffer who developed the outlines for several melodramatic radio series while calling most of the shots — as she appears to have done in real life. The mythical character also married the boss.

Keen in print accepted fees amounting to $5,000 and beyond before he found the girl of a young man's dreams. That would have been quite a tidy retainer a century ago. Yet, on radio, financial arrangements were handled altogether differently. Money was seldom mentioned between Keen and those who sought his services. Audiences understood that the aural sleuth was so well heeled that he could look into finding missing persons and maniacal killers for the mere sport of it. Funds seldom changed hands. While some of his clients offered to pay, the audio Keen seldom accepted more than their heartfelt gratitude. When, on rare occasions, he acquiesced to an insistent patron, he allowed that he would donate those earnings to charity. His resources were apparently endless; his personal satisfaction in achieving a desired ambition seemed to be payment enough.

Perhaps attempting to honor Chambers' fictional legacy, the Hummerts introduced the tracer to their radio audiences by adapting one of the author's own stories as the first tale presented on the air. Its theme boiled down to discovering the perfect mate for a young man from among the many Keen-employed stenographers pounding that barrage of typewriter keyboards beyond Mr. Keen's private sanctuary.

The series moved on from that debut to identify and locate people from all walks of life. But at the show's apex, the aural sleuth experienced a drastic transmutation, as he turned to solving murders. By then, Chambers' original character had evolved into something he never could have envisioned. The epigraph for the daily Hummert serial *Stella Dallas* referred to episodes "in the later life" of that soap opera queen, noting they were based on the heroine in Olive Higgins Prouty's "great novel." Keen was drawn from Chambers' book, but, just like Stella, most of the parallels ended there.

While one Mr. Keen dealt exclusively in matters of the heart, the other heartily threw himself into finding missing persons or those who caused friends, acquaintances, business associates and relatives to meet foul ends. The departure from the original was great, yet it undoubtedly sustained the tracer, netting a following that welcomed him into millions of American homes for nearly two decades. As little more than a matchmaker, he probably wouldn't have endured beyond an initial season on the ether.

One wag suggested that Mr. Keen might qualify as the grandfather of *Mr. Chameleon* ("The Man of Many Disguises"), another Hummert radio characterization and a property concerning a police homicide detective. *Keen* had been airing for 11 years when *Chameleon* arrived in 1948. Calling Keen a "blood brother" of Chameleon,[12] an observer of the sleuthing pair intimated that the progenitor was about 60 years of age by then. "Keen and Chameleon were almost exactly alike," the pundit allowed, "both drawn from the joint well of Frank and Anne Hummert, both working on the same kinds of murder cases, both using simple methods of catching killers and both using dumber-than-thou assistants."[13]

Ash-Tree Press reissued a pair of tales from *The Tracer of Lost Persons* in 2000 in a collection of Robert Chambers' turn-of-the-century fiction. Edited by Hugh Lamb, *Out of the Dark, Volume 2: Diversions* includes two tales featuring an "enigmatic and seemingly omniscient Westrel Keen," one reviewer claimed.[14] Citing critic E. F. Bleiler, the analyst branded the tracer's narratives "a peculiarly sentimental detective form ... in which occasional elements of the supernatural entered."[15] Concluding that Westrel Keen's omniscience is neither taxed nor the reader's interest retained, the reviewer opined: "Chambers' customary soppiness in the love scenes creeps in too, while in the absence of anything gruesome, some exchanges of unintentional humor here and there may be savored."[16]

The same year Ash-Tree released its volume of Chambers' works, Chaosium Publications introduced *The Yellow Sign and Other Tales*. It was billed as a "fantasy collection-omnibus of the complete short weird fiction of R. W. Chambers."[17] The volume includes the novel *In Search of the Unknown* and four chapters excerpted from *The Tracer of Lost Persons*.

Would such contemporary revivals even remotely hint that there could be renewed interest in Chambers' long-ago fictional detective? It certainly isn't out of the question.

Although Chambers' incarnation of the tracer of lost persons may have been overshadowed by the radio version, the mid–1980s saw an extension of sorts to Chambers' original theme.[18] Producer Aaron Spelling (creator of TV's *Fantasy Island* and *Love Boat*) took a few liberties with the Chambers premise and revived it for an ABC-TV series titled *Finder of Lost Loves*. The hour-long detective drama premiered on September 22, 1984.

In it, Tony Franciosa portrayed a well-heeled widower, Cary Maxwell, who operated an agency seeking to reunite star-crossed lovers and find old flames for would-be suitors. In an age in which advanced technology was rapidly becoming the accustomed norm, Maxwell regularly called upon the aid of a computer (which he simply dubbed "Oscar"). That electronic jewel offered choice tidbits, helping Maxwell piece together information on the whereabouts of the lost persons his clients hired him to locate.

The show must have sounded some peculiar ring of familiarity to viewers who perhaps recalled *Mr. Keen, Tracer of Lost Persons* in its early aural years, or possibly who had read the Chambers novel. While avoiding any allusion to the model created by Chambers, one TV critic curiously observed: "Creator Gail Parent got her inspiration for the show after reading about a real-life 'finder' on an airplane flight."[19] And one wonders, where might that real-life finder have found *his or her* inspiration?

Helping Maxwell restore romance to the lives of some folks who had lost it were his attractive assistant, Daisy Lloyd (Deborah Adair), who was also his late wife's sister; a young protégé, Brian Fletcher (Richard Kantor); office manager Rita Hargrove (Anne Jeffreys); and the firm's gofer and chauffeur, Lyman Whittaker (Larry Flash Jenkins). Pop vocalist Dionne Warwick warbled the show's theme.

Contemporary reflections of Chambers' theme continue to appear. In the 2002–2003 television season, CBS unveiled a modernized crime drama titled *Without a Trace*, in which a corps of skilled investigators attempt to locate individuals who have suddenly dropped out of sight. With Anthony Lapaglia in the lead role of Jack Malone, the series turned into an early ratings success. Supporting him are Poppy Montgomery as Samantha Spade, Marianne Jean-Baptiste as Vivian Johnson, Enrique Murciano as Danny Taylor and Eric Close as Martin Fitzgerald. It's a show that also gives the viewers an opportunity to acknowledge sighting *real* missing persons in an effort to return them home safely.

Subsequently, in early 2003 Moonstone Books announced plans to release a three-issue miniseries of *Mr. Keen* narratives penned by Justin Gray and illustrated by Lee Ferguson. According to a Moonstone official, "The content is about a man who specializes in finding people who don't want to be found. It's set in the present day, and has a lot of great character stuff." Sound familiar?

Currently, audio recordings of the vintage radio series *Mr. Keen, Tracer of*

Lost Persons continue in widespread circulation, distributed by old-time radio and nostalgia dealers. The prototype on which the show was based seems as intriguing to audiences now as when it was conceived. With network and cable television's voracious appetite for imaginative dramatic concepts, videos, computers, movies and future diversionary forms of electronic, live and print communications, who can unequivocally say that the theme — and possibly the *very character*— that Robert W. Chambers dreamed up a century ago won't be recycled over and over in the years to come? After all, it has been generously incorporated into a myriad of formats to date. It seems plausible that Mr. Keen could prosper by thrilling multiple generations of fans not yet born.

3

Lost and Found

When Irene Jenkins married millionaire socialite Wickstead Granville, magnate of the Great National Railroad, she lied to him about her upbringing. Claiming a heritage that derived from a prominent aristocratic Southern clan, she informed her spouse that her parents were deceased. In truth, they were still very much alive, although utterly impoverished.

Her dad, Sam Jenkins, was a hardworking, poorly educated, longtime employee at a remote rail yard belonging to the very line her husband owned. Quietly, Irene informed her parents that her newly acquired status on the social register prevented her from seeing them again.

Six years went by. After imbibing deeply from her newfound trappings of luxury and its oft-resulting superficial values, Irene Granville acquired a sudden change of heart. Sincerely regretting her mistakes of the past, she commissioned the famous missing persons investigator, Mr. Keen, to locate her mother and father. Through the able efforts of Mike Clancy, then termed Mr. Keen's "assistant," the pair surfaced rather quickly.

In the intervening time, Sam Jenkins had become a helpless cripple, the result of a work-related accident. Because his disability forced him off the job permanently, his wife, Nellie, sustained the couple by washing dishes in a small restaurant. In time they grew terribly bitter over the inexplicable change in their daughter's personality.

Finding the couple, Mr. Keen assured them that their child was heartbroken over what she had done. He persuaded the duo to travel with him to the opulent mansion the Granvilles occupied for a face-to-face reunion with their offspring. During an emotional encounter, Irene invited her folks to live under her own roof. In the midst of a touching reconciliation, Wickstead Granville returned home. Upon learning that his spouse had been living a lie, he ordered her parents off the estate. It took quick thinking, intervention and perseverance by the kindly old investigator to foster a softening of the wealthy railroad tycoon's heart. Harmony was restored and, presumably, the foursome lived happily together ever after.

That poignant narrative, "Mrs. Granville's Real Family," aired in five consecutive installments between June 23 and July 5, 1938. It was typical of the melodramatic plotting that transpired in the years that the namesake hero of *Mr. Keen, Tracer of Lost Persons* focused on the pursuits that the show's title implied. While there were occasional darker moments in the storyline between 1937 (the program's inception) and 1943 (which saw the start of an extensive overhaul and transition in the drama's course), only a handful of those tales bordered on the sinister themes that were to become the characteristic thesis of the show's final dozen years on the air. (Actually, the program evolved into the killer-pursuing drama for which it is best recalled in 1943, 1944 and early 1945, drawing elements from both motifs.)

A handful of repetitive theses, some quite shallow, tended to dominate the storyline during this embryonic epoch. The concept of the family member—usually a wife or mother—who became so ill that she left home so as to avoid becoming a burden to those left behind was played out to distraction. Can you imagine splitting from your loved ones for many years when you are simply too sick to continue? Unless that individual died (and that was rare), in the traditional happy ending she was invariably located, her motives accepted, her actions forgiven and the family reunited. The listener was to presume they'd all live in blissful harmony after the big bugaboo was exorcised.

Another theme employed ad infinitum was that of the individual who went under more than one moniker. The figure either posed as someone he wasn't (frequently for questionable motives) or forgot (or didn't know) who he was and so took an assumed name. As one of the writers would later point out, there were only a handful of premises available. Across so many installments, one could expect to encounter the basic plots again and again, often with only small variations from earlier incarnations.

The absorbing series was introduced to radio listeners over the NBC Blue network at 7:15 P.M. Eastern Standard Time on Tuesday, October 12, 1937. Announcer Ben Grauer, the precursor in a long line, exclaimed:

Ben Grauer (1908–1977), whom a pundit labeled "an aural identification mark for NBC," initially introduced *Mr. Keen, Tracer of Lost Persons* to radio listeners. Grauer announced the show in its first three years (1937–1940), terming himself "a utility man"—a special events reporter for all occasions. The National Academy of Vocal Arts dubbed his voice "the most authoritative in the world." Grauer remained a broadcast giant long past his days as *Mr. Keen*'s narrator. (*Photofest*)

We present for the first time on the air one of the most famous characters of American fiction and drama, *Mr. Keen, Tracer of Lost Persons*—the story of a man who believes everyone in the world has lost someone they'd like to find again—who guarantees to find any lost person anywhere in the world. He could be a great detective, but he fights heartbreak, not crime; he helps people no one else could perhaps ever help. Tonight, for the first time, we go behind the scenes with this man who discovered the most fascinating profession a man ever followed. We'll watch *Mr. Keen, Tracer of Lost Persons* at work.[1]

Mr. Keen's initial delving into his file of missing persons, beginning with that

During the first half-dozen years *Mr. Keen, Tracer of Lost Persons* was on the air, the kindly old investigator displayed an engaging personality. His geniality encouraged listeners to welcome him into their homes thrice weekly. That winsomeness was pushed into the background in succeeding years as an intense battle to find murderers affected his demeanor. Bennett Kilpack (left), in the namesake role, and Jim Kelly, who played Mike Clancy, rehearse. (**Photofest**)

broadcast, was titled "The Case of the Girl Who Couldn't Be Found." By the close of the series' fifth chapter, in what would prove to be a typical pattern, the kindly old investigator located a simple lass in his own employ to become the wife of a dashing young man having difficulty locating the girl of his dreams. It was fashioned after the original narrative of Robert W. Chambers' work *The Tracer of Lost Persons* that first circulated more than three decades earlier.

During those initial six years on the air, Mr. Keen maintained a much more engaging personality than what was to become emblematic of him later in the drama.

His winsome spirit, coupled with frequent laughter, an ability to interact in the lives of his patrons and those around them, and a demonstrated knack of avoiding taking himself too seriously, was obvious. This stood in stark contrast to the more pointed, professional interrogator he was to become later, when he transformed into an all-business, extremely focused private eye.

In those formative years, upon solving a romantic riddle, for instance, he might accept an invitation to an impending wedding. Possibly he would agree to give a bride away or stand in as a groom's best man. In November 1938 he was so beguiled by one charming feminine client that he even fancied himself being swept off his own feet. His usual cool, suave demeanor temporarily disappeared, and he disregarded the suspicions of his staff— which were later proven right when the young lady turned out to be a murderer. On occasion, Mr. Keen was observed to socialize at cafés, restaurants and watering holes with his clientele following the satisfying solution of a case. But such interchanges would almost never transpire in the years that he devoted to being a crime fighting detective.

In the early era, Mr. Keen's geniality undoubtedly encouraged listeners to welcome him into their homes thrice weekly. His tales were of the classically homespun variety. While he wasn't the drama's narrator, he exuded a caring, familiar presence that was occupied in guiding, shaping and developing individuals who were mired in human misery and conflict. During that prewar and wartime era, the nation habitually sought out sanguine entertainment that could distract it, for the moment at least, from the rigors of world tension that predominated most citizens' minds. In landing a sustained following, it seems that *Mr. Keen* supplied a diversion that satisfied a portion of that need.

Probably few who tuned into *Mr.*

Keen exclusively during the series' final dozen years—when it was to reach its zenith (and its largest audience) as a crime-solving detective mystery—would realize that the drama had ever been otherwise. Yet during its embryonic stage the central figure focused on why certain individuals dropped out of sight, or—just as often—where they had gone. He discovered that some of those subjects vanished of their own volition, ostensibly to fulfill as-yet-undisclosed purposes. On rare occasions he tackled cases hinting that some of those disappearing acts were fraught with foreboding undertones. This became especially true as the end of the Second World War approached and Americans appeared ready for more challenging and intriguing radio puzzlers.

As a tracer of lost persons, Keen had no equal. The show's fan mail in those days often requested his personal assistance in helping to find missing sweethearts, children, spouses and other relatives and acquaintances who had seemingly evaporated, just like the mythical figures in the radio play. Keen's work was deeply rooted in the model envisioned by Robert W. Chambers' 1906 novel, from which the aural series stemmed.[2]

The tracer's all-encompassing passion—to locate "the whereabouts of anybody on earth"—was briefly examined in the foregoing chapter. To that end, he was determined to avoid failure at all costs, never permitting any blemish to stain an untarnished reputation. He was unwavering, certain that he could ultimately locate or identify virtually any misplaced individual. As he pursued his quarry, the kindly old investigator weaved fascinating tales of his subjects' disappearances.

In a typical case of mistaken identity, he once encountered a lovelorn Air Force lieutenant. While home on leave, the officer had become entranced by the clever charms of a lonely woman whom he met at a masquerade ball. When she disappeared, he appealed to Mr. Keen, who summarily tracked her down. Keen also discovered that she was the wife of a prominent businessman. Lapsing into his earlier role as a matchmaker, Keen arranged a subsequent date for the serviceman and his woman of mystery. But for the big night out, the investigator substituted his own office assistant, Susie Hargraves, whose features were altogether similar to those of the millionaire's spouse.

The story concluded with the lieutenant telling Keen he intended to marry Hargraves when he returned from his next tour of duty. The outcome was anticipated and offered a warm, fuzzy ending. It was typical of the lighter fare that characterized the *Keen* series in its first half-dozen years on radio.

In "The Wife Who Grew Tired of Waiting," Mr. Keen reunited a mother, father and their four-year-old son. An unemployed father—taunted by his uncle who had taken the down-on-their-luck family in—at last stalked away defiantly while seeking work far beyond the confines of home. It took him three years to find a satisfactory job offering a living wage; by then his wife and son had left the kin's abode, unable to withstand any more of his constant derision. Mr. Keen masterminded a plan to locate the missing boy and his mom, then brought the family together, restoring unity to their shattered lives.

In "The Table for Two," a married couple that split three years earlier (so that neither partner's vocational aspirations would be hampered) discovered that genuine happiness existed for them only when they were together. In the meantime, their separate objectives had led them in diverse geographical directions. Mr. Keen was engaged by the wife to locate the husband, with whom she had lost touch. The tale's climax was an emotional renewal of their vows, coupled with a determination to put one another ahead of their personal careers.

In "Woman, Single, Forty-Five, Unemployed, Unwanted," at the behest of that woman's mother and father, Mr. Keen soon located a very despondent daughter. In secret she had been working as a nighttime cleaning lady in an office tower where formerly she was a private secretary. Viewed as "too old" for that secretarial duty, she was replaced, and subsequently plunged into emotional depths. Ashamed and unwilling to become a burden to anyone, she vanished from the home she shared with her aging parents. As a result of Mr. Keen's prodding, the lady was restored to her family and the position she had occupied earlier. And in the process she regained the dignity and self-respect she had lost.

The tales of scores of other displaced citizens who were found and returned to their accustomed stations by Mr. Keen presented thrilling chapters in the lives of various misfits. They usually offered listeners some satisfying resolution to tales of disenchanted, disenfranchised and dysfunctional individuals and their troubled relationships. Perpetuating the aura of the Keen mystique, a popular fanzine of that day, *Radio and Television Mirror*, began reprinting some of the famous tracer's stories about lost persons (starting with its January 1941 issue).

For all its warm and fuzzy memories, however, to be totally fair, the *Keen* series was saddled with occasional albatrosses that prevented it from flying to the heights of the aural literary epic. This was true in the show's earliest years and, regrettably, didn't improve for its later reincarnation. While the blame for its lapses is often laid at the feet of those who penned its scripts—and who certainly must stand in the accountability line—the ultimate responsibility for its shortcomings must rest with the show's producers. Indeed, they should have demanded higher standards of quality and excellence, and accepted nothing less. Yet, for all their capabilities, Frank and Anne Hummert appeared preoccupied with quantity rather than quality in the vast surfeit of radio productions they controlled. Invariably, they cut corners to boost the bottom line.

In some episodes of *Mr. Keen, Tracer of Lost Persons*, for example, minor (but important) factual details were overlooked, and glaring errors crept in. On an occasion in July 1939, Miss Maisie Ellis, Keen's private secretary, and his assistant Mike Clancy met a character who fed them foreboding details of an impending calamity about to strike Mr. Keen. Leaving the informant behind in New York, the pair jumped into a car and—as fast as they could drive—headed up the New England coast in pursuit of Keen, who was then riding with a suspected madman. Having stopped enroute overnight at a New Hampshire hotel, by the next morning Ellis and Clancy were conversing with their informant in person—the man who had stayed put in New York. He was in the car as they resumed their journey, with no mention of how he got there. At best it must have been somewhat disconcerting to the audience at home.

Conversations often became trite in *Keen* dialogue. On September 24, 1940, the narrator droned on in tortuous verbiage that surely confounded the listeners: "Learning there was nothing to the other-man angle, he [Keen] began to look for the person who must still be in touch with Rose in order to tell her when Howard had a job. And he found that person! Wherefore we now discover him in the hall of a tenement house up in Harlem, making use of the pay-station telephone installed there." Wow! They even got away with shifting tenses! What a convoluted fiasco.

Actually, there was a sustained period during the early episodes broadcast over

CBS (1942–1943) in which the dialogue, supplied by several scribes, was literally dreadful. Across the entire 18-year run, this deluge of drivel was surely the low point, and may have accounted in considerable measure for the subsequent transitioning of the show into a manhunting-crimefighter series. If ever the drama could be justifiably accused of spewing out banal dialogue, it certainly seemed to wallow in a solid concentration of it during that singular broadcast season.

Plots at times dissolved into meaningless messes. As a consequence, the drama never reached its potential, and fell well short of such contemporary crime radio standard-bearers as Sam Spade, Sherlock Holmes and Johnny Dollar. The opportunity was there, but it would have required an overhaul of the assembly-line methods that the Hummerts so firmly embraced. If such a thought ever crossed their minds, they obviously rejected it.

Speaking of the Hummerts, they weren't given to crediting their underlings consistently. During the early run of *Mr. Keen*, for example, the closing tag "Your announcer, Ben Grauer" (or whoever happened to be narrating a given performance) frequently would be crossed out in pencil on the scripts and never uttered on the air. Sometimes the name didn't show up in the scripts at all. There seemed to be no rhyme or reason to the pattern. Theoretically, it appeared that if the show was running long, that self-identification line was among the first to be cut. The decision was in line with a practice adopted by Frank and Anne Hummert on all their radio features.

Admittedly, the *Keen* series has often been the butt of jokes, both among well-intended collectors of old-time radio trivia and the professional, career-oriented pundits. Certainly the program could have become far more than it was. Despite that reality, let it be duly noted that the series was—and still is—admired by a band of steadfast fans. The author's intent in acknowledging some of its shortcomings is to offer a balanced, objective assessment of the program.

Had there been enough time in the rapidly-paced plots for listeners to seriously ponder some of the deficiencies that routinely surfaced, they would surely have wondered how such confusion could possibly exist. Deep-thinkers among them must have scratched their heads over some of it. But in so many instances the dialogue passed right over the baffling obstacles, especially those that made little sense. There follow a few examples of the common lapses during *Keen*'s early years. (Further instances that occurred in the crime-solving era will be highlighted in a later chapter.)

On March 16, 1944, Mr. Keen went to Buffalo to interview a department store personnel manager who had earlier allegedly employed a figure in Keen's present investigation. Now stop and consider this for a moment: Wouldn't a sane person have saved time, expense and effort by engaging the Buffalo contact on the telephone? Even if Keen felt the trip was necessary, he could have determined through a single call or wire (Western Union, to the uninitiated) if the interviewee was actually in his current capacity at the time Keen's subject was employed there. He could also have learned if that official would be available to speak with him upon his planned arrival in Buffalo. Inevitably, everything worked out in the tracer's favor without any of the expected hitches, despite a lack of advance communication. At times the tracer simply went to extreme lengths to advance his theories, following procedures that an actual investigator would find ridiculous due to obvious practical concerns.

A number of implausibles occurred in an episode aired later that same year, on

November 16, 1944, which clearly demonstrate some of the peculiarities found in the scripting.

When the police discovered a child who had been restrained for weeks in an abandoned warehouse, a night watchman confirmed to Keen that several times he thought he heard a child crying inside the structure. And he did absolutely *nothing* about it? Hel-lo-o-o-o. He was definitely a candidate for immediate dismissal, and perhaps even some kind of negligence charge, although this was never even *mentioned*.

Later, on meeting Mr. Keen for the first time, the child's mom was easily persuaded to check out of an upstate "rest home." Most such facilities wouldn't have allowed that except by prior notification and approval of the family or a physician, or possibly a court order. The woman immediately accompanied this heretofore unknown man (Keen) to New York to see if the boy who had disappeared—and was later locked in the warehouse—was her son. It wouldn't take much imagination to think what could happen to her if Keen hadn't been on the up-and-up. But there was little time for the lady to protest that he might simply be nothing more than a dirty old man.

Next, before a fashionable house party crowd, Keen—an uninvited guest—encouraged the child to confront another woman, the one who had actually imprisoned him in the warehouse. When he did, she freely confessed to her tainted deeds before a roomful of spectators, an appalling but typical scenario in *Keen* storylines. No problem with later court convictions there! In real life, of course, guilty parties seldom admit their misdeeds before swelled crowds of eyewitnesses, an obvious axiom that radio ignored.

Finally, an all-knowing tracer assured the party guests and his home audience that—for this unbalanced culprit—"a mental hospital will be her new home." How he invariably *knew* precisely what a judge and jury would decide was never disclosed. His perceptions were considered hallowed, however; and by no means could they be challenged.

On the broadcast of October 13, 1938, Vera Johnson pulled a similar stunt, paralleling the antics of the mother of the boy in the tale just described. Having uprooted from her Texas home five years earlier, leaving a spouse and daughter behind, Vera was situated 50 miles from New York in a "free sanitarium" (do they exist?) when Mr. Keen caught up with her. She chucked everything, defying physicians, common sense and a semblance of propriety to board a train with this stranger. The pair headed off to Texas to attend her daughter's wedding solely at the suggestion of Keen, whom she had never heard of. For two days they journeyed by rail. Talk about "strangers on a train." And what might the buzz have been when the pair alighted from their Pullman in that tiny hamlet she had departed so long ago? But there was no time for radio listeners to dwell on such matters, for the action continued moving along swiftly. Taboos were simply never to be broached.

A number of the plots throughout *Mr. Keen*'s long run on the ether could be considered quite thin. Ponder the domestic dispute in one home during the early years of the drama in which an autocratic father had a falling out with his teenage son, a not uncommon occurrence. That was followed by a characteristic response: the boy ran away from home. What did dad do? Instead of carefully weighing the natural options himself, or even filing a missing persons report with the proper authorities, he aired his dirty laundry with Mr. Keen. And what did Keen do? Learning the youth was an avid football fan, he summarily deduced that the lad would "probably" show up at a venerated high school football game staged annually in his community.

Keen and partner Mike Clancy arrived at the stadium before the game, met the rebellious young man, and encouraged him to accompany them back home. The boy departed with the dual strangers (not a good plan), and — at the home — Keen lightly chastised the father, opening his eyes to the error of his ways. End of problem. Unless, of course, the dysfunctional family issues that set up the circumstances in the first place was examined and sorted out. But that would more likely have been fodder for psychologist Dr. Joyce Brothers' show, not this one.

All Keen had to do was find a runaway at a logical venue and return him to the environment he so desperately sought to escape. Radio listeners had little time to dwell on the intricacies and implications beyond the feel-good endings that such shallow plotting provided. Regretfully, it was emblematic of many of the *Keen* dramas, and often lowered the bar for any respectable semblance of intermittent literary achievement.

The terminology in the *Keen* programs, both in the earlier and later eras, often reflected some of the idioms that characterized that period in American history. For instance, Mr. Keen was invariably bumping into *foundlings* (or individuals who had been led to believe they were of that heritage). The expression, without further elaboration, would almost assuredly send most modern listeners to their dictionaries. It describes an abandoned infant, a figure in those dramas that was viewed with less promise than outright adoptees. Then there were people who were either placed in or had escaped from an *asylum*, an archaic term for a mental institution. *Securities*, mentioned so often on the show, would be classified today as investments of varying types. A *ne'er-do-well* was an idle or worthless bum, while a *man-about-town* was a worldly, socially active chap. A *sweetheart* in that period took precedence over beaus, suitors, honeys, lovers, girlfriends and boyfriends. To be *gay* meant exuberant and carefree. And the common reference to *making love* had an altogether different meaning than it does in contemporary times. (On at least one occasion, a couple told Mr. Keen they had been making love in the backseat of a car; you may be certain that what they were doing never even raised the eyebrow of a network program censor.)

The subject of payment for Mr. Keen's services was a topic that surfaced frequently during the lost-and-found years. His reactions to the matter were more or less predictable.

When a dad inquired, after his kidnapped son was returned to him, "How can we ever thank you?" the kindly old investigator's response — following several days of intensive pursuit, including personal out-of-pocket expenses for an evidence-gathering trip to Chicago — was a sappy: "My own happiness is reward enough."

To a female client who asked, "How can I ever thank you?" Keen answered: "It's not necessary to thank me, my dear. The thanks I receive from seeing that justice is done is quite enough."

On one subsequent occasion he assured a family: "My reward is in seeing you all so happy."

When a lady in yet another case told him, "I have money and I can pay you whatever you charge," Keen replied: "The money is not important. I happen to have all I need for an old bachelor." That revelation should have been a siren song to hordes of gold diggers!

When Keen located an embezzler who had been in hiding for years, he covered the thief's $5,000 debt with a personal check of his own. "You can pay me back in installments over time," the trusting tracer

Florence Malone (Miss Maisie Ellis, Mr. Keen's private secretary), Bennett Kilpack (Mr. Keen) and Jim Kelly (Mike Clancy, his assistant) played three recurring figures during the first few years that *Mr. Keen, Tracer of Lost Persons* appeared on the ether. The trio is shown rehearsing a scene for a chapter to be aired shortly after the series shifted from NBC Blue to CBS late in 1942. At that juncture the serialized narrative was marking its fifth anniversary on the air. (*Photofest*)

assured the miscreant. It definitely took somebody with deep pockets and an extra large heart to extend such professional courtesies to non-paying clients — particularly those who got off without being tossed in the slammer for their criminal activities.

Let's face it: Keen may have possessed the wisdom of Solomon, but when it came to making practical financial decisions, you'd hardly want him to be in your employ.

Unfortunately, on occasion the plots were resolved by shallow — even risible — solutions.

When Keen turned up a missing man who was accused of slaying a hotel desk clerk, the man's description of the clerk's physical attributes — an impostor who had killed the real employee before he robbed the hotel safe — was enough for the tracer to suggest that the charlatan's bodily features could *only* fit one man, notorious safecracker Bugs Morelli. "Morelli's your man," Keen insisted to the cops. Based on Keen's word alone, the authorities released their eyewitness, the missing man whom Keen had only recently located. The private eye then drove the man to his waiting family. Their case solved for them, the police had only to pick up the murderer. If you thought that one through, it was laughable. But with time running out on the episode, it was an easy method of tying up the loose ends and bringing the narrative to a rapid conclusion. Regrettably, more than one *Keen* tale ground to a resounding halt via somewhat superficial explanations.

Aside from Mr. Keen, partner Mike Clancy, and infrequently appearing office assistant Susie Hargaves, the only other recurring figure in the story line this early in the series' life was Maisie Ellis, the investigator's private secretary. Listeners were often reminded that she was a spinster. Her presence generally offered little more than someone for Mr. Keen to dialogue with. During those summary conversations, details of previous actions were reiterated and subsequent plans announced. On at least one occasion, however, Miss Ellis (Keen always addressed her using the formal designation) was kidnapped, thereby becoming a missing person in her own right.

In passing, let it be noted, too, that Miss Ellis frequently accompanied the tracer on his many out-of-town adventures. The action in the early years is literally strewn with journeys that the pair made to hamlets and metropolises, secluded quiet spots and exotic far-flung locales, usually by train but occasionally by car, plane or cruise ship. A vacation to the West Indies and a holiday in Hollywood were typical of such fare. While it may have all been totally above board, the fact that the old man and his elderly feminine companion ran off together so often must have raised antennae among 1930s listeners. After all, what was her *real* contribution to those escapades—taking dictation? If so, why couldn't it wait until he got home?

On one occasion Mr. Keen vacationed with an old chum—a celebrated movie star—at the actor's West Coast digs. Miss Ellis accompanied him and stayed under the actor's roof, purportedly to "see some of the big names up close." Mr. Keen may have notified his host that he was bringing his secretary. But what kinds of messages might those arrangements have conveyed to his host? (Think manners and morals.) Did he really need someone along with whom he was personally acquainted in order to recap the details from previous episodes? It was a radical departure from the expected, well-understood, traditionally prudish Hummert stance (which will be explored in greater detail in a later chapter). At best it must have generated plenty of interesting mail from the audience at home.

The Hummerts maintained a predilection for selecting music for their shows from public domain. That way they avoided usage fees that would have lowered their net profits. While *Mr. Keen, Tracer of Lost Persons* debuted to the tune of Noel Coward's haunting refrain "Someday I'll Find You," by the early 1940s that ditty had been ditched in favor of Chopin's "Fantasie Impromptu," recalling the more familiar melody from it, "I'm Always Chasing Rainbows." But that tune soon got the ax, too. As the series ended its serialized episodic plots in late 1943, its theme of earlier days returned. "Someday I'll Find You" introduced the show to legions of waiting ears for the next dozen years, until the program left the airwaves forever. The latter melody was one of the most identifiable and durable musical scores among vintage radio series. It also seemed the perfect song; "Someday I'll Find You" expressed the spirit and optimism of the "tracer of lost persons" perhaps as well as any label could.

The melodic opening, closing and intervals (or bridges) between scenes on *Mr. Keen* utilized a console organ. This was also true nearly everywhere else in the early days of live audio dramatic productions. Virtually every network studio, no matter what its size, was equipped with such a revered instrument.

In particular, Hummert radio features were symbolized by a heavy reliance upon an organ to establish mood and emphasize reactions. This trend was to be supplanted by recorded music in the nighttime productions down the road. By then a blend of standardized musical scores, sometimes combined with an organ, were routinely offered. But until the late 1940s, when the national chains relaxed their longstanding policies against airing prerecorded material, the live organ was a crucial and intimate part of almost every dramatic series on the air.

For their part, the infamous Frank and Anne Hummert kept a firm grip on *Mr. Keen*, just as they did on all of the productions that bore their names. While they normally didn't suggest to their seasoned wordsmiths a direction that a specific case might take — including the action and dialogue, as they ordinarily might do with their glut of daytime soap operas— the couple certainly were kept fully apprised of an author's intentions. For many years each script was initialed with an "ASH" (Anne Schumacher Hummert) or "EFH" (Edward Frank Hummert) prior to broadcast, indicating their personal endorsement (or rejection, which would have been followed by an automatic rewrite) of everything that went out on the air under their names. Producing as many as 100 or more new episodes of women's and juvenile serials every week, and possibly another 10 programs that aired simultaneously, the couple faced a formidable task.

Their stable of scribes, who could be assigned to a specific Hummert mystery for a lengthy period, were required to submit two- or three-page typewritten "Story Lines" to the producers for an OK before final scripts were prepared. Such a proposal projected a case title, offered a central problem to be resolved, named and described the individual characters and how they were to interact with one another, explained how Mr. Keen and his staff were to be involved and, finally, pursued the tale to its natural conclusion.

While an "ASH" or "EFH" and the date appearing on such documents signified that a writer could proceed with a concept, handwritten suggestions for changes and improvement — and possibly outright rejection — might also appear. Authors knew that they *must* incorporate any alterations specified. The Hummerts ran a tight ship; there was little opportunity for a scriptwriter's thoughts to vary when they conflicted with those of their discerning producers.

In *Mr. Keen*'s first few years on the air, ASH, EFH and the name or initials of a sponsor's spokesperson were all collected on separate cover pages (designated a "Dramatic Flyleaf") of each individual script. While the client's OK was solicited throughout the run, after many years the Hummert initials disappeared. After all, they had already given approval to an author's proposed storyline before a script could be written, and that may have seemed sufficient.

One area that particularly suffered during the show's formative years was the naming of the various cases Mr. Keen pursued. More often than one might anticipate, the stories were allowed to begin under one title and proceed after an episode or two (or more) under an altered moniker — possibly throwing off listeners who kept track of such things, at least until they received some details of a familiar investigation in progress. After four episodes of "The Case of the XPBA Plans" in December 1937, for instance, a new title was substituted: "The Case of the Stolen Airplane Secrets." On the next broadcast it was altered to "The Case of the Stolen Airplane Plans." Apparently the writer grew tired of explaining that XPBA stood for Experimental Patrol Bomber of the Atgood Type at the start of every new chapter, admittedly quite a mouthful. What would have been wrong in applying the second or third appellation consistently? It was a little bewildering that they couldn't seem to get it right.

After "The Girl with the Lovely Eyes" began in February 1938, by March she was "The Girl with the Beautiful Eyes"—not a colossal change, but some purists may have wondered: did I miss an episode? Again in October 1938, "The Wife Who Ran Away" was introduced after two installments as "The Wife Who Ran Off to Die." Why?

As previously mentioned, Frank and Anne Hummert leaned heavily upon their handpicked program directors. That select little group was charged with auditioning and hiring support players. Seasoned thespians who could get by on little paid rehearsal time, thereby saving the organization considerable expense, were preferred. The directors were further expected to adhere to well publicized, stringent expectations for each performance, and to notify cast and crew of whatever the producers wished to communicate.

Program directors were required to enforce a myriad of limiting and often peculiar regulations considered by the Hummerts to be totally sacrosanct. The following caution appeared on the flyleaf of every *Mr. Keen* script, for instance: "Under no condition is any music to be played under the actual commercial credits on this show." Violation presumably was cause for immediate termination. There were numerous added edicts, some which made good sense, others that were seemingly without substance. As long as everybody played by the rules and held to the expectations of their employers, they fared well in the Hummert regime and may have continued to serve it for years. Offspring of actors who worked for them now recall that, if the Hummerts found favor in their parents, those thespians were habitually called upon for performances on the myriad of Hummert features.

The mailhook was a common practice employed by many radio series during the 1930s and 1940s. Not only was it a prime method of hyping interest in a show, it also gave a solid indication to sponsors of just how many listeners were tuning in to their program. The mailhook became an accepted byproduct of soap opera and juvenile adventure features, and it seeped over into other continuing programs as well.

Its concept was simple: Advertisers would shamelessly offer their audiences a packet of flower seeds, a piece of "genuine" imitation jewelry, a portrait or photograph of a star, a family album, a child's decoder ring or some other trinket hyped to the extreme and deemed to be of intrinsic value by the fans. These goodies were shipped in exchange for a box top or label from the sponsor's product, and were often accompanied by a dime. Fulfillment houses prepared to respond to hundreds of thousands of requests when such offers aired. Few were disappointed. On occasion, the demand was so great that announcements had to be made that the supplies were exhausted and no further orders could be processed.

The success of the mailhook ventures wasn't lost for a moment on the producers of *Mr. Keen, Tracer of Lost Persons*. The Hummerts, in fact, stood at the forefront of the mass hysteria that frequently resulted. Thus it wasn't a surprise when the same type of offers featured on their soap operas and juvenile adventure serials spilled over to their nighttime dramas. This one, aired in the late 1930s, was typical:

> *Attention, please! We have wonderful news for every young girl—every bride—every wife in America!... Through special arrangement with Mr. Keen, Tracer of Lost Persons, we are about to make one of the most remarkable offers ever made on the radio—a ... stunning piece of jewelry—a "Lover's Knot" pin so exquisitely fashioned—so dramatically original in design—that you will adore it and want to treasure it all your life.*

Here's what it looks like: Two 24-carat gold-washed strands over two inches in length, gracefully looped and tied in the center in a DOUBLE Lover's Knot — then fastened to a strong pin with a genuine safety catch on it....

Actually, this "Lover's Knot" pin is adapted from the kind your grandmother wore — for a touch of old-fashioned quaintness in jewelry is all the rage today. Your friends probably will think it is a family heirloom....

We make this offer you can't afford to miss in order to get thousands to try Kolynos — the amazing modern dentifrice used on a DRY brush — that brings out natural lightness and brightness in your teeth.

Now — to get this beautiful "Lover's Knot" pin — simply send one cardboard box from a regular size tube of Kolynos toothpaste — together with one dime — to "Mr. Keen" ... care of the National Broadcasting Company, New York City.

Be sure to send in for your "Lover's Knot" pin tonight, as the supply is limited — and you don't want to miss out![3]

During its lost-and-found epoch, *Mr. Keen, Tracer of Lost Persons* was broadcast in serialized form for a quarter-hour on three consecutive nights over two national chains, although never concurrently. Each individual narrative normally required four to six chapters before reaching its conclusion.

From October 12, 1937, through October 22, 1942, *Mr. Keen* presented a total of 789 original episodes at 7:15 P.M. Eastern Time on Tuesday, Wednesday and Thursday nights over the NBC Blue network. Beginning the very next week, from October 28, 1942, through November 26, 1943, an additional 171 chapters were aired at 7:45 P.M. Eastern Time on Wednesday, Thursday and Friday nights over CBS. In all, the kindly old tracer pursued 224 individual cases during that run of 960 chapters averaging slightly more than four installments before reaching each solution.

On Thursday, December 2, 1943, the series transitioned from the installment plan to an entirely new format. For the majority of the next dozen years the drama would occupy a half-hour at 8:30 P.M. Eastern Time, mostly on Thursday nights over two networks (principally CBS). The serialized episodes gave way to 25- or 30-minute self-contained narratives. And while some of the newly expanded tales delved into the macabre, at least for a while those lost-and-found acts continued to predominate.

By September 20, 1945, it was obvious that the formula that had previously worked so well had been discarded. In its place Mr. Keen became a fierce, resolute, competitive individual whose singular ambition was to ferret out cold-blooded murderers and bring them to justice. There wasn't to be much laughter from then on, nor much socializing with the clientele. Keen was totally preoccupied with a more somber agenda. No more Mr. Nice Guy; the fun and games were gone. Keen's prey demanded greater resolve. About the only lost people he'd be finding were those lurking in the shadows after they'd committed horrifyingly foul deeds.

The show went through a metamorphosis. In its new permutation, far more fans were tuning in, according to national ratings services. One reported an increase in *Mr. Keen*'s listenership from a modest 8.6 in mid-season 1944–1945, in which the final vestiges of the "tracer" mode aired, to an impressive 17.9 by mid-season 1949–1950, the peak of the succeeding "chaser" era.[3] It was a pretty fair indication that the *Keen* audience strongly approved of the series' ambitious overhaul. Could there be much doubt that the tracer's paramount epoch was to emerge in the years directly ahead?

4

The Tracer as Chaser

The shift to a less tolerant, more intense hero was accomplished gradually over time. The laid-back, genial investigator didn't suddenly transform into a resolute detective — one who wouldn't be satisfied by anything less than bringing vile evil-mongers to justice. Yet, while the tracer continued to seek displaced individuals in many episodes throughout 1944, by early 1945 he had clearly turned a corner and was usually hunting for bigger game. Instead of solely turning up lost persons, more often he was fingering cold-blooded killers. It started late in 1943 and intensified as time wore on. Eventually, that's all he would ever do.

The program progressively ratcheted up its tempo, gradually evolving into the narrative that was to characterize it for the remainder of its air life (then well beyond a decade away). Keen was clearly shedding his rather hackneyed image as a tracer of *lost* persons. Even though that sobriquet was still audibly expressed weekly, by the mid–1940s he had clearly become a chaser of homicidal maniacs.

Despite his single-mindedness of purpose, Mr. Keen carried over some familiar traits from his earlier life. In a typewritten memo to "Mr. Leonard" (Richard Leonard, the show's most enduring director) from "Mrs. Hummert" (notice the unwavering formality) dated February 21, 1952, Leonard was reminded: "Mr. Keen throughout is kindly, just, unruffled. He never indicates by voice that he suspects anyone. He is the soul of kindness and justice. ASH"

The subtle modifications soon marked the tracer as one of the foremost investigators in all of radio drama. Each week his audience tuned in to hear a murder committed; a friend or relative of the deceased approaching Mr. Keen to enlist his aid in finding the killer; and — in the ensuing investigation — Keen corralling three or four potential suspects before exposing the villain near the drama's close.

Discovering little tidbits of information as he interrogated witnesses (via a slip of the tongue; evidence he uncovered that the police had simply missed; and little clues that seemingly only he was capable of recognizing) Keen rattled several suspects before turning his full vengeance upon a killer. Exposing fabrications, he inevitably prompted the culprit to offer a full confession, often within hearing range of bystanders. More often than not the half-crazed individual then turned on the investigator and his partner, Mike Clancy, attempting to dispose of them, too, before a quick-acting Clancy overpowered the scoundrel. On occasion, a malefactor was

Mr. Keen possessed an uncanny ability to uncover clues that authorities had simply overlooked in their investigation of cold-blooded murders. Assisting is Keen's partner, Mike Clancy, played by Jim Kelly (standing). During the drama's later years (1950–1955), Philip Clarke appeared in the title role. (*Photofest*)

fatally silenced in the altercation that erupted.

Clancy's status is worth exploring. In the early narratives he is routinely referred to as Mr. Keen's "assistant" or his "lead assistant," or even his "primary assistant." But with the inception of the longer, non-serialized tales, Mr. Keen consistently introduces him to others as his "partner." The contemplative listener might wonder: Aren't partners usually of equal prominence in most organizations? Mike Clancy, meanwhile, speaking in a thick Irish brogue, constantly takes his cues and orders from Keen, and refers to him as "Boss" and "Mr. Keen, sir." Those who interact with Keen inadvertently brush Clancy aside. He doesn't possess the sterling reputation of "the great investigator." He's even labeled a nimble-headed buffoon by critics. While, in theory, Clancy is an integral part of every investigation, in practice he's a virtual nobody. He chats with the tracer of lost persons in order to advance the listeners' knowledge, but always lets the great one muse over his own suppositions about a crime. Clancy habitually gathers a few details and runs some errands for Keen — but little of it is of a substantive nature. Yet when a disgruntled killer is out for Keen's blood, Clancy assiduously steps in to rescue his "partner."

In 1949 the program, then in its heyday, arrived and departed the airwaves to the tune of a recorded orchestra, over which the traditional studio organ added a richer-sounding rendition of the drama's long-playing theme, "Someday I'll Find You." By then, *Mr. Keen*'s opening epigraph had been fine-tuned into an enticing piece of copy. Following the narrator's cold opening, "It's time now for *Mr. Keen, Tracer of Lost Persons*," and a few strains of the familiar theme melody, announcer Larry Elliott declared:

Ladies and gentlemen, Anacin and Kolynos present Mr. Keen, Tracer of Lost Persons, *one of the most famous characters of American fiction in one of radio's most thrilling dramas. Tonight and every Thursday at this same time the famous old investigator takes from his file and brings to us one of his most celebrated missing persons cases. Tonight's case is entitled* [whereupon Elliott would provide the name of that week's drama].

It was captivating stuff. Millions of devoted fans gathered around their radios every week to eavesdrop as the kindly old investigator took "from his file" and solved another of his "celebrated missing persons cases." Of course, the only thing actually *missing* — for a little while, at least — was the killer's identity. Undoubtedly plenty of Keen buffs were swept up in playing a guessing game, matching their wits with the eminent investigator's, figuring out on their own who among the myriad of suspects really was the guilty party. The idea in many quarters was to get it right before Keen revealed the name near the close of each narrative.

The following is an outline of a typical *Mr. Keen* feature broadcast during the series' halcyon days. The performance of "The Country Club Murder Case," aired on April 20, 1950, is emblematic of the program's weekly fare.

Premise: During a young persons' dance at a Westchester country club, well-heeled socialite Arlene Graham is strangled to death. Her partner, Alan Rogers, an investment advisor who hoped to marry Arlene, seeks Mr. Keen's help in locating her estranged spouse, Chester, whom she was suing for divorce, and who has subsequently dropped from sight. Rogers claims the victim was "gentle, kind and loyal to a worthless husband." He portrays Chester as a drunkard who lost $500,000 of his wife's money gambling; he also physically abused her while pursuing another woman — Eve Worthing — behind Arlene's back. An artist in Greenwich Village, Worthing had been Mrs. Graham's social secretary. Before her marriage, the victim resided with an uncle,

Hubert Parker, now devastated by her death. Rogers admits giving Mrs. Graham unsound financial advice once, but she dismissed it, though the matter recurs to Keen frequently.

Protocol: Keen and Mike Clancy begin their hunt at Worthing's studio, where they find Chester in hiding. When Parker arrives, he fires a gun at Chester. Clancy deflects the bullet, preventing further tragedy. Summoned to Keen's office, Rogers later attests that the victim had no accountant. The country club's membership is limited to 70 young people, he acknowledges, and thinks no affiliate is beyond age 40. Keen phones Parker to inform him they will search Arlene Graham's home. Inquiring about her finances, Keen learns that Parker handled her affairs when she was his ward, but there was no need for an accountant: her late father invested well and she received income from those securities.

Resolution: At Arlene's home, Keen and Clancy are perplexed to find Worthing present. From her knitting bag they recover canceled checks she had picked up, some apparently forgeries. It's an obvious attempt to protect Chester Graham, Keen surmises. Worthing says Arlene phoned her, trying to locate her spouse shortly before her death. She told Worthing she had found more than $50,000 in forged checks and believed Chester wrote them. When Parker arrives, he recalls that Arlene told him about some missing money. Keen produces the bad checks, and Parker intimates that this confirms Chester's guilt. Keen reminds him that no one saw Chester at the dance. Parker allows: "I saw him there." Parker says he was at the dance and affirms his affiliation with the country club. Keen had noted that Parker was left-handed when he fired shots at Graham, and now observes that a left-handed writer forged the checks. He also knew Parker lied when he said he was a country club member, for he is visibly past age 40. He lied about seeing Chester, and knew his niece found the forgeries and was going public about it. Her separation from her spouse, and Chester's blatant lifestyle, gave Parker a perfect cover to commit murder. While his niece discovered the forgeries, she missed the fact that a couple of checks were written while she lived with her uncle; instead, she believed her husband was the scoundrel. Parker helped himself to her fortune and she hadn't noticed. He confesses, and Keen assures him he will feel the full wrath of the law for his crimes.

Actually, many of the Hummert detectives (including Mr. Keen) took a particular delight in passing judgment on a culprit's fate in advance of a formal criminal prosecution for murder. With a tinge of euphoria in his voice, Mr. Keen, the kindly old tracer, routinely dispensed some foreboding missive to his quarry, like, "the state has an electric chair that will provide you with proper recompense for your ill-doing." Air Features investigators seldom deliberated about what a judge and jury would do; they reveled in announcing a culprit's fate.

The Hummerts were strenuously opposed to lawbreaking activity in any form. Anne Hummert assured an interviewer on one occasion: "Crime may appear [in the dramas we produce], but either the annihilation or change of heart of the unerring one must follow."[1] The writers stayed true to the dictates of their superiors that full punishment must be meted out for heinous transgressions. In Hummert melodrama crime didn't pay, and a day of reckoning was certain and swift for any who violated that basic canon.

Typical *Keen* investigations bore titles that were obviously written to motivate audiences to tune in at the same time the following week for a subsequent adventure. Among some of the more alluring appellations: "The Silver Candlestick Murder Case," "Murder and the Absent-Minded Professor," "The Case of Murder and a Thousand Witnesses," "Murder at a Mile a Minute," "The Quicksand Murder Case," "The Case of the Man Who Invented Death," "The Case of the Woman Who Married a Murderer," "The Photograph Album Murder Case," "The Forgotten Cave Murder Case," "The Bride and Groom

Murder Case" and "The Broken Window Murder Case." Each followed the same general pattern, allowing the audience to overhear the murder, the soliciting of Mr. Keen's help, his identification and interrogation of the suspects and, finally, Keen solving the crime by producing the killer. Few of those tales departed from that template in the narrative's final dozen years on the air.

Mr. Keen was purportedly so well known that, upon introducing himself to a character by stating "My name is Keen," he'd almost universally provoke the same quizzical retort: "Mr. Keen, the *great investigator*?" It seemed everybody in Gotham and its surrounding environs was intimately acquainted with the private detective's exploits.

When Keen listened to a character offering tidbits of information, "I see" or "Go on" were his characteristic rejoinders. Another frequently utilized expression would come shortly before Keen named a crime's perpetrator: "I think we'll put our hands on the killer within the hour," he'd announce.

Just as in the earlier *Keen* era, later scripts offered some noticeable idiosyncrasies. For one thing, Keen could break all the rules that everyone else was subject to in a murder investigation, yet never be questioned about it:

- He visited crime scenes that should have been cordoned off by the police, examined objects there with disregard for possible fingerprints, and even removed articles at will from the scene.
- He rarely reported conversations with suspects—and any knowledge he'd gained—to investigative authorities.
- He bypassed search warrants, forcing illegal entry into victims' or suspects' homes or businesses while searching for clues that the police might have overlooked. (He absolutely adored entering private residences through cellar doors, then hiding in people's basements—especially when they wouldn't allow him in through the front entrance.)
- In the end he arrested those he fingered as killers, ignoring the fact that he had no power to do so. "We usually work along with the police" was the prime justification given to anyone inquiring of Keen and Clancy's involvement in a murder case.

He did a lot of other things that—if you thought about it for a while—seemed downright fantastical.

He turned into a discerning handwriting expert when the situation warranted, for instance, even though such proficiency was never qualified. Invariably he could state with absolute conviction that a suspect's penmanship was irrefutably identical to a written clue he had unearthed.

Furthermore, he could look at a dead man, as he did on August 17, 1951, and testify unequivocally: "Judging by his color and the expression on his face, I would say he was poisoned." Instantly he announced that the contaminated food consumed by the deceased "smells of a highly poisonous chemical used in making or developing film." Keen could save the state a lot of wasted time and the expense of running lots of unnecessary tests. His deductive powers, put simply, knew no limit.

The tracer could also mystify his fans by displaying an ingenious ability to recognize people he had never met. In the episode of March 13, 1952—when he and Mike Clancy found a body stashed in a coal bin—he assured his partner that this was the missing person they had been seeking. Never mind that no evidence was offered to substantiate the assumption that the man had met with foul play. Recall, also, that Keen had never met the man, never seen his photograph nor read or heard a description of his physical form. He simply possessed such extraordinary intuitive powers that all doubt was removed when the kindly old investigator emphatically declared that a spade was a spade. And he certainly knew that no thinking individual would ever attempt to contradict him, which must have stroked his ego, although he didn't exhibit it.

The murder plots themselves were sometimes inexplicably convoluted.

Mr. Keen entered an abandoned cave during the broadcast of November 3, 1949, in the company of a taxi driver who knew the premises and served as his guide. The pair discovered what Keen anticipated — the body of a man who had been missing for a short while. At Keen's bidding, the cabbie returned to a nearby house where Mike Clancy and several suspects waited. The driver related Keen's verbal commands to Clancy, who then relayed to the group a message Keen wanted them to hear. Meanwhile, Keen waited alone (unless you count the stiff) in the darkened hole 30 feet below ground — a cave with slimy, damp, algae-covered walls and a perilously rocky pathway.

Clancy then left the mansion and joined Keen inside the cave, where the two sleuths waited for the anticipated arrival of the killer, a foregone conclusion. It could have all been simplified, of course, if Keen had returned to the house after finding the body, made his pronouncements himself, and slipped into the cave with Clancy to await their quarry's approach. But doing things the easy way was seldom Keen's style. Maybe he had a thing for biding his time with a corpse.

Plenty of other silly situations surfaced in the *Keen* dramatizations. Follow this dialogue exchange (which occurred at the door of a midtown Manhattan apartment) broadcast on February 22, 1955:

KEEN: Are you Miss Amy Fairchild?
FAIRCHILD: Yes, how do you know my name?

KEEN: It's right here, under your doorbell.

Did somebody say *dumbbell*?

To add insult to injury, when the uninvited guest, an unknown private detective, announced to Ms. Fairchild, "My name is Keen — may I come in?" she did nothing to prevent him from doing so. She didn't request any identification, didn't call the cops or ask anybody nearby to rescue her. Even in 1950s New York, would an old spinster in her right mind open her door to a total stranger and invite him in, even failing to ask up front the nature of his business? Hardly. In radio you simply had to accept things that wouldn't have transpired in real people's lives.

The housewives of New York apparently placed their utmost confidence in Mr. Keen. When he and his partner arrived at the home of Professor Graft on March 9, 1950, the music instructor wasn't at home. But his wife, Louella — who had never met nor heard of Keen or Clancy (one of the few Big Apple residents who hadn't) — invited the pair inside. Momentarily, she cautioned Clancy against snooping through her spouse's compositions, spread across a table, after Clancy appeared curiously drawn to them. She then exited the room, leaving the two strangers with a breezy: "I think I'd better get back to the kitchen. Make yourselves at home. My husband will be here shortly."

Who in the name of common sense assured her that these two weren't thieves, convicted rapists or escaped lunatics from the local asylum? Even though that would have immediately raised red flags in most quarters, such scenes were included in *Keen* story lines almost weekly. The twosome just *looked* like such decent gents!

And why on earth — in the episode aired June 9, 1949 — would young, affluent Kay Adams invite all of the suspects attending her late father's final dinner party (at which one of them murdered him) to remain overnight and enjoy the pleasure of her hospitality in her dad's mansion, each of them occupying separate guest rooms? In reality, such a thought would never occur to a grieving daughter, so recently orphaned, just hours after her pop's demise. Some of it really didn't make any sense at all.

There were some other troubling conditions in those plots that proved equally devoid of good judgment and common sense.

In the episode broadcast on September 22, 1949, the victim's throat was lacerated at midnight under mysterious circumstances: a yellow talon, or claw, was found near the body. Fourteen hours later, at 2 P.M., the victim's funeral was held, following an autopsy by a medical examiner in the nearby hamlet. Not only was that local official quick on the trigger, the funeral home was, too — a time improbability for most small town professionals fulfilling those duties.

After a victim — driving a "borrowed" automobile in the May 11, 1950, story — was shot to death as he sat behind the steering wheel of the parked vehicle, his body was stuffed into the car's trunk. The vehicle was left parked by the side of the road. Later, after the owner reported his car stolen, the police found his abandoned property, still unlocked and with the keys in it. (It was good there were no *other* thieves lurking nearby!) Of course, the authorities skipped dusting it for fingerprints or peering inside the trunk. Nor did they notice any splattered blood, bone or brains in the driver's seat (the assassin had sat in the back seat directly behind the driver). Instead, they merely drove the car to its owner, no questions asked. "Nothing appeared out of the ordinary," said the titleholder after Mr. Keen later discovered the body in the trunk. Saints preserve us! How incredibly inept did the thinking fans believe the New York Police Department really was?

As portrayed on this show, that law enforcement agency surely consisted of the most dimwitted cops in the nation. In one episode they missed finding a secret compartment in a desk, a matter of little consequence for Mr. Keen. It held "the greatest sapphire in existence," the ill-gotten gains of a heist, which its new "owner" intended to retrieve at a more opportune moment.

NYPD officers invariably overlooked personal articles at crime scenes, too — like jewelry, clothing, unusual cigarette and cigar butts, etc. — that a killer might leave behind, evidence that never escaped Mr. Keen's piercing eyes. Applying his keen mind (no pun intended), he'd naturally examine a victim's bank accounts and checkbooks, diary, tax records, telephone bills, investment accounts and legal papers — all things that New York's finest routinely missed.

Most new listeners, after tuning in for a few weeks, grasped why Mr. Keen's clientele bypassed official police investigators, engaging him instead to solve those dastardly crimes. While professional law enforcement authorities were supposedly qualified (given their training and experience) to remove killers from the Big Apple's boulevards, they seldom lived up to performance expectations. Instead, they appeared utterly inept, possibly lacking something upstairs that could help them bring heartless criminals to justice. Even when the cops did make an arrest, suspects often broke free of their captors, remaining on the loose. It was a pretty bum rap for the NYPD, but it permitted the halo around the tracer of lost persons to radiate unremittingly.

The dialogue in these dramas was often as stilted as the action.

When a key figure in the episode of January 13, 1944, learned that her fiancé had been fatally shot, her reaction was astonishing: In a rather blasé fashion, "Oh how utterly horrible" tumbled from her lips. Later, upon hearing who, among her acquaintances, had polished off her late lover, she cried: "Mr. Keen, how can I ever thank you?" At least the lady possessed some etiquette, even if she demonstrated no regrets.

Jenny Haines, on the other hand (the grieving widow featured on the broadcast of April 3, 1952) was visibly (or, more accurately, audibly) shaken and sobbed uncontrollably when Mr. Keen exposed her late husband's killer. The gumshoe had also earlier discovered that the dead man ran a narcotics operation, something his spouse knew nothing about. "It may help you to bear your sorrow, Mrs. Haines, to know that your husband was part of a dope ring, too," Keen offered as comfort to the unfortunate woman. (How in the hell was it to do that? It's surely one of the most ludicrous lines ever pitched to a mournful spouse.) And then, attempting to console her further, Keen added: "Your life will be better without him." That week's writer, incidentally, was none other than Frank Hummert himself. Did anyone ever tell him he should stick to his daytime job? In this author's humble opinion, that discourse easily won the prize for the weakest dialogue exchange aired during *Mr. Keen*'s long run.

Further incongruities became readily apparent to *Mr. Keen*'s ardent fans.

For some reason, the French surname Laf'ouge apparently entranced the drama's staff. In December 1938 Tom Laf'ouge surfaced after a 22-year absence, pretending to be a long-lost son returning to tap into his wealthy mom's investments. Was it mere coincidence that Jean Laf'ouge, an exporter of African curios, turned up in a 1949 episode, only to be followed a few months later by stage makeup artist Francois Laf'ouge? Laf'ouge isn't a particularly common moniker. Writer Larry Klee appeared to be enamored of all things French, for he sprinkled his scripts with Gallic references and frequently included characters with a French heritage. (Each year he took two-month sojourns to Europe and other far-flung lands.) The Hummerts, meanwhile, were also regular Parisian visitors, and Anne Hummert once lived there. So did the spouse of the actor then playing Mr. Keen. The French links were copious.

Yet another absurdity was how frequently the *Keen* drama reminded listeners that soap opera was the predominant product of the Hummert radio factory. There were some pretty strong indications that none of the apples in the Hummert orchard would ever fall far from that ancestral tree.

On July 20, 1951, the *Keen* narrative concerned a "handsome matinee idol" actor over whom millions of women drooled. Concurrently, every weekday afternoon, announcer Ford Bond offered this epigraph while introducing one of the Hummerts' most popular serials: "Now, we present once again *Backstage Wife*, the story of Mary Noble, a little Iowa girl who married one of America's most handsome actors, Larry Noble, matinee idol of a million other women — the story of what it means to be the wife of a famous star." The similarity in the singular *Keen* plot and the washboard weeper's premise was uncanny, yet unmistakable. And to hammer it home, the *Keen* cast that week included seasoned actor James Meighan as Don Taylor, the victim. For years Meighan portrayed beleaguered hero Larry Noble on *Backstage Wife*. In addition, *Keen*'s longtime director, Richard Leonard, had shouldered similar responsibilities on that soap opera; and Larry Klee, at varying intervals, penned *both* shows. No surprises there.

Such ties with the Hummert world before sundown were evident throughout *Mr. Keen*'s protracted run. Aside from the fact that many of the actors, directors and writers routinely traversed from the

Hummert daytime dramas to their nighttime features (readily moving across what might be seen as a great chasm to those not working in a dually-aligned system), there were many other instances of analogous plotting.

Jean Carroll authored the Hummerts' celebrated *Our Gal Sunday* in the final 14 years of that venerable serial's life. During a portion of that time, Carroll submitted some scripts for *Mr. Keen*, too. In the mystery of August 10, 1951, the great investigator inquired of Doris Crane about her connection to a wealthy male victim. "I intended to marry him — he was head over heels in love with me," she asserted, adding, "Of all the rotten luck for this [his death] to happen." Stunned by her admission, Keen noted that Crane didn't seem quite "grief stricken." She retorted: "I didn't say I *loved* Henry Kellogg. I wanted to be mistress of his estate — I wanted expensive clothes, jewelry and lots of money. He could have given me those things."

Longtime listeners of *Our Gal Sunday* may have instantly recalled a theme common in that heroine's ill-fated lot. The wily vamps of Virginia consistently sought the affections of an exceedingly prosperous Lord Henry Brinthrope, Sunday's husband. One madwoman after another moved heaven and earth to displace Lord Henry's beloved Sunday as "the new mistress of Black Swan Hall" (the Brinthropes' "lovely Virginia estate"). Genuine affection for Lord Henry rarely entered into the dishpan drama's story line; these vixens were after money and social standing. The same was true of the figure in Jean Carroll's script for *Mr. Keen*. If an idea worked satisfactorily in one place, it would often surface elsewhere.

One of the recurring discrepancies in the *Keen* plots (which surely annoyed many listeners) involved the proper designation of a specific character's domicile. The week of August 3, 1951, illustrates the point: A "wealthy society woman" reputedly resided in a stately manor in "a fashionable suburban section of the city." But her upscale digs were described only a short while later as an "apartment," a striking comedown that was subsequently altered in succeeding references. The dilemma, while perhaps a small one, occurred frequently in *Mr. Keen* scripts. It could be disconcerting to the aural purist whose ear was trained to absorb, file and recall important bits of trivia after years of exposure to the theater of the mind. Glaring inconsistencies like that one probably dimmed a story's fantasy for some patrons, jarring them back to reality while tersely reminding them that it was, in fact, only a play.

As mentioned earlier, Mr. Keen possessed extraordinary deductive powers that helped him find his prey every time out. He could be charming and persuasive, but his voice took on a harsh, sharp-edged tone when he identified and confronted his tainted targets.

The writers sustained an odd proclivity for injecting the murderer into their plots at a time when that individual didn't appear to have a natural occasion for surfacing. One might turn up for little reason — beyond expressing personal condolences, for instance — thereby gaining Mr. Keen's attention. Killers in this series instinctively emerged at inopportune moments. As a result, the slayer was introduced to the audience and Keen's suspicions were promptly aroused. A seemingly innocent remark or action in such chance meetings never escaped the great one's notice. Anything he deemed dubious would be filed away in his memory and recalled at the proper moment, as his examination moved toward its inevitable conclusion.

There could be little doubt that many of the show's fans attempted to guess the perpetrator of a crime themselves. Playing along with the famous tracer, they would match wits with him, seeing if their selection was the one he would grasp near the conclusion of a case. Over time, and because the scripts were derived by a mere handful of wordsmiths, those followers developed some formulas to help them make wise choices.

One clue that surfaced frequently (nearly weekly) proved to be a dead giveaway (again, no pun intended): the killer would single out flaws in other suspects, deriding them while possibly recounting each individual's damning ties to the deceased. By harping on a subject's weaknesses, the murderer intended, of course, to exonerate himself in Mr. Keen's eyes. On August 3, 1951, for instance, Peter Taylor, that week's perpetrator, embellished the tale of a violent argument that he allegedly witnessed between Vernon Phillips and the victim. Even if Keen had believed the story, after so many similar diatribes by previous villians, this one would likely have only increased his suspicions. The same thing had simply occurred too many times in too many previous investigations.

On many occasions, as-yet-unidentified killers offered their own suppositions as to why certain conditions existed or why certain actions were taken. At these pronouncements, Keen invariably advanced a theory or two of his own, in direct contrast to that of the murderer. Any time a suspect was in verbal disagreement with the investigator, that person's name usually could be moved to the top of the list of serious candidates.

Sometimes a murderer categorically fingered an individual as the culprit, leaving no room for doubt. This normally happened just before he or she was exposed as the guilty party. On August 3, 1951, a husband (the true killer) admitted to Mr. Keen that his wife had bumped off the victim. At the same time, he pled with the private detective to "be lenient" with her. It was a frequent ploy and an obvious tip-off to Keen and his listeners.

Yet another indicator of guilt was, perversely, the mounting of strong evidence against one or more alternate suspects. When it became apparent that a suspect possessed motive and opportunity to carry out a diabolical scheme, you could be fairly certain that those "most likely" nominees were *not* the actual schemers. The scriptwriters possessed an uncanny proclivity for building strong cases against individuals who invariably came out smelling like a rose.

The motives, by the way, generally involved a few basic circumstances. The most popular reasons for getting rid of someone were greed, jealousy and revenge, separately or in some combination. All of it ultimately boiled down to an overriding self-interest, of course. In addition to sequences dealing with theft of money, securities, jewels, real estate, business and identity, *Mr. Keen*'s storylines offered a neverending parade of suitors who suffered when a love affair went awry. There were also those whose romantic advances were thwarted. All of the speculation about why a murderer acted upon his or her homicidal impulses could probably be canvassed by six or eight hypotheses.

As an aside, it was common for murderers to meet their fate via the same methods they used to dispatch their victims. Upon exposure, some would go insane, threaten Keen and his partner and any onlookers, then topple over the wall of a high rise building, crash through a window, mistakenly consume poison, stumble on a knife or be bitten by a venomous reptile — dying the same way as their victims. It was always a fitting end, Keen observed, to unscrupulously clever and twisted minds.

While rarely did the individual who engaged Mr. Keen's services on a victim's behalf turn out to be the killer (though this did occasionally occur), plots involving business associates were common. And there was an excess of stories in which the victim was engaged or recently married. The scenario could be classified as falling into a rut if it involved newlyweds and betrothed couples. Sometimes such situational plotting was allowed to run for weeks on end.

The writers appeared to favor certain terms in titling their cases, calling upon a handful of preferred idioms again and again. Among the overworked expressions: *bloodstained, weird, ghost, phantom, sinister, corpse.* To wit: "The Case of the Phantom Who Lurked from the Deep" and others akin to it. They also loved to work in colors (green monsters, gray ghosts, a yellow apparition, a lady in blue, etc.). And the scribes employed creative means by which their antagonists would commit their crimes, using not just guns, but knives, fire, drowning, asphyxiation, strangulation, bombs and electrocution. In particular, poison seemed a favorite — on a teacup rim, in the ice poured into drinks, stored in a hatpin, in a pin hidden within a thimble, on a perfumed handkerchief, as well as the more traditional poisoned food, tainted beverage and a disturbed snake's venom. There was more than one way to slay a dragon, and *Mr. Keen*'s writers proved adept at hatching unusual ones as the series wore on.

Although Keen could be considered a man of means (as noted in earlier references to non-payment for his services), his pursuits, surprisingly, were almost entirely limited to the well heeled segment of New York City's populace. This was especially evident after he began to solve homicides. Nearly every one of his murder cases involved a "fashionable apartment in midtown Manhattan" or a manor, mansion or estate in an upscale setting, quite often in the countryside "not far from the city." Keen clearly limited his practice to the people who could best afford him, yet refused to charge them for his services. Those who approached him most often were there largely on behalf of recently deceased tycoons, socialites and other figures well connected in business, professional and cultural circles. They didn't plead very often on behalf of common laborers and paupers. Why so? There could be more than one explanation.

The individuals who brought the mythical investigator to the air tended to enjoy elegant living themselves. Thus they maintained familiarity with, and an affinity for, breeding, prestige and prosperity. Robert W. Chambers and Frank and Anne Hummert could hardly have been expected to stand in Gotham's soup lines (even as volunteers). Furthermore, at least some of the hacks deriving the concepts and penning the *Keen* storylines were rather handsomely compensated for their efforts. These folks could certainly be included among the upper crust (or at least upper middle class) of their day.

But the most plausible explanation as to why the *Keen* series routinely touted the moneyed ranks is that — just as the soap opera writers discovered earlier — a prosperous lifestyle was far more fetching than one experienced by, let us say, a retired salesclerk with nominal means of support beyond Social Security. The existences of commoners — who might be the salt of the earth and who would offer the shirts off their backs to anyone needing them — plainly weren't of interest to the masses of radio listeners. Their lives were drab by comparison, devoid of all-but-simple accouterments and the fascinating details that could be supplied by a world of fantasy. Hence, nearly every *Keen* homicide pertained to people of better-than-average means. It probably would have proven self-defeating to pursue its themes week after week any other way, even though featuring the affluent became laboriously repetitious at times. It wasn't that the rich liked to kill each other off — their deaths simply provided more appealing plot fodder!

As noted elsewhere, Frank and Anne Hummert ran a tight ship and exhibited many eccentricities. With few exceptions, they shunned the hundreds of individuals who worked in their employ, preferring to rely on a few well-placed intermediaries to deliver their directives and handle most of the business matters they didn't wish to be burdened with. Actors and crews were kept at arm's length, many never meeting or even seeing the people for whom they toiled. Those birds were a strange pair, reclusive to a fault and often out of public sight for extended periods while working 14-hour days at their ostentatious Greenwich, Connecticut, estate. All of this is recounted in delicious detail in the volume *Frank and Anne Hummerts' Radio Factory* by this author.

One of their idiosyncrasies was to take credit for work done by their minions. "Frank and Anne Hummert" by itself would be read over the air, crediting the duo as the producers of a series; the contributions of others were rarely mentioned. Yet as time advanced, the odd squad mellowed just a tad. On March 27, 1947, nearly nine-and-a-half years after *Mr. Keen*'s premiere, Bennett Kilpack finally was cited on the air for playing the lead. He had been doing so since day one. The only time he was acknowledged before that was during an extended period in 1946 when he was ill, and actor Arthur Hughes temporarily replaced him in the role. On that occasion the Hummerts undoubtedly anticipated that the show's loyal fans would notice the difference in the two men's dialects, which was considerable and distinguishable.

Perhaps that occasion was instrumental in persuading the head honchos to relax their stringent no-credit rules. Whatever the case, a week after Kilpack's name was revealed, on April 3, 1947, Lawrence M. Klee's name was read aloud for his function in penning the dialogue. He had been writing the show intermittently since September 17, 1942. Along with these others, then-director Richard Leonard also received his just due. The Hummerts were truly on a roll!

Although they never acknowledged the names of supporting cast members (those who appeared in one-time-only parts in the various dramatizations)— nor the musicians, sound technicians or engineers— the unforgivable omission (obviously not an oversight) was that Jim Kelly (who played Mike Clancy for the entire run of 18 years) was seldom credited on the air. On June 5, 1947, during the era in which the Hummerts appeared to be especially charitable, he *did* receive on-air recognition for playing the part of Clancy, but this was obviously due to the fact that for that one week Bennett Kilpack (Mr. Keen) was away on vacation. The following week Kelly faded back into the woodwork, his name never to be mentioned again except during brief spells when he was ill or vacationing (both exceptions rare), and someone else stood in for him. Such shoddy treatment wasn't justified. Kelly was, in fact, the only individual— beyond the Hummerts— to stay with the series for its entire run, including directors, leads, announcers, writers, musicians, sound techs, engineers, sponsors, agency reps and anyone else associated with the property. Who said life is fair?

Incidentally, Arthur Hughes (daytime radio's *Just Plain Bill*) filled in for Bennett Kilpack during several extended periods between 1946 and 1948 in which the latter was ill or vacationing. Kilpack remained in the part through the broadcast of October 26, 1950, having carried the title role for 13 years. Philip Clarke was introduced the following week, on November 2, 1950, "substituting for Bennett Kilpack," indicating that Kilpack was expected to return. For five weeks, in fact, Clarke substituted for Kilpack. But by the broadcast of December 7, 1950, Kilpack's name was no longer mentioned. "The part of Mr. Keen is played by Philip Clarke," informed the announcer. Clarke continued in the lead until the show left the air five years later.

What became of Kilpack? His illnesses may have been more than he — or the Hummerts — could manage. Perhaps his advancing age played a factor in his departure. Whatever the case, his voice was readily distinguishable to radio listeners for a very long stretch of time. After most listeners became used to Clarke, however, few would probably recall that somebody else was ever featured in the role.

Beginning with some of the longer episodes featured in the 1945–1946 radio season, Richard Leonard's master scripts included the names of many of the actors. Where this information has been preserved, it is included in the entries appearing in the series log at the end of this volume. A fascinating bonus for anyone personally examining the permanent script files is a chance to read (in Leonard's own handwriting) notes regarding cuts, timing, dialogue and other pertinent matters.

The all-in-one-episode murders began in earnest on Thursday evenings in 1945 (broadcast on CBS), although plenty of similar episodes aired in the two preceding years (launch date December 2, 1943). The half-hour format continued through the 1946–1947 season. Beginning August 28, 1947, the narrative was reduced to 25 minutes, but it still aired Thursdays on CBS, acquiring — for several years — a lock on the 8:30 P.M. timeslot. The following summer it was lengthened to a half-hour, beginning Thursday, June 24, 1948. The feature concluded its lengthy run on CBS (which was launched on October 28, 1942) with the broadcast of July 12, 1951, *Mr. Keen*'s 1351st outing.

The following week, on Friday, July 20, 1951, at 9:30 P.M., *Keen* resurfaced over the NBC airwaves as a half-hour mystery. A few weeks later, on September 6, the drama — still on NBC — reverted to its venerated 8:30 P.M. Thursday slot. It remained there through April 24, 1952.

At that juncture *Mr. Keen* made a final network leap, returning to CBS for the duration of its run. Starting Thursday, May 1, 1952, its half hours aired at 9:30 P.M. On June 5, 1952, it shifted to 8 P.M. Thursdays. The program aired in that time period through September 25, 1952; the following week, on October 3, it moved to Fridays at 8 P.M., remaining in that timeslot through June 25, 1954.

In the meantime, on Monday, June 21, 1954, a quarter-hour serialized Monday-through-Friday *Mr. Keen* feature debuted on the CBS schedule at 10 P.M. On Monday a murder was committed, with the kindly old investigator spending the rest of the week tracking clues. On Friday he identified the assassin from among several suspects. For a while, the drama-by-installment aired concurrently with the longer weekly series. The serialized episodes ended with the broadcast of January 14, 1955.

The complete weekly sequences reverted to a 25-minute format on July 2, 1954, but still aired Fridays at 8 P.M. That format continued through October 1 of that year.

After a brief absence (of the weekly drama), *Mr. Keen* returned to the air as a half-hour mystery heard over CBS on Tuesdays at 8:30 P.M., beginning February 22, 1955. It remained there through April 19, 1955. The following week, on April 25, it transferred to a final time period, a 25-minute slot at 8 P.M. Mondays on CBS.

The program persisted through the broadcast of September 26, 1955 — continuity number 1693. Purportedly there were 1693 scripts produced, but, preempted thrice, the series aired just 1690 times. Cancellations occurred on April 12, 1945, (upon the death of President Franklin D. Roosevelt), April 26, 1945 (during the first plenary session of the "San Francisco Conference," which laid the groundwork for the United Nations, and was broadcast live from the San Francisco Opera House), and November 1, 1954 (when national off-year election returns aired).

While almost all of the *Keen* scripts survive, the permanent files contain a few holes. Normally these gaps consist of the odd solitary show (or perhaps two consecutive programs). However, from the late 1943 and early 1944 transition period (as the drama went from thrice-weekly installments to half-hour complete narratives) the first 41 scripts remain unaccounted for. Even then, all is not lost, for 10 of those features, having aired live, have been preserved via the magic of recording tape and remain in widespread distribution. Nor are there scripts available for the eight-week period from July 12, 1945, through August 30, 1945. Luckily, *all* of these programs are on tape. Finally, a gap of two weeks exists at the end of the five-night-a-week installments (January 3–14, 1955) in which all scripts are missing, without benefit of recordings to supply data.

Sixty-four *Keen* dramas are thought to exist in recorded form, although five are believed to be in one individual's private collection and therefore unavailable to hobbyists. That leaves 59 shows in widespread circulation (labeled as "extant episodes" in this book's Radio Episode Guide). Of course, it's always possible that more programs will surface at a later date. Who knows what may be salted away in attics, in basements, in garages and on closet shelves of second and third generations who may have no notion of the significance of what they possess? Who knows what may turn up at flea markets, nostalgia shops, rummage sales and other obscure spots where radiophiles forage? Enthusiasts continue to search diligently for additional broadcasts, and probably always will.

While the mystery series frequently recycled plot ideas, to this author's knowledge only 14 of the crime cases solved by Mr. Keen were reprised, thus accounting for 1676 original scripts. For the repeats, sometimes the title was altered, sometimes the characters' names were changed and sometimes both were distorted, while the plot remained intact. On rare occasions, nothing was modified from one performance to the next. Repeats occurred on the following dates:

Original Broadcasts	*Reprised Broadcasts*
June 28, 1945	January 31, 1946
March 11, 1948	August 15, 1955
April 15, 1948	August 22, 1955
August 12, 1948	July 31, 1952
September 23, 1948	August 17, 1951
October 28, 1948	January 10, 1952
January 20, 1949	August 21, 1952
March 3, 1949	June 20, 1951
April 28, 1949	January 15, 1954
June 2, 1949	August 3, 1951
August 18, 1949	September 6, 1951
October 6, 1949	August 27, 1954
September 14, 1950	October 1, 1954
February 22, 1951	May 15, 1952

For the 25- and 30-minute dramatizations of *Mr. Keen*, rehearsals were usually confined to a two-day period—the day prior to broadcast and the day of the show. For example, the episode airing September 6, 1951, called for the cast to attend a preliminary practice session on Wednesday, September 5, from 5 to 7 P.M. On Thursday, September 6, the cast and crew were to be available from 6:30 to 9 P.M., the final half-hour being the actual live broadcast.

Ingrid Meighan Waldron, whose father, James Meighan, played continuing roles on a variety of Hummert daytime dramas (*Backstage Wife, Just Plain Bill, Lora Lawton, Our Gal Sunday* and a host of others), recalls some special occasions when she accompanied him to *Mr. Keen* rehearsals and broadcasts. (He appeared in numerous supporting roles over several years.) In the 1951–1952 season, when *Mr. Keen* aired over NBC, the show originated from an enormous two-story soundproofed theater used by *Just Plain Bill* and many other features. It was also on the route for Radio City guided tours. Waldron remembers: "It [the studio] had a separate, glassed-in audience seating area where NBC pages brought the tours to watch the shows live. I was about nine years old, and I felt terribly important and didn't dare to look up at the tour groups (that would have been unprofessional)."[2]

She characterizes the people she met in old-time radio as "extremely bright, clever and well read. They loved mind games and were sometimes just a little bit eccentric, too." Ingrid Waldron further recalls that — on radio's mystery and detective shows — the actors considered winning the part of the victim — referred to as the "brass ring" — a real prize. "You got paid the same AFTRA [American Federation of Television and Radio Actors] rates but could get off early," she explains. (Remember, the victim met his fate in the first three minutes of the half hour. Unless there were flashback sequences, he was finished for the night.) "Why it was called the brass ring I'm not sure, but maybe, like the carousel rider who pulls the brass ring, it was considered a lucky part."

James Meighan, incidentally, utilized a system common among radio actors. He'd take his script (Air Features scripts were 8-1/2" × 11" and approximately 30 pages in length, printed in purple ink), remove the staple and lay the pages on a music stand about chest high. In this way he quietly turned the pages without the rustle of paper distracting the listeners. But he suffered from the fear of what his daughter called a "periodic nightmare" — that the pages would somehow get out of order and he'd lose his place when his cue came. "It never happened, but he obsessed about it!" she remembers.

As many aural series approached the end of their long runs on the ether — with pressure intensifying to hold to the status quo and defy the television screens invading America's living rooms — the Hummerts handed down an edict banning a heretofore widely accepted practice: no longer would they allow replacements to stand in for seasoned actors during rehearsals of their dramatic series when an individual's schedule conflicted with the appointed practice time due to other on-air appearances. For years, scores of freelancing actors personally paid substitutes to take their place at rehearsals, reading their character's lines and making notes of cuts and words to be emphasized on the scripts they were handed as they arrived for a part in a supporting role (e.g., victim, suspect, killer). The Hummerts nixed the practice, virtually across the board on their dramatic series, as they stood their ground against encroaching television, knowing that their livelihood was tied solely to radio. Directors were told there could be few, if any, exceptions when a conflict in scheduling arose.

Until that juncture, which occurred in the early 1950s, stand-ins routinely augmented *Mr. Keen*'s rehearsals. A standard typewritten entry on director Richard Leonard's master copy of the script for May 10, 1951, referred to the rehearsal set for Wednesday, May 9, (5 to 7 P.M.): *FLORENCE WILLIAMS coming from "Front Page Farrell." Her stand-in until 6:10 P.M. will be Marion Carr. ARLINE BLACKBURN coming from "Lorenzo Jones." Her stand-in until 5:00 P.M. will be Barbara Bell Wright. RICHARD NEWTON coming from "Just Plain Bill." His stand-in until 6:00 P.M. will be Humphrey Davis.*

When the series left the air for the final time on September 26, 1955, announcer Harry Kramer — the last in a long line of well-seasoned, velvet-throated interlocutors—casually allowed: "This concludes our present *Mr. Keen* series." There was no mention that, after 18 years, this durable drama, closely charted by a loyal audience still estimated in the millions, might never return. The faithful would discover the finality of that last pronouncement in the months to follow.

The indomitable Frank and Anne Hummert, who at times evidenced a spirit of eternal optimism, hoped — and perhaps even anticipated — that a miracle might occur as *Mr. Keen* and other features of their radio dynasty left the air. Would their cancelled series ever return to enjoy extended lives in the hereafter? Unfortunately, they would not. As the fortunes of radio steadily ebbed, for *Mr. Keen, Tracer of Lost Persons,* this time there would be no reprise. The chaser of homicidal maniacs, who had intrigued multitudes for so many years, had finally solved his last case.

5

Funny Business

Despite the fact that there was little opportunity for levity in the crimefighting era of *Mr. Keen, Tracer of Lost Persons*, it's been duly noted that lighter moments—intentional or otherwise—crept into the plotting of the drama's storyline. The kindly old investigator realized not only the professional esteem that came with being an astute sage, he also appeared to relish whatever stature he earned as an aging, well-heeled bachelor, particularly during the first half-dozen years. His winsome spirit permitted him, on occasion, to hobnob socially with some of those early clients. Laughter was a natural by-product, and often was in at least moderate supply.

There were also plenty of times (several have been cited) when the program's action or dialogue dipped towards the ludicrous. Such occasions were usually a result of improbable situations or conversations that actually made very little sense and *Mr. Keen*'s critics had a field day with these, ridiculing their absurdity. Such lapses may have resulted from slipshod, fall-through-the-crack methods that the producers relied upon as they employed mass assembly-line production techniques. Regrettably, whenever quality could be sacrificed to hold expenses to a minimum, it was. The results were sometimes unintentionally hilarious.

Without taking anything away from the mystery's gratifying characteristics as a charismatic diversionary amusement, it can be freely admitted that the series unabashedly embraced the daytime melodrama that was hatched in the same shop. While *Mr. Keen* was never intended to be a comedic feature, at times it came off that way.

One of those infamous Frank and Anne Hummert dictates that regularly cascaded down from on high was that the audience must know at all times who was speaking and to whom. There could never be any hesitancy, no indecisiveness, no ambiguity about that. All of their programs—daytime *and* nighttime—featured annoyingly inane duplication as personal identifications resounded ad infinitum. A fictitious character named Ernest Green might, for example, state something like the following, emblematic of the dialogue on any Hummert series:

"Mr. Keen, my brother-in-law Peter Dowling was a very poor businessman. He kept Martha Green, my wife, in the dark about his financial dealings, even though he controlled interests that were of benefit not only to himself but to Martha and his brother, Richard Dowling."

Mr. Keen might respond: "Well, Ernest Green, your observations are most intriguing. I will ask my partner here, Mike Clancy, to look into the public records of your brother-in-law Peter Dowling and determine just how his business was being conducted."

To which the suspect might retort: "Thank you, Mr. Keen. I'm sure Richard Dowling, who is also my brother-in-law, and my wife, Martha, will be grateful to you."

Laughable? Without a doubt. If there was ever a moment's hesitation about who was speaking and who was being spoken to in a Hummert drama, somebody was asleep at the switch. Making sure this occurred was one of the notorious mandated duties assigned to the program directors. If such clichéd conversations were missed in the scripting and editing stages, a director could catch hell if the repetitious name-identification didn't get on the air.

To this day, there are still those who lambaste the show, claiming it was never on a par with its contemporaries. But beauty is in the eye of the beholder. No gumshoe was everybody's cup of tea. *Mr. Keen* brought hours of chilling fables to the ether and mesmerized audiences as he did so. The fact that we can still poke fun at it probably suggests it must have succeeded at something, even in the face of blatantly hackneyed dialogue.

Keen's demeanor turned into a vigilant, determined, pitiless stalker of murderers during the drama's last dozen years, diminishing most of the opportunities for levity. Yet there was at least one anticipated chance every week. In fact, it caused some of the die-hard fans to snicker to themselves and maybe even chuckle out loud, especially as others gathered around their radios to tune in alongside them.

As previously noted, Mr. Keen had an "assistant" in the early years who was later acknowledged as his "partner." Mike Clancy was an Irishman who spoke blarney with such an arrant Irish accent that you'd suspect he just got off the ship from Dublin. His dialect was in such marked contrast to Mr. Keen's and those actors in supporting roles that there could never be any doubt about who was speaking when you heard *him*!

That wasn't the biggest giveaway, however. It was the stuff he *said* that made it all so funny. In his most telling line, usually delivered just after the tracer exposed a killer, he'd exclaim: "Saints preserve us, Mr. Keen! He's got a gun!" Every time, his surprised cadence implied that this was a simply outrageous possibility, and one strikingly unexpected.

Clancy worked that "Saints preserve us" phrase to death. It turned up once, twice or thrice in every sequence. When an acquaintance of the deceased called at the office to enlist Mr. Keen's help in an investigation, the visitor might state innocently enough, "I came to report a murder." "A *murder*? Saints preserve us!" Clancy would bellow as an instant rejoinder. If you thought about it, that was absolutely hilarious, because investigating homicides was what he did for a living. It was as if, for the moment, he had sustained a temporary loss of memory.

As one might imagine, the pundits gleefully seized upon Clancy, suggesting he was placed in the storyline merely to relieve the tension and provide someone for Mr. Keen to banter with. While that could be true, a frail Keen habitually called upon the Irishman's brawn to restrain a just-revealed murderer.

A prominent radio historiographer explained that producers Frank and Anne Hummert maintained a penchant for saddling their private detectives with "dumber-than-thou assistants," of which Mike Clancy was a prime example.[1] "It was a trick dating back to Sherlock Holmes and Watson, perhaps beyond — that of giving the brilliant hero a none-too-bright sidekick to ask the dumb questions and make sure the

"This appears to be a weapon," Philip Clarke (Mr. Keen) seems to be telling his partner, Mike Clancy (portrayed by Jim Kelly), who undoubtedly will exclaim: "Saints preserve us! *It is!*" Clancy comes across as a bone-headed buffoon in the narratives of *Mr. Keen, Tracer of Lost Persons*. This was to allow the hero to shine by comparison. As a result, Clancy became the focus of derision leveled by critics of the series. (*Photofest*)

Great One had plugged all the holes," the critic averred.[2]

"Clancy was incredible," he observed. "'Saints preserve us, Mr. Keen, do you mean ... ?' he said, week after week. Ever the patient and kindly investigator, Mr. Keen replied sagely, 'Yes, Mike,' as though explaining the facts of life to his small child."[3] Maybe facetiously, this critic added: "One of the great portraits in the Radio Hall of Fame is of Mike Clancy — mouth open, scratching his head."[4]

Another old time radio enthusiast, pondering this unwavering figure, offered a discerning analyisis:

Mike Clancy may have felt like he was doing brain surgery on his brother when he sliced into his evening turnip, but he could be sure he was performing the rightful role of sidekick by being dumber than his kindly old boss.... Sidekicks are there to be explained to, never to explain. That's not such a bad job. I think Mike Clancy should be viewed as one of nature's stumbles; he was meant to be an Irish setter and came out as an Irish sap. I, for one, envy Mike the spiritual epiphany that put him in touch with his inner dog.[5]

While the role of Mike Clancy may not have been played for laughs, it surely came off that way in many episodes.

Two who chided *Mr. Keen* openly, and entertained millions of delighted followers with their biting satire, were radio comedians Bob (Elliott, left) and Ray (Goulding). Their parodies of the drama, under the titles "Mr. Treat, Chaser of Lost Persons" and "Mr. Trace, Keener Than Most Persons," were classic examples of clever humor that kept audiences coming back for more. *Mr. Keen, Tracer of Lost Persons* was but one of many radio features the duo lampooned. (*Photofest*)

Another aspect regarding *Mr. Keen* definitely *was* staged for laughs. And it achieved rollicking success, then and now (through surviving audio recordings). It involved a pair of unparalleled golden age radio comedians, Bob (Elliott) and Ray (Goulding). Their creative minds brought many voices to the microphone that netted instant and vociferous belly laughs.

Bob and Ray's specialized brand of unique humor included a long line of imitations. Together they parodied performers like Arthur Godfrey and repeatedly offered takeoffs on many popular radio series. Among their most requested vignettes were "Mary Backstayge, Noble Wife," "One Fella's Family," "Aunt Penny's Sunlit Kitchen," "Mister Science," "King Yukon of the Northwest," "Jack Armstrong, the All-American American" and "Our Fella Thursday."

They must have found that melodrama was easy to do because they performed so much of it. And one of their favorites—and that of their radio audiences—was a couple of recurring satirical diatribes based on *Mr. Keen* (played by Bob Elliott). At alternate times Bob and Ray labeled them "Mr. Treat, Chaser of Lost Persons" and "Mr. Trace, Keener Than Most Persons," with their humorous exchanges prefaced by a few bars of "Someday I'll Find You." As with almost any Bob and Ray creation, their mischievous repartee struck America's funnybone, this time at the private detective's expense—referred to in their jesting as "the surly old investigator."

For his part, Mike Clancy was teased to the hilt. In the Bob and Ray parodies he was renamed Spike Delancy, but there was never any doubt which character was being portrayed. Recall that Clancy often referred to his brilliant pal as "boss" on the genuine *Keen* series. On Bob and Ray's audio snippets, Ray Goulding grossly exaggerated the Irish brogue (and everything else). The bumbling chump repeatedly called his friend "*Buyce*," adding a sort of hissing echo to the appellation. Since it was all played for laughs, it really didn't make any difference whether he actually got it right. He also prefaced nearly every statement he made with "Saints preserve us, Buyce …" which would ratchet up the hilarity a few notches.

In one of the faux Keen's typical cases, "The Peg Leg Man Murder Clue," listeners heard the thump, thump, thump of the peg leg's approach as the man entered the offices of Keen and Delancy. The inspired duo made marvelous applications of sound effects to support their aural escapades.

"The Overdose of Very Fatal Poison Murder Clue," another classic sketch, opened in the luxurious New York penthouse apartment of wealthy Jacobus Pike, "famous backer of Broadway plays." (Daytime Hummert followers instantly recognized the reference to *Backstage Wife*, in which characters with similar names, relationships and responsibilities were then involved in a like imbroglio.)

Pike gave instructions to his valet: "Rudy, I want you to take this manuscript back to Greg Marlowe, the young playwright who's secretly in love with my sister Julia, who dreams of a career on the stage. There's a note inside which will explain my reasons for failing to back his play on Broadway."

After the valet departed, listeners overheard Pike mumbling to himself: "That young upstart thinks he can coerce me into putting up my money for any such ridiculous play as that—well, he's got another thing—what? How did *you* get in here? What do you want? No! No! Don't shoot me with that gun you're holding! I'll do anything! Don't come any closer! No! No! [*Sound of shots fired*] Ooooooh! You've murdered me!" [*Sound of body falling lingering a trifle too long*]

The scene shifted to Mr. Treat's office, where Spike Delancy ushered in a caller to his "Buyce," who explained to the surly old investigator: "Mr. Treat, I'm Gregory Marlowe, young playwright, secretly in love with wealthy Jacobus Pike's sister, Julia, who dreams of a career on the stage." He enlisted Treat's help, and the interrogation of witnesses ensued, leading to a farfetched, side-splitting conclusion.

Bob and Ray began their career as two staffers at a Boston radio station in the mid–1940s. Each went there to do something other than comedy, but in between shows they clowned around. Their inventive minds created a humorous duo that quickly earned favorable acclaim, landing them jobs in front of the microphones of the national radio chains in New York City in the 1950s. Their take-offs on *Mr. Keen* were among a surfeit of hilarious and memorable exchanges in two widely celebrated careers.

Mr. Keen, Tracer of Lost Persons began as a well-intended melodramatic series. In time, it evolved into a show about grisly murders investigated by a gruesome twosome who pursued their mission with absolute gravity. Somewhere along the way, however, it probably occurred to *Mr. Keen*'s legion of loyal listeners that their beloved progam contained numerous nonsensical—yet refreshing—elements, which elicited a knowing smile from the most rabid fanatic, if not an outright guffaw. It was often simply too much to be believed, and a titter was a logical response when unanswered questions and awkward circumstances were left to one's imagination. Frequently it simply dissolved into unintentionally funny business—and certainly that characterized one of the more compelling attractions of the show.

6

Hired Guns

The professionals who made up the Mr. Keen company—the writers, leads and (often recurring) supporting actors, announcers and musicians—were, for the most part, freelance artists. Sound technicians and engineers, on the other hand, were employed directly by the networks. (The national chains frowned upon their employees fraternizing with the artists supplied by the various agencies to fill their program time.[1])

The drama's producers, Frank and Anne Hummert, approved some of those freelancers for longterm service. The support roles were normally filled by seasoned thespians who were routinely selected by the program directors because of their ability, versatility and experience. In that way the Hummert regime—ever mindful of spiraling costs—saved money by holding the number of rehearsal hours to absolute minimums.

The Hummerts' organization (which went under the corporate moniker Air Features, Incorporated, or AFI) was well known within the industry for practicing a bare-bones approach to broadcasting. Whereas, for instance, some other producers' soap opera rehearsals were allotted as much as 90 minutes for a single quarter-hour episode, a Hummert serial *never* allowed more than 60 minutes of rehearsal time. And in the early days they were held to no more than 45 minutes. Such cardinal rules were never to be violated, for one simple reason: more hours spent in rehearsals incurred more out-of-pocket expenses.

The directors of *Mr. Keen* and many other Hummert features were not, themselves, bona fide freelancers, but agency staff. While they could never be considered members of any type of "inner circle"—for, indeed, none existed at AFI—they functioned to a large degree as emissaries. Among their tasks, these "on-duty managers" represented their normally absentee bosses by relaying instructions and implementing missives from the Hummerts' ivory tower. Despite such an inauspicious posture, the AFI contingent at that level could easily be considered among radio's most able directors.

Mr. Keen, Tracer of Lost Persons tended to keep its program leadership employed for long stretches. In fact, the 18-year run was overseen by only three directors. Each one excelled in a specific segment (format or time frame) of the long-lasting series.

As the drama began, Martha Atwell supervised those quarter-hour serialized features from 1937 to 1943. Richard Leonard was head honcho over the 25- and 30-minute mysteries between 1943 and 1955.

57

Edward Slattery directed most of the concurrently running weeknight installments in 1954–1955. Together this triumvirate shepherded virtually all of the 1690 *Mr. Keen* performances, likely achieving some type of record in the annals of radio broadcasting history.

Martha Atwell earned a reputation as one of the industry's most precise, unyielding and—according to some reactionaries—*feared* professionals. While soap opera heroine Mary Jane Higby found her to be a kind, gentle, warmhearted person, in her memoirs she observed that Atwell maintained "the stoniest face I had ever seen. She smiled rarely, and when she did it always seemed ... the smile of someone whose feet hurt."[2] George Ansbro, who announced long runs of several serials that Atwell directed, and who read cowcatcher (at a program's start) and hitchhike (at a program's end) commercials on many *Mr. Keen* shows, claimed her as a close friend, insisting, "Working with her was a delightful experience."[3]

Atwell, whose loyalty and shrewd business sense gained her respect and tenure in the Hummert organization, saw her stock rise as she implemented orders with a precision and style that gratified her employers. They rewarded her with several lengthy runs as director of some of their most venerated drainboard dramas: *Chaplain Jim U.S.A.*, *David Harum*, *Just Plain Bill*, *Lora Lawton*, *Mrs. Wiggs of the Cabbage Patch* and *Young Widder Brown*. After sundown she directed their *Mystery Theater*. Furthermore, she presided over a trio of syndicated washboard weepers beyond Air Features' reach: *The Editor's Daughter*, *Hearts in Harmony* and *Linda's First Love*.

While Atwell certainly could be kind, she was also resolute, especially on certain topics. For example, as noted earlier, if an actor appearing on one program expected to arrive late at a second, subsequent show's rehearsal, or to miss it altogether (known in the industry as a "conflict"), he might pay another to stand in (say his lines for him) until he could personally arrive at the studio. The one paying the fee anticipated being there for the actual performance, of course. While it was tradition in many camps for directors to approve of using substitutes in advance, Atwell was the *one* AFI official "whom I would never have dared ask for a conflict," recalled actress Mary Jane Higby.[4] There was no need to approach the all-business, stopwatch-toting director with such a request for it simply wouldn't have been granted.

While not much is known of Atwell's personal life, the smartly attired spinster was plainly depicted in the pages of Robert Hardy Andrew's novel *Legend of a Lady*, a fictional account of the life of Anne Hummert. On December 28, 1949, Atwell's secretary, Frances Von Bernhardt, and a physician who had been treating her for a recent illness, found her partially-submerged, negligee-clad body in a bathtub at Atwell's apartment at 65 East Fifty-Fifth Street in New York.[5] It was later determined that she had taken her own life.[6] Her unexpected death at age 49 sent shock waves rippling among her contemporaries.

The date Atwell began directing *Mr. Keen* cannot be verified with authenticity because, until the 206th episode (which occurred on February 1, 1939), the names of the cast members weren't printed on the Dramatic Flyleafs (cover pages) of *Mr. Keen* scripts. It's reasonable to assume that Atwell directed the very first broadcast on October 12, 1937. Without positive documentation, however, it can't be substantiated. She continued in that capacity—with exceedingly rare absences—through the 960 episodes that comprised *Keen*'s initial serialized run, ending with the broadcast of November 26, 1943.

The half-hour complete dramas then

ensued, starting December 2, 1943. Because no scripts of the first 41 longer shows have surfaced, to date it's uncertain when Richard Leonard replaced Martha Atwell as director. He was in that role early in 1944, to be sure, for tape recordings of the series acknowledge it. This would intimate that he likely took over the responsibility when the program switched from a quarter-hour to half-hour format in late 1943.

Leonard directed the longer features through the end of the run, culminating on September 26, 1955. The Hummerts utilized his talents still further by having him edit all of the *Mr. Keen* scripts submitted by the show's writers (including the weekly dramas as well as the weeknight broadcasts when that format was launched in 1954). Leonard continued to perform this extra task regularly, with the brief exception of a notable span in 1951–1952. At that juncture Frank Hummert took an active interest in approving (and even writing some of) the scripts.

The Hummerts obviously found Richard Leonard to their liking, or he wouldn't have prospered as well and as long as he did. They gave him many key assignments apart from *Mr. Keen*. At one time or other he also directed *Backstage Wife, Chaplain Jim U.S.A., Front Page Farrell, Mr. Chameleon, The Romance of Helen Trent, Stella Dallas* and *Young Widder Brown* for Air Features. He took over *Brown*, incidentally, upon the untimely demise of Martha Atwell.

In the mid–1940s Leonard penned the dialogue for another producer's soap opera, *Barry Cameron* (aka *The Soldier Who Came Home*). He was the final director for *Ma Perkins* when that hallowed drama finally left the air on November 25, 1960, generally considered by most vintage ether historians as "the day radio drama died." Furthermore, he produced the broadcasts of the NBC Symphony Orchestra conducted by Arturo Toscanini for a spell. To put it mildly, this well-rounded executive was certainly a busy boy.

Although Leonard could be considered a company man, he differed from Martha Atwell in at least one respect. While Atwell refused to grant a "conflict" status on the programs she directed, Leonard habitually approved actors' replacements for the rehearsals he supervised. The practice continued at least until radio's audiences began draining into TV like a sieve, resulting in exposed nerves in the aural medium. The fact that such consideration was granted perhaps indicated a more tolerant and casual approach on Leonard's part toward the people with whom he associated.

Little has been preserved about the career of Edward Slattery, who supervised the *Keen* quarter-hours that aired five nights a week late in the run. Slattery served in a similar capacity on two Hummert daytime serials, *Front Page Farrell* and *Young Widder Brown* (completing the trilogy of directors who served both *Brown* and *Keen*).

A myriad of wordsmiths freelanced under the Air Features umbrella while penning *Keen*'s scripts. (Their names are supplied alongside the broadcast data in the Appendix.) A handful sustained lengthy runs in writing the dialogue and action for the kindly old tracer. They included (with some of their other radio writing credits appearing in parentheses): Barbara Bates (*Just Plain Bill*), Marie Baumer (*Mr. Chameleon*), Stedman Coles (*Famous Jury Trials, Roger Kilgore—Public Defender, The Shadow*), David Davidson (*Aunt Jenny's Real Life Stories, Believe It or Not, Society Girl*), Jerome Ross (*Society Girl*) and Robert J. Shaw (*The Adventures of Christopher Wells, Mr. District Attorney, The Lone Ranger, Philo Vance*).

Without qualification, the name of Lawrence M. (Larry) Klee remains far better recognized among *Mr. Keen* fans than any of the others. The durable scribe penned the dialogue during the narrative's halcyon days, when the program sustained its largest audiences. He also wrote far more chapters than any other individual. Larry Klee offers an interesting character study all by himself.

Born in Manhattan, New York, on July 24, 1914, Klee was educated at the University of Wisconsin before enrolling for pre-med study at the University of Alabama. The son of a vaudevillian, Mel Klee, the lad joined his dad's act at age 10, and traipsed across the nation trading jokes with his pa and dancing the Charleston. Later, in medical school, when the fondness for greasepaint and stage lights tugged a tad too fiercely (and after he had gained notoriety producing a campus revue that was banned by Alabama's dean of women), Klee returned to show business.

He applied some reticent literary skills to gag writing for comedian Jack Gilford. But when he transferred that talent to radio serials, he hit his stride. Within a few years he was churning out scripts for *Aunt Jenny's Real Life Stories*, *Backstage Wife*, *Chaplain Jim U.S.A.*, *Front Page Farrell*, *Hearts in Harmony*, *The Romance of Helen Trent*, *Stella Dallas*, *Valiant Lady* and *Young Widder Brown*—with most of those washboard weepers produced by Air Features. The Hummerts were so impressed by his ability that they assigned him to troubleshoot on a number of their dramatic series. As a script doctor he improved the submissions of some other scribes, probably editing chiefly for clarity.

With a few serials under his belt, Klee branched out into mysteries, initially scripting *Mr. Keen, Tracer of Lost Persons*. That wouldn't be his last, however. Klee penned lengthy runs of *The Fat Man*, *Mr. and Mrs. North*, *The Clock* and several plays for *Mystery Theater*. He originated the premise of *The Line-Up*, although he never authored its scripts. (The series appeared on CBS Radio from 1950 to 1953 and on CBS-TV from 1954 to 1960.) He dialogued a dramatic adventure anthology, *The Chase*. He also gained some personal acclaim with a feature-length documentary film on the life of Franklin D. Roosevelt. *The Roosevelt Story* played in cinema houses around the globe, in fact. For his patriotic contributions, both the U. S. War and Treasury departments honored the fertile author.

By 1943 Klee was among radio's highest paid dramatic wordsmiths. At that point he collected $250 from World Broadcasting System for five *Hearts in Harmony* scripts weekly, plus $150 from the NBC Blue network for a half-hour *Chaplain Jim U.S.A.* script every week, and another $175 from AFI for three episodes of *Mr. Keen, Tracer of Lost Persons* per week.[7] If he wrote nothing else, his income would have approached $30,000 annually, a tidy sum for a freelancing scribe during the war years.

But things picked up. In early 1948 he signed a new contract with AFI that paid him $250 per half-hour episode of *Mr. Keen*. A key clause in that contract proved emblematic of what AFI required of its literary suppliers:

> As an integral part of this agreement, I [the writer] assign to you, exclusively, all right, title and interest that I may have in and to the scripts, story, future plot development, and all revisions thereof, including the right to edit, broadcast, televise, publish and copyright the same in your name throughout the world.

In doing so, Klee relinquished ownership to everything he wrote for AFI. In mid–1949 he signed with the William Esty Company for an added $1,000 a week. It encompassed 52 dramatic episodes of a premiering live simulcast radio–TV series, to star actor Ralph Bellamy, called *Man Against Crime*. Klee's 23-page contract included escalation clauses increasing his compensation to $1,500 weekly within four years. It was obvious he was an above-average wage earner, an indication of both his knack and resolve.

In a 1950 newspaper interview, Klee offered some fascinating personal perspectives into writing for a fictional broadcast detective:

> All murderers can be divided into three classifications by their motives: profit, passion, psychological. The problem is to find a novel way to murder in a new and unusual setting, which can be adequately represented in half an hour....
>
> If you do a regular show, you should try to arrange the sex of the murderer and the victim so that you don't get into too much of a rut. Often I've bet hundreds of dollars that no one could point out a type of murder that I hadn't committed through various characters on shows I have written. So far I haven't lost a bet... .
>
> The two questions most writers hear: How do you get your ideas? How far ahead are you?
>
> My answer to the first is, "Banging my head against the wall," which is literally true. To the second question the answer is, "I'm usually two or three weeks ahead."
>
> Often I sit for hours in front of the typewriter just thinking. I never get ideas from the newspapers. I don't believe that truth is stranger than fiction. Fiction may be different, but after turning out more than 5000 scripts, I know that truth doesn't offer much in the way of inspiration.

Klee married former stage and screen actress Jane Weldon, who retired from professional life to become a homemaker and mother. The couple had a daughter, Margaret, and a son, Paul, and lived in comfortable digs just outside Westport, Connecticut. Larry and Jane Klee toured the world for a couple of months every summer, visiting exotic locales in Europe, the Caribbean and South America.

A chain-smoking workaholic, Klee suffered a heart attack in 1953, and doctors assessed that he probably had less than a year to live. According to his daughter, he didn't alter his lifestyle. On New Year's Day 1957, at the age of 42, a second heart attack proved fatal. By then, *Mr. Keen*'s durable run had ended a mere 15 months earlier. And *Man Against Crime* had left the small screen on August 26, 1956 (having gone to film in 1952, it was syndicated under the banner *Follow That Man* for several more years).

Margaret Klee Lichtenberg and Paul Klee, the facile writer's offspring, ages 15 and 12 respectively when their dauntless father died, provided distinctive views of their lives while growing up in the Klee household.

Their pop's preoccupation with "thinking up the next episode of the next script" gave Margaret limited accessibility to her well-known dad.[8] "Talking to him when he came downstairs to take a break out of a seven- to eight-hour day didn't particularly seem an option," she remembers. There was a period when her parents spent three days every week in New York. She also recalls those two-month excursions her parents took every summer, although the family seldom vacationed together.

Starting as preschoolers, the children were dispatched to summer camp. At one point the family lived in Europe and the children went away to a Swiss boarding school. "We didn't have much of a connected family life while my father was alive," Margaret recalls, "so when he checked out, I was left feeling deeply saddened and truly gypped out of a father."

Their mother lived for three decades beyond their dad's death. "The regret is never having known this amazing man as an adult," Margaret reflects.

Paul F. Klee views the situation a little differently. Acknowledging that the siblings spent long periods away from home, resulting in homesickness, he suggests: "Overall, I never felt cheated of my father. He was, to be sure, extremely strict about his work time. We were never allowed into

Shown with his young daughter Margaret in 1951, Lawrence M. (Larry) Klee possessed one of the most fertile pens in the writing stable of producers Frank and Anne Hummert. For many years he authored *Mr. Keen, Tracer of Lost Persons*. While exceptionally gifted, the prolific Klee labored under managerial constraints that inhibited a writer's ability to create enhanced literary product. A workaholic, he died of a heart attack at age 42. (*Photo courtesy of Margaret Klee Lichtenberg*)

his study while he was working, nor could we disturb him. But his office was his office, and most children's fathers were commuting to— and working in — the city. It would be unfair to suggest he hadn't time for us because he spent long hours in his office."9

The younger Klee fondly recalls his father playing catch with him, and their many conversations about baseball as they compared their own boyhood heroes. Klee believes the exceptionally close ties between his parents naturally reduced the focus the youngsters might have otherwise anticipated. "So, if there was a lack of attention, I'm not sure that one can attribute it solely to workaholic tendencies," he surmises.

While he was too young to appreciate most of his dad's radio contributions, Paul Klee recalled sitting in the family living room in front of a Zenith console as they listened to *Mr. Keen, Tracer of Lost Persons* together. "In fact, that is the only program I actually do recall hearing," he states, "possibly because my father was especially proud of that one. My mother said it was his favorite."

As previously indicated, the Hummerts appeared genuinely pleased with Larry Klee and his contributions. Some inter-office memos and other correspondence in the permanent file offer astute perceptions on how they appraised him and his work at varying points, while simultaneously offering additional insights into the massive Hummert operation itself. In a memorandum dated December 31, 1945, to Maurice (Mickey) Scopp — one of their most trusted confidantes (who appeared to be temporarily in command on those fleeting occasions when the Hummerts were away) — Anne Hummert wrote:

Mr. Klee has finished writing BACKSTAGE WIFE scripts through January 15th and will mail them today, so that we can expect to receive them on Wednesday.

He has asked to have relief from writing a 5-times-a-week serial for the present, and will continue to write just MR. KEEN and CHAPLAIN JIM.

When Mr. Klee returns from his vacation in Cuba which, as I understand it, will be in about three weeks from now, he then wishes to let about six weeks elapse before he takes on any other work.

I have had a long talk with Mr. Klee and have told him that whenever he wants to do more work, he should let us know and that we shall do everything within our power to provide it for him instantly. For instance, he has said that it might be possible for him to write — every so often — a three-week case for FRONT PAGE FARRELL. This would be ideal for the show.

In the memo, Anne Hummert then turns her attention to the writing of several other programs, and who will be responsible for them at specific intervals. She ends with a statement that dialoguer Nancy Moore "should not be used on MR. KEEN, because Mr. Klee will now have more time to give us more KEEN scripts."

In a letter to Klee dated February 6, 1951, Richard Leonard, longtime director of *Mr. Keen*, was cautionary, representative of the communications he likely was instructed to relay:

Mrs. Hummert has asked me to pass on to you the following request: She and Mr. Hummert feel that we should be careful in the future not to have stories built around ideas that are difficult for the audience to visualize, and therefore need a lot of explaining. Particularly, she had in mind, scripts recently about a voodoo doll, a gorilla and a Swiss clock.

Our experience in the past has been that many listeners are confused, and we are apt to lose part of our audience when this happens. It seems to be best when we stick to our tried and true formula, without involving strange places and things in the plot.

Such "requests" became even more pointed when the ratings began to dip. On

July 17, 1953, an inter-office memo from the Hummerts (most likely composed by Anne) to Richard Leonard gives the impression that panic has started to set in:

> This concerns our conversation of this morning.
>
> We are very much alarmed by the drop in rating on MR. KEEN. The last rating shows that it controlled only 18.8% of the audience. Ordinarily MR. KEEN controls well over 30% of the audience.
>
> For that reason, we are returning the script "The Poison Pen Letter Murder Case" which we think requires re-writing in order to hold and build an audience.
>
> This script does not sound like Larry Klee for it lacks so many of the elements he usually puts into KEEN and which have gone to make it a success.
>
> We have felt that ever so often recently the scripts have tended to be static, with none of the color, movement and switches and surprises usually in KEEN. The result is that one usually knows who the killer is going to be from the start.
>
> In order for Larry to know what is wanted it is probably best to give him two examples from the past, which he has written, and which can serve as the best type guide we know of for him.
>
> We suggest that you send him the scripts which we repeated and recorded for August 7th and 14th. He wrote both of them and he will quickly see how *different* they are.
>
> As you know, the flash-back has been used very effectively on KEEN from time to time but recently we think it has been overused and it can be very confusing at times.
>
> Here are some suggestions we make to add interest and suspense to "The Poison Pen Letter Murder Case"—
>
> When young Irene Torrence comes to Mr. Keen, she not only tells him that the police are looking for Helen Prentiss as the writer of the poison pen letter found beside her mother's body but she also tells Mr. Keen in terror and dread that she is fearful her husband may have written the poisonous letter, the letter of threat to her mother following an argument in which she wouldn't give him money. She has not told this to the police. She adores her husband. She was a devoted daughter to her mother—can Mr. Keen please pull her out. This immediately adds new interest as you can see.

Lest the reader be persuaded that the Hummerts turned their once cordial relationship with Larry Klee into one of less tolerance, it should be pointed out that as the 1950s advanced, and advertisers and audiences switched their loyalties from radio to television, these aural-only producers witnessed their livelihood (and fiefdom) evaporating. An examination of the correspondence file concerning other Hummert-produced series clearly suggests that Larry Klee wasn't singled out for reprimand. All AFI writers—in fact, probably all who labored for that shop in any way— began to feel colossal pressure to perform to the very utmost of their abilities. After all, the empire's foundation was under siege. Its erosion would mean the loss of jobs for everybody, not just for the founding father and mother.

Over an 18-year run, only two actors portrayed Mr. Keen on a permanent basis, William Bennett Kilpack and Philip Clarke. Coincidentally, both of these leads were native Brits. A third thespian, Arthur Hughes, also filled the part on several occasions as situations warranted.

Any longevity award for the role must unquestionably go to Kilpack, who in 13 years (1937–1950) appeared on roughly 1300 of the nearly 1700 broadcasts. Because the Hummerts were loath to acknowledge their underlings' contributions to their own success, nearly a decade elapsed before Kilpack heard his name credited on the air. "Bennett Kilpack plays Mr. Keen" was announced for the first time on the broadcast of March 27, 1947. He had played the part for 10 years.

Born a minister's son in 1883, Kilpack embraced the stage at an early age, going all the way back to the amateur plays he regularly performed in at school. He simply couldn't get enough of it. Because his father insisted, "a Kilpack as an actor is a Kilpack better dead," Bennett temporarily diverted his vocational ambitions, studying electrical engineering at the English Finsbury Technical College.[10] By 1908 he headed for America, intending to land a job in the field for which he had trained. But encountering a surplus of electrical engineers, he followed his heart into acting. His first part was as Cassio in William Shakespeare's *Othello*. He toured with Sir Philip Ben Greet's Shakespearean players—which brought him profound satisfaction—and won prominent roles in several Broadway plays, among them Cornelia Otis Skinner's *Kismet*. In 1927 he drifted into radio, taking the lead in a brief serial in 1931, *Wayside Inn*.

Kilpack flourished in several of the Hummerts' daytime properties—*Doc Barclay's Daughters* (1939–1940), where he played the lead, and in recurring roles on *Alias Jimmy Valentine, David Harum, Mrs. Wiggs of the Cabbage Patch* and *Young Widder Brown*. He was featured in the casts of other producers' series, too, including *Believe It or Not, The Goldbergs* and *Seth Parker*. Sporadically he turned up in one-shot parts on dramas like *Gangbusters, Grand Central Station* and *Great Plays*.

Kilpack's marked English dialect could be readily distinguished in the audio roles he portrayed. Having already noted the Irishman Mike Clancy's distinct contributions to *Mr. Keen*, Kilpack's accent added yet another dimension to the mix.

Possibly the best example was his pronunciation of *records*, a term he used often. When he said it, it invariably sounded like two very precise, very distinct words: *wreck-chords*. In a typical dialogue exchange with Clancy, he once instructed his partner: "Mike, check the trip *wreck-chords* of every taxi company in town."

In young adulthood, Kilpack's private life included behavior that would seem un-

William Bennett Kilpack (1883–1962) appeared roughly 1300 times in the lead role of *Mr. Keen, Tracer of Lost Persons* during the years 1937 to 1950. This minister's son, born in England, loved acting as a youth but had to come to America to develop it, initially on the stage and eventually in radio. His hobbies included gardening, woodworking and cooking. Married twice, Kilpack was plagued by illness during his final few years as Mr. Keen. (*Photofest*)

conscionable to "the kindly old tracer" for whom he was to be recalled. In April 1909, within a few months of his arrival in the United States, Kilpack married Mabel Alice Cromer in Boston. The couple never had children. Sixteen years later, in Paris, Mabel Kilpack sued her husband for divorce and was granted it on grounds of desertion.[11] In February 1924, Kilpack, then living at 132 East Nineteenth Street in New York, dispatched his spouse to the French capital, promising to join her there shortly. He never did, and she alleged that he left her for three months without sustenance and did not communicate with her. Had

Kilpack been playing "the kindly old tracer" at the time — the ultimate missing persons investigator — the tabloids would undoubtedly have had a field day!

Kilpack remained unattached for the next 15 years, indicating to any who hadn't known him in his pre-radio days that he closely paralleled the confirmed bachelor epitomized on *Mr. Keen*. In fact, he probably surprised many when, in September 1940, at age 57, he once again went to the altar.

This time he married a young widow whose son he readily adopted, legally changing the boy's name to John Kilpack. After living in a city apartment for a while, the family acquired a 150-acre farm in the Green Mountains of southern Vermont near the village of East Dover. There Kilpack raised a massive garden, growing most of the fruits and vegetables the family consumed. Dorothy, his wife, canned, preserved, dried and pickled the produce.

Possibly because he had lived alone for so long, Kilpack was something of a gourmet chef. His specialties were two: steaks broiled out of doors, soaked in soy sauce the night before, and ham spiked with cloves, coated with brown sugar, baked in wine and served with gravy made from a secret recipe that he refused to divulge. He also had an affinity for woodworking, undoubtedly a throwback to his earlier technical training.[12]

There was but one obstacle to the Kilpacks' dream home in Vermont, but it ultimately became decisive. With *Mr. Keen* airing on Thursday nights for much of its run, each Wednesday Kilpack took a five-hour trip by train to New York City, arriving in time for rehearsals at 5 P.M., then spending a night in a hotel. On Thursdays he usually tended to a myriad of appointments and obligations before the 6:30 P.M. final rehearsals. After dual live performances (there were two through July 12, 1951, one at 8:30 P.M. and a repeat for the West Coast audience at 11:30 P.M.— until recording the live show and playing it back later for the Pacific time zone was allowed), he'd board an overnight sleeper for the return trip by rail to Vermont.

It simply got to be too much too often.

After much heart-wrenching agonizing, in the late 1940s the Kilpacks sold their farm and moved to a fenced, wooded estate near Ridgefield, Connecticut. Its size occupied only about three percent of the land they left behind in the Green Mountain State, but the commute to New York was comparatively brief. Kilpack continued to garden extensively and to fiddle in his woodworking shop.

By mid–1946, busy radio thespian Arthur Hughes was being called upon with some frequency to substitute for Kilpack as Mr. Keen. The regular actor was more often than not out of the lineup due to unexplained illness, sometimes for weeks at a time. It was a pattern that was to plague him for much of the remainder of his tenure. Hughes filled in for Kilpack a combined 22 weeks: June 20, 1946, through July 18, 1946 (five weeks, due to illness); August 8, 1946, through September 19, 1946 (seven weeks, illness); September 25, 1947 (one week, illness); and February 19, 1948, through April 15, 1948 (nine weeks, reason unstated). On October 26, 1950, the program's 1314th show, Kilpack — then 67 — played for the very last time the part of Mr. Keen.

There is very clear evidence that he intended to return. The following week, announcer Larry Elliott broadcast: "We thank Phil Clarke for appearing tonight in the role of Mr. Keen for Bennett Kilpack, who was unable to appear." He echoed that statement for five consecutive weeks, in fact. Starting December 7, 1950, Bennett Kilpack's name was never mentioned again, only that "Philip Clarke plays Mr. Keen." Clarke remained with the program though its final broadcast on September 26, 1955.

Within a short time, the Kilpacks sold their Ridgefield estate, left the East Coast forever and settled in Westchester, California. Kilpack lived to August 18, 1962, succumbing to cancer at Berkshire Sanitarium in Santa Monica. He was 79.[13] John Kilpack, his adopted son, survived him.

What prompted Kilpack's abrupt and unexplained departure from the *Keen* cast? One theory, though unsubstantiated, is that he was ill. That is certainly logical, since he was "unable to appear" those last few weeks. Furthermore, the Hummerts may have had enough of the on-again, off-again uncertainty of it all — possibly even if their actor-hero had sufficiently recovered from a malady to be well enough to continue. In any case, it remains uncertain just what transpired as his long reign drew to a close.

Philip N. Clarke, a second Englishman, brought another distinct accent to the role of Mr. Keen. Though Clarke's dialect differed significantly from that of Kilpack's, Clarke's intonations were much nearer those of the originator than was Arthur Hughes', whose whiny, high-pitched nasal twang distinguished the small town barber *Just Plain Bill*, whom he played on radio for 23 years (1932–1955).

Not much is known about Clarke. Born in London on August 4, 1904, he was the scion of a famous theatrical family. In the late 1920s he spent several years in India as a lieutenant in the British Army. He was presented to American stage audiences in a biblical production arranged by Sir Philip Ben Greet, *Joseph and His Brethren*. (Recall that Bennett Kilpack had earlier toured with Greet's Shakespearean company, a striking coincidence.) Clarke later performed on Broadway in major roles in *Native Son* and *On Whitman Avenue*.

Clark moved to radio in 1937 and eventually appeared on more than 10,000 broadcasts, encompassing all four major

Philip N. Clarke (1904–1985) followed Bennett Kilpack in the namesake role of *Mr. Keen, Tracer of Lost Persons*, appearing in the part from 1950 through 1955. Like his predecessor, Clarke was of British origin. He fought in his nation's military operations before leaving his homeland to pursue an interest in theater in America. By 1937 he was working in radio, eventually appearing on at least 10,000 shows. (*Photofest*)

chains. He sustained recurring parts in *Against the Storm* and *The Light of the World* (the latter a Hummert property, in which he played Adam, the first man). He was the "keeper of the book," a croaking, cackling hermit-type in the brief 1940s series *The Sealed Book*. No other permanent roles have been documented.

Clarke was married and raised three daughters. He died in September 1985, date unknown.

Arthur Hughes was not only *Just Plain Bill* for almost 6000 episodes, but he played the leads in *Fu Manchu* and *The Orange Lantern*, too.[14] He won recurring roles in *I Love Linda Dale*, *Jungle Jim* and *Stella Dallas*, and steadily turned up in the dramatic companies of *The Collier Hour, East of Cairo* and *X-Minus One*.

If any actor in the Hummert employ had ever had any kind of inside track with those infamous producers, it would probably have been Hughes. When radio's golden days ended, the duo sold their showplace in Greenwich, Connecticut, and moved to a posh apartment overlooking New York's Central Park. Arthur and Geneva (Harrison) Hughes (she was a former Broadway actress) resided nearby. The couples fraternized socially on several occasions, and the remaining trio remained in cordial contact following Frank Hummert's death in 1966. While it was never recorded that Hughes was the producers' preferred thespian, some industry insiders perceived it as such.

Born in Bloomington, Illinois, on June 14, 1893, Hughes' acting career was launched when he was only seven. A stage manager and family friend took him to the theater to perform in kids' roles. The bug bit him early and hard. Eventually he distinguished himself in Broadway productions like *Elizabeth the Queen, Golden Boy, Idiot's Delight* and *Mourning Becomes Elektra*.

Hughes was considered by radio colleagues to be "an actor's actor." He would take his script, mark his lines in red pencil and go off to a corner by himself to memorize those lines before airtime. When radio work ended, he continued his acting career, amusing audiences with his portrayal of an eccentric millionaire in the 1968 Broadway hit musical *How Now Dow Jones?* The accomplished thespian died at age 89 in New York City on December 28, 1982. A half-century had elapsed since he inaugurated his fabled role as the barber of Hartville.

If there is a certified unfortunate in the *Keen* milieu — one who seemed predestined to be denied his just due — it was James Kelly. For his 18-year run as Mike Clancy — making him the only person, aside from the show's producers, to remain with it from start to finish — about the only time Kelly heard his name read over the air was when he was absent. On those rare occasions, with the disparity in dialects so noticeable between himself and the actor who substituted for him, the announcer advised: "We wish to think Joe Blow [or whomever] for appearing as Mike Clancy in the absence of James Kelly."

And if that ill fortune wasn't enough, radio historians weren't particularly kind to the Irishman, either, failing to maintain much in the way of biographical details about him. Saints preserve us! The only other ongoing roles he is known to have held were in a couple of Hummert dishpan dramas, *David Harum* and the short-lived *Nona from Nowhere*. Regrettably, no other information on his professional or personal life appears to have survived.

One other character made a sustained, important contribution to the show's narrative during *Mr. Keen*'s formative years— Miss Maisie Ellis, the investigator's private secretary. Actress Florence Malone assumed the role of Keen's near-constant companion. Malone was active in several other radio series, including *The Adventures of Captain Diamond, Against the Storm, Amanda of Honeymoon Hill, Betty and Bob, By Kathleen Norris, Pretty Kitty Kelly, The Singing Story Lady, The Story of Bess Johnson* and *Young Widder Brown*. Among the drainboard dramas, *Amanda, Betty and Bob* and *Brown* were AFI productions. Malone also performed with acting companies on several other features, including *Great Plays* and *Wheatena Playhouse*. While her part on *Mr. Keen* ended by the mid–1940s, Malone lived until March 4, 1956, five months after the series left the air for the last time.

A large contingent of radio thespians filled the supporting roles on *Mr. Keen, Tracer of Lost Persons*. Some of those individuals appeared in the cast only once, while others turned up routinely. A company of seasoned actors was readily available for summoning to auditions called by the program directors. Many of them appeared sporadically on a myriad of other Hummert dramatic features.

It wasn't out of the ordinary, as a result, for some of those same people to be tapped week after week, month after month, year after year for Air Features series. Most of them intermingled throughout the day on various soap operas, then returned after sundown to the microphones for one-time parts in mystery dramas. Ardent fans could easily discern some of the more distinctive tongues they normally heard elsewhere when those voices appeared on *Mr. Keen*. They frequently included Charita Bauer, Anne Burr, Helen Claire, Toni Darnay, Anne Elstner, Florence Freeman, Mary Jane Higby, James Meighan, Jan Miner, Vivian Smolen, Guy Sorel, Julie Stevens, Lucille Wall, Gertrude Warner, Karl Weber, Ned Wever and many more.

Wever is representative of the actors whose careers spanned both daytime and nighttime dramatic series. For 17 years he portrayed the number one suitor of the beleaguered heroine of AFI's melodramatic malaise that was *Young Widder Brown*. The story of how he acquired that role, which he delighted in repeating, is a classic.

Clayton (Bud) Collyer, radio's *Superman*—who also appeared on numerous daytime serials as an actor or announcer, and who was destined to be a stunt and panel show host in the early days of TV (*Break the Bank, Beat the Clock, Feather Your Nest, To Tell the Truth*, et al.)—was Ellen Brown's beau when the soap opera debuted in 1938. Collyer appeared in the role of physician Peter Turner.

One of the inviolable laws in the Hummert canon was that there could never be any hanky-panky, or even a hint of anything immodest or improper, between genders on their shows. (When Helen Trent accepted one of her many suitors' marriage proposals, for instance, she sternly admonished: "Just because we're engaged doesn't give you the right to hold my hand!") With such unmistakable puritanical directives, one would assume no accidents could possibly occur. One did.

In 1939 the Hummerts took an extended European vacation, mistakenly leaving behind a neophyte wordsmith assigned to pen the *Young Widder Brown* series—a new scribe only vaguely familiar with some of the Hummert absolutes. Before long, during the Hummerts' overseas sojourn, Ellen Brown and Peter Turner were sipping coffee in their bathrobes at Ellen's home. When the Hummerts returned and learned what had transpired (although nothing really had), "all hell broke loose," according to Ned Wever, who recounted the story with glee to a TV audience some years later.[15]

The Hummerts were convinced that there was little hope of salvaging the show without an exhaustive cleansing. In a short while, Dr. Peter Turner (actor Collyer) was history and Dr. Anthony Loring (actor Wever) was introduced, thereby "redeeming" a serial that had lapsed into "utter degradation." Wever hung on through the final episode, aired on June 22, 1956, nine months after *Mr. Keen* departed the ether. He had acted on *Mr. Keen* many times, sometimes in back-to-back episodes as a victim, solicitor (enlisting Mr. Keen's involvement in a case), suspect or murderer.

This versatile artist was not only in demand as a radio thespian (he turned up in leads or character roles on *Angel of Mercy, Cavalcade of America, Gangbusters, Grand Central Station, Her Honor Nancy James, Inner Sanctum Mysteries, Lora Lawton, Manhattan Mother, Perry Mason, Two on a Clue, Valiant Lady* and *We the People*), he was also a gifted musician. Wever composed the lyrics to several popular

Ned Wever (1902–1984) was typical of a host of daytime radio thespians that turned up in support roles on *Mr. Keen, Tracer of Lost Persons* at night. He variously played the part of the victim, the contact involving Mr. Keen in an investigation, suspect or the malefactor. Wever's career took him to stage, screen, radio and television. He is probably best recalled as the durable suitor in *Young Widder Brown*, Dr. Anthony Loring. (**Photograph courtesy of Patti Wever Knoll**)

tunes, "Spellbound," "I Can't Resist You," "Trouble in Paradise" and "Trust in Me" among them.

The native New Yorker, born April 27, 1902, saw his acting talent embrace the stage, screen and television well beyond his radio days. The entertainer died at age 82 on May 6, 1984, at Laguna Hills, California. His accomplishments were typical of the scores of talented aural thespians who graced the *Mr. Keen* microphones across that show's extensive run.

A plethora of silver-tongued announcers introduced *Mr. Keen, Tracer of Lost Persons* over nearly two decades. While some made only brief appearances, at least seven earned berths qualifying them for enduring status: Ben Grauer (1937–1940), James Fleming (1940–1943), Ken Roberts (1943), Lawrence K. (Larry) Elliott (1943–1951), Jack Costello (1951–1952), Harry Kramer (1952–1955) and Stuart Metz (during the serialized overlap, 1954–1955). Three more substituted with some frequency — George Ansbro (in the Fleming era), Dick Dunham (for Elliott) and George Bryan (for Metz). All of these "regulars" were seasoned veterans, some with years of training and experience acquired from introducing many other programs on the air.

Of the lot, Larry Elliott is likely the best remembered by fans that still recall the show. He was not only enduring but was also present in the drama's halcyon days. Elliott probably accepted the *Keen* announcing chores when the show was reconfigured from a three-night-a-week quarter-hour serial to a weekly complete half-hour drama on December 2, 1943. (The first few scripts bearing those cast names, the reader will recall, are missing from the permanent records.) He remained the show's interlocutor through the CBS run, ending July 12, 1951. That was *Mr. Keen*'s heyday, during which it easily drew its largest audiences.

Born in Washington, D. C. on August 31, 1900, Elliott's entry into radio was entirely unanticipated. While selling cars for an automobile dealership, he developed a flair for singing. For five years, strictly as a sideline, he took voice lessons, unsure what he would do with his developing talent. At about the same time Elliot sold a car to a local WJSV radio official, the dealership failed and Elliott was tossed out on his ear. Taking pity, the radio man offered him an announcing spot.

Elliott was soon newscasting, and by the mid–1930s became CBS's chief White House reporter. He also frequently substituted for Arthur Godfrey when the Old Redhead failed to appear at the start of his local early morning disk jockey program, long before Godfrey became a national celebrity. Elliott once advised those early risers in the listening audience: "If you're silly enough to get out of a nice warm bed at this ungodly hour, it's your fault. Don't expect me to entertain you. I'm tired, too."[16] In 1938 he left the capital to launch his own early morning program in New York City.

As a freelance announcer, Elliott turned up in that capacity on numerous radio features, from dramas and comedies to music, quiz and variety. Included in his repertoire were *The Alan Young Show, The American Melody Hour* (a Hummert property), *Barry Cameron, The Bob Hawk Show, Boston Blackie, Front Page Farrell* (a Hummert serial), *The Music of Andre Kostelanetz, Rose of My Dreams, Saturday Night Bandwagon, The Strange Romance of Evelyn Winters* (another Hummert serial), *The Texaco Star Theater* and *Treasury Star Parade*. In the latter series he was the official voice of the U. S. Treasury, selling war bonds by pitching "Millions for Defense." He was also a regular performer in the casts of *The Fred Allen Show* and *Major Bowes' Shower of Stars*.

Married, and with two children, Elliott was tagged as having "more hobbies than anyone else in radio."[17] His favorite pastimes were making pipes for smokers and gardening at his home at Scarsdale (and later Port Chester, New York). Elliott's career surprisingly ended early. He was just 56 when he died at his Port Chester home of a heart attack on July 27, 1957. He had launched a video acting career the previous year, appearing on NBC-TV's *Kraft Theater*.

Incidentally, the number of parallels in the deaths of writer Lawrence M. (Larry) Klee and Lawrence K. (Larry) Elliott appear almost uncanny. In addition to possessing similar monikers, both men lived and died within a few months of each other at an early age at their homes just outside New York City, a region where they spent much of their lives. Both were victims of heart attacks. Each left behind a widow and two children — a daughter, the oldest, and a son. Both men had, only a short time before, launched promising career extensions into the attractive, beckoning, newer medium of television. And, of course, for so many years the two were simultaneously, inextricably bound to the *Mr. Keen* series.

Several musicians played the theme and musical bridges between scenes on *Mr. Keen, Tracer of Lost Persons*. Ironically reflecting the show's title, most of their names have been lost to history. The studio organ pealed out the familiar refrain "Someday I'll Find You" as the program arrived and departed from the airwaves during most of its long run. That was augmented in later years by a recorded orchestral arrangement enriched by the mellow tones of the organ played over the band's sonata. In the show's final few years, standardized, taped stock melodies aired. The networks were then relying heavily upon similar recurring ditties on most of their mystery series. It was a cheap method of establishing mood, changing scenes and filling in the time lapses where needed.

The best-known musical artists appearing on *Mr. Keen* were organist John Winters and musical conductor Al Rickey. Each had several other programs to his credit. Winters' included a quartet of daytime dramas — *Myrt and Marge, When a Girl Marries, Young Doctor Malone* and *Young Widder Brown*. Rickey also arranged and conducted for *The Beatrice Lillie Show* and *Folies de Paris*, the latter a Hummert presentation.

Sound technician Jack Amrhein provided the background noises heard on the *Mr. Keen* broadcasts for much of the drama's life. A contemporary suggested he was "one of the best sound-effects artists in radio."[18] Amrhein, who left Paramount Studios to move to the airwaves, fulfilled similar duties on *The Fred Allen Show, Inner Sanctum Mysteries, Mr. Chameleon, The Mysterious Traveler, The Philip Morris Playhouse* and *The Robert Q. Lewis Show*. Some others who stepped in to supply sound effects for *Mr. Keen* included Al Briney, Bill Brinkmeyer, Bill Brown, Bill Campbell, Jimmy Dwan, Jimmy Lynch, John McCloskey, John McDonald, Lloyd Morse and Byron Wingett.

A coincidence concerning *Mr. Keen* and another AFI production, *Young Widder Brown*, seems worth mentioning. Of the 11 long-term individuals associated with *Keen*— Martha Atwell, Philip Clarke, Larry Elliott, Anne Hummert, Frank Hummert, Bennett Kilpack, Larry Klee, Richard Leonard, Florence Malone, Edward Slattery and John Winters—all but two, Clarke and Elliott, were associated with that daytime saga over lengthy runs. And, of course, *Brown*'s two enduring leads, Florence Freeman and Ned Wever, frequently appeared in *Keen* supporting roles, along with several more from the matinee melodrama. In fact, there may have been no better visible evidence of the formidable connection between Hummert series that aired both in the sunshine and the moonlight hours than in this striking example.

Over its long run, *Mr. Keen, Tracer of Lost Persons* presented some of the most talented artists in radio. Only a few of them have been cited in this chapter. For many years these hired guns provided listeners with satisfying amusement. Their collective contributions resulted in *Mr. Keen, Tracer of Lost Persons* becoming the memorable feature that it inexorably did.

7

Sold on Radio

During radio's golden age, it was not unusual for the sponsors of daytime narratives to finance the same program for multiple years — in some cases doing so for decades. By comparison, the advertisers on the evening dramas were rare who subscribed to one series for a decade or longer. Yet a single sponsor of *Mr. Keen, Tracer of Lost Persons* was so enamored of the kindly old investigator, or — to put it bluntly — so satisfied with the response to its commercial messages on the program, that for nearly 14 years it exclusively underwrote the aural series, through July 12, 1951 (1349 performances). Even afterward it continued to support the program that had been so well received for so long, funding a portion of it for another nine months, through April 24, 1952 (another 51 broadcasts) before moving on to other commercial ventures.

According to the *International Directory of Company Histories*, *Mr. Keen*'s most enduring sponsor, American Home Products (AHP), is sometimes referred to as "Anonymous Home Products" or the "withdrawn corporate giant." One of the largest pharmaceutical conglomerates in the nation, AHP included food and household-product divisions in its portfolio, and, as of this writing, markets familiar brand names like Advil, Anacin, Anbesol, Centrum, ChapStick, Dimetapp, Dristan, Preparation H, Primatene and Robitussin.

Yet its corporate name never appears on its commodity labels. "Public relations is considered such a low priority that until recently switchboard operators answered the phone with the company phone number instead of the company name," the *International Directory* attests.

Thus it probably comes as no surprise that during all those years the firm underwrote *Mr. Keen, Tracer of Lost Persons*, along with radio's *Front Page Farrell*, *Just Plain Bill*, *Our Gal Sunday* and *The Romance of Helen Trent*— each of them an Air Features (Frank and Anne Hummert) property — there was never any public revelation that AHP was the bankroller behind them. For many years the commercials simply acknowledged that a particular show was being "brought to you by the makers of Bi-So-Dol analgesic tablets for upset stomach distress" or something similar. Listeners never really knew who those "makers" were.

Down the road a flicker of light eventually shed some illuminatin on the matter although it was more of a flashlight than spotlight. The firm began announcing that "the Whitehall Pharmacal Company, the makers of Anacin and many other dependable drug products" sponsored some of those programs. Whitehall Pharmacal (which was later changed to Whitehall Laboratories and then to Whitehall-Robins Healthcare), a branch of AHP, then produced such commodities as Kolynos toothpaste, Bi-So-Dol analgesic, Anacin pain-relieving tablets, Heet pain-relieving liniment, Infrarub pain-relieving balm, Neet hair remover, Dristan and Primatene cold remedies, Preparation H hemorrhoid reliever, Hill's cold medication, Kriptin antihistamine, Sleep-Eze calmative and Freezone corn remover. Simultaneously, AHP maintained a household products division, Boyle-Midway, that generated Aerowax and Olde English floor cleaners, Easy-Off oven cleaner, Easy-On starch, Black Flag and Fly-Ded insecticides, Wizard room deodorizer, Sani-Flush toilet cleanser and others. There was also a foodstuffs unit whose most prominent names included Chef Boyardee and Jiffy Pop (though that brand was trimmed in the late 1990s).

In the *Mr. Keen* days, however, the show's advertising primarily focused on three AHP products — Bi-So-Dol and Kolynos in its earliest years, and later Anacin (and Kolynos). Of the trio, Anacin received far more exposure than any of the other drugs.

The story of Anacin's creation is a fascinating one in the annals of American packaged goods.[1] The original formula was a mixture of four drugs widely consumed in the early twentieth century. The best known were caffeine and aspirin; quinine sulfate and acetanilide were the others. (By 1963, the latter two ingredients were dropped.) In 1915 a Minneapolis pharmacist, William M. Knight, invented his own analgesic brand that he called An-A-Cin, a capsule combining the four components. Three years later he gained a trademark for the product under the modified spelling Anacin. Sold by his Anacin Chemical Company, the capsules were initially marketed to dentists for relieving pain and inflammation resulting from tooth extractions. It was also pushed as a remedy for headaches and neuralgia.

Knight sold his Anacin brand in 1919, and it changed hands several times over the next few years. In 1926 Van Ess Laboratories, Inc., of Delaware purchased it. By then the American Dental Association was inquiring if Anacin's ingredient mixture was more effective than aspirin. Anacin makers capitalized on a popular notion that several components were "always better" than just one. This claim was to dominate much of the brand's advertising over the next half-century.

American Home Products, a large holding company, bought Van Ess in 1930. Formed in 1926 by a group of prominent businessmen, AHP's history was to be characterized by continuous acquisitions. Ironically, one of its founders, Albert Diebold, also co-founded Sterling Products, Inc., the U. S. owner of Bayer aspirin since 1918, which was destined to become one of radio's major sponsors (and who backed a surfeit of Hummert-produced series: *The American Album of Familiar Music, American Melody Hour, Backstage Wife, Lorenzo Jones, Manhattan Merry-Go-Round, Mr. Chameleon, Stella Dallas, Waltz Time* and *Young Widder Brown*). In 1935, as Sterling spent more than $750,000 on Bayer advertising, American Home Products budgeted but $200,000 for all its copious commodities. That wouldn't continue, however; in the next two years (when *Mr. Keen, Tracer of Lost Persons* debuted) Anacin's advertising budget increased fourfold and was heavily concentrated in radio. By 1941, Anacin out-spent Bayer.

Anacin's commercials continued to emphasize the company's more-ingredients-are-better advertising strategy. "Anacin is a combination of medically proven and tested ingredients — not just one," said one radio spot. "Like a doctor's prescription," another emphasized. The ads were reinforced by various marketing techniques. Anacin reps visited more than 500 doctors daily, while 65,000 samples were distributed monthly to physicians and dentists.

The AHP commercials that aired on *Mr. Keen, Tracer of Lost Persons* and its other radio series were nothing if not repetitious. Yet their singsong approach became so familiar to listeners that many could recite the familiar words right along with the announcer from week to week and broadcast to broadcast. This one was emblematic.

> The next time you're suffering from the pains of headache, neuritis or neuralgia, try Anacin. You'll bless the day you heard of this incredibly fast way to relieve these pains. Now the reason Anacin is so wonderfully fast acting and effective is this: Anacin is like a doctor's prescription. That is, Anacin contains not just one but a combination of medically proven active ingredients in easy-to-take tablet form. Thousands of people have received envelopes containing Anacin tablets from their own dentists or physicians and in this way have discovered the incredibly fast relief Anacin brings from pain of headache, neuritis or neuralgia. So next time such pain strikes take Anacin. For most effective relief, use only as directed. Your druggist has Anacin in handy boxes of 12 and 30, and economical family size bottles of 50 and 100. The name is Anacin. A-N-A-C-I-N.

By the early 1950s, as some major advertisers began shifting the bulk of their promotional budgets to the exciting new medium of television, the big radio networks introduced their own strategy to stave off impending doom — at least for a while. Instead of selling a quarter-hour, half-hour or hour-long show exclusively to an individual sponsor (as they had done for decades), networks offered to redistribute the advertising load. "Participating," "cooperative" or "multiple" sponsorship resulted. In this way, two or more traditionally non-competing operations aired their commercials on a single series. The plan had the effect of attracting more medium-sized firms to the market while continuing to entice major media buyers to spend a portion of their advertising revenues in radio.

Thus, when *Mr. Keen* transitioned from CBS to NBC on July 20, 1951, it embraced this new joint-advertising concept. Three corporations initially underwrote the program: American Home Products for Anacin, Liggett & Myers Tobacco Company for Chesterfield cigarettes and Radio Corporation of America for RCA Victor home entertainment appliances. As they departed, replacements were signed. Over the years *Mr. Keen*'s underwriters included the American Chicle Company for Dentyne, Chiclets and Beemans Pepsin gum; Eno-Scott and Bowne for Brylcreem men's hair preparations; The Murine Company, Inc. for Murine eye drops; The Nestle Company for Nescafe coffee; and the Procter & Gamble Company for Lava soap and Lilt home permanents. During the weeknight installments that began June 21, 1954, and on the weekly series starting July 2, 1954, *Mr. Keen* was aired on a sustaining (or unsponsored) basis.

One of the virtues that Frank and Anne Hummert displayed was a patriotic loyalty. They demonstrated it in a myriad of ways. During the Second World War, Anne Hummert was tapped as a special envoy to participate with the U. S. departments of War and Treasury in projecting ongoing communications to the general public. The Hummerts strongly evidenced their commitment to the nation by introducing wartime themes and figures into their storylines. They encouraged their audiences by sending some of the characters on their daytime serials to work in war plants and to serve in various voluntary capacities. They also provided a platform on their many programs for strategic appeals to the folks at home, enlisting them in conservation efforts while suggesting that they do without or be satisfied with less in order to support the war effort.

Their perseverance positively impacted the nation's morale. *Mr. Keen, Tracer of Lost Persons* was a prime vehicle for such messages, routinely airing one or more public service announcements virtually every night throughout the war years. This one from February 3, 1944, delivered by Bennett Kilpack, is typical.

> *This is Mr. Keen with one last word. I've been asked to bring to your attention the important fact that our country is still faced by a critical shortage of tires for civilian use. The tires you have now must last you indefinitely. Do not be misled by announcements that huge quantities of synthetic rubber are being made. They are but — they are required for military use. So do everything you can to make your tires last as long as possible. Drive only when necessary, under 35 miles an hour. Keep your tires properly inflated and inspected. Recap your tires as soon as they need it and — share your car with others. Goodnight and thank you all.*

In the years before the war and immediately following it, *Mr. Keen* provided generous opportunities for declarations that supported organizations like the Red Cross, the Scouts, the Community Chest, the March of Dimes, and various other civic and charitable organizations. Such sporadic warmhearted humanitarian appeals probably helped ingratiate the tracer of lost persons to the listening audience.

There was a lot sold on radio in those days. Thanks to *Mr. Keen* and similar programs, a great deal of it was of benefit to all humankind.

Radio Episode Guide

This log of the radio broadcasts of *Mr. Keen, Tracer of Lost Persons* is adapted from the scripts that encompass the *Mr. Keen* anthology in the Frank and Anne Hummert, and the Lawrence M. Klee collections at the American Heritage Center of the University of Wyoming. This repository offers the most comprehensive documents in existence embracing the radio show. More than 1600 of the 1693 sequentially numbered scripts are archived, in conjunction with limited but pertinent letters, memos and correspondence. While occasional lapses of continuity do occur, they are minimal (and are offset by the magnitude of data that does exist).

A resolute, painstaking effort has been made to craft an expansive, engaging and useful episode guide, which should be of interest to both the casual peruser and those who wish to validate their own knowledge and memory (or add to their individual trivia compilations) of *Mr. Keen, Tracer of Lost Persons*. Cast lists have been included when available. Where appropriate, notes have been added that call attention to items of special interest (e.g., extant episodes in circulation; rationale for not broadcasting on particular dates; shifts in networks, days and times; substitute voices and the reasons for them, etc.).

CONTINUITY #1
Tuesday, October 12, 1937
7:15–7:30 p.m. EST
NBC Blue
Ben Grauer, Announcer
American Home Products (Bi-So-Dol), Sponsor
"The Case of the Girl Who Couldn't Be Found"
　　Adapted from the theme of the 1906 *Tracer of Lost Persons* book, Mr. Keen's first aural case involves the pursuit of a girl who theoretically doesn't exist. He seeks the lass in Jack Gatewood's dreams.

CONTINUITY #2
Wednesday, October 13, 1937
7:15–7:30 p.m. EST
NBC Blue
Ben Grauer, Announcer
American Home Products (Bi-So-Dol), Sponsor
"The Case of the Girl Who Couldn't Be Found"
　　The girl in affluent, young, bored Jack Gatewood's dreams actually works for Mr. Keen! Gatewood falls in love with Marjorie Southerland, but has he lost her under false pretenses?

CONTINUITY #3
Thursday, October 14, 1937
7:15–7:30 p.m. EST
NBC Blue
Ben Grauer, Announcer
American Home Products (Bi-So-Dol), Sponsor
"The Case of the Girl Who Couldn't Be Found"
   A complex situation develops as investigator Marjorie seeks *herself*! Mr. Keen is well aware of what is transpiring, and planned for developments to occur just as they have.

CONTINUITY #4
Tuesday, October 19, 1937
7:15–7:30 p.m. EST
NBC Blue
Ben Grauer, Announcer
American Home Products (Bi-So-Dol), Sponsor
"The Case of the Girl Who Couldn't Be Found"
   Marjorie, learning that *she* is the girl she's been seeking, bolts from the office and tells Gatewood she'll never speak to him again (and, in fact, *hates* him!). Keen ponders the problem discussing it with Mike Clancy.

CONTINUITY #5
Wednesday, October 20, 1937
7:15–7:30 p.m. EST
NBC Blue
Ben Grauer, Announcer
American Home Products (Bi-So-Dol), Sponsor
"The Case of the Girl Who Couldn't Be Found"
   Mr. Keen works his magic, subduing opposing views. He helps Marjorie accept Gatewood as a potential lifelong companion. The challenged lovers appear headed toward eternal bliss.

CONTINUITY #6
Thursday, October 21, 1937
7:15–7:30 p.m. EST
NBC Blue
Ben Grauer, Announcer
American Home Products (Bi-So-Dol), Sponsor
"The Case of the Man Who Was Not"
   Mrs. Henry Edwards asks Mr. Keen to find her spouse, who, she claims, left with a woman in his office, Mildred Burton. But the latter refutes this, branding Mrs. Edwards a liar.

CONTINUITY #7
Tuesday, October 26, 1937
7:15–7:30 p.m. EST
NBC Blue
Announcer's name omitted
American Home Products (Bi-So-Dol), Sponsor
"The Case of the Man Who Was Not"
   Keen believes Miss Burton and not his client, accusing the wife of wanting to kill her spouse. He probes further, then mulls over the case with Miss Ellis, his spinster secretary.

CONTINUITY #8
Wednesday, October 27, 1937
7:15–7:30 p.m. EST
NBC Blue
Announcer's name omitted
American Home Products (Bi-So-Dol), Sponsor
"The Case of the Man Who Was Not"
   It turns out that Mr. Keen's suspicions were well placed. Henry Edwards was indeed murdered by his wife, who then attempted to pin the crime on a woman Henry had long adored.

CONTINUITY #9
Thursday, October 28, 1937
7:15–7:30 p.m. EST
NBC Blue
Announcer's name omitted
American Home Products (Bi-So-Dol), Sponsor
"The Case of the Father Who Crept into Darkness"
   At New York's palatial Vanderpool Hotel, Mr. Keen visits with movie queen Felicia Gray. She appeals to him to locate her dad, a gambler-alcoholic who deserted her mom a decade ago.

CONTINUITY #10
Tuesday, November 2, 1937
7:15–7:30 p.m. EST
NBC Blue
Announcer's name omitted
American Home Products (Bi-So-Dol), Sponsor

"The Case of the Father Who Crept into Darkness"

The trail to find the long-lost father leads Mr. Keen and Mike Clancy to the city's slums and flophouses. Now they approach a tumble-down roominghouse in the worst district.

CONTINUITY #11
Wednesday, November 3, 1937
7:15–7:30 p.m. EST
NBC Blue
Announcer's name omitted
American Home Products (Bi-So-Dol), Sponsor
"The Case of the Father Who Crept into Darkness"

Charles Gray, a vagrant "wreck of a man," is living in New York's slums. Because of his love for his daughter, he begs Mr. Keen not to reveal his plight, in order to avoid impacting her.

CONTINUITY #12
Thursday, November 4, 1937
7:15–7:30 p.m. EST
NBC Blue
Announcer's name omitted
American Home Products (Bi-So-Dol), Sponsor
"The Case of the Father Who Crept into Darkness"

Felicia Gray, without her dad's guidance, is about to marry Alex Rockhurst, whom Mr. Keen feels is unworthy of her. Keen made a promise to Charles Gray, however, and keeps it.

CONTINUITY #13
Tuesday, November 9, 1937
7:15–7:30 p.m. EST
NBC Blue
Announcer's name omitted
American Home Products (Bi-So-Dol), Sponsor
"The Case of the Boy Who Dreamed"

Robert Manley, 15, has run away from home. His parents enlist Mr. Keen's aid. The boy left a note — he couldn't stand his dad's rigid discipline and coldness any longer.

CONTINUITY #14
Wednesday, November 10, 1937
7:15–7:30 p.m. EST
NBC Blue
Announcer's name omitted
American Home Products (Bi-So-Dol), Sponsor
"The Case of the Boy Who Dreamed"

Clues lead Mr. Keen and Miss Ellis to the coast. A schooner is about to sail to the West Indies. They encounter Robert. After returning home, life will be easier, Keen promises.

CONTINUITY #15
Thursday, November 11, 1937
7:15–7:30 p.m. EST
NBC Blue
Announcer's name omitted
American Home Products (Bi-So-Dol), Sponsor
"The Case of the Boy Who Dreamed"

Returning to the office, Mr. Keen suggests that Robert's father alter his disposition and try to understand his son's needs. Father and son are then reconciled in an emotional meeting.

CONTINUITY #16
Tuesday, November 16, 1937
7:15–7:30 p.m. EST
NBC Blue
Announcer's name omitted
American Home Products (Bi-So-Dol), Sponsor
"The Case of the Dead Man Who May Be Living"

Eminent physician Robert Thornwald mysteriously disappears. His distracted wife seeks Mr. Keen's help. News arrives that Dr. Thornwald is dead, but Keen's suspicions have been aroused.

CONTINUITY #17
Wednesday, November 17, 1937
7:15–7:30 p.m. EST
NBC Blue
Announcer's name omitted
American Home Products (Bi-So-Dol), Sponsor
"The Case of the Dead Man Who May Be Living"

Keen learns that some large insurance policies were recently issued on the dead man. He wonders if Thornwald is dead. Pursuing it, he and Miss Ellis take a train to Valeboro.

CONTINUITY #18
Thursday, November 18, 1937
7:15–7:30 p.m. EST
NBC Blue
Announcer's name omitted
American Home Products (Bi-So-Dol), Sponsor
"The Case of the Dead Man Who May Be Living"

Keen learns Thornwald arrived in Valeboro transporting a bundle, perhaps a body. A man resembling the doc was seen *after* his fatal accident. Keen attends Thornwald's funeral.

CONTINUITY #19
Tuesday, November 23, 1937
7:15–7:30 p.m. EST
NBC Blue
Announcer's name omitted
American Home Products (Bi-So-Dol), Sponsor
"The Case of the Dead Man Who May Be Living"

Mr. Keen proves that the doctor is alive (the man even attends his own funeral!). The "late" wife was about to collect over a million dollars in insurance in the scam Mr. Keen exposes.

CONTINUITY #20
Wednesday, November 24, 1937
7:15–7:30 p.m. EST
NBC Blue
Announcer's name omitted
American Home Products (Bi-So-Dol), Sponsor
"The Case of the Lincoln Letter"

Mrs. Barnes seeks her twin sister, Marie Cooper, who left 25 years ago. Marie had in her possession a letter from Abraham Lincoln to a relative, one that Barnes recently saw for sale. She's worried about her long-lost sister's welfare.

CONTINUITY #21
Thursday, November 25, 1937
7:15–7:30 p.m. EST
NBC Blue
Announcer's name omitted
American Home Products (Bi-So-Dol), Sponsor
"The Case of the Lincoln Letter"

The trail leads from dealers in rare letters to a junkman who purchased the heirloom from a poor wreck, a drug addict named Agnes Harrigan, now in the Home of Refuge. Keen goes there.

CONTINUITY #22
Tuesday, November 30, 1937
7:15–7:30 p.m. EST
NBC Blue
Announcer's name omitted
American Home Products (Bi-So-Dol), Sponsor
"The Case of the Lincoln Letter"

Keen believes a wealthy, arrogant socialite, Mrs. Roger Kirkpatrick, is Marie Cooper, who denies any ties to a humble birth. Keen and Barnes arrive at the woman's palatial digs.

CONTINUITY #23
Wednesday, December 1, 1937
7:15–7:30 p.m. EST
NBC Blue
Announcer's name omitted
American Home Products (Bi-So-Dol), Sponsor
"The Case of the Lincoln Letter"

The haughty Mrs. Kirkpatrick *is* the missing woman, but she won't reunite with her twin. It appears that Mr. Keen can do nothing to induce her to recognize her modest beginnings.

CONTINUITY #24
Thursday, December 2, 1937
7:15–7:30 p.m. EST
NBC Blue
Announcer's name omitted
American Home Products (Bi-So-Dol), Sponsor
"The Case of the Lincoln Letter"

The scene shifts to Mr. Keen's office. Mrs. Kirkpatrick's young daughter Gloria delivers a surprise before Mr. Keen effects a reconciliation at last between mother and aunt.

CONTINUITY #25
Tuesday, December 7, 1937
7:15–7:30 p.m. EST
NBC Blue
Announcer's name omitted
American Home Products (Bi-So-Dol), Sponsor
"The Case of the Man in Search of Himself"

A phone call from Peter Denning involves Keen in a strange case — the caller has lost *himself*! Accompanied by fiancée Cynthia Wilson, Denning arrives at Keen's office, hoping to find his *other* self.

CONTINUITY #26
Wednesday, December 8, 1937
7:15–7:30 p.m. EST
NBC Blue
Announcer's name omitted
American Home Products (Bi-So-Dol), Sponsor
"The Case of the Man in Search of Himself"

A shell-shocked war veteran, Denning is an amnesiac. Currently betrothed to his nurse, he must learn if he is already wed. Keen pursues clues to the Haslett home in Winton, Maryland.

CONTINUITY #27
Thursday, December 9, 1937
7:15–7:30 p.m. EST
NBC Blue
Announcer's name omitted
American Home Products (Bi-So-Dol), Sponsor
"The Case of the Man in Search of Himself"

Madeline Haslett is a middle-aged woman with a daughter (Betty, 23) and son (Arthur, 22). Her husband, in the war, was declared missing in 1918. A photo of Denning matches that of her spouse.

CONTINUITY #28
Tuesday, December 14, 1937
7:15–7:30 p.m. EST
NBC Blue
Announcer's name omitted
American Home Products (Bi-So-Dol), Sponsor
"The Case of the Man in Search of Himself"

Mr. Keen brings Peter Denning face to face with Madeline Haslett, who says he's her missing husband. Denning has no recollection of this. Keen will try again to restore his memory.

CONTINUITY #29
Wednesday, December 15, 1937
7:15–7:30 p.m. EST
NBC Blue
Announcer's name omitted
American Home Products (Bi-So-Dol), Sponsor
"The Case of the Man in Search of Himself"

In a panic after hearing that her fiancé is already married, Cynthia Wilson runs away. Denning's marriage can be annulled after an absence of 20 years. To whom is he now morally bound?

CONTINUITY #30
Thursday, December 16, 1937
7:15–7:30 p.m. EST
NBC Blue
Announcer's name omitted
American Home Products (Bi-So-Dol), Sponsor
"The Case of the Man in Search of Himself"

Cynthia bravely and unselfishly steps aside after Denning's memory returns— and with it the love for his wife and family. The amnesiac is restored to his place in his former home.

CONTINUITY #31
Tuesday, December 21, 1937
7:15–7:30 p.m. EST
NBC Blue
Announcer's name omitted
American Home Products (Bi-So-Dol), Sponsor
"The Case of the XPBA Plans"

Simon Richards, chief engineer at Chicago's Atgood Brothers, is missing, along with designs for a new military defense plane, the XPBA (Experimental Patrol Bomber — Atgood Type).

CONTINUITY #32
Wednesday, December 22, 1937
7:15–7:30 p.m. EST
NBC Blue
Announcer's name omitted
American Home Products (Bi-So-Dol), Sponsor
"The Case of the XPBA Plans"

Richards' 21-year-old daughter Louisa is also missing. Marshall Atgood fears theft, espionage, and murder. An arms syndicate is after the XPBA. Now the original designs also go missing.

CONTINUITY #33
Thursday, December 23, 1937
7:15–7:30 p.m. EST
NBC Blue
Announcer's name omitted

American Home Products (Bi-So-Dol), Sponsor
"The Case of the XPBA Plans"
Is Simon Richards a traitor and his alleged "daughter" his accomplice? The actual Louisa Richards, who's attending school in Switzerland, returns home to help find her father.

CONTINUITY #34
Tuesday, December 28, 1937
7:15–7:30 p.m. EST
NBC Blue
Announcer's name omitted
American Home Products (Bi-So-Dol), Sponsor
"The Case of the XPBA Plans"
Simon Richards is found murdered. Mr. Keen thinks the girl posing as the daughter belongs to an international spy ring. An antique gold bracelet figures prominently in the plot.

CONTINUITY #35
Wednesday, December 29, 1937
7:15–7:30 p.m. EST
NBC Blue
Announcer's name omitted
American Home Products (Bi-So-Dol), Sponsor
"The Case of the XPBA Plans"
Mr. Keen and Miss Ellis travel to Washington, D.C. to infiltrate the ring. She is wearing the gold bracelet, the spy ring's identifying mark, as the two visit a restaurant.

CONTINUITY #36
Thursday, December 30, 1937
7:15–7:30 p.m. EST
NBC Blue
Announcer's name omitted
American Home Products (Bi-So-Dol), Sponsor
"The Case of the XPBA Plans"
Mr. Keen and Marshall Atgood intercept Theodora LeClerk a beautiful, notorious global spy who killed her partner after he stole the plans—before she can sail to Europe with them.

CONTINUITY #37
Tuesday, January 4, 1938
7:15–7:30 p.m. EST
NBC Blue
Announcer's name omitted
American Home Products (Bi-So-Dol), Sponsor
"The Case of the Mother Who Couldn't Forget"
Mr. Keen encounters a pitiful, forlorn, frail Mary Varnum, a scrubwoman who left her spouse and daughter 15 years ago to earn money on the stage (intending to improve her family's standard of living).

CONTINUITY #38
Wednesday, January 5, 1938
7:15–7:30 p.m. EST
NBC Blue
Announcer's name omitted
American Home Products (Bi-So-Dol), Sponsor
"The Case of the Mother Who Couldn't Forget"
Mary Varnum, age 45 but looking 60, collapses in Keen's office. He takes her to his apartment. She wants him to find her girl, Peggy. Remus, Keen's black butler, attends to her needs.

CONTINUITY #39
Thursday, January 6, 1938
7:15–7:30 p.m. EST
NBC Blue
Announcer's name omitted
American Home Products (Bi-So-Dol), Sponsor
"The Case of the Mother Who Couldn't Forget"
Mr. Keen locates Peggy Varnum, now 25, living with her dad (whom Mary deserted for a stage career). Keen and Miss Ellis visit Donald Varnum at his palatial New Jersey estate.

CONTINUITY #40
Tuesday, January 11, 1938
7:15–7:30 p.m. EST
NBC Blue
Announcer's name omitted
American Home Products (Bi-So-Dol), Sponsor
"The Case of the Mother Who Couldn't Forget"
Donald believes it wise that Mary keep out of her child's life (he told Peggy her mom had died). Peggy, in awe of an unpromising theatrical director, is also seeking stage fame.

CONTINUITY #41
Wednesday, January 12, 1938
7:15–7:30 p.m. EST
NBC Blue
Announcer's name omitted
American Home Products (Bi-So-Dol), Sponsor
"The Case of the Mother Who Couldn't Forget"
Keen senses Peggy's need for her mother's influence. He and Miss Ellis discuss it in his office. Mary and Donald Varnum arrive separately; they've not been together in 15 years.

CONTINUITY #42
Thursday, January 13, 1938
7:15–7:30 p.m. EST
NBC Blue
Announcer's name omitted
American Home Products (Bi-So-Dol), Sponsor
"The Case of the Mother Who Couldn't Forget"
Mr. Keen impresses upon Donald the notion that possibly only Mary can save Peggy from ruining her life. Mary is reunited with her family, proving a mother's love can survive years of misery.

CONTINUITY #43
Tuesday, January 18, 1938
7:15–7:30 p.m. EST
NBC Blue
Announcer's name omitted
American Home Products (Bi-So-Dol), Sponsor
"The Case of Mr. and Mrs. Blake's Golden Wedding"
An elderly farm couple visits Mr. Keen, asking him to find their two sons who left home 20 years ago. They are about to celebrate their 50th anniversary and want them there.

CONTINUITY #44
Wednesday, January 19, 1938
7:15–7:30 p.m. EST
NBC Blue
Announcer's name omitted
American Home Products (Bi-So-Dol), Sponsor
"The Case of Mr. and Mrs. Blake's Golden Wedding"
George had eloped with his brother Roger's fiancée. Then Roger vanished. Their sister, Justine, tells Keen that their parents don't know that Roger was implicated in bank embezzlement.

CONTINUITY #45
Thursday, January 20, 1938
7:15–7:30 p.m. EST
NBC Blue
Announcer's name omitted
American Home Products (Bi-So-Dol), Sponsor
"The Case of Mr. and Mrs. Blake's Golden Wedding"
Keen and Miss Ellis trace Roger, now a thriving banker, to Marwood in the Midwest. Keen reminds him his sis covered up his mistake, paying $2,000 for it. Keen searches for George.

CONTINUITY #46
Tuesday, January 25, 1938
7:15–7:30 p.m. EST
NBC Blue
Announcer's name omitted
American Home Products (Bi-So-Dol), Sponsor
"The Case of Mr. and Mrs. Blake's Golden Wedding"
In a small Midwest town, Mr. Keen locates George in a tenement building. Having eloped with his brother's former fiancée, Mary, George is now unemployed and destitute, and his wife has become an invalid.

CONTINUITY #47
Wednesday, January 26, 1938
7:15–7:30 p.m. EST
NBC Blue
Announcer's name omitted
American Home Products (Bi-So-Dol), Sponsor
"The Case of Mr. and Mrs. Blake's Golden Wedding"
Both sons have been persuaded to return for the celebration. Both are marked by a common guilt — parental neglect. An air of anticipation abounds, as friends gather at the farmhouse.

CONTINUITY #48
Thursday, January 27, 1938
7:15–7:30 p.m. EST

NBC Blue
Announcer's name omitted
American Home Products (Bi-So-Dol), Sponsor
"The Case of Mr. and Mrs. Blake's Golden Wedding"
    A renewal of family ties occurs as the two sons are welcomed and restored to their rightful places within the family, alongside their sister Justine. All is forgiven.

CONTINUITY #49
Tuesday, February 1, 1938
7:15–7:30 p.m. EST
NBC Blue
Announcer's name omitted
American Home Products (Bi-So-Dol), Sponsor
"The Case of Miss Cinderella"
    A pathetic Dorothy Mitchell, 15, asks Keen to find her *real* parents. She's convinced she's a foundling, not an orphan, and her folks may be alive. Her foster mom is cruel to her.

CONTINUITY #50
Wednesday, February 2, 1938
7:15–7:30 p.m. EST
NBC Blue
Announcer's name omitted
American Home Products (Bi-So-Dol), Sponsor
"The Case of Miss Cinderella"
    At the Mitchell home, Keen observes that Dorothy is a drudge, a slave to Mrs. Mitchell's every whim. Until her adoption seven years ago, the girl lived at Oakville Children's Home.

CONTINUITY #51
Thursday, February 3, 1938
7:15–7:30 p.m. EST
NBC Blue
Announcer's name omitted
American Home Products (Bi-So-Dol), Sponsor
"The Case of Miss Cinderella"
    At Oakville Children's Home, Mr. Keen and Miss Ellis learn that Mrs. Mitchell only *pretended* to adopt Dorothy — she *is* the child's real mother. The pair returns to Tyndale, New Jersey, and the Mitchell abode.

CONTINUITY #52
Tuesday, February 8, 1938
7:15–7:30 p.m. EST
NBC Blue
Announcer's name omitted
American Home Products (Bi-So-Dol), Sponsor
"The Case of Miss Cinderella"
    Mrs. Mitchell perpetrated the ruse in order to hide her unhappy first marriage from her current spouse. Dorothy runs away from home. Keen plans to inform Mr. Mitchell of the deception.

CONTINUITY #53
Wednesday, February 9, 1938
7:15–7:30 p.m. EST
NBC Blue
Announcer's name omitted
American Home Products (Bi-So-Dol), Sponsor
"The Case of Miss Cinderella"
    A "guilt complex" accounts for Mrs. Mitchell's inhumane treatment of her daughter. Her secret bared, Mrs. Mitchell wants the girl returned. They find her at the Children's Aid Society.

CONTINUITY #54
Thursday, February 10, 1938
7:15–7:30 p.m. EST
NBC Blue
Announcer's name omitted
American Home Products (Bi-So-Dol), Sponsor
"The Case of Miss Cinderella"
    With newfound love and understanding, Dorothy Mitchell is restored to her parents in an emotional reunion. Her mother promises to treat the child with proper respect from now on.

CONTINUITY #55
Tuesday, February 15, 1938
7:15–7:30 p.m. EST
NBC Blue
Announcer's name omitted
American Home Products (Bi-So-Dol), Sponsor
"The Case of the Sins of the Father"
    Mrs. Harry Malloy and son Joe, age 19, ask Keen's aid in finding Harry. He turned to crime 10 years back, deserting them. Joe has fallen in with a gang, and his mother thinks he'll listen to his dad.

CONTINUITY #56
Wednesday, February 16, 1938
7:15–7:30 p.m. EST
NBC Blue
Announcer's name omitted
American Home Products (Bi-So-Dol), Sponsor
"The Case of the Sins of the Father"
    Mr. Keen locates Harry Malloy, a petty crook with a prison record, who refuses to return to his family. Keen goes to visit Mrs. Malloy, who runs a small news-vending concern.

CONTINUITY #57
Thursday, February 17, 1938
7:15–7:30 p.m. EST
NBC Blue
Announcer's name omitted
American Home Products (Bi-So-Dol), Sponsor
"The Case of the Sins of the Father"
    Mrs. Malloy's fears come true: Joe is arrested for attempted burglary. But Mr. Keen has a plan. He has the dad picked up as a suspicious character and placed in his son's cell.

CONTINUITY #58
Tuesday, February 22, 1938
7:15–7:30 p.m. EST
NBC Blue
Announcer's name omitted
American Home Products (Bi-So-Dol), Sponsor
"The Case of the Sins of the Father"
    In a courtroom, Joe Malloy is found guilty as charged. Joe and his father are temporarily confined together. Mr. Keen visits the detective room at the precinct police station.

CONTINUITY #59
Wednesday, February 23, 1938
7:15–7:30 p.m. EST
NBC Blue
Announcer's name omitted
American Home Products (Bi-So-Dol), Sponsor
"The Case of the Sins of the Father"
    In court Joe pleads guilty to breaking into a warehouse. He's about to be sentenced. Keen is helpful in reuniting the broken family and seeing a light sentence meted out.

CONTINUITY #60
Thursday, February 24, 1938
7:15–7:30 p.m. EST
NBC Blue
Announcer's name omitted
American Home Products (Bi-So-Dol), Sponsor
"The Case of the Girl with the Lovely Eyes"
    Peter Gregory, 28, enlists Mr. Keen's aid in finding Laura Wheaton, his fiancée, who left six years ago. He was then a penniless painter; now he's on the brink of success.

CONTINUITY #61
Tuesday, March 1, 1938
7:15–7:30 p.m. EST
NBC Blue
Announcer's name omitted
American Home Products (Bi-So-Dol), Sponsor
"The Case of the Girl with the Lovely Eyes"
    Keen and Mike Clancy trace Laura from city to city until they find her in Whipple's Corner, Vermont. She's hidden there because she has gone blind. She won't listen to them.

CONTINUITY #62
Wednesday, March 2, 1938
7:15–7:30 p.m. EST
NBC Blue
Announcer's name omitted
American Home Products (Bi-So-Dol), Sponsor
"The Case of the Girl with the Lovely Eyes"
    Laura suffers deep fits of depression. Mr. Keen prevents her from taking her own life and summons Peter Gregory. They will converge at the farmhouse where Laura boards.

CONTINUITY #63
Thursday, March 3, 1938
7:15–7:30 p.m. EST
NBC Blue
Announcer's name omitted
American Home Products (Bi-So-Dol), Sponsor
"The Case of the Girl with the Lovely Eyes"
    Peter still wants to marry Laura, despite the tragic loss of her sight. Mr. Keen takes the star-crossed lovers to Dr. Frawley, eminent Boston surgeon, who examines Laura's eyes.

CONTINUITY #64
Tuesday, March 8, 1938
7:15–7:30 p.m. EST
NBC Blue
Announcer's name omitted
American Home Products (Bi-So-Dol), Sponsor
"The Case of the Girl with the Lovely Eyes"
   Dr. Frawley declares that an operation *might* restore the girl's sight, but makes no guarantees. She decides to try it. Peter Gregory and Mr. Keen anxiously await the outcome.

CONTINUITY #65
Wednesday, March 9, 1938
7:15–7:30 p.m. EST
NBC Blue
Announcer's name omitted
American Home Products (Bi-So-Dol), Sponsor
"The Case of the Girl with the Lovely Eyes"
   The operation is a success. The young lovers, whose affection for each other persevered despite their years of separation, are ready for a promising future together.

CONTINUITY #66
Thursday, March 10, 1938
7:15–7:30 p.m. EST
NBC Blue
Ben Grauer, Announcer
American Home Products (Bi-So-Dol), Sponsor
"The Case of the Man Who Deserted a Dream"
   Mrs. Krause, age 65, runs a bakery with an orphaned granddaughter, 15-year-old Rose. Fred Krause left a decade ago with $4,000 the couple had saved to retire on. Rose wants him back; grandma doesn't.

CONTINUITY #67
Tuesday, March 15, 1938
7:15–7:30 p.m. EST
NBC Blue
Announcer's name omitted
American Home Products (Bi-So-Dol), Sponsor
"The Case of the Man Who Deserted a Dream"
   Mr. Keen presses his Midwest agent, Herbert Maxwell, into service. Maxwell summons Keen to Barrowsford, Iowa, when he turns up evidence that Fred Krause, now 65, is living there.

CONTINUITY #68
Wednesday, March 16, 1938
7:15–7:30 p.m. EST
NBC Blue
Announcer's name omitted
American Home Products (Bi-So-Dol), Sponsor
"The Case of the Man Who Deserted a Dream"
   They find the man at a small commercial hotel. Losing the $4,000 has preyed upon his mind, turning Krause into an embittered, grouchy old man. He refuses to return home.

CONTINUITY #69
Thursday, March 17, 1938
7:15–7:30 p.m. EST
NBC Blue
Announcer's name omitted
American Home Products (Bi-So-Dol), Sponsor
"The Case of the Man Who Deserted a Dream"
   Before departing Barrowsford, Mr. Keen learns that the overworked Mrs. Krause has suffered an attack. He persuades Fred to accompany him. Rose stands vigil by her granny's bedside.

CONTINUITY #70
Tuesday, March 22, 1938
7:15–7:30 p.m. EST
NBC Blue
Announcer's name omitted
American Home Products (Bi-So-Dol), Sponsor
"The Case of the Man Who Deserted a Dream"
   Mr. Keen is successful in bringing the old couple together again, even though the restoration comes just moments before Mrs. Krause passes away. Krause will guide young Rose.

CONTINUITY #71
Wednesday, March 23, 1938
7:15–7:30 p.m. EST
NBC Blue
Announcer's name omitted
American Home Products (Bi-So-Dol), Sponsor
"The Case of the Man Whom the World Scorned"
   Garage mechanic Tad Barnett left his wife and vanished 12 years back. He designed a diesel engine he couldn't sell. Now two firms want it. Pal Jess Hewlitt appeals to Keen.

CONTINUITY #72
Thursday, March 24, 1938
7:15–7:30 p.m. EST
NBC Blue
Announcer's name omitted
American Home Products (Bi-So-Dol), Sponsor
"The Case of the Man Whom the World Scorned"
To avoid his being cheated out of his patent rights, Barnett will need to be located quickly by Mr. Keen. Mike Clancy and spinster secretary Miss Ellis are pressed into service.

CONTINUITY #73
Tuesday, March 29, 1938
7:15–7:30 p.m. EST
NBC Blue
Announcer's name omitted
American Home Products (Bi-So-Dol), Sponsor
"The Case of the Man Whom the World Scorned"
Barnett is a panhandler residing at a Bowery lodge house. A lawyer of dubious repute has contacted the inebriated inventor, presumably to purchase the patents at a price far below current value.

CONTINUITY #74
Wednesday, March 30, 1938
7:15–7:30 p.m. EST
NBC Blue
Announcer's name omitted
American Home Products (Bi-So-Dol), Sponsor
"The Case of the Man Whom the World Scorned"
Mr. Keen and Mike Clancy find Tad Barnett and tell him what has happened. Back at the office, Keen informs Jess Hewlitt and Mrs. Barnett of his success in locating the man.

CONTINUITY #75
Thursday, March 31, 1938
7:15–7:30 p.m. EST
NBC Blue
Announcer's name omitted
American Home Products (Bi-So-Dol), Sponsor
"The Case of the Man Whom the World Scorned"
Tad is brought into the equation. A former drunk and outcast who deserted his wife and business partner because no one liked his idea, Ted Barnett has now been vindicated and restored to respectability.

CONTINUITY #76
Tuesday, April 5, 1938
7:15–7:30 p.m. EST
NBC Blue
Announcer's name omitted
American Home Products (Bi-So-Dol), Sponsor
"The Case of the Lost Song"
A shabby Mr. and Mrs. Tyler ask Keen to hunt for ex-boarder Riccardo Vasari, who used to sing to their eight-year-old son Tommy. Tommy is ill, and doctors think the presence of Vasari might prompt a recovery.

CONTINUITY #77
Wednesday, April 6, 1938
7:15–7:30 p.m. EST
NBC Blue
Announcer's name omitted
American Home Products (Bi-So-Dol), Sponsor
"The Case of the Lost Song"
Vasari is now rich and famous. The tracer visits an Italian contractor for whom he once worked. Keen learns that today Vasari goes by the name of Riccardo Veronesco, a radio and opera star.

CONTINUITY #78
Thursday, April 7, 1938
7:15–7:30 p.m. EST
NBC Blue
Announcer's name omitted
American Home Products (Bi-So-Dol), Sponsor
"The Case of the Lost Song"
Mr. Keen and Miss Ellis go to Veronesco's palatial dwelling. Time has wrought great change. Rich and spoiled, the star refuses to visit Tommy, though that might pull him through.

CONTINUITY #79
Tuesday, April 12, 1938
7:15–7:30 p.m. EST
NBC Blue

Ben Grauer, Announcer
American Home Products (Bi-So-Dol), Sponsor
"The Case of the Lost Song"
    Interrupting one of the great singer's lavish champagne parties, Mr. Keen at last persuades him to change his mind. A pampered Veronesco agrees to visit the sick little boy.

CONTINUITY #80
Wednesday, April 13, 1938
7:15–7:30 p.m. EST
NBC Blue
Ben Grauer, Announcer
American Home Products (Bi-So-Dol), Sponsor
"The Case of the Lost Song"
    Riccardo Veronesco comes to the bedside of the gravely ill child. It works wonders. Mr. Keen earns plaudits from Mrs. Tyler, for she believes he literally saved her son's life.

CONTINUITY #81
Thursday, April 14, 1938
7:15–7:30 p.m. EST
NBC Blue
Announcer's name omitted
American Home Products (Bi-So-Dol), Sponsor
"The Case of the Ladies Sewing Circle"
    Mrs. Tippit, Mrs. Longwell and Mrs. Finch of Rosebud Manor enlist Mr. Keen to seek neighbor Lydia Hatfield. She left abruptly five months ago, and her spouse claims she's on a global trip.

CONTINUITY #82
Tuesday, April 19, 1938
7:15–7:30 p.m. EST
NBC Blue
Announcer's name omitted
American Home Products (Bi-So-Dol), Sponsor
"The Case of the Ladies Sewing Circle"
    Lydia Hatfield left quite suddenly, without a word to anyone. Posing as a salesman, Keen questions Hugo Hatfield. Like the women, he too is alarmed by the man's answers.

CONTINUITY #83
Wednesday, April 20, 1938
7:15–7:30 p.m. EST
NBC Blue
Announcer's name omitted
American Home Products (Bi-So-Dol), Sponsor
"The Case of the Ladies Sewing Circle"
    The trio of women meets Keen at the Tippit home next to the Hatfields. They spy on Hugo—he puts barbed wire fencing around his garage, then welcomes a heavily veiled woman.

CONTINUITY #84
Thursday, April 21, 1938
7:15–7:30 p.m. EST
NBC Blue
Announcer's name omitted
American Home Products (Bi-So-Dol), Sponsor
"The Case of the Ladies Sewing Circle"
    Hugo is summoned to Mr. Keen's office. Mrs. Tippit has told the tracer that Hugo is madly in love with Madame Valeria, a "gay foreign widow" who runs a suburban beauty salon.

CONTINUITY #85
Tuesday, April 26, 1938
7:15–7:30 p.m. EDST
NBC Blue
Announcer's name omitted
American Home Products (Bi-So-Dol), Sponsor
"The Case of the Ladies Sewing Circle"
    Returning to the Tippit home, Mr. Keen locates the missing woman, who was murdered and buried by her spouse. It turns out the suspicions of gossiping housewives were well placed.

CONTINUITY #86
Wednesday, April 27, 1938
7:15–7:30 p.m. EDST
NBC Blue
Announcer's name omitted
American Home Products (Bi-So-Dol), Sponsor
"The Case of the Two Mrs. Marvins"
    Herbert and Dora Marvin, age 35 and 25 respectively, visit Mr. Keen for help in finding Herbert's mother, who vanished last week while Herbert was away on business. Dora is too calm to suit Keen.

CONTINUITY #87
Thursday, April 28, 1938
7:15–7:30 p.m. EDST
NBC Blue
Announcer's name omitted
American Home Products (Bi-So-Dol), Sponsor
"The Case of the Two Mrs. Marvins"
   In Tyndale, Ohio, Keen questions friends of the elderly lady. Dora's ill treatment of her mother-in-law prompted Agnes Marvin to leave their home and move in with Clara Richards.

CONTINUITY #88
Tuesday, May 3, 1938
7:15–7:30 p.m. EDST
NBC Blue
Announcer's name omitted
American Home Products (Bi-So-Dol), Sponsor
"The Case of the Two Mrs. Marvins"
   At Mrs. Richards' shabby bungalow in Santa Ramona, California, Mr. Keen finds an atmosphere of love and joy generated by the homeowner and her 7-year-old child, Peggy. He sends for Herbert Marvin.

CONTINUITY #89
Wednesday, May 4, 1938
7:15–7:30 p.m. EDST
NBC Blue
Announcer's name omitted
American Home Products (Bi-So-Dol), Sponsor
"The Case of the Two Mrs. Marvins"
   Fearful of more fighting with Dora, Agnes Marvin disappears a second time. Later, at the Marvin home in Ohio, Mr. Keen is an overnight guest. Herbert and Dora discuss the events.

CONTINUITY #91
Tuesday, May 10, 1938
7:15–7:30 p.m. EDST
NBC Blue
Announcer's name omitted
American Home Products (Bi-So-Dol), Sponsor
"The Case of the Girl Who Learned How to Live"
   The palatial Long Island estate of Colonel Hubert Van Doren is the backdrop for this tale of dissatisfaction among the rich. Sylvia Van Doren, heiress to millions, is missing. Her mother fears kidnapping; her father wants the cops.

CONTINUITY #92
Wednesday, May 11, 1938
7:15–7:30 p.m. EDST
NBC Blue
Announcer's name omitted
American Home Products (Bi-So-Dol), Sponsor
"The Case of the Girl Who Learned How to Live"
   Mr. Keen starts a search by questioning a Van Doren aide, Jarvis. Keen thinks Sylvia tired of her luxurious lifestyle and ran away. An ex-chauffeur had taunted her about getting a job.

CONTINUITY #93
Thursday, May 12, 1938
7:15–7:30 p.m. EDST
NBC Blue
Announcer's name omitted
American Home Products (Bi-So-Dol), Sponsor
"The Case of the Girl Who Learned How to Live"
   Sylvia's working in a bottling plant in Rexley, New Jersey, put up to it by collegian Roddy Matthews, the ex-chauffeur. He and Keen go to the home she occupies with two factory girls.

CONTINUITY #94
Tuesday, May 17, 1938
7:15–7:30 p.m. EDST
NBC Blue
Announcer's name omitted
American Home Products (Bi-So-Dol), Sponsor
"The Case of the Girl Who Learned How to Live"
   Keen and Matthews meet Sylvia and her housemates, Jenny and Paula. Sylvia *is* fed up with the pampering and formality at home. She and Roddy are in love, even though he's jobless.

CONTINUITY #95
Wednesday, May 18, 1938
7:15–7:30 p.m. EDST
NBC Blue

Announcer's name omitted
American Home Products (Bi-So-Dol), Sponsor
"The Case of the Girl Who Learned How to Live"
    Oil and rail baron Van Doren, and his "silly society-loving wife," go to Keen's office. Keen assures them that money isn't everything. They acquiesce and accept Sylvia and Roddy.

CONTINUITY #96
Thursday, May 19, 1938
7:15–7:30 p.m. EDST
NBC Blue
Announcer's name omitted
American Home Products (Bi-So-Dol), Sponsor
"The Case of Two Men, a Girl and a Violin"
    Keen and Miss Ellis attend a concert given by brilliant violinist Martin Rex. They meet a beggar, Felix Clermont, who had been a renowned violinist, and who's now searching for a missing son.

CONTINUITY #97
Tuesday, May 24, 1938
7:15–7:30 p.m. EDST
NBC Blue
Announcer's name omitted
American Home Products (Bi-So-Dol), Sponsor
"The Case of Two Men, a Girl and a Violin"
    Clermont, seeing Rex's news photos, thinks he's Francois, his lost son. His wife left him for another man 20 years ago, taking their son, and landing him in poverty and obscurity.

CONTINUITY #98
Wednesday, May 25, 1938
7:15–7:30 p.m. EDST
NBC Blue
Announcer's name omitted
American Home Products (Bi-So-Dol), Sponsor
"The Case of Two Men, a Girl and a Violin"
    Mr. Keen buys a suit of clothes for Clermont and takes him to the concert hall to hear Rex play. Keen interviews the genius, who indignantly denies he could be the beggar's son.

CONTINUITY #99
Thursday, May 26, 1938
7:15–7:30 p.m. EDST
NBC Blue
Announcer's name omitted
American Home Products (Bi-So-Dol), Sponsor
"The Case of Two Men, a Girl and a Violin"
    From debutante Eveline Crowley, Rex's fiancée, Keen learns that Rex really *is* the missing lad. She assures the tracer that she will find a way to bring father and son together.

CONTINUITY #100
Tuesday, May 31, 1938
7:15–7:30 p.m. EDST
NBC Blue
Announcer's name omitted
American Home Products (Bi-So-Dol), Sponsor
"The Case of Two Men, a Girl and a Violin"
    Martin Rex performs for guests at a party. Eveline is at his side. Keen and Felix Clermont attend. All is revealed, and this portion of the family is reunited, thanks to Keen.

CONTINUITY #101
Wednesday, June 1, 1938
7:15–7:30 p.m. EDST
NBC Blue
Announcer's name omitted
American Home Products (Bi-So-Dol), Sponsor
"The Case of the Man Who Threw Away His Chance"
    Tim Bernard, age 13, and his sister, Ginny (age 11) ask Keen to find their father, Adam Bernard. Their folks divorced. They're wary of their mom's new intended, believing he plans to seize her livelihood.

CONTINUITY #102
Thursday, June 2, 1938
7:15–7:30 p.m. EDST
NBC Blue
Announcer's name omitted
American Home Products (Bi-So-Dol), Sponsor
"The Case of the Man Who Threw Away His Chance"
    Jack Fletcher manages Adele Bernard's roadhouse. Mr. Keen traces Adam Bernard to a Manhattan hotel. Rich widow Anna Lawson is ready to stake Bernard to a Florida hotel venture.

CONTINUITY #103
Tuesday, June 7, 1938
7:15–7:30 p.m. EDST
NBC Blue
Announcer's name omitted
American Home Products (Bi-So-Dol), Sponsor
"The Case of the Man Who Threw Away His Chance"
    Keen urges Bernard to return and keep his ex from marrying a bounder who's only after her property. He refuses. Life with Anna seems far more appealing. Keen takes Tim and Ginny to the hotel.

CONTINUITY #104
Wednesday, June 8, 1938
7:15–7:30 p.m. EDST
NBC Blue
Announcer's name omitted
American Home Products (Bi-So-Dol), Sponsor
"The Case of the Man Who Threw Away His Chance"
    Bernard isn't impressed. Mr. Keen drives Tim and Ginny home from New York after their pleas fall on deaf ears. In the meantime, Adele and Jack are conversing at the roadhouse.

CONTINUITY #105
Thursday, June 9, 1938
7:15–7:30 p.m. EDST
NBC Blue
Announcer's name omitted
American Home Products (Bi-So-Dol), Sponsor
"The Case of the Man Who Threw Away His Chance"
    Adam Bernard has second thoughts. He realizes that his love and future happiness rests with Adele, his ex-wife, and their two children. There is the hint of wedding bells.

CONTINUITY #106
Tuesday, June 14, 1938
7:15–7:30 p.m. EDST
NBC Blue
Ben Grauer, Announcer
American Home Products (Kolynos), Sponsor
"The Case of the Man Who Was Found Before He Disappeared"
    Keen is to find *where* Arnold Brockton will vanish *before* he does. A once-rich famous athlete, he's now in dire financial straits. He insured himself for $1 million.

CONTINUITY #107
Wednesday, June 15, 1938
7:15–7:30 p.m. EDST
NBC Blue
Ben Grauer, Announcer
American Home Products (Kolynos), Sponsor
"The Case of the Man Who Was Found Before He Disappeared"
    The ex–swim champ may intend to vanish in a windstorm on Mallard Lake in the Adirondacks. People will think he drowned. Keen and Clancy are among the spectators watching the risky long-distance swim.

CONTINUITY #108
Thursday, June 16, 1938
7:15–7:30 p.m. EDST
NBC Blue
Ben Grauer, Announcer
American Home Products (Kolynos), Sponsor
"The Case of the Man Who Was Found Before He Disappeared"
    A storm breaks during Brockton's swim, and he is lost. The public is sure he drowned, but Keen believes otherwise. He's certain Brockton is hiding in a sanatorium across the lake.

CONTINUITY #109
Tuesday, June 21, 1938
7:15–7:30 p.m. EDST
NBC Blue
Ben Grauer, Announcer
American Home Products (Kolynos), Sponsor
"The Case of the Man Who Was Found Before He Disappeared"
    Keen and Clancy pursue Brockton to the sanatorium, only to find he really *has* vanished! It appears the insurer will have to pay.

CONTINUITY #110
Wednesday, June 22, 1938
7:15–7:30 p.m. EDST
NBC Blue
Ben Grauer, Announcer
American Home Products (Kolynos), Sponsor
"The Case of the Man Who Was Found Before He Disappeared"

Keen's brilliant deductive powers reveal that Mr. Rutherford, the insurance VP who hired Keen, is in on the swindle. Brockton is located and their scam exposed.

CONTINUITY #111
Thursday, June 23, 1938
7:15–7:30 p.m. EDST
NBC Blue
Ben Grauer, Announcer
American Home Products (Kolynos), Sponsor
"The Case of Mrs. Granville's Real Family"

Irene Granville, wife of a snobbish millionaire, seeks her parents. She lied about her lower-class family, claimed her folks had died. But after six years she's weary of playing games.

CONTINUITY #112
Tuesday, June 28, 1938
7:15–7:30 p.m. EDST
NBC Blue
Ben Grauer, Announcer
American Home Products (Bi-So-Dol), Sponsor
"The Case of Mrs. Granville's Real Family"

Irene's dad, Sam Jenkins, now a cripple, had been among the minions employed by Irene's rail magnate spouse. Irene's mother, Nellie, is a dishwasher. Embittered, the couple lives in abject poverty.

CONTINUITY #113
Wednesday, June 29, 1938
7:15–7:30 p.m. EDST
NBC Blue
Ben Grauer, Announcer
American Home Products (Bi-So-Dol), Sponsor
"The Case of Mrs. Granville's Real Family"

Mr. Keen locates the impoverished couple and induces them to make up with their daughter, reporting her change of heart. The two accompany him to the luxurious Granville estate.

CONTINUITY #114
Thursday, June 30, 1938
7:15–7:30 p.m. EDST
NBC Blue
Ben Grauer, Announcer
American Home Products (Bi-So-Dol), Sponsor
"The Case of Mrs. Granville's Real Family"

Irene welcomes her folks with open arms. She wants them to live there. During their celebration, Wickstead Granville enters. He becomes furious with his wife, and orders her parents to leave.

CONTINUITY #115
Tuesday, July 5, 1938
7:15–7:30 p.m. EDST
NBC Blue
Ben Grauer, Announcer
American Home Products (Bi-So-Dol), Sponsor
"The Case of Mrs. Granville's Real Family"

Wickstead Granville rethinks his position. Irene was rich and arrogant, but still felt the need of her parents' simple goodness and love. She could change, and now so can he.

CONTINUITY #116
Wednesday, July 6, 1938
7:15–7:30 p.m. EDST
NBC Blue
Ben Grauer, Announcer
American Home Products (Bi-So-Dol), Sponsor
"The Case of the Wife Who Grew Tired of Waiting"

Keen seeks Betty Bradford, age 25, and son Herbert, age four. Betty and her spouse Duncan lived in Tramville, Indiana, when he lost his job four years ago. His uncle, Herbert Craig, took them in.

CONTINUITY #117
Thursday, July 7, 1938
7:15–7:30 p.m. EDST
NBC Blue
Ben Grauer, Announcer
American Home Products (Bi-So-Dol), Sponsor
"The Case of the Wife Who Grew Tired of Waiting"

Craig taunted his nephew, who left. A year ago Betty took Herbert and departed the Craig house. Duncan now has a job but no family. Now residing in Random City, Illinois, Betty serves Duncan with divorce papers.

CONTINUITY #118
Tuesday, July 12, 1938

7:15–7:30 p.m. EDST
NBC Blue
Ben Grauer, Announcer
American Home Products (Bi-So-Dol), Sponsor
"The Case of the Wife Who Grew Tired of Waiting"
    Mr. Keen and Duncan Bradford visit Random City. They find Betty Bradford snubbing their appeals to return home. Her employer, Mr. Tompkins, though twice her age, has grown quite fond of her.

CONTINUITY #119
Wednesday, July 13, 1938
7:15–7:30 p.m. EDST
NBC Blue
Ben Grauer, Announcer
American Home Products (Bi-So-Dol), Sponsor
"The Case of the Wife Who Grew Tired of Waiting"
    Mr. Keen and Duncan Bradford visit the Tompkins Coal Company where Betty is employed. They meet the owner. Efforts to persuade her not to divorce and remarry fall on deaf ears.

CONTINUITY #120
Thursday, July 14, 1938
7:15–7:30 p.m. EDST
NBC Blue
Ben Grauer, Announcer
American Home Products (Bi-So-Dol), Sponsor
"The Case of the Wife Who Grew Tired of Waiting"
    In a typical feel-good ending, Betty returns to her husband. Keen tells them hardship, hurt and humiliation are nothing compared to lasting affection. They head for eternal bliss.

CONTINUITY #121
Tuesday, July 19, 1938
7:15–7:30 p.m. EDST
NBC Blue
Ben Grauer, Announcer
American Home Products (Bi-So-Dol), Sponsor
"The Case of the Actor Who Lived His Part"
    Actor Ronald Wintringham asks Keen to locate Diane Lorimer, whom he played opposite of in "Romeo and Juliet" seven years ago. He was madly in love with her, but his fickleness drove her away.

CONTINUITY #122
Wednesday, July 20, 1938
7:15–7:30 p.m. EDST
NBC Blue
Ben Grauer, Announcer
American Home Products (Bi-So-Dol), Sponsor
"The Case of the Actor Who Lived His Part"
    Wintringham opened last week in the same play, and memories cascaded over him. He received an unsigned note from Diane. Keen traces the girl to a shabby theatrical boarding house.

CONTINUITY #123
Thursday, July 21, 1938
7:15–7:30 p.m. EDST
NBC Blue
Ben Grauer, Announcer
American Home Products (Bi-So-Dol), Sponsor
"The Case of the Actor Who Lived His Part"
    Desperate for money and unable to get back on the stage, Diane Lorimer has taken a job in a cheap roadhouse. She opens tonight. Keen and Wintringham will go to see her.

CONTINUITY #124
Tuesday, July 26, 1938
7:15–7:30 p.m. EDST
NBC Blue
Ben Grauer, Announcer
American Home Products (Bi-So-Dol), Sponsor
"The Case of the Actor Who Lived His Part"
    At Giovanni's Venetian Gardens the men watch Diane's parody impersonations. Aghast at her fall from legitimate theater, Wintringham makes his presence known. She runs away, and the press touts the story.

CONTINUITY #125
Wednesday, July 27, 1938
7:15–7:30 p.m. EDST
NBC Blue
Ben Grauer, Announcer
American Home Products (Bi-So-Dol), Sponsor

"The Case of the Actor Who Lived His Part"

Mr. Keen locates Diane Lorimer a second time and returns her to Ronald Wintringham. He concludes that real life often holds as much romance as the love stories acted on the stage.

CONTINUITY #126
Thursday, July 28, 1938
7:15–7:30 p.m. EDST
NBC Blue
Ben Grauer, Announcer
American Home Products (Bi-So-Dol), Sponsor
"The Case of the Man Whose Story Didn't Ring True"

Ralph Potter, an art treasures dealer, lost his wife and infant daughter 22 years ago. Returning from a long trip, his family simply was gone. Mr. Keen seems skeptical of his tale.

CONTINUITY #127
Tuesday, August 2, 1938
7:15–7:30 p.m. EDST
NBC Blue
Ben Grauer, Announcer
American Home Products (Bi-So-Dol), Sponsor
"The Case of the Man Whose Story Didn't Ring True"

Keen finds that eight years ago Louise Potter, now living with her 24-year-old daughter in Cloverly, Pennsylvania, had her husband declared dead. Louise married Samuel Haywood, a merchant.

CONTINUITY #128
Wednesday, August 3, 1938
7:15–7:30 p.m. EDST
NBC Blue
Ben Grauer, Announcer
American Home Products (Bi-So-Dol), Sponsor
"The Case of the Man Whose Story Didn't Ring True"

Did Louise run away from her first spouse? Keen goes to Cloverly to find out. Louise's daughter, Linda, knows nothing of her real dad. Sam Haywood offers to tell Keen a great deal about Ralph Potter.

CONTINUITY #129
Thursday, August 4, 1938
7:15–7:30 p.m. EDST
NBC Blue
Ben Grauer, Announcer
American Home Products (Bi-So-Dol), Sponsor
"The Case of the Man Whose Story Didn't Ring True"

Potter deserted his family, rather than them deserting him. He has been blackmailing Haywood, threatening to "turn up alive in court" and contest the validity of the second marriage.

CONTINUITY #130
Tuesday, August 9, 1938
7:15–7:30 p.m. EDST
NBC Blue
Ben Grauer, Announcer
American Home Products (Bi-So-Dol), Sponsor
"The Case of the Man Whose Story Didn't Ring True"

Sam Haywood loves Linda as his own child. He hasn't called the police because he wants to avoid scandalizing his family. Mr. Keen rebukes his client and restores peace in the Haywood home.

CONTINUITY #131
Wednesday, August 10, 1938
7:15–7:30 p.m. EDST
NBC Blue
Ben Grauer, Announcer
American Home Products (Bi-So-Dol), Sponsor
"The Case of the Cowardice of Captain Hardy"

A freighter sank 25 years ago. Captain Will Hardy was saved but faced charges of deserting his crew. Found guilty, and branded a coward in seaports everywhere, he vanished.

CONTINUITY #132
Thursday, August 11, 1938
7:15–7:30 p.m. EDST
NBC Blue
Ben Grauer, Announcer
American Home Products (Bi-So-Dol), Sponsor
"The Case of the Cowardice of Captain Hardy"

Hardy's innocence having since been proven, Eric Pickering III (the son of Hardy's former employer and current owner of the steamship line) presses Mr. Keen into service to find the captain. Keen starts at the Sailor's Aid Society at New York's waterfront. Interviews lead to Hardy.

CONTINUITY #133
Tuesday, August 16, 1938
7:15–7:30 p.m. EDST
NBC Blue
Ben Grauer, Announcer
American Home Products (Bi-So-Dol), Sponsor
"The Case of the Cowardice of Captain Hardy"
The Hardys occupy a shabby flat. He has faced torment, jeers, insults and innuendo. Sailors haven't forgotten his "failing." When recognized, he even lost menial sailing jobs.

CONTINUITY #134
Wednesday, August 17, 1938
7:15–7:30 p.m. EDST
NBC Blue
Ben Grauer, Announcer
American Home Products (Bi-So-Dol), Sponsor
"The Case of the Cowardice of Captain Hardy"
Keen and Clancy visit the Hardys. They find a broken man with a seafaring career in ruins. Hardy attempts suicide but is stopped in time. Keen urges him to visit his ex-employer's son.

CONTINUITY #135
Thursday, August 18, 1938
7:15–7:30 p.m. EDST
NBC Blue
Ben Grauer, Announcer
American Home Products (Bi-So-Dol), Sponsor
"The Case of the Cowardice of Captain Hardy"
Eric Pickering III, owner of Pickering Steamship Lines, rejoices at a meeting with Will Hardy. Other sea captains join in. Restitution is made and his good name restored.

CONTINUITY #136
Tuesday, August 23, 1938
7:15–7:30 p.m. EDST
NBC Blue
Andre Baruch, Announcer
American Home Products (Bi-So-Dol), Sponsor
"The Case of the Three Sisters"
Keen and Miss Ellis drive to an old Washington, D.C. mansion fallen into disrepair. The Marbury spinster sisters (Laura, age 80, and Theresa, age 75), a late senator's daughters, sent for them.

CONTINUITY #137
Wednesday, August 24, 1938
7:15–7:30 p.m. EDST
NBC Blue
Andre Baruch, Announcer
American Home Products (Bi-So-Dol), Sponsor
"The Case of the Three Sisters"
Peters, an elderly butler, cares for the recluses. They want Keen to find another sister, Edith, now 60, who ran off 40 years ago. Keen thinks they're hiding a secret from him.

CONTINUITY #138
Thursday, August 25, 1938
7:15–7:30 p.m. EDST
NBC Blue
Andre Baruch, Announcer
American Home Products (Bi-So-Dol), Sponsor
"The Case of the Three Sisters"
Edith eloped with the family coachman, Tom Wheelock. Keen locates her in Everly, Indiana. Tom has since died. The VP of a local bank, Mr. Crozier, is with her as Mr. Keen arrives.

CONTINUITY #139
Tuesday, August 30, 1938
7:15–7:30 p.m. EDST
NBC Blue
Andre Baruch, Announcer
American Home Products (Bi-So-Dol), Sponsor
"The Case of the Three Sisters"
Bitter about the past, Edith wants nothing to do with her family. Hounded by creditors, the Marbury spinsters auction their home and contents. A greedy crowd attends the sale.

CONTINUITY #140
Wednesday, August 31, 1938
7:15–7:30 p.m. EDST
NBC Blue
Andre Baruch, Announcer

American Home Products (Bi-So-Dol), Sponsor
"The Case of the Three Sisters"
   Mr. Keen notes that somebody bids very high prices for items of sentimental value. By proxy, Edith has bid on family heirlooms. A change of heart restores her to her family and her home.

CONTINUITY #141
Thursday, September 1, 1938
7:15–7:30 p.m. EDST
NBC Blue
Andre Baruch, Announcer
American Home Products (Bi-So-Dol), Sponsor
"The Case of Grandfather Gilbert"
   In Gilbertsville, South Dakota, a former thriving mining camp, wealthy Fred Gilbert, father of prominent banker Martin Gilbert, disappears. We learn that Martin's wife Gladys is spoiled and self-centered.

CONTINUITY #142
Tuesday, September 6, 1938
7:15–7:30 p.m. EDST
NBC Blue
Ben Grauer, Announcer
American Home Products (Bi-So-Dol), Sponsor
"The Case of Grandfather Gilbert"
   Fred, enamored of past eras, frequently embarrasses his socially-driven family. There are deep bonds between Fred and grandson Jed, age 10, now missing from an exclusive Eastern military academy.

CONTINUITY #143
Wednesday, September 7, 1938
7:15–7:30 p.m. EDST
NBC Blue
Ben Grauer, Announcer
American Home Products (Bi-So-Dol), Sponsor
"The Case of Grandfather Gilbert"
   Staying at the Gilbert home, Keen must solve both mysteries. Fred infected his grandson with the romance of bygone Indian days. The tracer follows the pair to Fred's hunting camp.

CONTINUITY #144
Thursday, September 8, 1938
7:15–7:30 p.m. EDST
NBC Blue
Ben Grauer, Announcer
American Home Products (Bi-So-Dol), Sponsor
"The Case of Grandfather Gilbert"
   The duo is fed up with the formality of modern life. Keen stays overnight at the cabin and persuades both generations that the way to enjoy life is to conquer it, not flee from it.

CONTINUITY #145
Tuesday, September 13, 1938
7:15–7:30 p.m. EDST
NBC Blue
Ben Grauer, Announcer
American Home Products (Bi-So-Dol), Sponsor
"The Case of the Girl Who Went to Hollywood"
   Keen and Miss Ellis fly to a Hollywood retreat hosted by one of Keen's movie star pals, Stuart Whitby. Keen is seeking Ella Ramsey, too, an aspiring actress who left Illinois months ago.

CONTINUITY #146
Wednesday, September 14, 1938
7:15–7:30 p.m. EDST
NBC Blue
Ben Grauer, Announcer
American Home Products (Bi-So-Dol), Sponsor
"The Case of the Girl Who Went to Hollywood"
   While Miss Ellis meets movie stars, Keen learns that Ella Ramsey fell into a dishonest promoter's hands. She's at an L.A. tenement, her money gone and jobs as an "extra" sparse.

CONTINUITY #147
Thursday, September 15, 1938
7:15–7:30 p.m. EDST
NBC Blue
Ben Grauer, Announcer
American Home Products (Bi-So-Dol), Sponsor
"The Case of the Girl Who Went to Hollywood"
   Stuart Whitby drives Keen to Ella Ramsey's address. They find her broke and hungry. She doesn't want to go home just yet, however;

and Keen prevails on Whitby to test her acting potential.

CONTINUITY #148
Tuesday, September 20, 1938
7:15–7:30 p.m. EDST
NBC Blue
Ben Grauer, Announcer
American Home Products (Bi-So-Dol), Sponsor
"The Case of the Girl Who Went to Hollywood"
At Whitby's palatial Beverly Hills digs, the star has become intrigued by farm girl Ella's natural beauty and charm. The typically pampered, sophisticated women of Hollywood bore him.

CONTINUITY #149
Wednesday, September 21, 1938
7:15–7:30 p.m. EDST
NBC Blue
George Ansbro, Announcer
American Home Products (Bi-So-Dol), Sponsor
"The Case of the Girl Who Went to Hollywood"
Ella has fallen for Whitby, who claims that he cares for her. Keen doesn't think so, and wires for Amos Ramsey, the girl's father, to rush out and fetch Ella home. Mr. Ramsey goes to her flat.

CONTINUITY #150
Thursday, September 22, 1938
7:15–7:30 p.m. EDST
NBC Blue
Ben Grauer, Announcer
American Home Products (Bi-So-Dol), Sponsor
"The Case of the Girl Who Went to Hollywood"
The case concludes with Ella Ramsey, the little Illinois farm girl who ran off to Hollywood and a career in pictures, becoming engaged to leading actor Stuart Whitby, Mr. Keen's host.

CONTINUITY #151
Tuesday, September 27, 1938
7:15–7:30 p.m. EST
NBC Blue
Ben Grauer, Announcer
American Home Products (Bi-So-Dol), Sponsor
"The Case of the Witness Who Wasn't Afraid"
A bitter upstate D. A. election pits lawyer Perry Webster against dirty politico Sam Brogan, who frames Webster on a bomb charge. Brogan's man Ted Fellows, now in hiding, knows the truth.

CONTINUITY #152
Wednesday, September 28, 1938
7:15–7:30 p.m. EST
NBC Blue
George Ansbro, Announcer
American Home Products (Bi-So-Dol), Sponsor
"The Case of the Witness Who Wasn't Afraid"
Keen goes to Wembley, New York. He interviews bartender Mary Fellows, wife of the missing man, who refuses to divulge her husband's location. Keen also watches Sam Brogan and the men around him.

CONTINUITY #153
Thursday, September 29, 1938
7:15–7:30 p.m. EST
NBC Blue
Ben Grauer, Announcer
American Home Products (Bi-So-Dol), Sponsor
"The Case of the Witness Who Wasn't Afraid"
Perry Webster addresses a street corner election rally. Mr. Keen is on the platform. It's obvious Fellows is deathly afraid of boss Brogan. Some of Brogan's henchmen show up.

CONTINUITY #154
Tuesday, October 4, 1938
7:15–7:30 p.m. EST
NBC Blue
Ben Grauer, Announcer
American Home Products (Bi-So-Dol), Sponsor
"The Case of the Witness Who Wasn't Afraid"
Mr. Keen finds frightened Ted Fellows but can't persuade him to return and clear Perry Webster. Webster's trial begins at Ted's hideout the young man tunes in a newscast.

CONTINUITY #155
Wednesday, October 5, 1938

7:15–7:30 p.m. EST
NBC Blue
Ben Grauer, Announcer
American Home Products (Bi-So-Dol), Sponsor
"The Case of the Witness Who Wasn't Afraid"
   Keen sits with Mary Fellows in a court presided over by a corrupt judge, and featuring Sam Brogan's lying witnesses. Just then, Ted Fellows shows up and testifies against the crooks.

CONTINUITY #156
Thursday, October 6, 1938
7:15–7:30 p.m. EST
NBC Blue
Ben Grauer, Announcer
American Home Products (Bi-So-Dol), Sponsor
"The Case of the Wife Who Ran Off to Die"
   Five years ago Vera Johnson left spouse David Johnson and daughter Sally, age 15, heading for New York. She said her husband couldn't adequately support her there in Texas. Now she can't be found.

CONTINUITY #157
Tuesday, October 11, 1938
7:15–7:30 p.m. EST
NBC Blue
Ben Grauer, Announcer
American Home Products (Bi-So-Dol), Sponsor
"The Case of the Wife Who Ran Off to Die"
   About to marry, Sally wants her mom at the wedding. Vera has written to them, but they discover that she wasn't at any of the places mentioned. Keen traces her to a sanitarium 50 miles away.

CONTINUITY #158
Wednesday, October 12, 1938
7:15–7:30 p.m. EST
NBC Blue
Ben Grauer, Announcer
American Home Products (Bi-So-Dol), Sponsor
"The Case of the Wife Who Ran Off to Die"
   Keen meets Vera at the free sanitarium for consumptives, where she went to spare her family the truth. She and Keen go to Ft. Thomas, Texas, by train. She will maintain the deception.

CONTINUITY #159
Thursday, October 13, 1938
7:15–7:30 p.m. EST
NBC Blue
Ben Grauer, Announcer
American Home Products (Bi-So-Dol), Sponsor
"The Case of the Wife Who Ran Off to Die"
   Vera collapses from nervousness and excitement. Her family hears the truth. The nuptials occur. Vera rests in bed at the ranch. Sally and her spouse Larry delay the honeymoon.

CONTINUITY #160
Tuesday, October 18, 1938
7:15–7:30 p.m. EST
NBC Blue
Ben Grauer, Announcer
American Home Products (Bi-So-Dol), Sponsor
"The Case of the Wife Who Ran Off to Die"
   The tracer impresses upon Vera Johnson the fact that problems and burdens must be shared in order to hold families close together. The family rejoices in having her back.

CONTINUITY #161
Wednesday, October 19, 1938
7:15–7:30 p.m. EST
NBC Blue
Ben Grauer, Announcer
American Home Products (Bi-So-Dol), Sponsor
"The Case of the Man They All Hated"
   Keen is asked to find Hugo Radcliffe — financier, Wall Street gambler and ruthless speculator — hated by all for crushing any in his way. He left on a yacht cruise and never returned.

CONTINUITY #162
Thursday, October 20, 1938
7:15–7:30 p.m. EST
NBC Blue
Ben Grauer, Announcer
American Home Products (Bi-So-Dol), Sponsor
"The Case of the Man They All Hated"
   Winifred, Hugo's wife, admits she doesn't love her spouse. Keen suspects a link between her and the man's secretary, Thomas Ames. Hugo was last seen in Teddiwickport, Maine.

CONTINUITY #163
Tuesday, October 25, 1938
7:15–7:30 p.m. EST
NBC Blue
Ben Grauer, Announcer
American Home Products (Bi-So-Dol), Sponsor
"The Case of the Man They All Hated"
    Keen and Miss Ellis take a train to Maine. They find Hugo a changed man, living under the assumed name "Brown" in the fishing town. Locals call him "the Good Samaritan" for his deeds.

CONTINUITY #164
Wednesday, October 26, 1938
7:15–7:30 p.m. EST
NBC Blue
Ben Grauer, Announcer
American Home Products (Bi-So-Dol), Sponsor
"The Case of the Man They All Hated"
    Keen observes Radcliffe's altered lifestyle and questions him during a visit to his cottage. Radcliffe was tired of being hated. Keen hopes to reconcile him and his wife, and sends for her.

CONTINUITY #165
Thursday, October 27, 1938
7:15–7:30 p.m. EST
NBC Blue
Ben Grauer, Announcer
American Home Products (Bi-So-Dol), Sponsor
"The Case of the Man They All Hated"
    Radcliffe thinks his wife is infatuated with his secretary, Thomas Ames. Ames arrives in the fishing village. Keen and Miss Ellis prepare to return home, having done all they can.

CONTINUITY #166
Tuesday, November 1, 1938
7:15–7:30 p.m. EST
NBC Blue
Ben Grauer, Announcer
American Home Products (Bi-So-Dol), Sponsor
"The Case of the Man They All Hated"
    Keen makes a final attempt to convince the one-time pirate of finance, now reformed, that his place is back at home with his wife, where he can set an example for others. And he pulls it off.

CONTINUITY #167
Wednesday, November 2, 1938
7:15–7:30 p.m. EST
NBC Blue
Ben Grauer, Announcer
American Home Products (Bi-So-Dol), Sponsor
"The Case of the Delightful Mrs. Raine"
    Department store owner Herbert Raine disappeared five years ago. A comprehensive search did no good. His wife, Mary, began managing the store. She asks Keen for help in finding him.

CONTINUITY #168
Thursday, November 3, 1938
7:15–7:30 p.m. EST
NBC Blue
Ben Grauer, Announcer
American Home Products (Bi-So-Dol), Sponsor
"The Case of the Delightful Mrs. Raine"
    Is Keen in love with the charming Mary Raine? Other clients haven't touched him like this. The pair go to theaters and restaurants. Miss Ellis and Mike Clancy become suspicious.

CONTINUITY #169
Tuesday, November 8, 1938
7:15–7:30 p.m. EST
NBC Blue
Ben Grauer, Announcer
American Home Products (Bi-So-Dol), Sponsor
"The Case of the Delightful Mrs. Raine"
    His staff's reaction angers Keen. He rebukes Hilda Raine, Herbert's offspring, who casts figurative stones at her stepmother. Mary is with slick Barry Bromwell, a man she easily dominates.

CONTINUITY #170
Wednesday, November 9, 1938
7:15–7:30 p.m. EST
NBC Blue
Ben Grauer, Announcer
American Home Products (Bi-So-Dol), Sponsor
"The Case of the Delightful Mrs. Raine"

Miss Ellis and Clancy think they have proof that Mary Raine is involved in her spouse's disappearance. After a heated quarrel with Mr. Keen, however, Ellis abruptly resigns.

CONTINUITY #171
Thursday, November 10, 1938
7:15–7:30 p.m. EST
NBC Blue
Ben Grauer, Announcer
American Home Products (Bi-So-Dol), Sponsor
"The Case of the Delightful Mrs. Raine"
   Keen refuses to believe that Mary Raine is dangerous, yet soon discovers that he's wrong. Barry Bromwell claims that Mary killed her spouse, and Keen will try to trap her into confessing.

CONTINUITY #172
Tuesday, November 15, 1938
7:15–7:30 p.m. EST
NBC Blue
Ben Grauer, Announcer
American Home Products (Bi-So-Dol), Sponsor
"The Case of the Delightful Mrs. Raine"
   Keen begs Miss Ellis to return. She does. Mary Raine's past is exposed and she's handed over to the police. Keen is deeply dejected by the turn of events, emotionally drained.

CONTINUITY #173
Wednesday, November 16, 1938
7:15–7:30 p.m. EST
NBC Blue
Ben Grauer, Announcer
American Home Products (Bi-So-Dol), Sponsor
"The Case of Miss Wicks and Her Daughter"
   The Louis Wheelers, arriving from a 12-year stay abroad, find that they officially became guardians of niece Betty Raymond four years ago. She and nurse Emily Wicks vanished en-route to them.

CONTINUITY #174
Thursday, November 17, 1938
7:15–7:30 p.m. EST
NBC Blue
Ben Grauer, Announcer
American Home Products (Bi-So-Dol), Sponsor
"The Case of Miss Wicks and Her Daughter"
   Keen and Clancy begin at Griggs Ferry, Iowa, the Raymonds' hometown. Spinster Emily Wicks cared for Betty from birth and adored her. She may have taken her to Withington, Wisconsin.

CONTINUITY #175
Tuesday, November 22, 1938
7:15–7:30 p.m. EST
NBC Blue
Ben Grauer, Announcer
American Home Products (Bi-So-Dol), Sponsor
"The Case of Miss Wicks and Her Daughter"
   At Withington, Keen meets a tired, hard-working washerwoman, Mrs. Henderson, and her child Betty, age 10. The pair are Emily Wicks and Betty Raymond. They're soon furiously packing.

CONTINUITY #176
Wednesday, November 23, 1938
7:15–7:30 p.m. EST
NBC Blue
Ben Grauer, Announcer
American Home Products (Bi-So-Dol), Sponsor
"The Case of Miss Wicks and Her Daughter"
   Emily Wicks is frantic, afraid she may lose the child she loves as her own. Mr. Keen summons the legal guardians, Mr. and Mrs. Wheeler, to Withington, who arrive there promptly.

CONTINUITY #177
Thursday, November 24, 1938
7:15–7:30 p.m. EST
NBC Blue
Ben Grauer, Announcer
American Home Products (Bi-So-Dol), Sponsor
"The Case of Miss Wicks and Her Daughter"
   Betty is united with her guardians. Emily Wicks, her lifelong nurse, will continue to figure in her life, for she is virtually the only "mother" the child has ever known.

CONTINUITY #178
Tuesday, November 29, 1938
7:15–7:30 p.m. EST
NBC Blue
Ben Grauer, Announcer

American Home Products (Bi-So-Dol), Sponsor
"The Case of the Loved One Who Never Came Back"

Wealthy widow Lynne McIntyre is reunited with a son, Edgar Morehouse, from her first union. She left that spouse years ago. Roberta, a daughter from Lynn's second marriage, thinks Edgar is an imposter.

CONTINUITY #179
Wednesday, November 30, 1938
7:15–7:30 p.m. EST
NBC Blue
Ben Grauer, Announcer
American Home Products (Bi-So-Dol), Sponsor
"The Case of the Loved One Who Never Came Back"

Jefferson Neidig, Mrs. McIntyre's attorney, has helped convince her that the illiterate, rude, uncouth youth is indeed her long-lost son. Keen feels neither Edgar nor the lawyer can be trusted.

CONTINUITY #180
Thursday, December 1, 1938
7:15–7:30 p.m. EST
NBC Blue
Ben Grauer, Announcer
American Home Products (Bi-So-Dol), Sponsor
"The Case of the Loved One Who Never Came Back"

At Mr. Keen's request, Roberta plants a piece of dictating equipment in the McIntyre mansion, hoping to trap the presumed Edgar. Jefferson Neidig has a meeting with Edgar.

CONTINUITY #181
Tuesday, December 6, 1938
7:15–7:30 p.m. EST
NBC Blue
Ben Grauer, Announcer
American Home Products (Bi-So-Dol), Sponsor
"The Case of the Loved One Who Never Came Back"

Mr. Keen uncovers a conspiracy between lawyer and alleged son. Neidig has instigated a plot to gain control of Mrs. McIntyre's estate. Keen summons the youth to his office.

CONTINUITY #182
Wednesday, December 7, 1938
7:15–7:30 p.m. EST
NBC Blue
Ben Grauer, Announcer
American Home Products (Bi-So-Dol), Sponsor
"The Case of the Loved One Who Never Came Back"

Imposter Tom LaForge, by mistake, confirms that the real son died years ago, giving LaForge some personal memorabilia to take to Edgar's mother. LaForge is arrested; now Keen goes to Neidig's office.

CONTINUITY #183
Thursday, December 8, 1938
7:15–7:30 p.m. EST
NBC Blue
Ben Grauer, Announcer
American Home Products (Bi-So-Dol), Sponsor
"The Case of the Loved One Who Never Came Back"

Keen relays the sad news to Mrs. McIntyre that her son, the boy she spent years and a fortune looking for, is dead. The revelation brings mother and daughter closer together.

CONTINUITY #184
Tuesday, December 13, 1938
7:15–7:30 p.m. EST
NBC Blue
Ben Grauer, Announcer
American Home Products (Bi-So-Dol), Sponsor
"The Case of John Leroy's Best Friend"

Teacher John Leroy lost his sight and then cut ties with everyone. Given a seeing-eye dog, he eventually returned and resumed his life. A week ago, however, Champ was stolen. Keen is called in to find the dog.

CONTINUITY #185
Wednesday, December 14, 1938
7:15–7:30 p.m. EST
NBC Blue
Ben Grauer, Announcer
American Home Products (Bi-So-Dol), Sponsor
"The Case of John Leroy's Best Friend"

Two men stole Champ. Wounded and

suffering, the animal is soon left to die. Keen oversees a statewide search. Fifty miles away, Dickey Wilson, age 10, finds Champ and hides him in a barn.

CONTINUITY #186
Thursday, December 15, 1938
7:15–7:30 p.m. EST
NBC Blue
Ben Grauer, Announcer
American Home Products (Bi-So-Dol), Sponsor
"The Case of John Leroy's Best Friend"

The wounded dog is the first ray of sunshine in orphaned Dickey's life. His aunt, Mrs. Wilson, knows nothing of the dog. John Leroy again becomes despondent and stops teaching.

CONTINUITY #187
Tuesday, December 20, 1938
7:15–7:30 p.m. EST
NBC Blue
Ben Grauer, Announcer
American Home Products (Bi-So-Dol), Sponsor
"The Case of John Leroy's Best Friend"

Mr. Keen visits Leroy at home. The aunt now knows about the dog. Learning of the reward offered, she contacts Keen. The tracer goes to the Wilson farm, but Dickey hides in the attic with Champ.

CONTINUITY #188
Wednesday, December 21, 1938
7:15–7:30 p.m. EST
NBC Blue
Ben Grauer, Announcer
American Home Products (Bi-So-Dol), Sponsor
"The Case of John Leroy's Best Friend"

Dickey is heartbroken when Mr. Keen tries to take his newfound pet away. Mr. Keen wisely gives the lad until Christmas to take Champ back to his rightful owner of his own free will.

CONTINUITY #189
Thursday, December 22, 1938
7:15–7:30 p.m. EST
NBC Blue
Ben Grauer, Announcer
American Home Products (Bi-So-Dol), Sponsor
"The Case of John Leroy's Best Friend"

On Christmas Eve, John Leroy, without his dog, feels utterly depressed. Dickey Wilson arrives with Champ, Leroy's lost companion, delivering the best Christmas present possible.

CONTINUITY #190
Tuesday, December 27, 1938
7:15–7:30 p.m. EST
NBC Blue
Ben Grauer, Announcer
American Home Products (Bi-So-Dol), Sponsor
"The Case of the Author Who Lost His Soul"

Jane Merrill asks Keen to locate her ex, Stephen Giddings, a struggling author. An unpublished novel he wrote years ago is now in demand. Giddings left Jane to wed affluent Rita Sanford.

CONTINUITY #191
Wednesday, December 28, 1938
7:15–7:30 p.m. EST
NBC Blue
Ben Grauer, Announcer
American Home Products (Bi-So-Dol), Sponsor
"The Case of the Author Who Lost His Soul"

Rita could support Giddings' writing lifestyle. Jane still loves him and wants to see the book succeed. Keen finds the Giddings living in Bermuda, and flies down to urge Stephen to return to writing.

CONTINUITY #192
Thursday, December 29, 1938
7:15–7:30 p.m. EST
NBC Blue
Ben Grauer, Announcer
American Home Products (Bi-So-Dol), Sponsor
"The Case of the Author Who Lost His Soul"

Giddings has changed. He and Rita live wasted, lazy existences. He hasn't written in years. Disillusioned, he's fed up with his marriage. Keen reports this to Jane.

CONTINUITY #193
Tuesday, January 3, 1939
7:15–7:30 p.m. EST
NBC Blue
Ben Grauer, Announcer

American Home Products (Bi-So-Dol), Sponsor

"The Case of the Author Who Lost His Soul"

Mr. Keen takes Giddings, a beaten failure, back to his first wife, Jane. Giddings realizes that all his achievement sprang from the devotion and encouragement of this woman.

CONTINUITY #194
Wednesday, January 4, 1939
7:15–7:30 p.m. EST
NBC Blue
Ben Grauer, Announcer
American Home Products (Bi-So-Dol), Sponsor

"The Case of Lucy Daire's Real Family"

Lucy Daire, heiress to a fortune, is engaged to socialite David Baxter. When Baxter's mother gave Lucy pearls worth $35,000, Lucy burst into tears and fled, leaving behind a note: she's adopted.

CONTINUITY #195
Thursday, January 5, 1939
7:15–7:30 p.m. EST
NBC Blue
Ben Grauer, Announcer
American Home Products (Bi-So-Dol), Sponsor

"The Case of Lucy Daire's Real Family"

The Daires adopted Lucy from a foundling home. Keen and Baxter go there. At a Boston roominghouse, Lucy receives James Lockhart, who claims he's her uncle and tries to blackmail her.

CONTINUITY #196
Tuesday, January 10, 1939
7:15–7:30 p.m. EST
NBC Blue
Ben Grauer, Announcer
American Home Products (Bi-So-Dol), Sponsor

"The Case of Lucy Daire's Real Family"

Lucy learns she's the child of unmarried Grant Lockhart and factory girl Mary Deming. Lucy shields her fiancé and foster parents. Alicia Lockhart, James' sister, is helping Mr. Keen.

CONTINUITY #197
Wednesday, January 11, 1939
7:15–7:30 p.m. EST
NBC Blue
Ben Grauer, Announcer
American Home Products (Bi-So-Dol), Sponsor

"The Case of Lucy Daire's Real Family"

Her uncle torments Lucy. Her folks *were* wed, but she doesn't know that. She thinks she's not good enough for David and his family. Lockhart finally confesses the truth, and takes Keen and David to Lucy.

CONTINUITY #198
Thursday, January 12, 1939
7:15–7:30 p.m. EST
NBC Blue
Ben Grauer, Announcer
American Home Products (Bi-So-Dol), Sponsor

"The Case of Lucy Daire's Real Family"

Everything is out in the open now. David and Lucy are reunited, and past mistakes and misunderstandings are all forgiven. It appears there will be a wedding after all!

CONTINUITY #199
Tuesday, January 17, 1939
7:15–7:30 p.m. EST
NBC Blue
Ben Grauer, Announcer
American Home Products (Bi-So-Dol), Sponsor

"The Case of the Husband Who Didn't Believe His Wife Was Dead"

Vaudevillian Charley McBride is booed off the stage. Years ago, "McBride and Lindine" had many fans. Wife Jenny Lindine took ill and left to avoid becoming a burden, and now Charley is drunk more often than not.

CONTINUITY #200
Wednesday, January 18, 1939
7:15–7:30 p.m. EST
NBC Blue
Ben Grauer, Announcer
American Home Products (Bi-So-Dol), Sponsor

"The Case of the Husband Who Didn't Believe His Wife Was Dead"

McBride's only hope is to find Jenny. Mr. Keen learns that she recovered and is now known as Jeanette Linden. She's opening in Nolly Parker's Broadway Revue. Keen attends a rehearsal.

CONTINUITY #201
Thursday, January 19, 1939
7:15–7:30 p.m. EST
NBC Blue
Ben Grauer, Announcer
American Home Products (Bi-So-Dol), Sponsor
"The Case of the Husband Who Didn't Believe His Wife Was Dead"

Jeanette keeps company with millionaire playboy Larry Withington. She refuses to see McBride again. Her ankle is injured during a rehearsal mishap. Can she still dance?

CONTINUITY #202
Tuesday, January 24, 1939
7:15–7:30 p.m. EST
NBC Blue
Ben Grauer, Announcer
American Home Products (Bi-So-Dol), Sponsor
"The Case of the Husband Who Didn't Believe His Wife Was Dead"

Keen and Miss Ellis go to Jeanette's apartment. She was dropped from the show due to her injury. The playboy loses interest. Keen urges her to see McBride, but she refuses.

CONTINUITY #203
Wednesday, January 25, 1939
7:15–7:30 p.m. EST
NBC Blue
Ben Grauer, Announcer
American Home Products (Bi-So-Dol), Sponsor
"The Case of the Husband Who Didn't Believe His Wife Was Dead"

McBride is in New York. The couple meet. Keen not only reunites them, but sees that the stage act of McBride and Lindine will re-form, to the delight of audiences everywhere.

CONTINUITY #204
Thursday, January 26, 1939
7:15–7:30 p.m. EST
NBC Blue
Ben Grauer, Announcer
American Home Products (Bi-So-Dol), Sponsor
"The Case of the Mind That Wanted to Slumber"

For over a year Dr. Applegate and college professor Hartley tried to restore the memory of a ragged amnesiac (since labeled "Tom") found in Indiana. Now they've summoned Mr. Keen.

CONTINUITY #205
Tuesday, January 31, 1939
7:15–7:30 p.m. EST
NBC Blue
Ben Grauer, Announcer
American Home Products (Bi-So-Dol), Sponsor
"The Case of the Mind That Wanted to Slumber"

The two professionals in Ferringdale, Indiana, share some clues with Mr. Keen. The tracer sets out to locate an individual from Tom's past who might possibly have been his other self.

CONTINUITY #206
Wednesday, February 1, 1939
7:15–7:30 p.m. EST
NBC Blue
Martha Atwell, Director
Jerome D. Ross, Writer
Mildred Fenton, Editor
Ben Grauer, Announcer
American Home Products (Bi-So-Dol), Sponsor
"The Case of the Mind That Wanted to Slumber"

Through his agents, Keen unearths the tale of a young surgeon in a Pittsburgh auto crash. Thinking his fiancée had been killed, his mind cracked. Mr. Keen believes Tom is Dr. Ronald Burke.

Starting with this episode, the scripts begin crediting additional members of the show's production staff. Their names are not announced on the air, however.

CONTINUITY #207
Thursday, February 2, 1939
7:15–7:30 p.m. EST
NBC Blue
Martha Atwell, Director
Jerome D. Ross, Writer
Mildred Fenton, Editor
Ben Grauer, Announcer
American Home Products (Bi-So-Dol), Sponsor

"The Case of the Mind That Wanted to Slumber"

Brilliant surgeon Dr. Ronald Burke and fiancée Grace Lawrence were in an accident. Thinking Grace dead and himself to blame, Burke suffered a mental collapse. Now he's his real self again.

CONTINUITY #208
Tuesday, February 7, 1939
7:15–7:30 p.m. EST
NBC Blue
Martha Atwell, Director
Jerome D. Ross, Writer
Mildred Fenton, Editor
Ben Grauer, Announcer
American Home Products (Bi-So-Dol), Sponsor
"The Case of the Mind That Wanted to Slumber"

Mr. Keen succeeds in reuniting Dr. Burke with his fiancée, Grace Lawrence, and in returning the brilliant young surgeon to his medical career. Burke has many people to thank.

CONTINUITY #209
Wednesday, February 8, 1939
7:15–7:30 p.m. EST
NBC Blue
Martha Atwell, Director
Jerome D. Ross, Writer
Mildred Fenton, Editor
Ben Grauer, Announcer
American Home Products (Bi-So-Dol), Sponsor
"The Case of the Disappearance of Mr. Waters"

Gordon Waters, head of Cleveland's Waters Department Store, never arrived home from work three days ago. His odd family seems upset because this disrupts their Palm Beach vacation.

CONTINUITY #210
Thursday, February 9, 1939
7:15–7:30 p.m. EST
NBC Blue
Martha Atwell, Director
Jerome D. Ross, Writer
Mildred Fenton, Editor
Ben Grauer, Announcer
American Home Products (Bi-So-Dol), Sponsor
"The Case of the Disappearance of Mr. Waters"

Keen thinks Waters left to escape the nagging and bickering at home. He dreaded the family trip, and so replied to a young couple that advertised for a paying rider to go to Florida.

CONTINUITY #211
Tuesday, February 14, 1939
7:15–7:30 p.m. EST
NBC Blue
Martha Atwell, Director
Jerome D. Ross, Writer
Mildred Fenton, Editor
Ben Grauer, Announcer
American Home Products (Bi-So-Dol), Sponsor
"The Case of the Disappearance of Mr. Waters"

Traveling as "Jones," Waters goes to Florida with Joe and Ellen Blanton. He learns that Joe worked in his store and was fired by Waters' son, Franklin. Keen travels to Florida, too.

CONTINUITY #212
Wednesday, February 15, 1939
7:15–7:30 p.m. EST
NBC Blue
Martha Atwell, Director
Jerome D. Ross, Writer
Mildred Fenton, Editor
Ben Grauer, Announcer
American Home Products (Bi-So-Dol), Sponsor
"The Case of the Disappearance of Mr. Waters"

Keen finds Waters. When the Blantons learn who he is, they want nothing to do with him. At the cheap tourist camp where they've been staying, Keen talks with Joe and Ellen.

CONTINUITY #213
Thursday, February 16, 1939
7:15–7:30 p.m. EST
NBC Blue
Martha Atwell, Director
Jerome D. Ross, Writer
Mildred Fenton, Editor
Ben Grauer, Announcer
American Home Products (Bi-So-Dol), Sponsor
"The Case of the Disappearance of Mr. Waters"

Gordon Waters returns to his family. On Mr. Keen's advice, Waters intends to rule his selfish family with an iron hand. The young couple he traveled with will continue as friends.

CONTINUITY #214
Tuesday, February 21, 1939
7:15–7:30 p.m. EST
NBC Blue
Martha Atwell, Director
Jerome D. Ross, Writer
Mildred Fenton, Editor
Ben Grauer, Announcer
American Home Products (Bi-So-Dol), Sponsor
"The Case of the Woman Who Dreamed Strange Dreams"
   Keen seeks Billy Trudeau, who was in trouble eight years ago and ran away. His mom, a hard-working widow, is ill. She has tortured dreams about him calling from prison.

CONTINUITY #215
Wednesday, February 22, 1939
7:15–7:30 p.m. EST
NBC Blue
Martha Atwell, Director
Jerome D. Ross, Writer
Mildred Fenton, Editor
Ben Grauer, Announcer
American Home Products (Bi-So-Dol), Sponsor
"The Case of the Woman Who Dreamed Strange Dreams"
   The possibly dying widow describes the prison as it appears in her dreams to Mr. Keen. She's convinced that Billy, now 25, is in big trouble. Keen reviews it all with Miss Ellis.

CONTINUITY #216
Thursday, February 23, 1939
7:15–7:30 p.m. EST
NBC Blue
Martha Atwell, Director
Jerome D. Ross, Writer
Mildred Fenton, Editor
Ben Grauer, Announcer
American Home Products (Bi-So-Dol), Sponsor
"The Case of the Woman Who Dreamed Strange Dreams"
   Keen learns of a prison out West that fits the description in Mrs. Trudeau's dream. It houses a young man about to die for his part in a murder. He has maintained his innocence all along.

CONTINUITY #217
Tuesday, February 28, 1939
7:15–7:30 p.m. EST
NBC Blue
Martha Atwell, Director
Jerome D. Ross, Writer
Mildred Fenton, Editor
Ben Grauer, Announcer
American Home Products (Bi-So-Dol), Sponsor
"The Case of the Woman Who Dreamed Strange Dreams"
   Keen goes to the pen in a Western state. He persuades the governor to grant a stay of execution. Ten days later Keen produces proof of Billy's innocence and gains a full pardon, for the boy.

CONTINUITY #218
Wednesday, March 1, 1939
7:15–7:30 p.m. EST
NBC Blue
Martha Atwell, Director
Jerome D. Ross, Writer
Mildred Fenton, Editor
Ben Grauer, Announcer
American Home Products (Bi-So-Dol), Sponsor
"The Case of the Woman Who Dreamed Strange Dreams"
   Billy is released. As he is returned to his mother's arms, she dies. Her passing isn't in vain, however, for the smile on her face encourages Billy to live a better, more productive life.

CONTINUITY #219
Thursday, March 2, 1939
7:15–7:30 p.m. EST
NBC Blue
Martha Atwell, Director
Jerome D. Ross, Writer
Mildred Fenton, Editor
Ben Grauer, Announcer
American Home Products (Bi-So-Dol), Sponsor
"The Case of the Wife Who Was Found Before She Disappeared"

Keen goes to North Carolina's Great Smokies. Spencer Kennicott, age 50, says his wife Anne, age 30, is demented and about to run off with Tom Carswell. Keen hears her shriek.

CONTINUITY #220
Tuesday, March 7, 1939
7:15–7:30 p.m. EST
NBC Blue
Martha Atwell, Director
Jerome D. Ross, Writer
Mildred Fenton, Editor
Ben Grauer, Announcer
American Home Products (Bi-So-Dol), Sponsor
"The Case of the Wife Who Was Found Before She Disappeared"
   Keen, convinced by Spencer's story, promises to prevent Anne's flight. Carswell arrives. Anne accuses Spencer of insanity. Keen ascribes her charges to her demented state.

CONTINUITY #221
Wednesday, March 8, 1939
7:15–7:30 p.m. EST
NBC Blue
Martha Atwell, Director
Jerome D. Ross, Writer
Mildred Fenton, Editor
Ben Grauer, Announcer
American Home Products (Bi-So-Dol), Sponsor
"The Case of the Wife Who Was Found Before She Disappeared"
   From Carswell, Keen learns it is Spencer who's the crazy one. He's kept Anne locked up for months in the remote mountain camp. Spencer induces Carswell to go shoot rabbits with him.

CONTINUITY #222
Thursday, March 9, 1939
7:15–7:30 p.m. EST
NBC Blue
Martha Atwell, Director
Jerome D. Ross, Writer
Mildred Fenton, Editor
Ben Grauer, Announcer
American Home Products (Bi-So-Dol), Sponsor
"The Case of the Wife Who Was Found Before She Disappeared"

Spencer goes totally mad and attempts to murder Carswell. Spencer fires a shot and injures Anne. The next morning, Keen sends for mountaineers to come, neighbors of the reclusive couple.

CONTINUITY #223
Tuesday, March 14, 1939
7:15–7:30 p.m. EST
NBC Blue
Martha Atwell, Director
Jerome D. Ross, Writer
Mildred Fenton, Editor
Ben Grauer, Announcer
American Home Products (Bi-So-Dol), Sponsor
"The Case of the Wife Who Was Found Before She Disappeared"
   The case is resolved following the near tragedy caused by the insane man. His delicate, nerve-wracked wife goes over to the man she truly loves, Tom Carswell, to start a new life.

CONTINUITY #224
Wednesday, March 15, 1939
7:15–7:30 p.m. EST
NBC Blue
Martha Atwell, Director
Jerome D. Ross, Writer
Mildred Fenton, Editor
Announcer's name omitted
American Home Products (Bi-So-Dol), Sponsor
"The Case of Mrs. Lovelace of Greenway Hall"
   Miss Lancaster restores and converts the old Waynethorpe plantation at Charleston, South Carolina, to Greenway Hall School for Young Ladies. Keen is asked to find a missing housemother.

CONTINUITY #225
Thursday, March 16, 1939
7:15–7:30 p.m. EST
NBC Blue
Martha Atwell, Director
Jerome D. Ross, Writer
Mildred Fenton, Editor
Announcer's name omitted
American Home Products (Bi-So-Dol), Sponsor
"The Case of Mrs. Lovelace of Greenway Hall"
   Only Betty Lou Dayton isn't upset by the

disappearance of Mrs. Lovelace. Keen is wary of headmistress Lancaster. He approaches Sally Ann Roberts, the student who requested him.

CONTINUITY #226
Tuesday, March 21, 1939
7:15–7:30 p.m. EST
NBC Blue
Martha Atwell, Director
Jerome D. Ross, Writer
Mildred Fenton, Editor
Ben Grauer, Announcer
American Home Products (Bi-So-Dol), Sponsor
"The Case of Mrs. Lovelace of Greenway Hall"
   Mrs. Lovelace was dismissed at the insistence of Dayton, a rich, unpopular coed, Keen learns. Dayton won't reveal why she dislikes the woman, however, and Keen investigates the matter further.

CONTINUITY #227
Wednesday, March 22, 1939
7:15–7:30 p.m. EST
NBC Blue
Martha Atwell, Director
Jerome D. Ross, Writer
Mildred Fenton, Editor
George Ansbro, Announcer
American Home Products (Bi-So-Dol), Sponsor
"The Case of Mrs. Lovelace of Greenway Hall"
   An idle clan owns nearby Tempeston Manor. Son Randy is in jail for murder. Mrs. Lovelace stopped Dayton from eloping with him. After a change of heart, Dayton begins helping Keen.

CONTINUITY #228
Thursday, March 23, 1939
7:15–7:30 p.m. EST
NBC Blue
Martha Atwell, Director
Jerome D. Ross, Writer
Mildred Fenton, Editor
Ben Grauer, Announcer
American Home Products (Bi-So-Dol), Sponsor
"The Case of Mrs. Lovelace of Greenway Hall"
   Mrs. Lovelace hides in a rooming house. She was Magnolia Waynethorpe, aristocratic mistress of Greenway Hall. A bad marriage and kin hurt her. Her grandson is Randy Tempeston.

CONTINUITY #229
Tuesday, March 28, 1939
7:15–7:30 p.m. EST
NBC Blue
Martha Atwell, Director
Jerome D. Ross, Writer
Mildred Fenton, Editor
Ben Grauer, Announcer
American Home Products (Bi-So-Dol), Sponsor
"The Case of Mrs. Lovelace of Greenway Hall"
   Once more Mr. Keen works his magic to restore a distraught woman to her position. He convinces Mrs. Lovelace that her place today is at Greenway Hall, where she is deeply loved.

CONTINUITY #230
Wednesday, March 29, 1939
7:15–7:30 p.m. EST
NBC Blue
Martha Atwell, Director
Jerome D. Ross, Writer
Mildred Fenton, Editor
Ben Grauer, Announcer
American Home Products (Bi-So-Dol), Sponsor
"The Case of the Man Who Was Once a Hero"
   Civil engineer David Hodge, missing for two years, acted like a hero during the floods that hit New Trent in 1936. But his wife drowned. He had long advocated flood prevention plans, but to no avail.

CONTINUITY #231
Thursday, March 30, 1939
7:15–7:30 p.m. EST
NBC Blue
Martha Atwell, Director
Jerome D. Ross, Writer
Mildred Fenton, Editor
Ben Grauer, Announcer
American Home Products (Bi-So-Dol), Sponsor
"The Case of the Man Who Was Once a Hero"
   In New Trent, Mr. Keen views a badly needed flood control plan. David Hodge's ideas have been vindicated, and the city wants to honor him again. Mr. Keen visits Mayor Bingham.

CONTINUITY #232
Tuesday, April 4, 1939
7:15–7:30 p.m. EST
NBC Blue
Martha Atwell, Director
Jerome D. Ross, Writer
Mildred Fenton, Editor
Ben Grauer, Announcer
American Home Products (Bi-So-Dol), Sponsor
"The Case of the Man Who Was Once a Hero"
 The hamlet is about to launch a flood prevention system — dams, reservoirs, levees. Keen locates Hodge, now a drunken anti-social wreck. Keen summons Mayor Bingham to join him.

CONTINUITY #233
Wednesday, April 5, 1939
7:15–7:30 p.m. EST
NBC Blue
Martha Atwell, Director
Jerome D. Ross, Writer
Mildred Fenton, Editor
Ben Grauer, Announcer
American Home Products (Bi-So-Dol), Sponsor
"The Case of the Man Who Was Once a Hero"
 Keen urges the desolate Hodge to return for the unveiling of the dam, an idea he once envisioned. On the big day, scandal shakes New Trent. Lawmakers may end the flood control plan.

CONTINUITY #234
Thursday, April 6, 1939
7:15–7:30 p.m. EST
NBC Blue
Martha Atwell, Director
Jerome D. Ross, Writer
Mildred Fenton, Editor
Ben Grauer, Announcer
American Home Products (Bi-So-Dol), Sponsor
"The Case of the Man Who Was Once a Hero"
 When his native city needs him again, David Hodge goes to bat for it. His fighting spirit returns, and he crusades for the flood control plan, winning over the misguided politicians.

CONTINUITY #235
Tuesday, April 11, 1939
7:15–7:30 p.m. EST
NBC Blue
Martha Atwell, Director
Jerome D. Ross, Writer
Mildred Fenton, Editor
Ben Grauer, Announcer
American Home Products (Bi-So-Dol), Sponsor
"The Case of the Woman Who Vanished Into Thin Air"
 Several housewives in one neighborhood have been fleeced of gems, cash and securities by foreign gypsy fortune-teller Madame Lenya. Dora Little, a beauty parlor operator, recommended Lenya.

CONTINUITY #236
Wednesday, April 12, 1939
7:15–7:30 p.m. EST
NBC Blue
Martha Atwell, Director
Jerome D. Ross, Writer
Mildred Fenton, Editor
Ben Grauer, Announcer
American Home Products (Bi-So-Dol), Sponsor
"The Case of the Woman Who Vanished Into Thin Air"
 Posing as an affluent out-of-town widow, Miss Ellis visits Dora's shop, informing her she has money to invest. At once the beauty parlor operator mentions the mysterious Madame Lenya.

CONTINUITY #237
Thursday, April 13, 1939
7:15–7:30 p.m. EST
NBC Blue
Martha Atwell, Director
Jerome D. Ross, Writer
Mildred Fenton, Editor
Ben Grauer, Announcer
American Home Products (Bi-So-Dol), Sponsor
"The Case of the Woman Who Vanished Into Thin Air"
 Mr. Keen calls at every domicile where Dora says the missing fortune-teller lived. Posing as Mrs. Brown, Ellis is lodged in an expensive hotel. She keeps in touch with Dora Little.

CONTINUITY #238
Tuesday, April 18, 1939

7:15–7:30 p.m. EST
NBC Blue
Martha Atwell, Director
Jerome D. Ross, Writer
Mildred Fenton, Editor
Ben Grauer, Announcer
American Home Products (Bi-So-Dol), Sponsor
"The Case of the Woman Who Vanished Into Thin Air"
 Dora falls for the trick and arranges for Miss Ellis to meet Madame Lenya in a small park opposite Dora's beauty parlor. Mr. Keen can't figure the connection between Dora and Lenya.

CONTINUITY #239
Wednesday, April 19, 1939
7:15–7:30 p.m. EST
NBC Blue
Martha Atwell, Director
Jerome D. Ross, Writer
Mildred Fenton, Editor
Ben Grauer, Announcer
American Home Products (Bi-So-Dol), Sponsor
"The Case of the Woman Who Vanished Into Thin Air"
 Keen, Ellis and a detective wait in a doorway a short way from Dora's shop. Lenya escapes, taking refuge in the beauty parlor. A search turns up only Dora on the premises.

CONTINUITY #240
Thursday, April 20, 1939
7:15–7:30 p.m. EST
NBC Blue
Martha Atwell, Director
Jerome D. Ross, Writer
Mildred Fenton, Editor
Ben Grauer, Announcer
American Home Products (Bi-So-Dol), Sponsor
"The Case of the Woman Who Vanished Into Thin Air"
 Keen, Ellis and the detective question Dora Little. They finally put it all together: Madame Lenya simply *doesn't exist*. She's Dora in disguise, a most imaginative swindler.

CONTINUITY #241
Tuesday, April 25, 1939
7:15–7:30 p.m. EST
NBC Blue
Martha Atwell, Director
Jerome D. Ross, Writer
Mildred Fenton, Editor
Ben Grauer, Announcer
American Home Products (Bi-So-Dol), Sponsor
"The Case of the Table for Two"
 Jim and Bonny Anderson parted three years ago at Pierre Fleury's Greenwich bistro. Feeling imprisoned by their marriage, he wanted to quit work and start over; she wanted a career. Now she's hunting for him.

CONTINUITY #242
Wednesday, April 26, 1939
7:15–7:30 p.m. EST
NBC Blue
Martha Atwell, Director
Jerome D. Ross, Writer
Mildred Fenton, Editor
Ben Grauer, Announcer
American Home Products (Bi-So-Dol), Sponsor
"The Case of the Table for Two"
 Bitter, sad and disappointed, Bonny hopes to find Jim. She has achieved security but knows her happiness lies with Jim. He didn't keep their date. The bistro owners call in Mr. Keen.

CONTINUITY #243
Thursday, April 27, 1939
7:15–7:30 p.m. EST
NBC Blue
Martha Atwell, Director
Jerome D. Ross, Writer
Mildred Fenton, Editor
Ben Grauer, Announcer
American Home Products (Bi-So-Dol), Sponsor
"The Case of the Table for Two"
 She's an artist; he runs a press in Massachusetts and is now a stuffed shirt "yes man" to his boss. He blames her for their plight. She decides to wed ne'er-do-well Tommy Diggs.

CONTINUITY #244
Tuesday, May 2, 1939
7:15–7:30 p.m. EDST
NBC Blue

Martha Atwell, Director
Jerome D. Ross, Writer
Mildred Fenton, Editor
Ben Grauer, Announcer
American Home Products (Bi-So-Dol), Sponsor
"The Case of the Table for Two"
 The tracer cooks up a scheme in which Bonny sends art samples to Jim under an assumed name. He likes them and plans to interview her. Keen meets with Pierre Fleury, café owner.

CONTINUITY #245
Wednesday, May 3, 1939
7:15–7:30 p.m. EDST
NBC Blue
Martha Atwell, Director
Jerome D. Ross, Writer
Mildred Fenton, Editor
Ben Grauer, Announcer
American Home Products (Bi-So-Dol), Sponsor
"The Case of the Table for Two"
 Amid the gay festivities at the little French restaurant in Greenwich Village, Mr. Keen reunites Bonny and former husband Jim Anderson. Keen is obviously a matchmaker made in heaven.

CONTINUITY #246
Thursday, May 4, 1939
7:15–7:30 p.m. EDST
NBC Blue
Martha Atwell, Director
Jerome D. Ross, Writer
Mildred Fenton, Editor
Ben Grauer, Announcer
American Home Products (Bi-So-Dol), Sponsor
"The Case of the Parents Who Gave Their Daughter Everything"
 Captain and Mrs. MacDonald ask Mr. Keen to find their daughter Vivian, now age 25. She ran away four years ago. Mike Clancy locates her in Templewood, New Jersey. She has wed Fred Blair.

CONTINUITY #247
Tuesday, May 9, 1939
7:15–7:30 p.m. EDST
NBC Blue
Martha Atwell, Director
Jerome D. Ross, Writer
Mildred Fenton, Editor
Ben Grauer, Announcer
American Home Products (Bi-So-Dol), Sponsor
"The Case of the Parents Who Gave Their Daughter Everything"
 It's a classic case of overindulging. Vivian couldn't take it, and says she hates her parents and never wants to see them again. She told Fred they were dead. Clancy is wary of her folks.

CONTINUITY #248
Wednesday, May 10, 1939
7:15–7:30 p.m. EDST
NBC Blue
Martha Atwell, Director
Jerome D. Ross, Writer
Mildred Fenton, Editor
Ben Grauer, Announcer
American Home Products (Bi-So-Dol), Sponsor
"The Case of the Parents Who Gave Their Daughter Everything"
 Vivian tells Keen that the MacDonalds aren't her real parents, nor are they kind and charming. They're swindlers, cardsharps. They adopted her at 15 and forced her to participate in crooked schemes.

CONTINUITY #249
Thursday, May 11, 1939
7:15–7:30 p.m. EDST
NBC Blue
Martha Atwell, Director
Jerome D. Ross, Writer
Mildred Fenton, Editor
Ben Grauer, Announcer
American Home Products (Bi-So-Dol), Sponsor
"The Case of the Parents Who Gave Their Daughter Everything"
 Hearing of Vivian's past, Fred leaves. Keen wants the parents to pay for their crimes. He calls the cops and they go to jail. He asks Vivian to reveal everything about her foster parents.

CONTINUITY #250
Tuesday, May 16, 1939

7:15–7:30 p.m. EDST
NBC Blue
Martha Atwell, Director
Jerome D. Ross, Writer
Mildred Fenton, Editor
Ben Grauer, Announcer
American Home Products (Bi-So-Dol), Sponsor
"The Case of the Parents Who Gave Their Daughter Everything"

Vivian Blair tells all and puts her crooked foster parents "where they belong." Keen is instrumental in reuniting Fred with Vivian, helping him see that the past doesn't matter.

CONTINUITY #251
Wednesday, May 17, 1939
7:15–7:30 p.m. EDST
NBC Blue
Martha Atwell, Director
Jerome D. Ross, Writer
Mildred Fenton, Editor
George Ansbro, Announcer
American Home Products (Bi-So-Dol), Sponsor
"The Case of the Story Book Romance"

Joe Wheeler, the elevator operator in Keen's office building, met a girl named Peggy at Coney Island last Sunday. They had a good time, but she vanished. He has a photo and is in love.

CONTINUITY #252
Thursday, May 18, 1939
7:15–7:30 p.m. EDST
NBC Blue
Martha Atwell, Director
Jerome D. Ross, Writer
Mildred Fenton, Editor
Ben Grauer, Announcer
American Home Products (Bi-So-Dol), Sponsor
"The Case of the Story Book Romance"

When a pretty girl visits Keen, seeking a young man and telling him she met him at Coney Island, Keen decides to stage a reunion "by accident" the next Sunday at Coney Island.

CONTINUITY #253
Tuesday, May 23, 1939
7:15–7:30 p.m. EDST
NBC Blue
Martha Atwell, Director
Jerome D. Ross, Writer
Mildred Fenton, Editor
Ben Grauer, Announcer
American Home Products (Bi-So-Dol), Sponsor
"The Case of the Story Book Romance"

The storybook romance with a boy-meets-girl theme draws to a satisfying conclusion for Joe Wheeler and Peggy Collins when they are brought together through the efforts of Mr. Keen.

CONTINUITY #254
Wednesday, May 24, 1939
7:15–7:30 p.m. EDST
NBC Blue
Martha Atwell, Director
Jerome D. Ross, Writer
Mildred Fenton, Editor
Ben Grauer, Announcer
American Home Products (Bi-So-Dol), Sponsor
"The Case of the Woman Who Lived in a Glass House"

Loretta Trumbull, child rearing and domestic issues expert, rules son Robert, age 25, with an iron fist. When she tried to end his engagement to Frances Dana a month ago, he finally rebelled and left.

CONTINUITY #255
Thursday, May 25, 1939
7:15–7:30 p.m. EDST
NBC Blue
Martha Atwell, Director
Jerome D. Ross, Writer
Mildred Fenton, Editor
Announcer's name omitted
American Home Products (Bi-So-Dol), Sponsor
"The Case of the Woman Who Lived in a Glass House"

Robert intends to find work and send for Frances. She is frantic, however, so Mr. Keen appeals to Mrs. Trumbull to help find her son. She's on a tour and hasn't admitted publicly that he's missing.

CONTINUITY #256
Tuesday, May 30, 1939
7:15–7:30 p.m. EDST

NBC Blue
Martha Atwell, Director
Jerome D. Ross, Writer
Mildred Fenton, Editor
Ben Grauer, Announcer
American Home Products (Bi-So-Dol), Sponsor
"The Case of the Woman Who Lived in a Glass House"
Keen learns that the youth contacted his father, separated from his mother for 10 years. Pop offered Robert the chance to live on a Vermont farm, but he has disappeared from the farmhouse.

CONTINUITY #257
Wednesday, May 31, 1939
7:15–7:30 p.m. EDST
NBC Blue
Martha Atwell, Director
Jerome D. Ross, Writer
Mildred Fenton, Editor
Ben Grauer, Announcer
American Home Products (Bi-So-Dol), Sponsor
"The Case of the Woman Who Lived in a Glass House"
Several days have passed. Keen, Robert's father Amos, and Frances locate Robert in Chicago. Unable to find work, and afraid to be on his own, he took poison. He's in critical condition in a hospital.

CONTINUITY #258
Thursday, June 1, 1939
7:15–7:30 p.m. EDST
NBC Blue
Martha Atwell, Director
Jerome D. Ross, Writer
Mildred Fenton, Editor
Ben Grauer, Announcer
American Home Products (Bi-So-Dol), Sponsor
"The Case of the Woman Who Lived in a Glass House"
Keen reunites the Trumbulls, including mother, recovered son and father. He brings about a new and deeper understanding between them. It appears Frances will be Robert's bride, after all.

CONTINUITY #259
Tuesday, June 6, 1939
7:15–7:30 p.m. EDST
NBC Blue
Martha Atwell, Director
Jerome D. Ross, Writer
Mildred Fenton, Editor
Ben Grauer, Announcer
American Home Products (Kolynos), Sponsor
"The Case of the Player with Two Strikes on Him"
Titans rookie pitcher Speedy Rackham, team star, disappears. Manager Matty Evans is keeping it out of the press. He thinks "Rackham" is an alias, as the boy won't speak of his past.

CONTINUITY #260
Wednesday, June 7, 1939
7:15–7:30 p.m. EDST
NBC Blue
Martha Atwell, Director
Jerome D. Ross, Writer
Mildred Fenton, Editor
Ben Grauer, Announcer
American Home Products (Kolynos), Sponsor
"The Case of the Player with Two Strikes on Him"
Keen discovers that Speedy's name is Brand, and that he's from a small Texas town. Keen and Evans drive there and learn that Speedy was promptly arrested upon his earlier arrival. The pair visits the county seat.

CONTINUITY #261
Thursday, June 8, 1939
7:15–7:30 p.m. EDST
NBC Blue
Martha Atwell, Director
Jerome D. Ross, Writer
Mildred Fenton, Editor
Ben Grauer, Announcer
American Home Products (Kolynos), Sponsor
"The Case of the Player with Two Strikes on Him"
Speedy once worked for auto thieves without knowing it. A victim saw his photo. To avoid a team scandal, Speedy gave himself up. Keen tries to get the victim to drop the case.

CONTINUITY #262
Tuesday, June 13, 1939
7:15–7:30 p.m. EDST
NBC Blue

Martha Atwell, Director
Jerome D. Ross, Writer
Mildred Fenton, Editor
Ben Grauer, Announcer
American Home Products (Kolynos), Sponsor
"The Case of the Player with Two Strikes on Him"

Keen fails in his efforts to convince the bigoted victim to aid in Speedy's release, and the man insists on a trial. At a Chicago stadium, Keen and Evans watch a Titans game aired nationwide.

CONTINUITY #263
Wednesday, June 14, 1939
7:15–7:30 p.m. EDST
NBC Blue
Martha Atwell, Director
Jerome D. Ross, Writer
Mildred Fenton, Editor
Ben Grauer, Announcer
American Home Products (Kolynos), Sponsor
"The Case of the Player with Two Strikes on Him"

A nation of baseball fans is grateful to Keen for locating Speedy Rackham. It turns out that Keen was indirectly responsible for the rookie's return when the victim finally dropped the unwarranted charges.

CONTINUITY #264
Thursday, June 15, 1939
7:15–7:30 p.m. EDST
NBC Blue
Martha Atwell, Director
Jerome D. Ross, Writer
Mildred Fenton, Editor
Ben Grauer, Announcer
American Home Products (Kolynos), Sponsor
"The Case of the Man Whose Life Was a Grand Adventure"

Marjorie Brice, a wealthy widow, visits Keen following a breakdown upon her spouse's demise. She's looking for an old friend, Robert Gray. Her nephew and lawyer say Gray doesn't exist.

CONTINUITY #265
Tuesday, June 20, 1939
7:15–7:30 p.m. EDST
NBC Blue
Martha Atwell, Director
Jerome D. Ross, Writer
Mildred Fenton, Editor
Ben Grauer, Announcer
American Home Products (Kolynos), Sponsor
"The Case of the Man Whose Life Was a Grand Adventure"

Robert Gray adored Marjorie. He was sane, and she needs him to talk to her now. Nephew Ward Brice, she believes, is after her money. Mr. Keen finds Grey living in Rutherford, Iowa.

CONTINUITY #266
Wednesday, June 21, 1939
7:15–7:30 p.m. EDST
NBC Blue
Martha Atwell, Director
Jerome D. Ross, Writer
Mildred Fenton, Editor
Ben Grauer, Announcer
American Home Products (Kolynos), Sponsor
"The Case of the Man Whose Life Was a Grand Adventure"

Grey runs a traveling Punch and Judy show in the Midwest. He refuses to see Marjorie, but Keen sends for her anyway. Tonight he's staging a puppet show at a country school.

CONTINUITY #267
Thursday, June 22, 1939
7:15–7:30 p.m. EDST
NBC Blue
Martha Atwell, Director
Jerome D. Ross, Writer
Mildred Fenton, Editor
Ben Grauer, Announcer
American Home Products (Kolynos), Sponsor
"The Case of the Man Whose Life Was a Grand Adventure"

Keen and Mrs. Brice watch the performance, surrounded by excited youngsters. Later, a school where Gray was to perform again for poverty-stricken rural kids catches on fire.

CONTINUITY #268
Tuesday, June 27, 1939
7:15–7:30 p.m. EDST
NBC Blue
Martha Atwell, Director
Jerome D. Ross, Writer
Mildred Fenton, Editor

Ben Grauer, Announcer
American Home Products (Kolynos), Sponsor
"The Case of the Man Whose Life Was a Grand Adventure"

Keen succeeds in bringing Marjorie Brice and her old friend Robert Gray together. She had all the money in the world and little contentment. He was a poor man who knew how to live.

CONTINUITY #269
Wednesday, June 28, 1939
7:15–7:30 p.m. EDST
NBC Blue
Martha Atwell, Director
Jerome D. Ross, Writer
Mildred Fenton, Editor
Ben Grauer, Announcer
American Home Products (Kolynos), Sponsor
"The Case of Mr. Keen's Holiday Cruise"

Keen and Miss Ellis cruise to the West Indies. Aboard ship are wheelchair-bound financier Cyrus Egstrom, his valet and his beautiful secretary. Yet Keen saw Egstrom walk without aid.

CONTINUITY #270
Thursday, June 29, 1939
7:15–7:30 p.m. EDST
NBC Blue
Martha Atwell, Director
Jerome D. Ross, Writer
Mildred Fenton, Editor
Ben Grauer, Announcer
American Home Products (Kolynos), Sponsor
"The Case of Mr. Keen's Holiday Cruise"

Egstrom is aloof, keeping to himself. He gives indications of being an invalid. Keen becomes highly suspicious; something unsavory is transpiring here. The liner heads into a fog.

CONTINUITY #271
Tuesday, July 4, 1939
7:15–7:30 p.m. EDST
NBC Blue
Martha Atwell, Director
Jerome D. Ross, Writer
Mildred Fenton, Editor
Ben Grauer, Announcer
American Home Products (Kolynos), Sponsor
"The Case of Mr. Keen's Holiday Cruise"

Word is sent to the ocean liner that Egstrom is wanted for larceny at home. Philip, his valet, and Miss Devereux, his secretary, claim he jumped overboard, leaving a note.

CONTINUITY #272
Wednesday, July 5, 1939
7:15–7:30 p.m. EDST
NBC Blue
Martha Atwell, Director
Jerome D. Ross, Writer
Mildred Fenton, Editor
Ben Grauer, Announcer
American Home Products (Kolynos), Sponsor
"The Case of Mr. Keen's Holiday Cruise"

The captain delivers a funeral eulogy. Keen doesn't think Egstrom committed suicide, and remains unimpressed by the farewell note he left. The ocean liner ploughs on toward Havana.

CONTINUITY #273
Thursday, July 6, 1939
7:15–7:30 p.m. EDST
NBC Blue
Martha Atwell, Director
Jerome D. Ross, Writer
Mildred Fenton, Editor
Ben Grauer, Announcer
American Home Products (Kolynos), Sponsor
"The Case of Mr. Keen's Holiday Cruise"

Keen's investigation reveals that Egstrom didn't jump overboard and is quite alive. The employees accompanying him plan to leave the ship at Havana. The liner is just arriving there.

CONTINUITY #274
Tuesday, July 11, 1939
7:15–7:30 p.m. EDST
NBC Blue
Martha Atwell, Director
Jerome D. Ross, Writer
Mildred Fenton, Editor
Ben Grauer, Announcer
American Home Products (Kolynos), Sponsor
"The Case of Mr. Keen's Holiday Cruise"

Keen forestalls Egstrom's escape, and the fugitive is turned over to the Havana police. His valet and secretary were in on the phony scheme to help him get away.

CONTINUITY #275
Wednesday, July 12, 1939
7:15–7:30 p.m. EDST

NBC Blue
Martha Atwell, Director
Jerome D. Ross, Writer
Mildred Fenton, Editor
Ben Grauer, Announcer
American Home Products (Kolynos), Sponsor
"The Case of Miss Ellis, Tracer of Mr. Keen"

Former movie star Carmella Flores vanishes. Henry Cotton, Flores' fiancé, fears lunatic asylum escapee Tom Wingate, her ex, holds her in Maine. He asks Keen to go with him.

CONTINUITY #276
Thursday, July 13, 1939
7:15–7:30 p.m. EDST
NBC Blue
Martha Atwell, Director
Jerome D. Ross, Writer
Mildred Fenton, Editor
Ben Grauer, Announcer
American Home Products (Kolynos), Sponsor
"The Case of Miss Ellis, Tracer of Mr. Keen"

Miss Ellis is uneasy as the two men drive off to the Maine hunting lodge. The *real* Cotton turns up. Ellis and Clancy realize Wingate is *posing* as Cotton. Keen is with a madman.

CONTINUITY #277
Tuesday, July 18, 1939
7:15–7:30 p.m. EDST
NBC Blue
Martha Atwell, Director
Jerome D. Ross, Writer
Mildred Fenton, Editor
Ben Grauer, Announcer
American Home Products (Kolynos), Sponsor
"The Case of Miss Ellis, Tracer of Mr. Keen"

Miss Ellis and Clancy speed toward Maine along the route that Keen and Wingate supposedly traveled a day earlier. They hope to warn Keen of his peril before it's too late.

CONTINUITY #278
Wednesday, July 19, 1939
7:15–7:30 p.m. EDST
NBC Blue
Martha Atwell, Director
Jerome D. Ross, Writer
Mildred Fenton, Editor
Ben Grauer, Announcer
American Home Products (Kolynos), Sponsor
"The Case of Miss Ellis, Tracer of Mr. Keen"

The followers learn that Wingate's car skidded and overturned. A telegram names a hotel the men were at on the New Hampshire coast. Clancy and Ellis stop there overnight; Keen is gone.

CONTINUITY #279
Thursday, July 20, 39
7:15–7:30 p.m. EDST
NBC Blue
Martha Atwell, Director
Jerome D. Ross, Writer
Mildred Fenton, Editor
Ben Grauer, Announcer
American Home Products (Kolynos), Sponsor
"The Case of Miss Ellis, Tracer of Mr. Keen"

En-route, the pursuers hear that Keen is acting strange, as if he has been drugged. Soon Clancy and Miss Ellis approach Carmella Flores' summer lodge on Rango Lake at Rango, Maine.

CONTINUITY #280
Tuesday, July 25, 1939
7:15–7:30 p.m. EDST
NBC Blue
Martha Atwell, Director
Jerome D. Ross, Writer
Mildred Fenton, Editor
Ben Grauer, Announcer
American Home Products (Kolynos), Sponsor
"The Case of Miss Ellis, Tracer of Mr. Keen"

Wingate is holding Carmella and Keen as prisoners. The pursuers cross the lake to the lodge in a motorboat, speeding to the aid of the captured pair held by a madman.

CONTINUITY #281
Wednesday, July 26, 1939
7:15–7:30 p.m. EDST
NBC Blue
Martha Atwell, Director
Jerome D. Ross, Writer
Mildred Fenton, Editor
Ben Grauer, Announcer
American Home Products (Kolynos), Sponsor
"The Case of Miss Ellis, Tracer of Mr. Keen"

The timely appearance of the two assistants saves Mr. Keen's life, enabling him to save Carmella Flores. Tom Wingate is returned to the lunatic asylum from which he had escaped.

CONTINUITY #282
Thursday, July 27, 1939
7:15–7:30 p.m. EDST
NBC Blue
Martha Atwell, Director
Jerome D. Ross, Writer
Mildred Fenton, Editor
Ben Grauer, Announcer
American Home Products (Kolynos), Sponsor
"The Case of the Twin Sister Team"

Twins Dottie and Sue Hopkins went to New York to seek radio talent jobs. Sue sustained them as a saleslady. Dot fell for theatrical agent Harry Lorimer. Then Sue disappeared.

CONTINUITY #283
Tuesday, August 1, 1939
7:15–7:30 p.m. EDST
NBC Blue
Martha Atwell, Director
Jerome D. Ross, Writer
Mildred Fenton, Editor
Ben Grauer, Announcer
American Home Products (Kolynos), Sponsor
"The Case of the Twin Sister Team"

Keen wonders if Lorimer is involved in the disappearance. Sue and Harry, Dot's beau, left together. Keen doesn't tell Dot, who is headed for a radio audition Keen will attend.

CONTINUITY #284
Wednesday, August 2, 1939
7:15–7:30 p.m. EDST
NBC Blue
Martha Atwell, Director
Jerome D. Ross, Writer
Mildred Fenton, Editor
Ben Grauer, Announcer
American Home Products (Kolynos), Sponsor
"The Case of the Twin Sister Team"

Dot learns the truth. It upsets her and she fails miserably at her audition. Mike Clancy traces Sue Hopkins and Harry Lorimer to a hotel near Niagara Falls. Keen arrives there.

CONTINUITY #285
Thursday, August 3, 1939
7:15–7:30 p.m. EDST
NBC Blue
Martha Atwell, Director
Jerome D. Ross, Writer
Mildred Fenton, Editor
Ben Grauer, Announcer
American Home Products (Kolynos), Sponsor
"The Case of the Twin Sister Team"

The pair eloped and married. Despondent, Dot has run away in the meantime. The newlyweds are conscience stricken. Sue goes to Keen's office to talk over their next move.

CONTINUITY #286
Tuesday, August 8, 1939
7:15–7:30 p.m. EDST
NBC Blue
Martha Atwell, Director
Jerome D. Ross, Writer
Mildred Fenton, Editor
Ben Grauer, Announcer
American Home Products (Kolynos), Sponsor
"The Case of the Twin Sister Team"

Keen proves himself a wizard once again, by bringing together the feuding Hopkins twins. Jealousy and misunderstanding tore them apart; with the tracer to advise them, they make up.

CONTINUITY #287
Wednesday, August 9, 1939
7:15–7:30 p.m. EDST
NBC Blue
Martha Atwell, Director
Jerome D. Ross, Writer
Mildred Fenton, Editor
Ben Grauer, Announcer
American Home Products (Kolynos), Sponsor
"The Case of the Man Who Lived in the Clouds"

Airline executive Phil Driscoll seeks Red and Lola Huston. Years ago the men were pals, until Red wed Lola, Phil's fiancée. Phil thinks the couple are in trouble, for Red sold a plane the men used to fly.

CONTINUITY #288
Thursday, August 10, 1939
7:15–7:30 p.m. EDST
NBC Blue
Martha Atwell, Director
Jerome D. Ross, Writer
Mildred Fenton, Editor
Ben Grauer, Announcer
American Home Products (Kolynos), Sponsor
"The Case of the Man Who Lived in the Clouds"

Keen and Phil go to an airport near Kansas

City where the men worked, making inquiries. It turns out that Red treated Lola miserably. He's an alcoholic, and hasn't held down a good pilot job in years.

CONTINUITY #289
Tuesday, August 15, 1939
7:15–7:30 p.m. EDST
NBC Blue
Martha Atwell, Director
Jerome D. Ross, Writer
Mildred Fenton, Editor
Ben Grauer, Announcer
American Home Products (Kolynos), Sponsor
"The Case of the Man Who Lived in the Clouds"

Keen and Phil find the Hustons living in poverty. Phil promises his friend a job if he reforms. Two weeks go by. Red is staying in the country trying to rehabilitate.

CONTINUITY #290
Wednesday, August 16, 1939
7:15–7:30 p.m. EDST
NBC Blue
Martha Atwell, Director
Jerome D. Ross, Writer
Mildred Fenton, Editor
Ben Grauer, Announcer
American Home Products (Kolynos), Sponsor
"The Case of the Man Who Lived in the Clouds"

Phil summons Keen to his office at Peerless Air Lines. Red was turned down. Years of inebriation have left their mark. Drunk, Red leaves in the old plane he used to own, now owned by Phil.

CONTINUITY #291
Thursday, August 17, 1939
7:15–7:30 p.m. EDST
NBC Blue
Martha Atwell, Director
Jerome D. Ross, Writer
Mildred Fenton, Editor
Tom Shirley, Announcer
American Home Products (Kolynos), Sponsor
"The Case of the Man Who Lived in the Clouds"

Red Huston deliberately crashes the airplane in order to step out of the eternal triangle that bound their three lives. It appears Phil and Lola will have a life together after all.

CONTINUITY #292
Tuesday, August 22, 1939
7:15–7:30 p.m. EDST
NBC Blue
Norman Sweetser, Director
Jerome D. Ross, Writer
Mildred Fenton, Editor
Tom Shirley, Announcer
American Home Products (Kolynos), Sponsor
"The Case of the Boy Who Wanted Parents"

Peter Blythe, age 10, left a summer boys' camp. Aunt Chauncey, a socialite, is his guardian (Peter's mother is dead, and dad takes no interest). Peter's father and stepmother visited him just before he fled.

CONTINUITY #293
Wednesday, August 23, 1939
7:15–7:30 p.m. EDST
NBC Blue
Norman Sweetser, Director
Jerome D. Ross, Writer
Mildred Fenton, Editor
Tom Shirley, Announcer
American Home Products (Kolynos), Sponsor
"The Case of the Boy Who Wanted Parents"

Keen and Mrs. Chauncey visit the camp. They learn that Peter was ashamed of his dad's neglect. Keen intends to discover the reason for the father's sudden, belated interest in his son.

CONTINUITY #294
Thursday, August 24, 1939
7:15–7:30 p.m. EDST
NBC Blue
Norman Sweetser, Director
Jerome D. Ross, Writer
Mildred Fenton, Editor
Tom Shirley, Announcer
American Home Products (Kolynos), Sponsor
"The Case of the Boy Who Wanted Parents"

Mr. Keen thinks the boy ran off to join his father. So far he's found no link between the boy and the dad who neglected him. Mr. Keen returns to the Adirondacks camp for boys.

CONTINUITY #295
Tuesday, August 29, 1939
7:15–7:30 p.m. EDST
NBC Blue
Norman Sweetser, Director
Jerome D. Ross, Writer
Mildred Fenton, Editor

Tom Shirley, Announcer
American Home Products (Kolynos), Sponsor
"The Case of the Boy Who Wanted Parents"

Keen learns that Richard Blythe and wife Shirley took Peter to a Canadian fishing camp. Pop's reasons were mercenary: he wants control of the boy's $3 million inheritance.

CONTINUITY #296
Wednesday, August 30, 1939
7:15–7:30 p.m. EDST
NBC Blue
Norman Sweetser, Director
Jerome D. Ross, Writer
Mildred Fenton, Editor
Tom Shirley, Announcer
American Home Products (Kolynos), Sponsor
"The Case of the Boy Who Wanted Parents"

In the woods of Quebec the trio casts fishing lines into a brook. Keen arrives and returns Peter to his aunt, whom the boy despises. Days later the scene shifts to a courthouse.

CONTINUITY #297
Thursday, August 31, 1939
7:15–7:30 p.m. EDST
NBC Blue
Norman Sweetser, Director
Jerome D. Ross, Writer
Mildred Fenton, Editor
Tom Shirley, Announcer
American Home Products (Kolynos), Sponsor
"The Case of the Boy Who Wanted Parents"

With Mr. Keen's assistance, Peter, a poor little rich boy, finds happiness and contentment as he is reunited with his father and stepmother. The boy's dream — to have parents — comes true.

CONTINUITY #298
Tuesday, September 5, 1939
7:15–7:30 p.m. EDST
NBC Blue
Martha Atwell, Director
Jerome D. Ross, Writer
Mildred Fenton, Editor
Ben Grauer, Announcer
American Home Products (Bi-So-Dol), Sponsor
"The Case of Miss Willow of the Public Library"

Mr. Hale, chief librarian in Center City, wants to find aide Parthenia Willow, who vanished a week ago. She spoke incessantly of spies—characters who hung around the reading room.

CONTINUITY #299
Wednesday, September 6, 1939
7:15–7:30 p.m. EDST
NBC Blue
Martha Atwell, Director
Jerome D. Ross, Writer
Mildred Fenton, Editor
Ben Grauer, Announcer
American Home Products (Bi-So-Dol), Sponsor
"The Case of Miss Willow of the Public Library"

At Central City, Keen questions Miss Willow's landlady. The town is shaken by a foreign spy scare. Keen tries to link the spy scandal with the lady's disappearance. He goes to see Mr. Hale.

CONTINUITY #300
Thursday, September 7, 1939
7:15–7:30 p.m. EDST
NBC Blue
Martha Atwell, Director
Jerome D. Ross, Writer
Mildred Fenton, Editor
Ben Grauer, Announcer
American Home Products (Bi-So-Dol), Sponsor
"The Case of Miss Willow of the Public Library"

Government agents uncovered a ring of foreign agents present in Central City. The spies use the public library as a base of operations. Keen calls Mr. Compton of the Justice Department to aid him.

CONTINUITY #301
Tuesday, September 12, 1939
7:15–7:30 p.m. EDST
NBC Blue
Martha Atwell, Director
Jerome D. Ross, Writer
Mildred Fenton, Editor
Ben Grauer, Announcer
American Home Products (Bi-So-Dol), Sponsor
"The Case of Miss Willow of the Public Library"

Keen and Compton learn that the spies use books to concoct a code communication. Miss Willow had discovered this and vanished. The sleuths arrest Mrs. Temple, a member of the spy ring.

CONTINUITY #302
Wednesday, September 13, 1939
7:15–7:30 p.m. EDST
NBC Blue
Martha Atwell, Director
Jerome D. Ross, Writer
Mildred Fenton, Editor
Ben Grauer, Announcer
American Home Products (Bi-So-Dol), Sponsor
"The Case of Miss Willow of the Public Library"
The ring steals data from munitions and airplane factories. The sleuths grill Mrs. Temple, then go to a house where Willow was held. There they find a cryptic code on a wall. Another spy is caught.

CONTINUITY #303
Thursday, September 14, 1939
7:15–7:30 p.m. EDST
NBC Blue
Martha Atwell, Director
Jerome D. Ross, Writer
Mildred Fenton, Editor
Ben Grauer, Announcer
American Home Products (Bi-So-Dol), Sponsor
"The Case of Miss Willow of the Public Library"
The charade comes to an end as the spies are either shot to death or imprisoned. Miss Willow is found and taken safely to her home. Central City returns to its former quiet calm.

CONTINUITY #304
Tuesday, September 19, 1939
7:15–7:30 p.m. EDST
NBC Blue
Martha Atwell, Director
Jerome D. Ross, Writer
Mildred Fenton, Editor
Ben Grauer, Announcer
American Home Products (Bi-So-Dol), Sponsor
"The Case of the Girl Who Sang About Yesterday"
Stage director Stanley Thompson asks Keen to find Barb Lewis, whom he loved before she chose actor Ken Mowbray. She subsequently left Ken, and now lives in poverty somewhere in New York. Ken asks Keen to find her, too.

CONTINUITY #305
Wednesday, September 20, 1939
7:15–7:30 p.m. EDST
NBC Blue
Martha Atwell, Director
Jerome D. Ross, Writer
Mildred Fenton, Editor
Ben Grauer, Announcer
American Home Products (Bi-So-Dol), Sponsor
"The Case of the Girl Who Sang About Yesterday"
The bitter rivals quarrel, but Keen makes them shake hands. He will find Lewis for *both* of them; then they can battle it out. Unbeknownst to the trio, Barb Lewis is arrested for panhandling.

CONTINUITY #306
Thursday, September 21, 1939
7:15–7:30 p.m. EDST
NBC Blue
Martha Atwell, Director
Jerome D. Ross, Writer
Mildred Fenton, Editor
Ben Grauer, Announcer
American Home Products (Bi-So-Dol), Sponsor
"The Case of the Girl Who Sang About Yesterday"
Aspiring actress Lewis had turned down two lovers in favor of a career. Now having been tried in Magistrates Court, she has been given a job by a woman. From the court clerk Keen obtains the woman's address.

CONTINUITY #307
Tuesday, September 26, 1939
7:15–7:30 p.m. EST
NBC Blue
Martha Atwell, Director
Jerome D. Ross, Writer
Mildred Fenton, Editor
Ben Grauer, Announcer
American Home Products (Bi-So-Dol), Sponsor

"The Case of the Girl Who Sang About Yesterday"

Keen reunites Lewis with the two young men in love with her. We are left to wonder whom she picked, if either. Keen did what he said he would do, leaving the details to the trio.

CONTINUITY #308
Wednesday, September 27, 1939
7:15–7:30 p.m. EST
NBC Blue
Martha Atwell, Director
Jerome D. Ross, Writer
Mildred Fenton, Editor
Ben Grauer, Announcer
American Home Products (Bi-So-Dol), Sponsor
"The Case of the Wife Who Wagered Her Love"

Young attorney Roger Bentham hires Mr. Keen to find his wife Alice, who ran away. Alice believes her husband loves Ethel Holloway, his secretary. Holloway admits to taunting Alice.

CONTINUITY #309
Thursday, September 28, 1939
7:15–7:30 p.m. EST
NBC Blue
Martha Atwell, Director
Jerome D. Ross, Writer
Mildred Fenton, Editor
Ben Grauer, Announcer
American Home Products (Bi-So-Dol), Sponsor
"The Case of the Wife Who Wagered Her Love"

Bentham's efforts to find his wife seem half-hearted. It's obvious to Keen that Miss Holloway isn't on the level, either. Keen assigns Mike Clancy to shadow her and report her actions.

CONTINUITY #310
Tuesday, October 3, 1939
7:15–7:30 p.m. EST
NBC Blue
Martha Atwell, Director
Jerome D. Ross, Writer
Mildred Fenton, Editor
Ben Grauer, Announcer
American Home Products (Bi-So-Dol), Sponsor
"The Case of the Wife Who Wagered Her Love"

Mike Clancy reports on Ethel Holloway. Mr. Keen catches up with Alice Bentham. Is it too late to effect reconciliation between husband and wife? Keen contemplates his next move.

CONTINUITY #311
Wednesday, October 4, 1939
7:15–7:30 p.m. EST
NBC Blue
Martha Atwell, Director
Jerome D. Ross, Writer
Mildred Fenton, Editor
Ben Grauer, Announcer
American Home Products (Bi-So-Dol), Sponsor
"The Case of the Wife Who Wagered Her Love"

Keen informs Roger Bentham that Ethel Holloway is married. She and her spouse planned to blackmail him. This ends his infatuation. Alice is hiding at a friend's home in Virginia.

CONTINUITY #312
Thursday, October 5, 1939
7:15–7:30 p.m. EST
NBC Blue
Martha Atwell, Director
Jerome D. Ross, Writer
Mildred Fenton, Editor
Ben Grauer, Announcer
American Home Products (Bi-So-Dol), Sponsor
"The Case of the Wife Who Wagered Her Love"

Alice and Roger Bentham are brought together again. Roger realizes that his rightful place is with his wife. She has been waiting in Virginia for him to come to his senses.

CONTINUITY #313
Tuesday, October 10, 1939
7:15–7:30 p.m. EST
NBC Blue
Martha Atwell, Director
Jerome D. Ross, Writer
Mildred Fenton, Editor
Ben Grauer, Announcer
American Home Products (Bi-So-Dol), Sponsor
"The Case of the a la Carte Menu"

At Chicago's Hotel Luxuria Mr. Keen seeks chef Gustav. Hotel manager McDermott says a sinister man ordered a dish — Chicken a la Jeanette — and the chef became excited and left.

CONTINUITY #314
Wednesday, October 11, 1939
7:15–7:30 p.m. EST
NBC Blue
Martha Atwell, Director
Jerome D. Ross, Writer
Mildred Fenton, Editor
Ben Grauer, Announcer
American Home Products (Bi-So-Dol), Sponsor
"The Case of the a la Carte Menu"
  Years ago, Gustav served Jordon Keerwellen, a European banking family heir who died mysteriously. Mrs. Gustav is evasive to Keen. He asks a news pal to dig up dope on the Keerwellens.

CONTINUITY #315
Thursday, October 12, 1939
7:15–7:30 p.m. EST
NBC Blue
Martha Atwell, Director
Jerome D. Ross, Writer
Mildred Fenton, Editor
Ben Grauer, Announcer
American Home Products (Bi-So-Dol), Sponsor
"The Case of the a la Carte Menu"
  Chicago Daily Standard reporter Ned Billings provides helpful information. Keen now thinks Keerwellen didn't die, but is posing as Gustav. Keen goes to question Mrs. Gustav again.

CONTINUITY #316
Tuesday, October 17, 1939
7:15–7:30 p.m. EST
NBC Blue
Martha Atwell, Director
Jerome D. Ross, Writer
Mildred Fenton, Editor
Ben Grauer, Announcer
American Home Products (Bi-So-Dol), Sponsor
"The Case of the a la Carte Menu"
  Keen finds Gustav, who *is* Keerwellen. He ran a Monte Carlo gambling ring that tried to kill him but hit his chef instead. A marked man, Keerwellen fled. His butler, Jacques, now receives hush money.

CONTINUITY #317
Wednesday, October 18, 1939
7:15–7:30 p.m. EST
NBC Blue
Martha Atwell, Director
Jerome D. Ross, Writer
Mildred Fenton, Editor
Ben Grauer, Announcer
American Home Products (Bi-So-Dol), Sponsor
"The Case of the a la Carte Menu"
  Jacques Cassade, the only person other than Mrs. Gustav to know the full story, is poisoned in the hotel's dining room. Did Gustav Keerwellen kill him? Police inspector Mallory questions the chef.

CONTINUITY #318
Thursday, October 19, 1939
7:15–7:30 p.m. EST
NBC Blue
Martha Atwell, Director
Jerome D. Ross, Writer
Mildred Fenton, Editor
Ben Grauer, Announcer
American Home Products (Bi-So-Dol), Sponsor
"The Case of the a la Carte Menu"
  Mr. Keen finds the answer to blackmailer Jacques Cassade's death. Keerwellen continues in his new life, with the world none the wiser about his real identity and strange heritage.

CONTINUITY #319
Tuesday, October 24, 1939
7:15–7:30 p.m. EST
NBC Blue
Martha Atwell, Director
Jerome D. Ross, Writer
Mildred Fenton, Editor
Ben Grauer, Announcer
American Home Products (Bi-So-Dol), Sponsor
"The Case of the Girl with Red Hair"
  Keen's pal Oliver Sinclair says a woman must be alluring. Oliver's "practical" secretary isn't suitable. Keen will teach him! They go to a masquerade ball, where they meet a stunning redhead.

CONTINUITY #320
Wednesday, October 25, 1939
7:15–7:30 p.m. EST

NBC Blue
Martha Atwell, Director
Jerome D. Ross, Writer
Mildred Fenton, Editor
Ben Grauer, Announcer
American Home Products (Bi-So-Dol), Sponsor
"The Case of the Girl with Red Hair"
    Affluent, spoiled Oliver tries to find the redhead. Oliver doesn't know it, but Margie Hamilton, his secretary, loves him. Mr. Keen summons her to help carry out his plans.

CONTINUITY #321
Thursday, October 26, 1939
7:15–7:30 p.m. EST
NBC Blue
Martha Atwell, Director
Jerome D. Ross, Writer
Mildred Fenton, Editor
Ben Grauer, Announcer
American Home Products (Bi-So-Dol), Sponsor
"The Case of the Girl with Red Hair"
    Margie will be useful in curing Oliver of his flippant attitude toward life. Keen provides a disguise that Oliver hasn't, as yet, seen through. But he's getting suspicious.

CONTINUITY #322
Tuesday, October 31, 1939
7:15–7:30 p.m. EST
NBC Blue
Martha Atwell, Director
Jerome D. Ross, Writer
Mildred Fenton, Editor
Ben Grauer, Announcer
American Home Products (Bi-So-Dol), Sponsor
"The Case of the Girl with Red Hair"
    The ruse ends as Oliver's eyes are opened to his pretty young secretary, Margie Hamilton. He falls head over heels for her. That old matchmaker Mr. Keen has done it again!

CONTINUITY #323
Wednesday, November 1, 1939
7:15–7:30 p.m. EST
NBC Blue
Martha Atwell, Director
Jerome D. Ross, Writer
Mildred Fenton, Editor
Ben Grauer, Announcer
American Home Products (Bi-So-Dol), Sponsor
"The Case of the Beating Drums"
    Keen and Miss Ellis go to a cinema. The audience agitatedly calls for Johnny Jeepers, the drummer and leader of his own swing band, to appear. But he and pretty Elise Mathews have gone missing.

CONTINUITY #324
Thursday, November 2, 1939
7:15–7:30 p.m. EST
NBC Blue
Martha Atwell, Director
Jerome D. Ross, Writer
Mildred Fenton, Editor
Ben Grauer, Announcer
American Home Products (Bi-So-Dol), Sponsor
"The Case of the Beating Drums"
    Billy Bruce, Johnny's manager, talks with Keen. The drummer eloped with Elise. He's tired and overworked. Keen learns that Johnny has developed a morbid interest in primitive Indian music.

CONTINUITY #325
Tuesday, November 7, 1939
7:15–7:30 p.m. EST
NBC Blue
Martha Atwell, Director
Jerome D. Ross, Writer
Mildred Fenton, Editor
Ben Grauer, Announcer
American Home Products (Bi-So-Dol), Sponsor
"The Case of the Beating Drums"
    The Kublas, a primitive Indian tribe, are currently observing their sacred harvest celebration. The tracer believes that Johnny and his bride are heading for the Kubla village — and for trouble.

CONTINUITY #326
Wednesday, November 8, 1939
7:15–7:30 p.m. EST
NBC Blue
Martha Atwell, Director
Jerome D. Ross, Writer
Mildred Fenton, Editor
Ben Grauer, Announcer

American Home Products (Bi-So-Dol), Sponsor
"The Case of the Beating Drums"
   Johnny is cracking up. For days he has confined Elise in a hillside cave while pounding crazily on drums. The Kubla overseer fears that the Indians will kill the intruders.

CONTINUITY #327
Thursday, November 9, 1939
7:15–7:30 p.m. EST
NBC Blue
Martha Atwell, Director
Jerome D. Ross, Writer
Mildred Fenton, Editor
Ben Grauer, Announcer
American Home Products (Bi-So-Dol), Sponsor
"The Case of the Beating Drums"
   Joe Sun Dust guides Keen to Johnny and Elise. Johnny, who has suffered a nervous breakdown, is put under a doctor's care. Johnny's pretty wife will help him recover.

CONTINUITY #328
Tuesday, November 14, 1939
7:15–7:30 p.m. EST
NBC Blue
Martha Atwell, Director
Jerome D. Ross, Writer
Mildred Fenton, Editor
Ben Grauer, Announcer
American Home Products (Bi-So-Dol), Sponsor
"The Case of the Schoolmarm Who Learned a Lesson"
   Pretty Irene Leslie is sick of her family — sick of slavishly supporting them and of their pointed questions about her spinsterhood. She tells Keen she's running away and not to look for her.

CONTINUITY #329
Wednesday, November 15, 1939
7:15–7:30 p.m. EST
NBC Blue
Martha Atwell, Director
Jerome D. Ross, Writer
Mildred Fenton, Editor
Ben Grauer, Announcer
American Home Products (Bi-So-Dol), Sponsor
"The Case of the Schoolmarm Who Learned a Lesson"
   Irene does disappear, going to a hotel on Nantucket Island off the Massachusetts coast. She meets David Draper. Her family appeals to Mr. Keen for help, just as she had predicted.

CONTINUITY #330
Thursday, November 16, 1939
7:15–7:30 p.m. EST
NBC Blue
Martha Atwell, Director
Jerome D. Ross, Writer
Mildred Fenton, Editor
Ben Grauer, Announcer
American Home Products (Bi-So-Dol), Sponsor
"The Case of the Schoolmarm Who Learned a Lesson"
   Trying to build herself up in David's eyes, Irene tells him she's an actress. She fabricates a glamorous life, which only serves to scare him off. Keen knows where she is but won't tell her folks.

CONTINUITY #331
Tuesday, November 21, 1939
7:15–7:30 p.m. EST
NBC Blue
Martha Atwell, Director
Jerome D. Ross, Writer
Mildred Fenton, Editor
Ben Grauer, Announcer
American Home Products (Bi-So-Dol), Sponsor
"The Case of the Schoolmarm Who Learned a Lesson"
   David loves Irene, but, thinking she's laughing at him, plans to leave the island. Mr. Keen arrives just in time. He urges her not to give David up so easily. She hears him.

CONTINUITY #332
Wednesday, November 22, 1939
7:15–7:30 p.m. EST
NBC Blue
Martha Atwell, Director
Jerome D. Ross, Writer
Mildred Fenton, Editor
Ben Grauer, Announcer
American Home Products (Bi-So-Dol), Sponsor

"The Case of the Schoolmarm Who Learned a Lesson"

Mr. Keen persuades Irene Leslie to return to her selfish, demanding family after he helps her find happiness and love away from that family. It appears that now everybody is happy.

CONTINUITY #333
Thursday, November 23, 1939
7:15–7:30 p.m. EST
NBC Blue
Martha Atwell, Director
Jerome D. Ross, Writer
Mildred Fenton, Editor
Ben Grauer, Announcer
American Home Products (Bi-So-Dol), Sponsor
"The Case of the Master Mind"

Charlie Beecher and Bill Henley share a home and an interest in a mail order detective course. When school owner Leonard Chickering vanishes, they call Mr. Keen.

CONTINUITY #334
Tuesday, November 28, 1939
7:15–7:30 p.m. EST
NBC Blue
Martha Atwell, Director
Jerome D. Ross, Writer
Mildred Fenton, Editor
Ben Grauer, Announcer
American Home Products (Bi-So-Dol), Sponsor
"The Case of the Master Mind"

Chickering showed a peculiar interest in the "perfect" crime — one that couldn't be solved — before dropping from sight. Bill and Charlie read about a shipload of art treasures.

CONTINUITY #335
Wednesday, November 29, 1939
7:15–7:30 p.m. EST
NBC Blue
Martha Atwell, Director
Jerome D. Ross, Writer
Mildred Fenton, Editor
Ben Grauer, Announcer
American Home Products (Bi-So-Dol), Sponsor
"The Case of the Master Mind"

Keen thinks Chickering — an erratic, conceited ex-gumshoe — plans to commit the perfect crime: stealing the priceless Bouvary art collection that recently arrived from wartorn Europe.

CONTINUITY #336
Thursday, November 30, 1939
7:15–7:30 p.m. EST
NBC Blue
Martha Atwell, Director
Jerome D. Ross, Writer
Mildred Fenton, Editor
Ben Grauer, Announcer
American Home Products (Bi-So-Dol), Sponsor
"The Case of the Master Mind"

Keen apprehends the missing detective, Leonard Chickering, just as he's about to commit the perfect crime. Bill and Charlie, while amateurs, contribute heavily to solving the case.

CONTINUITY #337
Tuesday, December 5, 1939
7:15–7:30 p.m. EST
NBC Blue
Martha Atwell, Director
Al Scheuer, Writer
Mildred Fenton, Editor
Ben Grauer, Announcer
American Home Products (Bi-So-Dol), Sponsor
"The Case of the Long Distance Telephone Call"

Nan Conway left a chilling message for husband Jack at his hotel — she's taking their young son and leaving New Haven forever. John wants to find her and file for divorce; he loves someone else.

CONTINUITY #338
Wednesday, December 6, 1939
7:15–7:30 p.m. EST
NBC Blue
Martha Atwell, Director
Al Scheuer, Writer
Mildred Fenton, Editor
Ben Grauer, Announcer
American Home Products (Bi-So-Dol), Sponsor
"The Case of the Long Distance Telephone Call"

Keen notes that all communication between the two consisted of phone messages.

The PBX operator observed that Nan often refused John's calls. Keen finds Nan in Boston. She was told Jack wouldn't take *her* calls.

CONTINUITY #339
Thursday, December 7, 1939
7:15–7:30 p.m. EST
NBC Blue
Martha Atwell, Director
Jerome D. Ross, Writer
Mildred Fenton, Editor
Ben Grauer, Announcer
American Home Products (Bi-So-Dol), Sponsor
"The Case of the Long Distance Telephone Call"
Could the phone messages have been tampered with? Keen is starting to think so.

CONTINUITY #340
Tuesday, December 12, 1939
7:15–7:30 p.m. EST
NBC Blue
Martha Atwell, Director
Ernest R. Shenkin, Writer
Mildred Fenton, Editor
Ben Grauer, Announcer
American Home Products (Bi-So-Dol), Sponsor
"The Case of the Long Distance Telephone Call"
It appears that the switchboard girl at Jack's hotel, Doris, is the culprit. Keen arranges for little Johnny Conway to phone his dad at 7:15 p.m. In the hotel lobby Keen watches.

CONTINUITY #341
Wednesday, December 13, 1939
7:15–7:30 p.m. EST
NBC Blue
Martha Atwell, Director
Ernest R. Shenkin, Writer
Mildred Fenton, Editor
Ben Grauer, Announcer
American Home Products (Bi-So-Dol), Sponsor
"The Case of the Long Distance Telephone Call"
Keen learns that Doris is Joan Evans, the woman with whom Jack has become infatuated. This puts a new spin on everything and reunites the Conways.

CONTINUITY #342
Thursday, December 14, 1939
7:15–7:30 p.m. EST
NBC Blue
Martha Atwell, Director
Allan Leonard, Writer
Mildred Fenton, Editor
James Fleming, Announcer
American Home Products (Bi-So-Dol), Sponsor
"The Case of the Man in Search of Christmas"
Famous actress Adrienne Lee asks Keen to find film writer Adam Blake. Blake left California for New York but never arrived in the Big Apple. A note from Vermonter Mrs. Knox, inviting Blake for Christmas, puts Keen on the trail.

CONTINUITY #343
Tuesday, December 19, 1939
7:15–7:30 p.m. EST
NBC Blue
Martha Atwell, Director
Allan Leonard, Writer
Mildred Fenton, Editor
Ben Grauer, Announcer
American Home Products (Bi-So-Dol), Sponsor
"The Case of the Man in Search of Christmas"
At Shaftesbury, Vermont, Keen locates Blake, hiding from New York and Hollywood sophisticates. Blake crashes through the ice on the river but is saved by Keen and Knox's 12-year-old granddaughter.

CONTINUITY #344
Wednesday, December 20, 1939
7:15–7:30 p.m. EST
NBC Blue
Martha Atwell, Director
Allan Leonard, Writer
Mildred Fenton, Editor
Ben Grauer, Announcer
American Home Products (Bi-So-Dol), Sponsor
"The Case of the Man in Search of Christmas"
Adrienne Lee loves Blake. Keen learns that Adrienne and Blake both think that the other prefers a career and cash. Blake has contracted pneumonia. Unbeknownst to the ailing writer, Keen sends for Adrienne.

CONTINUITY #345
Thursday, December 21, 1939
7:15–7:30 p.m. EST
NBC Blue
Martha Atwell, Director
Allan Leonard, Writer
Mildred Fenton, Editor
Ben Grauer, Announcer
American Home Products (Bi-So-Dol), Sponsor
"The Case of the Man in Search of Christmas"
On Christmas day at the Knox home, Blake is on the mend. He receives a big surprise when Adrienne appears. Keen leaves them to work out their futures together.

CONTINUITY #346
Tuesday, December 26, 1939
7:15–7:30 p.m. EST
NBC Blue
Martha Atwell, Director
Allan Leonard, Writer
Mildred Fenton, Editor
Ben Grauer, Announcer
American Home Products (Bi-So-Dol), Sponsor
"The Case of the Girl Who Wanted to Disappear"
In 1937 (as the radio series began) Mr. Keen united Jack Gatewood and an aide, Marjorie Southerland. Keen celebrates with them. Marjorie's friend, Dorothy Webb, now needs Keen's help.

CONTINUITY #347
Wednesday, December 27, 1939
7:15–7:30 p.m. EST
NBC Blue
Martha Atwell, Director
Allan Leonard, Writer
Mildred Fenton, Editor
Ben Grauer, Announcer
American Home Products (Bi-So-Dol), Sponsor
"The Case of the Girl Who Wanted to Disappear"
Model Dorothy Webb is frantic because playboy Gerald Hare, her lover, is engaged to another. Unable to go home and face her father, Dorothy wants Keen to help her vanish and start over.

CONTINUITY #348
Thursday, December 28, 1939
7:15–7:30 p.m. EST
NBC Blue
Martha Atwell, Director
Allan Leonard, Writer
Mildred Fenton, Editor
Ben Grauer, Announcer
American Home Products (Bi-So-Dol), Sponsor
"The Case of the Girl Who Wanted to Disappear"
Gerald Hare gets into a brawl with Ken Griffin. Ken had earlier impressed Mr. Keen with his unselfish interest in Dorothy Webb. The two appear to be headed toward a future together.

CONTINUITY #349
Tuesday, January 2, 1940
7:15–7:30 p.m. EST
NBC Blue
Martha Atwell, Director
Allan Leonard, Writer
Mildred Fenton, Editor
Announcer's name omitted
American Home Products (Bi-So-Dol), Sponsor
"The Case of the Missing Clown"
Mr. Keen and Miss Ellis go to a circus as guests of Captain Wallace, the circus' owner and Keen's friend. The clown Bobo vanishes. Suicide is ruled out when Keen finds clues to suggest otherwise.

CONTINUITY #350
Wednesday, January 3, 1940
7:15–7:30 p.m. EST
NBC Blue
Martha Atwell, Director
Allan Leonard, Writer
Mildred Fenton, Editor
Ben Grauer, Announcer
American Home Products (Bi-So-Dol), Sponsor
"The Case of the Missing Clown"
Bobo went to Inglewood, New Jersey, where a boy Keen thinks is Bobo's grandson, Henry Wadsworth, age nine, goes to school. Keen figures a tragic tale is behind it all, and calls in Al Wadsworth, Henry's father.

CONTINUITY #351
Thursday, January 4, 1940
7:15–7:30 p.m. EST
NBC Blue
Martha Atwell, Director
Allan Leonard, Writer
Mildred Fenton, Editor
Ben Grauer, Announcer
American Home Products (Bi-So-Dol), Sponsor
"The Case of the Missing Clown"
  Bobo's wife left him years ago, taking their daughter. When he later found the girl, she had wed a society man and had a son. Ashamed of her father, she rejected him and later died. But Bobo loves his longlost grandson Henry.

CONTINUITY #352
Tuesday, January 9, 1940
7:15–7:30 p.m. EST
NBC Blue
Martha Atwell, Director
Allan Leonard, Writer
Mildred Fenton, Editor
Ben Grauer, Announcer
American Home Products (Bi-So-Dol), Sponsor
"The Case of the Missing Clown"
  Mr. Keen seeks to bring boy and grandfather together. Keen visits Captain Wallace and has his friend schedule a circus performance at Henry's school, so that the boy can see Bobo perform. Henry doesn't know Bobo is kin.

CONTINUITY #353
Wednesday, January 10, 1940
7:15–7:30 p.m. EST
NBC Blue
Martha Atwell, Director
Allan Leonard, Writer
Mildred Fenton, Editor
Ben Grauer, Announcer
American Home Products (Bi-So-Dol), Sponsor
"The Case of the Missing Clown"
  Mr. Keen and Miss Ellis attend the performance at Henry's military academy. The connection between grandpa and grandson is established, and their lives forever reordered.

CONTINUITY #354
Thursday, January 11, 1940
7:15–7:30 p.m. EST
NBC Blue
Martha Atwell, Director
Allan Leonard, Writer
Mildred Fenton, Editor
Ben Grauer, Announcer
American Home Products (Bi-So-Dol), Sponsor
"The Case of the Girl Who Wanted Glamour"
  Cranky society maven Amelia Devereaux calls Keen to her Long Island estate. Her secretary, Elizabeth Fuller, is gone. Nephew Taylor, who loves Elizabeth, thinks the old lady sent her away.

CONTINUITY #355
Tuesday, January 16, 1940
7:15–7:30 p.m. EST
NBC Blue
Martha Atwell, Director
Allan Leonard, Writer
Mildred Fenton, Editor
James Fleming, Announcer
American Home Products (Bi-So-Dol), Sponsor
"The Case of the Girl Who Wanted Glamour"
  Amelia tells Keen she hopes Taylor and Elizabeth will wed but tested them by acting otherwise. Since transformed into a glamour girl, Elizabeth refuses to return to marry Taylor.

CONTINUITY #356
Wednesday, January 17, 1940
7:15–7:30 p.m. EST
NBC Blue
Martha Atwell, Director
Allan Leonard, Writer
Mildred Fenton, Editor
Ben Grauer, Announcer
American Home Products (Bi-So-Dol), Sponsor
"The Case of the Girl Who Wanted Glamour"
  In a Cinderella twist, the rich clan wants the poor girl but she snubs them. Taylor's social rank and Amelia's controlling nature turns her off. Amelia disowns Taylor and throws him out.

CONTINUITY #357
Thursday, January 18, 1940
7:15–7:30 p.m. EST

NBC Blue
Martha Atwell, Director
Allan Leonard, Writer
Mildred Fenton, Editor
James Fleming, Announcer
American Home Products (Bi-So-Dol), Sponsor
"The Case of the Girl Who Wanted Glamour"

Keen is behind Amelia's actions. He convinces Elizabeth and Taylor that love and marriage have nothing to do with money and prestige. The couple plan to devote their lives to one another.

CONTINUITY #358
Tuesday, January 23, 1940
7:15–7:30 p.m. EST
NBC Blue
Martha Atwell, Director
Allan Leonard, Writer
Mildred Fenton, Editor
James Fleming, Announcer
American Home Products (Bi-So-Dol), Sponsor
"The Case of the Lost Mother"

Keen and Clancy visit Lydia Crossett, head of an exclusive girls' school. The mother of pupil Nancy Darrell, age six, has deserted the girl. Nancy, very ill with appendicitis, is crying for her mom.

CONTINUITY #359
Wednesday, January 24, 1940
7:15–7:30 p.m. EST
NBC Blue
Martha Atwell, Director
Allan Leonard, Writer
Mildred Fenton, Editor
James Fleming, Announcer
American Home Products (Bi-So-Dol), Sponsor
"The Case of the Lost Mother"

Nancy receives a magnificent doll from her mother. Keen and Clancy visit a major New York department store to trace the doll. This leads them to an address in Palm Beach, Florida.

CONTINUITY #360
Thursday, January 25, 1940
7:15–7:30 p.m. EST
NBC Blue
Martha Atwell, Director
Allan Leonard, Writer
Mildred Fenton, Editor
James Fleming, Announcer
American Home Products (Bi-So-Dol), Sponsor
"The Case of the Lost Mother"

Nancy's mother is Lady Stevane, a British tycoon's wife and mistress of a huge estate. She denies kinship to Nancy. Told of her child's illness, Lady Stevane drops the pretense and flies to Nancy's bedside.

CONTINUITY #361
Tuesday, January 30, 1940
7:15–7:30 p.m. EST
NBC Blue
Martha Atwell, Director
Allan Leonard, Writer
Mildred Fenton, Editor
James Fleming, Announcer
American Home Products (Kolynos), Sponsor
"The Case of the Lost Mother"

Nancy's father had died before her birth. Her mother met and wed Lord Stevane but didn't tell him about her daughter. Nancy, now enveloped by her mother's arms, improves. Lord Stevane is on his way, and Nancy's mother flees.

CONTINUITY #362
Wednesday, January 31, 1940
7:15–7:30 p.m. EST
NBC Blue
Martha Atwell, Director
Allan Leonard, Writer
Mildred Fenton, Editor
James Fleming, Announcer
American Home Products (Kolynos), Sponsor
"The Case of the Lost Mother"

Lord Stevane meets Keen. He's sympathetic yet perplexed that his wife's faith in him was not strong enough to trust him with her secret. She attempts suicide, but Keen puts the family back together.

CONTINUITY #363
Thursday, February 1, 1940
7:15–7:30 p.m. EST
NBC Blue
Martha Atwell, Director
Ernest R. Shenkin, Writer

Mildred Fenton, Editor
James Fleming, Announcer
American Home Products (Kolynos), Sponsor
"The Case of the Runaway Boy"

Mary Kelly asks Mr. Keen to find her brother Jimmy, age 15. He left a note saying that he wants to avoid becoming a burden to her. She has raised him since their parents' deaths six years ago.

CONTINUITY #364
Tuesday, February 6, 1940
7:15–7:30 p.m. EST
NBC Blue
Martha Atwell, Director
Ernest R. Shenkin, Writer
Mildred Fenton, Editor
James Fleming, Announcer
American Home Products (Kolynos), Sponsor
"The Case of the Runaway Boy"

Mary lives in a shabby, but tidy, apartment. She's a salesclerk. Jimmy fears a social worker, who claims Mary is unfit to care for him, will take him away. Keen discovers that Jimmy hopped a freight train.

CONTINUITY #365
Wednesday, February 7, 1940
7:15–7:30 p.m. EST
NBC Blue
Martha Atwell, Director
Ernest R. Shenkin, Writer
Mildred Fenton, Editor
James Fleming, Announcer
American Home Products (Kolynos), Sponsor
"The Case of the Runaway Boy"

Jimmy is found in a hospital in a small town in upstate New York. He maintains that his name is Joe Riley and that Keen has made a mistake. Keen is unable to shake the youth's story.

CONTINUITY #366
Thursday, February 8, 1940
7:15–7:30 p.m. EST
NBC Blue
Martha Atwell, Director
Ernest R. Shenkin, Writer
Mildred Fenton, Editor
James Fleming, Announcer
American Home Products (Kolynos), Sponsor
"The Case of the Runaway Boy"

Keen persuades Jimmy to return home only to learn that the welfare worker has sworn out a deposition stating that Jimmy has no fit guardian and should be sent to an orphan asylum.

CONTINUITY #367
Tuesday, February 13, 1940
7:15–7:30 p.m. EST
NBC Blue
Martha Atwell, Director
Ernest R. Shenkin, Writer
Mildred Fenton, Editor
James Fleming, Announcer
American Home Products (Kolynos), Sponsor
"The Case of the Runaway Boy"

In court Mr. Keen convinces the judge and social worker that Jimmy is better off in his sister's care than in a state facility. Thanks to Keen, Mary will also now have a better job.

CONTINUITY #368
Wednesday, February 14, 1940
7:15–7:30 p.m. EST
NBC Blue
Martha Atwell, Director
Ernest R. Shenkin, Writer
Mildred Fenton, Editor
James Fleming, Announcer
American Home Products (Kolynos), Sponsor
"The Case of the Missing Cop"

Irish cop Terry O'Flynn vanishes. He's accused of taking a bribe from racketeer Rudy Ravenna. Janie Grogan had refused to marry him without more dough; now she sports a costly fur.

CONTINUITY #369
Thursday, February 15, 1940
7:15–7:30 p.m. EST
NBC Blue
Martha Atwell, Director
Allan Leonard, Writer
Mildred Fenton, Editor
James Fleming, Announcer
American Home Products (Kolynos), Sponsor
"The Case of the Missing Cop"

Keen and Clancy go to the dive where Janie waits tables. Ravenna's gang killed Terry's best friend. He took the cash to infiltrate the gang and find the culprit. A shot hits Janie.

CONTINUITY #370
Tuesday, February 20, 1940
7:15–7:30 p.m. EST
NBC Blue
Martha Atwell, Director
Allan Leonard, Writer
Mildred Fenton, Editor
James Fleming, Announcer
American Home Products (Kolynos), Sponsor
"The Case of the Missing Cop"

Mr. Keen finds Terry at Rudy's roadhouse. Terry shows Keen evidence that Rudy is the murderer. Rudy overhears them and summons two thugs to take the two investigators for a ride.

CONTINUITY #371
Wednesday, February 21, 1940
7:15–7:30 p.m. EST
NBC Blue
Martha Atwell, Director
Allan Leonard, Writer
Mildred Fenton, Editor
James Fleming, Announcer
American Home Products (Kolynos), Sponsor
"The Case of the Missing Cop"

Mr. Keen saves himself and Terry O'Flynn from the dangerous predicament in which they find themselves. Rudy Ravenna and his gang are put away. They'll take no revenge on Terry.

CONTINUITY #372
Thursday, February 22, 1940
7:15–7:30 p.m. EST
NBC Blue
Martha Atwell, Director
Allan Leonard, Writer
Mildred Fenton, Editor
James Fleming, Announcer
American Home Products (Kolynos), Sponsor
"The Case of the Girl Who Didn't Believe in Love"

Neophyte actress Beulah Ross won a part in a film thanks to Barry Carewe, now a star. She vanishes before finishing the picture. She writes her mother that she knows a secret so bad she can't bear it.

CONTINUITY #373
Tuesday, February 27, 1940
7:15–7:30 p.m. EST
NBC Blue
Martha Atwell, Director
Allan Leonard, Writer
Mildred Fenton, Editor
James Fleming, Announcer
American Home Products (Kolynos), Sponsor
"The Case of the Girl Who Didn't Believe in Love"

Keen and Clancy fly to L.A. where they learn that Barry and Beulah had dreams of stardom. Knowing that he loved her, when Barry received his big break, he gave Beulah a break as well. But co-star Lydia Vale maliciously told Beulah that she and Barry had wed. Heartbroken, Beulah left.

CONTINUITY #374
Wednesday, February 28, 1940
7:15–7:30 p.m. EST
NBC Blue
Martha Atwell, Director
Allan Leonard, Writer
Mildred Fenton, Editor
James Fleming, Announcer
American Home Products (Kolynos), Sponsor
"The Case of the Girl Who Didn't Believe in Love"

Beulah flees to an orange ranch at Redlands, owned by narrow-minded Joe Anderson, age 50. Keen tells her of Lydia's lie and Barry's intent to marry her. But she's now been promised to Joe.

CONTINUITY #375
Thursday, February 29, 1940
7:15–7:30 p.m. EST
NBC Blue
Martha Atwell, Director
Allan Leonard, Writer
Mildred Fenton, Editor
James Fleming, Announcer
American Home Products (Kolynos), Sponsor
"The Case of the Girl Who Didn't Believe in Love"

Keen and Clancy return to New York, content that their visit to the West Coast convinced Beulah Ross and Barry Carewe that love really does exist and that it can triumph over falsehood.

CONTINUITY #376
Tuesday, March 5, 1940
7:15–7:30 p.m. EST

NBC Blue
Martha Atwell, Director
Allan Leonard, Writer
Mildred Fenton, Editor
James Fleming, Announcer
American Home Products (Kolynos), Sponsor
"The Case of the Dragon Fly"

Miss Ellis receives a wire, purportedly from Keen, luring her away. Keen realizes that gangsters intend to stop him testifying at Rudy Ravenna's murder trial, so they hold Ellis hostage.

CONTINUITY #377
Wednesday, March 6, 1940
7:15–7:30 p.m. EST
NBC Blue
Martha Atwell, Director
Allan Leonard, Writer
Mildred Fenton, Editor
James Fleming, Announcer
American Home Products (Kolynos), Sponsor
"The Case of the Dragon Fly"

Keen receives a note Miss Ellis put in a bottle and threw into the river telling him she is being held on a boat called *Annie K*. In heavy fog, Keen and the D.A. use a police boat to search for the *Annie K*.

CONTINUITY #378
Thursday, March 7, 1940
7:15–7:30 p.m. EST
NBC Blue
Martha Atwell, Director
Allan Leonard, Writer
Mildred Fenton, Editor
James Fleming, Announcer
American Home Products (Kolynos), Sponsor
"The Case of the Dragon Fly"

Miss Ellis has been spirited away from the *Annie K*. Owner Mr. Bardow is the Dragon Fly. Keen plans to meet with him. Bardow deceptively appears to be a pillar of the community.

CONTINUITY #379
Tuesday, March 12, 1940
7:15–7:30 p.m. EST
NBC Blue
Martha Atwell, Director
Allan Leonard, Writer
Mildred Fenton, Editor
James Fleming, Announcer
American Home Products (Kolynos), Sponsor
"The Case of the Dragon Fly"

Keen sees Mrs. Bardow, an ex–chorus girl, as a chink in Bardow's armor. Keen accuses her of being the Dragon Fly's wife. She admits it and calls her chauffeur, who shoots Mr. Keen.

CONTINUITY #380
Wednesday, March 13, 1940
7:15–7:30 p.m. EST
NBC Blue
Martha Atwell, Director
Allan Leonard, Writer
Mildred Fenton, Editor
James Fleming, Announcer
American Home Products (Kolynos), Sponsor
"The Case of the Dragon Fly"

The D. A. and Clancy visit Keen at the hospital. Ellis is freed and the gang rounded up. Law and order are restored. Keen's arm is in a sling, but it was nothing more than a flesh wound.

CONTINUITY #381
Thursday, March 14, 1940
7:15–7:30 p.m. EST
NBC Blue
Martha Atwell, Director
Allan Leonard, Writer
Mildred Fenton, Editor
James Fleming, Announcer
American Home Products (Kolynos), Sponsor
"The Case of the Lost Sword"

Frenchwoman Madame Verdurin says her partner in an antique shop, Edmund Baker, has vanished. A couple of theories are bandied about, but Keen is skeptical. He and Clancy go to Baker's home.

CONTINUITY #382
Tuesday, March 19, 1940
7:15–7:30 p.m. EST
NBC Blue
Martha Atwell, Director
Allan Leonard, Writer
Mildred Fenton, Editor
James Fleming, Announcer
American Home Products (Kolynos), Sponsor
"The Case of the Lost Sword"

The Soo-Chan Sword, reputed to bring bad luck, disappeared from the shop that same night. In a diary, Baker accuses the father of fiancée Gloria Thomas of killing his own father. A secret passageway is found.

CONTINUITY #383
Wednesday, March 20, 1940
7:15–7:30 p.m. EST
NBC Blue
Martha Atwell, Director
Allan Leonard, Writer
Mildred Fenton, Editor
James Fleming, Announcer
American Home Products (Kolynos), Sponsor
"The Case of the Lost Sword"
  Keen and Clancy find Baker badly wounded in a vault. Madame Verdurin was at the house the night he was attacked. Unsatisfied, Keen calls Verdurin to his office for a conference the next day.

CONTINUITY #384
Thursday, March 21, 1940
7:15–7:30 p.m. EST
NBC Blue
Martha Atwell, Director
Allan Leonard, Writer
Mildred Fenton, Editor
James Fleming, Announcer
American Home Products (Kolynos), Sponsor
"The Case of the Lost Sword"
  Mr. Keen learns that profit, not the curse that supposedly follows the sword's owner, was behind the attempted murder of Edmund Baker. Keen ties the loose ends together.

CONTINUITY #385
Tuesday, March 26, 1940
7:15–7:30 p.m. EST
NBC Blue
Martha Atwell, Director
Allan Leonard, Writer
Mildred Fenton, Editor
James Fleming, Announcer
American Home Products (Kolynos), Sponsor
"The Case of the Missing Pilot"
  Val Burton's wife doesn't think Val died in an air crash in Canada; she received a note from him mailed two days after the accident. She tries to kill herself. Keen and Clancy go to St. Marie, Canada.

CONTINUITY #386
Wednesday, March 27, 1940
7:15–7:30 p.m. EST
NBC Blue
Martha Atwell, Director
Allan Leonard, Writer
Mildred Fenton, Editor
James Fleming, Announcer
American Home Products (Kolynos), Sponsor
"The Case of the Missing Pilot"
  A blind man hiding in a deserted cabin might be Val. Keen heads out with French Canadian trapper Francois Jarvais and village nurse Celeste, crossing the snow in a blizzard.

CONTINUITY #387
Thursday, March 28, 1940
7:15–7:30 p.m. EST
NBC Blue
Martha Atwell, Director
Allan Leonard, Writer
Mildred Fenton, Editor
James Fleming, Announcer
American Home Products (Kolynos), Sponsor
"The Case of the Missing Pilot"
  The man in the cabin *is* famous pilot Val Burton. He went blind and planned to commit suicide, but bailed out in a parachute instead. He's taken to a Quebec hospital and his wife is sent for.

CONTINUITY #388
Tuesday, April 2, 1940
7:15–7:30 p.m. EST
NBC Blue
Martha Atwell, Director
Allan Leonard, Writer
Mildred Fenton, Editor
James Fleming, Announcer
American Home Products (Bi-So-Dol), Sponsor
"The Case of the Missing Pilot"
  The arrival of his loving wife restores Val Burton's faith in life. Mr. Keen is confident that now he will go on to make a new life for himself through service to others.

CONTINUITY #389
Wednesday, April 3, 1940
7:15–7:30 p.m. EST
NBC Blue
Martha Atwell, Director
Allan Leonard, Writer
Mildred Fenton, Editor

James Fleming, Announcer
American Home Products (Bi-So-Dol), Sponsor
"The Case of the Wife Who Lacked Faith"
　　Mrs. Jennifer asks Keen to shadow her spouse, Lee. Is he having an affair with Bernice Roberts? Lee tells Keen he embezzled from Bernice's aunt and will jump from a bridge. The police are called.

CONTINUITY #390
Thursday, April 4, 1940
7:15–7:30 p.m. EST
NBC Blue
Martha Atwell, Director
Allan Leonard, Writer
Mildred Fenton, Editor
James Fleming, Announcer
American Home Products (Bi-So-Dol), Sponsor
"The Case of the Wife Who Lacked Faith"
　　There's no proof that Lee took his own life. His wife says he left with Bernice to start a new life. The aunt arrives and reports the stolen cash. Keen goes to Bernice's apartment.

CONTINUITY #391
Tuesday, April 9, 1940
7:15–7:30 p.m. EST
NBC Blue
Martha Atwell, Director
Allan Leonard, Writer
Mildred Fenton, Editor
James Fleming, Announcer
American Home Products (Bi-So-Dol), Sponsor
"The Case of the Wife Who Lacked Faith"
　　Keen traces Lee to Leadville, Colorado. Bernice saved him from suicide, then sent him to check on a mine to perform a service for her aunt and thus make restitution. Keen follows him.

CONTINUITY #392
Wednesday, April 10, 1940
7:15–7:30 p.m. EST
NBC Blue
Martha Atwell, Director
Allan Leonard, Writer
Mildred Fenton, Editor
James Fleming, Announcer
American Home Products (Bi-So-Dol), Sponsor
"The Case of the Wife Who Lacked Faith"
　　At the mine, Lee poses as Tom Walker. Keen helps him admit what he did, and restores him to the wife who thought he didn't love her. Bernice loves him, so Keen goes to see her.

CONTINUITY #393
Thursday, April 11, 1940
7:15–7:30 p.m. EST
NBC Blue
Martha Atwell, Director
Allan Leonard, Writer
Mildred Fenton, Editor
James Fleming, Announcer
American Home Products (Bi-So-Dol), Sponsor
"The Case of the Wife Who Lacked Faith"
　　Keen is now satisfied that all the people involved in this situation have come out content—even Bernice Roberts, who, through providing assistance to others, finds happiness and love.

CONTINUITY #394
Tuesday, April 16, 1940
7:15–7:30 p.m. EST
NBC Blue
Martha Atwell, Director
Allan Leonard, Writer
Mildred Fenton, Editor
James Fleming, Announcer
American Home Products (Bi-So-Dol), Sponsor
"The Case of the New Citizen"
　　Cobbler Anton Eslavski drops from sight before his efforts to become a United States citizen come to fruitron. His daughter Rose, with whom Anton argued recently, fears he killed himself. But Anton had his U. S. history books with him.

CONTINUITY #395
Wednesday, April 17, 1940
7:15–7:30 p.m. EST
NBC Blue
Martha Atwell, Director
Allan Leonard, Writer
Mildred Fenton, Editor
James Fleming, Announcer
American Home Products (Bi-So-Dol), Sponsor
"The Case of the New Citizen"

Keen finds Eslavski wallowing in despair, for he feels he cannot answer the citizenship questions. Mr. Keen is impressed with his decency and kindness, and promises to testify as a witness.

CONTINUITY #396
Thursday, April 18, 1940
7:15–7:30 p.m. EST
NBC Blue
Martha Atwell, Director
Allan Leonard, Writer
Mildred Fenton, Editor
James Fleming, Announcer
American Home Products (Bi-So-Dol), Sponsor
"The Case of the New Citizen"

Mr. Keen puts in a good word for Anton Eslavski, the emigrant shoemaker, at the Federal Building. Through Keen's intervention, Eslavski becomes a full-fledged American citizen.

CONTINUITY #397
Tuesday, April 23, 1940
7:15–7:30 p.m. EST
NBC Blue
Martha Atwell, Director
Jerome D. Ross, Writer
Mildred Fenton, Editor
James Fleming, Announcer
American Home Products (Bi-So-Dol), Sponsor
"The Case of the Missing Parents"

Hank and Grace Benson farm in Illinois. Two weeks ago they headed for New York to visit son Larry and his wife Edna, but vanished. Larry says they were welcome, but Keen is dubious.

CONTINUITY #398
Wednesday, April 24, 1940
7:15–7:30 p.m. EST
NBC Blue
Martha Atwell, Director
Jerome D. Ross, Writer
Mildred Fenton, Editor
James Fleming, Announcer
American Home Products (Bi-So-Dol), Sponsor
"The Case of the Missing Parents"

Keen goes to Rand's Corners, Illinois, the missing couple's home town. Keen learns that, far from planning to care for his parents, Larry and Edna Benson planned to separate them.

CONTINUITY #399
Thursday, April 25, 1940
7:15–7:30 p.m. EST
NBC Blue
Martha Atwell, Director
Jerome D. Ross, Writer
Mildred Fenton, Editor
Announcer's name omitted
American Home Products (Bi-So-Dol), Sponsor
"The Case of the Missing Parents"

Larry planned to put his mom in an old folks' home. Keen locates the couple in Kelceyville, Indiana, where they met 50 years ago. Keen pays a visit to Tom Nolan, the town's leading citizen.

CONTINUITY #400
Tuesday, April 30, 1940
7:15–7:30 p.m. EDST
NBC Blue
Martha Atwell, Director
Jerome D. Ross, Writer
Mildred Fenton, Editor
James Fleming, Announcer
American Home Products (Bi-So-Dol, Kolynos), Sponsor
"The Case of the Missing Parents"

Keen tells the old couple that their son and daughter-in-law regret their cruelty. The pair is doubtful and willing never to see them again. Nolan takes them under his care.

CONTINUITY #401
Wednesday, May 1, 1940
7:15–7:30 p.m. EDST
NBC Blue
Martha Atwell, Director
Jerome D. Ross, Writer
Mildred Fenton, Editor
James Fleming, Announcer
American Home Products (Bi-So-Dol, Kolynos), Sponsor
"The Case of the Missing Parents"

Mr. Keen brings the matter to a happy conclusion. Hank and Grace Benson are reunited with their son and daughter-in-law. They anticipate a good life on a Kelceyville farm.

CONTINUITY #402
Thursday, May 2, 1940
7:15–7:30 p.m. EDST
NBC Blue
Martha Atwell, Director
Willard Wiener, Writer
Mildred Fenton, Editor
James Fleming, Announcer
American Home Products (Bi-So-Dol, Kolynos), Sponsor
"The Case of the Missing Doll"
   Cathy Barnes, age nine, pleads with Keen to find her doll. Her mom is also missing. Innkeeper Mrs. Walters cares for Cathy, who thinks her mother will return — and doesn't know she's suicidal.

CONTINUITY #403
Tuesday, May 7, 1940
7:15–7:30 p.m. EDST
NBC Blue
Martha Atwell, Director
Willard Wiener, Writer
Mildred Fenton, Editor
James Fleming, Announcer
American Home Products (Bi-So-Dol, Kolynos), Sponsor
"The Case of the Missing Doll"
   Keen sets out to find Mrs. Barnes before it is too late. In a shabby roominghouse where Cathy and her mother live he finds a clue, a doll's dress, leading him to a doll factory.

CONTINUITY #404
Wednesday, May 8, 1940
7:15–7:30 p.m. EDST
NBC Blue
Martha Atwell, Director
Willard Wiener, Writer
Mildred Fenton, Editor
James Fleming, Announcer
American Home Products (Bi-So-Dol, Kolynos), Sponsor
"The Case of the Missing Doll"
   A doll police fish from the river turns out to be the one Cathy lost. The mystery of her mother's disappearance is no nearer solution, however. Keen, Mike Clancy and Miss Ellis review the case.

CONTINUITY #405
Thursday, May 9, 1940
7:15–7:30 p.m. EDST
NBC Blue
Martha Atwell, Director
Willard Wiener, Writer
Mildred Fenton, Editor
James Fleming, Announcer
American Home Products (Bi-So-Dol, Kolynos), Sponsor
"The Case of the Missing Doll"
   Keen sees a lady watching Cathy. He chases her, and she runs to the subway. He reaches her as a train arrives. She runs to the platform edge; Keen calls out "Mrs. Barnes," and she screams.

CONTINUITY #406
Tuesday, May 14, 1940
7:15–7:30 p.m. EDST
NBC Blue
Martha Atwell, Director
Willard Wiener, Writer
Mildred Fenton, Editor
James Fleming, Announcer
American Home Products (Bi-So-Dol, Kolynos), Sponsor
"The Case of the Missing Doll"
   Mrs. Barnes is spared. Mr. Keen returns her to little Cathy, who never realizes that her mother was ever missing.

CONTINUITY #407
Wednesday, May 15, 1940
7:15–7:30 p.m. EDST
NBC Blue
Martha Atwell, Director
Allan Leonard, Writer
Mildred Fenton, Editor
James Fleming, Announcer
American Home Products (Bi-So-Dol, Kolynos), Sponsor
"The Case of the Girl with Crutches"
   Helen Blake, a beautiful young crippled girl, disappears. Bob Stevens, an intern at City Hospital, begs Mr. Keen to find her. He's in love with Helen, but she thinks he only pities her.

CONTINUITY #408
Thursday, May 16, 1940
7:15–7:30 p.m. EDST
NBC Blue
Martha Atwell, Director
Eric Arthur, Writer

Mildred Fenton, Editor
James Fleming, Announcer
American Home Products (Bi-So-Dol, Kolynos), Sponsor
"The Case of the Girl with Crutches"

Keen traces Helen to Philadelphia Hospital, where Lawrence Gordon operated on her in a dangerous procedure that offered her one chance in a hundred that she'd walk again. Keen goes to Philly.

CONTINUITY #409
Tuesday, May 21, 1940
7:15–7:30 p.m. EDST
NBC Blue
Martha Atwell, Director
Eric Arthur, Writer
Mildred Fenton, Editor
James Fleming, Announcer
American Home Products (Bi-So-Dol, Kolynos), Sponsor
"The Case of the Girl with Crutches"

The surgery is successful. Helen's recovery, however, is complicated by depression and self-pity. But Keen is with her.

CONTINUITY #410
Wednesday, May 22, 1940
7:15–7:30 p.m. EDST
NBC Blue
Martha Atwell, Director
Eric Arthur, Writer
Mildred Fenton, Editor
James Fleming, Announcer
American Home Products (Bi-So-Dol, Kolynos), Sponsor
"The Case of the Girl with Crutches"

Helen is reunited with young Dr. Bob Stevens, who loves her and will marry her as soon as she leaves the hospital. She will walk without crutches or cane.

CONTINUITY #411
Thursday, May 23, 1940
7:15–7:30 p.m. EDST
NBC Blue
Martha Atwell, Director
Allan Leonard and Mildred Fenton, Writers
Mildred Fenton, Editor
James Fleming, Announcer
American Home Products (Bi-So-Dol, Kolynos), Sponsor
"The Case of Murder and the Night Club Singer"

Jim Ford is in prison for murder. He escaped to find singer Lorraine McKenzie, who can clear him. Failing that, he returned to jail. Keen hears that McKenzie is in San Francisco.

CONTINUITY #412
Tuesday, May 28, 1940
7:15–7:30 p.m. EDST
NBC Blue
Martha Atwell, Director
Allan Leonard, Writer
Mildred Fenton, Editor
James Fleming, Announcer
American Home Products (Bi-So-Dol, Kolynos), Sponsor
"The Case of Murder and the Night Club Singer"

McKenzie now goes by the name of Lori Macken. She signs a statement that Fred Chase, the murdered man, turned the gun on himself and wasn't shot by Jim Ford. Keen takes this to the D.A.

CONTINUITY #413
Wednesday, May 29, 1940
7:15–7:30 p.m. EDST
NBC Blue
Martha Atwell, Director
Willard Wiener, Writer
Mildred Fenton, Editor
James Fleming, Announcer
American Home Products (Bi-So-Dol, Kolynos), Sponsor
"The Case of Murder and the Night Club Singer"

Through his persistence, Mr. Keen has obtained the evidence to free Jim Ford of a murder charge and to insure the future happiness of Lori Macken and Jim, who are in love.

CONTINUITY #414
Thursday, May 30, 1940
7:15–7:30 p.m. EDST
NBC Blue
Martha Atwell, Director
Willard Wiener, Writer
Mildred Fenton, Editor
James Fleming, Announcer
American Home Products (Bi-So-Dol, Kolynos), Sponsor

"The Case of the Woman Who Wasn't Needed"
Wealthy merchant Henry Frank asks Keen to locate his wife. Given every luxury, she had no reason to leave. She may be on her way to Florida; her car is found in North Carolina.

CONTINUITY #415
Tuesday, June 4, 1940
7:15–7:30 p.m. EDST
NBC Blue
Martha Atwell, Director
Willard Wiener, Writer
Mildred Fenton, Editor
James Fleming, Announcer
American Home Products (Kolynos, Fly-Ded), Sponsor
"The Case of the Woman Who Wasn't Needed"
In North Carolina Keen finds Mrs. Frank, a counselor at an orphans' camp. She's lonely, having left her family because she became convinced that they didn't need her. Keen induces her to return home with him.

CONTINUITY #416
Wednesday, June 5, 1940
7:15–7:30 p.m. EDST
NBC Blue
Martha Atwell, Director
Willard Wiener, Writer
Mildred Fenton, Editor
James Fleming, Announcer
American Home Products (Kolynos, Fly-Ded), Sponsor
"The Case of the Woman Who Wasn't Needed"
(*Extant Episode*)
The Frank clan awaits Mrs. Frank's return. Keen effects a reunion, and tells Mrs. Frank she is needed and appreciated. He mentions that charitable groups exist nearby that can use her services.

CONTINUITY #417
Thursday, June 6, 1940
7:15–7:30 p.m. EDST
NBC Blue
Martha Atwell, Director
John M. Young, Writer
Mildred Fenton, Editor
James Fleming, Announcer
American Home Products (Kolynos, Fly-Ded), Sponsor
"The Case of the Vanishing Bride"
Heiress Martha Hudson, brilliant sculptor-instructor Alec Chalmers' fiancée, disappeared on their wedding day. On a hunch, Keen flies to Washington, D.C., where Alec has an exhibit.

CONTINUITY #418
Tuesday, June 11, 1940
7:15–7:30 p.m. EDST
NBC Blue
Martha Atwell, Director
John M. Young, Writer
Mildred Fenton, Editor
James Fleming, Announcer
American Home Products (Kolynos, Fly-Ded), Sponsor
"The Case of the Vanishing Bride"
Keen finds Martha. She says Alec didn't love her and was marrying her for money. She refuses to return. Keen is hard pressed to know why she believes Alec has deceived her.

CONTINUITY #419
Wednesday, June 12, 1940
7:15–7:30 p.m. EDST
NBC Blue
Martha Atwell, Director
John M. Young, Writer
Mildred Fenton, Editor
James Fleming, Announcer
American Home Products (Kolynos, Fly-Ded), Sponsor
"The Case of the Vanishing Bride"
Keen learns that a bridesmaid informed Martha that Alec was marrying for money. Martha returns. A cousin tells Alec that Martha has run off to marry Harry Barlow. Alec says he will "get" Barlow.

CONTINUITY #420
Thursday, June 13, 1940
7:15–7:30 p.m. EDST
NBC Blue
Martha Atwell, Director
John M. Young, Writer
Mildred Fenton, Editor
James Fleming, Announcer
American Home Products (Kolynos, Fly-Ded), Sponsor
"The Case of the Vanishing Bride"
Mr. Keen clears up the misunderstanding that separated Martha Hudson and Alec

Chalmers. It involves gossip and deception perpetrated by more than one person. The wedding proceeds.

CONTINUITY #421
Tuesday, June 18, 1940
7:15–7:30 p.m. EDST
NBC Blue
Martha Atwell, Director
Francis Winikus, Writer
Mildred Fenton, Editor
James Fleming, Announcer
American Home Products (Kolynos, Fly-Ded), Sponsor
"The Case of Doctor Bruce's Son"

Rick Warner, foster son and bright aide to Dr. Steve Bruce, disappears. Nurse Kathy Ryder relays rumors that Dr. Bruce is incompetent and often takes credit for Rick's work.

CONTINUITY #422
Wednesday, June 19, 1940
7:15–7:30 p.m. EDST
NBC Blue
Martha Atwell, Director
Francis Winikus, Writer
Mildred Fenton, Editor
James Fleming, Announcer
American Home Products (Kolynos, Fly-Ded), Sponsor
"The Case of Doctor Bruce's Son"

Keen learns that Rick left after being offered his foster father's post as head surgeon. Dr. Bruce has lost his ability and is to be retired. Rick and Kathy are engaged, but Bruce disapproves.

CONTINUITY #423
Thursday, June 20, 1940
7:15–7:30 p.m. EDST
NBC Blue
Martha Atwell, Director
Francis Winikus, Writer
Mildred Fenton, Editor
James Fleming, Announcer
American Home Products (Kolynos, Fly-Ded), Sponsor
"The Case of Doctor Bruce's Son"

Mr. Keen brings Dr. Rick Warner back to Central Memorial Hospital and the post of head surgeon. Like his foster father before him, he'll serve, heal and offer courage to many.

CONTINUITY #424
Tuesday, June 25, 1940
7:15–7:30 p.m. EDST
NBC Blue
Martha Atwell, Director
John M. Young, Writer
Mildred Fenton, Editor
George Ansbro, Announcer
American Home Products (Kolynos, Fly-Ded), Sponsor
"The Case of the Young Couple Who Couldn't Get Married"

Office clerk George Ogden, who doesn't make enough to marry Madeline Richards, leaves when his employer refuses his request for a raise. Keen finds a letter offering George a job in Providence, Rhode Island.

CONTINUITY #425
Wednesday, June 26, 1940
7:15–7:30 p.m. EDST
NBC Blue
Martha Atwell, Director
John M. Young, Writer
Mildred Fenton, Editor
George Ansbro, Announcer
American Home Products (Kolynos, Fly-Ded), Sponsor
"The Case of the Young Couple Who Couldn't Get Married"

At Bates Machine Company in Providence, George works as a machinist's helper. This job pays no more than the last, but he loves the work. He has given up the idea of marriage; his in-laws wouldn't accept a mechanic.

CONTINUITY #426
Thursday, June 27, 1940
7:15–7:30 p.m. EDST
NBC Blue
Martha Atwell, Director
John M. Young, Writer
Mildred Fenton, Editor
George Ansbro, Announcer
American Home Products (Kolynos, Fly-Ded), Sponsor
"The Case of the Young Couple Who Couldn't Get Married"

Keen induces George to return, and impresses upon the Richardses that George is helping in national defense. But the parents say no to their daughter marrying him. Keen tries a new plan.

CONTINUITY #427
Tuesday, July 2, 1940
7:15–7:30 p.m. EDST
NBC Blue
Martha Atwell, Director
John M. Young, Writer
Mildred Fenton, Editor
George Ansbro, Announcer
American Home Products (Kolynos, Fly-Ded), Sponsor
"The Case of the Young Couple Who Couldn't Get Married"
   Keen shows George Ogden and Madeline Richards how they can live outside New York on his small salary, making marriage possible. The principals, including the parents, reconcile.

CONTINUITY #428
Wednesday, July 3, 1940
7:15–7:30 p.m. EDST
NBC Blue
Martha Atwell, Director
John M. Young, Writer
Mildred Fenton, Editor
James Fleming, Announcer
American Home Products (Kolynos, Fly-Ded), Sponsor
"The Case of the Wayward Brothers"
   Widowed invalid Mrs. Cochran asks Keen to find son Bert, who left two years ago. Mrs. Cochran hopes that Bert can talk his brother Jim out of joining a group of racketeers. Jim tells Keen that Bert is a criminal.

CONTINUITY #429
Thursday, July 4, 1940
7:15–7:30 p.m. EDST
NBC Blue
Martha Atwell, Director
John M. Young, Writer
Mildred Fenton, Editor
James Fleming, Announcer
American Home Products (Kolynos, Fly-Ded), Sponsor
"The Case of the Wayward Brothers"
   Mom and Jim's wife Edna don't know about Bert's record. Bert follows the horses—going south in winter, north in summer. Keen wires police forces at Northern tracks. He finds Bert and goes to his box.

CONTINUITY #430
Tuesday, July 9, 1940
7:15–7:30 p.m. EDST
NBC Blue
Martha Atwell, Director
John M. Young, Writer
Mildred Fenton, Editor
James Fleming, Announcer
American Home Products (Kolynos, Fly-Ded), Sponsor
"The Case of the Wayward Brothers"
   Bert is arrested for bribery. Keen posts $5,000 bail so Bert can return home. Bert, with wife Mabel, instead plans to escape enroute. The couple and Keen board a train home.

CONTINUITY #431
Wednesday, July 10, 1940
7:15–7:30 p.m. EDST
NBC Blue
Martha Atwell, Director
John M. Young, Writer
Mildred Fenton, Editor
James Fleming, Announcer
American Home Products (Kolynos, Fly-Ded), Sponsor
"The Case of the Wayward Brothers"
   Keen prevents the escape. Bert dissuades Jim from a life of crime. Bert resolves to go straight after serving his time. Keen keeps this disgrace and heartbreak from Mrs. Cochran and Edna.

CONTINUITY #432
Thursday, July 11, 1940
7:15–7:30 p.m. EDST
NBC Blue
Martha Atwell, Director
John M. Young, Writer
Mildred Fenton, Editor
James Fleming, Announcer
American Home Products (Kolynos, Fly-Ded), Sponsor
"The Case of the Man Who Didn't Know He Was Lost"
   Bill Stanton is gone. Mr. Balfour, his father-in-law and boss, dislikes him. Miriam Stanton fears for her spouse's safety. She and Keen go the firm's explosives test site.

CONTINUITY #433
Tuesday, July 16, 1940

7:15–7:30 p.m. EDST
NBC Blue
Martha Atwell, Director
John M. Young, Writer
Mildred Fenton, Editor
George Ansbro, Announcer
American Home Products (Kolynos, Fly-Ded), Sponsor
"The Case of the Man Who Didn't Know He Was Lost"

Keen and Miriam find Bill Stanton conducting some dangerous tests in Colorado. But he won't take extra precautions. Keen and Miriam view four blasts, one of which buries Bill under an avalanche.

CONTINUITY #434
Wednesday, July 17, 1940
7:15–7:30 p.m. EDST
NBC Blue
Martha Atwell, Director
John M. Young, Writer
Mildred Fenton, Editor
George Ansbro, Announcer
American Home Products (Kolynos, Fly-Ded), Sponsor
"The Case of the Man Who Didn't Know He Was Lost"

Bill is in the hospital, convinced his father-in-law, whom Mr. Keen has wired to come West, was directly responsible. Bill makes sure he has his gun ready for Balfour's arrival.

CONTINUITY #435
Thursday, July 18, 1940
7:15–7:30 p.m. EDST
NBC Blue
Martha Atwell, Director
John M. Young, Writer
Mildred Fenton, Editor
George Ansbro, Announcer
American Home Products (Kolynos, Fly-Ded), Sponsor
"The Case of the Man Who Didn't Know He Was Lost"

Keen works through the delicate situation that involves Bill, Miriam and her father, Mr. Balfour. At last they gain a new appreciation of one another.

CONTINUITY #436
Tuesday, July 23, 1940
7:15–7:30 p.m. EDST
NBC Blue
Martha Atwell, Director
John M. Young, Writer
Mildred Fenton, Editor
James Fleming, Announcer
American Home Products (Kolynos, Fly-Ded), Sponsor
"The Case of the Little Girl Left Alone"

Miss Ellis returns early from her vacation. She and a companion found a houseboat in a wooded cove off Haven Island. Libby Lee, age nine, whose folks left five days ago, was on the boat by herself.

CONTINUITY #437
Wednesday, July 24, 1940
7:15–7:30 p.m. EDST
NBC Blue
Martha Atwell, Director
Doris Halman, Writer
Mildred Fenton, Editor
George Ansbro, Announcer
American Home Products (Kolynos, Fly-Ded), Sponsor
"The Case of the Little Girl Left Alone"

Keen believes Libby's folks are actually an aunt and uncle. Libby's dying mother asked them to keep Libby away from her brutal father, Patterson Tryling. He was awarded custody of Libby, but the kin fled with her.

CONTINUITY #438
Thursday, July 25, 1940
7:15–7:30 p.m. EDST
NBC Blue
Martha Atwell, Director
Doris Halman, Writer
Mildred Fenton, Editor
James Fleming, Announcer
American Home Products (Kolynos, Fly-Ded), Sponsor
"The Case of the Little Girl Left Alone"

Tryling's yacht arrived at Haven Island on the very day "Mummy" and "Daddy" vanished! Clancy notices a P.I. from New York watching a boardinghouse. Keen goes there.

CONTINUITY #439
Tuesday, July 30, 1940
7:15–7:30 p.m. EDST
NBC Blue

Martha Atwell, Director
Doris Halman, Writer
Mildred Fenton, Editor
James Fleming, Announcer
American Home Products (Kolynos, Fly-Ded), Sponsor
"The Case of the Little Girl Left Alone"

Keen locates Mr. and Mrs. James Grant, Libby's kin. Tryling's men monitor the boardinghouse constantly in an effort to locate Libby. Keen obtains evidence that can be used in court to prove that Tryling is an unfit dad.

CONTINUITY #440
Wednesday, July 31, 1940
7:15–7:30 p.m. EDST
NBC Blue
Martha Atwell, Director
Doris Halman, Writer
Mildred Fenton, Editor
James Fleming, Announcer
American Home Products (Kolynos, Fly-Ded), Sponsor
"The Case of the Little Girl Left Alone"

Mike Clancy tips off Keen that Tryling is on his way to the houseboat. The Grants and Keen hurry to the boat. The Grants will apply for legal guardianship. Tryling is now defeated.

CONTINUITY #441
Thursday, August 1, 1940
7:15–7:30 p.m. EDST
NBC Blue
Martha Atwell, Director
Doris Halman, Writer
Mildred Fenton, Editor
James Fleming, Announcer
American Home Products (Kolynos, Fly-Ded), Sponsor
"The Case of the Man Who Was Seen in Two Places at Once"

Simon Penny has been missing for two weeks. An acrobat, he started West by train on a journey to a vaudeville booking for a Western theater chain. He never arrived. Mr. Keen goes to Chicago.

CONTINUITY #442
Tuesday, August 6, 1940
7:15–7:30 p.m. EDST
NBC Blue
Martha Atwell, Director
Doris Halman, Writer
Mildred Fenton, Editor
James Fleming, Announcer
American Home Products (Kolynos, Fly-Ded), Sponsor
"The Case of the Man Who Was Seen in Two Places at Once"

A conductor says Penny rode a coach car. Another says he had a drawing room and sent wires to a New York mining firm. The firm's staff, shown his photo, identifies him as the company's president.

CONTINUITY #443
Wednesday, August 7, 1940
7:15–7:30 p.m. EDST
NBC Blue
Martha Atwell, Director
Doris Halman, Writer
Mildred Fenton, Editor
James Fleming, Announcer
American Home Products (Kolynos, Fly-Ded), Sponsor
"The Case of the Man Who Was Seen in Two Places at Once"

Simon Penny and Peter Vandergriff (the real head of the Silver Streak Mining Corporation) are twins, although neither knew about the other. An accident victim dying in a Nevada hospital is identified as Penny.

CONTINUITY #444
Thursday, August 8, 1940
7:15–7:30 p.m. EDST
NBC Blue
Martha Atwell, Director
Doris Halman, Writer
Mildred Fenton, Editor
James Fleming, Announcer
American Home Products (Kolynos, Fly-Ded), Sponsor
"The Case of the Man Who Was Seen in Two Places at Once"

Mr. Keen and Mrs. Penny fly to Nevada. She doesn't believe Keen's insistence that the dying man is *not* her spouse. They go to the hospital. Keen is proven right.

CONTINUITY #445
Tuesday, August 13, 1940
7:15–7:30 p.m. EDST
NBC Blue
Martha Atwell, Director
Doris Halman, Writer
Mildred Fenton, Editor
Announcer's name omitted
American Home Products (Kolynos, Fly-Ded), Sponsor
"The Case of the Lawyer Whose Conscience Hurt Him"
 Keen is traveling abroad. Mr. and Mrs. Smith hope that their family's black sheep, John Smith, won't surface and disinherit them from a relative's will. Their lawyer is compelled to ask Keen's firm to find Smith.

CONTINUITY #446
Wednesday, August 14, 1940
7:15–7:30 p.m. EDST
NBC Blue
Martha Atwell, Director
Doris Halman, Writer
Mildred Fenton, Editor
James Fleming, Announcer
American Home Products (Kolynos, Fly-Ded), Sponsor
"The Case of the Lawyer Whose Conscience Hurt Him"
 Attorney Bertram De Vaux doesn't inform the Smiths that he's working both sides. The missing man must show up within three days. Smith is a poor inventor living near Boston.

CONTINUITY #447
Thursday, August 15, 1940
7:15–7:30 p.m. EDST
NBC Blue
Martha Atwell, Director
Doris Halman, Writer
Mildred Fenton, Editor
James Fleming, Announcer
American Home Products (Kolynos, Fly-Ded), Sponsor
"The Case of the Lawyer Whose Conscience Hurt Him"
 John Smith rushes to his ancestral home in Mapletree, New Jersey, to find both home and residents gone! Now De Vaux has vanished! Smith threatens to sue Keen's firm upon Keen's return.

CONTINUITY #448
Tuesday, August 20, 1940
7:15–7:30 p.m. EDST
NBC Blue
Martha Atwell, Director
Doris Halman, Writer
Mildred Fenton, Editor
James Fleming, Announcer
American Home Products (Kolynos, Fly-Ded), Sponsor
"The Case of the Lawyer Whose Conscience Hurt Him"
 A clever crook had tricked Keen's staff into luring John Smith, an inventor, from his home so that his latest invention could be stolen. Keen catches the crook and retrieves the invention.

CONTINUITY #449
Wednesday, August 21, 1940
7:15–7:30 p.m. EDST
NBC Blue
Martha Atwell, Director
Doris Halman, Writer
Mildred Fenton, Editor
James Fleming, Announcer
American Home Products (Kolynos, Fly-Ded), Sponsor
"The Case of the Husband Who Asked Himself, 'Why Did My Wife Marry Me?'"
 Caroline Brockton confides in Keen that her husband, Walter, purportedly on a business trip, has left her. She says his secretary Helen Ross knows where he is but won't divulge the information.

CONTINUITY #450
Thursday, August 22, 1940
7:15–7:30 p.m. EDST
NBC Blue
Martha Atwell, Director
Doris Halman, Writer
Mildred Fenton, Editor
James Fleming, Announcer
American Home Products (Kolynos, Fly-Ded), Sponsor
"The Case of the Husband Who Asked Himself, 'Why Did My Wife Marry Me?'"
 Ross doesn't know Walter's location after all. A waitress points Keen to the man's birthplace, a farm in Nicolin, Maine. Keen drives up to a barren farmhouse and is met by an old woman.

CONTINUITY #451
Tuesday, August 27, 1940
7:15–7:30 p.m. EDST
NBC Blue
Martha Atwell, Director
Doris Halman, Writer
Mildred Fenton, Editor
James Fleming, Announcer
American Home Products (Kolynos, Fly-Ded), Sponsor
"The Case of the Husband Who Asked Himself, 'Why Did My Wife Marry Me?'"

Keen finds Walter in hiding. He refuses to return — all his wife wants is money, he says. At Keen's suggestion, Caroline leaves her opulent digs and goes to work. Several weeks pass.

CONTINUITY #452
Wednesday, August 28, 1940
7:15–7:30 p.m. EDST
NBC Blue
Martha Atwell, Director
Doris Halman, Writer
Mildred Fenton, Editor
James Fleming, Announcer
American Home Products (Kolynos, Fly-Ded), Sponsor
"The Case of the Husband Who Asked Himself, 'Why Did My Wife Marry Me?'"

Keen proves to Walter that, though Caroline indeed married him for security 20 years ago, she long ago learned to love him. It takes time to sink in, but the embittered man finally returns to her.

CONTINUITY #453
Thursday, August 29, 1940
7:15–7:30 p.m. EDST
NBC Blue
Martha Atwell, Director
Doris Halman, Writer
Mildred Fenton, Editor
James Fleming, Announcer
American Home Products (Kolynos, Fly-Ded), Sponsor
"The Case of a Mother's Place in the Life of Her Son"

Louella Rennselaer leaves a suicide note. Son Martin says she couldn't face it when fiancée Julie Cobb came between mother and son. Julie says Lovella is selfish and would do anything to hold onto Martin.

CONTINUITY #454
Tuesday, September 3, 1940
7:15–7:30 p.m. EDST
NBC Blue
Martha Atwell, Director
Doris Halman, Writer
Mildred Fenton, Editor
James Fleming, Announcer
American Home Products (Bi-So-Dol, Kolynos), Sponsor
"The Case of a Mother's Place in the Life of Her Son"

Martin breaks his engagement to Julie. Dr. Garrick Trevelyan, Lovella's doctor, says she isn't the invalid she claims to be. He won't divulge more. Keen finds Lovella in Moose Crag Falls, Pennsylvania.

CONTINUITY #455
Wednesday, September 4, 1940
7:15–7:30 p.m. EDST
NBC Blue
Martha Atwell, Director
Doris Halman, Writer
Mildred Fenton, Editor
James Fleming, Announcer
American Home Products (Bi-So-Dol, Kolynos), Sponsor
"The Case of a Mother's Place in the Life of Her Son"

Keen and Clancy pursue. Louella expects to return home upon hearing the news of her son's broken vow. Keen doesn't tell her, leaving her there instead. In New York Keen mends Martin and Julie's rift.

CONTINUITY #456
Thursday, September 5, 1940
7:15–7:30 p.m. EDST
NBC Blue
Martha Atwell, Director
Doris Halman, Writer
Mildred Fenton, Editor
James Fleming, Announcer
American Home Products (Bi-So-Dol, Kolynos), Sponsor
"The Case of a Mother's Place in the Life of Her Son"

Two weeks go by. Keen, Martin and Julie drive to Moose Crag Falls for an emotional reunion. Keen tells Lovella what her place should be in Martin's life. Happy nuptials will follow.

CONTINUITY #457
Tuesday, September 10, 1940
7:15–7:30 p.m. EDST
NBC Blue
Martha Atwell, Director
Doris Halman, Writer
Mildred Fenton, Editor
James Fleming, Announcer
American Home Products (Bi-So-Dol, Kolynos), Sponsor
"The Case of the Girl Who Didn't Come to Her Own Wedding"

Ian Lang works for millionaire J. Bruce Cameron. Lang and Margaret Cameron plan to marry against her father's wishes. She vanishes. Dad says she's ill; a maid says she's gone.

CONTINUITY #458
Wednesday, September 11, 1940
7:15–7:30 p.m. EDST
NBC Blue
Martha Atwell, Director
Doris Halman, Writer
Mildred Fenton, Editor
James Fleming, Announcer
American Home Products (Bi-So-Dol, Kolynos), Sponsor
"The Case of the Girl Who Didn't Come to Her Own Wedding"

Ian thinks Cameron is detaining the girl. Keen learns that a waterfront saloon pickpocket, Lighthouse Maggie, has a jagged forehead scar just like Margaret's. Clancy will watch Maggie.

CONTINUITY #459
Thursday, September 12, 1940
7:15–7:30 p.m. EDST
NBC Blue
Martha Atwell, Director
Doris Halman, Writer
Mildred Fenton, Editor
James Fleming, Announcer
American Home Products (Bi-So-Dol, Kolynos), Sponsor
"The Case of the Girl Who Didn't Come to Her Own Wedding"

Keen, convinced it's a case of split personality, intends to cure Margaret/Maggie of her affliction. He will introduce Ian to Maggie at the waterfront dive. But Margaret comes home just then.

CONTINUITY #460
Tuesday, September 17, 1940
7:15–7:30 p.m. EDST
NBC Blue
Martha Atwell, Director
Doris Halman, Writer
Mildred Fenton, Editor
James Fleming, Announcer
American Home Products (Bi-So-Dol, Kolynos), Sponsor
"The Case of the Girl Who Didn't Come to Her Own Wedding"

Keen is still able to cure Margaret of her split personality disorder through a dangerous but successful experiment. The two lovers will marry, with or without the father's blessing.

CONTINUITY #461
Wednesday, September 18, 1940
7:15–7:30 p.m. EDST
NBC Blue
Martha Atwell, Director
Doris Halman, Writer
Mildred Fenton, Editor
James Fleming, Announcer
American Home Products (Bi-So-Dol, Kolynos), Sponsor
"The Case of the Wife Who Refused to Support Her Husband and Ran Away"

Howard Forbes, unemployed for four years, tries to kill himself at Keen's office. He wed Rose Gilman, whose career has continued to rise. She just left him, he thinks, for Porter Brandon.

CONTINUITY #462
Thursday, September 19, 1940
7:15–7:30 p.m. EDST
NBC Blue
Martha Atwell, Director
Doris Halman, Writer
Mildred Fenton, Editor
James Fleming, Announcer
American Home Products (Bi-So-Dol, Kolynos), Sponsor
"The Case of the Wife Who Refused to Support Her Husband and Ran Away"

Keen calls on Brandon and learns that there is no other man in Rose's life. He looks for someone who might be in touch with Rose. This sends him to a tenement house in Harlem.

CONTINUITY #463
Tuesday, September 24, 1940
7:15–7:30 p.m. EDST
NBC Blue
Martha Atwell, Director
Doris Halman, Writer
Mildred Fenton, Editor
James Fleming, Announcer
American Home Products (Bi-So-Dol, Kolynos), Sponsor
"The Case of the Wife Who Refused to Support Her Husband and Ran Away"

Rose is working in a New Haven, Connecticut, shop. Learning that Howard threatens suicide if she isn't back by their fifth wedding anniversary, she promises to return on that day. And she does.

CONTINUITY #464
Wednesday, September 25, 1940
7:15–7:30 p.m. EDST
NBC Blue
Martha Atwell, Director
Doris Halman, Writer
Mildred Fenton, Editor
James Fleming, Announcer
American Home Products (Bi-So-Dol, Kolynos), Sponsor
"The Case of the Wife Who Refused to Support Her Husband and Ran Away"

Keen works through the emotional trauma Howard and Rose Forbes experienced. She ran away to motivate him to look for work. Now he has a steady job and can support her.

CONTINUITY #465
Thursday, September 26, 1940
7:15–7:30 p.m. EDST
NBC Blue
Martha Atwell, Director
Doris Halman, Writer
Mildred Fenton, Editor
James Fleming, Announcer
American Home Products (Bi-So-Dol, Kolynos), Sponsor
"The Case of the Convict's Fortune"

There were three Herricks kids in Castleton, New York, 60 years ago—Charles, Sam and Abigail. Sam went to prison for robbery. The clan disowned him, changed their surname and moved away.

CONTINUITY #466
Tuesday, October 1, 1940
7:15–7:30 p.m. EST
NBC Blue
Martha Atwell, Director
Doris Halman, Writer
Mildred Fenton, Editor
James Fleming, Announcer
American Home Products (Bi-So-Dol, Kolynos), Sponsor
"The Case of the Convict's Fortune"

Sam is now Cyrus Newday. He went straight, never wed, and made millions. He wants Keen to find his kin, judge them, and help him decide to whom he'll leave his fortune. Abigail in Kansas City is rich and rotten.

CONTINUITY #467
Wednesday, October 2, 1940
7:15–7:30 p.m. EST
NBC Blue
Martha Atwell, Director
Doris Halman, Writer
Mildred Fenton, Editor
James Fleming, Announcer
American Home Products (Bi-So-Dol, Kolynos), Sponsor
"The Case of the Convict's Fortune"

Abigail's only nephew, Fred Bates, son of the late Charles, lives in a Pennsylvania shack. Keen goes to visit Newday, the feeble old president of Coastwise Continental Railroad.

CONTINUITY #468
Thursday, October 3, 1940
7:15–7:30 p.m. EST
NBC Blue
Martha Atwell, Director
Doris Halman, Writer
Mildred Fenton, Editor
James Fleming, Announcer
American Home Products (Bi-So-Dol, Kolynos), Sponsor
"The Case of the Convict's Fortune"

Keen did what he was asked to do, defining how Newday's millions will be distributed. They agree that the money will go to Fred Bates and his three children, who live in poverty.

CONTINUITY #469
Tuesday, October 8, 1940

7:15–7:30 p.m. EST
NBC Blue
Martha Atwell, Director
Doris Halman, Writer
Mildred Fenton, Editor
James Fleming, Announcer
American Home Products (Bi-So-Dol, Kolynos), Sponsor
"The Case of Woman, Single, Forty-Five, Unemployed, Unwanted"
    Pauline Markham worked for a firm 12 years and then was replaced by a younger girl. She lived with her aged parents and looked for work endlessly, then vanished, taking a want ad along.

CONTINUITY #470
Wednesday, October 9, 1940
7:15–7:30 p.m. EST
NBC Blue
Martha Atwell, Director
Doris Halman, Writer
Mildred Fenton, Editor
James Fleming, Announcer
American Home Products (Bi-So-Dol, Kolynos), Sponsor
"The Case of Woman, Single, Forty-Five, Unemployed, Unwanted"
    The employment agency placing the ad turned Pauline down due to her age. She was presently directed to a downtown office complex seeking a cleaning lady. Keen goes to the facility.

CONTINUITY #471
Thursday, October 10, 1940
7:15–7:30 p.m. EST
NBC Blue
Martha Atwell, Director
Doris Halman, Writer
Mildred Fenton, Editor
James Fleming, Announcer
American Home Products (Bi-So-Dol, Kolynos), Sponsor
"The Case of Woman, Single, Forty-Five, Unemployed, Unwanted"
    Pauline now cleans the building where she was once a secretary. She reads things in her old office — now in a bad way — which she could improve. Keen suggests she leave some unsigned notes.

CONTINUITY #472
Tuesday, October 15, 1940
7:15–7:30 p.m. EST
NBC Blue
Martha Atwell, Director
Doris Halman, Writer
Mildred Fenton, Editor
James Fleming, Announcer
American Home Products (Bi-So-Dol, Kolynos), Sponsor
"The Case of Woman, Single, Forty-Five, Unemployed, Unwanted"
    Three weeks pass, and Pauline is welcomed back to her old post. The tracer has shown her how to win her way back into the business world and regain the confidence she had lost.

CONTINUITY #473
Wednesday, October 16, 1940
7:15–7:30 p.m. EST
NBC Blue
Martha Atwell, Director
Doris Halman, Writer
Mildred Fenton, Editor
James Fleming, Announcer
American Home Products (Bi-So-Dol, Kolynos), Sponsor
"The Case of the Third Sermon"
    The Reverend Roger Patterson visited a Southern factory town to hear a classmate, the Rev. Steven McGrue, preach his third sermon. But the minister — using Steven's name — was *someone else*!

CONTINUITY #474
Thursday, October 17, 1940
7:15–7:30 p.m. EST
NBC Blue
Martha Atwell, Director
Doris Halman, Writer
Mildred Fenton, Editor
James Fleming, Announcer
American Home Products (Bi-So-Dol, Kolynos), Sponsor
"The Case of the Third Sermon"
    McGrue is dead. An imposter, gang leader Baby Face Craven, a minister's son who stole sermons from his dad, had him killed. Keen goes to the War Department in Washington.

CONTINUITY #475
Tuesday, October 22, 1940

7:15–7:30 p.m. EST
NBC Blue
Martha Atwell, Director
Doris Halman, Writer
Mildred Fenton, Editor
George Ansbro, Announcer
American Home Products (Bi-So-Dol, Kolynos), Sponsor
"The Case of the Third Sermon"

Craven stole six sermons, so he'll only last six weeks. Keen figures the gang plans to steal the factory payroll just after it expands (with defense orders now three times normal size).

CONTINUITY #476
Wednesday, October 23, 1940
7:15–7:30 p.m. EST
NBC Blue
Martha Atwell, Director
Doris Halman, Writer
Mildred Fenton, Editor
George Ansbro, Announcer
American Home Products (Bi-So-Dol, Kolynos), Sponsor
"The Case of the Third Sermon"

Keen poses as Arthur Blanchard. He becomes friendly with factory owner Pollard, whose daughter is engaged to the bogus McGrue. The leader and gang are exposed and go to prison.

CONTINUITY #477
Thursday, October 24, 1940
7:15–7:30 p.m. EST
NBC Blue
Martha Atwell, Director
Doris Halman, Writer
Mildred Fenton, Editor
James Fleming, Announcer
American Home Products (Bi-So-Dol, Kolynos), Sponsor
"The Case of the Little Girl Who Didn't Want Her Mother and Father to Be Divorced"

Jennie Edwards, age 14, tells Keen that both her parents voluntarily vanished on the same day, neither knowing the other's plan, thinking the child would be happier with one parent.

CONTINUITY #478
Tuesday, October 29, 1940
7:15–7:30 p.m. EST
NBC Blue
Martha Atwell, Director
Doris Halman, Writer
Mildred Fenton, Editor
James Fleming, Announcer
American Home Products (Bi-So-Dol, Kolynos), Sponsor
"The Case of the Little Girl Who Didn't Want Her Mother and Father to Be Divorced"

Jennie's dad, Paul, was smitten by Althea Scott, his fiancée from years before. Wife Beth protested. Jennie wanted no split; each left separately. Keen locates both and sends for them.

CONTINUITY #479
Wednesday, October 30, 1940
7:15–7:30 p.m. EST
NBC Blue
Martha Atwell, Director
Doris Halman, Writer
Mildred Fenton, Editor
James Fleming, Announcer
American Home Products (Bi-So-Dol, Kolynos), Sponsor
"The Case of the Little Girl Who Didn't Want Her Mother and Father to Be Divorced"

Keen's housekeeper is caring for Jennie at his home. Keen mends the marriage. Paul and Beth Edwards will not divorce or separate, remaining together for Jennie's sake. But now Jennie has vanished!

CONTINUITY #480
Thursday, October 31, 1940
7:15–7:30 p.m. EST
NBC Blue
Martha Atwell, Director
Doris Halman, Writer
Mildred Fenton, Editor
James Fleming, Announcer
American Home Products (Bi-So-Dol, Kolynos), Sponsor
"The Case of the Little Girl Who Didn't Want Her Mother and Father to Be Divorced"

At last Jennie is found and returned to her parents. They realize that both their duty and their own happiness lies in staying together and making a normal home for their dear child.

CONTINUITY #481
Tuesday, November 5, 1940
7:15–7:30 p.m. EST

NBC Blue
Martha Atwell, Director
Doris Halman, Writer
Mildred Fenton, Editor
James Fleming, Announcer
American Home Products (Bi-So-Dol, Kolynos), Sponsor
"The Case of the Girl with the Lonely Heart"

It surprises everybody when homely Molly Thurlow, age 25, of Wanatee Falls, Connecticut, disappears. Her best friend, Charlotte Robinson, can't help, she says, but Keen thinks otherwise.

CONTINUITY #482

Wednesday, November 6, 1940
7:15–7:30 p.m. EST
NBC Blue
Martha Atwell, Director
Doris Halman, Writer
Mildred Fenton, Editor
James Fleming, Announcer
American Home Products (Bi-So-Dol, Kolynos), Sponsor
"The Case of the Girl with the Lonely Heart"

Though Molly had never had a beau, it looks like elopement. Keen learns that she joined a Lonely Hearts club and received a marriage proposal from "V. J." of Oakton, Wisconsin. Keen follows.

CONTINUITY #483

Thursday, November 7, 1940
7:15–7:30 p.m. EST
NBC Blue
Martha Atwell, Director
Doris Halman, Writer
Mildred Fenton, Editor
James Fleming, Announcer
American Home Products (Bi-So-Dol, Kolynos), Sponsor
"The Case of the Girl with the Lonely Heart"

Molly wed Verne Jellison in Chicago. In Oakton she learns he is a rascal who uses the club to prey on women with money. Molly will inherit $40,000. She runs from him — to Chicago.

CONTINUITY #484

Tuesday, November 12, 1940
7:15–7:30 p.m. EST
NBC Blue
Martha Atwell, Director
Doris Halman, Writer
Mildred Fenton, Editor
James Fleming, Announcer
American Home Products (Bi-So-Dol, Kolynos), Sponsor
"The Case of the Girl with the Lonely Heart"

Keen finds the girl in Chicago and rescues her from the consequences of her secret actions. He returns Molly to her frantic and appreciative parents. She is older and wiser.

CONTINUITY #485

Wednesday, November 13, 1940
7:15–7:30 p.m. EST
NBC Blue
Martha Atwell, Director
Doris Halman, Writer
Mildred Fenton, Editor
James Fleming, Announcer
American Home Products (Bi-So-Dol, Kolynos), Sponsor
"The Case of the Lost Violin"

Violin prodigy Robbie Cray, age 10, is gone; financier Severard Bannister took him into his home for training. Robbie's mother is dead, and he had been living with drunken stepdad Jake Mellick and a new wife.

CONTINUITY #486

Thursday, November 14, 1940
7:15–7:30 p.m. EST
NBC Blue
Martha Atwell, Director
Doris Halman, Writer
Mildred Fenton, Editor
James Fleming, Announcer
American Home Products (Bi-So-Dol, Kolynos), Sponsor
"The Case of the Lost Violin"

Keen isn't content with the Mellicks' claim of ignorance about the boy's disappearance. He visits them and learns that the boy was in their flat the day he left, running away after a clash when his violin was broken.

CONTINUITY #487

Tuesday, November 19, 1940
7:15–7:30 p.m. EST
NBC Blue
Martha Atwell, Director
Doris Halman, Writer

Mildred Fenton, Editor
James Fleming, Announcer
American Home Products (Bi-So-Dol, Kolynos), Sponsor
"The Case of the Lost Violin"

Keen finds Robbie with a beggar, Minch, in the slums. Mellick enlisted thug Heeler Finn to rob Bannister, with Robbie as an accessory. Keen leads Finn's gang there, walking into a likely death trap.

CONTINUITY #488
Wednesday, November 20, 1940
7:15–7:30 p.m. EST
NBC Blue
Martha Atwell, Director
Doris Halman, Writer
Mildred Fenton, Editor
James Fleming, Announcer
American Home Products (Bi-So-Dol, Kolynos), Sponsor
"The Case of the Lost Violin"

Keen almost loses his life. But the tables are suddenly turned and the tormentors take a dose of their own medicine. Severard Bannister adopts young Robbie Cray as his own son.

CONTINUITY #489
Thursday, November 21, 1940
7:15–7:30 p.m. EST
NBC Blue
Martha Atwell, Director
Doris Halman, Writer
Mildred Fenton, Editor
James Fleming, Announcer
American Home Products (Bi-So-Dol, Kolynos), Sponsor
"The Case of the Young Draftee"

George Winter left his wife Sarah and son Ned 20 years ago, embittered about his poor health that kept him from the war and work. Ned is going off to war now. Could George heal if he knew it?

CONTINUITY #490
Tuesday, November 26, 1940
7:15–7:30 p.m. EST
NBC Blue
Martha Atwell, Director
Doris Halman, Writer
Mildred Fenton, Editor
James Fleming, Announcer
American Home Products (Bi-So-Dol, Kolynos), Sponsor
"The Case of the Young Draftee"

Winter is a cab driver. He won't go home, ashamed to reveal he's still a physical wreck and poor. He once met Ned, who called him "Grouchy." Keen asks him to watch Ned's departure.

CONTINUITY #491
Wednesday, November 27, 1940
7:15–7:30 p.m. EST
NBC Blue
Martha Atwell, Director
Doris Halman, Writer
Mildred Fenton, Editor
James Fleming, Announcer
American Home Products (Bi-So-Dol, Kolynos), Sponsor
"The Case of the Young Draftee"

George Winter is among the crowd at his son's departure. He decides to try to make up the 20 years that he lost with his family, thanks to Mr. Keen's intervention in their lives.

CONTINUITY #492
Thursday, November 28, 1940
7:15–7:30 p.m. EST
NBC Blue
Martha Atwell, Director
Doris Halman, Writer
Mildred Fenton, Editor
James Fleming, Announcer
American Home Products (Bi-So-Dol, Kolynos), Sponsor
"The Case of the Man Who Went Out to Smoke Between Acts"

Neighbors Mr. and Mrs. Jarvis Parr and Keen attend a benefit play. Patron Blair Gregory goes out to smoke between acts and doesn't return. His newlywed wife Philippa is frantic.

CONTINUITY #493
Tuesday, December 3, 1940
7:15–7:30 p.m. EST
NBC Blue
Martha Atwell, Director
Doris Halman, Writer
Mildred Fenton, Editor
James Fleming, Announcer
American Home Products (Bi-So-Dol, Kolynos), Sponsor

"The Case of the Man Who Went Out to Smoke Between Acts"

Blair went backstage at the end of intermission, but no one saw him leave. He doesn't turn up. The producer is giving a private supper party onstage, so Keen and Philippa go out.

CONTINUITY #494
Wednesday, December 4, 1940
7:15–7:30 p.m. EST
NBC Blue
Martha Atwell, Director
Doris Halman, Writer
Mildred Fenton, Editor
James Fleming, Announcer
American Home Products (Bi-So-Dol, Kolynos), Sponsor
"The Case of the Man Who Went Out to Smoke Between Acts"

A photo of an old actress in the theater lobby upset Blair. Billed as Mary Hunter, she didn't know him. Keen recognizes her as a former famous star who vanished after a scandal.

CONTINUITY #495
Thursday, December 5, 1940
7:15–7:30 p.m. EST
NBC Blue
Martha Atwell, Director
Doris Halman, Writer
Mildred Fenton, Editor
James Fleming, Announcer
American Home Products (Bi-So-Dol, Kolynos), Sponsor
"The Case of the Man Who Went Out to Smoke Between Acts"

Keen and Philippa go to a newspaper morgue. There they solve the puzzle. Blair is found, and he and Philippa are reunited. The honeymooners then return home to Cleveland.

CONTINUITY #496
Tuesday, December 10, 1940
7:15–7:30 p.m. EST
NBC Blue
Martha Atwell, Director
Doris Halman, Writer
Mildred Fenton, Editor
James Fleming, Announcer
American Home Products (Bi-So-Dol, Kolynos), Sponsor
"The Case of the Girl Who Hated to Say Good-Bye"

Kay Morrell vanishes, abandoning love, a thriving career and a huge salary. She leaves a farewell note for fiancé Miles Waring, and later writes to her boss, Acheson McKnight, at *Milady* magazine.

CONTINUITY #497
Wednesday, December 11, 1940
7:15–7:30 p.m. EST
NBC Blue
Martha Atwell, Director
Doris Halman, Writer
Mildred Fenton, Editor
James Fleming, Announcer
American Home Products (Bi-So-Dol, Kolynos), Sponsor
"The Case of the Girl Who Hated to Say Good-Bye"

Keen visits McKnight. He learns that Kay's disappearance was meticulously planned (she even left written instructions for her successor). Her checkbook is missing monthly checks, with the stubs never having been filled out.

CONTINUITY #498
Thursday, December 12, 1940
7:15–7:30 p.m. EST
NBC Blue
Martha Atwell, Director
Doris Halman, Writer
Mildred Fenton, Editor
James Fleming, Announcer
American Home Products (Bi-So-Dol, Kolynos), Sponsor
"The Case of the Girl Who Hated to Say Good-Bye"

The mystery checks went to Connecticut's Crandall Sanitarium for the incurably insane. Kay's father is there. Mistaking overwork for insanity, she's hiding in Vermont, awaiting her own end.

CONTINUITY #499
Tuesday, December 17, 1940
7:15–7:30 p.m. EST
NBC Blue
Martha Atwell, Director
Doris Halman, Writer
Mildred Fenton, Editor

James Fleming, Announcer
American Home Products (Bi-So-Dol, Kolynos), Sponsor
"The Case of the Girl Who Hated to Say Good-Bye"
   Keen must prove that Kay's father's mental trouble is due to an accident and can't be inherited. He does so by going to a Canadian fishing village where the man was staying just before going insane.

CONTINUITY #500
Wednesday, December 18, 1940
7:15–7:30 p.m. EST
NBC Blue
Martha Atwell, Director
Doris Halman, Writer
Mildred Fenton, Editor
James Fleming, Announcer
American Home Products (Bi-So-Dol, Kolynos), Sponsor
"The Case of the Christmas Toy"
   Jewelry vanishes from a department store. Dan Bredon goes there to buy a costly teddy bear for his motherless child, six-year-old Lulie, but can't afford it. Lulie cries into delirium.

CONTINUITY #501
Thursday, December 19, 1940
7:15–7:30 p.m. EST
NBC Blue
Martha Atwell, Director
Doris Halman, Writer
Mildred Fenton, Editor
James Fleming, Announcer
American Home Products (Bi-So-Dol, Kolynos), Sponsor
"The Case of the Christmas Toy"
   Bredon is told by a doctor to get the bear, but it has been sold to Mrs. Fenwick. Since her own child recently died, Mrs. Fenwick gave the bear to a New Orleans nephew. She'll have it returned.

CONTINUITY #502
Tuesday, December 24, 1940
7:15–7:30 p.m. EST
NBC Blue
Martha Atwell, Director
Doris Halman, Writer
Mildred Fenton, Editor
James Fleming, Announcer
American Home Products (Bi-So-Dol, Kolynos), Sponsor
"The Case of the Christmas Toy"
   Marshall Fenwick, bitter at the loss of his child, won't let another in his home. His wife takes the bear to Keen, who finds the stolen jewelry in it. He sets a trap for Bredon.

CONTINUITY #503
Wednesday, December 25, 1940
7:15–7:30 p.m. EST
NBC Blue
Martha Atwell, Director
Doris Halman, Writer
Mildred Fenton, Editor
James Fleming, Announcer
American Home Products (Bi-So-Dol, Kolynos), Sponsor
"The Case of the Christmas Toy"
   The crime is solved and several people are happy. The store detective, who lost his job over the theft, is reinstated. Lulie goes to a good home with a sad couple whose child had died.

CONTINUITY #504
Thursday, December 26, 1940
7:15–7:30 p.m. EST
NBC Blue
Martha Atwell, Director
Doris Halman, Writer
Mildred Fenton, Editor
James Fleming, Announcer
American Home Products (Bi-So-Dol, Kolynos), Sponsor
"The Case of the Unclaimed Bank Account"
   Keen's aged servants, James and Sarah, offer a challenge to Keen: find someone in a week with only a name and an old address. Helga Larssen — with unclaimed funds waiting — is the subject.

CONTINUITY #505
Tuesday, December 31, 1940
7:15–7:30 p.m. EST
NBC Blue
Martha Atwell, Director
Doris Halman, Writer
Mildred Fenton, Editor
James Fleming, Announcer
American Home Products (Bi-So-Dol, Kolynos), Sponsor
"The Case of the Unclaimed Bank Account"

Norwegian immigrant Helga was a maid at Middleview Towers Hotel, where she lived. She saved money regularly. At age 60 (20 years ago), she stopped making deposits, quit work and vanished.

CONTINUITY #506
Wednesday, January 1, 1941
7:15–7:30 p.m. EST
NBC Blue
Martha Atwell, Director
Doris Halman, Writer
Mildred Fenton, Editor
James Fleming, Announcer
American Home Products (Bi-So-Dol), Sponsor
"The Case of the Unclaimed Bank Account"

Helga was kind to a sick guest 20 years ago. The rich lady gave her a job as housekeeper at her Maine seacoast estate. Helga told pastor Borgstad, who can't recall where she went.

CONTINUITY #507
Thursday, January 2, 1941
7:15–7:30 p.m. EST
NBC Blue
Martha Atwell, Director
Doris Halman, Writer
Mildred Fenton, Editor
James Fleming, Announcer
American Home Products (Bi-So-Dol, Kolynos), Sponsor
"The Case of the Unclaimed Bank Account"

Within a year at Kent Harbor, Maine, Helga died, leaving an heir she didn't know — a young, crippled Norwegian sailor who can use the $10,000 she left. Keen secures his claim to it.

CONTINUITY #508
Tuesday, January 7, 1941
7:15–7:30 p.m. EST
NBC Blue
Martha Atwell, Director
Doris Halman, Writer
Mildred Fenton, Editor
James Fleming, Announcer
American Home Products (Bi-So-Dol, Kolynos), Sponsor
"The Case of the Young Man Who Promised to Work All Night"

An old recluse dies, leaving a revealing manuscript. A book publisher acquires it. Film agent Elsa Wyatt, hoping it can be turned into a movie, needs to see it. An intricate plan is set in motion.

CONTINUITY #509
Wednesday, January 8, 1941
7:15–7:30 p.m. EST
NBC Blue
Martha Atwell, Director
Doris Halman, Writer
Mildred Fenton, Editor
James Fleming, Announcer
American Home Products (Bi-So-Dol, Kolynos), Sponsor
"The Case of the Young Man Who Promised to Work All Night"

Working for Elsa, Bob Sanford takes the manuscript home for an overnight reading. He and it disappear. Elsa calls Mr. Keen. Bob was lured from his home with the document by a fake call.

CONTINUITY #510
Thursday, January 9, 1941
7:15–7:30 p.m. EST
NBC Blue
Martha Atwell, Director
Doris Halman, Writer
Mildred Fenton, Editor
Announcer's name omitted
American Home Products (Bi-So-Dol, Kolynos), Sponsor
"The Case of the Young Man Who Promised to Work All Night"

The solution lies in the unknown contents of the manuscript. Keen meets Horace Tandy, the book publisher, at a literary reception at a hotel. He must learn what the manuscript holds.

CONTINUITY #511
Tuesday, January 14, 1941
7:15–7:30 p.m. EST
NBC Blue
Martha Atwell, Director
Doris Halman, Writer
Mildred Fenton, Editor
Announcer's name omitted
American Home Products (Bi-So-Dol, Kolynos), Sponsor
"The Case of the Young Man Who Promised to Work All Night"

Keen learns that the text is an exposé of aged tycoon Augustus P. Greneker. Keen rescues Bob Sanford from gangsters hired by Greneker to steal the book and deliver it to him in Florida.

CONTINUITY #512
Wednesday, January 15, 1941
7:15–7:30 p.m. EST
NBC Blue
Martha Atwell, Director
Doris Halman, Writer
Mildred Fenton, Editor
Announcer's name omitted
American Home Products (Bi-So-Dol, Kolynos), Sponsor
"The Case of the Young Man Who Promised to Work All Night"

Keen saves the reputations of three young people when he stops an unscrupulous old multimillionaire from destroying a document that exposes the evil methods by which he made his fortune.

CONTINUITY #513
Thursday, January 16, 1941
7:15–7:30 p.m. EST
NBC Blue
Martha Atwell, Director
Doris Halman, Writer
Mildred Fenton, Editor
James Fleming, Announcer
American Home Products (Bi-So-Dol, Kolynos), Sponsor
"The Case of the Lost Baby"

The tenement burns where Harry Sakas lives with wife Elena and their week-old baby. Trapped by flames, Harry tosses the boy to a man below. When they get out, the man and their baby are gone!

CONTINUITY #514
Tuesday, January 21, 1941
7:15–7:30 p.m. EST
NBC Blue
Martha Atwell, Director
Doris Halman, Writer
Mildred Fenton, Editor
James Fleming, Announcer
American Home Products (Bi-So-Dol, Kolynos), Sponsor
"The Case of the Lost Baby"

Keen is with Harry, window washer for the building housing Keen and Co., at 5 a.m. By 5:30 Mike Clancy joins them. At six o'clock two men approach each other under a streetlamp.

CONTINUITY #515
Wednesday, January 22, 1941
7:15–7:30 p.m. EST
NBC Blue
Martha Atwell, Director
Doris Halman, Writer
Mildred Fenton, Editor
James Fleming, Announcer
American Home Products (Bi-So-Dol, Kolynos), Sponsor
"The Case of the Lost Baby"

By 7 a.m. Keen knows who they're after — Hardy Johnson, an unemployed vet whose newborn died hours ago as he carried it to a doctor. His poor blind wife lies dying in their shack.

CONTINUITY #516
Thursday, January 23, 1941
7:15–7:30 p.m. EST
NBC Blue
Martha Atwell, Director
Doris Halman, Writer
Mildred Fenton, Editor
James Fleming, Announcer
American Home Products (Bi-So-Dol, Kolynos), Sponsor
"The Case of the Lost Baby"

Hardy Johnson placed the Sakas baby in the arms of his dying blind wife to keep her from learning what happened to her own baby. Keen decides against prosecution and finds Johnson a job.

CONTINUITY #517
Tuesday, January 28, 1941
7:15–7:30 p.m. EST
NBC Blue
Martha Atwell, Director
Doris Halman, Writer
Mildred Fenton, Editor
James Fleming, Announcer
American Home Products (Bi-So-Dol, Kolynos), Sponsor
"The Case of the Unfinished Picture"

Prosperity ruined Natalie and Peter Carey after he achieved success. She left him in Frisco.

In New York she just saw him on a street, a filthy panhandler. He recognized her and ran.

CONTINUITY #518
Wednesday, January 29, 1941
7:15–7:30 p.m. EST
NBC Blue
Martha Atwell, Director
Doris Halman, Writer
Mildred Fenton, Editor
George Ansbro, Announcer
American Home Products (Bi-So-Dol, Kolynos), Sponsor
"The Case of the Unfinished Picture"

When Natalie left Peter he was a commercial artist, a genius with too much money, fast friends and harmful pleasures. It's snowing now. Carey makes a few bucks shoveling snow.

CONTINUITY #519
Thursday, January 30, 1941
7:15–7:30 p.m. EST
NBC Blue
Martha Atwell, Director
Doris Halman, Writer
Mildred Fenton, Editor
James Fleming, Announcer
American Home Products (Bi-So-Dol, Kolynos), Sponsor
"The Case of the Unfinished Picture"

Keen locates Peter Carey, but Keen sends Natalie back to her job without that news. He takes Carey, sick and penniless, into his home and begins to rehabilitate him. Two weeks go by.

CONTINUITY #520
Tuesday, February 4, 1941
7:15–7:30 p.m. EST
NBC Blue
Martha Atwell, Director
Doris Halman, Writer
Mildred Fenton, Editor
George Ansbro, Announcer
American Home Products (Bi-So-Dol, Kolynos), Sponsor
"The Case of the Unfinished Picture"

Keen is successful in restoring Peter Carey's self-respect and desire to work his way up again to the position in life he held prior to his downfall. He reconnects with Natalie.

CONTINUITY #521
Wednesday, February 5, 1941
7:15–7:30 p.m. EST
NBC Blue
Martha Atwell, Director
Doris Halman, Writer
Mildred Fenton, Editor
George Ansbro, Announcer
American Home Products (Bi-So-Dol, Hill's cold tablets), Sponsor
"The Case of the Ghost Which Appeared at Midnight"

Keen visits a friend, the Reverend Matthew Briggs, in Chariton, Pennsylvania. Parishioner Lavinia Walton is plagued by the appearance of her late husband's ghost. There must be a human agent at work.

CONTINUITY #522
Thursday, February 6, 1941
7:15–7:30 p.m. EST
NBC Blue
Martha Atwell, Director
Doris Halman, Writer
Mildred Fenton, Editor
Announcer's name omitted
American Home Products (Bi-So-Dol, Hill's cold tablets), Sponsor
"The Case of the Ghost Which Appeared at Midnight"

The tracer summons Miss Ellis and Mike Clancy, who he intends to plant in the Walton house as a companion and handyman, respectively. He'll use them to expose the "ghost."

CONTINUITY #523
Tuesday, February 11, 1941
7:15–7:30 p.m. EST
NBC Blue
Martha Atwell, Director
Doris Halman, Writer
Mildred Fenton, Editor
George Ansbro, Announcer
American Home Products (Bi-So-Dol, Kolynos), Sponsor
"The Case of the Ghost Which Appeared at Midnight"

Keen learns that a young doctor, Coleman — at the request of Lavinia's neighbor, Edmund Varley — wrote the Waltons that Lavinia is insane. Liggett Walton, a nephew by marriage, intends to have Lavinia committed.

CONTINUITY #524
Wednesday, February 12, 1941
7:15–7:30 p.m. EST
NBC Blue
Martha Atwell, Director
Doris Halman, Writer
Mildred Fenton, Editor
George Ansbro, Announcer
American Home Products (Bi-So-Dol, Kolynos), Sponsor
"The Case of the Ghost Which Appeared at Midnight"
   On Ellis and Clancy's first night in the house, Mr. Keen conducts a test to catch the ghost and prevent its escape. Ellis actually lays hands on it — and ends up holding nothing!

CONTINUITY #525
Thursday, February 13, 1941
7:15–7:30 p.m. EST
NBC Blue
Martha Atwell, Director
Doris Halman, Writer
Mildred Fenton, Editor
George Ansbro, Announcer
American Home Products (Bi-So-Dol, Kolynos), Sponsor
"The Case of the Ghost Which Appeared at Midnight"
   Keen and the Reverend Briggs go to the Walton home. Varley, from an adjacent farm, is there. Liggett Walton arrives, and Keen exposes his scheme to commit the old lady and steal away her fortune.

CONTINUITY #526
Tuesday, February 18, 1941
7:15–7:30 p.m. EST
NBC Blue
Martha Atwell, Director
Doris Halman, Writer
Mildred Fenton, Editor
James Fleming, Announcer
American Home Products (Bi-So-Dol, Kolynos), Sponsor
"The Case of the Frightened Stepmother"
   Hester Norris Blake, age 28, a Keen and Co. staffer from 10 years ago, returns to visit. All are glad to see her. She married her boss, whose wife died. Her stepson hates her and ran away.

CONTINUITY #527
Wednesday, February 19, 1941
7:15–7:30 p.m. EST
NBC Blue
Martha Atwell, Director
Doris Halman, Writer
Mildred Fenton, Editor
James Fleming, Announcer
American Home Products (Bi-So-Dol, Kolynos), Sponsor
"The Case of the Frightened Stepmother"
   Jim Blake, Hester's spouse, worked hard to pay his late wife's debts. They could no longer afford a lavish lifestyle, so Hester economized. Ronnie, age 15, had to give up private school — and took it out on Hester.

CONTINUITY #528
Thursday, February 20, 1941
7:15–7:30 p.m. EST
NBC Blue
Martha Atwell, Director
Doris Halman, Writer
Mildred Fenton, Editor
James Fleming, Announcer
American Home Products (Bi-So-Dol, Kolynos), Sponsor
"The Case of the Frightened Stepmother"
   Aubrey Castleman, who loaned money to his late mom, tells Ronnie of her unfaithfulness to his dad. Ronnie flees to Serena Browning, their housekeeper until Hester had to let her go.

CONTINUITY #529
Tuesday, February 25, 1941
7:15–7:30 p.m. EST
NBC Blue
Martha Atwell, Director
Doris Halman, Writer
Mildred Fenton, Editor
James Fleming, Announcer
American Home Products (Bi-So-Dol, Kolynos), Sponsor
"The Case of the Frightened Stepmother"
   Keen visits Serena's room at a big Long Island estate. He is able to reconcile the family members and prove to the runaway that his resentment of Hester is without cause.

CONTINUITY #530
Wednesday, February 26, 1941

7:15–7:30 p.m. EST
NBC Blue
Martha Atwell, Director
Doris Halman, Writer
Mildred Fenton, Editor
James Fleming, Announcer
American Home Products (Bi-So-Dol, Kolynos), Sponsor
"The Case of the Glass Slipper"

Nineteen-year-old Melanie Benard, bakery owner Victor Benard's daughter, leaves home with most of her father's savings. They argued at 3 a.m. when she came home from a night out with best friend Kitty Shane.

CONTINUITY #531

Thursday, February 27, 1941
7:15–7:30 p.m. EST
NBC Blue
Martha Atwell, Director
Doris Halman, Writer
Mildred Fenton, Editor
James Fleming, Announcer
American Home Products (Bi-So-Dol, Kolynos), Sponsor
"The Case of the Glass Slipper"

Kitty left Melanie at a Broadway dance hall at 11 o'clock. A boy saved her from a lousy pickup, danced with her until 1 a.m. and took her to her "home," chic Middleview Towers Hotel.

CONTINUITY #532

Tuesday, March 4, 1941
7:15–7:30 p.m. EST
NBC Blue
Martha Atwell, Director
Doris Halman, Writer
Mildred Fenton, Editor
James Fleming, Announcer
American Home Products (Kolynos, Bi-So-Dol), Sponsor
"The Case of the Glass Slipper"

Keen finds the girl living a storybook romance for a week — posing as an heiress in gorgeous clothes, and dating handsome, affluent law student Gavin Carmichael. Keen takes her to her father.

CONTINUITY #533

Wednesday, March 5, 1941
7:15–7:30 p.m. EST
NBC Blue
Martha Atwell, Director
Doris Halman, Writer
Mildred Fenton, Editor
James Fleming, Announcer
American Home Products (Kolynos, Bi-So-Dol), Sponsor
"The Case of the Glass Slipper"

Imagining herself a modern Cinderella, the young runaway is in for a big surprise: Prince Charming, it seems, is merely a shipping clerk, far from the law student of a well-off clan he claims to be.

CONTINUITY #534

Thursday, March 6, 1941
7:15–7:30 p.m. EST
NBC Blue
Martha Atwell, Director
Doris Halman, Writer
Mildred Fenton, Editor
George Ansbro, Announcer
American Home Products (Kolynos, Bi-So-Dol), Sponsor
"The Case of the Seventh Juror"

Eight years ago Zach Warner of Chicago served as the seventh juror in a murder case. Found guilty, the defendant was executed in March 1934. Every year since then, one of the jurors has died in March — each expiring in the order of their selection for the jury. Zach is sure he's next.

CONTINUITY #535

Tuesday, March 11, 1941
7:15–7:30 p.m. EST
NBC Blue
Martha Atwell, Director
Doris Halman, Writer
Mildred Fenton, Editor
James Fleming, Announcer
American Home Products (Kolynos, Bi-So-Dol), Sponsor
"The Case of the Seventh Juror"

Keen and Clancy go to Chicago. Due to the crisis, Zach doesn't dare propose marriage to wealthy widow Petrella Morival, a new Chicagoan. He hasn't even told her what's happening.

CONTINUITY #536

Wednesday, March 12, 1941

7:15–7:30 p.m. EST
NBC Blue
Martha Atwell, Director
Doris Halman, Writer
Mildred Fenton, Editor
James Fleming, Announcer
American Home Products (Kolynos, Bi-So-Dol), Sponsor
"The Case of the Seventh Juror"

A woman has figured in all the previous six deaths. Now there's one in Zach's life. Garth Deverett, adopted in infancy, was Petrella Morival's son. He was also the man convicted by the jury!

CONTINUITY #537
Thursday, March 13, 1941
7:15–7:30 p.m. EST
NBC Blue
Martha Atwell, Director
Doris Halman, Writer
Mildred Fenton, Editor
James Fleming, Announcer
American Home Products (Kolynos, Bi-So-Dol), Sponsor
"The Case of the Seventh Juror"

Mr. Keen puts it all together and exposes the killer, saving the lives of Zach Warner and the five jurors selected after him.

CONTINUITY #538
Tuesday, March 18, 1941
7:15–7:30 p.m. EST
NBC Blue
Martha Atwell, Director
Doris Halman, Writer
Mildred Fenton, Editor
Announcer's name omitted
American Home Products (Kolynos, Bi-So-Dol), Sponsor
"The Case of the Rich Young Man in an Ivory Tower"

Denny Frank vanished from New York after falling under the influence of a cult focusing on pleasure and beauty. Karen Atwater, who loves him, says he wasn't happy.

CONTINUITY #539
Wednesday, March 19, 1941
7:15–7:30 p.m. EST
NBC Blue
Martha Atwell, Director
Doris Halman, Writer
Mildred Fenton, Editor
James Fleming, Announcer
American Home Products (Kolynos, Bi-So-Dol), Sponsor
"The Case of the Rich Young Man in an Ivory Tower"

Keen goes to the small town Denny Frank hailed from. He learns that the cult reveals itself only to a few rich and lonely folks. Keen pretends to retire, remaining at home for over a week.

CONTINUITY #540
Thursday, March 20, 1941
7:15–7:30 p.m. EST
NBC Blue
Martha Atwell, Director
Doris Halman, Writer
Mildred Fenton, Editor
James Fleming, Announcer
American Home Products (Kolynos, Bi-So-Dol), Sponsor
"The Case of the Rich Young Man in an Ivory Tower"

The cult whisks its converts away to a new earthly paradise after gaining control of their fortunes. Keen learns that Mrs. Darnell leaves for the mysterious destination by air from Flushing Field at dawn.

CONTINUITY #541
Tuesday, March 25, 1941
7:15–7:30 p.m. EST
NBC Blue
Martha Atwell, Director
Doris Halman, Writer
Mildred Fenton, Editor
James Fleming, Announcer
American Home Products (Kolynos, Bi-So-Dol), Sponsor
"The Case of the Rich Young Man in an Ivory Tower"

Keen meets an aviatrix, and they follow the victim in her plane. They land in the Sierras and go to town for aid. The state police won't interfere; the plane is at an insane asylum.

CONTINUITY #542
Wednesday, March 26, 1941
7:15–7:30 p.m. EST

NBC Blue
Martha Atwell, Director
Doris Halman, Writer
Mildred Fenton, Editor
Announcer's name omitted
American Home Products (Kolynos, Bi-So-Dol), Sponsor
"The Case of the Rich Young Man in an Ivory Tower"

Keen turns to the D.A. in New York for help. He gets it. The cult takes control people's assets and then puts them in a place from which they could never return. The group is put away.

CONTINUITY #543
Thursday, March 27, 1941
7:15–7:30 p.m. EST
NBC Blue
Martha Atwell, Director
Doris Halman, Writer
Mildred Fenton, Editor
Announcer's name omitted
American Home Products (Kolynos, Bi-So-Dol), Sponsor
"The Case of the Faithful Heart"

Marchmont Colby tracks a rare witchcraft pamphlet to the High Banks, New Jersey, library. Librarian Effie Dunwood goes to fetch it but fails to return. The pamphlet is gone, too.

CONTINUITY #544
Tuesday, April 1, 1941
7:15–7:30 p.m. EST
NBC Blue
Martha Atwell, Director
Doris Halman, Writer
Mildred Fenton, Editor
James Fleming, Announcer
American Home Products (Kolynos, Bi-So-Dol), Sponsor
"The Case of the Faithful Heart"

Mr. Cabot, who died, once owned the pamphlet. He told son Loren to give his books to Harvey Black, a foster son. Black sold them to the library. Effie loves Loren Cabot.

CONTINUITY #545
Wednesday, April 2, 1941
7:15–7:30 p.m. EST
NBC Blue
Martha Atwell, Director
Doris Halman, Writer
Mildred Fenton, Editor
James Fleming, Announcer
American Home Products (Kolynos, Bi-So-Dol), Sponsor
"The Case of the Faithful Heart"

Effie hid until nightfall, then took a bus to New York. Her motive was to keep Colby from finding a will hidden in the pamphlet favoring Harvey over Loren.

CONTINUITY #546
Thursday, April 3, 1941
7:15–7:30 p.m. EST
NBC Blue
Martha Atwell, Director
Doris Halman, Writer
Mildred Fenton, Editor
James Fleming, Announcer
American Home Products (Kolynos, Bi-So-Dol), Sponsor
"The Case of the Faithful Heart"

Effie resurfaces. It comes to light that she silently loved Loren Cabot all her life and wanted to protect the man she loves from a will she felt unjust. A happy ending ensues.

CONTINUITY #547
Tuesday, April 8, 1941
7:15–7:30 p.m. EST
NBC Blue
Martha Atwell, Director
Doris Halman, Writer
Mildred Fenton, Editor
James Fleming, Announcer
American Home Products (Kolynos, Bi-So-Dol), Sponsor
"The Case of the Closed Keyboard"

Pianist Tony Vala, protégé of composer Mirskoff, vanished 10 years ago after his wife died in childbirth during his New York concert debut. Mirskoff is coming to the U.S., where he'll be honored at a special event.

CONTINUITY #548
Wednesday, April 9, 1941
7:15–7:30 p.m. EST
NBC Blue
Martha Atwell, Director
Doris Halman, Writer
Mildred Fenton, Editor
James Fleming, Announcer

American Home Products (Kolynos, Bi-So-Dol), Sponsor
"The Case of the Closed Keyboard"

Manager Saul Garnett wants Vala to appear at Mirskoff's testimonial. Keen learns that Vala took up carpentry, his father's trade. He goes by the name "Bill Jones," and lives in Forgeville.

CONTINUITY #549
Thursday, April 10, 1941
7:15–7:30 p.m. EST
NBC Blue
Martha Atwell, Director
Doris Halman, Writer
Mildred Fenton, Editor
James Fleming, Announcer
American Home Products (Kolynos, Bi-So-Dol), Sponsor
"The Case of the Closed Keyboard"

The ex-concert artist and Edith Wells are initially attracted to one another. However, she is a piano teacher, which causes Vala to back away from a potential romance. He's shingling her house as Keen arrives in their Midwest hamlet.

CONTINUITY #550
Tuesday, April 15, 1941
7:15–7:30 p.m. EST
NBC Blue
Martha Atwell, Director
Doris Halman, Writer
Mildred Fenton, Editor
James Fleming, Announcer
American Home Products (Kolynos, Bi-So-Dol), Sponsor
"The Case of the Closed Keyboard"

Post Office clerk Rudge Saunders is jealous of Vala. He concocts a tale to make Edith think Vala is a criminal. She believes him. Keen persuades Vala to return to New York.

CONTINUITY #551
Wednesday, April 16, 1941
7:15–7:30 p.m. EST
NBC Blue
Martha Atwell, Director
Doris Halman, Writer
Mildred Fenton, Editor
James Fleming, Announcer
American Home Products (Kolynos, Bi-So-Dol), Sponsor
"The Case of the Closed Keyboard"

Keen is instrumental in bringing Edith and Vala together, revealing the deception caused by the postal clerk. Vala returns to music with a new vision and outlook on life.

CONTINUITY #552
Thursday, April 17, 1941
7:15–7:30 p.m. EST
NBC Blue
Martha Atwell, Director
Doris Halman, Writer
Mildred Fenton, Editor
James Fleming, Announcer
American Home Products (Kolynos, Bi-So-Dol), Sponsor
"The Case of the Young Husband Who Thought His Wife Failed Him"

Successful salesman Donald Craigie asks Keen to find his wife Sheila. Resenting city life, she left six months ago after they moved from Vermont. He seeks a divorce in order to remarry.

CONTINUITY #553
Tuesday, April 22, 1941
7:15–7:30 p.m. EST
NBC Blue
Martha Atwell, Director
Doris Halman, Writer
Mildred Fenton, Editor
James Fleming, Announcer
American Home Products (Kolynos, Bi-So-Dol), Sponsor
"The Case of the Young Husband Who Thought His Wife Failed Him"

Keen finds Sheila working in a day nursery. Donald plans to marry sophisticated writer Rosalind Prescott. Mr. Keen goes to Prescott's domicile, wanting to know her before he acts.

CONTINUITY #554
Wednesday, April 23, 1941
7:15–7:30 p.m. EST
NBC Blue
Martha Atwell, Director
Doris Halman, Writer
Mildred Fenton, Editor
James Fleming, Announcer
American Home Products (Kolynos, Bi-So-Dol), Sponsor

"The Case of the Young Husband Who Thought His Wife Failed Him"

Keen fakes a dim view of Prescott, and so decides to test both women. He attends a house party at Donald's Connecticut summer place. Donald is injured in a fight with Prescott's previous (jilted) suitor.

CONTINUITY #555
Thursday, April 24, 1941
7:15–7:30 p.m. EST
NBC Blue
Martha Atwell, Director
Doris Halman, Writer
Mildred Fenton, Editor
James Fleming, Announcer
American Home Products (Kolynos, Bi-So-Dol), Sponsor
"The Case of the Young Husband Who Thought His Wife Failed Him"

Keen proves to Donald Craigie that old rules about hard work and saving for a rainy day are worth more than "keeping up with the Joneses." Donald reunites with estranged wife Sheila.

CONTINUITY #556
Tuesday, April 29, 1941
7:15–7:30 p.m. EDST
NBC Blue
Martha Atwell, Director
Doris Halman, Writer
Mildred Fenton, Editor
James Fleming, Announcer
American Home Products (Kolynos, Bi-So-Dol), Sponsor
"The Case of the Little Girl from England"

Six-year-old Gillian Standish, of Southampton, England, visiting kin in New York, vanishes from Gramercy Park. A doorman took her there when her aunt and uncle, now frantic, went to work.

CONTINUITY #557
Wednesday, April 30, 1941
7:15–7:30 p.m. EDST
NBC Blue
Martha Atwell, Director
Doris Halman, Writer
Mildred Fenton, Editor
James Fleming, Announcer
American Home Products (Kolynos, Bi-So-Dol), Sponsor
"The Case of the Little Girl from England"

The park has a high iron fence and locked gates. Other kids tell Keen that one of them gave Gillian money. She started for Southampton, Long Island, confusing it with Southampton, England.

CONTINUITY #558
Thursday, May 1, 1941
7:15–7:30 p.m. EDST
NBC Blue
Martha Atwell, Director
Doris Halman, Writer
Mildred Fenton, Editor
James Fleming, Announcer
American Home Products (Kolynos, Bi-So-Dol), Sponsor
"The Case of the Little Girl from England"

Keen and Clancy trace the route to a railroad station. At Southampton Gillian was last seen trudging toward closed summer estates. They hire a car and search the streets.

CONTINUITY #559
Tuesday, May 6, 1941
7:15–7:30 p.m. EDST
NBC Blue
Martha Atwell, Director
Doris Halman, Writer
Mildred Fenton, Editor
James Fleming, Announcer
American Home Products (Kolynos, Bi-So-Dol), Sponsor
"The Case of the Little Girl from England"

The sleuths find the child unharmed. She left the park in search of her mother at Southampton. She goes back to New York and delivers a radio greeting to anxious parents across the sea.

CONTINUITY #560
Wednesday, May 7, 1941
7:15–7:30 p.m. EDST
NBC Blue
Martha Atwell, Director
Doris Halman, Writer
Mildred Fenton, Editor
James Fleming, Announcer
American Home Products (Kolynos, Bi-So-Dol), Sponsor
"The Case of the Five Kinsmen"

When a dinner guest fails to appear at his

club, Ben Fantrell is upset. James Fantrell of Hawaii had agreed to meet Ben; James is in town to determine if five Fantrells in the phone book are his kin.

CONTINUITY #561
Thursday, May 8, 1941
7:15–7:30 p.m. EDST
NBC Blue
Martha Atwell, Director
Doris Halman, Writer
Mildred Fenton, Editor
James Fleming, Announcer
American Home Products (Kolynos, Bi-So-Dol), Sponsor
"The Case of the Five Kinsmen"
   On a hunch, Keen looks up the other four local Fantrells. None of them have seen James. Each of five letters James wrote begin the same but have different second paragraphs. Keen takes the five notes to work.

CONTINUITY #562
Tuesday, May 13, 1941
7:15–7:30 p.m. EDST
NBC Blue
Martha Atwell, Director
Doris Halman, Writer
Mildred Fenton, Editor
James Fleming, Announcer
American Home Products (Kolynos, Bi-So-Dol), Sponsor
"The Case of the Five Kinsmen"
   Keen learns that James Fantrell vanished just as Feds from the West Coast closed in on the trail of narcotics smuggler Digney. The letters hold a clue: Fantrell (Digney) is in Springfield, Massachusetts.

CONTINUITY #563
Wednesday, May 14, 1941
7:15–7:30 p.m. EDST
NBC Blue
Martha Atwell, Director
Doris Halman, Writer
Mildred Fenton, Editor
James Fleming, Announcer
American Home Products (Kolynos, Bi-So-Dol), Sponsor
"The Case of the Five Kinsmen"
   Digney was driven into hiding by pursuing agents of the law. Mr. Keen leads those agents to him and thereby brings an end to one of the "wickedest rackets in the world."

CONTINUITY #564
Thursday, May 15, 1941
7:15–7:30 p.m. EDST
NBC Blue
Martha Atwell, Director
Doris Halman, Writer
Mildred Fenton, Editor
James Fleming, Announcer
American Home Products (Kolynos, Bi-So-Dol), Sponsor
"The Case of the Sacred Trust"
   Apartment manager Amy Clark, with a crippled spouse and two kids, holds a costly relic for a tenant who moved to Peru 11 years ago. She asks Keen to keep it until the owner returns.

CONTINUITY #565
Tuesday, May 20, 1941
7:15–7:30 p.m. EDST
NBC Blue
Martha Atwell, Director
Doris Halman, Writer
Mildred Fenton, Editor
James Fleming, Announcer
American Home Products (Kolynos, Bi-So-Dol), Sponsor
"The Case of the Sacred Trust"
   Keen visits the Peruvian Legation in Washington, D.C. He traces owner Marie Bracken from Peru — where her spouse had died — to Mexico. She wed planter Ramon Valdez. Keen takes the object to her.

CONTINUITY #566
Wednesday, May 21, 1941
7:15–7:30 p.m. EDST
NBC Blue
Martha Atwell, Director
Doris Halman, Writer
Mildred Fenton, Editor
James Fleming, Announcer
American Home Products (Kolynos, Bi-So-Dol), Sponsor
"The Case of the Sacred Trust"
   Caretaker Amy Clark was too honest to convert the object she held into cash, though she could have used it. Mr. Keen delivers the ornament to a wealthy plantation owner's wife.

CONTINUITY #567
Thursday, May 22, 1941
7:15–7:30 p.m. EDST
NBC Blue
Martha Atwell, Director
Doris Halman, Writer
Mildred Fenton, Editor
James Fleming, Announcer
American Home Products (Kolynos, Bi-So-Dol), Sponsor
"The Case of the Sacred Trust"
  For keeping the sacred trust through years of poverty, hard work and illness, Amy Clark is substantially rewarded by the relic's owner. She won't ever have financial worries again.

CONTINUITY #568
Tuesday, May 27, 1941
7:15–7:30 p.m. EDST
NBC Blue
Martha Atwell, Director
Doris Halman, Writer
John Hunter, Editor
James Fleming, Announcer
American Home Products (Kolynos, Bi-So-Dol), Sponsor
"The Case of the Boyhood Hero"
  Derek Ford, age 12, asks Mr. Keen to find his hero, lame Lance McCrae, missing a month. McCrae was at the boy's home so often, recalling his sea adventures, that Mr. Ford became jealous.

CONTINUITY #569
Wednesday, May 28, 1941
7:15–7:30 p.m. EDST
NBC Blue
Martha Atwell, Director
Doris Halman, Writer
John Hunter, Editor
James Fleming, Announcer
American Home Products (Kolynos, Bi-So-Dol), Sponsor
"The Case of the Boyhood Hero"
  Mr. Keen is touched by Derek's distress. He interviews the parents. Ford had asked McCrae to go, but McCrae, knowing the jealousy to be unfounded, refused. Keen investigates further.

CONTINUITY #570
Thursday, May 29, 1941
7:15–7:30 p.m. EDST
NBC Blue
Martha Atwell, Director
Doris Halman, Writer
John Hunter, Editor
James Fleming, Announcer
American Home Products (Kolynos, Bi-So-Dol), Sponsor
"The Case of the Boyhood Hero"
  Keen learns that Lance McCrae was an escaped convict whose real name is John Tyndall. He went to New York to buy Derek a birthday present, where he was re-arrested and sent back to prison.

CONTINUITY #571
Tuesday, June 3, 1941
7:15–7:30 p.m. EDST
NBC Blue
Martha Atwell, Director
Doris Halman, Writer
John Hunter, Editor
James Fleming, Announcer
American Home Products (Kolynos, Bi-So-Dol), Sponsor
"The Case of the Boyhood Hero"
  Keen returns to the Ford home. He doesn't tell Derek that his hero was an escaped con who's now back in jail. Instead, Keen helps forge a closer bond between a busy father and his son.

CONTINUITY #572
Wednesday, June 4, 1941
7:15–7:30 p.m. EDST
NBC Blue
Martha Atwell, Director
Doris Halman, Writer
John Hunter, Editor
James Fleming, Announcer
American Home Products (Kolynos, Bi-So-Dol), Sponsor
"The Case of the Rainbow Pins"
  A shabby old lady, called "Mother" by many, who sells gardenias at a department store entrance disappears. Keen starts investigating at a downtown wholesale flower market.

CONTINUITY #573
Thursday, June 5, 1941
7:15–7:30 p.m. EDST
NBC Blue

Martha Atwell, Director
Doris Halman, Writer
John Hunter, Editor
James Fleming, Announcer
American Home Products (Kolynos, Bi-So-Dol), Sponsor
"The Case of the Rainbow Pins"

Keen learns that the lady's name is Mrs. Wheary. She lived in an East Side tenement. She left there in a big car with a fine looking middle-aged man two weeks ago. Keen must find him.

CONTINUITY #574
Tuesday, June 10, 1941
7:15–7:30 p.m. EDST
NBC Blue
Martha Atwell, Director
Doris Halman, Writer
John Hunter, Editor
James Fleming, Announcer
American Home Products (Kolynos, Bi-So-Dol), Sponsor
"The Case of the Rainbow Pins"

Mrs. Wheary's son, affluent manufacturer Steven Wainwright, found his mom and snatched her from poverty. Keen discovers that she has become isolated and lonely. She wishes she was poor in New York again.

CONTINUITY #575
Wednesday, June 11, 1941
7:15–7:30 p.m. EDST
NBC Blue
Martha Atwell, Director
Doris Halman, Writer
John Hunter, Editor
James Fleming, Announcer
American Home Products (Kolynos, Bi-So-Dol), Sponsor
"The Case of the Rainbow Pins"

Keen visits Steven Wainwright. He convinces him that his mother yearns for her old life. She is returned to it and is now happy as a lark.

CONTINUITY #576
Thursday, June 12, 1941
7:15–7:30 p.m. EDST
NBC Blue
Martha Atwell, Director
Doris Halman, Writer
John Hunter, Editor
James Fleming, Announcer
American Home Products (Kolynos, Bi-So-Dol), Sponsor
"The Case of the Man She Might Have Married"

Jane Wingate agreed to play the lead in a pageant at a Boston high school. In New York she boarded a boat that makes no stops before reaching Boston, yet she never arrived. Mr. Keen goes to Boston.

CONTINUITY #577
Tuesday, June 17, 1941
7:15–7:30 p.m. EDST
NBC Blue
Martha Atwell, Director
Doris Halman, Writer
John Hunter, Editor
James Fleming, Announcer
American Home Products (Kolynos, Bi-So-Dol), Sponsor
"The Case of the Man She Might Have Married"

Gilbert Forrester, a man who had once been engaged to Jane Wingate and jilted her to marry someone else, may have been on the boat, Keen learns. Keen goes to the high school.

CONTINUITY #578
Wednesday, June 18, 1941
7:15–7:30 p.m. EDST
NBC Blue
Martha Atwell, Director
Doris Halman, Writer
John Hunter, Editor
James Fleming, Announcer
American Home Products (Kolynos, Bi-So-Dol), Sponsor
"The Case of the Man She Might Have Married"

Gilbert, on the boat, realized he was duped into marrying a selfish woman. He considered divorcing her for Jane, but Jane said no. She fled to Maine after the boat docked. Keen follows her.

CONTINUITY #579
Thursday, June 19, 1941
7:15–7:30 p.m. EDST
NBC Blue

Martha Atwell, Director
Doris Halman, Writer
John Hunter, Editor
James Fleming, Announcer
American Home Products (Kolynos, Bi-So-Dol), Sponsor
"The Case of the Man She Might Have Married"
    Mr. Keen straightens out Jane Wingate's life by proving to her that she no longer loves Gilbert Forrester. She seems content with that knowledge and returns to New York.

CONTINUITY #580
Tuesday, June 24, 1941
7:15–7:30 p.m. EDST
NBC Blue
Martha Atwell, Director
Doris Halman, Writer
John Hunter, Editor
James Fleming, Announcer
American Home Products (Kolynos, Bi-So-Dol), Sponsor
"The Case of the Mother Who Thought Her Son Would Never Make Good"
    Widow Mrs. O'Rourke, who cleans Keen and Co.'s offices, asks Mr. Keen to find son Sean, age 20. Headstrong, scrappy, and jobless, he rejected Mary Donovan, his mother's choice for him, to pursue Lily Wick.

CONTINUITY #581
Wednesday, June 25, 1941
7:15–7:30 p.m. EDST
NBC Blue
Martha Atwell, Director
Doris Halman, Writer
John Hunter, Editor
James Fleming, Announcer
American Home Products (Kolynos, Bi-So-Dol), Sponsor
"The Case of the Mother Who Thought Her Son Would Never Make Good"
    Wick introduced Sean to dubious cohorts like Harry Lucchino. When mom reads that Harry was arrested for auto theft, and that police are searching for an accessory, she thinks of Sean. Keen continues his investigation at the jail.

CONTINUITY #582
Thursday, June 26, 1941
7:15–7:30 p.m. EDST
NBC Blue
Martha Atwell, Director
Doris Halman, Writer
John Hunter, Editor
Announcer's name omitted
American Home Products (Kolynos, Bi-So-Dol), Sponsor
"The Case of the Mother Who Thought Her Son Would Never Make Good"
    The police seek Chip Magoon. Discovering that his pals were crooks, Sean broke with them. In Atlantic City he became a bus boy at a cafeteria. He was fired for arguing with a G.I.

CONTINUITY #583
Tuesday, July 1, 1941
7:15–7:30 p.m. EDST
NBC Blue
Martha Atwell, Director
Doris Halman, Writer
John Hunter, Editor
James Fleming, Announcer
American Home Products (Kolynos, Bi-So-Dol), Sponsor
"The Case of the Mother Who Thought Her Son Would Never Make Good"
    Keen finds Sean at an Army training post in the South, happy among new friends and proudly serving his nation. He returns home on leave, giving his mom the biggest shock of her life.

CONTINUITY #584
Wednesday, July 2, 1941
7:15–7:30 p.m. EDST
NBC Blue
Martha Atwell, Director
Doris Halman, Writer
John Hunter, Editor
James Fleming, Announcer
American Home Products (Kolynos, Bi-So-Dol), Sponsor
"The Case of the Man with the Loving Wife"
    Three weeks ago criminal lawyer Christopher Powell left to go on a business trip. He never returned. No one at the firm knows any details of the trip. Wife Millicent is hysterical.

CONTINUITY #585
Thursday, July 3, 1941
7:15–7:30 p.m. EDST

NBC Blue
Martha Atwell, Director
Doris Halman, Writer
John Hunter, Editor
James Fleming, Announcer
American Home Products (Kolynos, Bi-So-Dol), Sponsor
"The Case of the Man with the Loving Wife"

Following the unlikeliest of clues, Keen goes to New Hampshire's Lake Manitago, where Powell's daughter Christina, age 15, is at a girls' camp. He approaches the office of a head counselor.

CONTINUITY #586
Tuesday, July 8, 1941
7:15–7:30 p.m. EDST
NBC Blue
Martha Atwell, Director
Doris Halman, Writer
John Hunter, Editor
James Fleming, Announcer
American Home Products (Kolynos, Bi-So-Dol), Sponsor
"The Case of the Man with the Loving Wife"

From Millicent, Christina and co-workers, Keen pieces together the truth: Powell disappeared because of his wife's excessive love. It stifled both his independence and their daughter's hopes.

CONTINUITY #587
Wednesday, July 9, 1941
7:15–7:30 p.m. EDST
NBC Blue
Martha Atwell, Director
Doris Halman, Writer
John Hunter, Editor
James Fleming, Announcer
American Home Products (Kolynos, Bi-So-Dol), Sponsor
"The Case of the Man with the Loving Wife"

Keen traces Powell to a small town in the Illinois mountains where he was raised, but Keen leaves Powell undisturbed. In New York Keen begins an interesting experiment. Weeks pass.

CONTINUITY #588
Thursday, July 10, 1941
7:15–7:30 p.m. EDST
NBC Blue
Martha Atwell, Director
Doris Halman, Writer
John Hunter, Editor
James Fleming, Announcer
American Home Products (Kolynos, Bi-So-Dol), Sponsor
"The Case of the Man with the Loving Wife"

Keen has taught Millicent to think and act for herself in the intervening weeks. Her devotion was overbearing. Keen then concludes his experiment and reunites the family.

CONTINUITY #589
Tuesday, July 15, 1941
7:15–7:30 p.m. EDST
NBC Blue
Martha Atwell, Director
Doris Halman, Writer
John Hunter, Editor
James Fleming, Announcer
American Home Products (Kolynos, Bi-So-Dol), Sponsor
"The Case of the Girl Who Screamed in the Dark"

Calling from Coney Island, Miss Ellis tells Keen that a girl who stepped into a car with her on a ride isn't the one who exited at the end of it, although they were dressed similarly.

CONTINUITY #590
Wednesday, July 16, 1941
7:15–7:30 p.m. EDST
NBC Blue
Martha Atwell, Director
Doris Halman, Writer
Philip Thorn, Editor
James Fleming, Announcer
American Home Products (Kolynos, Bi-So-Dol), Sponsor
"The Case of the Girl Who Screamed in the Dark"

Keen and Clancy learn that one girl *did* replace another on the ride. The first girl must be hidden in the building somewhere. The sleuths ride in the rear seat of the last car at closing time.

CONTINUITY #591
Thursday, July 17, 1941
7:15–7:30 p.m. EDST
NBC Blue
Martha Atwell, Director

Doris Halman, Writer
Philip Thorn, Editor
James Fleming, Announcer
American Home Products (Kolynos, Bi-So-Dol), Sponsor
"The Case of the Girl Who Screamed in the Dark"

Inventor's secretary Susan Baker is being held captive. A crooked gang intends to force her to reveal the combination of her employer's safe. Ellis calls the cops, and the crooks flee with the girl.

CONTINUITY #592
Tuesday, July 22, 1941
7:15–7:30 p.m. EDST
NBC Blue
Martha Atwell, Director
Doris Halman, Writer
Philip Thorn, Editor
Announcer's name omitted
American Home Products (Kolynos, Bi-So-Dol), Sponsor
"The Case of the Girl Who Screamed in the Dark"

Mr. Keen and Clancy are locked in a dark soundproof room upstairs. Extricated, they pursue the crooks, free the girl, capture the baddies and secure the inventor's work.

CONTINUITY #593
Wednesday, July 23, 1941
7:15–7:30 p.m. EDST
NBC Blue
Martha Atwell, Director
Doris Halman, Writer
Philip Thorn, Editor
Announcer's name omitted
American Home Products (Kolynos, Bi-So-Dol), Sponsor
"The Case of Lord Bountiful"

Linda and Andy Moore grew up in an orphanage and later wed. He fell ill. A doctor suggested Arizona. Needing $1,000, Linda asked a philanthropist for help. He refused, but she had better luck inquiring at the hall.

CONTINUITY #594
Thursday, July 24, 1941
7:15–7:30 p.m. EDST
NBC Blue
Martha Atwell, Director
Doris Halman, Writer
Philip Thorn, Editor
James Fleming, Announcer
American Home Products (Kolynos, Bi-So-Dol), Sponsor
"The Case of Lord Bountiful"

"Lord Bountiful" gave Linda the cash. Two years later the couple wanted to repay him, but learned he was an imposter. The real Lord has a black sheep brother he gave $1,000 to two years ago.

CONTINUITY #595
Tuesday, July 29, 1941
7:15–7:30 p.m. EDST
NBC Blue
Martha Atwell, Director
Doris Halman, Writer
Philip Thorn, Editor
James Fleming, Announcer
American Home Products (Kolynos, Bi-So-Dol), Sponsor
"The Case of Lord Bountiful"

Aging actor Rodney Vanbrugh was told by his sibling not to ask for any money. Rodney gave it all to Linda and vanished. Keen finds him in the lower East Side working as a sandwich man.

CONTINUITY #596
Wednesday, July 30, 1941
7:15–7:30 p.m. EDST
NBC Blue
Martha Atwell, Director
Doris Halman, Writer
Philip Thorn, Editor
James Fleming, Announcer
American Home Products (Kolynos, Bi-So-Dol), Sponsor
"The Case of Lord Bountiful"

Before Keen reaches him, Rodney collapses and is carried to a hospital his wealthy brother had built. Linda and Andy join Keen there. They open their home to him, and the two brothers reconcile.

CONTINUITY #597
Thursday, July 31, 1941
7:15–7:30 p.m. EDST
NBC Blue
Martha Atwell, Director
Doris Halman, Writer

Philip Thorn, Editor
James Fleming, Announcer
American Home Products (Kolynos, Bi-So-Dol), Sponsor
"The Case Mr. Keen Recorded as His Only Failure"

Invalid Augusta Valliance summons Mr. Keen to her Wisconsin home. Keen and Clancy learn that Augusta's 17-year-old niece, Joan Tower, ran into the woods at the walled estate and never emerged.

CONTINUITY #598
Tuesday, August 5, 1941
7:15–7:30 p.m. EDST
NBC Blue
Martha Atwell, Director
Doris Halman, Writer
Philip Thorn, Editor
James Fleming, Announcer
American Home Products (Kolynos, Bi-So-Dol), Sponsor
"The Case Mr. Keen Recorded as His Only Failure"

They comb the grounds. Keen learns that an Army bomber made a forced landing on the day Joan disappeared. She stowed away on the plane, telling the pilot of the intense anguish inflicted upon her by her aunt. He dropped her off in Illinois.

CONTINUITY #599
Wednesday, August 6, 1941
7:15–7:30 p.m. EDST
NBC Blue
Martha Atwell, Director
Doris Halman, Writer
Philip Thorn, Editor
James Fleming, Announcer
American Home Products (Kolynos, Bi-So-Dol), Sponsor
"The Case Mr. Keen Recorded as His Only Failure"

Keen charters a plane in Chicago and locates Joan on a farm. She has become like a daughter to an old couple. Terrified, she begs Keen not to reveal her whereabouts to her aunt.

CONTINUITY #600
Thursday, August 7, 1941
7:15–7:30 p.m. EDST
NBC Blue
Martha Atwell, Director
Doris Halman, Writer
Philip Thorn, Editor
James Fleming, Announcer
American Home Products (Kolynos, Bi-So-Dol), Sponsor
"The Case Mr. Keen Recorded as His Only Failure"

For the first and only time, Keen claims to have failed on a case he actually solved, sacrificing his reputation so that a pathetic young girl can stay safely hidden from a cruel, mentally ill guardian.

CONTINUITY #601
Tuesday, August 12, 1941
7:15–7:30 p.m. EDST
NBC Blue
Martha Atwell, Director
Doris Halman, Writer
Philip Thorn, Editor
James Fleming, Announcer
American Home Products (Kolynos, Bi-So-Dol), Sponsor
"The Case of the Spinster Who Put Her Pride in Her Pocket"

It appears Miss Ellis has been stood up when — two hours past a date with long-time beau Abernethy — the old gent doesn't arrive. He was seen at the subway near his home, where she now goes.

CONTINUITY #602
Wednesday, August 13, 1941
7:15–7:30 p.m. EDST
NBC Blue
Martha Atwell, Director
Doris Halman, Writer
Philip Thorn, Editor
James Fleming, Announcer
American Home Products (Kolynos, Bi-So-Dol), Sponsor
"The Case of the Spinster Who Put Her Pride in Her Pocket"

Miss Ellis traces her missing boyfriend to a floral shop. There he purchased an expensive orchid and then went to the home of Poppy Murgatroyd in a shabby downtown district.

CONTINUITY #603
Thursday, August 14, 1941
7:15–7:30 p.m. EDST

NBC Blue
Martha Atwell, Director
Doris Halman, Writer
Philip Thorn, Editor
James Fleming, Announcer
American Home Products (Kolynos, Bi-So-Dol), Sponsor
"The Case of the Spinster Who Put Her Pride in Her Pocket"

Unknown to Miss Ellis, Mike Clancy — in touch with Mr. Keen by telephone — has also taken up the search. He follows her taxi from the floral shop. A detective calls on Mr. Keen.

CONTINUITY #604
Tuesday, August 19, 1941
7:15–7:30 p.m. EDST
NBC Blue
Martha Atwell, Director
Doris Halman, Writer
Philip Thorn, Editor
James Fleming, Announcer
American Home Products (Kolynos, Bi-So-Dol), Sponsor
"The Case of the Spinster Who Put Her Pride in Her Pocket"

Abernethy is about to be ferried away by jewel thieves, with whom he by chance crossed paths. Ellis and Clancy are included. Keen arrives, finds clues, recovers the gems and follows them.

CONTINUITY #605
Wednesday, August 20, 1941
7:15–7:30 p.m. EDST
NBC Blue
Martha Atwell, Director
Doris Halman, Writer
Philip Thorn, Editor
James Fleming, Announcer
American Home Products (Kolynos, Bi-So-Dol), Sponsor
"The Case of the Spinster Who Put Her Pride in Her Pocket"

Mr. Keen and the detective pursue the gang down a Long Island highway. The pair catches up to the crooks, safely frees the hostages and puts the criminals where they can do no wrong.

CONTINUITY #606
Thursday, August 21, 1941
7:15–7:30 p.m. EDST
NBC Blue
Martha Atwell, Director
Doris Halman, Writer
Philip Thorn, Editor
James Fleming, Announcer
American Home Products (Kolynos, Bi-So-Dol), Sponsor
"The Case of the Wheel That Rolled Downhill"

Judge Truesdell drives Keen along a road above a deep ravine when a tire goes flat. They spot the burned-out wreck of a car, with the skeletons of a man and woman inside. The car's serial number is the only clue to the mystery.

CONTINUITY #607
Tuesday, August 26, 1941
7:15–7:30 p.m. EDST
NBC Blue
Martha Atwell, Director
Doris Halman, Writer
Philip Thorn, Editor
James Fleming, Announcer
American Home Products (Kolynos, Bi-So-Dol), Sponsor
"The Case of the Wheel That Rolled Downhill"

The car was first sold in St. Louis in 1928; the buyer drove it to California. His widow sold it to a secondhand dealer. Movie star Floria Fane bought it, but it was stolen from her.

CONTINUITY #608
Wednesday, August 27, 1941
7:15–7:30 p.m. EDST
NBC Blue
Martha Atwell, Director
Doris Halman, Writer
Philip Thorn, Editor
James Fleming, Announcer
American Home Products (Kolynos, Bi-So-Dol), Sponsor
"The Case of the Wheel That Rolled Downhill"

Aided by the L.A. police, Keen continues his investigation. He learns that in 1933 Sadie James owned the car. She left her family in Florida and ran away with a traveling man from Boston, Chester Pringle.

CONTINUITY #609
Thursday, August 28, 1941
7:15–7:30 p.m. EDST
NBC Blue

Martha Atwell, Director
Doris Halman, Writer
Philip Thorn, Editor
James Fleming, Announcer
American Home Products (Kolynos, Bi-So-Dol), Sponsor
"The Case of the Wheel That Rolled Downhill"

A Boston dentist helps determine that the couple who died in the car *were* Chester Pringle and Sadie James. Through perseverance Mr. Keen solves yet another tragic mystery.

CONTINUITY #610
Tuesday, September 2, 1941
7:15–7:30 p.m. EDST
NBC Blue
Martha Atwell, Director
Doris Halman, Writer
Philip Thorn, Editor
James Fleming, Announcer
American Home Products (Kolynos, Bi-So-Dol), Sponsor
"The Case of the Wedding of Mary Blair"

Mary Blair, whose folks are old friends of Keen, invited him to her wedding to chemist Alan Maxwell at Watchford, Connecticut. On the big day, Mary leaves a note that she has changed her mind.

CONTINUITY #611
Wednesday, September 3, 1941
7:15–7:30 p.m. EDST
NBC Blue
Martha Atwell, Director
Doris Halman, Writer
Philip Thorn, Editor
James Fleming, Announcer
American Home Products (Kolynos, Bi-So-Dol), Sponsor
"The Case of the Wedding of Mary Blair"

At the Blair house Keen finds two clues—proof she'd had a secret meeting with a man and, also, that she believed she shouldn't marry and raise a family in these difficult times.

CONTINUITY #612
Thursday, September 4, 1941
7:15–7:30 p.m. EDST
NBC Blue
Martha Atwell, Director
Doris Halman, Writer
Philip Thorn, Editor
James Fleming, Announcer
American Home Products (Kolynos, Bi-So-Dol), Sponsor
"The Case of the Wedding of Mary Blair"

Knowing Keen would look for her, Mary covered her tracks so well it took a week for him to trace her to Philadelphia. Keen and Alan consult the back files of newspapers there.

CONTINUITY #613
Tuesday, September 9, 1941
7:15–7:30 p.m. EDST
NBC Blue
Martha Atwell, Director
Doris Halman, Writer
Philip Thorn, Editor
James Fleming, Announcer
American Home Products (Kolynos, Bi-So-Dol), Sponsor
"The Case of the Wedding of Mary Blair"

Children figure in the resolution of this story. In the end, Mary and Alan will wed, thanks to Mr. Keen's ability to help Mary put in proper perspective her questions about family.

CONTINUITY #614
Wednesday, September 10, 1941
7:15–7:30 p.m. EDST
NBC Blue
Martha Atwell, Director
Doris Halman, Writer
Philip Thorn, Editor
James Fleming, Announcer
American Home Products (Kolynos, Bi-So-Dol), Sponsor
"The Case of the Perfumed Handkerchief"

Carlotta Ransom is arrested for her husband's murder. He dipped a hankie in a bottle of perfume he had given her and dabbed it to a shaving cut. It was laced with snake venom.

CONTINUITY #615
Thursday, September 11, 1941
7:15–7:30 p.m. EDST
NBC Blue
Martha Atwell, Director
Doris Halman, Writer
Philip Thorn, Editor
James Fleming, Announcer
American Home Products (Kolynos, Bi-So-Dol), Sponsor

"The Case of the Perfumed Handkerchief"

Criminal lawyer Christopher Powell, Carlotta's defense attorney, enlists Mr. Keen to investigate the murder. Keen and Powell visit her at the prison where she's being held.

CONTINUITY #616
Tuesday, September 16, 1941
7:15–7:30 p.m. EDST
NBC Blue
Martha Atwell, Director
Doris Halman, Writer
Philip Thorn, Editor
James Fleming, Announcer
American Home Products (Kolynos, Bi-So-Dol), Sponsor
"The Case of the Perfumed Handkerchief"

Carlotta's best friend, jealous Lorraine Valentine, poisoned her perfume to kill her. Keen arranges for Lorraine to be absent from her home while he searches it. But she returns unexpectedly!

CONTINUITY #617
Wednesday, September 17, 1941
7:15–7:30 p.m. EDST
NBC Blue
Martha Atwell, Director
Doris Halman, Writer
Philip Thorn, Editor
James Fleming, Announcer
American Home Products (Kolynos, Bi-So-Dol), Sponsor
"The Case of the Perfumed Handkerchief"

Mr. Keen obtains enough evidence at the Valentine apartment to pin the murder on Carlotta Ransom's supposed best friend. The intended victim escaped death, while her spouse met it.

CONTINUITY #618
Thursday, September 18, 1941
7:15–7:30 p.m. EDST
NBC Blue
Martha Atwell, Director
Doris Halman, Writer
Philip Thorn, Editor
James Fleming, Announcer
American Home Products (Kolynos, Bi-So-Dol), Sponsor
"The Case of the Captain Who Didn't Like Fog"

Captain Asa Drew disappeared 15 years ago after an Atlantic crossing. He didn't know his daughter and new son-in-law drowned during that last voyage. Drew's land may be sold.

CONTINUITY #619
Tuesday, September 23, 1941
7:15–7:30 p.m. EDST
NBC Blue
Martha Atwell, Director
Doris Halman, Writer
Philip Thorn, Editor
James Fleming, Announcer
American Home Products (Kolynos, Bi-So-Dol), Sponsor
"The Case of the Captain Who Didn't Like Fog"

Keen finds that, upon reaching port, Drew learned that his daughter was aboard a foundering schooner to which he failed to provide aid. Is Drew still alive? Keen asks at a mariners' club.

CONTINUITY #620
Wednesday, September 24, 1941
7:15–7:30 p.m. EDST
NBC Blue
Martha Atwell, Director
Doris Halman, Writer
Philip Thorn, Editor
James Fleming, Announcer
American Home Products (Kolynos, Bi-So-Dol), Sponsor
"The Case of the Captain Who Didn't Like Fog"

Asa Drew is now in his late 50s, though he appears older. He is embittered, half-crazed, penniless and hopeless. Mr. Keen finds him and sets in motion a plan to "rescue" him.

CONTINUITY #621
Thursday, September 25, 1941
7:15–7:30 p.m. EDST
NBC Blue
Martha Atwell, Director
Doris Halman, Writer
Philip Thorn, Editor
James Fleming, Announcer
American Home Products (Kolynos, Bi-So-Dol), Sponsor
"The Case of the Captain Who Didn't Like Fog"

Drew resurfaced as Foggy Harper, eccentric tugboat captain in the New York harbor. In an eerie climax involving the dead girl's voice calling through the fog, Keen helps Drew put the past behind him.

CONTINUITY #622
Tuesday, September 30, 1941
7:15–7:30 p.m. EST
NBC Blue
Martha Atwell, Director
Doris Halman, Writer
Philip Thorn, Editor
James Fleming, Announcer
American Home Products (Kolynos, Bi-So-Dol), Sponsor
"The Case of the Silver Pencil in the Sky"

At Ararat, Missouri, Keen finds denizens cut off from the world, living like their ancestors. Suicides are prompted by messages in clouds written by a silver pencil. A skywriter is at fault.

CONTINUITY #623
Wednesday, October 1, 1941
7:15–7:30 p.m. EST
NBC Blue
Martha Atwell, Director
Doris Halman, Writer
Philip Thorn, Editor
James Fleming, Announcer
American Home Products (Kolynos, Bi-So-Dol), Sponsor
"The Case of the Silver Pencil in the Sky"

During a visit to the village, Mr. Keen meets blind old patriarch Nahum Grover, who receives the first of the fateful warnings intended for him. These messages always arrive in threes.

CONTINUITY #624
Thursday, October 2, 1941
7:15–7:30 p.m. EST
NBC Blue
Martha Atwell, Director
Doris Halman, Writer
Philip Thorn, Editor
James Fleming, Announcer
American Home Products (Kolynos, Bi-So-Dol), Sponsor
"The Case of the Silver Pencil in the Sky"

Besides the old patriarch, only a few women and children are still alive. Grover receives a second warning. The identity of the skywriter is revealed, but he hasn't yet been located.

CONTINUITY #625
Tuesday, October 7, 1941
7:15–7:30 p.m. EST
NBC Blue
Martha Atwell, Director
Doris Halman, Writer
Philip Thorn, Editor
James Fleming, Announcer
American Home Products (Kolynos, Bi-So-Dol), Sponsor
"The Case of the Silver Pencil in the Sky"

Keen hires pilot Dwight Fennimore to take him to search for the criminal's hideout. They find Eliphalet Hawkes, a fanatical madman. Though dying, he's still capable of violence.

CONTINUITY #626
Wednesday, October 8, 1941
7:15–7:30 p.m. EST
NBC Blue
Martha Atwell, Director
Doris Halman, Writer
Philip Thorn, Editor
James Fleming, Announcer
American Home Products (Kolynos, Bi-So-Dol), Sponsor
"The Case That the Visiting Nurse Brought to Mr. Keen"

Nurse Catherine Hannan asks Keen's help on behalf of a slum family. Tom Lunt requested a raise and was fired. His child fell ill, he wasn't rehired, and his boss was murdered. Upon becoming a suspect, Tom left.

CONTINUITY #627
Thursday, October 9, 1941
7:15–7:30 p.m. EST
NBC Blue
Martha Atwell, Director
Doris Halman, Writer
Philip Thorn, Editor
James Fleming, Announcer
American Home Products (Kolynos, Bi-So-Dol), Sponsor
"The Case That the Visiting Nurse Brought to Mr. Keen"

Keen tells Tom's wife Etta that she's harming him by keeping his whereabouts a secret. She reveals that Tom is staying on a farm. Keen finds him doing outdoor work at the farm.

CONTINUITY #628
Tuesday, October 14, 1941
7:15–7:30 p.m. EST
NBC Blue
Martha Atwell, Director
Doris Halman, Writer
Philip Thorn, Editor
James Fleming, Announcer
American Home Products (Kolynos, Bi-So-Dol), Sponsor
"The Case That the Visiting Nurse Brought to Mr. Keen"
Keen hears the fugitive's story and persuades him to save his family from further misery by surrendering. Keen sets out to find the murderer, going to a dingy lodging house.

CONTINUITY #629
Wednesday, October 15, 1941
7:15–7:30 p.m. EST
NBC Blue
Martha Atwell, Director
Doris Halman, Writer
Philip Thorn, Editor
James Fleming, Announcer
American Home Products (Kolynos, Bi-So-Dol), Sponsor
"The Case That the Visiting Nurse Brought to Mr. Keen"
It doesn't take Keen long to point the finger of guilt at Sidney Gideon, a flashy, smooth-tongued devil who is the actual killer. The Lunts' situation improves significantly.

CONTINUITY #630
Thursday, October 16, 1941
7:15–7:30 p.m. EST
NBC Blue
Martha Atwell, Director
Doris Halman, Writer
Philip Thorn, Editor
James Fleming, Announcer
American Home Products (Kolynos, Bi-So-Dol), Sponsor
"The Case of the Mystery of My Cousin Maria"
When old bachelor Septimus Blaikie died, his sister, Countess Fanny de Larme, inherited a fortune. But estate manager Bartley Groff robbed her of the money and tried to blackmail her.

CONTINUITY #631
Tuesday, October 21, 1941
7:15–7:30 p.m. EST
NBC Blue
Martha Atwell, Director
Doris Halman, Writer
Philip Thorn, Editor
James Fleming, Announcer
American Home Products (Kolynos, Bi-So-Dol), Sponsor
"The Case of the Mystery of My Cousin Maria"
The Countess prefers poverty to blackmail. She sends Keen looking for scandalous Maria Corvelin, whom her brother loved and whom Fanny drove away decades ago, now his presumed heir.

CONTINUITY #632
Wednesday, October 22, 1941
7:15–7:30 p.m. EST
NBC Blue
Martha Atwell, Director
Doris Halman, Writer
Philip Thorn, Editor
James Fleming, Announcer
American Home Products (Kolynos, Bi-So-Dol), Sponsor
"The Case of the Mystery of My Cousin Maria"
Maria went to jail for working a badger game. She used many aliases in the U.S. and Europe. Later she worked a confidence game on ocean liners, and finally disappeared abroad.

CONTINUITY #633
Thursday, October 23, 1941
7:15–7:30 p.m. EST
NBC Blue
Martha Atwell, Director
Doris Halman, Writer
Philip Thorn, Editor
James Fleming, Announcer
American Home Products (Kolynos, Bi-So-Dol), Sponsor
"The Case of the Mystery of My Cousin Maria"
Countess Fanny de Larme's fears about the legitimacy of the fortune she inherited are put to rest. Mr. Keen solves the mystery of the ill-fated woman presumed to have been an heir.

CONTINUITY #634
Tuesday, October 28, 1941
7:15–7:30 p.m. EST
NBC Blue
Martha Atwell, Director
Doris Halman, Writer
Philip Thorn, Editor
James Fleming, Announcer
American Home Products (Kolynos, Bi-So-Dol), Sponsor
"The Case of the Neglected Parents"
    Brilliant engineer Willard Chase, of New York café society and engaged to a Broadway star, avoids acknowledging his humble heritage. He sends his folks large checks but never writes or visits them.

CONTINUITY #635
Wednesday, October 29, 1941
7:15–7:30 p.m. EST
NBC Blue
Martha Atwell, Director
David Davidson, Writer
Philip Thorn, Editor
James Fleming, Announcer
American Home Products (Kolynos, Bi-So-Dol), Sponsor
"The Case of the Neglected Parents"
    Heartbroken, the Chases left their home at Raineyville. Keen is alarmed to learn that they carried a gun with them. They went to Buffalo and booked a steamer trip to Cleveland. But the boat sank!

CONTINUITY #636
Thursday, October 30, 1941
7:15–7:30 p.m. EST
NBC Blue
Martha Atwell, Director
David Davidson, Writer
Philip Thorn, Editor
James Fleming, Announcer
American Home Products (Kolynos, Bi-So-Dol), Sponsor
"The Case of the Neglected Parents"
    Clues lead Keen to Heightsville, Massachusetts. It is late afternoon there. Lamps have already twinkled on, and the street is filled with homeward-bound workers. He heads for a cottage.

CONTINUITY #637
Tuesday, November 4, 1941
7:15–7:30 p.m. EST
NBC Blue
Martha Atwell, Director
David Davidson, Writer
Philip Thorn, Editor
James Fleming, Announcer
American Home Products (Kolynos, Bi-So-Dol), Sponsor
"The Case of the Neglected Parents"
    Working deliberately and tenaciously, Mr. Keen straightens out Willard Chase's perspective. He puts the lives of Sam and Eva Chase together with Willard and fiancée Winnie Riggs.

CONTINUITY #638
Wednesday, November 5, 1941
7:15–7:30 p.m. EST
NBC Blue
Martha Atwell, Director
David Davidson, Writer
Philip Thorn, Editor
James Fleming, Announcer
American Home Products (Kolynos, Bi-So-Dol), Sponsor
"The Case of the Haunted Client"
    Wealthy Arthur Romney, certain that his insane half-brother Jason—an asylum escapee—is following him, vanishes. Keen follows a clue to Huto's auction room, where he trips over Jason's body!

CONTINUITY #639
Thursday, November 6, 1941
7:15–7:30 p.m. EST
NBC Blue
Martha Atwell, Director
David Davidson, Writer
Philip Thorn, Editor
James Fleming, Announcer
American Home Products (Kolynos, Bi-So-Dol), Sponsor
"The Case of the Haunted Client"
    Behind this is a securities fortune the eccentric father of the two men kept hidden, with jingles as the only clues. One is stolen from Keen. Keen is poisoned while dining with Arthur's wife Grace.

CONTINUITY #640
Tuesday, November 11, 1941
7:15–7:30 p.m. EST
NBC Blue

Martha Atwell, Director
David Davidson, Writer
Philip Thorn, Editor
James Fleming, Announcer
American Home Products (Kolynos, Bi-So-Dol), Sponsor
"The Case of the Haunted Client"

A recovered Mr. Keen finds the hiding place, but the securities are gone, taken by a dangerous adversary whom he knows only as "Mr. X." He fears that Arthur Romney doesn't have long to live.

CONTINUITY #641
Wednesday, November 12, 1941
7:15–7:30 p.m. EST
NBC Blue
Martha Atwell, Director
David Davidson, Writer
Philip Thorn, Editor
James Fleming, Announcer
American Home Products (Kolynos, Bi-So-Dol), Sponsor
"The Case of the Haunted Client"

Crooked asylum orderly George Raven is at last identified as the murderer and thief. He's suave, clever and dangerous. Mr. Keen and Mike Clancy capture him, sparing Romney's life.

CONTINUITY #642
Thursday, November 13, 1941
7:15–7:30 p.m. EST
NBC Blue
Martha Atwell, Director
David Davidson, Writer
Philip Thorn, Editor
James Fleming, Announcer
American Home Products (Kolynos, Bi-So-Dol), Sponsor
"The Case of the Famous Wife"

Using her maiden name, Rhoda Lewis edits a fashion magazine. Her spouse, bank clerk Tom Cooper, sacrifices to help her career. He disappears, and so does $5,000 of the bank's funds.

CONTINUITY #643
Tuesday, November 18, 1941
7:15–7:30 p.m. EST
NBC Blue
Martha Atwell, Director
David Davidson, Writer
Philip Thorn, Editor
James Fleming, Announcer
American Home Products (Kolynos, Bi-So-Dol), Sponsor
"The Case of the Famous Wife"

Mr. Keen interviews the bank manager. A clue sends the tracer to Key West, Florida. There he learns that Tom hired a boat to take him to Cuba. Keen and Mike Clancy review the details.

CONTINUITY #644
Wednesday, November 19, 1941
7:15–7:30 p.m. EST
NBC Blue
Martha Atwell, Director
David Davidson, Writer
Philip Thorn, Editor
James Fleming, Announcer
American Home Products (Kolynos, Bi-So-Dol), Sponsor
"The Case of the Famous Wife"

Mr. Keen believes that Tom did *not* steal the money, but left on a sudden impulse to try and make good in his own right. Keen and Clancy arrive at the American Consulate in Havana.

CONTINUITY #645
Thursday, November 20, 1941
7:15–7:30 p.m. EST
NBC Blue
Martha Atwell, Director
David Davidson, Writer
Philip Thorn, Editor
James Fleming, Announcer
American Home Products (Kolynos, Bi-So-Dol), Sponsor
"The Case of the Famous Wife"

Keen's hunch was right, Tom is found, and the bank manager satisfactorily explains the missing money. Tom and Rhoda reunite, and both now have a new outlook on life.

CONTINUITY #646
Tuesday, November 25, 1941
7:15–7:30 p.m. EST
NBC Blue
Martha Atwell, Director
David Davidson, Writer
Philip Thorn, Editor

James Fleming, Announcer
American Home Products (Kolynos, Bi-So-Dol), Sponsor
"The Case of the Girl Who Flirted"
Art student Peggy Arden flirted with a visitor at an art museum and went to lunch with him, but never returned. Museum staffer Dick Edwards, in love with her, asks Keen's help.

CONTINUITY #647
Wednesday, November 26, 1941
7:15–7:30 p.m. EST
NBC Blue
Martha Atwell, Director
David Davidson, Writer
Philip Thorn, Editor
James Fleming, Announcer
American Home Products (Kolynos, Bi-So-Dol), Sponsor
"The Case of the Girl Who Flirted"
Peggy was sketching at the museum. Keen notices that from her vantage point in the museum she could always view a priceless Italian painting. He suggests the work be examined thoroughly.

CONTINUITY #648
Thursday, November 27, 1941
7:15–7:30 p.m. EST
NBC Blue
Martha Atwell, Director
David Davidson, Writer
Philip Thorn, Editor
James Fleming, Announcer
American Home Products (Kolynos, Bi-So-Dol), Sponsor
"The Case of the Girl Who Flirted"
It turns out that the priceless work was stolen and a copy substituted. Keen finds the original in the museum. Thieves hid it, to be removed later. Peggy is bound and held captive inside an East River house.

CONTINUITY #649
Tuesday, December 2, 1941
7:15–7:30 p.m. EST
NBC Blue
Martha Atwell, Director
David Davidson, Writer
Philip Thorn, Editor
James Fleming, Announcer
American Home Products (Kolynos, Bi-So-Dol), Sponsor
"The Case of the Girl Who Flirted"
Mr. Keen is successful in rounding up culprits Bolton and Sankey, and in rescuing Peggy. Dick Edwards is overjoyed. Peggy learns an important lesson about flirting.

CONTINUITY #650
Wednesday, December 3, 1941
7:15–7:30 p.m. EST
NBC Blue
Martha Atwell, Director
David Davidson, Writer
Philip Thorn, Editor
Announcer's name omitted
American Home Products (Kolynos, Bi-So-Dol), Sponsor
"The Case of the Man Who Never Laughed"
Affluent Daniel Strong hid himself away on his Long Island estate seven years ago after his daughter eloped. Driven by his butler, Joe, to see a doctor, Strong vanishes enroute.

CONTINUITY #651
Thursday, December 4, 1941
7:15–7:30 p.m. EST
NBC Blue
Martha Atwell, Director
David Davidson, Writer
Philip Thorn, Editor
James Fleming, Announcer
American Home Products (Kolynos, Bi-So-Dol), Sponsor
"The Case of the Man Who Never Laughed"
Housekeeper Mrs. Benton calls Keen. It appears that Joe allowed Strong to be abducted. Now Joe has left rather than face questioning. Keen and Clancy confer at the Strong estate.

CONTINUITY #652
Tuesday, December 9, 1941
7:15–7:30 p.m. EST
NBC Blue
Martha Atwell, Director
David Davidson, Writer
Philip Thorn, Editor
James Fleming, Announcer
American Home Products (Kolynos, Bi-So-Dol), Sponsor
"The Case of the Man Who Never Laughed"
Mr. Keen establishes that the abduction

was the work of Strong's daughter and her husband. He knows where the man is being held, too. Keen is hesitant to proceed, however.

CONTINUITY #653
Wednesday, December 10, 1941
7:15–7:30 p.m. EST
NBC Blue
Martha Atwell, Director
David Davidson, Writer
Philip Thorn, Editor
James Fleming, Announcer
American Home Products (Kolynos, Bi-So-Dol), Sponsor
"The Case of the Man Who Never Laughed"
Daniel Strong resurfaces at last. He and Mr. Keen face his abductors, Helen and Oliver Wells, his daughter and son-in-law. Wells went from being a waiter to a big hotel manager.

CONTINUITY #654
Thursday, December 11, 1941
7:15–7:30 p.m. EST
NBC Blue
Martha Atwell, Director
David Davidson, Writer
Philip Thorn, Editor
James Fleming, Announcer
American Home Products (Kolynos, Bi-So-Dol), Sponsor
"The Case of the Door Marked Private"
Secretary Laura Whipple entered the private office of Edgar Blake, her boss. Fiancé Frank Morley waited outside to go to lunch with her. She never came out, but Blake claims she did.

CONTINUITY #655
Tuesday, December 16, 1941
7:15–7:30 p.m. EST
NBC Blue
Martha Atwell, Director
David Davidson, Writer
Philip Thorn, Editor
James Fleming, Announcer
American Home Products (Kolynos, Bi-So-Dol), Sponsor
"The Case of the Door Marked Private"
Blake says that Laura intended to break her engagement. Laura wanders into the lobby in front of Keen and Frank; she is dazed and injured, and mumbling strangely. Keen takes her home for care.

CONTINUITY #656
Wednesday, December 17, 1941
7:15–7:30 p.m. EST
NBC Blue
Martha Atwell, Director
David Davidson, Writer
Philip Thorn, Editor
James Fleming, Announcer
American Home Products (Kolynos, Bi-So-Dol), Sponsor
"The Case of the Door Marked Private"
Behind the private door of Edgar Blake lurks a murderer. Laura barely escaped death there. Blake goes to dine at his partner's home. Keen follows and finds the house in flames.

CONTINUITY #657
Thursday, December 18, 1941
7:15–7:30 p.m. EST
NBC Blue
Martha Atwell, Director
David Davidson, Writer
Philip Thorn, Editor
James Fleming, Announcer
American Home Products (Kolynos, Bi-So-Dol), Sponsor
"The Case of the Door Marked Private"
Detective Williams whisks Edgar Blake away once his crimes are exposed. The love of Laura Whipple and Frank Morley grows stronger as a result of the incidents that transpired.

CONTINUITY #658
Tuesday, December 23, 1941
7:15–7:30 p.m. EST
NBC Blue
Martha Atwell, Director
David Davidson, Writer
Philip Thorn, Editor
James Fleming, Announcer
American Home Products (Kolynos, Bi-So-Dol), Sponsor
"The Case of the Little Girl Who Asked Mr. Keen to Find Her Mother for Christmas"
Wendy Lawrence, age 10, is wise and sad beyond her years. Though wealthy, she's frail and must spend much of her time in bed. She watches others prepare for Christmas from her window.

CONTINUITY #659
Wednesday, December 24, 1941

7:15–7:30 p.m. EST
NBC Blue
Martha Atwell, Director
David Davidson, Writer
Philip Thorn, Editor
James Fleming, Announcer
American Home Products (Kolynos, Bi-So-Dol), Sponsor
"The Case of the Little Girl Who Asked Mr. Keen to Find Her Mother for Christmas"

Wendy's mother left three years ago. Her father and grandfather refuse to discuss it. Wendy took her mom's photo to Keen. Grandpa orders Keen to stay out of it, but Keen thinks he has seen Wendy's mother working as a cigar store clerk.

CONTINUITY #660
Thursday, December 25, 1941
7:15–7:30 p.m. EST
NBC Blue
Martha Atwell, Director
David Davidson, Writer
Philip Thorn, Editor
George Ansbro, Announcer
American Home Products (Kolynos, Bi-So-Dol), Sponsor
"The Case of the Little Girl Who Asked Mr. Keen to Find Her Mother for Christmas"

Keen finds Wendy's mom. She left after her temper flared and she crossed her well-heeled father-in-law. To avoid custody notoriety, she left. On Christmas she and Wendy have a moving reunion.

CONTINUITY #661
Tuesday, December 30, 1941
7:15–7:30 p.m. EST
NBC Blue
Martha Atwell, Director
David Davidson, Writer
Philip Thorn, Editor
George Ansbro, Announcer
American Home Products (Kolynos, Bi-So-Dol), Sponsor
"The Case of the Little Girl Who Asked Mr. Keen to Find Her Mother for Christmas"

Five days after mother and child meet in secret, Keen reunites the entire family, including grandfather and James Lawrence, Wendy's father. It's a heartwarming occasion!

CONTINUITY #662
Wednesday, December 31, 1941
7:15–7:30 p.m. EST
NBC Blue
Martha Atwell, Director
David Davidson, Writer
Philip Thorn, Editor
George Ansbro, Announcer
American Home Products (Kolynos, Bi-So-Dol), Sponsor
"The Case of the Man Who Lost His Faith"

Draftsman Sam Tyler attempts suicide, but Keen stops him. The death of Sam's wife left him alone, and New Year's Eve makes it worse. Keen will prove to Sam his own worth. Sam, stays overnight with Keen.

CONTINUITY #663
Thursday, January 1, 1942
7:15–7:30 p.m. EST
NBC Blue
Martha Atwell, Director
David Davidson, Writer
Philip Thorn, Editor
George Ansbro, Announcer
American Home Products (Kolynos, Bi-So-Dol), Sponsor
"The Case of the Man Who Lost His Faith"

On New Year's Day Keen outlines his strategy to Sam. Keen brings in several people—Mrs. Holton, Mr. Van Kruger, Jimmy Reed—who have a positive influence on Sam and reinforce his worth.

CONTINUITY #664
Tuesday, January 6, 1942
7:15–7:30 p.m. EST
NBC Blue
Martha Atwell, Director
David Davidson, Writer
Philip Thorn, Editor
James Fleming, Announcer
American Home Products (Kolynos, Bi-So-Dol), Sponsor
"The Case of the Message that Came in the Night"

Mr. Smiley, a Pennsylvania farmer who raises carrier pigeons, is upset that a cohort, Joe Booth, has disappeared. Keen finds signs of a fracas at Joe's house behind his snack bar.

CONTINUITY #665
Wednesday, January 7, 1942
7:15–7:30 p.m. EST
NBC Blue
Martha Atwell, Director
David Davidson, Writer
Philip Thorn, Editor
James Fleming, Announcer
American Home Products (Kolynos, Bi-So-Dol), Sponsor
"The Case of the Message That Came in the Night"

Joe's fiancée, Susan Ward, fears that he's been forced back into a life of crime; Joe's old gang is active. Joe tried to reach Smiley, but he and his car were taken. The Post Office safe is robbed.

CONTINUITY #666
Thursday, January 8, 1942
7:15–7:30 p.m. EST
NBC Blue
Martha Atwell, Director
David Davidson, Writer
Philip Thorn, Editor
James Fleming, Announcer
American Home Products (Kolynos, Bi-So-Dol), Sponsor
"The Case of the Message That Came in the Night"

Joe is an ex-safecracker who was going straight. Mr. Keen thinks he's still holding out against the gang's pressure. Keen meets with Susan and Smiley at the latter's farmhouse.

CONTINUITY #667
Tuesday, January 13, 1942
7:15–7:30 p.m. EST
NBC Blue
Martha Atwell, Director
David Davidson, Writer
Philip Thorn, Editor
James Fleming, Announcer
American Home Products (Kolynos, Bi-So-Dol), Sponsor
"The Case of the Message That Came in the Night"

Joe Booth is freed, and Mr. Keen gathers evidence to put the culprits behind bars. It being a federal crime, they won't have a chance to intimidate Joe again for a very long while.

CONTINUITY #668
Wednesday, January 14, 1942
7:15–7:30 p.m. EST
NBC Blue
Martha Atwell, Director
David Davidson, Writer
Philip Thorn, Editor
James Fleming, Announcer
American Home Products (Kolynos, Bi-So-Dol), Sponsor
"The Case of the Girl Whose Mother Didn't Care"

Arrogant society matron Mrs. Spencer Marville frets about status and neglects her thrill-crazy daughter Barbara. The girl vanishes after dining with socialite Donald Kennicut.

CONTINUITY #669
Thursday, January 15, 1942
7:15–7:30 p.m. EST
NBC Blue
Martha Atwell, Director
David Davidson, Writer
Philip Thorn, Editor
James Fleming, Announcer
American Home Products (Kolynos, Bi-So-Dol), Sponsor
"The Case of the Girl Whose Mother Didn't Care"

Donald and Barbara frequented a shady café called the Runaround Club. Keen is angered by Mrs. Marville's negligence. He learns that Donald was tied to a gang of nefarious bond swindlers.

CONTINUITY #670
Tuesday, January 20, 1942
7:15–7:30 p.m. EST
NBC Blue
Martha Atwell, Director
David Davidson, Writer
Philip Thorn, Editor
James Fleming, Announcer
American Home Products (Kolynos, Bi-So-Dol), Sponsor
"The Case of the Girl Whose Mother Didn't Care"

The gang flees town, with the young couple (who fail to realize what is in store for them) in tow. They are held captive in a place far from New York City. Keen thinks he knows where.

CONTINUITY #671
Wednesday, January 21, 1942
7:15–7:30 p.m. EST
NBC Blue
Martha Atwell, Director
David Davidson, Writer
Philip Thorn, Editor
James Fleming, Announcer
American Home Products (Kolynos, Bi-So-Dol), Sponsor
"The Case of the Girl Whose Mother Didn't Care"
   The ruthless swindlers and their hostages are ensconced in Donald's oceanfront cottage at Palm Beach, Florida. Mr. Keen and Mike Clancy scout the situation before taking action.

CONTINUITY #672
Thursday, January 22, 1942
7:15–7:30 p.m. EST
NBC Blue
Martha Atwell, Director
David Davidson, Writer
Philip Thorn, Editor
James Fleming, Announcer
American Home Products (Kolynos, Bi-So-Dol), Sponsor
"The Case of the Girl Whose Mother Didn't Care"
   The sleuths close in. Nick Dexter, the tough, murderous leader of the gang, is captured. Donald and Barbara are safe. They return to New York, and Mrs. Marville mends her neglectful ways.

CONTINUITY #673
Tuesday, January 27, 1942
7:15–7:30 p.m. EST
NBC Blue
Martha Atwell, Director
David Davidson, Writer
Philip Thorn, Editor
Announcer's name omitted
American Home Products (Kolynos, Bi-So-Dol), Sponsor
"The Case of the Young Man Who Lost Himself Because He Lost His Courage"
   Tom Ellis, age 21, is an average, eager, wholesome American youth. He's also the nephew of Miss Ellis, Keen's spinster secretary. Flashbacks feature Tom as a baby and at age 18.

CONTINUITY #674
Wednesday, January 28, 1942
7:15–7:30 p.m. EST
NBC Blue
Martha Atwell, Director
David Davidson, Writer
Philip Thorn, Editor
James Fleming, Announcer
American Home Products (Kolynos, Bi-So-Dol), Sponsor
"The Case of the Young Man Who Lost Himself Because He Lost His Courage"
   Mr. Keen brings this short sequence to its swift conclusion. Tom Ellis, who saw his valor fail him and thereby lost his zest for life, has his confidence restored by the tracer.

CONTINUITY #675
Thursday, January 29, 1942
7:15–7:30 p.m. EST
NBC Blue
Martha Atwell, Director
David Davidson, Writer
Philip Thorn, Editor
James Fleming, Announcer
American Home Products (Kolynos, Bi-So-Dol), Sponsor
"The Case of the Tragedy of Malicious Gossip"
   Lovers Frank Martin and Mary Casey work at the same firm. Idle gossip suggested that the boss had the hots for her. Frank stays late to confront the boss, who's found dead. His alibi vanishes.

CONTINUITY #676
Tuesday, February 3, 1942
7:15–7:30 p.m. EST
NBC Blue
Martha Atwell, Director
David Davidson, Writer
Philip Thorn, Editor
James Fleming, Announcer
American Home Products (Kolynos, Bi-So-Dol), Sponsor
"The Case of the Tragedy of Malicious Gossip"
   Frank was miles away on a bus when his boss died. But the bus driver disappears. Now he's found dead, too. Mr. Keen talks with Mary and Frank's lawyer at Louisville, New York.

CONTINUITY #677
Wednesday, February 4, 1942

7:15–7:30 p.m. EST
NBC Blue
Martha Atwell, Director
David Davidson, Writer
Philip Thorn, Editor
James Fleming, Announcer
American Home Products (Kolynos, Bi-So-Dol), Sponsor
"The Case of the Tragedy of Malicious Gossip"
Lying witness Peter Corey caused Frank's arrest. The scene shifts to the courtroom at Louisville, where Frank stands trial for murder. During a brief recess he talks to Mary.

CONTINUITY #678
Thursday, February 5, 1942
7:15–7:30 p.m. EST
NBC Blue
Martha Atwell, Director
David Davidson, Writer
Philip Thorn, Editor
James Fleming, Announcer
American Home Products (Kolynos, Bi-So-Dol), Sponsor
"The Case of the Tragedy of Malicious Gossip"
The bus driver isn't really dead after all. Mr. Keen proves that Peter Corey, the supposed witness, is the ruthless murderer. Frank is free, and it appears he will marry Mary.

CONTINUITY #679
Tuesday, February 10, 1942
7:15–7:30 p.m. EWT
NBC Blue
Martha Atwell, Director
David Davidson, Writer
Philip Thorn, Editor
James Fleming, Announcer
American Home Products (Kolynos, Bi-So-Dol), Sponsor
"The Case of the Army Aviation Cadet"
Betty Young and Linda Wells spot a lonely Army aviation cadet whom they want to find and cheer up with letters and gifts. Keen assigns young researcher Larry Harper to the case.

CONTINUITY #680
Wednesday, February 11, 1942
7:15–7:30 p.m. EWT
NBC Blue
Martha Atwell, Director
David Davidson, Writer
Philip Thorn, Editor
James Fleming, Announcer
American Home Products (Kolynos, Bi-So-Dol), Sponsor
"The Case of the Army Aviation Cadet"
Harper decides to follow up the various stages in recruiting a cadet. Suddenly he disappears at Pennsylvania Station, to everyone's dismay. Betty and Linda go to see Mr. Keen.

CONTINUITY #681
Thursday, February 12, 1942
7:15–7:30 p.m. EWT
NBC Blue
Martha Atwell, Director
David Davidson, Writer
Philip Thorn, Editor
James Fleming, Announcer
American Home Products (Kolynos, Bi-So-Dol), Sponsor
"The Case of the Army Aviation Cadet"
The matter is resolved when Larry resurfaces. Betty, goddaughter to the indulgent Mr. Keen, and Linda find a solution to their dilemma in one of Keen's more lightweight cases.

CONTINUITY #682
Tuesday, February 17, 1942
7:15–7:30 p.m. EWT
NBC Blue
Martha Atwell, Director
David Davidson, Writer
Philip Thorn, Editor
James Fleming, Announcer
American Home Products (Kolynos, Bi-So-Dol), Sponsor
"The Case of the Secret of Professor Grove"
For years Professor Grove, science instructor at Cranville University, has gone on secret weekend trips. He failed to return from his last. Daughter Marjorie enlists Mr. Keen.

CONTINUITY #683
Wednesday, February 18, 1942
7:15–7:30 p.m. EWT
NBC Blue
Martha Atwell, Director
David Davidson, Writer
Philip Thorn, Editor
James Fleming, Announcer

American Home Products (Kolynos, Bi-So-Dol), Sponsor

"The Case of the Secret of Professor Grove"

Keen finds a pair of leads: cryptic notes locked in the prof's desk, and the fact that a scientific periodical is missing from his library. Keen surprises an intruder, who runs off.

CONTINUITY #684
Thursday, February 19, 1942
7:15–7:30 p.m. EWT
NBC Blue
Martha Atwell, Director
David Davidson, Writer
Philip Thorn, Editor
James Fleming, Announcer
American Home Products (Kolynos, Bi-So-Dol), Sponsor

"The Case of the Secret of Professor Grove"

The secret is out: in a hidden lab the professor has been conducting innovative chemical experiments. Now unscrupulous interests seeking to steal his work are apparently holding him there.

CONTINUITY #685
Tuesday, February 24, 1942
7:15–7:30 p.m. EWT
NBC Blue
Martha Atwell, Director
David Davidson, Writer
Philip Thorn, Editor
James Fleming, Announcer
American Home Products (Kolynos, Bi-So-Dol), Sponsor

"The Case of the Secret of Professor Grove"

Keen consults with Marjorie and track star Jimmy Hunter, her sweetheart. Keen secures the professor's release, exposing Kelton, the professor's assistant, and Phipps, who plotted against him, as the culprits.

CONTINUITY #686
Wednesday, February 25, 1942
7:15–7:30 p.m. EWT
NBC Blue
Martha Atwell, Director
David Davidson, Writer
Philip Thorn, Editor
James Fleming, Announcer
American Home Products (Kolynos, Bi-So-Dol), Sponsor

"The Case of the Wife Who Suffered in Silence"

After his wife's death, Walter Long married his secretary, Martha. She was always affectionate with his son Bobby, now 10. A year later she left home. Mr. Keen may know why.

CONTINUITY #687
Thursday, February 26, 1942
7:15–7:30 p.m. EWT
NBC Blue
Martha Atwell, Director
David Davidson, Writer
Philip Thorn, Editor
James Fleming, Announcer
American Home Products (Kolynos, Bi-So-Dol), Sponsor

"The Case of the Wife Who Suffered in Silence"

Bobby is devoted to the memory of his dead mother. Martha kept her troubles a secret from her husband. In despair she left home. Keen learns that she took a taxi to the Hudson River.

CONTINUITY #688
Tuesday, March 3, 1942
7:15–7:30 p.m. EWT
NBC Blue
Martha Atwell, Director
David Davidson, Writer
Philip Thorn, Editor
James Fleming, Announcer
American Home Products (Kolynos, Bi-So-Dol), Sponsor

"The Case of the Wife Who Suffered in Silence"

Following a lengthy search, the tracer makes his way to a Philadelphia hospital where Martha Long was taken, suffering pneumonia. He speaks with a doctor in a hallway.

CONTINUITY #689
Wednesday, March 4, 1942
7:15–7:30 p.m. EWT
NBC Blue
Martha Atwell, Director
David Davidson, Writer
Philip Thorn, Editor
James Fleming, Announcer
American Home Products (Kolynos, Bi-So-Dol), Sponsor

"The Case of the Wife Who Suffered in Silence"

Walter, Martha and Bobby Long are reunited. Mr. Keen helps Walter understand what has happened in his home and assures Bobby that his stepmom loves him and won't replace his mother.

CONTINUITY #690
Thursday, March 5, 1942
7:15–7:30 p.m. EWT
NBC Blue
Martha Atwell, Director
David Davidson, Writer
Philip Thorn, Editor
James Fleming, Announcer
American Home Products (Kolynos, Bi-So-Dol), Sponsor
"The Case of the Fortune of Titus Drake"
Eccentric old bachelor Titus Drake called four kinsmen to his Hudson River home to announce he would leave them his fortune. He went for a walk by the river and never returned.

CONTINUITY #691
Tuesday, March 10, 1942
7:15–7:30 p.m. EWT
NBC Blue
Martha Atwell, Director
David Davidson, Writer
Philip Thorn, Editor
James Fleming, Announcer
American Home Products (Kolynos, Bi-So-Dol), Sponsor
"The Case of the Fortune of Titus Drake"
Grandniece Helen Drake asks Keen for help. By the river, Keen finds signs of a scuffle. Thick, broken glasses point to nearsighted grandnephew Herbert Drake. A thrown knife barely misses Keen.

CONTINUITY #692
Wednesday, March 11, 1942
7:15–7:30 p.m. EWT
NBC Blue
Martha Atwell, Director
David Davidson, Writer
Philip Thorn, Editor
James Fleming, Announcer
American Home Products (Kolynos, Bi-So-Dol), Sponsor
"The Case of the Fortune of Titus Drake"
As Mr. Keen and Mike Clancy leave their room, a luncheon tray vanishes into thin air. Now the two sleuths are prowling down a dark corridor in the old Drake house.

CONTINUITY #693
Thursday, March 12, 1942
7:15–7:30 p.m. EWT
NBC Blue
Martha Atwell, Director
David Davidson, Writer
Philip Thorn, Editor
James Fleming, Announcer
American Home Products (Kolynos, Bi-So-Dol), Sponsor
"The Case of the Fortune of Titus Drake"
The tracer and his partner locate Titus Drake, alive and well, and solve the mystery of his disappearance. Another grandnephew, Oliver Drake, is exposed as the would-be murderer.

CONTINUITY #694
Tuesday, March 17, 1942
7:15–7:30 p.m. EWT
NBC Blue
Martha Atwell, Director
Doris Halman, Writer
Philip Thorn, Editor
James Fleming, Announcer
American Home Products (Kolynos, Bi-So-Dol), Sponsor
"The Case of the Wife Who Was Jealous of Her Husband's Work"
Twenty-two-year-old Francia left California to marry painter Edward Wile, age 42, in New York. She was intensely jealous of his work. They quarreled and she took off, leaving a suicide note.

CONTINUITY #695
Wednesday, March 18, 1942
7:15–7:30 p.m. EWT
NBC Blue
Martha Atwell, Director
Doris Halman, Writer
Philip Thorn, Editor
James Fleming, Announcer
American Home Products (Kolynos, Bi-So-Dol), Sponsor
"The Case of the Wife Who Was Jealous of Her Husband's Work"
Edward is frantic. He and Keen follow Francia to Fairfax, site of a war industries plant. They know she purchased poison there. They proceed down a row of lodging houses.

CONTINUITY #696
Thursday, March 19, 1942

7:15–7:30 p.m. EWT
NBC Blue
Martha Atwell, Director
Doris Halman, Writer
Philip Thorn, Editor
James Fleming, Announcer
American Home Products (Kolynos, Bi-So-Dol), Sponsor
"The Case of the Wife Who Was Jealous of Her Husband's Work"

Francia — "with new courage born of her extreme hour" — is working night shift at a war industries plant. The tracer and Edward Wile approach the factory gates as dawn breaks.

CONTINUITY #697
Tuesday, March 24, 1942
7:15–7:30 p.m. EWT
NBC Blue
Martha Atwell, Director
Doris Halman, Writer
Philip Thorn, Editor
James Fleming, Announcer
American Home Products (Kolynos, Bi-So-Dol), Sponsor
"The Case of the Wife Who Was Jealous of Her Husband's Work"

Francia and Edward come face to face. Mr. Keen helps her understand that Edward cares for her deeply, that she is the most important thing in the world to him. They reunite.

CONTINUITY #698
Wednesday, March 25, 1942
7:15–7:30 p.m. EWT
NBC Blue
Martha Atwell, Director
Carl A. Buss, Writer
Philip Thorn, Editor
James Fleming, Announcer
American Home Products (Kolynos, Bi-So-Dol), Sponsor
"The Case of the Girl Who Had Only Herself to Fear"

Why did Hannah Wright disappear from her home the night before she was to marry handsome George Hawkins, whom she loved? Her sister, Shirley Wright, puts that question to Mr. Keen.

CONTINUITY #699
Thursday, March 26, 1942
7:15–7:30 p.m. EWT
NBC Blue
Martha Atwell, Director
Carl A. Buss, Writer
Philip Thorn, Editor
James Fleming, Announcer
American Home Products (Kolynos, Bi-So-Dol), Sponsor
"The Case of the Girl Who Had Only Herself to Fear"

Keen traces Hannah to New York City. He and Mike Clancy believe they have found her. In the foyer of an office building, Clancy waits while Keen phones.

CONTINUITY #700
Tuesday, March 31, 1942
7:15–7:30 p.m. EWT
NBC Blue
Martha Atwell, Director
Carl A. Buss, Writer
Philip Thorn, Editor
James Fleming, Announcer
American Home Products (Kolynos, Bi-So-Dol), Sponsor
"The Case of the Girl Who Had Only Herself to Fear"

Hannah, under the alias Hattie Wilson, is a servant for wealthy Henry Van Slyke. His wife is insanely jealous of the new maid. While Keen is there, the wife fires a gun at Hannah.

CONTINUITY #701
Wednesday, April 1, 1942
7:15–7:30 p.m. EWT
NBC Blue
Martha Atwell, Director
Carl A. Buss, Writer
Philip Thorn, Editor
James Fleming, Announcer
American Home Products (Kolynos, Bi-So-Dol), Sponsor
"The Case of the Girl Who Had Only Herself to Fear"

Thanks to Keen, Hannah, Shirley and George Hawkins reconnect. It's obvious that Henry and Irene Van Slyke have greater problems than any experienced by that trio.

CONTINUITY #702
Thursday, April 2, 1942
7:15–7:30 p.m. EWT

NBC Blue
Martha Atwell, Director
Ben Brady, Writer
Philip Thorn, Editor
Announcer's name omitted
American Home Products (Kolynos, Bi-So-Dol), Sponsor
"The Case of the Suspicious Playboy"

Archie Patterson left one day and didn't return. His rich uncle, Magnus, isn't upset, saying that it's merely another escapade. Archie's wife Enid, however, *is* concerned. Magnus receives a $50,000 ransom note.

CONTINUITY #703
Tuesday, April 7, 1942
7:15–7:30 p.m. EWT
NBC Blue
Martha Atwell, Director
Ben Brady, Writer
Philip Thorn, Editor
James Fleming, Announcer
American Home Products (Kolynos, Bi-So-Dol), Sponsor
"The Case of the Suspicious Playboy"

Keen traces Archie's actions to a phone call made from Magnus's home. Magnus is startled in mid-call when Keen telephones. There's a shriek and they are cut off. The sleuths hurry to Magnus's residence.

CONTINUITY #704
Wednesday, April 8, 1942
7:15–7:30 p.m. EWT
NBC Blue
Martha Atwell, Director
Ben Brady, Writer
Philip Thorn, Editor
James Fleming, Announcer
American Home Products (Kolynos, Bi-So-Dol), Sponsor
"The Case of the Suspicious Playboy"

Mr. Ashley, an aide to Magnus, is indicted for the murder of his employer. Keen goes to a deserted farmhouse and finds Archie a prisoner. Archie tells him of gambler Tom Grogan.

CONTINUITY #705
Thursday, April 9, 1942
7:15–7:30 p.m. EWT
NBC Blue
Martha Atwell, Director
Ben Brady, Writer
Philip Thorn, Editor
James Fleming, Announcer
American Home Products (Kolynos, Bi-So-Dol), Sponsor
"The Case of the Suspicious Playboy"

Keen catches up to the sinister, crude professional gambler Grogan, who is a conspirator in the plot to extort money from wealthy Magnus Patterson. Magnus turns up alive and well.

CONTINUITY #706
Tuesday, April 14, 1942
7:15–7:30 p.m. EWT
NBC Blue
Martha Atwell, Director
Doris Halman, Writer
Philip Thorn, Editor
James Fleming, Announcer
American Home Products (Kolynos, Bi-So-Dol), Sponsor
"The Case of the Lie That Love Told"

Chicago millionaire Jared Potter disowned nephew David when he wed a poor girl 25 years ago. Jared is now receiving notes intended for David. Jared asks Keen to trace the sender and stop it.

CONTINUITY #707
Wednesday, April 15, 1942
7:15–7:30 p.m. EWT
NBC Blue
Martha Atwell, Director
Doris Halman, Writer
Philip Thorn, Editor
James Fleming, Announcer
American Home Products (Kolynos, Bi-So-Dol), Sponsor
"The Case of the Lie That Love Told"

Gay, David's child, is the sender. Now a helpless invalid, David told Gay that he and Jared reconciled, and he now lives with his uncle. Gay married poor boy Jock Anderson, whom she loved. Keen is in Chicago.

CONTINUITY #708
Thursday, April 16, 1942
7:15–7:30 p.m. EWT
NBC Blue
Martha Atwell, Director
Doris Halman, Writer
Philip Thorn, Editor

James Fleming, Announcer
American Home Products (Kolynos, Bi-So-Dol), Sponsor
"The Case of the Lie That Love Told"

David saw Gay wed and then disappeared in Chicago, without funds or any prospect of earning a living. Mr. Keen calls on Chicago banker Andrew Forsythe, once David's best friend.

CONTINUITY #709
Tuesday, April 21, 1942
7:15–7:30 p.m. EWT
NBC Blue
Martha Atwell, Director
Doris Halman, Writer
Philip Thorn, Editor
James Fleming, Announcer
American Home Products (Kolynos, Bi-So-Dol), Sponsor
"The Case of the Lie That Love Told"

Keen finds David. In a waiting room at the Keen and Co. Chicago office, Gay Anderson and her father again see one another. The breach between Jared and David is healed.

CONTINUITY #710
Wednesday, April 22, 1942
7:15–7:30 p.m. EWT
NBC Blue
Martha Atwell, Director
John Martin, Writer
Philip Thorn, Editor
James Fleming, Announcer
American Home Products (Kolynos, Bi-So-Dol), Sponsor
"The Case of the Girl with a Secret Fear"

Rich, beautiful New York debutante Elaine Hamilton vanishes while on horseback on the bridle path in Central Park. Her father George and fiancé Lt. Richard Calkins contact Keen.

CONTINUITY #711
Thursday, April 23, 1942
7:15–7:30 p.m. EWT
NBC Blue
Martha Atwell, Director
John Martin, Writer
Philip Thorn, Editor
James Fleming, Announcer
American Home Products (Kolynos, Bi-So-Dol), Sponsor
"The Case of the Girl with a Secret Fear"

Elaine feared Harry Jasper. A photo convinces Keen that Jasper was at the riding academy when her horse returned without her. A cabbie had earlier picked up some of Elaine's street clothes from the house.

CONTINUITY #712
Tuesday, April 28, 1942
7:15–7:30 p.m. EWT
NBC Blue
Martha Atwell, Director
John Martin, Writer
Philip Thorn, Editor
James Fleming, Announcer
American Home Products (Kolynos, Bi-So-Dol), Sponsor
"The Case of the Girl with a Secret Fear"

Jasper knocks out Mike Clancy. Keen boards a plane to Pennsylvania to see Mary Blodget, Elaine's former nurse. He thinks Mary is the key to solving the mystery.

CONTINUITY #713
Wednesday, April 29, 1942
7:15–7:30 p.m. EWT
NBC Blue
Martha Atwell, Director
John Martin, Writer
Philip Thorn, Editor
James Fleming, Announcer
American Home Products (Kolynos, Bi-So-Dol), Sponsor
"The Case of the Girl with a Secret Fear"

Keen finds Elaine Hamilton and restores her to Lt. Richard Calkins. It turns out that Harry Jasper was a fortune hunter who would go to any lengths to secure an opportunity to live on a grand scale.

CONTINUITY #714
Thursday, April 30, 1942
7:15–7:30 p.m. EWT
NBC Blue
Martha Atwell, Director
Ben Brady, Writer
Philip Thorn, Editor
James Fleming, Announcer
American Home Products (Kolynos, Bi-So-Dol), Sponsor
"The Case of the Soldier Who Didn't Return"

Soldier Ted Fellowes vanishes from Emma

Harlan's estate in northern New Jersey. Janet Finchley, Emma's social secretary, summons Mr. Keen to investigate. He and Mike Clancy drive to New Jersey.

CONTINUITY #715
Tuesday, May 5, 1942
7:15–7:30 p.m. EWT
NBC Blue
Martha Atwell, Director
Ben Brady, Writer
Philip Thorn, Editor
James Fleming, Announcer
American Home Products (Kolynos, Bi-So-Dol), Sponsor
"The Case of the Soldier Who Didn't Return"
   Ted went to visit Janet once more before she wed Emma's son William. The Harlans went away for the weekend. Ted and Janet argued, and he disappeared shortly thereafter.

CONTINUITY #716
Wednesday, May 6, 1942
7:15–7:30 p.m. EWT
NBC Blue
Martha Atwell, Director
Ben Brady, Writer
Philip Thorn, Editor
James Fleming, Announcer
American Home Products (Kolynos, Bi-So-Dol), Sponsor
"The Case of the Soldier Who Didn't Return"
   The Harlans return and claim they've never met any of Janet's friends. Keen encounters several mysterious situations that defy explanation — situations that cast the Harlans in a suspicious light.

CONTINUITY #717
Thursday, May 7, 1942
7:15–7:30 p.m. EWT
NBC Blue
Martha Atwell, Director
Ben Brady, Writer
Philip Thorn, Editor
James Fleming, Announcer
American Home Products (Kolynos, Bi-So-Dol), Sponsor
"The Case of the Soldier Who Didn't Return"
   Keen learns that William isn't Emma Harlan's son at all. William surprises Keen, firing a gun at him. Mike Clancy breaks in. Ted is found safe, and it seems that Janet will shift fiancés.

CONTINUITY #718
Tuesday, May 12, 1942
7:15–7:30 p.m. EWT
NBC Blue
Martha Atwell, Director
Ben Brady, Writer
Philip Thorn, Editor
James Fleming, Announcer
American Home Products (Kolynos, Bi-So-Dol), Sponsor
"The Case of the Broken Promise"
   In Philadelphia Mr. Keen and Miss Ellis meet ex–Keen and Co. operative Tom Kennedy. Tom's daughter Evelyn has vanished, leaving a farewell note. He's ailing, and she has been his caretaker.

CONTINUITY #719
Wednesday, May 13, 1942
7:15–7:30 p.m. EWT
NBC Blue
Martha Atwell, Director
Ben Brady, Writer
Philip Thorn, Editor
James Fleming, Announcer
American Home Products (Kolynos, Bi-So-Dol), Sponsor
"The Case of the Broken Promise"
   Evelyn borrowed sister Sylvia's car. Sylvia had told her that she would take Tom into their home soon, but her spouse opposed it. Evelyn and beau Ed Benton had a fight. The car is found in the bay.

CONTINUITY #720
Thursday, May 14, 1942
7:15–7:30 p.m. EWT
NBC Blue
Martha Atwell, Director
Ben Brady, Writer
Editor's name omitted
James Fleming, Announcer
American Home Products (Kolynos, Bi-So-Dol), Sponsor
"The Case of the Broken Promise"
   Keen learns that when Sylvia's spouse refused to let Tom live with them, Evelyn couldn't accept Ed's proposal. Sylvia claims

that Ed never intended to marry Evelyn, but he states otherwise.

CONTINUITY #721
Tuesday, May 19, 1942
7:15–7:30 p.m. EWT
NBC Blue
Martha Atwell, Director
Ben Brady, Writer
Philip Thorn, Editor
James Fleming, Announcer
American Home Products (Kolynos, Bi-So-Dol), Sponsor
"The Case of the Broken Promise"
 The truth comes to light. Mr. Keen and Ed visit a government office in Washington. Evelyn reappears and is restored to her place in the family — and with Edward.

CONTINUITY #722
Wednesday, May 20, 1942
7:15–7:30 p.m. EWT
NBC Blue
Martha Atwell, Director
Jerome D. Ross, Writer
Philip Thorn, Editor
James Fleming, Announcer
American Home Products (Kolynos, Bi-So-Dol), Sponsor
"The Case of the People Who Didn't Exist"
 Eccentric Jeremy Cartwright, age 82, lives in a weird castle by the Hudson. He thought daughter Kathryn died, but people arrive to tell him she's alive. A nephew says he's nuts.

CONTINUITY #723
Thursday, May 21, 1942
7:15–7:30 p.m. EWT
NBC Blue
Martha Atwell, Director
Jerome D. Ross, Writer
Philip Thorn, Editor
James Fleming, Announcer
American Home Products (Kolynos, Bi-So-Dol), Sponsor
"The Case of the People Who Didn't Exist"
 The old man's daughter *is* dead, so Keen drops the case, believing him to be senile. Now, in Keen's office, Jeremy's nephew Henry, and his wife Leona, clarify their future plans.

CONTINUITY #724
Tuesday, May 26, 1942
7:15–7:30 p.m. EWT
NBC Blue
Martha Atwell, Director
Jerome D. Ross, Writer
Philip Thorn, Editor
James Fleming, Announcer
American Home Products (Kolynos, Bi-So-Dol), Sponsor
"The Case of the People Who Didn't Exist"
 Keen and Mike Clancy learn that Jeremy is sane after all, and that Henry intends to obtain the old man's fortune by faking various incidents that make him appear crazy. Henry holds the sleuths prisoner.

CONTINUITY #725
Wednesday, May 27, 1942
7:15–7:30 p.m. EWT
NBC Blue
Martha Atwell, Director
Jerome D. Ross, Writer
Philip Thorn, Editor
James Fleming, Announcer
American Home Products (Kolynos, Bi-So-Dol), Sponsor
"The Case of the People Who Didn't Exist"
 In court, a legal hearing is under way to adjudge Jeremy's sanity. Henry testifies. Keen and Clancy free themselves and expose the nefarious plot. The court declares Jeremy sane.

CONTINUITY #726
Thursday, May 28, 1942
7:15–7:30 p.m. EWT
NBC Blue
Martha Atwell, Director
Jerome D. Ross, Writer
Philip Thorn, Editor
James Fleming, Announcer
American Home Products (Kolynos, Bi-So-Dol), Sponsor
"The Case of the Worst Boy in Town"
 Ronny Henderson, age 14, vanishes. His mother says he's a good kid, but his father claims he's the worst boy in town — a school bully who runs with a gang of toughs. The father thinks Ronny was involved in a robbery.

CONTINUITY #727
Tuesday, June 2, 1942

7:15–7:30 p.m. EWT
NBC Blue
Martha Atwell, Director
Jerome D. Ross, Writer
Philip Thorn, Editor
James Fleming, Announcer
American Home Products (Kolynos, Bi-So-Dol), Sponsor
"The Case of the Worst Boy in Town"

Keen goes to Killsboro Falls. He thinks Ronny has reformed and abandoned his wild ways. Keen goes to Ronny's dad's office, where he meets with Marvin Brown, owner of the robbed warehouse.

CONTINUITY #728
Wednesday, June 3, 1942
7:15–7:30 p.m. EWT
NBC Blue
Martha Atwell, Director
Jerome D. Ross, Writer
Philip Thorn, Editor
James Fleming, Announcer
American Home Products (Kolynos, Bi-So-Dol), Sponsor
"The Case of the Worst Boy in Town"

Keen proves Ronny innocent and fingers the culprits, Joe and Rusty, a pair of tough East End kids. They return the stolen goods, and Keen draws a neat conclusion about Ronny's whereabouts.

CONTINUITY #729
Thursday, June 4, 1942
7:15–7:30 p.m. EWT
NBC Blue
Martha Atwell, Director
Jerome D. Ross, Writer
Philip Thorn, Editor
James Fleming, Announcer
American Home Products (Kolynos, Bi-So-Dol), Sponsor
"The Case of the Worst Boy in Town"

Keen thinks Ronny will join the Navy after a teacher he admired was killed in action. Keen notifies Naval authorities. Ronny offers himself in San Francisco, proving he did indeed reform.

CONTINUITY #730
Tuesday, June 9, 1942
7:15–7:30 p.m. EWT
NBC Blue
Martha Atwell, Director
Ben Brady, Writer
Philip Thorn, Editor
James Fleming, Announcer
American Home Products (Kolynos, Bi-So-Dol), Sponsor
"The Case of the Perfect Alibi"

Cynthia Masters, traveling from Boston to New York to settle her late foster father's will, vanishes. Toby Craig, Cynthia's sweetheart, left her at an uncle's home; but the relative denies it. Keen finds proof that she was there.

CONTINUITY #731
Wednesday, June 10, 1942
7:15–7:30 p.m. EWT
NBC Blue
Martha Atwell, Director
Ben Brady, Writer
Philip Thorn, Editor
James Fleming, Announcer
American Home Products (Kolynos, Bi-So-Dol), Sponsor
"The Case of the Perfect Alibi"

Keen learns that Uncle Clarence Masters has boarded a plane for New York. Toby takes a long-distance phone call from her that Keen traces to New York.

CONTINUITY #732
Thursday, June 11, 1942
7:15–7:30 p.m. EWT
NBC Blue
Martha Atwell, Director
Ben Brady, Writer
Philip Thorn, Editor
James Fleming, Announcer
American Home Products (Kolynos, Bi-So-Dol), Sponsor
"The Case of the Perfect Alibi"

At lawyer Warren Hobson's office Keen asks permission to inspect some stock certificates. Hobson hedges. Hobson invites Keen and Toby to attend a play as his guests.

CONTINUITY #733
Tuesday, June 16, 1942
7:15–7:30 p.m. EWT
NBC Blue
Martha Atwell, Director
Ben Brady, Writer

Philip Thorn, Editor
James Fleming, Announcer
American Home Products (Kolynos, Bi-So-Dol), Sponsor
"The Case of the Perfect Alibi"

Keen realizes that there is something important behind Hobson's invitation to see a play. He finds Cynthia and unravels the story of her disappearance. It isn't what it appeared.

CONTINUITY #734
Wednesday, June 17, 1942
7:15–7:30 p.m. EWT
NBC Blue
Martha Atwell, Director
Ben Brady, Writer
Philip Thorn, Editor
James Fleming, Announcer
American Home Products (Kolynos, Bi-So-Dol), Sponsor
"The Case of the Unwanted Career"

Actor Wellsley Carter vanishes. Actress Jeanne Pancoast says her sister Lenore loves him. Jeanne asks Keen's help. Lenore collapses and tells Keen that Jeanne took Wellsley away from her.

CONTINUITY #735
Thursday, June 18, 1942
7:15–7:30 p.m. EWT
NBC Blue
Martha Atwell, Director
Ben Brady, Writer
Philip Thorn, Editor
James Fleming, Announcer
American Home Products (Kolynos, Bi-So-Dol), Sponsor
"The Case of the Unwanted Career"

Keen chastises Jeanne for failing to disclose the condition of her affair. When he threatens to discontinue the case, she implores him to listen, for she's anxious to confess.

CONTINUITY #736
Tuesday, June 23, 1942
7:15–7:30 p.m. EWT
NBC Blue
Martha Atwell, Director
Ben Brady, Writer
Philip Thorn, Editor
James Fleming, Announcer
American Home Products (Kolynos, Bi-So-Dol), Sponsor
"The Case of the Unwanted Career"

Wellsley had experienced a change in attitude toward Lenore, prompting her collapse. Lenore thought Jeanne was behind his change of heart, but Keen traces the reason to producer John Stillman.

CONTINUITY #737
Wednesday, June 24, 1942
7:15–7:30 p.m. EWT
NBC Blue
Martha Atwell, Director
Ben Brady, Writer
Philip Thorn, Editor
James Fleming, Announcer
American Home Products (Kolynos, Bi-So-Dol), Sponsor
"The Case of the Unwanted Career"

Mr. Keen visits Stillman's office. He straightens out all the complicated pieces of the puzzle, and restores the lives of the two sisters and Carter, who finally surfaces.

CONTINUITY #738
Thursday, June 25, 1942
7:15–7:30 p.m. EWT
NBC Blue
Martha Atwell, Director
Ben Brady, Writer
Philip Thorn, Editor
James Fleming, Announcer
American Home Products (Kolynos, Bi-So-Dol), Sponsor
"The Case of the Doctor and the Mummy"

Dr. Carson Lundeen vanishes after buying a mummy from a museum. A month ago a friend did the same thing — and likewise disappeared. Museum operator Frohlich claims this is the result of a curse on mummy owners.

CONTINUITY #739
Tuesday, June 30, 1942
7:15–7:30 p.m. EWT
NBC Blue
Martha Atwell, Director
Ben Brady, Writer
Philip Thorn, Editor
James Fleming, Announcer
American Home Products (Kolynos, Bi-So-Dol), Sponsor

"The Case of the Doctor and the Mummy"

Paul Redman, suitor of Polly Lundeen (Dr. Lundeen's daughter), won't accept this malarkey. Mrs. Dillon, wife of the friend who vanished a month ago, saw the mummy and said it had her spouse's face.

CONTINUITY #740
Wednesday, July 1, 1942
7:15–7:30 p.m. EWT
NBC Blue
Martha Atwell, Director
Ben Brady, Writer
Philip Thorn, Editor
James Fleming, Announcer
American Home Products (Kolynos, Bi-So-Dol), Sponsor
"The Case of the Doctor and the Mummy"

Keen obtains entrance to the museum and examines the mummy. He finds evidence that implicates Frohlich. When Keen later visits Frohlich, the villain serves him poisoned tea. Keen becomes dizzy, chokes and collapses.

CONTINUITY #741
Thursday, July 2, 1942
7:15–7:30 p.m. EWT
NBC Blue
Martha Atwell, Director
Ben Brady, Writer
Philip Thorn, Editor
James Fleming, Announcer
American Home Products (Kolynos, Bi-So-Dol), Sponsor
"The Case of the Doctor and the Mummy"

The tables are turned when Keen revives. Frohlich is put away, and Dr. Lundeen, appearing thin and weak, is found alive.

CONTINUITY #742
Tuesday, July 7, 1942
7:15–7:30 p.m. EWT
NBC Blue
Martha Atwell, Director
John T. W. Martin, Writer
Philip Thorn, Editor
James Fleming, Announcer
American Home Products (Kolynos, Bi-So-Dol), Sponsor
"The Case of the Bottomless Lake"

Dr. Alfred Tompkins, of Grand Mountain in the Adirondacks, is missing. Daughter Nancy says that both her stepmother and her own beau, Robert Allen, oppose her father's secret lab tests. To complicate matters, Dr. Tompkins had argued with Joe Daly.

CONTINUITY #743
Wednesday, July 8, 1942
7:15–7:30 p.m. EWT
NBC Blue
Martha Atwell, Director
John T. W. Martin, Writer
Philip Thorn, Editor
James Fleming, Announcer
American Home Products (Kolynos, Bi-So-Dol), Sponsor
"The Case of the Bottomless Lake"

Allen warns Keen to back off. Keen confronts Daly, who says the lake is bottomless and never gives up what it receives. Keen hears some strange tales. He chats with Mike Clancy.

CONTINUITY #744
Thursday, July 9, 1942
7:15–7:30 p.m. EWT
NBC Blue
Martha Atwell, Director
John T. W. Martin, Writer
Philip Thorn, Editor
James Fleming, Announcer
American Home Products (Kolynos, Bi-So-Dol), Sponsor
"The Case of the Bottomless Lake"

Keen finds a bleached spot on Tompkins' boat and — across the lake — a bush with bleached leaves. A chemical that bleached the two is in the doctor's lab. Allen removes the chemical.

CONTINUITY #745
Tuesday, July 14, 1942
7:15–7:30 p.m. EWT
NBC Blue
Martha Atwell, Director
John T. W. Martin, Writer
Philip Thorn, Editor
James Fleming, Announcer
American Home Products (Kolynos, Bi-So-Dol), Sponsor
"The Case of the Bottomless Lake"

It takes a while, but the tracer establishes what happened to the gentle, kindly Dr. Tompkins, the small-town physician involved in research. Keen rescues him from his predicament.

CONTINUITY #746
Wednesday, July 15, 1942
7:15–7:30 p.m. EWT
NBC Blue
Martha Atwell, Director
Ben Brady, Writer
Philip Thorn, Editor
James Fleming, Announcer
American Home Products (Kolynos, Bi-So-Dol), Sponsor
"The Case of the Killer Who Struck Again"
   Helen Wilson vanishes from a Tulsa, Oklahoma, ranch her spouse and his sister Cora own. Someone tried to kill Helen. For an instant, Keen and Mitch see Helen in a window. A gun fires.

CONTINUITY #747
Thursday, July 16, 1942
7:15–7:30 p.m. EWT
NBC Blue
Martha Atwell, Director
Ben Brady, Writer
Philip Thorn, Editor
James Fleming, Announcer
American Home Products (Kolynos, Bi-So-Dol), Sponsor
"The Case of the Killer Who Struck Again"
   In Helen's room Keen and Clancy find Cora and supervisor Philip Ensley. Foreman Lud Kilgore enters. Keen finds a .22 caliber bullet that was fired earlier. It fits Cora's gun.

CONTINUITY #748
Tuesday, July 21, 1942
7:15–7:30 p.m. EWT
NBC Blue
Martha Atwell, Director
Ben Brady, Writer
Philip Thorn, Editor
James Fleming, Announcer
American Home Products (Kolynos, Bi-So-Dol), Sponsor
"The Case of the Killer Who Struck Again"
   Keen wants to know more about Ensley and Kilgore. He and Clancy search Lud's bunkhouse and find a locked duffle bag. They open it and, to their amazement, discover a woman's head.

CONTINUITY #749
Wednesday, July 22, 1942
7:15–7:30 p.m. EWT
NBC Blue
Martha Atwell, Director
Ben Brady, Writer
Philip Thorn, Editor
James Fleming, Announcer
American Home Products (Kolynos, Bi-So-Dol), Sponsor
"The Case of the Killer Who Struck Again"
   The mystery of the woman's head and Helen Wilson's strange disappearance is solved when the tracer finds Helen very much alive. He's able to explain a number of weird events.

CONTINUITY #750
Thursday, July 23, 1942
7:15–7:30 p.m. EWT
NBC Blue
Martha Atwell, Director
Ben Brady, Writer
Philip Thorn, Editor
James Fleming, Announcer
American Home Products (Kolynos, Bi-So-Dol), Sponsor
"The Case of the Inherited Fear"
   Keen attends the launch of a Naval ship named for the late father of Captain Arnold Bradley, his friend. Five Bradley sons served in the Navy. Released from the service because of his claustrophobia, Ken, Arnold Bradley's son, disappears.

CONTINUITY #751
Tuesday, July 28, 1942
7:15–7:30 p.m. EWT
NBC Blue
Martha Atwell, Director
Ben Brady, Writer
Philip Thorn, Editor
James Fleming, Announcer
American Home Products (Kolynos, Bi-So-Dol), Sponsor
"The Case of the Inherited Fear"
   Ken's mother says he inherited his condition from her. Uncle Edmond Bradley had criticized him for tainting the legacy. Edmond claims that Ken was killed when a car and train collided.

CONTINUITY #752
Wednesday, July 29, 1942

7:15–7:30 p.m. EWT
NBC Blue
Martha Atwell, Director
Ben Brady, Writer
Philip Thorn, Editor
James Fleming, Announcer
American Home Products (Kolynos, Bi-So-Dol), Sponsor
"The Case of the Inherited Fear"

To everyone's surprise, Ken is alive. Gloria Linton, his sweetheart, and Mr. Keen find him trying to overcome his fear by working underground in a Pennsylvania mining camp.

CONTINUITY #753
Thursday, July 30, 1942
7:15–7:30 p.m. EWT
NBC Blue
Martha Atwell, Director
Ben Brady, Writer
Philip Thorn, Editor
James Fleming, Announcer
American Home Products (Kolynos, Bi-So-Dol), Sponsor
"The Case of the Inherited Fear"

An alarm sounds—there has been a cave-in; 140 men are trapped below. Keen tells Ken that he must go save the men. Ken overcomes his fear and does what must be done, saving all the miners.

CONTINUITY #754
Tuesday, August 4, 1942
7:15–7:30 p.m. EWT
NBC Blue
Martha Atwell, Director
Ben Brady, Writer
Philip Thorn, Editor
James Fleming, Announcer
American Home Products (Kolynos, Bi-So-Dol), Sponsor
"The Case of the Girl Who Never Forgot"

Sixteen-year-old Linda Pine, adopted by her overbearing grandmother, Mrs. Nelson, is gone. She had visited the town wastrel, Milo Kenyon, since picked up for robbing Nelson's factory. Did Linda get away?

CONTINUITY #755
Wednesday, August 5, 1942
7:15–7:30 p.m. EWT
NBC Blue
Martha Atwell, Director
Ben Brady, Writer
Philip Thorn, Editor
James Fleming, Announcer
American Home Products (Kolynos, Bi-So-Dol), Sponsor
"The Case of the Girl Who Never Forgot"

Linda's father served a year in prison for theft. Grandma thinks she picked up his habits. Roger Hamilton, manager of Nelson's company, provides bail money for Milo's release.

CONTINUITY #756
Thursday, August 6, 1942
7:15–7:30 p.m. EWT
NBC Blue
Martha Atwell, Director
Ben Brady, Writer
Philip Thorn, Editor
James Fleming, Announcer
American Home Products (Kolynos, Bi-So-Dol), Sponsor
"The Case of the Girl Who Never Forgot"

Linda's mother died from the shock of her husband's theft from his mother-in-law's firm. Mr. Keen discusses the details of the case and its many ramifications with assistant Mike Clancy.

CONTINUITY #757
Tuesday, August 11, 1942
7:15–7:30 p.m. EWT
NBC Blue
Martha Atwell, Director
Ben Brady, Writer
Philip Thorn, Editor
Announcer's name omitted
American Home Products (Kolynos, Bi-So-Dol), Sponsor
"The Case of the Girl Who Never Forgot"

Mr. Keen is successful in locating Linda Pine and restoring her to her family. He identifies the guilty party in the theft at Mrs. Nelson's business. Justice is meted out.

CONTINUITY #758
Wednesday, August 12, 1942
7:15–7:30 p.m. EWT
NBC Blue
Martha Atwell, Director
Ben Brady, Writer
Philip Thorn, Editor

James Fleming, Announcer
American Home Products (Kolynos, Bi-So-Dol), Sponsor
"The Case of the Grieving Cat"
   Reamer Vander Horn, age 78, vanished from his estate. Daughter Dora thinks that butler Haven cast a spell, giving the old man a cat. Haven thinks Dora is to blame. Her sister Pam agrees with him.

CONTINUITY #759
Thursday, August 13, 1942
7:15–7:30 p.m. EWT
NBC Blue
Martha Atwell, Director
Ben Brady, Writer
Philip Thorn, Editor
James Fleming, Announcer
American Home Products (Kolynos, Bi-So-Dol), Sponsor
"The Case of the Grieving Cat"
   Pam, a tad off, claims that Dora has a room in which "she puts people she doesn't like." Mr. Keen finds it and becomes locked in with Pam, who handcuffs him to a wall. She then attempts to kill him.

CONTINUITY #760
Tuesday, August 18, 1942
7:15–7:30 p.m. EWT
NBC Blue
James Church, Director
Ben Brady, Writer
Philip Thorn, Editor
James Fleming, Announcer
American Home Products (Kolynos, Bi-So-Dol), Sponsor
"The Case of the Grieving Cat"
   Only Reamer and Haven are aware of a tunnel that leads to a tree-covered knoll—upon which 12 blighted trees were filled with cement to save them. Keen meets Reamer's nephew, who threatens to kill him.

CONTINUITY #761
Wednesday, August 19, 1942
7:15–7:30 p.m. EWT
NBC Blue
James Church, Director
Ben Brady, Writer
Philip Thorn, Editor
James Fleming, Announcer
American Home Products (Kolynos, Bi-So-Dol), Sponsor
"The Case of the Grieving Cat"
   Reamer Vander Horn does *not* return alive in the exciting finish. Mr. Keen finds him in one of the hollow trees.
   (Note: This plot was reprised years later as a half-hour episode.)

CONTINUITY #762
Thursday, August 20, 1942
7:15–7:30 p.m. EWT
NBC Blue
James Church, Director
Ben Brady, Writer
Philip Thorn, Editor
James Fleming, Announcer
American Home Products (Kolynos, Bi-So-Dol), Sponsor
"The Case of the Highest Calling"
   Mr. and Mrs. Henry Nesibit ask Keen to find daughter Natalie, age 18. She went to Kenosha, New York, a week ago, and left by train three days later for home—but never arrived. They've had one letter from her since.

CONTINUITY #763
Tuesday, August 25, 1942
7:15–7:30 p.m. EWT
NBC Blue
James Church, Director
Ben Brady, Writer
Philip Thorn, Editor
James Fleming, Announcer
American Home Products (Kolynos, Bi-So-Dol), Sponsor
"The Case of the Highest Calling"
   Natalie's note said not to worry, that she might never come back. She went to see a girlfriend but applied for—and got—a job in an airplane factory. Then she was injured while on the job.

CONTINUITY #764
Wednesday, August 26, 1942
7:15–7:30 p.m. EWT
NBC Blue
James Church, Director
Ben Brady, Writer
Philip Thorn, Editor
James Fleming, Announcer
American Home Products (Kolynos, Bi-So-Dol), Sponsor

"The Case of the Highest Calling"
 Natalie boarded a train, then hurried off, taking a taxi to a tourist camp. Enroute, the cabbie left the car briefly to offer help at an accident scene; he came back and she was gone.

CONTINUITY #765
Thursday, August 27, 1942
7:15–7:30 p.m. EWT
NBC Blue
James Church, Director
Ben Brady, Writer
Philip Thorn, Editor
James Fleming, Announcer
American Home Products (Kolynos, Bi-So-Dol), Sponsor
"The Case of the Highest Calling"
 Natalie is found. The reasons for her erratic moves of the last week are examined. She is reconciled with her parents, who are deeply thankful to Keen for returning her safely.

CONTINUITY #766
Tuesday, September 1, 1942
7:15–7:30 p.m. EWT
NBC Blue
James Church, Director
John T. W. Martin, Writer
Philip Thorn, Editor
James Fleming, Announcer
American Home Products (Kolynos, Bi-So-Dol), Sponsor
"The Case of the Daily Flowers"
 While trying to decode a secret explosive our government has acquired, engineer George Randall disappears. Meanwhile, Randall talks to Al Borden in a mansion just north of New York.

CONTINUITY #767
Wednesday, September 2, 1942
7:15–7:30 p.m. EWT
NBC Blue
James Church, Director
John T. W. Martin, Writer
Philip Thorn, Editor
James Fleming, Announcer
American Home Products (Kolynos, Bi-So-Dol), Sponsor
"The Case of the Daily Flowers"
 Randall was lured away by a forged letter from a competitor. He is working tenaciously on breaking the coded formula. Al Borden is with him, but has no idea he's taking part in seditious activity.

CONTINUITY #768
Thursday, September 3, 1942
7:15–7:30 p.m. EWT
NBC Blue
James Church, Director
John T. W. Martin, Writer
Philip Thorn, Editor
James Fleming, Announcer
American Home Products (Kolynos, Bi-So-Dol), Sponsor
"The Case of the Daily Flowers"
 Keen reports to the employer from a drug store phone booth. The line goes dead. Clancy trails Borden to a nearby house. Clancy is knocked unconscious, bound, gagged, and locked in a closet.

CONTINUITY #769
Tuesday, September 8, 1942
7:15–7:30 p.m. EWT
NBC Blue
Martha Atwell, Director
John T. W. Martin, Writer
Philip Thorn, Editor
James Fleming, Announcer
American Home Products (Kolynos, Bi-So-Dol), Sponsor
"The Case of the Daily Flowers"
 Mr. Keen locates George Randall before the code secrets fall into the opposition's hands. Mrs. Randall is reunited with George, who never even realized the danger.

CONTINUITY #770
Wednesday, September 9, 1942
7:15–7:30 p.m. EWT
NBC Blue
Martha Atwell, Director
Ben Brady, Writer
Philip Thorn, Editor
James Fleming, Announcer
American Home Products (Kolynos, Bi-So-Dol), Sponsor
"The Case of the Soldier and His Bride"
 Ellen Carstairs weds GI Tod Driscoll, goes to pack for their trip and fails to meet him as planned. Her stepmother serves him with annulment papers and puts their home up for sale.

CONTINUITY #771
Thursday, September 10, 1942
7:15–7:30 p.m. EWT
NBC Blue
Martha Atwell, Director
Ben Brady, Writer
Philip Thorn, Editor
James Fleming, Announcer
American Home Products (Kolynos, Bi-So-Dol), Sponsor
"The Case of the Soldier and His Bride"
   Through a ruse, Keen has Mrs. Carstairs' lawyer lead him to the home of Alva Colby, a career blackmailer. Keen and Clancy wait in a cab for the attorney to depart.

CONTINUITY #772
Tuesday, September 15, 1942
7:15–7:30 p.m. EWT
NBC Blue
Martha Atwell, Director
Ben Brady, Writer
Philip Thorn, Editor
James Fleming, Announcer
American Home Products (Kolynos, Bi-So-Dol), Sponsor
"The Case of the Soldier and His Bride"
   Through executing an intricate plan, Mr. Keen discovers that Desmond, the lawyer, engineered the scheming scenario. Threatened by implication, Mrs. Carstairs agrees to tell the whole story.

CONTINUITY #773
Wednesday, September 16, 1942
7:15–7:30 p.m. EWT
NBC Blue
Martha Atwell, Director
Ben Brady, Writer
Philip Thorn, Editor
James Fleming, Announcer
American Home Products (Kolynos, Bi-So-Dol), Sponsor
"The Case of the Soldier and His Bride"
   Ellen is found unharmed and returned safely to her spouse, Tod Driscoll, who loves her dearly. Desmond is held accountable for his conniving and using Mrs. Carstairs as his pawn.

CONTINUITY #774
Thursday, September 17, 1942
7:15–7:30 p.m. EWT
NBC Blue
Martha Atwell, Director
Lawrence M. Klee, Writer
Philip Thorn, Editor
James Fleming, Announcer
American Home Products (Kolynos, Bi-So-Dol), Sponsor
"The Case of the Second Marriage"
   Lorna Haydon, 13-year-old daughter of wealthy lawyer John Haydon, is missing. Last seen in the garden at home, she resented her dad's recent second marriage, perhaps accounting for her disappearance.
   Note: This episode is the first to be penned by Lawrence M. Klee, who was destined to become the most prolific and infamous Mr. Keen author in the program's long history. With infrequent exceptions, Klee continued writing the series until it left the air forever on September 26, 1955.

CONTINUITY #775
Tuesday, September 22, 1942
7:15–7:30 p.m. EWT
NBC Blue
Martha Atwell, Director
Lawrence M. Klee, Writer
Philip Thorn, Editor
James Fleming, Announcer
American Home Products (Kolynos, Bi-So-Dol), Sponsor
"The Case of the Second Marriage"
   John Haydon continues telling his story to Mr. Keen in his office. The major focus is on Lorna's antipathy toward her stepmom. It appears to be a strong motive for her departure.

CONTINUITY #776
Wednesday, September 23, 1942
7:15–7:30 p.m. EWT
NBC Blue
Martha Atwell, Director
Lawrence M. Klee, Writer
Philip Thorn, Editor
James Fleming, Announcer
American Home Products (Kolynos, Bi-So-Dol), Sponsor
"The Case of the Second Marriage"
   At dawn Mr. Keen and Mike Clancy approach the caretaker's cottage at Larchdale Cemetery. Lorna is there visiting her mother's

grave. Stepmother Fran Haydon comforts the grieving child.

CONTINUITY #777
Thursday, September 24, 1942
7:15–7:30 p.m. EWT
NBC Blue
Martha Atwell, Director
Lawrence M. Klee, Writer
Philip Thorn, Editor
James Fleming, Announcer
American Home Products (Kolynos, Bi-So-Dol), Sponsor
"The Case of Mr. Keen's Disguise"

Peter Hendricks, a farmer's son, disappears. Neighbor Silas Bender says he stole silver from him, the goods are returned and Hendricks' farm is sold to him for peanuts, so he might forget the crime.

CONTINUITY #778
Tuesday, September 29, 1942
7:15–7:30 p.m. EWT
NBC Blue
Martha Atwell, Director
Lawrence M. Klee, Writer
Philip Thorn, Editor
James Fleming, Announcer
American Home Products (Kolynos, Bi-So-Dol), Sponsor
"The Case of Mr. Keen's Disguise"

A heart ailment earns Peter a Four F classification from his draft board, disappointing the young man, who wants to enter the Armed Forces. Keen and Clancy are busy contacting recruiting stations.

CONTINUITY #779
Wednesday, September 30, 1942
7:15–7:30 p.m. EWT
NBC Blue
Martha Atwell, Director
Lawrence M. Klee, Writer
Philip Thorn, Editor
James Fleming, Announcer
American Home Products (Kolynos, Bi-So-Dol), Sponsor
"The Case of Mr. Keen's Disguise"

The sleuths catch up to Peter Hendricks in the hamlet of Allentown, at an Army Recruiting office. Keen offers several suggestions as to how he might contribute to his country.

CONTINUITY #780
Thursday, October 1, 1942
7:15–7:30 p.m. EWT
NBC Blue
Martha Atwell, Director
Lawrence M. Klee, Writer
Philip Thorn, Editor
James Fleming, Announcer
American Home Products (Kolynos, Bi-So-Dol), Sponsor
"The Case of the Gentle People"

John and Emma Higgins, elderly friends of Miss Ellis, disappear. Today is their 40th wedding anniversary. Mr. Keen talks with their children, Pamela and Charles, about it.

CONTINUITY #781
Tuesday, October 6, 1942
7:15–7:30 p.m. EWT
NBC Blue
Martha Atwell, Director
Lawrence M. Klee, Writer
Philip Thorn, Editor
James Fleming, Announcer
American Home Products (Kolynos, Bi-So-Dol), Sponsor
"The Case of the Gentle People"

Mr. Keen's only clue to the old couple's whereabouts is a book of mementoes the kindly couple kept for 40 years. Meanwhile, Pamela and Charles seem to exude animosity.

CONTINUITY #782
Wednesday, October 7, 1942
7:15–7:30 p.m. EWT
NBC Blue
Martha Atwell, Director
Lawrence M. Klee, Writer
Philip Thorn, Editor
James Fleming, Announcer
American Home Products (Kolynos, Bi-So-Dol), Sponsor
"The Case of the Gentle People"

Believing they were a burden to their kids, John and Emma Higgins left their home in Brooklyn. Just as Keen catches up with them in a small Fifth Avenue hotel, they slip away.

CONTINUITY #783
Thursday, October 8, 1942
7:15–7:30 p.m. EWT
NBC Blue

Martha Atwell, Director
Lawrence M. Klee, Writer
Philip Thorn, Editor
James Fleming, Announcer
American Home Products (Kolynos, Bi-So-Dol), Sponsor
"The Case of the Gentle People"

Two days later Keen goes to the home of Pamela Bridges, the married daughter, with some startling and not-so-pleasant news. The parents are located and return to their home.

CONTINUITY #784
Tuesday, October 13, 1942
7:15–7:30 p.m. EWT
NBC Blue
Martha Atwell, Director
Lawrence M. Klee, Writer
Philip Thorn, Editor
James Fleming, Announcer
American Home Products (Kolynos, Bi-So-Dol), Sponsor
"The Case of the Laughing Woman"

Edna Hillory, whose features were scarred in a train accident, disappears. Dora Thorgasen, her loyal cook and housekeeper, appeals to Mr. Keen to locate her.

CONTINUITY #785
Wednesday, October 14, 1942
7:15–7:30 p.m. EWT
NBC Blue
Martha Atwell, Director
Lawrence M. Klee, Writer
Philip Thorn, Editor
James Fleming, Announcer
American Home Products (Kolynos, Bi-So-Dol), Sponsor
"The Case of the Laughing Woman"

The disappearance is blamed on a man Edna met often on a park bench near her home. Mr. Keen locates the man, a famous surgeon who gave up his practice after going blind.

CONTINUITY #786
Thursday, October 15, 1942
7:15–7:30 p.m. EWT
NBC Blue
Martha Atwell, Director
Lawrence M. Klee, Writer
Philip Thorn, Editor
James Fleming, Announcer
American Home Products (Kolynos, Bi-So-Dol), Sponsor
"The Case of the Laughing Woman"

Edna fell in love with Dr. John Courtland, but she comes to believe that he had only led her on (a misunderstanding). Mr. Keen hopes to bring her back to the joy she thought she could never have.

CONTINUITY #787
Tuesday, October 20, 1942
7:15–7:30 p.m. EWT
NBC Blue
Martha Atwell, Director
Lawrence M. Klee, Writer
Philip Thorn, Editor
James Fleming, Announcer
American Home Products (Kolynos, Bi-So-Dol), Sponsor
"The Case of the Laughing Woman"

Still tracing Edna Hillory, Mr. Keen goes to the West Fifties in New York City, a street lined with warehouses and garages. He is determined to improve her circumstances.

CONTINUITY #788
Wednesday, October 21, 1942
7:15–7:30 p.m. EWT
NBC Blue
Martha Atwell, Director
Lawrence M. Klee, Writer
Philip Thorn, Editor
James Fleming, Announcer
American Home Products (Kolynos, Bi-So-Dol), Sponsor
"The Case of the Laughing Woman"

From New York the tracer is directed to the post office in the little town of Bentonville, New Jersey. There at last he finds Edna Hillory. He has good news to share with her.

CONTINUITY #789
Thursday, October 22, 1942
7:15–7:30 p.m. EWT
NBC Blue
Martha Atwell, Director
Lawrence M. Klee, Writer
Philip Thorn, Editor
James Fleming, Announcer
American Home Products (Kolynos, Bi-So-Dol), Sponsor
"The Case of the Laughing Woman"

Mr. Keen, Mike Clancy and Edna Hillory hurry back to New York. She's still impassive — has Keen won only a temporary victory? She's reunited with John and everything improves.

Note: This sequence is the final episode to be aired over the Blue network. The show will be heard on different days and at a different time starting the following week.

CONTINUITY #790
Wednesday, October 28, 1942
7:45–8:00 p.m. EWT
CBS
Martha Atwell, Director
Lawrence M. Klee, Writer
Philip Thorn, Editor
James Fleming, Announcer
American Home Products (Kolynos, Aerowax), Sponsor
"The Case of the Solitary Witness"

The murder of Frankie Vince, a hoodlum of long standing, brings the trial and conviction of William James. James' daughter Evelyn tells Keen that a witness saw the crime and the real murderer.

Note: This sequence was the first to be aired over the CBS network on different days and at a new time. The regular cast and sponsor remained unchanged.

CONTINUITY #791
Thursday, October 29, 1942
7:45–8:00 p.m. EWT
CBS
Martha Atwell, Director
Lawrence M. Klee, Writer
Philip Thorn, Editor
James Fleming, Announcer
American Home Products (Kolynos, Aerowax), Sponsor
"The Case of the Solitary Witness"

Mr. Keen will attempt to locate the witness and save James' life. He and Miss Ellis review the court testimony. Keen and Mike Clancy go to the street where the murder was committed.

CONTINUITY #792
Friday, October 30, 1942
7:45–8:00 p.m. EWT
CBS
Martha Atwell, Director
Lawrence M. Klee, Writer
Philip Thorn, Editor
James Fleming, Announcer
American Home Products (Kolynos, Aerowax), Sponsor
"The Case of the Solitary Witness"

The tracer is trapped in Lola Morgan's apartment, chief witness for the state. Tied to a chair, Keen faces Morgan and an accomplice, Duke, who just made an ominous phone call.

CONTINUITY #793
Wednesday, November 4, 1942
7:45–8:00 p.m. EWT
CBS
Martha Atwell, Director
Lawrence M. Klee, Writer
Philip Thorn, Editor
James Fleming, Announcer
American Home Products (Kolynos, Aerowax), Sponsor
"The Case of the Solitary Witness"

Mike Clancy rescues Mr. Keen, and, to save herself, Lola fingers the real murderer, Duke. An innocent William James will be spared and freed as the result of her testimony.

CONTINUITY #794
Thursday, November 5, 1942
7:45–8:00 p.m. EWT
CBS
Martha Atwell, Director
Lawrence M. Klee, Writer
Philip Thorn, Editor
James Fleming, Announcer
American Home Products (Kolynos, Aerowax), Sponsor
"The Case of the Father Who Didn't Understand"

After a misunderstanding and quarrel with his father, 17-year-old Ralph Hanley disappears from home. Keen finds Frank Hanley difficult to reason with, but the tracer patiently persists.

CONTINUITY #795
Friday, November 6, 1942
7:45–8:00 p.m. EWT
CBS
Martha Atwell, Director
Lawrence M. Klee, Writer
Philip Thorn, Editor
James Fleming, Announcer

American Home Products (Kolynos, Aerowax), Sponsor
"The Case of the Father Who Didn't Understand"
Knowing of the boy's love of football, Mr. Keen and Mike Clancy arrive at Cooper Stadium an hour before the annual Tate-Cooper football game. Keen thinks Ralph may be nearby.

CONTINUITY #796
Wednesday, November 11, 1942
7:45–8:00 p.m. EWT
CBS
Martha Atwell, Director
Lawrence M. Klee, Writer
Philip Thorn, Editor
James Fleming, Announcer
American Home Products (Kolynos, Aerowax), Sponsor
"The Case of the Father Who Didn't Understand"
Keen's hunch is right. He finds Ralph with Chick Donovan, a genial, athletic type who's an inspiration to Ralph. Mr. Keen facilitates some acceptance between the boy and his father.

CONTINUITY #797
Thursday, November 12, 1942
7:45–8:00 p.m. EWT
CBS
Martha Atwell, Director
Lawrence M. Klee, Writer
Philip Thorn, Editor
James Fleming, Announcer
American Home Products (Kolynos, Aerowax), Sponsor
"The Case of the Unexpected Wedding"
Philip Lawson's second marriage brings tragedy to his home. It results in the disappearance of his 14-year-old daughter, Karen, who dislikes the new union. He and new wife Marsha appeal to Mr. Keen.

CONTINUITY #798
Friday, November 13, 1942
7:45–8:00 p.m. EWT
CBS
Martha Atwell, Director
Lawrence M. Klee, Writer
Philip Thorn, Editor
James Fleming, Announcer
American Home Products (Kolynos, Aerowax), Sponsor
"The Case of the Unexpected Wedding"
Mr. Keen goes to the Lawson home in Philadelphia. Marsha tried desperately to win Karen over, but to no avail. Keen visits the home of Joan Reynolds, Karen's closest friend.

CONTINUITY #799
Wednesday, November 18, 1942
7:45–8:00 p.m. EWT
CBS
Martha Atwell, Director
Lawrence M. Klee, Writer
Philip Thorn, Editor
Announcer's name omitted
American Home Products (Kolynos, Aerowax), Sponsor
"The Case of the Unexpected Wedding"
Following clues about the disappearance of Karen Lawson, Mr. Keen and Mike Clancy proceed to Huntsville, Long Island. The two men hold a consultation at the local post office.

CONTINUITY #800
Thursday, November 19, 1942
7:45–8:00 p.m. EWT
CBS
Martha Atwell, Director
Lawrence M. Klee, Writer
Philip Thorn, Editor
James Fleming, Announcer
American Home Products (Kolynos, Aerowax), Sponsor
"The Case of the Unexpected Wedding"
Keen clears up the matter. He finds Karen, and brings a new understanding to the relationship between her and Marsha Lawson, whose marriage to Karen's father was something of a surprise.

CONTINUITY #801
Friday, November 20, 1942
7:45–8:00 p.m. EWT
CBS
Martha Atwell, Director
Lawrence M. Klee, Writer
Philip Thorn, Editor
James Fleming, Announcer
American Home Products (Kolynos, Aerowax), Sponsor

"The Case of Mr. Tweed"
Mr. Tweed, a kindly, generous philanthropist who has helped countless people, disappears. Nick Alapoupolis asks Mr. Keen to find him. A few missing stamp albums are the only clues.

CONTINUITY #802
Wednesday, November 25, 1942
7:45–8:00 p.m. EWT
CBS
Martha Atwell, Director
Lawrence M. Klee, Writer
Philip Thorn, Editor
James Fleming, Announcer
American Home Products (Kolynos, Aerowax), Sponsor
"The Case of Mr. Tweed"
In Manhattan's Chinatown several folks tell Keen of how Tweed has helped them. Knowing Tweed's love for stamp collecting, Keen places an ad in newspapers announcing a rare stamp for sale.

CONTINUITY #803
Thursday, November 26, 1942
7:45–8:00 p.m. EWT
CBS
Martha Atwell, Director
Lawrence M. Klee, Writer
Philip Thorn, Editor
James Fleming, Announcer
American Home Products (Kolynos, Aerowax), Sponsor
"The Case of Mr. Tweed"
The advertisement brings Mr. Tweed out into the open when he answers it, and his reasons for disappearing are revealed. He is overwhelmed by the public acclaim bestowed upon him by so many.

CONTINUITY #804
Friday, November 27, 1942
7:45–8:00 p.m. EWT
CBS
Martha Atwell, Director
Lawrence M. Klee, Writer
Philip Thorn, Editor
James Fleming, Announcer
American Home Products (Kolynos, Aerowax), Sponsor
"The Case of the Boy Who Whistled"
Biff Stanton, age 15, disappears following a robbery in which a grocery clerk is seriously wounded. Biff's mother asks Keen to find her son. Keen's only lead is that the boy loves to whistle.

CONTINUITY #805
Wednesday, December 2, 1942
7:45–8:00 p.m. EWT
CBS
Martha Atwell, Director
Lawrence M. Klee, Writer
Philip Thorn, Editor
James Fleming, Announcer
American Home Products (Kolynos, Aerowax), Sponsor
"The Case of the Boy Who Whistled"
Mr. Keen has good reason to think Biff is involved in the crime, with seasoned criminal Tony Grimes. Mike Clancy hurries to Keen on a shabby side street in lower Manhattan.

CONTINUITY #806
Thursday, December 3, 1942
7:45–8:00 p.m. EWT
CBS
Martha Atwell, Director
Lawrence M. Klee, Writer
Philip Thorn, Editor
James Fleming, Announcer
American Home Products (Kolynos, Aerowax), Sponsor
"The Case of the Boy Who Whistled"
Keen locates Biff Stanton and reveals the facts behind the robbery. Biff's tendency to walk on the wild side will be tempered by Rev. Alton, who will play a major role in his rehabilitation.

CONTINUITY #807
Friday, December 4, 1942
7:45–8:00 p.m. EWT
CBS
Martha Atwell, Director
Lawrence M. Klee, Writer
Philip Thorn, Editor
James Fleming, Announcer
American Home Products (Kolynos, Aerowax), Sponsor
"The Case of the Disappearance of Marcia Blair"
When Marcia Blair learns her fiancé is

missing in action, she vanishes. Her mother objected to Marcia marrying a Marine lieutenant after a brief courtship, and now Mrs. Blair seeks Mr. Keen's help in finding her daughter.

CONTINUITY #808
Wednesday, December 9, 1942
7:45–8:00 p.m. EWT
CBS
Martha Atwell, Director
Lawrence M. Klee, Writer
Philip Thorn, Editor
James Fleming, Announcer
American Home Products (Kolynos, Aerowax), Sponsor
"The Case of the Disappearance of Marcia Blair"
Marcia, bitter and resentful because her mother argued against marriage so soon, decides the course of her future. She applies at an Army Recruiting Office for enlistment.

CONTINUITY #809
Thursday, December 10, 1942
7:45–8:00 p.m. EWT
CBS
Martha Atwell, Director
Lawrence M. Klee, Writer
Philip Thorn, Editor
James Fleming, Announcer
American Home Products (Kolynos, Aerowax), Sponsor
"The Case of the Two Sisters"
Amy Travis leaves home believing the man she loves jilted her. Mrs. Travis, Amy's grandmother, and Amy's younger sister Maxine, make frantic attempts to locate the girl.

CONTINUITY #810
Friday, December 11, 1942
7:45–8:00 p.m. EWT
CBS
Martha Atwell, Director
Lawrence M. Klee, Writer
Philip Thorn, Editor
James Fleming, Announcer
American Home Products (Kolynos, Aerowax), Sponsor
"The Case of the Two Sisters"
The case becomes even more complex when Maxine vanishes, too. She stole the affections of Lt. Barry Walsh, whom Amy loves. Mr. Keen discusses it with Mrs. Travis, the grandmother.

CONTINUITY #811
Wednesday, December 16, 1942
7:45–8:00 p.m. EWT
CBS
Martha Atwell, Director
Lawrence M. Klee, Writer
Philip Thorn, Editor
Announcer's name omitted
American Home Products (Kolynos, Aerowax), Sponsor
"The Case of the Two Sisters"
The tracer learns of the death of a woman who might be Amy Travis. Thus, late in the evening Mr. Keen appears at the City Morgue.

CONTINUITY #812
Thursday, December 17, 1942
7:45–8:00 p.m. EWT
CBS
Martha Atwell, Director
Lawrence M. Klee, Writer
Philip Thorn, Editor
James Fleming, Announcer
American Home Products (Kolynos, Aerowax), Sponsor
"The Case of the Two Sisters"
Amy isn't dead. Keen finds her and tries to persuade her to return home. Maxine appears at Amy's small hotel room in downtown New York. The two estranged sisters now face each other.

CONTINUITY #813
Friday, December 18, 1942
7:45–8:00 p.m. EWT
CBS
Martha Atwell, Director
Lawrence M. Klee, Writer
Philip Thorn, Editor
James Fleming, Announcer
American Home Products (Kolynos, Aerowax), Sponsor
"The Case of the Two Sisters"
A throng of characters appears—Mr. Keen, Miss Ellis, Mike Clancy, Amy, Maxine, Mrs. Travis and Barry Walsh. The big mess is straightened out, and the two sisters reconnect.

CONTINUITY #814
Wednesday, December 23, 1942

7:45–8:00 p.m. EWT
CBS
Martha Atwell, Director
Lawrence M. Klee, Writer
Philip Thorn, Editor
James Fleming, Announcer
American Home Products (Kolynos, Aerowax), Sponsor
"The Case of Mr. Keen's Dilemma"
　　Eight-year-old Betty B. Robinson asks Mr. Keen to locate Santa Claus. She and Willie Green, age 9, who also lives at the Crandall Street Orphanage, say the gentleman has been missing a long time.

CONTINUITY #815
Thursday, December 24, 1942
7:45–8:00 p.m. EWT
CBS
Martha Atwell, Director
Lawrence M. Klee, Writer
Philip Thorn, Editor
James Fleming, Announcer
American Home Products (Kolynos, Aerowax), Sponsor
"The Case of Mr. Keen's Dilemma"
　　On Christmas Eve Keen and Clancy visit one of the large department stores shortly before closing time. Later at home, Keen puts the finishing touches on a well-known costume.

CONTINUITY #816
Friday, December 25, 1942
7:45–8:00 p.m. EWT
CBS
Martha Atwell, Director
Lawrence M. Klee, Writer
Philip Thorn, Editor
James Fleming, Announcer
American Home Products (Kolynos), Sponsor
"The Case of Mr. Keen's Dilemma"
　　Mr. Keen, disguised as Santa Claus, royally entertains the residents at the Crandall Street Orphanage, doling out gifts to each boy and girl. Mike Clancy assists "Santa."

CONTINUITY #817
Wednesday, December 30, 1942
7:45–8:00 p.m. EWT
CBS
Martha Atwell, Director
Lawrence M. Klee, Writer
Philip Thorn, Editor
James Fleming, Announcer
American Home Products (Kolynos, Aerowax), Sponsor
"The Case of the Magician's Assistant"
　　Zorostro the Magnificent puts his helper, Diana Larue, in a large box at a performance at the Royal Theater. With a wave of his wand she disappears. Only ... she doesn't come back.

CONTINUITY #818
Thursday, December 31, 1942
7:45–8:00 p.m. EWT
CBS
Martha Atwell, Director
Lawrence M. Klee, Writer
Philip Thorn, Editor
James Fleming, Announcer
American Home Products (Kolynos, Aerowax), Sponsor
"The Case of the Magician's Assistant"
　　Zorostro and a piccolo player, Mr. Pappas, are both madly in love with Diana. Mr. Keen attends a New Year's Eve party where Pappas is playing, thinking Diana will be there.

CONTINUITY #819
Friday, January 1, 1943
7:45–8:00 p.m. EWT
CBS
Martha Atwell, Director
Lawrence M. Klee, Writer
Philip Thorn, Editor
James Fleming, Announcer
American Home Products (Kolynos, Aerowax), Sponsor
"The Case of the Magician's Assistant"
　　Mr. Keen, Mike Clancy and Miss Ellis enjoy the music revue. Zorostro the Magnificent, Mr. Pappas and Diana, the ditzy, disappearing babe, all surface, too, as the tale climaxes.

CONTINUITY #820
Wednesday, January 6, 1943
7:45–8:00 p.m. EWT
CBS
Martha Atwell, Director
Lawrence M. Klee, Writer
Philip Thorn, Editor
James Fleming, Announcer
American Home Products (Kolynos, Aerowax), Sponsor

"The Case of the Yellow Parrot"
Keen recalls a case he pursued shortly before Mike joined him. A paralytic, Craig, refused to sell his home, even at three times its value. Louise, his niece, had been missing for four months.

CONTINUITY #821
Thursday, January 7, 1943
7:45–8:00 p.m. EWT
CBS
Martha Atwell, Director
Lawrence M. Klee, Writer
Philip Thorn, Editor
James Fleming, Announcer
American Home Products (Kolynos, Aerowax), Sponsor
"The Case of the Yellow Parrot"
Craig was a con artist of sorts. For his own purposes, he merely appeared to be a helpless invalid. It was only a cover that helped him carry out his sinister plots.

CONTINUITY #822
Friday, January 8, 1943
7:45–8:00 p.m. EWT
CBS
Martha Atwell, Director
Lawrence M. Klee, Writer
Philip Thorn, Editor
James Fleming, Announcer
American Home Products (Kolynos, Aerowax), Sponsor
"The Case of the Yellow Parrot"
Craig owned a yellow parrot. Keen went to the police with the tale of the niece's peculiar disappearance. The parrot was the key to revealing that Craig assisted her in leaving.

CONTINUITY #823
Wednesday, January 13, 1943
7:45–8:00 p.m. EWT
CBS
Martha Atwell, Director
Lawrence M. Klee, Writer
Philip Thorn, Editor
James Fleming, Announcer
American Home Products (Kolynos, Aerowax), Sponsor
"The Case of Stonehaven Hall"
Stonehaven Hall is in an area of the Catskills with few residents. It is gloomy, forbidding and impregnable, ruled with an iron hand by builder Montague Stonehaven.

CONTINUITY #824
Thursday, January 14, 1943
7:45–8:00 p.m. EWT
CBS
Martha Atwell, Director
Lawrence M. Klee, Writer
Philip Thorn, Editor
James Fleming, Announcer
American Home Products (Kolynos, Aerowax), Sponsor
"The Case of Stonehaven Hall"
Montague's 19-year-old daughter, Pamela Stonehaven, has vanished. The grim appearance of Stonehaven's rambling acres and medieval walls is reflected in both the children who live there and its stern, unrelenting owner.

CONTINUITY #825
Friday, January 15, 1943
7:45–8:00 p.m. EWT
CBS
Martha Atwell, Director
Lawrence M. Klee, Writer
Philip Thorn, Editor
James Fleming, Announcer
American Home Products (Kolynos, Aerowax), Sponsor
"The Case of Stonehaven Hall"
Montague Stonehaven strongly disapproves of his daughter's attraction to Private Toby Wilton, surely a prime factor in her decision to leave. Keen knows that reconciliation may be thorny.

CONTINUITY #826
Wednesday, January 20, 1943
7:45–8:00 p.m. EWT
CBS
Martha Atwell, Director
Lawrence M. Klee, Writer
Philip Thorn, Editor
James Fleming, Announcer
American Home Products (Kolynos, Aerowax), Sponsor
"The Case of Stonehaven Hall"
Pamela's brother Jeffrey, age 24, leaves home, too. Mr. Keen catches up to Jeffrey and his sister, and tries to sort the situation out.

Their unyeilding father fails to appear, yet they make choices about the future.

CONTINUITY #827
Thursday, January 21, 1943
7:45–8:00 p.m. EWT
CBS
Martha Atwell, Director
Lawrence M. Klee, Writer
Philip Thorn, Editor
James Fleming, Announcer
American Home Products (Kolynos, Aerowax), Sponsor
"The Case of the Woman Who Wouldn't Die"
Myra Blake disappears. Her husband appeals to Mr. Keen to find her. What Mr. Keen doesn't know is that Martin Blake has poisoned his wife, making Keen part of a nefarious cover-up.

CONTINUITY #828
Friday, January 22, 1943
7:45–8:00 p.m. EWT
CBS
Martha Atwell, Director
Lawrence M. Klee, Writer
Philip Thorn, Editor
James Fleming, Announcer
American Home Products (Kolynos, Aerowax), Sponsor
"The Case of the Woman Who Wouldn't Die"
The tracer finds himself embroiled in a situation that has far graver implications than he initially imagined. Slowly the finger of suspicion starts to point toward Martin Blake.

CONTINUITY #829
Wednesday, January 27, 1943
7:45–8:00 p.m. EWT
CBS
Martha Atwell, Director
Lawrence M. Klee, Writer
Philip Thorn, Editor
James Fleming, Announcer
American Home Products (Kolynos, Aerowax), Sponsor
"The Case of the Woman Who Wouldn't Die"
Mr. Keen contacts a lady known only as Dolores, who has taken great interest in the Blake clan. Posing as a workman, Mike Clancy goes to her apartment in a fashionable neighborhood.

CONTINUITY #830
Thursday, January 28, 1943
7:45–8:00 p.m. EWT
CBS
Martha Atwell, Director
Lawrence M. Klee, Writer
Philip Thorn, Editor
James Fleming, Announcer
American Home Products (Kolynos, Aerowax), Sponsor
"The Case of the Woman Who Wouldn't Die"
Blake tells Dolores that his wife's body was fished from a New Jersey river. At a prearranged meeting site, Keen and Clancy wait for Dolores. Does this spell the end for Blake?

CONTINUITY #831
Friday, January 29, 1943
7:45–8:00 p.m. EWT
CBS
Martha Atwell, Director
Lawrence M. Klee, Writer
Philip Thorn, Editor
James Fleming, Announcer
American Home Products (Kolynos, Aerowax), Sponsor
"The Case of the Woman Who Wouldn't Die"
The supposedly dead Myra Blake makes a surprise appearance. Her cruel spouse is held accountable for his inhumane actions. Figuring in the climax are Lt. Grogan, Dolores and a doctor.

CONTINUITY #832
Wednesday, February 3, 1943
7:45–8:00 p.m. EWT
CBS
Martha Atwell, Director
Lawrence M. Klee, Writer
Philip Thorn, Editor
James Fleming, Announcer
American Home Products (Kolynos, Aerowax), Sponsor
"The Case of the Million Dollar Girl"
Joanna Lane, a wealthy heiress known as "the million dollar girl," vanishes. Reporter Ray Wilson of *The New York Star* asks Mr. Keen's help. His career depends on the story.

CONTINUITY #833
Thursday, February 4, 1943
7:45–8:00 p.m. EWT

CBS
Martha Atwell, Director
Lawrence M. Klee, Writer
Philip Thorn, Editor
James Fleming, Announcer
American Home Products (Kolynos, Aerowax), Sponsor
"The Case of the Million Dollar Girl"

Thinking her attorney knows Joanna's whereabouts, Keen and Wilson board a train for Bangor, Me., following lawyer Harrison. In Hartford he eludes them while they are forced to proceed.

CONTINUITY #834
Friday, February 5, 1943
7:45–8:00 p.m. EWT
CBS
Martha Atwell, Director
Lawrence M. Klee, Writer
Philip Thorn, Editor
James Fleming, Announcer
American Home Products (Kolynos, Aerowax), Sponsor
"The Case of the Million Dollar Girl"

Harrison arrives. Keen and Wilson suspect him of involvement in the disappearance. They corner him at his Maine house and — over his protests — answer his phone.

CONTINUITY #835
Wednesday, February 10, 1943
7:45–8:00 p.m. EWT
CBS
Martha Atwell, Director
Lawrence M. Klee, Writer
Philip Thorn, Editor
James Fleming, Announcer
American Home Products (Kolynos, Aerowax), Sponsor
"The Case of the Million Dollar Girl"

The pair trace Joanna to a Bangor restaurant, where she's working as a waitress.

CONTINUITY #836
Thursday, February 11, 1943
7:45–8:00 p.m. EWT
CBS
Martha Atwell, Director
Lawrence M. Klee, Writer
Philip Thorn, Editor
James Fleming, Announcer
American Home Products (Kolynos, Aerowax), Sponsor
"The Case of the Million Dollar Girl"

Two days later, B. F. Garnett, city editor of *The New York Star*, has an uninvited guest. Ray Wilson arrives to hit him up for a long-awaited appointment as Washington correspondent.

CONTINUITY #837
Friday, February 12, 1943
7:45–8:00 p.m. EWT
CBS
Martha Atwell, Director
Lawrence M. Klee, Writer
Philip Thorn, Editor
James Fleming, Announcer
American Home Products (Kolynos, Aerowax), Sponsor
"The Case of Murder by the Clock"

When John Russel, a mild-mannered inventor, disappears, his wife suspects foul play. The tracer is unaware that a band of professional killers has been hired to murder Russel.

CONTINUITY #838
Wednesday, February 17, 1943
7:45–8:00 p.m. EWT
CBS
Martha Atwell, Director
Lawrence M. Klee, Writer
Philip Thorn, Editor
James Fleming, Announcer
American Home Products (Kolynos, Aerowax), Sponsor
"The Case of Murder by the Clock"

The corpse that turns up in the Russel home is not that of the missing man, but of a gunman. At police headquarters Mr. Keen reviews the facts with his friend Lieutenant Grogan.

CONTINUITY #839
Thursday, February 18, 1943
7:45–8:00 p.m. EWT
CBS
Martha Atwell, Director
Lawrence M. Klee, Writer
Philip Thorn, Editor
James Fleming, Announcer
American Home Products (Kolynos, Aerowax), Sponsor

"The Case of Murder by the Clock"
Suspecting that the victim is a member of a group making a business of murder, Mr. Keen lays out plans that he hopes will secure John Russel and bring the killers to justice.

CONTINUITY #840
Friday, February 19, 1943
7:45–8:00 p.m. EWT
CBS
Martha Atwell, Director
Lawrence M. Klee, Writer
Philip Thorn, Editor
James Fleming, Announcer
American Home Products (Kolynos, Aerowax), Sponsor
"The Case of Murder by the Clock"
The first part of Keen's plan comes to fruition when he finds Russel in an obscure rooming house. Unfortunately, gangsters Pike and Al trap them there, leaving the pair to die in a room with an open gas jet.

CONTINUITY #841
Wednesday, February 24, 1943
7:45–8:00 p.m. EWT
CBS
Martha Atwell, Director
Lawrence M. Klee, Writer
Philip Thorn, Editor
James Fleming, Announcer
American Home Products (Kolynos, Aerowax), Sponsor
"The Case of Murder by the Clock"
An hour later, in the cigar store that fronts as Pike's headquarters, he, Al and Morgan are rounded up by Lt. Grogan. Grogan earlier found Keen and Russel, saving their lives.

CONTINUITY #842
Thursday, February 25, 1943
7:45–8:00 p.m. EWT
CBS
Martha Atwell, Director
Lawrence M. Klee, Writer
Philip Thorn, Editor
James Fleming, Announcer
American Home Products (Kolynos, Aerowax), Sponsor
"The Case of Eight Hours Leave"
Army Private Bob Hagen disappears. His buddy Jerry enlists Mr. Keen's aid. If Bob doesn't return to camp in a few hours he'll be declared A.W.O.L. and disgraced in the eyes of his friends.

CONTINUITY #843
Friday, February 26, 1943
7:45–8:00 p.m. EWT
CBS
Martha Atwell, Director
Lawrence M. Klee, Writer
Philip Thorn, Editor
James Fleming, Announcer
American Home Products (Kolynos, Aerowax), Sponsor
"The Case of Eight Hours Leave"
Jerry telephones his friend Francine from a booth opposite her boarding house. Telling her roommate to get in touch with Mr. Keen at once, Francine quickly leaves the house.

CONTINUITY #844
Wednesday, March 3, 1943
7:45–8:00 p.m. EWT
CBS
Martha Atwell, Director
Lawrence M. Klee, Writer
Philip Thorn, Editor
James Fleming, Announcer
American Home Products (Kolynos, Aerowax), Sponsor
"The Case of Eight Hours Leave"
Mr. Keen, Francine, Bob and Jerry see action in the exciting finish to this tale. Bob Hagen reappears just in time to avoid becoming A.W.O.L. and suffering all its attendant humiliation.

CONTINUITY #845
Thursday, March 4, 1943
7:45–8:00 p.m. EWT
CBS
Martha Atwell, Director
Lawrence M. Klee, Writer
Philip Thorn, Editor
James Fleming, Announcer
American Home Products (Kolynos, Aerowax), Sponsor
"The Case of the Lady in the Pullman"
Mr. Keen boards an express train bound for Chicago on business. An elderly lady aboard disappears. The train has not stopped since Horten Junction, where she was last seen.

CONTINUITY #846
Friday, March 5, 1943
7:45–8:00 p.m. EWT
CBS
Martha Atwell, Director
Lawrence M. Klee, Writer
Philip Thorn, Editor
James Fleming, Announcer
American Home Products (Kolynos, Aerowax), Sponsor
"The Case of the Lady in the Pullman"
   A Pullman porter subsequently vanishes. With the aid of another passenger, Mr. Olive, Keen tries to make sense of it. He's with conductor Rumsey in the Pullman.

CONTINUITY #847
Wednesday, March 10, 1943
7:45–8:00 p.m. EWT
CBS
Martha Atwell, Director
Lawrence M. Klee, Writer
Philip Thorn, Editor
James Fleming, Announcer
American Home Products (Kolynos, Aerowax), Sponsor
"The Case of the Lady in the Pullman"
   Now the conductor has disappeared — along with another passenger, too! Mr. Keen finds an important clue — a gray wig stashed in the men's smoking room.

CONTINUITY #848
Thursday, March 11, 1943
7:45–8:00 p.m. EWT
CBS
Martha Atwell, Director
Lawrence M. Klee, Writer
Philip Thorn, Editor
James Fleming, Announcer
American Home Products (Kolynos, Aerowax), Sponsor
"The Case of the Lady in the Pullman"
   Mike Clancy and Miss Ellis work on the case back in New York. The mysteries of those strange disappearances aboard the train are solved, partly due to Mr. Keen's perseverance.

CONTINUITY #849
Friday, March 12, 1943
7:45–8:00 p.m. EWT
CBS
Martha Atwell, Director
Lawrence M. Klee, Writer
Philip Thorn, Editor
James Fleming, Announcer
American Home Products (Kolynos, Aerowax), Sponsor
"The Case of the Unsigned Letters"
   Fifteen-year-old Judy Randall disappears. Her stepmother, Ellen, appeals to Mr. Keen to find her. She knows why Judy left: the girl is trying to create a rift between Ellen and Judy's father.

CONTINUITY #850
Wednesday, March 17, 1943
7:45–8:00 p.m. EWT
CBS
Martha Atwell, Director
Lawrence M. Klee, Writer
Philip Thorn, Editor
James Fleming, Announcer
American Home Products (Kolynos, Aerowax), Sponsor
"The Case of the Unsigned Letters"
   Judy held an unjustified grudge against her stepmother. After a phone call from Mr. Keen telling her Judy has been found, Ellen Randall prepares to leave their home forever.

CONTINUITY #851
Thursday, March 18, 1943
7:45–8:00 p.m. EWT
CBS
Martha Atwell, Director
Lawrence M. Klee, Writer
Philip Thorn, Editor
James Fleming, Announcer
American Home Products (Kolynos, Aerowax), Sponsor
"The Case of the Unsigned Letters"
   Mr. Keen is instrumental in bringing reconciliation to the Randall home. He returns Judy there, and seeks to restore harmony in her life and in those of Ellen and Steven Randall.

CONTINUITY #852
Friday, March 19, 1943
7:45–8:00 p.m. EWT
CBS
Martha Atwell, Director
Lawrence M. Klee, Writer
Philip Thorn, Editor

James Fleming, Announcer
American Home Products (Kolynos, Aerowax), Sponsor
"The Case of a Fresh Flower Every Day"
   The sudden disappearance of Helen Kincaid brings her very attractive and emotional young daughter Paula to Mr. Keen's office. Could this possibly be part of a larger pattern?

CONTINUITY #853
Wednesday, March 24, 1943
7:45–8:00 p.m. EWT
CBS
Martha Atwell, Director
Lawrence M. Klee, Writer
Philip Thorn, Editor
James Fleming, Announcer
American Home Products (Kolynos, Aerowax), Sponsor
"The Case of a Fresh Flower Every Day"
   Somehow Paula Kincaid connects her fears for her missing mother with a series of murders of women that have occurred in the city in the past few weeks. Mr. Keen is aware of this.

CONTINUITY #854
Thursday, March 25, 1943
7:45–8:00 p.m. EWT
CBS
Martha Atwell, Director
Lawrence M. Klee, Writer
Philip Thorn, Editor
Ken Roberts, Announcer
American Home Products (Kolynos, Aerowax), Sponsor
"The Case of a Fresh Flower Every Day"
   Studying Helen Kincaid's diary, Mr. Keen and Mike Clancy uncover a potential clue in a mention of Jason Applegate, whom the lady has been seeing. Jason is partial to fresh flowers.

CONTINUITY #855
Friday, March 26, 1943
7:45–8:00 p.m. EWT
CBS
Martha Atwell, Director
Lawrence M. Klee, Writer
Philip Thorn, Editor
Ken Roberts, Announcer
American Home Products (Kolynos, Aerowax), Sponsor
"The Case of a Fresh Flower Every Day"
   It comes to light that the unknown serial killer wears a fresh flower in his lapel during every murder. An envelope in Jason Applegate's hotel room contains damning evidence.

CONTINUITY #856
Wednesday, March 31, 1943
7:45–8:00 p.m. EWT
CBS
Martha Atwell, Director
Lawrence M. Klee, Writer
Philip Thorn, Editor
Ed Fleming, Announcer
American Home Products (Kolynos, Aerowax), Sponsor
"The Case of a Fresh Flower Every Day"
   While searching Applegate's room, Keen and Clancy are surprised by the guest's sudden appearance. The maniacal Applegate *is* the man. And the unfortunate Helen won't be coming home.

CONTINUITY #857
Thursday, April 1, 1943
7:45–8:00 p.m. EWT
CBS
Martha Atwell, Director
Lawrence M. Klee, Writer
Philip Thorn, Editor
Ken Roberts, Announcer
American Home Products (Kolynos, Aerowax), Sponsor
"The Case of the Girl in Gingham"
   Amy Lawson, as simple in thought and emotion as the gingham dresses she wears, disappears. Her mother-in-law, Nora Lawson, enlists the tracer's help in finding her.

CONTINUITY #858
Friday, April 2, 1943
7:45–8:00 p.m. EWT
CBS
Martha Atwell, Director
Lawrence M. Klee, Writer
Philip Thorn, Editor
Ken Roberts, Announcer
American Home Products (Kolynos, Aerowax), Sponsor
"The Case of the Girl in Gingham"
   Suspecting that Amy Lawson's bitter and jealous sister Harriet could have something to

do with her disappearance, Mr. Keen goes to Harriet's apartment to interrogate her.

CONTINUITY #859
Wednesday, April 7, 1943
7:45–8:00 p.m. EWT
CBS
Martha Atwell, Director
Lawrence M. Klee, Writer
Philip Thorn, Editor
Ken Roberts, Announcer
American Home Products (Kolynos, Aerowax), Sponsor
"The Case of the Girl in Gingham"
   Amy vanished only a few days before her husband Ralph is scheduled to return home on furlough. An emotional scene takes place between the sisters in Harriet's tiny flat.

CONTINUITY #860
Thursday, April 8, 1943
7:45–8:00 p.m. EWT
CBS
Martha Atwell, Director
Lawrence M. Klee, Writer
Philip Thorn, Editor
Ken Roberts, Announcer
American Home Products (Kolynos, Aerowax), Sponsor
"The Case of Rings on Her Fingers"
   After 20 years of drudgery and work, Milly Bricker leaves home and a spouse who refuses to help support them. Flo Stanton, a friend of Milly's, comes to Mr. Keen for help.

CONTINUITY #861
Friday, April 9, 1943
7:45–8:00 p.m. EWT
CBS
Martha Atwell, Director
Lawrence M. Klee, Writer
Philip Thorn, Editor
Ken Roberts, Announcer
American Home Products (Kolynos, Aerowax), Sponsor
"The Case of Rings on Her Fingers"
   Milly left right after meeting with Charlie Haines and his wife. Milly might have married Charlie. His success seems mirrored in the clothes and jewelry he has given his wife.

CONTINUITY #862
Wednesday, April 14, 1943
7:45–8:00 p.m. EWT
CBS
Martha Atwell, Director
Lawrence M. Klee, Writer
Philip Thorn, Editor
Ken Roberts, Announcer
American Home Products (Kolynos, Aerowax), Sponsor
"The Case of Rings on Her Fingers"
   In a midtown hotel suite Mr. Keen questions Gloria Haines, Charlie's wife, about Milly's disappearance. He follows a hunch, and awaits subsequent developments.

CONTINUITY #863
Thursday, April 15, 1943
7:45–8:00 p.m. EWT
CBS
Martha Atwell, Director
Lawrence M. Klee, Writer
Philip Thorn, Editor
Ken Roberts, Announcer
American Home Products (Kolynos, Aerowax), Sponsor
"The Case of Rings on Her Fingers"
   Keen solves the mystery the following day at the Haineses' expensive hotel suite. Milly resurfaces, and Gloria, Flo and Joe are all present when Mr. Keen ties up the loose ends.

CONTINUITY #864
Friday, April 16, 1943
7:45–8:00 p.m. EWT
CBS
Martha Atwell, Director
Lawrence M. Klee, Writer
Philip Thorn, Editor
Ken Roberts, Announcer
American Home Products (Kolynos, Aerowax), Sponsor
"The Case of the Smiling Buckaroo"
   Tex Dawson, the movie star known as the Smiling Buckaroo, is the victim of a practical joke. His manager, Mr. Rivkin, goes to Keen for help, believing his client has disappeared.

CONTINUITY #865
Wednesday, April 21, 1943
7:45–8:00 p.m. EWT
CBS
Martha Atwell, Director
Lawrence M. Klee, Writer

Philip Thorn, Editor
Ken Roberts, Announcer
American Home Products (Kolynos, Aerowax), Sponsor
"The Case of the Smiling Buckaroo"

Overhearing a phone conversation in the lobby of the Walton Hotel in New York City, the tracer believes Tex is being held captive in room 719. He and Mike Clancy proceed there.

CONTINUITY #866
Thursday, April 22, 1943
7:45–8:00 p.m. EWT
CBS
Martha Atwell, Director
Lawrence M. Klee, Writer
Philip Thorn, Editor
Ken Roberts, Announcer
American Home Products (Kolynos, Aerowax), Sponsor
"The Case of the Smiling Buckaroo"

The charade — involving a Hollywood director and a cameraman — plays out. A conceited Tex Dawson (aka Smiling Buckaroo) is located, albeit a bit more humble now than he was before.

CONTINUITY #867
Friday, April 23, 1943
7:45–8:00 p.m. EWT
CBS
Martha Atwell, Director
Lawrence M. Klee, Writer
Philip Thorn, Editor
Ken Roberts, Announcer
American Home Products (Kolynos, Aerowax), Sponsor
"The Case of the Girl Who Couldn't Remember"

While being taken to an aunt's home by a neighbor, Mrs. Richards, 14-year-old Barbara Conway disappears following her mother's sudden death. Mr. Keen calls on her aunt, Bess Hanley.

CONTINUITY #868
Wednesday, April 28, 1943
7:45–8:00 p.m. EWT
CBS
Martha Atwell, Director
Lawrence M. Klee, Writer
Philip Thorn, Editor
Ken Roberts, Announcer
American Home Products (Kolynos, Aerowax), Sponsor
"The Case of the Girl Who Couldn't Remember"

The late Marian Conway wasn't the girl's real mother. Mrs. Conway adopted Barbara when her mother died in an auto crash that also wiped out the child's memory of many things.

CONTINUITY #869
Thursday, April 29, 1943
7:45–8:00 p.m. EWT
CBS
Martha Atwell, Director
Lawrence M. Klee, Writer
Philip Thorn, Editor
Ken Roberts, Announcer
American Home Products (Kolynos, Aerowax), Sponsor
"The Case of the Girl Who Couldn't Remember"

Barbara wants to be an opera star, unaware that her real mother had won a Met contract. Keen finds a notice in the girl's scrapbook about an audition for opera hopefuls at the Artist's Theater.

CONTINUITY #870
Friday, April 30, 1943
7:45–8:00 p.m. EWT
CBS
Martha Atwell, Director
Lawrence M. Klee, Writer
Philip Thorn, Editor
Ken Roberts, Announcer
American Home Products (Kolynos, Aerowax), Sponsor
"The Case of the Girl Who Couldn't Remember"

Keen and Clancy appear at the theater late in the evening, but learn from a charwoman that the child hasn't been there. Despite that, they eventually find her and help Barbara come to terms.

CONTINUITY #871
Wednesday, May 5, 1943
7:45–8:00 p.m. EWT
CBS
Martha Atwell, Director
Lawrence M. Klee, Writer

Philip Thorn, Editor
Ken Roberts, Announcer
American Home Products (Kolynos, Aerowax), Sponsor
"The Case of the Soldier Who Wanted to Disappear"

Sgt. Keith Winston, honorably discharged from the U.S. Army after heroic action on the battlefield, disappears. Cathy Hillyard thinks her fiancé wants her to believe he is dead.

CONTINUITY #872
Thursday, May 6, 1943
7:45–8:00 p.m. EWT
CBS
Martha Atwell, Director
Lawrence M. Klee, Writer
Philip Thorn, Editor
Ken Roberts, Announcer
American Home Products (Kolynos, Aerowax), Sponsor
"The Case of the Soldier Who Wanted to Disappear"

Mr. Keen and Mike Clancy go to Boston, where Keith was last seen. They learn that he has lost his sight, and has enrolled in a Boston school for the blind. Keen sends for Cathy.

CONTINUITY #873
Friday, May 7, 1943
7:45–8:00 p.m. EWT
CBS
Martha Atwell, Director
Lawrence M. Klee, Writer
Philip Thorn, Editor
Ken Roberts, Announcer
American Home Products (Kolynos, Aerowax), Sponsor
"The Case of the Soldier Who Wanted to Disappear"

Cathy and Keith meet for the first time since he went blind. In an effort to relieve her of his burden, he decided to slip away quietly. Mr. Keen helps them work through it.

CONTINUITY #874
Wednesday, May 12, 1943
7:45–8:00 p.m. EWT
CBS
Martha Atwell, Director
Lawrence M. Klee, Writer
Philip Thorn, Editor
Ken Roberts, Announcer
American Home Products (Kolynos, Aerowax), Sponsor
"The Case of the Unknown Correspondent"

Mortimer Himmer asks Keen to find Masha, whom he corresponded with but never met. Actually, it was reporter Terry Barton who sent a letter from "Masha" to Jean Page, the "Advice to the Lovelorn" columnist.

CONTINUITY #875
Thursday, May 13, 1943
7:45–8:00 p.m. EWT
CBS
Martha Atwell, Director
Lawrence M. Klee, Writer
Philip Thorn, Editor
Ken Roberts, Announcer
American Home Products (Kolynos, Aerowax), Sponsor
"The Case of the Unknown Correspondent"

The joke threatens to put Jean in an awkward spot. Himmer goes to Keen to find Masha when Jean, now aware of the hoax, tells him she vanished. Barton is in a difficult situation.

CONTINUITY #876
Friday, May 14, 1943
7:45–8:00 p.m. EWT
CBS
Martha Atwell, Director
Lawrence M. Klee, Writer
Philip Thorn, Editor
Ken Roberts, Announcer
American Home Products (Kolynos, Aerowax), Sponsor
"The Case of the Unknown Correspondent"

Terry Barton, who's in love with Jean Page, tried to impress her by appealing for romantic advice in the form of a fake letter. His charade earns him a rebuke at the paper's office.

CONTINUITY #877
Wednesday, May 19, 1943
7:45–8:00 p.m. EWT
CBS
Martha Atwell, Director
Lawrence M. Klee, Writer
Philip Thorn, Editor
Ken Roberts, Announcer
American Home Products (Kolynos, Aerowax), Sponsor

"The Case of the Polka Dotted Mask"
Pvt. Chick Hayes, member of a wealthy family, asks Mr. Keen to find a girl named Sue that he met at a masquerade ball for servicemen. Sue disappeared an hour after he met her.

CONTINUITY #878
Thursday, May 20, 1943
7:45–8:00 p.m. EWT
CBS
Martha Atwell, Director
Lawrence M. Klee, Writer
Philip Thorn, Editor
Ken Roberts, Announcer
American Home Products (Kolynos, Aerowax), Sponsor
"The Case of the Polka Dotted Mask"
Mr. Keen meets with Mrs. Bingham, who sponsored the ball. Keen and Clancy are startled to find that they have trailed the girl to the Howard Building, location of Keen and Co.

CONTINUITY #879
Friday, May 21, 1943
7:45–8:00 p.m. EWT
CBS
Martha Atwell, Director
Lawrence M. Klee, Writer
Philip Thorn, Editor
Ken Roberts, Announcer
American Home Products (Kolynos, Aerowax), Sponsor
"The Case of the Polka Dotted Mask"
The mysterious Sue, who wore a polka dotted mask during the masquerade ball, not only works in the Howard Building but at Keen and Co. She's Keen's own receptionist, Susie!

CONTINUITY #880
Wednesday, May 26, 1943
7:45–8:00 p.m. EWT
CBS
Martha Atwell, Director
Lawrence M. Klee, Writer
Philip Thorn, Editor
Ken Roberts, Announcer
American Home Products (Kolynos, Aerowax), Sponsor
"The Case of Murder in the Air"
Alone in his study at home during a thunderstorm, Mr. Keen finds a stranger in his closet. She's Renee Beaupaine, and she claims someone is trying to kill her, having already made three attempts.

CONTINUITY #881
Thursday, May 27, 1943
7:45–8:00 p.m. EWT
CBS
Martha Atwell, Director
Lawrence M. Klee, Writer
Philip Thorn, Editor
Ken Roberts, Announcer
American Home Products (Kolynos, Aerowax), Sponsor
"The Case of Murder in the Air"
To insure her safety, Keen lets Renee share a room with Mrs. Ryan, his housekeeper, in his home. Later he takes a phone call from Renee's brother-in-law, whom he invites over.

CONTINUITY #882
Friday, May 28, 1943
7:45–8:00 p.m. EWT
CBS
Martha Atwell, Director
Lawrence M. Klee, Writer
Philip Thorn, Editor
Ken Roberts, Announcer
American Home Products (Kolynos, Aerowax), Sponsor
"The Case of Murder in the Air"
The arrival of Chester Arnold alters the tracer's plans. Arnold claims Renee is losing her mind. Keen has another theory, which he subsequently shares with Renee and Mike Clancy.

CONTINUITY #883
Wednesday, June 2, 1943
7:45–8:00 p.m. EWT
CBS
Martha Atwell, Director
Lawrence M. Klee, Writer
Philip Thorn, Editor
Ken Roberts, Announcer
American Home Products (Kolynos, Black Flag), Sponsor
"The Case of Murder in the Air"
Keen lays a complex trap. Renee boards a New Jersey–bound ferry, and Mike hovers nearby. Keen and Arnold, waiting at Keen's office, are soon called to the ferry to meet police.

CONTINUITY #884
Thursday, June 3, 1943
7:45–8:00 p.m. EWT
CBS
Martha Atwell, Director
Lawrence M. Klee, Writer
Philip Thorn, Editor
Ken Roberts, Announcer
American Home Products (Kolynos, Black Flag), Sponsor
"The Case of Murder in the Air"
   The mystery is solved as police Lt. Jackson reveals an intricate scheme behind the threats on Renee Beaupaine's life. Chester Arnold is present, along with Keen and Mike Clancy.

CONTINUITY #885
Friday, June 4, 1943
7:45–8:00 p.m. EWT
CBS
Martha Atwell, Director
Lawrence M. Klee, Writer
Philip Thorn, Editor
Ken Roberts, Announcer
American Home Products (Kolynos, Black Flag), Sponsor
"The Case of the Girl in Red"
   Suspected of murder, hardened Boots Maddox, age 16, disappears. Feeling sorry for the young delinquent, and believing her innocent, Mr. Keen searches for her.

CONTINUITY #886
Wednesday, June 9, 1943
7:45–8:00 p.m. EWT
CBS
Martha Atwell, Director
Lawrence M. Klee, Writer
Philip Thorn, Editor
Ken Roberts, Announcer
American Home Products (Kolynos, Black Flag), Sponsor
"The Case of the Girl in Red"
   On the third floor of a shabby tenement, Mrs. Maddox, Boots' mother, has an unexpected visitor, Mr. Keen. Later, Keen goes to the home of 15-year-old Diz Henson, friend of the missing girl.

CONTINUITY #887
Thursday, June 10, 1943
7:45–8:00 p.m. EWT
CBS
Martha Atwell, Director
Lawrence M. Klee, Writer
Philip Thorn, Editor
Ken Roberts, Announcer
American Home Products (Kolynos, Black Flag), Sponsor
"The Case of the Girl in Red"
   Boots is drawn into the murder of a candy store proprietor. She realizes that Tony Marina, her erstwhile pal, has framed her. She goes to Diz's home, then lets an intruder inside.

CONTINUITY #888
Friday, June 11, 1943
7:45–8:00 p.m. EWT
CBS
Martha Atwell, Director
Lawrence M. Klee, Writer
Philip Thorn, Editor
Ken Roberts, Announcer
American Home Products (Kolynos, Black Flag), Sponsor
"The Case of the Girl in Red"
   Fortunately for Boots, Mr. Keen and police Lt. Jackson show up at just the right moment. A tough, wily Tony and his pal Biff, a hardened criminal, will pay for their foul deeds.

CONTINUITY #889
Wednesday, June 16, 1943
7:45–8:00 p.m. EWT
CBS
Martha Atwell, Director
Lawrence M. Klee, Writer
Philip Thorn, Editor
Ken Roberts, Announcer
American Home Products (Kolynos, Black Flag), Sponsor
"The Case of the Vindictive Wife"
   Seeking revenge for what she considers an injustice, the bitter Vivian Wade asks Mr. Keen to find her missing husband. Keen doesn't like her attitude, but will look for Joe Wade anyhow.

CONTINUITY #890
Thursday, June 17, 1943
7:45–8:00 p.m. EWT
CBS
Martha Atwell, Director
Lawrence M. Klee, Writer

Philip Thorn, Editor
Ken Roberts, Announcer
American Home Products (Kolynos, Black Flag), Sponsor
"The Case of the Vindictive Wife"

Keen knows that unless Vivian's attitude changes, Joe Wade's return may be only a temporary reunion and could be followed by more domestic tragedy. He says he's quitting the case.

CONTINUITY #891
Friday, June 18, 1943
7:45–8:00 p.m. EWT
CBS
Martha Atwell, Director
Lawrence M. Klee, Writer
Philip Thorn, Editor
Ken Roberts, Announcer
American Home Products (Kolynos, Black Flag), Sponsor
"The Case of the Vindictive Wife"

Mr. Keen locates Joe Wade. He's still uncertain whether he can affect a happy reunion between Joe and a bitter Vivian. Harry and Charley, Joe's friends, help arrange a meeting.

CONTINUITY #892
Wednesday, June 23, 1943
7:45–8:00 p.m. EWT
CBS
Martha Atwell, Director
Lawrence M. Klee, Writer
Philip Thorn, Editor
Ken Roberts, Announcer
American Home Products (Kolynos, Black Flag), Sponsor
"The Case of the Vindictive Wife"

With Barry and Charley's cooperation, Keen stages a reunion between Joe and Vivian Wade. Mr. Keen is instrumental in helping to smooth over the past and turning them towards a more forgiving future.

CONTINUITY #893
Thursday, June 24, 1943
7:45–8:00 p.m. EWT
CBS
Martha Atwell, Director
Lawrence M. Klee, Writer
Philip Thorn, Editor
Ken Roberts, Announcer
American Home Products (Kolynos, Black Flag), Sponsor
"The Case in Studio Nine"

The disappearance of Howie, a radio vocalist, comes as a blow to his adoring public—and especially to students at Simpson High School. Two girls ask Mr. Keen to help find the crooner.

CONTINUITY #894
Friday, June 25, 1943
7:45–8:00 p.m. EWT
CBS
Martha Atwell, Director
Lawrence M. Klee, Writer
Philip Thorn, Editor
Ken Roberts, Announcer
American Home Products (Kolynos, Aerowax), Sponsor
"The Case in Studio Nine"

The sudden disappearance of Howie, the idol of teenage girls everywhere, so disturbs the students of Simpson High that a mass meeting is called in the gymnasium to deal with it.

CONTINUITY #895
Wednesday, June 30, 1943
7:45–8:00 p.m. EWT
CBS
Martha Atwell, Director
Lawrence M. Klee, Writer
Philip Thorn, Editor
Ken Roberts, Announcer
American Home Products (Kolynos, Black Flag), Sponsor
"The Case in Studio Nine"

Howie's trail leads Mr. Keen to a small suite in an unpretentious midtown hotel. There he ends his search by finding a harassed, worried Howie.

CONTINUITY #896
Thursday, July 1, 1943
7:45–8:00 p.m. EWT
CBS
Martha Atwell, Director
Lawrence M. Klee, Writer
Philip Thorn, Editor
Ken Roberts, Announcer
American Home Products (Kolynos, Black Flag), Sponsor
"The Case of the Twelfth Juror"

Mr. Keen is one of 11 jurors favoring a guilty verdict for Lorraine Frame, on trial for murder. Helen Courtney, the sole juror holding out for acquittal, suddenly disappears.

CONTINUITY #897
Friday, July 2, 1943
7:45–8:00 p.m. EWT
CBS
Martha Atwell, Director
Lawrence M. Klee, Writer
Philip Thorn, Editor
Announcer's name omitted
American Home Products (Kolynos, Black Flag), Sponsor
"The Case of the Twelfth Juror"

The court appoints a new jury. Jean Courtney, the missing woman's daughter, enlists Mr. Keen's aid in finding her. Jean's brother, Peter, is a bitter, cynical wheelchair-bound man.

CONTINUITY #898
Wednesday, July 7, 1943
7:45–8:00 p.m. EWT
CBS
Martha Atwell, Director
Lawrence M. Klee, Writer
Philip Thorn, Editor
Ken Roberts, Announcer
American Home Products (Kolynos, Black Flag), Sponsor
"The Case of the Twelfth Juror"

The trail of Helen Courtney leads Mr. Keen to the private office of a well-known metropolitan surgeon, Dr. Woolton. The information Keen gains there leads him to Helen.

CONTINUITY #899
Thursday, July 8, 1943
7:45–8:00 p.m. EWT
CBS
Martha Atwell, Director
Lawrence M. Klee, Writer
Philip Thorn, Editor
Ken Roberts, Announcer
American Home Products (Kolynos, Black Flag), Sponsor
"The Case of the Twelfth Juror"

Helen Courtney thought Lorraine Frame innocent of murder. Mr. Keen knows she has proof, if she will submit it. Her silence shields her children, who will be affected if she speaks.

CONTINUITY #900
Friday, July 9, 1943
7:45–8:00 p.m. EWT
CBS
Martha Atwell, Director
Lawrence M. Klee, Writer
Philip Thorn, Editor
Ken Roberts, Announcer
American Home Products (Kolynos, Black Flag), Sponsor
"The Case of the Twelfth Juror"

Helen Courtney faces her responsibility and finally steps up to the plate. She offers her secret evidence to District Attorney Hanlon, the prosecutor in the murder case, and frees an innocent woman.

CONTINUITY #901
Wednesday, July 14, 1943
7:45–8:00 p.m. EWT
CBS
Stephen Gross, Director
Lawrence M. Klee, Writer
Philip Thorn, Editor
Ken Roberts, Announcer
American Home Products (Kolynos, Black Flag), Sponsor
"The Case of Shore Leave"

After only knowing one another for two weeks, Mary Roberts and Jim Haines, a sailor, decide to marry. On the day they are to obtain a license, Jim disappears. Mary appeals to Mr. Keen.

CONTINUITY #902
Thursday, July 15, 1943
7:45–8:00 p.m. EWT
CBS
Stephen Gross, Director
Lawrence M. Klee, Writer
Philip Thorn, Editor
Ken Roberts, Announcer
American Home Products (Kolynos, Black Flag), Sponsor
"The Case of Shore Leave"

Jim's pal Harry says Jim's ship sailed under sealed orders the night before he and Mary were to meet. He couldn't tell her. Harry and Keen go to Mary's rooming house, but she's gone.

CONTINUITY #903
Friday, July 16, 1943

7:45–8:00 p.m. EWT
CBS
Stephen Gross, Director
Lawrence M. Klee, Writer
Philip Thorn, Editor
Ken Roberts, Announcer
American Home Products (Kolynos, Black Flag), Sponsor
"The Case of Shore Leave"
   Deciding Jim has deserted her, Mary packs up and vacates the rooming house to return to Milwaukee and wed someone there. Mr. Keen works with Officer Kelly to reunite Mary and Jim.

CONTINUITY #904
Wednesday, July 21, 1943
7:45–8:00 p.m. EWT
CBS
Stephen Gross, Director
Lawrence M. Klee, Writer
Philip Thorn, Editor
Ken Roberts, Announcer
American Home Products (Kolynos, Black Flag), Sponsor
"The Case of From the Halls of Montezuma"
   Lefty Jenks and Benny Pine run a novelty concession. Marine Sgt. Texas Gilroy buys something with a hundred dollar bill but forgets to retrieve his change. The owners ask Keen to find him.

CONTINUITY #905
Thursday, July 22, 1943
7:45–8:00 p.m. EWT
CBS
Stephen Gross, Director
Lawrence M. Klee, Writer
Philip Thorn, Editor
Ken Roberts, Announcer
American Home Products (Kolynos, Black Flag), Sponsor
"The Case of From the Halls of Montezuma"
   Texas, who loves to whistle the Marine fighting song, is the father of a new baby boy — and doesn't know it. Keen places an ad in a Houston paper hoping Texas might pick it up at a New York newsstand offering out-of-town papers.

CONTINUITY #906
Friday, July 23, 1943
7:45–8:00 p.m. EWT
CBS
Stephen Gross, Director
Lawrence M. Klee, Writer
Philip Thorn, Editor
Ken Roberts, Announcer
American Home Products (Kolynos, Black Flag), Sponsor
"The Case of From the Halls of Montezuma"
   The connection is successfully made. Texas is found, his money is returned, he gets the news, and he beams like a very proud papa.

CONTINUITY #907
Wednesday, July 28, 1943
7:45–8:00 p.m. EWT
CBS
Stephen Gross, Director
Lawrence M. Klee, Writer
Philip Thorn, Editor
Ken Roberts, Announcer
American Home Products (Kolynos, Black Flag), Sponsor
"The Case of the Perfect Crime"
   Cora Lance, the half-sister of Randall and Jonathan Lance, disappears. Jonathan suspects his half-brother of foul play. Jonathan and Mr. Keen proceed to the Lance home.

CONTINUITY #908
Thursday, July 29, 1943
7:45–8:00 p.m. EWT
CBS
Stephen Gross, Director
Lawrence M. Klee, Writer
Philip Thorn, Editor
Ken Roberts, Announcer
American Home Products (Kolynos, Black Flag), Sponsor
"The Case of the Perfect Crime"
   Randall Lance is killed in the living room of his own home. The evidence strongly points to Cora, who returned to the house and argued with Randall just before he met his fate.

CONTINUITY #909
Friday, July 30, 1943
7:45–8:00 p.m. EWT
CBS
Stephen Gross, Director
Lawrence M. Klee, Writer
Philip Thorn, Editor

Ken Roberts, Announcer
American Home Products (Kolynos, Black Flag), Sponsor
"The Case of the Perfect Crime"
So who is the murderer? Police inspector Hix asks pointed questions of both Jonathan and Cora Lance. Of course, it's up to Mr. Keen, the hero, to finally uncover the offender.

CONTINUITY #910
Wednesday, August 4, 1943
7:45–8:00 p.m. EWT
CBS
Martha Atwell, Director
Lawrence M. Klee, Writer
Philip Thorn, Editor
Ken Roberts, Announcer
American Home Products (Kolynos, Black Flag), Sponsor
"The Case of the Red-Headed Runaway"
Alec Sprague, age 13, disappears. Mr. Keen suspects he may be the victim of a group of child labor black market racketeers. Aiding in the hunt is Miss Evans, Alec's summer school teacher.

CONTINUITY #911
Thursday, August 5, 1943
7:45–8:00 p.m. EWT
CBS
Martha Atwell, Director
Lawrence M. Klee, Writer
Philip Thorn, Editor
Ken Roberts, Announcer
American Home Products (Kolynos, Black Flag), Sponsor
"The Case of the Red-Headed Runaway"
Mr. Keen is convinced that something nefarious has befallen Alec. He's aware that certain profit-seeking interests are taking kids away and putting them to work.

CONTINUITY #912
Friday, August 6, 1943
7:45–8:00 p.m. EWT
CBS
Martha Atwell, Director
Lawrence M. Klee, Writer
Philip Thorn, Editor
Ken Roberts, Announcer
American Home Products (Kolynos, Black Flag), Sponsor
"The Case of the Red-Headed Runaway"
A clue leads Mr. Keen to the town of Baylor. In a poolroom on the outskirts of town, he catches up to Alec and Mullens, a toughie in his mid-thirties, who spirited the boy away.

CONTINUITY #913
Wednesday, August 11, 1943
7:45–8:00 p.m. EWT
CBS
Martha Atwell, Director
Lawrence M. Klee, Writer
Philip Thorn, Editor
Ken Roberts, Announcer
American Home Products (Kolynos, Black Flag), Sponsor
"The Case of the Mayor of Libbyville"
Lou Bassett challenges George Pixl, mayor of Libbyville, for that office. On election eve Pixl disappears. His wife and Harry Petrie, Pixl's campaign manager, ask Keen's help.

CONTINUITY #914
Thursday, August 12, 1943
7:45–8:00 p.m. EWT
CBS
Martha Atwell, Director
Lawrence M. Klee, Writer
Philip Thorn, Editor
Ken Roberts, Announcer
American Home Products (Kolynos, Black Flag), Sponsor
"The Case of the Mayor of Libbyville"
Mayor George Pixl had argued with his wife Beulah shortly before his disappearance. His hat is found floating in the river, possibly indicating a frightful tragedy.

CONTINUITY #915
Friday, August 13, 1943
7:45–8:00 p.m. EWT
CBS
Martha Atwell, Director
Lawrence M. Klee, Writer
Philip Thorn, Editor
Ken Roberts, Announcer
American Home Products (Kolynos, Black Flag), Sponsor
"The Case of the Mayor of Libbyville"
Keen persuades Beulah Pixl to run for mayor in her husband's stead in today's election. Lou Bassett and Harry Petrie await the re-

turns. George resurfaces, and the chicanery is revealed.

CONTINUITY #916
Wednesday, August 18, 1943
7:45–8:00 p.m. EWT
CBS
Martha Atwell, Director
Lawrence M. Klee, Writer
Philip Thorn, Editor
Ken Roberts, Announcer
American Home Products (Kolynos, Black Flag), Sponsor
"The Case of a Handful of Diamonds"
    Following a short friendship with widowed Stella Smith, George Grafton, debonair man-about-town, disappears—and so do the diamonds that were left to Stella by her husband.

CONTINUITY #917
Thursday, August 19, 1943
7:45–8:00 p.m. EWT
CBS
Martha Atwell, Director
Lawrence M. Klee, Writer
Philip Thorn, Editor
Ken Roberts, Announcer
American Home Products (Kolynos, Black Flag), Sponsor
"The Case of a Handful of Diamonds"
    Doris Belnord, a friend of Stella's who introduced Grafton to her, appeals to Mr. Keen for help in finding Grafton and recovering the stolen diamonds.

CONTINUITY #918
Friday, August 20, 1943
7:45–8:00 p.m. EWT
CBS
Martha Atwell, Director
Lawrence M. Klee, Writer
Philip Thorn, Editor
Ken Roberts, Announcer
American Home Products (Kolynos, Black Flag), Sponsor
"The Case of a Handful of Diamonds"
    Mr. Keen learns that Grafton, claiming to be a member of the famous Diamond Syndicate, assumed the identity of a trusted diamond dealer.

CONTINUITY #919
Wednesday, August 25, 1943
7:45–8:00 p.m. EWT
CBS
Martha Atwell, Director
Lawrence M. Klee, Writer
Philip Thorn, Editor
Ken Roberts, Announcer
American Home Products (Kolynos, Black Flag), Sponsor
"The Case of a Handful of Diamonds"
    The debonair Grafton's apparent friendship with Stella Smith was simply a ruse. Mr. Keen confers with Mike Clancy. They develop a plan to trap the imposter.

CONTINUITY #920
Thursday, August 26, 1943
7:45–8:00 p.m. EWT
CBS
Martha Atwell, Director
Lawrence M. Klee, Writer
Philip Thorn, Editor
Ken Roberts, Announcer
American Home Products (Kolynos, Black Flag), Sponsor
"The Case of a Handful of Diamonds"
    Grafton's real name is Carter. He's situated in a Boston hotel as the scene opens. Stella Smith is there when Mr. Keen and Mike Clancy at last put their hands on the thief.

CONTINUITY #921
Friday, August 27, 1943
7:45–8:00 p.m. EWT
CBS
Martha Atwell, Director
Lawrence M. Klee, Writer
Philip Thorn, Editor
Ken Roberts, Announcer
American Home Products (Kolynos, Black Flag), Sponsor
"The Case of Two Soldiers and a Girl"
    Mike Clancy and Susie Hargrave, the receptionist at Keen and Co., help Mr. Keen prepare for a journey to the West Coast to see Miss Ellis, who has suddenly fallen ill.

CONTINUITY #922
Wednesday, September 1, 1943
7:45–8:00 p.m. EWT
CBS

Martha Atwell, Director
Lawrence M. Klee, Writer
Philip Thorn, Editor
Announcer's name omitted
American Home Products (Kolynos, Aerowax), Sponsor
"The Case of Two Soldiers and a Girl"

After Keen departs, a man arrives telling of his fiancée's disappearance. A second man soon tells the same story about *his* fiancée. They are brothers, both engaged to the same girl.

CONTINUITY #923
Thursday, September 2, 1943
7:45–8:00 p.m. EWT
CBS
Martha Atwell, Director
Lawrence M. Klee, Writer
Philip Thorn, Editor
Ken Roberts, Announcer
American Home Products (Kolynos, Aerowax), Sponsor
"The Case of Two Soldiers and a Girl"

Engaged to Sgt. Don Heming, Elaine Barrett fell in love with his brother, Frank. Don has returned on furlough, and she has the unhappy task of telling him the awful truth.

CONTINUITY #924
Friday, September 3, 1943
7:45–8:00 p.m. EWT
CBS
Martha Atwell, Director
Lawrence M. Klee, Writer
Philip Thorn, Editor
Ken Roberts, Announcer
American Home Products (Kolynos, Aerowax), Sponsor
"The Case of Two Soldiers and a Girl"

Don, on furlough, and Frank meet for the first time at Mr. Keen's home. Don still doesn't have a clue.

CONTINUITY #925
Wednesday, September 8, 1943
7:45–8:00 p.m. EWT
CBS
Martha Atwell, Director
Lawrence M. Klee, Writer
Philip Thorn, Editor
Ken Roberts, Announcer
American Home Products (Kolynos, Aerowax), Sponsor
"The Case of Two Soldiers and a Girl"

Mr. Keen returns from his visit to Miss Ellis on the West Coast. The love triangle involving two brothers comes to a head, and Elaine, their object of affection, reappears. The future is set.

CONTINUITY #926
Thursday, September 9, 1943
7:45–8:00 p.m. EWT
CBS
Martha Atwell, Director
Lawrence M. Klee, Writer
Philip Thorn, Editor
Ken Roberts, Announcer
American Home Products (Kolynos, Aerowax), Sponsor
"The Case of a Suggestion for Murder"

Keen is summoned to a house on River Avenue. There he meets a man calling himself Dr. Manners, and a woman who's his nurse. Keen thinks that Helene Emerson, who called him, is Manners' unwilling patient.

CONTINUITY #927
Friday, September 10, 1943
7:45–8:00 p.m. EWT
CBS
Martha Atwell, Director
Lawrence M. Klee, Writer
Philip Thorn, Editor
Ken Roberts, Announcer
American Home Products (Kolynos, Aerowax), Sponsor
"The Case of a Suggestion for Murder"

Upon leaving the premises, Mr. Keen goes back again to make another check. This time he is told abruptly to leave. The scene opens in the gathering dusk outside 27 River Avenue.

CONTINUITY #928
Wednesday, September 15, 1943
7:45–8:00 p.m. EWT
CBS
Martha Atwell, Director
Lawrence M. Klee, Writer
Philip Thorn, Editor
Ken Roberts, Announcer
American Home Products (Kolynos, Aerowax), Sponsor

"The Case of a Suggestion for Murder"

Keen and Mike Clancy aren't fooled by the so-called doctor's smooth professional manner. Upon checking the premises, they find an unlocked window in the rear and enter a dark room.

CONTINUITY #929
Thursday, September 16, 1943
7:45–8:00 p.m. EWT
CBS
Martha Atwell, Director
Lawrence M. Klee, Writer
Philip Thorn, Editor
Ken Roberts, Announcer
American Home Products (Kolynos, Aerowax), Sponsor
"The Case of a Suggestion for Murder"

Trying to rescue Helene, who is marked for murder, Keen, Clancy and she are trapped in a windowless room in Helene's home. The sleuths soon overpower Dr. Manners and the lady named Hawks.

CONTINUITY #930
Friday, September 17, 1943
7:45–8:00 p.m. EWT
CBS
Martha Atwell, Director
Lawrence M. Klee, Writer
Philip Thorn, Editor
Ken Roberts, Announcer
American Home Products (Kolynos, Aerowax), Sponsor
"The Case of Home-Run Henry"

On the eve of an important baseball series, Henry Finch, star batter for the Striped Sox, disappears. Donahue, Henry's manager, asks Mr. Keen for help in finding the right-hander.

CONTINUITY #931
Wednesday, September 22, 1943
7:45–8:00 p.m. EWT
CBS
Martha Atwell, Director
Lawrence M. Klee, Writer
Philip Thorn, Editor
Ken Roberts, Announcer
American Home Products (Kolynos, Aerowax), Sponsor
"The Case of Home-Run Henry"

Donahue tells Mr. Keen about a gambler named Sykes who might be connected with Home-Run Henry's disappearance. Or Henry may have vanished over a quarrel with fiancée Gertie.

CONTINUITY #932
Thursday, September 23, 1943
7:45–8:00 p.m. EWT
CBS
Martha Atwell, Director
Lawrence M. Klee, Writer
Philip Thorn, Editor
Ken Roberts, Announcer
American Home Products (Kolynos, Aerowax), Sponsor
"The Case of Home-Run Henry"

Keen favors the theory involving the wily gambler Sykes, and goes to a midtown barbershop frequented by Sykes. Keen learns that Henry's absence will result in his team losing the big series.

CONTINUITY #933
Friday, September 24, 1943
7:45–8:00 p.m. EWT
CBS
Martha Atwell, Director
Lawrence M. Klee, Writer
Philip Thorn, Editor
Ken Roberts, Announcer
American Home Products (Kolynos, Aerowax), Sponsor
"The Case of Home-Run Henry"

Sykes has demonstrated more than a casual interest in the upcoming series. He owns a boat, currently in dry dock, that serves as his headquarters. The scene shifts there.

CONTINUITY #934
Wednesday, September 29, 1943
7:45–8:00 p.m. EWT
CBS
Martha Atwell, Director
Lawrence M. Klee, Writer
Philip Thorn, Editor
Ken Roberts, Announcer
American Home Products (Kolynos, Aerowax), Sponsor
"The Case of Home-Run Henry"

Henry Finch is located with Sykes. To get Henry away—knowing he's being detained against his will — Gertie, his fiancée, follows a plan set forth by Mr. Keen. The action has a boomerang effect.

CONTINUITY #935
Thursday, September 30, 1943
7:45–8:00 p.m. EWT
CBS
Martha Atwell, Director
Lawrence M. Klee, Writer
Philip Thorn, Editor
Ken Roberts, Announcer
American Home Products (Kolynos, Aerowax), Sponsor
"The Case of the Man Who Changed"

Helen Lacey, secretary to kindly philanthropist Frank Brent, tells Mr. Keen that her employer has changed radically overnight. The generous man has suddenly become self-centered and cruel.

CONTINUITY #936
Friday, October 1, 1943
7:45–8:00 p.m. EWT
CBS
Martha Atwell, Director
Lawrence M. Klee, Writer
Philip Thorn, Editor
Ken Roberts, Announcer
American Home Products (Kolynos, Aerowax), Sponsor
"The Case of the Man Who Changed"

Digging into Frank Brent's character, Keen places his own secretary, Susie Hargrave, in Brent's office at his home. After one day she meets Keen in order to relate some startling facts.

CONTINUITY #937
Wednesday, October 6, 1943
7:45–8:00 p.m. EWT
CBS
Martha Atwell, Director
Lawrence M. Klee, Writer
Philip Thorn, Editor
Ken Roberts, Announcer
American Home Products (Kolynos, Aerowax), Sponsor
"The Case of the Man Who Changed"

Keen follows the trail of clues to Brent's behavior shift to a shabby tenement in Philadelphia, where it ends abruptly. Susie, meanwhile, learns the truth and is in a very dangerous spot.

CONTINUITY #938
Thursday, October 7, 1943
7:45–8:00 p.m. EWT
CBS
Martha Atwell, Director
Lawrence M. Klee, Writer
Philip Thorn, Editor
Ken Roberts, Announcer
American Home Products (Kolynos, Aerowax), Sponsor
"The Case of the Man Who Changed"

Mr. Keen and Mike Clancy, back in the office, await word from Susie. Fortunately for her, they react quickly to remove her from the precarious position she finds herself in.

CONTINUITY #939
Friday, October 8, 1943
7:45–8:00 p.m. EWT
CBS
Martha Atwell, Director
Lawrence M. Klee, Writer
Philip Thorn, Editor
Ken Roberts, Announcer
American Home Products (Kolynos, Aerowax), Sponsor
"The Case of the Meanest Man"

Keen investigates a dilemma at the upstate home of the Anderson clan: a government allotment check failed to arrive this month — one that has come regularly ever since Jim joined the Army.

CONTINUITY #940
Wednesday, October 13, 1943
7:45–8:00 p.m. EWT
CBS
Martha Atwell, Director
Lawrence M. Klee, Writer
Philip Thorn, Editor
Ken Roberts, Announcer
American Home Products (Kolynos, Aerowax), Sponsor
"The Case of the Meanest Man"

Keen thinks a thief/forger is at work. A lodger in the home, Mr. Killian, falls under suspicion after he burns some papers in his room. Keen looks for evidence that will either confirm his guilt or prove his innocence.

CONTINUITY #941
Thursday, October 14, 1943

7:45–8:00 p.m. EWT
CBS
Martha Atwell, Director
Lawrence M. Klee, Writer
Philip Thorn, Editor
Ken Roberts, Announcer
American Home Products (Kolynos, Aerowax), Sponsor
"The Case of the Meanest Man"
    Mr. Keen and Mr. Bingham, a U.S. Secret Service agent, suspect Mr. Killian. They decide to wait and watch a short distance from the rural mailbox near the Anderson farmhouse.

CONTINUITY #942
Friday, October 15, 1943
7:45–8:00 p.m. EWT
CBS
Martha Atwell, Director
Lawrence M. Klee, Writer
Philip Thorn, Editor
Ken Roberts, Announcer
American Home Products (Kolynos, Aerowax), Sponsor
"The Case of the Meanest Man"
    Ah ha! Got 'em! Hands up — you're under arrest! Keen and Bingham put an end to the scheming of the perpetrator of this audacious crime. A whopping nine characters appear in this episode.

CONTINUITY #943
Wednesday, October 20, 1943
7:45–8:00 p.m. EWT
CBS
Martha Atwell, Director
Lawrence M. Klee, Writer
Philip Thorn, Editor
Ken Roberts, Announcer
American Home Products (Kolynos, Aerowax), Sponsor
"The Case of the Voice"
    Wealthy broker Herbert Manning goes to Mr. Keen for help in identifying a mysterious voice that threatens to kill him. Before he can tell more, the phone rings and the voice asks for Manning.

CONTINUITY #944
Thursday, October 21, 1943
7:45–8:00 p.m. EWT
CBS
Martha Atwell, Director
Lawrence M. Klee, Writer
Philip Thorn, Editor
Ken Roberts, Announcer
American Home Products (Kolynos, Aerowax), Sponsor
"The Case of the Voice"
    Keen seeks to uncover the identity of the mysterious menacing voice. Keen thinks that the guilty individual must be aware of Manning's every movement.

CONTINUITY #945
Friday, October 22, 1943
7:45–8:00 p.m. EWT
CBS
Martha Atwell, Director
Lawrence M. Klee, Writer
Philip Thorn, Editor
Ken Roberts, Announcer
American Home Products (Kolynos, Aerowax), Sponsor
"The Case of the Voice"
    The ingenuity displayed by this unknown assailant appears almost miraculous. The tracer is quite convinced that the person possesses some method of foreseeing Manning's every move.

CONTINUITY #946
Wednesday, October 27, 1943
7:45–8:00 p.m. EWT
CBS
Martha Atwell, Director
Lawrence M. Klee, Writer
Philip Thorn, Editor
Ken Roberts, Announcer
American Home Products (Kolynos, Aerowax), Sponsor
"The Case of the Voice"
    The charade comes ringing down when the voice actually makes an appearance, unknown to Mr. Keen, who arrives at Manning's house after a startling discovery. It's now all out in the open.

CONTINUITY #947
Thursday, October 28, 1943
7:45–8:00 p.m. EWT
CBS
Martha Atwell, Director
Lawrence M. Klee, Writer

Philip Thorn, Editor
Ken Roberts, Announcer
American Home Products (Kolynos, Aerowax), Sponsor
"The Case of the Broken Promise"

After announcing to her parents that she intends to marry Corporal Don Standish, a soldier she has known for only a few weeks, Janey Walsh disappears. The family appeals to Mr. Keen.

CONTINUITY #948
Friday, October 29, 1943
7:45–8:00 p.m. EWT
CBS
Martha Atwell, Director
Lawrence M. Klee, Writer
Philip Thorn, Editor
Ken Roberts, Announcer
American Home Products (Kolynos, Aerowax), Sponsor
"The Case of the Broken Promise"

Mr. Keen goes South to interview Don at his training camp. Don seems sincere when he tells Keen that he has no knowledge of Janey's whereabouts. Keen will follow a lead involving an un-posted letter Don received from Janey.

CONTINUITY #949
Wednesday, November 3, 1943
7:45–8:00 p.m. EWT
CBS
Martha Atwell, Director
Lawrence M. Klee, Writer
Philip Thorn, Editor
Ken Roberts, Announcer
American Home Products (Kolynos, Aerowax), Sponsor
"The Case of the Broken Promise"

In a hotel in Hillburgh, a nearby city, Keen locates the missing Janey Walsh, an impulsive girl. Mr. Keen reunites her with her mom and dad. Don, it appears, may be history.

CONTINUITY #950
Thursday, November 4, 1943
7:45–8:00 p.m. EWT
CBS
Martha Atwell, Director
Lawrence M. Klee, Writer
Philip Thorn, Editor
Ken Roberts, Announcer
American Home Products (Kolynos, Aerowax), Sponsor
"The Case of the Understanding Heart"

Mrs. Withers and Mr. Griggs, two people in the twilight years of their lives, disappear simultaneously. Their children, Margo Rodney and Hubert Griggs, ask Mr. Keen for assistance.

CONTINUITY #951
Friday, November 5, 1943
7:45–8:00 p.m. EWT
CBS
Martha Atwell, Director
Lawrence M. Klee, Writer
Philip Thorn, Editor
Ken Roberts, Announcer
American Home Products (Kolynos, Aerowax), Sponsor
"The Case of the Understanding Heart"

Mr. Keen's investigation reveals that Maybelle Withers and Harry Griggs met in 1901. That early meeting undoubtedly has a great deal to do with their present circumstances.

CONTINUITY #952
Wednesday, November 10, 1943
7:45–8:00 p.m. EWT
CBS
Martha Atwell, Director
Lawrence M. Klee, Writer
Philip Thorn, Editor
Ken Roberts, Announcer
American Home Products (Kolynos, Aerowax), Sponsor
"The Case of the Understanding Heart"

As Mr. Keen pursues the case of the disappearance of the two elderly people, he uncovers several startling revelations.

CONTINUITY #953
Thursday, November 11, 1943
7:45–8:00 p.m. EWT
CBS
Martha Atwell, Director
Lawrence M. Klee, Writer
Philip Thorn, Editor
Ken Roberts, Announcer
American Home Products (Kolynos, Aerowax), Sponsor
"The Case of the Understanding Heart"

The tune "In the Good Old Summertime" plays an important and nostalgic part in this episode. Mrs. Withers and Mr. Griggs return, and are reunited with their respective children.

CONTINUITY #954
Friday, November 12, 1943
7:45–8:00 p.m. EWT
CBS
Martha Atwell, Director
Lawrence M. Klee, Writer
Philip Thorn, Editor
Ken Roberts, Announcer
American Home Products (Kolynos, Aerowax), Sponsor
"The Case of the Smiling Mourner"
Mr. Keen hears a strange story about the late Charles Merkle from erstwhile secretary Vera Willard. Charles ostensibly died in a bus crash, but Vera suspects that he's alive and that someone else was buried in his stead.

CONTINUITY #955
Wednesday, November 17, 1943
7:45–8:00 p.m. EWT
CBS
Martha Atwell, Director
Lawrence M. Klee, Writer
Philip Thorn, Editor
Ken Roberts, Announcer
American Home Products (Kolynos, Aerowax), Sponsor
"The Case of the Smiling Mourner"
Vera believes that a smiling, bearded man attending the funeral was actually Charles in disguise. Keen plans to attend an auction sale at Charles' home, featuring Charles' watercolor paintings. Will curiosity tempt him?

CONTINUITY #956
Thursday, November 18, 1943
7:45–8:00 p.m. EWT
CBS
Martha Atwell, Director
Lawrence M. Klee, Writer
Philip Thorn, Editor
Ken Roberts, Announcer
American Home Products (Kolynos, Aerowax), Sponsor
"The Case of the Smiling Mourner"
Charles Merkle *does* make an appearance during the auction. His (figuratively) going underground was prompted by the depression and bitterness he felt after declaring bankruptcy.

CONTINUITY #957
Friday, November 19, 1943
7:45–8:00 p.m. EWT
CBS
Martha Atwell, Director
Lawrence M. Klee, Writer
Philip Thorn, Editor
Ken Roberts, Announcer
American Home Products (Kolynos, Aerowax), Sponsor
"The Case of the Young Marine"
For one year young Steve Harding has been missing from home. His sister goes to Mr. Keen in the hope that he may find him. The only clue is a postcard sent from Dawson, Virginia.

CONTINUITY #958
Wednesday, November 24, 1943
7:45–8:00 p.m. EWT
CBS
Martha Atwell, Director
Lawrence M. Klee, Writer
Philip Thorn, Editor
Ken Roberts, Announcer
American Home Products (Kolynos, Aerowax), Sponsor
"The Case of the Young Marine"
Before Mr. Keen can proceed with his investigation, Mrs. Harding, Steve's mother, receives word of her son's accidental death in Virginia. Keen and Mike Clancy seek more details.

CONTINUITY #959
Thursday, November 25, 1943
7:45–8:00 p.m. EWT
CBS
Martha Atwell, Director
Lawrence M. Klee, Writer
Philip Thorn, Editor
Ken Roberts, Announcer
American Home Products (Kolynos, Aerowax), Sponsor
"The Case of the Young Marine"
By a stroke of unusual luck, Mr. Keen discovers that the young man is now in San Francisco, a member of the Marine Corps on furlough. Mr. Keen takes a plane to the coast.

CONTINUITY #960
Friday, November 26, 1943
7:45–8:00 p.m. EWT

CBS
Martha Atwell, Director
Lawrence M. Klee, Writer
Philip Thorn, Editor
Ken Roberts, Announcer
American Home Products (Kolynos, Aerowax), Sponsor
"The Case of the Young Marine"

Mr. Keen catches up to the young recruit in California. The reason he kept out of sight for a year is revealed. Keen's multi-part adventures draw to a close with this episode, as the series subsequently takes on a new format.

NOTE: With the conclusion of the multi-part quarter-hour chapters aired three times weekly for over six years, Mr. Keen, Tracer of Lost Persons becomes a weekly feature, offering a self-contained story line in every broadcast. The scripts' continuity numbers restart at number 1 under the new format. Though I list these episodes using their new numbering system, I have included in brackets the number the episode would have carried had the system continued unchanged. In this way the reader may remain apprised of how many times the show aired from its inception, regardless of changes in formats. (During 1954 it reverts to multi-part episodes five nights weekly, while the self-contained plots continue simultaneously as a separate weekly feature.)

Regrettably, scripts for the initial 41 episodes in the self-contained storyline format, beginning December 2, 1943, have not been preserved. Continuity broadcast #42 (or #1002 since the show's debut) is the first extant script under that format. Luckily, 10 episodes from the 41 missing scripts have been discovered, providing some constructive data.

CONTINUITY #6 [966]
Thursday, January 6, 1944
7:30–8:00 p.m. EWT
CBS
Director's name omitted
Writer's name omitted
Editor's name omitted
Larry Elliott, Announcer
American Home Products (Kolynos, Aerowax), Sponsor
"The Case of the Moonless Night" (*Extant Episode*)

When Uncle Adam Meade disappears, Dorothea Meade summons Keen and Clancy to an antebellum plantation. The laws of inheritance come into play, and black walnut trees offer a hidden clue.

CONTINUITY #7 [967]
Thursday, January 13, 1944
7:30–8:00 p.m. EWT
CBS
Director's name omitted
Writer's name omitted
Editor's name omitted
Larry Elliott, Announcer
American Home Products (Kolynos, Aerowax), Sponsor
"The Case of the Missing Witness" (*Extant Episode*)

At a fashion show with Miss Ellis, Keen hears of the murder of Eric Plummer from Bunny Blaine, daughter of fashion designer Mary Blaine. Eric was Mary's fiancé; Bunny was smitten, too.

CONTINUITY #8 [968]
Thursday, January 20, 1944
7:30–8:00 p.m. EWT
CBS
Director's name omitted
Writer's name omitted
Editor's name omitted
Larry Elliott, Announcer
American Home Products (Kolynos, Aerowax), Sponsor
"The Case of the Girl Who Sang Too Well" (*Extant Episode*)

Skip Gordon's *Revue*, starring Lola Bennett, winds down after drawing sell-out Broadway crowds. Bennett disappears. Gordon hires Mr. Keen, admitting he secretly loves her.

CONTINUITY #9 [969]
Thursday, January 27, 1944
7:30–8:00 p.m. EWT
CBS
"The Case of the Man Who Didn't Come Home"

This title is mentioned at the conclusion of the previous week's episode, but no further information about it is available.

CONTINUITY #10 [970]
Thursday, February 3, 1944
7:30–8:00 p.m. EWT
CBS

Director's name omitted
Writer's name omitted
Editor's name omitted
Larry Elliott, Announcer
American Home Products (Kolynos, Aerowax), Sponsor
"The Case of the Girl Who Flirted" (*Extant Episode*)
 Museum officer Robert Colby involves Keen in the disappearance of art apprentice Elizabeth March, who refused to marry him. She had accepted a lunch date with a man she just met.

CONTINUITY #11 [971]
Thursday, February 10, 1944
7:30–8:00 p.m. EWT
CBS
Director's name omitted
Writer's name omitted
Editor's name omitted
Larry Elliott, Announcer
American Home Products (Kolynos, Aerowax), Sponsor
"The Case of the Boy Who Used Big Words" (*Extant Episode*)
 Young Jimmy Harmon, possessing a high IQ, tells Mr. Keen that something appalling is about to happen, and reports an encounter with a sinister figure in black that panicked Uncle Bill Harmon.

CONTINUITY #12 [972]
Thursday, February 17, 1944
7:30–8:00 p.m. EWT
CBS
Director's name omitted
Writer's name omitted
Editor's name omitted
Larry Elliott, Announcer
American Home Products (Kolynos, Aerowax), Sponsor
"The Case of Mr. Trevor's Secret" (*Extant Episode*)
 Keen and Clancy are summoned to a Connecticut plant critical to war production. Head chemical engineer Henry Trevor is missing. Has he fallen into enemy agent hands?

CONTINUITY #13 [973]
Thursday, February 24, 1944
7:30–8:00 p.m. EWT
CBS
Director's name omitted
Writer's name omitted
Editor's name omitted
Larry Elliott, Announcer
American Home Products (Kolynos, Aerowax), Sponsor
"The Case of Murder in the Air" (*Extant Episode*)
 Mr. Keen finds a very frightened Barbara Halliday in his office closet. She says she's marked for murder. She came to New York from Cleveland, and tells of three attempts on her life.

CONTINUITY #14 [974]
Thursday, March 2, 1944
7:30–8:00 p.m. EWT
CBS
"The Case of the Lady Who Didn't Want to be Found"
 This title is mentioned at the conclusion of the previous week's episode, but no further information is available.

CONTINUITY #16 [976]
Thursday, March 16, 1944
7:30–8:00 p.m. EWT
CBS
Director's name omitted
Writer's name omitted
Editor's name omitted
Larry Elliott, Announcer
American Home Products (Kolynos), Sponsor
"The Case of the Strange Display" (*Extant Episode*)
 Sally Wilson seeks Keen's aid in locating fiancé Jeff Jones, a window dresser, after he's accused of murdering his superior, Wendell Barton. Barton constantly rode him.

CONTINUITY #17 [977]
Thursday, March 23, 1944
7:30–8:00 p.m. EWT
CBS
"The Case of the Room That Vanished"
 This title is mentioned at the conclusion of the previous week's episode, but no further information is available.

CONTINUITY #20 [980]
Thursday, April 13, 1944

7:30–8:00 p.m. EWT
CBS
Director's name omitted
Writer's name omitted
Editor's name omitted
Larry Elliott, Announcer
American Home Products (Kolynos), Sponsor
"The Case of the Leaping Dog" (*Extant Episode*)

Keen and Clancy are drawn to a Belgian Shepherd baying outside the window of an apartment building near the office. The dog repeatedly leaps in the air and falls backward.

CONTINUITY #21 [981]
Thursday, April 20, 1944
7:30–8:00 p.m. EWT
CBS
"The Case of the Little Black Book"

This title is mentioned at the conclusion of the previous week's episode, but no further information is available.

CONTINUITY #29 [989]
Thursday, June 15, 1944
7:30–8:00 p.m. EWT
CBS
Director's name omitted
Writer's name omitted
Editor's name omitted
Larry Elliott, Announcer
American Home Products (Kolynos, Bi-So-Dol, Black Flag), Sponsor
"The Case of the Woman in Blue" (*Extant Episode*)

Air Force Lt. Don Lanson, home on leave, enlists Mr. Keen's help in finding a lady he just met and with whom he fell in love. He met Francia Jones at a masquerade ball.

CONTINUITY #30 [990]
Thursday, June 22, 1944
7:30–8:00 p.m. EWT
CBS
"The Case of the Hidden Motive"

This title is mentioned at the conclusion of the previous week's episode, but no further information is available.

NOTE: While the next episode for which a script currently exists is #42, only 41 weeks had passed from the documented inception of the longer, self-contained format on December 2, 1943, until #42's broadcast. The explanation for this incongruity remains unknown; one broadcast may have been omitted, or two shows might have aired in one week.

CONTINUITY #42 [1002]
Thursday, September 7, 1944
7:30–8:00 p.m. EWT
CBS
Richard Leonard, Director
David Davidson, Writer
Anne Hummert, Editor
Larry Elliott, Announcer
American Home Products (Kolynos, Anacin, Aerowax), Sponsor
"The Case of the Voices from the Past"

Mr. Keen and Mike Clancy are led into an intriguing tale involving several members of the same family with the surname French: Marian, Victoria, George and Wadsworth.

This is the first script available featuring Larry Elliott as announcer, Mr. Keen's most durable spokesman. Because his voice can be readily distinguished in the extant episodes broadcast earlier in the year, it may be presumed that he joined the cast with the format change on December 2, 1943.

CONTINUITY #43 [1003]
Thursday, September 14, 1944
7:30–8:00 p.m. EWT
CBS
Richard Leonard, Director
Marie Baumer, Writer
Anne Hummert, Editor
Larry Elliott, Announcer
American Home Products (Kolynos, Anacin, Aerowax), Sponsor
"The Case of the Siamese Cat"

As the tale opens in Mr. Keen's office, the kindly old tracer is grinning with amusement at Mike Clancy and Miss Ellis. However, neither of *them* is smiling, and both speak indignantly.

CONTINUITY #44 [1004]
Thursday, September 21, 1944
7:30–8:00 p.m. EWT
CBS
Richard Leonard, Director
Marie Baumer, Writer
Anne Hummert, Editor
Larry Elliott, Announcer

American Home Products (Kolynos, Anacin, Aerowax), Sponsor
"The Case of the Painted Horse"

The story begins on a gaudy midway that enlivens state and county fairs. On a sunny afternoon a young couple stand hand-in-hand at the merry-go-round.

CONTINUITY #45 [1005]
Thursday, September 28, 1944
7:30–8:00 p.m. EWT
CBS
Richard Leonard, Director
David Davidson, Writer
Anne Hummert, Editor
Larry Elliott, Announcer
American Home Products (Kolynos, Anacin, Aerowax), Sponsor
"The Case of the Landlocked Sailor"

Twelve characters are featured in this week's cast. Along with Mr. Keen and Mike Clancy are Inspector Lonsdale, Pierre Morrel, Carol Peters, Herr Vogel and a half-dozen more.

CONTINUITY #46 [1006]
Thursday, October 5, 1944
7:30–8:00 p.m. EWT
CBS
Richard Leonard, Director
David Davidson, Writer
Anne Hummert, Editor
Larry Elliott, Announcer
American Home Products (Kolynos, Anacin, Aerowax), Sponsor
"The Case of the Missing Motive"

Flanking Mr. Keen and Mike Clancy this week are Captain Thomas, Langley Drew, Mr. Horton, Rhoda Martin, Miss Gordon, Mrs. Lynch, a taxi driver and a page.

CONTINUITY #47 [1007]
Thursday, October 12, 1944
7:30–8:00 p.m. EWT
CBS
Richard Leonard, Director
David Davidson, Writer
Anne Hummert, Editor
Larry Elliott, Announcer
American Home Products (Kolynos, Anacin, Aerowax), Sponsor
"The Case of the Man Who Sent Flowers"

Along with the tracer and his assistant, we find Helen and Robert Porter, John Barlow, Alice Gardner, a prosecutor, a prison warden, a clerk, a girl, Jackson and sundry voices.

CONTINUITY #48 [1008]
Thursday, October 19, 1944
7:30–8:00 p.m. EWT
CBS
Richard Leonard, Director
Marie Baumer, Writer
Anne Hummert, Editor
Larry Elliott, Announcer
American Home Products (Kolynos, Anacin, Aerowax), Sponsor
"The Case of the Jeweled Hat Pin"

The story line features such figures as Mr. and Mrs. Andrews, Tom Hathaway, Police Lieutenant Evans, a prison guard and several others in addition to, of course, Keen and Clancy.

CONTINUITY #49 [1009]
Thursday, October 26, 1944
7:30–8:00 p.m. EWT
CBS
Richard Leonard, Director
Bennett Kilpack, Writer
Anne Hummert, Editor
Larry Elliott, Announcer
American Home Products (Kolynos, Anacin, Aerowax), Sponsor
"The Case of the Marked Hand"

David Perry vanishes after the cab in which he is riding with fiancée June Mason crashes. Found by Keen, Perry learns that his brother and another fellow have been rubbed out.

CONTINUITY #50 [1010]
Thursday, November 2, 1944
7:30–8:00 p.m. EWT
CBS
Richard Leonard, Director
Stedman Coles, Writer
Anne Hummert, Editor
Larry Elliott, Announcer
American Home Products (Kolynos, Anacin, Aerowax), Sponsor
"The Case of the Loaded Suitcase"

Harold and Marjorie Phillips are the focus of this investigation conducted by Keen and Clancy. Others in the company include Mark

Baldwin, Walter Conrad, Joyce Lipton and more.

CONTINUITY #51 [1011]
Thursday, November 9, 1944
7:30–8:00 p.m. EWT
CBS
Richard Leonard, Director
Marie Baumer, Writer
Anne Hummert, Editor
Larry Elliott, Announcer
American Home Products (Kolynos, Anacin, Aerowax), Sponsor
"The Case of the Girl and the Lost Violin"
    There's a dog in this adventure, along with Sheila Wayne and her mother, Toby Masters, Mrs. Sutherland, Norton and three Keen and Co. staff members—Keen, Clancy and Miss Ellis.

CONTINUITY #52 [1012]
Thursday, November 16, 1944
7:30–8:00 p.m. EWT
CBS
Richard Leonard, Director
Marie Baumer, Writer
Anne Hummert, Editor
Larry Elliott, Announcer
American Home Products (Kolynos, Anacin, Aerowax), Sponsor
"The Case of the Frightened Child" (*Extant Episode*)
    Joel is one frightened child in a mystery that also features Edith, Philip, George and Agnes Brandon, along with Lt. Evans and Clark. Mr. Keen and Mike Clancy do the fancy footwork.

CONTINUITY #53 [1013]
Thursday, November 23, 1944
7:30–8:00 p.m. EWT
CBS
Richard Leonard, Director
Bob Shaw, Writer
Anne Hummert, Editor
Larry Elliott, Announcer
American Home Products (Kolynos, Anacin, Aerowax), Sponsor
"The Case of the Two Strange and Beautiful Sisters"
    And those sisters are Julia and Hattie Best. Muriel Manson calls Mr. Keen and Mike Clancy into the case that also includes Dr. John Carson, George Prynne and Edward Manson.

CONTINUITY #54 [1014]
Thursday, November 30, 1944
7:30–8:00 p.m. EWT
CBS
Richard Leonard, Director
Marie Baumer, Writer
Anne Hummert, Editor
Larry Elliott, Announcer
American Home Products (Kolynos, Anacin, Aerowax), Sponsor
"The Case of the Stone That Was Worth a Fortune"
    There's mystery in the air when Keen, Clancy and Susie Hargrave follow the trail of a missing gem. Carl Lindquist, Mr. and Mrs. Peter Brant, Lieutenant Evans and others appear.

CONTINUITY #55 [1015]
Thursday, December 7, 1944
7:30–8:00 p.m. EWT
CBS
Richard Leonard, Director
Marie Baumer, Writer
Anne Hummert, Editor
Larry Elliott, Announcer
American Home Products (Kolynos, Anacin, Aerowax), Sponsor
"The Strange Case of the Guilty Woman"
    How is it to have a client who's admittedly guilty? Keen and Clancy will find out. Principals Martha and Edith Mitchell surface, along with others impacted by the "guilty" party.

CONTINUITY #56 [1016]
Thursday, December 14, 1944
7:30–8:00 p.m. EWT
CBS
Richard Leonard, Director
Bennett Kilpack, Writer
Anne Hummert, Editor
Larry Elliott, Announcer
American Home Products (Kolynos, Anacin, Aerowax), Sponsor
"The Nightmare Murder Case" (*Extant Episode*)
    Here's a murder case (not just a disappearing act) related by the killer himself! Keen, Clancy and Susie cross paths with Jim, Mary and Helen Nolan, John Olson and others.

CONTINUITY #57 [1017]
Thursday, December 21, 1944
7:30–8:00 p.m. EWT
CBS
Richard Leonard, Director
Edward Jurist, Writer
Anne Hummert, Editor
Larry Elliott, Announcer
American Home Products (Kolynos, Anacin, Aerowax), Sponsor
"The Case of the Rainbow Butterfly"
  In this plot we run across such figures as Professor and Eileen Manners, Mr. and Mrs. Rupert, a reporter, a sheriff, a postal clerk, an agent, and, of course, Keen and Mike Clancy.

CONTINUITY #58 [1018]
Thursday, December 28, 1944
7:30–8:00 p.m. EWT
CBS
Richard Leonard, Director
David Davidson, Writer
Anne Hummert, Editor
Larry Elliott, Announcer
American Home Products (Kolynos, Anacin, Aerowax), Sponsor
"The Case of the Man Who Wanted to Murder"
  Does that sound strange? Not for this show, especially considering *Mr. Keen*'s future focus. Keen, Clancy and Ellis meet John Weeks, Ginger Harvey, a prison guard, a warden, a cop and several other characters.

CONTINUITY #59 [1019]
Thursday, January 4, 1945
7:30–8:00 p.m. EWT
CBS
Richard Leonard, Director
Marie Baumer, Writer
Anne Hummert, Editor
Larry Elliott, Announcer
American Home Products (Kolynos, Hill's Cold Tablets, Aerowax), Sponsor
"The Case of the Guilty Conscience"
  Keen and Clancy encounter a small circle during this outing. They include Mrs. Williams, Mr. Winslow, Louise Winslow and a fellow known simply as David — a most intimate crowd.

CONTINUITY #60 [1020]
Thursday, January 11, 1945
7:30–8:00 p.m. EWT
CBS
Richard Leonard, Director
Marie Baumer, Writer
Anne Hummert, Editor
Larry Elliott, Announcer
American Home Products (Kolynos, Hill's, Aerowax), Sponsor
"The Case of Mr. Keen Takes a Partner"
  Mr. Keen as a vocalist? He is tonight when he sings a few bars of "A Bicycle Built for Two." Appearing also are staffers Clancy, Ellis, Hargrave and a passel of folks with trouble.

CONTINUITY #61 [1021]
Thursday, January 18, 1945
7:30–8:00 p.m. EWT
CBS
Richard Leonard, Director
David Davidson, Writer
Anne Hummert, Editor
Larry Elliott, Announcer
American Home Products (Kolynos, Hill's, Aerowax), Sponsor
"The Case of the Barber Shop Quartet"
  More music is in the air! Flanking a male quartet are Mrs. Shaw, Bill Hollis, Kid Knockout, Harry Roberts, a postal clerk and more, along with Mr. Keen, Mike Clancy and Miss Ellis.

CONTINUITY #62 [1022]
Thursday, January 25, 1945
7:30–8:00 p.m. EWT
CBS
Richard Leonard, Director
Lawrence M. Klee, Writer
Anne Hummert, Editor
Larry Elliott, Announcer
American Home Products (Kolynos, Hill's, Aerowax), Sponsor
"The Case of the Death Train"
  This intriguing melodrama features characters named Chip, Brock, Lewis, Diane Wilson, Mrs. Sydney and the conductor. There's Keen and Clancy, too.

CONTINUITY #63 [1023]
Thursday, February 1, 1945
7:30–8:00 p.m. EWT
CBS
Richard Leonard, Director

Marie Baumer, Writer
Anne Hummert, Editor
Larry Elliott, Announcer
American Home Products (Kolynos, Hill's, Aerowax), Sponsor
"The Case of the Evil Spirit"
    Who's mixing with the spirits? Keen and Clancy try to determine if it's Molly Keck, Josef Brant, a taxi driver, a dog or three members of the Ritter clan — Howard, Ida and Old Man Ritter.

CONTINUITY #64 [1024]
Thursday, February 8, 1945
7:30–8:00 p.m. EWT
CBS
Richard Leonard, Director
Lawrence M. Klee, Writer
Anne Hummert, Editor
Larry Elliott, Announcer
American Home Products (Kolynos, Hill's, Old English No-Rubbing Wax), Sponsor
"The Case of the Corpse Who Talked"
    This is eerie territory indeed! With Keen and Clancy this time out are Lance Hewitt, Inspector Poole, Mr. Targus, Olive, Robinson and Al. The theme should curdle one's blood.

CONTINUITY #65 [1025]
Thursday, February 15, 1945
7:30–8:00 p.m. EWT
CBS
Richard Leonard, Director
Edward Jurist, Writer
Anne Hummert, Editor
Larry Elliott, Announcer
American Home Products (Kolynos, Hill's, Old English), Sponsor
"The Case of the Man in the Tower"
    Along with Mr. Keen, Mike Clancy and Susie Hargrave, we find Mortimer Barrows, three from the Rumson family (Alex, Polly and John), Shelton, Lupari and two unidentified girls' voices.

CONTINUITY #66 [1026]
Thursday, February 22, 1945
7:30–8:00 p.m. EWT
CBS
Richard Leonard, Director
Marie Baumer, Writer
Anne Hummert, Editor
Larry Elliott, Announcer
American Home Products (Kolynos, Hill's, Old English), Sponsor
"The Case of the Music Box That Wouldn't Stop Playing"
    Here's some more music, this time from a music box! Keen and Clancy interact with Carter Dawson, Phoebe Atwater, Ellen Clark, Joe Edwards, Miss Wilson and a phone operator.

CONTINUITY #67 [1027]
Thursday, March 1, 1945
7:30–8:00 p.m. EWT
CBS
Richard Leonard, Director
Marie Baumer, Writer
Anne Hummert, Editor
Larry Elliott, Announcer
American Home Products (Kolynos, Hill's, Old English), Sponsor
"The Case of the Cross-Eyed Cat"
    How's that for an unusual topic? Here's a set of oddities: a cat, an old woman, an inspector, a detective, Sir Brouman-Jones, Ethel and George Thatcher, Keen, Clancy and Susie.

CONTINUITY #68 [1028]
Thursday, March 8, 1945
7:30–8:00 p.m. EWT
CBS
Richard Leonard, Director
Frank Kane, Writer
Anne Hummert, Editor
Announcer's name omitted
American Home Products (Kolynos, Hill's, Old English), Sponsor
"The Case of the Hidden Voice"
    Mr. Keen and Mike Clancy meet Ann Laramie, Earl Morton, Al Young, Hanson, Lipton, a page and a voice. The last guy isn't the hero of the drama, incidentally. Guess who is.

CONTINUITY #69 [1029]
Thursday, March 15, 1945
7:30–8:00 p.m. EWT
CBS
Richard Leonard, Director
David Davidson, Writer
Anne Hummert, Editor
Larry Elliott, Announcer
American Home Products (Kolynos, Hill's, Old English), Sponsor

"The Case of the Absent-Minded Professor" (*Extant Episode*)
Professor Roland Barton fits the description perfectly. Does he have something to hide? Mr. Keen and Mike Clancy investigate, and bring in professors Murray and Roberts with him.

CONTINUITY #70 [1030]
Thursday, March 22, 1945
7:30–8:00 p.m. EWT
CBS
Richard Leonard, Director
Marie Baumer, Writer
Anne Hummert, Editor
Larry Elliott, Announcer
American Home Products (Kolynos, Hill's, Old English), Sponsor
"The Case of the Bloodstained Piece of Tin"
Now there's a fascinating topic! We have a watchman but no sheriff. This episode features a very small cast of characters, including Miss Hall, Joe Dixon, Edie Carson and Mr. Peters (and Keen and Clancy, of course).

CONTINUITY #71 [1031]
Thursday, March 29, 1945
7:30–8:00 p.m. EWT
CBS
Richard Leonard, Director
David Davidson, Writer
Anne Hummert, Editor
Larry Elliott, Announcer
American Home Products (Kolynos, Hill's, Old English), Sponsor
"The Case of the Girl at the Switchboard"
Did she vanish? Her callers know for sure! And so, ultimately, do Mr. Keen and Mike Clancy, who meet 12 other players in this little farce, some of them merely voices on the phone line.

CONTINUITY #72 [1032]
Thursday, April 5, 1945
7:30–8:00 p.m. EWT
CBS
Richard Leonard, Director
Lawrence M. Klee, Writer
Anne Hummert, Editor
Larry Elliott, Announcer
American Home Products (Kolynos, Anacin, Old English), Sponsor
"The Case of the Walking Corpse"

Talk about your chilling tales—this *is* one! Keen and Clancy encounter Constable Jenkins (who's quite alive), along with Palmer, Dolly Dingle and Knight, a cozy trio involved in murder.

CONTINUITY #73 [1033]
The episode scheduled for April 12, 1945, continuity #73, was not aired due to President Franklin Delano Roosevelt's death, which occurred that day. The planned episode was withheld until the following week.

CONTINUITY #74 [1034]
Thursday, April 19, 1945
7:30–8:00 p.m. EWT
CBS
Richard Leonard, Director
David Davidson, Writer
Anne Hummert, Editor
Larry Elliott, Announcer
American Home Products (Kolynos, Anacin, Old English), Sponsor
"The Case of the Dangerous Wedding"
Mrs. Morgan Grenley, Alice and Roger Duncan, Mary Brent, Jane and those mysterious voices that seem to appear so frequently join Mr. Keen and Mike Clancy for this outing.

CONTINUITY #75 [1035]
The episode scheduled for April 26, 1945, continuity #75, was preempted by a live broadcast (from the San Francisco Opera House) of the first plenary session of the "San Francisco Conference," which laid the groundwork for the formation of the United Nations. The planned episode was withheld until the following week.

CONTINUITY #76 [1036]
Thursday, May 3, 1945
7:30–8:00 p.m. EWT
CBS
Richard Leonard, Director
David Davidson, Writer
Anne Hummert, Editor
Larry Elliott, Announcer
American Home Products (Kolynos, Anacin, Old English), Sponsor
"The Case of the Man with the Scar"
There are 15 (count 'em, 15!) roles in this story about a disfigured man. Keen and Clancy set out on a merry chase to solve the mystery.

CONTINUITY #77 [1037]
Thursday, May 10, 1945
7:30–8:00 p.m. EWT
CBS
Richard Leonard, Director
Bennett Kilpack, Writer
Anne Hummert, Editor
Larry Elliott, Announcer
American Home Products (Kolynos, Anacin, Old English), Sponsor
"The Case of the House on Washington Square"
　　Is the house on Washington Square haunted? Leave it to Keen, Clancy and Susie to find out. In yet another thriller, Calvin Meek, Philip and Wanda Van Steed, and a raft of others are along for the ride.

CONTINUITY #78 [1038]
Thursday, May 17, 1945
7:30–8:00 p.m. EWT
CBS
Richard Leonard, Director
Lawrence M. Klee, Writer
Anne Hummert, Editor
Larry Elliott, Announcer
American Home Products (Kolynos, Anacin, Old English), Sponsor
"The Footlight Murder Case"
　　Things become rather eerie in this tale involving Roberts, Conroy, Inspector Thompson, Darcy, Elaine Roberts, Cliff and Peggy. It's up to Keen and Clancy to sort it out.

CONTINUITY #79 [1039]
Thursday, May 24, 1945
7:30–8:00 p.m. EWT
CBS
Richard Leonard, Director
Frank Kane, Writer
Anne Hummert, Editor
Larry Elliott, Announcer
American Home Products (Kolynos, Anacin, Old English), Sponsor
"The Case of the Black Sheep"
　　It doesn't take three guesses to discern the nation of this story line. Helen Harris, Dr. Ed Matthews, Ace Daly, Inspector Thompson, Gloria Devon and others provide a challenge to Keen and Clancy.

CONTINUITY #80 [1040]
Thursday, May 31, 1945
7:30–8:00 p.m. EWT
CBS
Richard Leonard, Director
Frank Dahm, Writer
Anne Hummert, Editor
Larry Elliott, Announcer
American Home Products (Kolynos, Anacin, Old English), Sponsor
"The Case of the Missing Shoes"
　　Mr. Keen, Mike Clancy and Inspector Thompson investigate Alice Matthews, Paul Ames, Mrs. Greer, Bushels Belden and others. The shoes, incidentally, are the key to solving a major crime.

CONTINUITY #81 [1041]
Thursday, June 7, 1945
7:30–8:00 p.m. EWT
CBS
Richard Leonard, Director
Lillian Schoen, Writer
Anne Hummert, Editor
Larry Elliott, Announcer
American Home Products (Kolynos, Anacin, Black Flag), Sponsor
"The Case of Room 501"
　　What do Margery Sawyer, Danny, Russell, a watchman, a policeman and a cashier all have in common? They're involved with Mr. Keen and Mike Clancy, and the sinister plot in room 501.

CONTINUITY #82 [1042]
Thursday, June 14, 1945
7:30–8:00 p.m. EWT
CBS
Richard Leonard, Director
Latham Ovens, Writer
Anne Hummert, Editor
Larry Elliott, Announcer
American Home Products (Kolynos, Anacin, Black Flag), Sponsor
"The Case of the 20,000 Alibis"
　　Could the title contain something of an exaggeration? Mr. Keen and Mike Clancy are quick to the rescue in a tale featuring Matt Matson, Duke Williams, Marty McDonald and Doris Dineen.

CONTINUITY #83 [1043]
Thursday, June 21, 1945
7:30–8:00 p.m. EWT

CBS
Richard Leonard, Director
Frank Kane, Writer
Anne Hummert, Editor
Larry Elliott, Announcer
American Home Products (Kolynos, Anacin, Black Flag), Sponsor
"The Case of the Missing Spectacles"
    If seeing is believing, this case should be an eye-opener for Mr. Keen and Mike Clancy, who faced off against Harry and Ann Davies, Lopez, Ramirez, Tom Merrill, Captain Bale and others.

CONTINUITY #84 [1044]
Thursday, June 28, 1945
7:30–8:00 p.m. EWT
CBS
Richard Leonard, Director
Marie Baumer, Writer
Frank Dahm and Anne Hummert, Editors
Larry Elliott, Announcer
American Home Products (Kolynos, Anacin, Black Flag), Sponsor
"The Case of the Lonely Road"
    Here's a chiller that listeners won't soon forget. Maureen and Colin Shea, Mary Jarvis, Miss Richards, Adams and a nameless voice provide Keen and Clancy with some well-earned goose bumps.
    This episode was later repeated, with a new continuity number, for the broadcast of January 31, 1946.

CONTINUITY #85 [1045]
Thursday, July 5, 1945
7:30–8:00 p.m. EWT
CBS
Richard Leonard, Director
Lawrence M. Klee, Writer
Richard Leonard, Editor
Larry Elliott, Announcer
American Home Products (Kolynos, Anacin, Black Flag), Sponsor
"The Case of Murder on the Beach"
    Is this thriller a frightening nightmare or little more than a wet scream? Pat Downing, Laura, Jay and Carpenter provide suspects for the tracer and his partner ... and no shell games.

CONTINUITY #86–93 [1046–1053]
    Apparently none of these scripts have survived, although it is assumed that each of these chapters was broadcast during the time period of July 12 to August 30, 1945.

CONTINUITY #94 [1054]
Thursday, September 6, 1945
7:30–8:00 p.m. EWT
CBS
Richard Leonard, Director
Marie Baumer, Writer
Richard Leonard, Editor
Larry Elliott, Announcer
American Home Products (Kolynos, Anacin, Aerowax), Sponsor
"The Amazing Case of the Broadway Columnist"
    Miss Ellis reappears in the lineup with Keen and Clancy. Pete Hanson, Muriel Whitcomb, John Hartley, Ray Clark and Captain Thomas contribute to a journalistic-themed tale.

CONTINUITY #95 [1055]
Thursday, September 13, 1945
7:30–8:00 p.m. EWT
CBS
Richard Leonard, Director
Lawrence M. Klee, Writer
Richard Leonard, Editor
Larry Elliott, Announcer
American Home Products (Kolynos, Anacin, Aerowax), Sponsor
"The Case of Murder by Candlelight"
    Dinner by candlelight turns into something else. Keen and Clancy investigate a saga inolving a host of singularly-named characters: Kate, Ethel, Laura, Luther, Clara, John and Claude.

CONTINUITY #96 [1056]
Thursday, September 20, 1945
7:30–8:00 p.m. EWT
CBS
Richard Leonard, Director
Lawrence M. Klee, Writer
Richard Leonard, Editor
Larry Elliott, Announcer
American Home Products (Kolynos, Anacin, Aerowax), Sponsor
"The Case of the Necktie Murders"
    When Lane finds himself drugged at dinner, his host tightens the necktie he's wearing,

choking the life out of him. It's only the first of this perpetrator's dastardly deeds.

CONTINUITY #97 [1057]
Thursday, September 27, 1945
7:30–8:00 p.m. EWT
CBS
Richard Leonard, Director
Marie Baumer, Writer
Richard Leonard, Editor
Larry Elliott, Announcer
American Home Products (Kolynos, Anacin, Aerowax), Sponsor
"The Weird Case of the Girl Named Ethel"
　　Would you believe Ethel has no speaking role? But Arthur Lynch, Lucy Dibble, Flavius and Agnes Karns, a hotel clerk, a postmaster, a postmistress, a parrot and a mountain lion all do!

CONTINUITY #98 [1058]
Thursday, October 4, 1945
7:30–8:00 p.m. EWT
CBS
Richard Leonard, Director
Lawrence M. Klee, Writer
Richard Leonard, Editor
Larry Elliott, Announcer
American Home Products (Kolynos, Hill's, Aerowax), Sponsor
"The Case of the Smiling Corpse"
　　In a dressing room following an onstage theater show, movie idol Dean Fairchild laughs heartily. A guest rewards him with a pair of bullets. Keen and Mike Clancy have the job of identifying the culprit.

CONTINUITY #99 [1059]
Thursday, October 11, 1945
7:30–8:00 p.m. EST
CBS
Richard Leonard, Director
Lawrence M. Klee, Writer
Richard Leonard, Editor
Larry Elliott, Announcer
American Home Products (Kolynos, Hill's, Aerowax), Sponsor
"The Case of the Hidden Room"
　　Once more Keen writers provide a new treatment for an old, recurring subject. Keen and Clancy meet Florence Harrison, Mr. and Mrs. Carl Andrews, and others who harbor a secret hideaway.

CONTINUITY #100 [1060]
Thursday, October 18, 1945
7:30–8:00 p.m. EST
CBS
Richard Leonard, Director
Lawrence M. Klee, Writer
Richard Leonard, Editor
Larry Elliott, Announcer
American Home Products (Kolynos, Hill's, Aerowax), Sponsor
"The Case of the Perfect Murder"
　　Calling herself Gladys Revere, a runaway, Gladys Bell, age 23, is found shot to death in a rooming house on West 48th Street. Her father had asked Mr. Keen to find her only yesterday.

CONTINUITY #101 [1061]
Thursday, October 25, 1945
7:30–8:00 p.m. EST
CBS
Richard Leonard, Director
Lawrence M. Klee, Writer
Richard Leonard, Editor
Larry Elliott, Announcer
American Home Products (Kolynos, Hill's, Aerowax), Sponsor
"The Case of the Jealous Sister"
　　When sisters argue over the same man, things don't bode well for one of them. Shortly after Helen Wilson told Nancy she hated her, Nancy's car went over a cliff and burst into flames.

CONTINUITY #102 [1062]
Thursday, November 1, 1945
7:30–8:00 p.m. EST
CBS
Richard Leonard, Director
Lawrence M. Klee, Writer
Richard Leonard, Editor
Larry Elliott, Announcer
American Home Products (Kolynos, Hill's, Aerowax), Sponsor
"The Strange Case of Anna Norton"
　　Anna Norton is the victim of a heinous poisoning, sending her friend Mary Adams to Mr. Keen for help. Mary thinks the girl merely vanished, but will soon learn the awful truth.

CONTINUITY #103 [1063]
Thursday, November 8, 1945
7:30–8:00 p.m. EST

CBS
Richard Leonard, Director
Lawrence M. Klee, Writer
Richard Leonard, Editor
Larry Elliott, Announcer
American Home Products (Kolynos, Hill's, Aerowax), Sponsor
"The Case of the Man with the Twisted Mouth"
While John Arthur telephones Mr. Keen, someone strangles him, leaving slash marks all over his face. Is the guilty party Audrey Anderson, Dr. Denning or Mrs. Decker?

CONTINUITY #104 [1064]
Thursday, November 15, 1945
7:30–8:00 p.m. EST
CBS
Richard Leonard, Director
Marie Baumer, Writer
Richard Leonard, Editor
Larry Elliott, Announcer
American Home Products (Kolynos, Hill's, Aerowax), Sponsor
"The Case of the Missing Bridegroom"
Talk about standing up one's intended at the altar; it's worse when one party is murdered. Keen and Clancy delve into the unsettling scenario as they hunt for the missing person.

CONTINUITY #105 [1065]
Thursday, November 22, 1945
7:30–8:00 p.m. EST
CBS
Richard Leonard, Director
Lawrence M. Klee, Writer
Richard Leonard, Editor
Larry Elliott, Announcer
American Home Products (Kolynos, Hill's, Aerowax), Sponsor
"The Case of the Daring Young Man on the Flying Trapeze"
When a star circus performer comes crashing down to earth, Mr. Keen learns that a main guy rope was cut clean through. Which competitive colleague did it — Hank, Olga or Charles?

CONTINUITY #106 [1066]
Thursday, November 29, 1945
7:30–8:00 p.m. EST
CBS
Richard Leonard, Director
Lawrence M. Klee, Writer
Richard Leonard, Editor
Larry Elliott, Announcer
American Home Products (Kolynos, Hill's, Aerowax), Sponsor
"The Strange Case of Charley Lorimer"
Two men walking through some deserted woods run across a body. Has the local legend about people disappearing in those woods just become reality? And who is the dead man?

CONTINUITY #107 [1067]
Thursday, December 6, 1945
7:30–8:00 p.m. EST
CBS
Richard Leonard, Director
Lawrence M. Klee, Writer
Richard Leonard, Editor
Larry Elliott, Announcer
American Home Products (Kolynos, Hill's, Aerowax), Sponsor
"The Ballet Murder Case"
Guess what they find in ballerina Louisa's dressing room? Louisa — with a sword piercing her heart. Who could have done the dastardly deed? Barlov? Philip Ransom? Gwen Starling? Mr. Swade?

CONTINUITY #108 [1068]
Thursday, December 13, 1945
7:30–8:00 p.m. EST
CBS
Richard Leonard, Director
Marie Baumer, Writer
Richard Leonard, Editor
Larry Elliott, Announcer
American Home Products (Kolynos, Hill's, Aerowax), Sponsor
"The Weird Case of the Tolling Bell"
This is a story about ding-dongs: Charity, Faith and Hope Hopkins (such *cute* names!). The bell may toll for one of them. Whodunit? Hopkins, Asa Lumley or Ben Wilson?

CONTINUITY #109 [1069]
Thursday, December 20, 1945
7:30–8:00 p.m. EST
CBS
Richard Leonard, Director
Lawrence M. Klee, Writer
Richard Leonard, Editor

Larry Elliott, Announcer
American Home Products (Kolynos, Hill's, Aerowax), Sponsor
"The Case of the Man Who Confessed"

Pete Bartlett was laid off several months ago. His savings quickly depleted, he turned to Luther Craven, who loaned him cash at 30 percent interest. Now Craven is dead and Bartlett has confessed.

CONTINUITY #110 [1070]
Thursday, December 27, 1945
7:30–8:00 p.m. EST
CBS
Richard Leonard, Director
Lawrence M. Klee, Writer
Richard Leonard, Editor
Larry Elliott, Announcer
American Home Products (Kolynos, Hill's, Aerowax), Sponsor
"The Case of the Forecast of Death"

Mrs. Horn tells Keen she knows of several who'll welcome the news of Lois' (the victim's) demise. Lois received an unsigned note — "You will die tonight" — before a taxi struck her.

CONTINUITY #111 [1071]
Thursday, January 3, 1946
7:30–8:00 p.m. EST
CBS
Richard Leonard, Director
Marie Baumer, Writer
Richard Leonard, Editor
Larry Elliott, Announcer
American Home Products (Kolynos, Hill's, Aerowax), Sponsor
"The Sinister Case of the Talking Bird"

Was Max Darwin pecked to death by a parrot? Facial marks suggest so. Max's brother, pet shop owner Pete, and Betty Harrison, Pete's girlfriend and assistant, appeal to Keen.

CONTINUITY #112 [1072]
Thursday, January 10, 1946
7:30–8:00 p.m. EST
CBS
Richard Leonard, Director
Lawrence M. Klee, Writer
Richard Leonard, Editor
Larry Elliott, Announcer
American Home Products (Kolynos, Hill's, Aerowax), Sponsor
"The Case of the Disappearing Corpses"

Ice company night watchman Joe finds stiffs that vanish. Before long, Joe himself is murdered. What to make of this? Mr. Bolen, Hank Gow, Helen English, and John Bolen are all suspects.

CONTINUITY #113 [1073]
Thursday, January 17, 1946
7:30–8:00 p.m. EST
CBS
Richard Leonard, Director
Marie Baumer, Writer
Richard Leonard, Editor
Larry Elliott, Announcer
American Home Products (Kolynos, Hill's, Aerowax), Sponsor
"The Strange Case of the Sound of Death"

Finding Ed Carter dead (from a fatal blow to the head), Walter Hansen announces, "We've never had anything like this!" Mr. Keen responds, "Well, you've got it now." Award-winning dialogue!

CONTINUITY #114 [1074]
Thursday, January 24, 1946
7:30–8:00 p.m. EST
CBS
Richard Leonard, Director
Lawrence M. Klee, Writer
Richard Leonard, Editor
Larry Elliott, Announcer
American Home Products (Kolynos, Hill's, Aerowax), Sponsor
"The Strange Case of the Baldheaded Man"

When her stepmother and she can't get along, Lorna Higby, age 17, moves out of her home. Now Lorna's father is accused of murder. Lorna pleads for Mr. Keen to prove his innocence.

CONTINUITY #115 [1075]
Thursday, January 31, 1946
7:30–8:00 p.m. EST
CBS
Richard Leonard, Director
Marie Baumer, Writer
Richard Leonard, Editor
Larry Elliott, Announcer
American Home Products (Kolynos, Hill's, Aerowax), Sponsor
"The Case of the Lonely Road"

A horse-drawn cart pulls up in front of a home — with a dead man still holding the reins. And Maureen Shea's father has disappeared. How are the two events connected? It's Mr. Keen to the rescue.

This sequence aired previously, under a different continuity number, on June 28, 1945.

CONTINUITY #116 [1076]
Thursday, February 7, 1946
7:30–8:00 p.m. EST
CBS
Richard Leonard, Director
Lawrence M. Klee, Writer
Richard Leonard, Editor
Larry Elliott, Announcer
American Home Products (Kolynos, Hill's, Aerowax), Sponsor
"The Case of the Murdered Bride"

When Louise Reading is shot to death on her wedding day, her betrothed, Keith Travers, is devastated. What clues will Keen turn up to point a finger at the crime's perpetrator?

Actors in this episode include Helen Claire, Vinton Hayworth, Julie Stevens, Francis DeSales, Charles Webster, Ken Lynch, Flora Campbell and John Brewster.

CONTINUITY #117 [1077]
Thursday, February 14, 1946
7:30–8:00 p.m. EST
CBS
Richard Leonard, Director
Lawrence M. Klee, Writer
Richard Leonard, Editor
Larry Elliott, Announcer
American Home Products (Kolynos, Hill's, Aerowax), Sponsor
"The Strange Case of Nancy Rodgers"

When Nancy Rodgers can't recall driving a car with her dead fiancé in it, there's a logical explanation — she inherited an amnesia-like disease that results in temporary memory loss.

Actors in this episode include Bill Zuckert, Elaine Kent, Betty Garde, and James Van Dyk.

CONTINUITY #118 [1078]
Thursday, February 21, 1946
7:30–8:00 p.m. EST
CBS
Richard Leonard, Director
Lawrence M. Klee, Writer
Richard Leonard, Editor
Larry Elliott, Announcer
American Home Products (Kolynos, Hill's, Aerowax), Sponsor
"The Amazing Case of the Shrunken Head"

Lucy Prescott had a dilemma. Peter Harris fell in love with her, but she felt fonder towards Allen Robinson. Allen was stabbed to death with a hatpin. Now, no more dilemma!

Actors in this episode include Mary Jane Higby, Paul Potter, Donald Briggs, and Audrey Egan.

CONTINUITY #119 [1079]
Thursday, February 28, 1946
7:30–8:00 p.m. EST
CBS
Richard Leonard, Director
Lawrence M. Klee, Writer
Richard Leonard, Editor
Larry Elliott, Announcer
American Home Products (Kolynos, Hill's, Aerowax), Sponsor
"The Case of the Scarboro Murders"

Artie Hicks is shot to death in suburban Scarboro. A pair of newcomers to the neighborhood, newlyweds at that, are about to ruin two innocent people's lives with accusations.

Actors in this episode include Bess Johnson, Bob Reddick, Larry Haines, Frances Robinson, and Vivian Smolen.

CONTINUITY #120 [1080]
Thursday, March 7, 1946
7:30–8:00 p.m. EST
CBS
Richard Leonard, Director
Lawrence M. Klee, Writer
Richard Leonard, Editor
Larry Elliott, Announcer
American Home Products (Kolynos, Hill's, Aerowax), Sponsor
"The Case of the Golden Palm"

Fifty people watch as Mrs. Bender drowns in the pool at the Golden Palm, the hotel she inherited from her first spouse. But no post mortem is performed. Keen suspects poison.

CONTINUITY #121 [1081]
Thursday, March 14, 1946
7:30–8:00 p.m. EST
CBS

Richard Leonard, Director
Lawrence M. Klee, Writer
Richard Leonard, Editor
Larry Elliott, Announcer
American Home Products (Kolynos, Hill's, Aerowax), Sponsor
"The Case of the Twisted Ring"
   While Alice Porter, Mr. Keen and Mike Clancy await the impending appearance of Alice's father, two shots ring out. The sleuths find Porter inside, with two bullets in the brain.

CONTINUITY #122 [1082]
Thursday, March 21, 1946
7:30–8:00 p.m. EST
CBS
Richard Leonard, Director
Lawrence M. Klee, Writer
Richard Leonard, Editor
Larry Elliott, Announcer
American Home Products (Kolynos, Hill's, Aerowax), Sponsor
"The Case of the Candid Cameraman"
   "I usually deal only with missing people, Mr. Bruce, missing people — and murder," Keen says. Then Bruce hears that his friend Hank Russell has been murdered; and Keen has a new client.

CONTINUITY #123 [1083]
Thursday, March 28, 1946
7:30–8:00 p.m. EST
CBS
Richard Leonard, Director
Lawrence M. Klee, Writer
Richard Leonard, Editor
Larry Elliott, Announcer
American Home Products (Kolynos, Hill's, Aerowax), Sponsor
"The Case of the Blackstone Mansion"
   When a client relays his suspicion that a murder has been committed in a mansion he owns, Mike Clancy scoops up crumbled cement with his bare hands. He soon finds a woman who has been strangled to death.

CONTINUITY #124 [1084]
Thursday, April 4, 1946
7:30–8:00 p.m. EST
CBS
Richard Leonard, Director
Lawrence M. Klee, Writer

Richard Leonard, Editor
Larry Elliott, Announcer
American Home Products (Kolynos, Anacin, Aerowax), Sponsor
"The Case of the Poisoned Quill"
   Is Jill Adams jinxed? Boyfriend Ned dies in a tragic fire. Boyfriend Bruce leans over a pier too far, falls and drowns. Boyfriend Henry falls from a window and dies. Coincidence?
   Actors in this episode include Vivian Smolen, Elsie Hitz, Ann Shepherd, William Smith, Boyd Crawford, and Winston O'Keefe.

CONTINUITY #125 [1085]
Thursday, April 11, 1946
7:30–8:00 p.m. EST
CBS
Richard Leonard, Director
Lawrence M. Klee, Writer
Richard Leonard, Editor
Larry Elliott, Announcer
American Home Products (Kolynos, Anacin, Aerowax), Sponsor
"The Case of the Talking Mummy"
   Egyptian archeologist Albert Coppersmith is stabbed in the back (literally), and the gems he kept with the King Helmut mummy disappear. But son Ralph thinks the motive isn't theft.

CONTINUITY #126 [1086]
Thursday, April 18, 1946
7:30–8:00 p.m. EST
CBS
Richard Leonard, Director
Lawrence M. Klee, Writer
Richard Leonard, Editor
Larry Elliott, Announcer
American Home Products (Kolynos, Anacin, Aerowax), Sponsor
"The Case of the Runaway Horse"
   People say Philip Harlan died when his mount, Betsy, threw him. But ex-jockey Henry Jackson knows horses, he assures Keen, and says Betsy can be trusted: Harlan was murdered.

CONTINUITY #127 [1087]
Thursday, April 25, 1946
7:30–8:00 p.m. EST
CBS
Richard Leonard, Director

Marie Baumer, Writer
Richard Leonard, Editor
Larry Elliott, Announcer
American Home Products (Kolynos, Anacin, Old English No-Rubbing Wax), Sponsor
"The Sinister Case of the Wandering Singer"

When Harry Kimball dies, siblings Alfred and Stephen — who owned a chain of restaurants with him — label it suicide. But others aren't convinced, and neither is Mr. Keen.

CONTINUITY #128 [1088]
Thursday, May 2, 1946
7:30–8:00 p.m. EDST
CBS
Richard Leonard, Director
Marie Baumer, Writer
Richard Leonard, Editor
Larry Elliott, Announcer
American Home Products (Kolynos, Anacin, Old English), Sponsor
"The Case of the Sea Cove Strangler"

When her friend Elsie is strangled to death on the shore, Flora tells Mr. Keen that Elsie was the killer's third victim. Mr. Keen investigates.

CONTINUITY #129 [1089]
Thursday, May 9, 1946
7:30–8:00 p.m. EDST
CBS
Richard Leonard, Director
Lawrence M. Klee, Writer
Richard Leonard, Editor
Larry Elliott, Announcer
American Home Products (Kolynos, Anacin, Old English), Sponsor
"The Case of the Fabulous Necklace"

When a retail jeweler, Howard Pool, is found dead in his shop, jewel importer Mr. McCoy appeals to Mr. Keen to find his murderer. McCoy claims the death will hurt his reputation.

Actors in this episode include David Gothard, Eleanor Sherman, Paul McGrath, Martin Rudy, Flora Campbell and Karl Weber.

CONTINUITY #130 [1090]
Thursday, May 16, 1946
7:30–8:00 p.m. EDST
CBS
Richard Leonard, Director
Lawrence M. Klee, Writer

Richard Leonard, Editor
Larry Elliott, Announcer
American Home Products (Kolynos, Anacin, Old English), Sponsor
"The Case of Death in the Park"

A farmer rides a Ferris wheel at a county fair. When the ride ends, he's found sitting up, but dead. A heart attack is blamed, but his daughter doesn't buy it.

CONTINUITY #131 [1091]
Thursday, May 23, 1946
7:30–8:00 p.m. EDST
CBS
Richard Leonard, Director
Lawrence M. Klee, Writer
Richard Leonard, Editor
Larry Elliott, Announcer
American Home Products (Kolynos, Anacin, Old English), Sponsor
"The Case of the Glamorous Widow" (*Extant Episode*)

Addie Thompson, Doris Carlyle's personal maid, asks Keen to find her employer's murderer. An overdose of sleeping pills is thought to have killed her, but Addie says Doris never took them.

CONTINUITY #132 [1092]
Thursday, May 30, 1946
7:30–8:00 p.m. EDST
CBS
Richard Leonard, Director
Lawrence M. Klee, Writer
Richard Leonard, Editor
Larry Elliott, Announcer
American Home Products (Kolynos, Anacin, Old English), Sponsor
"The Case of the Golden Scorpion"

When her father is murdered with a poisoned dart, Sally Blake leaves her Pennsylvania home to go to New York with a golden scorpion that she's certain the killer will kill again in order to obtain.

CONTINUITY #133 [1093]
Thursday, June 6, 1946
7:30–8:00 p.m. EDST
CBS
Richard Leonard, Director
Lawrence M. Klee, Writer
Richard Leonard, Editor

Larry Elliott, Announcer
American Home Products (Kolynos, Anacin, Bi-So-Dol), Sponsor
"The Case of the House of Death"

Roy and Mary Holden rent a home in New Jersey. The last thing they expect to find are charred human bones stashed in the cellar. But when they do, they carry the box of proof to Keen.

CONTINUITY #134 [1094]

Thursday, June 13, 1946
7:30–8:00 p.m. EDST
CBS
Richard Leonard, Director
Marie Baumer, Writer
Richard Leonard, Editor
Larry Elliott, Announcer
American Home Products (Kolynos, Anacin, Bi-So-Dol), Sponsor
"The Tragic Case of the Chiming Watch"

Muriel Sheldon tells Barbara Marshall she's having dinner with a man called "John" (an alias) at the Blue Peacock. Later she is found stabbed in the alley behind the place.

CONTINUITY #135 [1095]

Thursday, June 20, 1946
7:30–8:00 p.m. EDST
CBS
Richard Leonard, Director
Lawrence M. Klee, Writer
Richard Leonard, Editor
Larry Elliott, Announcer
American Home Products (Kolynos, Anacin, Bi-So-Dol), Sponsor
"The Case of the Unfinished Portrait"

The police reason that the wife of artist's model Bob Stanley is the only person to profit from Bob's death. So when he dies by poison, they arrest her. But Stanley's agent, Jimmy Larribee, argues differently.

Arthur Hughes substitutes as Mr. Keen in this episode, filling in for Bennett Kilpack, who is ill.

CONTINUITY #136 [1096]

Thursday, June 27, 1946
7:30–8:00 p.m. EDST
CBS
Richard Leonard, Director
Lawrence M. Klee, Writer
Richard Leonard, Editor
Larry Elliott, Announcer
American Home Products (Kolynos, Anacin, Bi-So-Dol), Sponsor
"The Case of the Stuffed Kangaroo"

When he last saw Florence Erwin — wife of taxidermist George, who runs a shop opposite his small grocery — Mr. Wilbur says she was very unhappy. That was three weeks ago. Where is she now?

Arthur Hughes again substitutes as Mr. Keen in this episode, filling in for Bennett Kilpack, who is ill.

CONTINUITY #137 [1097]

Thursday, July 4, 1946
7:30–8:00 p.m. EDST
CBS
Richard Leonard, Director
William Morwood, Writer
Richard Leonard, Editor
Larry Elliott, Announcer
American Home Products (Kolynos, Anacin, Bi-So-Dol), Sponsor
"The Case of the Whimpering Dog"

It's déjà vu for Keen. He investigates the disappearance of Philip R. Mason, who left for his office one day but never arrived. Six weeks have gone by, and his wife is frantic.

Arthur Hughes substitutes as Mr. Keen in this episode, filling in for Bennett Kilpack, who is ill.

CONTINUITY #138 [1098]

Thursday, July 11, 1946
7:30–8:00 p.m. EDST
CBS
Richard Leonard, Director
Lawrence M. Klee, Writer
Richard Leonard, Editor
Larry Elliott, Announcer
American Home Products (Kolynos, Anacin, Bi-So-Dol), Sponsor
"The Case of the Phantom Killer"

Lillian Hall's father and aunt have been murdered in broad daylight, prompting newspapers to dub the culprit "the Phantom Killer." Lillian convinces herself that she's next on the hit list.

Arthur Hughes substitutes as Mr. Keen in this episode, filling in for Bennett Kilpack, who is ill.

CONTINUITY #139 [1099]
Thursday, July 18, 1946
7:30–8:00 p.m. EDST
CBS
Richard Leonard, Director
Lawrence M. Klee, Writer
Richard Leonard, Editor
Larry Elliott, Announcer
American Home Products (Kolynos, Anacin, Bi-So-Dol), Sponsor
"The Case of the Scar-faced Stoker"
 When an expensive antiques dealer books passage from Lima, Peru, to New York, but is never seen aboard and has been missing for weeks, it sounds a little fishy to daughter Marjorie.
 Arthur Hughes substitutes as Mr. Keen in this segment, filling in for Bennett Kilpack, who is ill.

CONTINUITY #140 [1100]
Thursday, July 25, 1946
7:30–8:00 p.m. EDST
CBS
Richard Leonard, Director
Marie Baumer, Writer
Richard Leonard, Editor
Larry Elliott, Announcer
American Home Products (Kolynos, Anacin, Bi-So-Dol), Sponsor
"The Weird Case of the Roaring Lion"
 Was Howard Greenleaf, in a plaster cast and thus immobile, frightened to death when a lion roared outside his house? With no mark on him, could death have been due to a heart attack?

CONTINUITY #141 [1101]
Thursday, August 1, 1946
7:30–8:00 p.m. EDST
CBS
Richard Leonard, Director
Lawrence M. Klee, Writer
Richard Leonard, Editor
Larry Elliott, Announcer
American Home Products (Kolynos, Anacin, Bi-So-Dol), Sponsor
"The Case of the Straw-Hat Murder"
 Aspiring actresses (and sisters) Ginny and Doris Fawcett play the straw-hat circuit (Broadway plays staged in rural areas). Ginny is killed with a blunt object, and Doris could be next.

CONTINUITY #142 [1102]
Thursday, August 8, 1946
7:30–8:00 p.m. EDST
CBS
Martha Atwell, Director
Lawrence M. Klee, Writer
Mr. Nobbs, Editor
Larry Elliott, Announcer
American Home Products (Kolynos, Anacin, Bi-So-Dol), Sponsor
"The Case of the Fatal Ruby"
 Ralph Cotton is positive someone tried to kill him twice, and is afraid his luck won't hold out much longer. It started as he walked home from work in a "rough neighborhood" on Fourth Street.
 Arthur Hughes substitutes as Mr. Keen in this episode, filling in for Bennett Kilpack, who is ill.

CONTINUITY #143 [1103]
Thursday, August 15, 1946
7:30–8:00 p.m. EDST
CBS
Richard Leonard, Director
Marie Baumer, Writer
Richard Leonard, Editor
Larry Elliott, Announcer
American Home Products (Kolynos, Anacin, Bi-So-Dol), Sponsor
"The Case of the Sinister Room"
 Kimball Stewart obtains the key to a locked gun closet from sibling Dick in order to kill a fox who's after his chickens. But Kimball winds up shot dead himself after sleeping in a terrifying room.
 Arthur Hughes substitutes as Mr. Keen in this episode, filling in for Bennett Kilpack, who is ill. Other actors in this epidsode include David Gothard, Bartlett Robinson, William J. Smith, Vera Allen, and Charita Bauer.

CONTINUITY #144 [1104]
Thursday, August 22, 1946
7:30–8:00 p.m. EDST
CBS
Richard Leonard, Director
Lawrence M. Klee, Writer
Richard Leonard, Editor
Larry Elliott, Announcer
American Home Products (Kolynos, Anacin, Bi-So-Dol), Sponsor

"The Case of the Mapleton Murder"

Mrs. Lawson, a licensed practical nurse and caretaker for kindly, wealthy, retired invalid Henry Carpenter of Mapleton, Delaware, tells Mr. Keen about the night he was murdered.

Arthur Hughes substitutes as Mr. Keen in this episode, filling in for Bennett Kilpack, who is ill.

CONTINUITY #145 [1105]
Thursday, August 29, 1946
7:30–8:00 p.m. EDST
CBS
Richard Leonard, Director
Lawrence M. Klee, Writer
Richard Leonard, Editor
Larry Elliott, Announcer
American Home Products (Kolynos, Anacin, Bi-So-Dol), Sponsor
"The Case of the Prelude to Death"

Joan Patterson went to Professor Martin's room for a piano lesson, but the maestro wasn't there. Martin's granddaughter heard a scream and came running, only to find Joan on the floor with her neck broken.

Arthur Hughes substitutes as Mr. Keen in this episode, filling in for Bennett Kilpack, who is ill.

CONTINUITY #146 [1106]
Thursday, September 5, 1946
7:30–8:00 p.m. EDST
CBS
Richard Leonard, Director
Lawrence M. Klee, Writer
Richard Leonard, Editor
Larry Elliott, Announcer
American Home Products (Kolynos, Anacin, Bi-So-Dol), Sponsor
"The Case of the Pinpoint Murder"

An autopsy performed on Lucy Prescott's mother indicates that the woman died of snakebite poisoning. But Lucy isn't satisfied. She presses the matter with Keen, who looks into it further.

Arthur Hughes substitutes as Mr. Keen in this episode, filling in for Bennett Kilpack, who is ill. Additional actors in this sequence include Joy Hathaway, Mitzi Gould, Ned Wever, Frank Dane, and Robert Haag.

CONTINUITY #147 [1107]
Thursday, September 12, 1946
7:30–8:00 p.m. EDST
CBS
Richard Leonard, Director
Lawrence M. Klee, Writer
Richard Leonard, Editor
Larry Elliott, Announcer
American Home Products (Kolynos, Anacin, Bi-So-Dol), Sponsor
"The Case of the Yellow Envelope"

Bill Shelley receives a yellow envelope containing a live white moth. Wife Louise takes this as some kind of death omen. Bill hides in their apartment while she pleads to Keen.

Arthur Hughes substitutes as Mr. Keen in this episode, filling in for Bennett Kilpack, who is ill.

CONTINUITY #148 [1108]
Thursday, September 19, 1946
7:30–8:00 p.m. EDST
CBS
Richard Leonard, Director
Lawrence M. Klee, Writer
Richard Leonard, Editor
Larry Elliott, Announcer
American Home Products (Kolynos, Anacin, Bi-So-Dol), Sponsor
"The Case of the Leaping Shark"

What does a gambling ship named the *Leaping Shark*, sailing outside the 12-mile limit off the New Jersey coast, have to do with the disappearance of Philip King? Keen is about to find out.

Arthur Hughes substitutes as Mr. Keen in this episode, filling in for Bennett Kilpack, who is ill. Other actors in this sequence include Toni Darnay, Spencer Bentley, Joe Julian, Grant Richards, Eleanor Sherman, Louis Hall, and Frank Richards.

CONTINUITY #149 [1109]
Thursday, September 26, 1946
7:30–8:00 p.m. EDST
CBS
Richard Leonard, Director
Lawrence M. Klee, Writer
Richard Leonard, Editor
Larry Elliott, Announcer
American Home Products (Kolynos, Hill's, Bi-So-Dol), Sponsor

"The Case of the Great Montclair"

A stage magician places a girl, Lola Richards, in a box to make her disappear before an audience. But when he opens the box, she's still there — with a knife in her back!

CONTINUITY #150 [1110]
Thursday, October 3, 1946
7:30–8:00 p.m. EST
CBS
Richard Leonard, Director
Lawrence M. Klee, Writer
Richard Leonard, Editor
Larry Elliott, Announcer
American Home Products (Kolynos, Bi-So-Dol, Hill's), Sponsor
"The Case of the Vanishing Strangler"

Burton Rivers insists on Mr. Keen's intervention when Laura Anderson's body is found in a park after she missed their date there. She's the third victim in a string of similar murders, and Rivers is a suspect.

CONTINUITY #151 [1111]
Thursday, October 10, 1946
7:30–8:00 p.m. EST
CBS
Richard Leonard, Director
Lawrence M. Klee, Writer
Richard Leonard, Editor
Larry Elliott, Announcer
American Home Products (Kolynos, Bi-So-Dol, Hill's), Sponsor
"The Case of the Man Who Repented"

Thinking it is he who's to blame for business partner Raymond Garrett's death, James Harris admits his foul deed to Keen. He accused Garrett of debauchery before "killing" him.

CONTINUITY #152 [1112]
Thursday, October 17, 1946
7:30–8:00 p.m. EST
CBS
Richard Leonard, Director
Lawrence M. Klee, Writer
Richard Leonard, Editor
Larry Elliott, Announcer
American Home Products (Kolynos, Bi-So-Dol, Hill's), Sponsor
"The Sedan Murder Case"

Cliff Ridley's father is found slumped beside his car in the garage. The hood was raised and the motor running, but the garage door was closed. The police call it an accident, but Cliff thinks otherwise.

CONTINUITY #153 [1113]
Thursday, October 24, 1946
7:30–8:00 p.m. EST
CBS
Richard Leonard, Director
Lawrence M. Klee, Writer
Richard Leonard, Editor
Larry Elliott, Announcer
American Home Products (Kolynos, Bi-So-Dol, Hill's), Sponsor
"The Case of the Crowded Cemetery"

Elsie Taylor goes to Mr. Keen with the request that he locate fiancé Frank Sills' father. Though the elder Sills opposed her and Frank's planned nuptials, she's certain he wouldn't have run away.

CONTINUITY #154 [1114]
Thursday, October 31, 1946
7:30–8:00 p.m. EST
CBS

This script is missing from the permanent repository file.

CONTINUITY #155 [1115]
Thursday, November 7, 1946
7:30–8:00 p.m. EST
CBS
Richard Leonard, Director
Lawrence M. Klee, Writer
Richard Leonard, Editor
Larry Elliott, Announcer
American Home Products (Kolynos, Bi-So-Dol, Hill's), Sponsor
"The Case of the Corpse Who Struck Back"

Helen Corning wed in New York and moved to California. Days later her father, a bed-ridden invalid, died "accidentally." No, it was "calculated murder," Helen claims.

CONTINUITY #156 [1116]
Thursday, November 14, 1946
7:30–8:00 p.m. EST
CBS
Richard Leonard, Director
Lawrence M. Klee, Writer
Richard Leonard, Editor
Larry Elliott, Announcer

American Home Products (Kolynos, Bi-So-Dol, Hill's), Sponsor
"The Case of the White Carnation Murder"

Lester Craig is engaged to David Nelson's mother. Craig says he will fund David's law school education and set him up in a practice. Still, bitter about the marriage, David leaves—and Craig dies.

CONTINUITY #157 [1117]
Thursday, November 21, 1946
7:30–8:00 p.m. EST
CBS
Richard Leonard, Director
Marie Baumer, Writer
Richard Leonard, Editor
Larry Elliott, Announcer
American Home Products (Kolynos, Bi-So-Dol, Hill's), Sponsor
"The Case of the Bloodstained Calendar"

While cooking, Hilda Harrison thinks she's using sugar but it's actually insect powder. She dies. Elizabeth Loomis announces that it is *she* the murderer hoped to silence.

CONTINUITY #158 [1118]
Thursday, November 28, 1946
7:30–8:00 p.m. EST
CBS
Richard Leonard, Director
Lawrence M. Klee, Writer
Richard Leonard, Editor
Larry Elliott, Announcer
American Home Products (Kolynos, Bi-So-Dol, Hill's), Sponsor
"The Case of the Murder Mansion"

Brad Lawson, possessing a shady history, runs a gambling house on New York's East Side in a brownstone mansion. Ellen Todd meets him and vanishes. Her father thinks she's probably dead.

CONTINUITY #159 [1119]
Thursday, December 5, 1946
7:30–8:00 p.m. EST
CBS
Richard Leonard, Director
Lawrence M. Klee, Writer
Richard Leonard, Editor
Larry Elliott, Announcer
American Home Products (Kolynos, Bi-So-Dol, Hill's), Sponsor
"The Case of the Missing Teacup"

Douglas Sprague points out to Keen and Clancy the body of Wallace Young lying on the floor. Keen assesses: "By the agonized expression of his face, I'd say he died of poison."

CONTINUITY #160 [1120]
Thursday, December 12, 1946
7:30–8:00 p.m. EST
CBS
Richard Leonard, Director
Marie Baumer, Writer
Richard Leonard, Editor
Larry Elliott, Announcer
American Home Products (Kolynos, Bi-So-Dol, Hill's), Sponsor
"The Case of the Wife Who Dreamed of Murder"

At the insistence of Alicia Grant, Isabel Dayton sees a fortune teller, who predicts precisely what she has dreamed for a month: that Bob, her spouse, will be strangled in their library.

CONTINUITY #161 [1121]
Thursday, December 19, 1946
7:30–8:00 p.m. EST
CBS
Richard Leonard, Director
Lawrence M. Klee, Writer
Richard Leonard, Editor
Larry Elliott, Announcer
American Home Products (Kolynos, Bi-So-Dol, Hill's), Sponsor
"The Case of the Lead-Lined Capsule"

Would a doctor in shirtsleeves risk pneumonia in cold winter weather by stepping out onto a high balcony to admire the view after he said he had no intention of doing so, then topple to his death?

CONTINUITY #162 [1122]
Thursday, December 26, 1946
7:30–8:00 p.m. EST
CBS
Richard Leonard, Director
Lawrence M. Klee, Writer
Richard Leonard, Editor
Larry Elliott, Announcer
American Home Products (Kolynos, Bi-So-Dol, Hill's), Sponsor
"The Case of Murder and the Double Mystery"

Lucy Andrews and Frank Gordon broke their engagement. Three months later she drops by to see him, but he has vanished. She doesn't realize — in this life, anyway — that he's never coming back.

CONTINUITY #163 [1123]
Thursday, January 2, 1947
7:30–8:00 p.m. EST
CBS
Richard Leonard, Director
Marie Baumer, Writer
Richard Leonard, Editor
Larry Elliott, Announcer
American Home Products (Kolynos, Anacin, Hill's), Sponsor
"The Case of the Telephone That Would Not Stop Ringing"
Hubert Marlowe can't get anyone to speak when he answers the incessant calls to his phone. Neither can Mrs. Peabody, his aide. Now he has vanished — does that portend a familiar ring?

CONTINUITY #164 [1124]
Thursday, January 9, 1947
7:30–8:00 p.m. EST
CBS
Richard Leonard, Director
Lawrence M. Klee, Writer
Richard Leonard, Editor
Larry Elliott, Announcer
American Home Products (Kolynos, Anacin, Hill's), Sponsor
"The Case of the Goat Woman"
Somebody gets Floyd Arnold's goat — at least his goat milk (good for "ailing adults") — and poisons it. The milk comes from Mrs. Barlow's Long Island farm. Now she's looking sheepish.

CONTINUITY #165 [1125]
Thursday, January 16, 1947
7:30–8:00 p.m. EST
CBS
Richard Leonard, Director
Lawrence M. Klee, Writer
Richard Leonard, Editor
Larry Elliott, Announcer
American Home Products (Kolynos, Anacin, Bi-So-Dol), Sponsor
"The Case of the Walking Death"
In this atypical triangle tale, three gals are roommates. Ethel Traynor is murdered, Sue Ronson is hauled to jail for it and Joan Franklyn appeals to Mr. Keen on Ronson's behalf.
Actors in this sequence include Stanley Harris, Audrey Egan, Helen Claire, Vivian Smolen and Chuck Webster.

CONTINUITY #166 [1126]
Thursday, January 23, 1947
7:30–8:00 p.m. EST
CBS
Richard Leonard, Director
Lawrence M. Klee, Writer
Richard Leonard, Editor
Larry Elliott, Announcer
American Home Products (Kolynos, Anacin, Bi-So-Dol), Sponsor
"The Case of the Phantom Bugler"
Mr. Keen and Mike Clancy go to the tiny village of Haversham in upstate New York. While there they discover the body of handyman Peter Gantry and report it to local authorities.
Actors in this sequence include Bill Lipton, Karl Swenson, and Ralph Bell.

CONTINUITY #167 [1127]
Thursday, January 30, 1947
7:30–8:00 p.m. EST
CBS
Richard Leonard, Director
Lawrence M. Klee, Writer
Richard Leonard, Editor
Larry Elliott, Announcer
American Home Products (Kolynos, Anacin, Bi-So-Dol), Sponsor
"The Good Samaritan Murder Case"
When Herbert Clinton picks up his morning paper and sees his own death notice among the obits, he's frightened to death. Well, not quite — but sufficiently so to take it to Mr. Keen.

CONTINUITY #168 [1128]
Thursday, February 6, 1947
7:30–8:00 p.m. EST
CBS
Richard Leonard, Director
Lawrence M. Klee, Writer
Richard Leonard, Editor
Larry Elliott, Announcer

American Home Products (Kolynos, Anacin, Bi-So-Dol), Sponsor
"The Case of the Velvet Park Jewel Murder"
Residents in or near Velvet Park have been living in fear since a jewel thief began targeting her neighborhood. Robbery has advanced to murder, and Ann Randolph tells Keen, "There goes the neighborhood."

CONTINUITY #169 [1129]
Thursday, February 13, 1947
7:30–8:00 p.m. EST
CBS
Richard Leonard, Director
Lawrence M. Klee, Writer
Richard Leonard, Editor
Larry Elliott, Announcer
American Home Products (Kolynos, Anacin, Bi-So-Dol), Sponsor
"The Case of the Ghost of Anita Marlowe"
Cabbie Jimmy Holland swears to Mrs. Kelvin that he picked up a fare at Madison Ave. and 44th St.—and the woman (her daughter) in a photo she shows him is that fare. But Mrs. Kelvin's daughter died at that corner 20 years ago!

CONTINUITY #170 [1130]
Thursday, February 20, 1947
7:30–8:00 p.m. EST
CBS
Richard Leonard, Director
Marie Baumer, Writer
Richard Leonard, Editor
Larry Elliott, Announcer
American Home Products (Kolynos, Anacin, Bi-So-Dol), Sponsor
"The Weird Case of the Glass-Topped Coffin"
Helen Stewart didn't know a lot about her intended when she married him after a month's courtship. Her spouse was handsome, reserved and wealthy. Now she's convinced that she killed him.

CONTINUITY #171 [1131]
Thursday, February 27, 1947
7:30–8:00 p.m. EST
CBS
Richard Leonard, Director
Lawrence M. Klee, Writer
Richard Leonard, Editor
Larry Elliott, Announcer
American Home Products (Kolynos, Anacin, Bi-So-Dol), Sponsor
"The Weird Case of the Gulf Stream Horror"
Leaving for Palm Beach, Clancy notes, "This is our first experience with a murderin' fish!" Keen perceptively adds: "Our fish may turn out to be remarkable—resemble a man."

CONTINUITY #172 [1132]
Thursday, March 6, 1947
7:30–8:00 p.m. EST
CBS
Richard Leonard, Director
Lawrence M. Klee, Writer
Richard Leonard, Editor
Larry Elliott, Announcer
American Home Products (Kolynos, Anacin, Bi-So-Dol), Sponsor
"The Enoch Arden Murder Case"
Lucy Garrett's father is about to wed millinery retailer Ellen Crawford. But Lucy has just received a note from her late mother—who was washed out to sea years ago—saying she's coming back.

CONTINUITY #173 [1133]
Thursday, March 13, 1947
7:30–8:00 p.m. EST
CBS
Richard Leonard, Director
Lawrence M. Klee, Writer
Richard Leonard, Editor
Larry Elliott, Announcer
American Home Products (Kolynos, Anacin, Bi-So-Dol), Sponsor
"The Case of the Hidden Corpse"
A distraught Elsie Winston appears before Keen begging his help in finding her fiancé, model Larry Nash, missing for a week. She's also jealous of model Joan Craig, the last known person to see Larry.

CONTINUITY #174 [1134]
Thursday, March 20, 1947
7:30–8:00 p.m. EST
CBS
Richard Leonard, Director
Lawrence M. Klee, Writer
Richard Leonard, Editor
Larry Elliott, Announcer
American Home Products (Kolynos, Anacin, Bi-So-Dol), Sponsor

"The Weird Case of William Hunter"
The killer who stabbed George Hunter's father took a circuitous route to avoid detection—from a study (the murder site) to a library to a hallway to the cellar and out of the house.

CONTINUITY #175 [1135]
Thursday, March 27, 1947
7:30–8:00 p.m. EST
CBS
Richard Leonard, Director
Lawrence M. Klee, Writer
Richard Leonard, Editor
Larry Elliott, Announcer
American Home Products (Kolynos, Anacin, Bi-So-Dol), Sponsor
"The Case of the Bloodstained Bookmark"
Medical librarian Jean Sheppard is convinced missing Anthony Vail, her good friend, is in some type of danger. Jean sometimes provides medical data to Mr. Keen about a case.

For the first time in the history of the series Bennett Kilpack's name is credited on the air for playing the lead.

CONTINUITY #176 [1136]
Thursday, April 3, 1947
7:30–8:00 p.m. EST
CBS
Richard Leonard, Director
Lawrence M. Klee, Writer
Richard Leonard, Editor
Larry Elliott, Announcer
American Home Products (Kolynos, Anacin, Bi-So-Dol), Sponsor
"The Case of the Jealous Husband"
They've not found a body, but Helen Gifford is sure that her spouse shot Ralph Caldwell to death in a jealous rage. He fired a shot and she heard a gasp afterward, then silence.

For the first time in the history of the series Lawrence M. Klee's name is credited on the air for writing the dialogue.

CONTINUITY #177 [1137]
Thursday, April 10, 1947
7:30–8:00 p.m. EST
CBS
Richard Leonard, Director
Lawrence M. Klee, Writer
Richard Leonard, Editor
Larry Elliott, Announcer
American Home Products (Kolynos, Bi-So-Dol), Sponsor
"The Case of the Faded Sapphire"
Thirty-six hours after Harvey and Caroline Duncan argue over some jewels, and he subsequently disappears, his mother is in Mr. Keen's office expressing fear over the possibility of foul play.

CONTINUITY #178 [1138]
Thursday, April 17, 1947
7:30–8:00 p.m. EST
CBS
Richard Leonard, Director
Marie Baumer, Writer
Richard Leonard, Editor
Larry Elliott, Announcer
American Home Products (Anacin, Bi-So-Dol), Sponsor
"The Terrifying Case of the Riderless Horse"
A horse races up to the Cox's farmhouse door at night. Jed Cox leaves his wife Emily to go out and investigate. She finds him moments later trampled to death by the horse's hooves.

Actors in this episode include Paul McGrath, Helen Claire, Frank Thomas, Edgar Stehli, Frank Behrens and Jeannette Dowling.

CONTINUITY #179 [1139]
Thursday, April 24, 1947
7:30–8:00 p.m. EST
CBS
Richard Leonard, Director
Lawrence M. Klee, Writer
Richard Leonard, Editor
Larry Elliott, Announcer
American Home Products (Anacin, Bi-So-Dol), Sponsor
"The Terrifying Case of the Unhappy Bridegroom"
Two weeks after his nuptials to Helen Driscoll, husband Roger Winston admits he really didn't know much about her. Her first spouse died in a train crash. And now she's missing.

CONTINUITY #180 [1140]
Thursday, May 1, 1947
7:30–8:00 p.m. EDST
CBS
Richard Leonard, Director

Lawrence M. Klee, Writer
Richard Leonard, Editor
Larry Elliott, Announcer
American Home Products (Anacin, Bi-So-Dol), Sponsor
"The Case of the Man Who Was Killed Twice"

Two weeks ago the business partner of Nancy Evans' father died in an accident. Now her father has received threatening letters that mention murder. They are both frightened.

Actors in this episode include Audrey Egan, Helen Choate, Vinton Hayworth, Cameron Prud'homme and Alice Frost.

CONTINUITY #181 [1141]
Thursday, May 8, 1947
7:30–8:00 p.m. EDST
CBS
Richard Leonard, Director
Marie Baumer, Writer
Richard Leonard, Editor
Larry Elliott, Announcer
American Home Products (Anacin, Kolynos, Bi-So-Dol), Sponsor
"The Case of the Living Dead"

Wealthy Jerry Thatcher, age 19, is overcome with grief when his twin sister Suzanne is killed. He lost his mother in childbirth, and his father was murdered two years later. Suzanne died at the same spot as his father.

CONTINUITY #182 [1142]
Thursday, May 15, 1947
7:30–8:00 p.m. EDST
CBS
Richard Leonard, Director
Marie Baumer, Writer
Richard Leonard, Editor
Larry Elliott, Announcer
American Home Products (Anacin, Bi-So-Dol), Sponsor
"The Case of the Beckoning Voices"

Dr. Richard Mott calls on Mr. Keen in regard to the Million Dollar Babies, two children — orphaned at ages five and seven — who will inherit a fortune "if they live to receive it."

Actors in this episode include Ned Wever, Dorothy Sands, Mary Jane Higby, Edgar Stehli, Joan Lazer and Bobby White.

CONTINUITY #183 [1143]
Thursday, May 22, 1947
7:30–8:00 p.m. EDST
CBS
Richard Leonard, Director
Lawrence M. Klee, Writer
Richard Leonard, Editor
Larry Elliott, Announcer
American Home Products (Anacin, Bi-So-Dol), Sponsor
"The Case of Murder and the Mental Marvel"

Watching a performance by the Mental Marvel, Penny Waldron's father leaves for a moment to make a call at a telephone booth. Penny finds him slumped over, a knife jutting from his back.

Actors in this episode include Charita Bauer, James Meighan, Elaine Kent, Ted Osborne, Florence Williams, Paul Potter and Henry Neeley.

CONTINUITY #184 [1144]
Thursday, May 29, 1947
7:30–8:00 p.m. EDST
CBS
Richard Leonard, Director
Lawrence M. Klee, Writer
Richard Leonard, Editor
Larry Elliott, Announcer
American Home Products (Anacin, Kolynos, Bi-So-Dol), Sponsor
"The Case of the Bargain for Murder"

When Mrs. Burke, an overnight cleaning woman in a downtown office building, overhears what she thinks is a plot to murder someone, she takes the matter directly to Mr. Keen.

Actors in this episode include Anne Elstner, Joseph Curtin, Chuck Webster, Anne Burr and Helen Claire.

CONTINUITY #185 [1145]
Thursday, June 5, 1947
7:30–8:00 p.m. EDST
CBS
Richard Leonard, Director
Lawrence M. Klee, Writer
Richard Leonard, Editor
Larry Elliott, Announcer
American Home Products (Anacin, Bi-So-Dol), Sponsor
"The Case of the Flower of Death"

Five days after Keen goes to Rhode Island to see Alelaide Crawford, who has received threatening letters demanding money, she comes to New York—to tell Mike Clancy that Mr. Keen never showed up!

Actors in this episode include Mary Jane Higby, William Podmore, Vinton Hayworth and Vivian Smolen. Jim Kelly receives his first on-air credit for playing the part of Mike Clancy, obviously due to the fact that Bennett Kilpack (Mr. Keen) is absent. This marks a rare occurrence, seldom repeated, except for the few times someone else played the part of Clancy when Kelly was ill or vacationing.

CONTINUITY #186 [1146]

Thursday, June 12, 1947
7:30–8:00 p.m. EDST
CBS
Richard Leonard, Director
Lawrence M. Klee, Writer
Richard Leonard, Editor
Larry Elliott, Announcer
American Home Products (Anacin, Kolynos, Bi-So-Dol), Sponsor
"The Case of the Iron Lady"

Clancy and Keen pry open the rusty-hinged door of the Iron Lady, and Mr. Keen announces: "It looks as if the Iron Lady has done another job." Inside is the body of Jimmy Spear.

CONTINUITY #187 [1147]

Thursday, June 19, 1947
7:30–8:00 p.m. EDST
CBS
Richard Leonard, Director
Lawrence M. Klee, Writer
Richard Leonard, Editor
Larry Elliott, Announcer
American Home Products (Anacin, Kolynos, Bi-So-Dol), Sponsor
"The Case of the Poisoned Glass"

David Boyd has had a weak heart for years. He takes a brown liquid for it. Someone substituted poison for today's dose. Now he's lying on the floor, dead. No more heart problems.

Actors in this episode include Julie Stevens, Alice Frost, Bartlett Robinson and Joy Hathaway.

CONTINUITY #188 [1148]

Thursday, June 26, 1947
7:30–8:00 p.m. EDST
CBS
Richard Leonard, Director
Lawrence M. Klee, Writer
Richard Leonard, Editor
Larry Elliott, Announcer
American Home Products (Anacin, Kolynos, Bi-So-Dol), Sponsor
"The Case of the Park Drive Murders"

Mrs. Dixon appears to be in a precarious spot. As a cleaning lady, she has worked for three young women who were all strangled to death and then robbed.

Actors in this episode include Betty Garde, Bill Lipton, Bill Smith, Fran Carlon and Joan Tompkins. Bennett Kilpack as Mr. Keen announces that the program will leave the air for the summer, returning August 28 at a new time. This is the first time the series has been off the ether in nearly a decade.

CONTINUITY #189 [1149]

Thursday, August 28, 1947
8:30–8:55 p.m. EDST
CBS
Richard Leonard, Director
Lawrence M. Klee, Writer
Richard Leonard, Editor
Larry Elliott, Announcer
American Home Products (Anacin, Kolynos, Bi-So-Dol), Sponsor
"The Case of the Man Who Traveled with Death"

Robert Hobson tells Keen that he had plenty to live for until last night, when a man was murdered. "Right now, I think my whole future—my life itself—depends on you."

Actors in this episode include John Raby, Vivian Smolen, Walter Greaza, William Zuckert, Florence Freeman and Joseph Curtin. Beginnig with this episode, live repeats of the series aired for the West Coast audience from 11:30 to 11:55 p.m. EDST.

CONTINUITY #190 [1150]

Thursday, September 4, 1947
8:30–8:55 p.m. EDST
CBS
Richard Leonard, Director
Lawrence M. Klee, Writer
Richard Leonard, Editor
Larry Elliott, Announcer
American Home Products (Anacin, Kolynos, Bi-So-Dol), Sponsor
"The Case of the Hatpin Murders"

"He's been stabbed through the heart with

an eight-inch hatpin," observes Clancy (who instantly and expertly deduces such things).

CONTINUITY #191 [1151]
Thursday, September 11, 1947
8:30–8:55 p.m. EDST
CBS
Richard Leonard, Director
Lawrence M. Klee, Writer
Richard Leonard, Editor
Larry Elliott, Announcer
American Home Products (Anacin, Kolynos, Bi-So-Dol), Sponsor
"The Auction Sale Murder Case"

The man in the Panama hat may be sorry that he didn't outbid Mrs. Lovett at the auction, but he didn't have long to dwell on it. Keen and Clancy find that his head sports two bullet holes.

Actors in this episode include Betty Garde, Bob Donnelly, Frank Readick, Anne Burr and Mandel Kramer.

CONTINUITY #192 [1152]
Thursday, September 18, 1947
8:30–8:55 p.m. EDST
CBS
Richard Leonard, Director
Lawrence M. Klee, Writer
Richard Leonard, Editor
Larry Elliott, Announcer
American Home Products (Anacin, Kolynos, Bi-So-Dol), Sponsor
"The Case of the Perpetual Widow"

Arnold Wayne and Elinor Corey wed at 4 p.m. By 5 o'clock, Arnold is dead, killed in an automobile wreck. But then this isn't the first time Elinor has lost spouses to death.

CONTINUITY #193 [1153]
Thursday, September 25, 1947
8:30–8:55 p.m. EDST
CBS
Richard Leonard, Director
Lawrence M. Klee, Writer
Richard Leonard, Editor
Larry Elliott, Announcer
American Home Products (Anacin, Kolynos, Bi-So-Dol), Sponsor
"The Spiny Ridge Murder Case"

"Look at those marks on the girl's throat, Mike," says Mr. Keen. "Laura [Greer] may have been killed by a beast. But it was the kind of a beast who walks upright on two legs."

Arthur Hughes substitutes as Mr. Keen in this episode, filling in for an ill Bennett Kilpack.

CONTINUITY #194 [1154]
Thursday, October 2, 1947
8:30–8:55 p.m. EST
CBS
Richard Leonard, Director
Lawrence M. Klee, Writer
Richard Leonard, Editor
Larry Elliott, Announcer
American Home Products (Anacin, Kolynos, Bi-So-Dol), Sponsor
"The Case of the Bloodstained Nail File"

Lewis Martin, admitting he's a murderer, persuades Mr. Keen and Mike Clancy to drop everything and accompany him to his apartment. He has just killed his friend Jerry Henshaw there.

CONTINUITY #195 [1155]
Thursday, October 9, 1947
8:30–8:55 p.m. EST
CBS
Richard Leonard, Director
Marie Baumer, Writer
Richard Leonard, Editor
Larry Elliott, Announcer
American Home Products (Anacin, Kolynos, Bi-So-Dol), Sponsor
"The Sinister Case of the Yellow Roses"

Ruth Clark, hopelessly in love with her boss, lawyer David James, while despising his fiancée, Helene Meredith, winds up poisoned to death. Keen has four suspects to interview.

Actors in this episode include Mitzi Gould, Florence Williams, Mary Jane Higby, Ned Wever and Larry Haines.

CONTINUITY #196 [1156]
Thursday, October 16, 1947
8:30–8:55 p.m. EST
CBS
Richard Leonard, Director
Lawrence M. Klee, Writer
Richard Leonard, Editor
Larry Elliott, Announcer
American Home Products (Anacin, Kolynos, Bi-So-Dol), Sponsor
"The Case of the Talking Corpse"

Astronomy professor Winthrop of Lauren University in Lauren, about 200 miles from New York, was murdered a week ago. Now his daughter Amy has come to Mr. Keen on urgent business.

Actors in this episode include John Brewster, Vivian Smolen, Helen Claire, Bill Lipton, Arthur Maitland and Guy Sorel.

CONTINUITY #197 [1157]
Thursday, October 23, 1947
8:30–8:55 p.m. EST
CBS
Richard Leonard, Director
Lawrence M. Klee, Writer
Richard Leonard, Editor
Larry Elliott, Announcer
American Home Products (Anacin, Kolynos, Bi-So-Dol), Sponsor
"The Case of the Appointment with Death"

Henry Raymond asks Keen to turn him in to the police. He murdered Philip Brandon five years ago and married Philip's wife. He can't stand it any longer. (But is he referring to the guilt — or the wife?)

CONTINUITY #198 [1158]
Thursday, October 30, 1947
8:30–8:55 p.m. EST
CBS
Richard Leonard, Director
Lawrence M. Klee, Writer
Richard Leonard, Editor
Larry Elliott, Announcer
American Home Products (Anacin, Kolynos, Bi-So-Dol), Sponsor
"The Case of the Teletype Murder"

Keen mentions that he's carrying a gun for the very first time in years. It sounds as if he might need it. He and Lewis Byron find Ann Page with a bullet through her head.

Actors in this episode include Bartlett Robinson, Alexander Scourby, Arline Blackburn and Patricia Wheel.

CONTINUITY #199 [1159]
Thursday, November 6, 1947
8:30–8:55 p.m. EST
CBS
Richard Leonard, Director
Lawrence M. Klee, Writer
Richard Leonard, Editor
Larry Elliott, Announcer
American Home Products (Anacin, Kolynos, Bi-So-Dol), Sponsor
"The Crossword Murder Case"

Architect Alfred Paine sat in his chair, "defenseless," while, son Fredric claims, "a cold blooded killer put a bullet in Dad's head." They had been close since his mother passed away.

Actors in this episode include Albert Aley, Ken Daigneau, Barbara Weeks, Katherine Emmet and Martin Blaine.

CONTINUITY #200 [1160]
Thursday, November 13, 1947
8:30–8:55 p.m. EST
CBS
Richard Leonard, Director
Lawrence M. Klee, Writer
Richard Leonard, Editor
Larry Elliott, Announcer
American Home Products (Anacin, Kolynos, Bi-So-Dol), Sponsor
"The Case of the Bulletproof Vest"

Gil Stevens worked hard to construct the perfect bulletproof vest. Testing it, Bob Cole wore the vest during a demonstration. Gil fired three shots at Bob, who fell over dead. It's back to the drawing board.

Actors in this episode include Craig McDonnell, John Raby, Florence Williams, Bill Smith and Julie Stevens.

CONTINUITY #201 [1161]
Thursday, November 20, 1947
8:30–8:55 p.m. EST
CBS
Richard Leonard, Director
Lawrence M. Klee, Writer
Richard Leonard, Editor
Larry Elliott, Announcer
American Home Products (Anacin, Kolynos, Bi-So-Dol), Sponsor
"The Case of the Poisoned Well"

Mrs. Chester calls at the Barrows place. She's told to look for the family in the dining room. They're there, all right, all sitting in their chairs — as dead as the meat on the table.

Actors in this episode include Athena Lorde, Warren Bryan, Donald Briggs and Dorothy Sands.

CONTINUITY #202 [1162]
Thursday, November 27, 1947

8:30–8:55 p.m. EST
CBS
Richard Leonard, Director
Lawrence M. Klee, Writer
Richard Leonard, Editor
Larry Elliott, Announcer
American Home Products (Anacin, Kolynos, Bi-So-Dol), Sponsor
"The Ferryboat Murder Case"

Mr. Baron calls Mr. Keen's office to speak to Elizabeth, his stepdaughter, who won't talk with him. He asks Keen to tell her that her friend Frank Carroll washed up on the Jersey shore.

CONTINUITY #203 [1163]
Thursday, December 4, 1947
8:30–8:55 p.m. EST
CBS

The script for this date is missing from the permanent file.

CONTINUITY #204 [1164]
Thursday, December 11, 1947
8:30–8:55 p.m. EST
CBS
Richard Leonard, Director
Lawrence M. Klee, Writer
Richard Leonard, Editor
Larry Elliott, Announcer
American Home Products (Anacin, Kolynos, Bi-So-Dol), Sponsor
"The Case of the Murdered Author"

Reacting to a phone call from Leslie Poole, and hearing shots, Keen and Clancy race to his home. Monica Poole, also just arriving, unlocks the door. Somebody has been shooting Poole.

Actors in this episode include James Monks, Helen Claire, Francis DeSales and Karl Swenson.

CONTINUITY #205 [1165]
Thursday, December 18, 1947
8:30–8:55 p.m. EST
CBS
Richard Leonard, Director
Lawrence M. Klee, Writer
Richard Leonard, Editor
Larry Elliott, Announcer
American Home Products (Anacin, Kolynos, Bi-So-Dol), Sponsor
"The Case of the Spider Killer"

Opera singer Loretta Carlson has sung her last aria. Three nights ago somebody drove a knife into her throat while she slept in her room.

Actors in this episode include Betty Garde, Bartlett Robinson, Fran Carlon and James Meighan.

CONTINUITY #206 [1166]
Thursday, December 25, 1947
8:30–8:55 p.m. EST
CBS
Richard Leonard, Director
Marie Baumer, Writer
Richard Leonard, Editor
Larry Elliott, Announcer
American Home Products (Anacin, Kolynos), Sponsor
"The Strange Case of the Christmas Bells"

In a return to melodramatic moments of the past, Keen searches for a lost child whom he believes may be dying. Mrs. Fielding is the key to finding him in time — if she'll talk.

CONTINUITY #207 [1167]
Thursday, January 1, 1948
8:30–8:55 p.m. EST
CBS
Richard Leonard, Director
Noel B. Gerson, Writer
Richard Leonard, Editor
Larry Elliott, Announcer
American Home Products (Anacin, Kolynos, Bi-So-Dol), Sponsor
"The Case of the Tin Pan Alley Killing"

Vicki Barbour left the Midwest for New York two months ago. Last week she and composer Monty Steiner became engaged. Monty was shot last night.

Actors in this episode include Paul Potter, John Monks, Vivian Smolen, Helen Claire, John Raby, Frank Thomas Sr. and William Zuckert.

CONTINUITY #208 [1168]
Thursday, January 8, 1948
8:30–8:55 p.m. EST
CBS
Richard Leonard, Director
Lawrence M. Klee, Writer
Richard Leonard, Editor
Larry Elliott, Announcer

American Home Products (Anacin, Kolynos, Bi-So-Dol), Sponsor
"The Case of the Broken Glass"

A dog belonging to Larry Trumbull, Mary Cole's friend, collapses and dies at the feet of Keen and Clancy as they stand outside the Archer house, where Louise Cole was murdered.

CONTINUITY #209 [1169]
Thursday, January 15, 1948
8:30–8:55 p.m. EST
CBS
Richard Leonard, Director
Lawrence M. Klee, Writer
Richard Leonard, Editor
Larry Elliott, Announcer
American Home Products (Anacin, Kolynos, Bi-So-Dol), Sponsor
"The Case of the Man Who Was Buried"

As Lt. Hale and others exhume the body of a murder victim identified as Mr. Johnson, Keen visits Mary Smith, who has been searching for her missing husband, Henry Smith.

Actors in this episode include Donald Briggs, Florence Freeman and Ruth Russell.

CONTINUITY #210 [1170]
Thursday, January 22, 1948
8:30–8:55 p.m. EST
CBS
Richard Leonard, Director
Lawrence M. Klee, Writer
Richard Leonard, Editor
Larry Elliott, Announcer
American Home Products (Anacin, Kolynos, Heet), Sponsor
"The Case of the Frozen Body Murder"

After Leona Graham visits Keen and Clancy to tell them of a skiing accident that took Bob Graham's life, the two sleuths fly to Canada and arrive at her hotel by horse-drawn sleigh.

Actors in this episode include Joy Hathaway, Spencer Bentley, Lamont Johnson, Walter Vaughn and Lawson Zerbe.

CONTINUITY #211 [1171]
Thursday, January 29, 1948
8:30–8:55 p.m. EST
CBS
Richard Leonard, Director
Lawrence M. Klee, Writer
Richard Leonard, Editor
Larry Elliott, Announcer
American Home Products (Anacin, Kolynos, Bi-So-Dol), Sponsor
"The Case of the Creeping Death"

Keen calls Lt. Hale after finding Philip Blackwell dead, his arm severely swollen from two wrist punctures. Snake bite, says Keen, tying it to letters to Philip from "the Snake."

CONTINUITY #212 [1172]
Thursday, February 5, 1948
8:30–8:55 p.m. EST
CBS
Richard Leonard, Director
Lawrence M. Klee, Writer
Richard Leonard, Editor
Larry Elliott, Announcer
American Home Products (Anacin, Kolynos, Heet), Sponsor
"The Double Death Murder Case"

Mr. Keen and Mike Clancy go to jail to interview a man named Garrett, who confessed to robbing the home of Mary Ball. She was found strangled to death, but he says he didn't do it.

Actors in this episode include Ned Wever, James Meighan, Warren Bryan, Anne-Marie Gayer, Frank Dane, James Van Dyk and Julie Stevens.

CONTINUITY #213 [1173]
Thursday, February 12, 1948
8:30–8:55 p.m. EST
CBS
Richard Leonard, Director
Lawrence M. Klee, Writer
Richard Leonard, Editor
Larry Elliott, Announcer
American Home Products (Anacin, Kolynos, Bi-So-Dol), Sponsor
"The Weird Case of Death and the Shoplifter"

Mr. Keen visits the apartment shared by Joan Waters and Cecily Nelson, the apartment where Clark Dawson, well-known theatrical producer, met his death at the hands of a murderer.

CONTINUITY #214 [1174]
Thursday, February 19, 1948
8:30–8:55 p.m. EST

CBS
Richard Leonard, Director
Lawrence M. Klee, Writer
Richard Leonard, Editor
Larry Elliott, Announcer
American Home Products (Anacin, Kolynos, Heet), Sponsor
"The Case of the Vanishing Murderer"

After hearing her story, Mr. Keen and Mike Clancy go with Lois Roth to her home in the suburbs. She told them of the sudden death of her father and an attempt on her own life.

Arthur Hughes appears in the role of Mr. Keen in this episode, in the absence of Bennett Kilpack.

CONTINUITY #215 [1175]
Thursday, February 26, 1948
8:30–8:55 p.m. EST
CBS
Richard Leonard, Director
Lawrence M. Klee, Writer
Richard Leonard, Editor
Larry Elliott, Announcer
American Home Products (Anacin, Kolynos, Bi-So-Dol), Sponsor
"The Case of the Dripping Candlestick"

Louise Simmons tells Keen she saw Betsy Hobson come and go from her brother's house before he was found with a knife in his heart. Keen interrogates Betsy and Martin, her spouse.

Arthur Hughes appears in the role of Mr. Keen in this episode, in the absence of Bennett Kilpack.

CONTINUITY #216 [1176]
Thursday, March 4, 1948
8:30–8:55 p.m. EST
CBS
Richard Leonard, Director
Lawrence M. Klee, Writer
Richard Leonard, Editor
Larry Elliott, Announcer
American Home Products (Anacin, Kolynos, Heet), Sponsor
"The Case of the Picture of Death"

Well-known brain surgeon Dr. Robert Bligh is murdered in an x-ray room. At the request of his nurse, Miss Carrol, Keen and Clancy investigate the death.

Arthur Hughes appears in the role of Mr. Keen in this episode, in the absence of Bennett Kilpack.

CONTINUITY #217 [1177]
Thursday, March 11, 1948
8:30–8:55 p.m. EST
CBS
Richard Leonard, Director
Lawrence M. Klee, Writer
Richard Leonard, Editor
Larry Elliott, Announcer
American Home Products (Anacin, Kolynos, Bi-So-Dol), Sponsor
"The Case of the Secret Murder"

The sleuths find an entry in Jeffrey Norton's diary hinting that his mother, Helen Barker, may have murdered his father, Kenneth, her first husband. The pair confront her.

Arthur Hughes appears in the role of Mr. Keen in this episode, in the absence of Bennett Kilpack. With some slight variation in names (but using the same title), this episode was later reprised for the broadcast of August 15, 1955.

CONTINUITY #218 [1178]
Thursday, March 18, 1948
8:30–8:55 p.m. EST
CBS
Richard Leonard, Director
Jerome D. Ross, Writer
Richard Leonard, Editor
Larry Elliott, Announcer
American Home Products (Anacin, Kolynos, Heet), Sponsor
"The Case of the Terror Over the Telephone"

Hit with evidence linking him to Mrs. Merryman's murder, Albert Francisco bolts from the dead lady's apartment. Keen and Clancy remain with the dead woman's neice, Betty Tilford, also a suspect.

Arthur Hughes appears in the role of Mr. Keen in this episode, in the absence of Bennett Kilpack.

CONTINUITY #219 [1179]
Thursday, March 25, 1948
8:30–8:55 p.m. EST
CBS
Richard Leonard, Director
Lawrence M. Klee, Writer
Richard Leonard, Editor
Larry Elliott, Announcer

American Home Products (Anacin, Kolynos, Bi-So-Dol), Sponsor
"The Case of the Emerald of Death"
Four hours have elapsed since the tracer and his partner found the body of beautiful Isabel Carter, who was shot to death. Still in the Carter home, Keen ponders the case.

Arthur Hughes appears in the role of Mr. Keen in this episode, in the absence of Bennett Kilpack.

CONTINUITY #220 [1180]
Thursday, April 1, 1948
8:30–8:55 p.m. EST
CBS
Richard Leonard, Director
Lawrence M. Klee, Writer
Richard Leonard, Editor
Larry Elliott, Announcer
American Home Products (Anacin, Kolynos, Bi-So-Dol), Sponsor
"The Case of the Death Train"
Mr. Keen and Mike Clancy search a train for the missing body of Elliot Simpson. He was murdered on this New York to Chicago line.

Arthur Hughes appears in the role of Mr. Keen in this episode, in the absence of Bennett Kilpack.

CONTINUITY #221 [1181]
Thursday, April 8, 1948
8:30–8:55 p.m. EST
CBS
Richard Leonard, Director
Marie Baumer, Writer
Richard Leonard, Editor
Larry Elliott, Announcer
American Home Products (Anacin, Kolynos, Bi-So-Dol), Sponsor
"The Case of the Deadly Perfume"
In the gloomy Markham library, Mr. Keen and his partner, Mike Clancy, are with the three Markham brothers—Jim, Brad and Chase. He questions them in regard to a poisoned scent.

Arthur Hughes appears in the role of Mr. Keen in this episode, in the absence of Bennett Kilpack.

CONTINUITY #222 [1182]
Thursday, April 15, 1948
8:30–8:55 p.m. EST
CBS
Richard Leonard, Director
Lawrence M. Klee, Writer
Richard Leonard, Editor
Larry Elliott, Announcer
American Home Products (Anacin, Kolynos, Bi-So-Dol), Sponsor
"The Case of the Broken Mirror"
The protesting, terrified voice of Stephen Crawford, and the sound of two shots on his office Dictaphone, convince the tracer of lost persons that he is a victim of foul play.

Actors in this episode include Florence Williams, Mary Jane Higby, Karl Weber, Warren Stevens and Teri Keane. Arthur Hughes appears in the role of Mr. Keen, in the absence of Bennett Kilpack. This episode, under a slightly modified title, was reprised for the broadcast of August 22, 1955.

CONTINUITY #223 [1183]
Thursday, April 22, 1948
8:30–8:55 p.m. EST
CBS
Richard Leonard, Director
Lawrence M. Klee, Writer
Richard Leonard, Editor
Larry Elliott, Announcer
American Home Products (Anacin, Kolynos, Bi-So-Dol), Sponsor
"The Case of the Murder and the Sharp Scissors"
Mrs. Copping brings to Keen's attention a case involving her peer, seamstress Grace Higgins. Grace was stabbed to death with scissors in a fashionable retail dress shop's workroom.

Actors in this episode include Julie Stevens, Ned Wever, Cathleen Cordell, Anne Elstner and Charles Webster.

CONTINUITY #224 [1184]
Thursday, April 29, 1948
8:30–8:55 p.m. EDST
CBS
Richard Leonard, Director
Lawrence M. Klee, Writer
Richard Leonard, Editor
Larry Elliott, Announcer
American Home Products (Anacin, Kolynos, Bi-So-Dol), Sponsor
"The Case of the Rehearsal of Death"
Stage star Lois Shelby is murdered. Keen goes to see Cathy Roberts, who's taking over

Lois' role. While Keen is at Cathy's midtown apartment, Howard Shelby, the dead woman's spouse, appears.

CONTINUITY #225 [1185]
Thursday, May 6, 1948
8:30–8:55 p.m. EDST
CBS
Richard Leonard, Director
Lawrence M. Klee, Writer
Richard Leonard, Editor
Larry Elliott, Announcer
American Home Products (Anacin, Kolynos, Bi-So-Dol), Sponsor
"The Case of the Motion Picture Murder"
  Arriving at the Summerville Art School to investigate the disappearance of student Loretta Wilson, Keen and Clancy receive news of the murder of another co-ed, Eloise Farrow.

CONTINUITY #226 [1186]
Thursday, May 13, 1948
8:30–8:55 p.m. EDST
CBS
Richard Leonard, Director
Marie Baumer, Writer
Richard Leonard, Editor
Larry Elliott, Announcer
American Home Products (Anacin, Kolynos, Bi-So-Dol), Sponsor
"The Case of Murder on a May Afternoon"
  Larry Hill is sure it was no accident that resulted in his wife Marilyn's body washing ashore. She had inherited her mother Eunice's estate from a grandfather who hated Eunice.

CONTINUITY #227 [1187]
Thursday, May 20, 1948
8:30–8:55 p.m. EDST
CBS
Richard Leonard, Director
Lawrence M. Klee, Writer
Richard Leonard, Editor
Larry Elliott, Announcer
American Home Products (Anacin, Kolynos, Bi-So-Dol), Sponsor
"The Case of the Letter of Death"
  Mr. Keen, tracer of lost persons, discovers the body of Robert Craven, who has been stabbed to death. A short time later Mr. Keen is in the office of Police Lieutenant Hale.

CONTINUITY #228 [1188]
Thursday, May 27, 1948
8:30–8:55 p.m. EDST
CBS
Richard Leonard, Director
Lawrence M. Klee, Writer
Richard Leonard, Editor
Larry Elliott, Announcer
American Home Products (Anacin, Kolynos, Bi-So-Dol), Sponsor
"The Case of the Elephant Gun Murder"
  The gumshoes visit the spot where gardener Henry Lockwood found a blood and oil-smeared handkerchief. The elephant gun that killed Parker Creighton was wiped clean of fingerprints.

CONTINUITY #229 [1189]
Thursday, June 3, 1948
8:30–8:55 p.m. EDST
CBS
Richard Leonard, Director
Lawrence M. Klee, Writer
Richard Leonard, Editor
Larry Elliott, Announcer
American Home Products (Anacin, Kolynos, Bi-So-Dol), Sponsor
"The Case of Murder in Room Three Twenty Seven"
  Several hours after Mr. Keen and Mike Clancy discover the body of Fred Bellows in room 327 of the Hotel Creighton, the investigators review the case details in the victim's room.
  Actors in this episode include Kenneth Williams, Julie Stevens, Lawson Zerbe, Vinton Hayworth, Ken Lynch and Ruth Yorke.

CONTINUITY #230 [1190]
Thursday, June 10, 1948
8:30–8:55 p.m. EDST
CBS
Richard Leonard, Director
Lawrence M. Klee, Writer
Richard Leonard, Editor
Larry Elliott, Announcer
American Home Products (Anacin, Kolynos, Bi-So-Dol), Sponsor
"The Case of the Omen of Death"
  Accompanied by Harlan Sawyer, Mr. Keen and Mike Clancy discover the body of Alice Sawyer, Harlan's wife, in the Sawyer home.

Keen inspects the premises while Clancy calls the police.

Actors in this episode include Florence Freeman, Bartlett Robinson, Joy Hathaway and Joseph Curtin.

CONTINUITY #231 [1191]
Thursday, June 17, 1948
8:30–8:55 p.m. EDST
CBS
Richard Leonard, Director
Lawrence M. Klee, Writer
Richard Leonard, Editor
Larry Elliott, Announcer
American Home Products (Anacin, Kolynos, Bi-So-Dol), Sponsor
"The Case of the Murder Monster"

Interrogating Mrs. Cotter about the murder of two young neighbors, Keen and Clancy receive an emergency phone call from Lois Pierce. Someone is trying to break into her house.

Actors in this episode include Mary Jane Higby, Toni Darnay, Betty Garde, Karl Swenson and James Monks.

CONTINUITY #232 [1192]
Thursday, June 24, 1948
8:30–9:00 p.m. EDST
CBS
Richard Leonard, Director
Lawrence M. Klee, Writer
Richard Leonard, Editor
Larry Elliott, Announcer
American Home Products (Anacin, Kolynos, Bi-So-Dol), Sponsor
"The Case of the Murder in the House of Horrors"

While Mr. Keen and Mike Clancy notify the police that they have found the body of George Blake in the House of Horrors at a local amusement park, said body mysteriously vanishes.

Actors in this episode include Anne Elstner, Anne-Marie Gayer, Lawson Zerbe, Charles Webster and Mary Maron. Beginning with this broadcast, the series' air time was lengthened by five minutes.

CONTINUITY #233 [1193]
Thursday, July 1, 1948
8:30–9:00 p.m. EDST
CBS
Richard Leonard, Director
Lawrence M. Klee, Writer
Richard Leonard, Editor
Larry Elliott, Announcer
American Home Products (Anacin, Kolynos, Bi-So-Dol), Sponsor
"The Case of the Prophecy of Death"

Mr. Keen and Mike Clancy find the body of Madame LeBaron, a fortune-teller, in her home. A short time later Keen meets with the homicide squad's Lieutenant Hale to consider the case.

CONTINUITY #234 [1194]
Thursday, July 8, 1948
8:30–9:00 p.m. EDST
CBS
Richard Leonard, Director
Lawrence M. Klee, Writer
Richard Leonard, Editor
Larry Elliott, Announcer
American Home Products (Anacin, Kolynos, Bi-So-Dol), Sponsor
"The Case of the Murder in the Zoo"

Investigating the strange death of importer Philip Dacey, Mr. Keen and his partner Mike Clancy drive to the business area of Manhattan that is frequented by importers.

CONTINUITY #235 [1195]
Thursday, July 15, 1948
8:30–9:00 p.m. EDST
CBS
Richard Leonard, Director
Jean Carroll, Writer
Richard Leonard, Editor
Larry Elliott, Announcer
American Home Products (Anacin, Kolynos, Bi-So-Dol), Sponsor
"The Case of Death and the Weird Music"

Keen and Clancy probe the murder of Marge Clark. When they talk with her sister Evelyn in the bathhouse on the Clark estate, a thrown knife embeds itself in the wall between them.

CONTINUITY #236 [1196]
Thursday, July 22, 1948
8:30–9:00 p.m. EDST
CBS
Richard Leonard, Director

Lawrence M. Klee, Writer
Richard Leonard, Editor
Larry Elliott, Announcer
American Home Products (Anacin, Kolynos, Bi-So-Dol), Sponsor
"The Case of the Murder, Old and New"

In the hamlet of Brookville in upstate New York, Mr. Keen and Mike Clancy are on the trail of a woman who murdered her spouse, then murdered the police detective who cornered her.

CONTINUITY #237 [1197]
Thursday, July 29, 1948
8:30–9:00 p.m. EDST
CBS
Richard Leonard, Director
Lawrence M. Klee, Writer
Richard Leonard, Editor
Larry Elliott, Announcer
American Home Products (Anacin, Kolynos, Bi-So-Dol), Sponsor
"The Case of the Death on Coral Beach"

Keen and Clancy probe the murder of socially prominent Mrs. Courtney at fashionable Coral Beach. Meanwhile, daughter Lois Courtney collapses suddenly. What's behind this turn of events?

CONTINUITY #238 [1198]
Thursday, August 5, 1948
8:30–9:00 p.m. EDST
CBS
Richard Leonard, Director
Lawrence M. Klee, Writer
Richard Leonard, Editor
Announcer's name omitted
American Home Products (Anacin, Kolynos, Bi-So-Dol), Sponsor
"The Case of the Figure of Death"

Herbert Bradley receives a small doll just before his death. A female doll is discovered in his desk. Mr. Keen wonders if this spells danger for Elsie Bradley, his sister.

CONTINUITY #239 [1199]
Thursday, August 12, 1948
8:30–9:00 p.m. EDST
CBS
Richard Leonard, Director
Lawrence M. Klee, Writer
Richard Leonard, Editor

Larry Elliott, Announcer
American Home Products (Anacin, Kolynos, Bi-So-Dol), Sponsor
"The Engagement Party Murder"

Tom Bestor's fiancée Lucille is murdered in the garden of affluent Mrs. Bestor's home during an engagement party. The guests are questioned, one of whom lost a diamond necklace.

This story was reprised under another title, and with different characters' names, for the broadcast aired July 31, 1952.

CONTINUITY #240 [1200]
Thursday, August 19, 1948
8:30–9:00 p.m. EDST
CBS
Richard Leonard, Director
Lawrence M. Klee, Writer
Richard Leonard, Editor
Larry Elliott, Announcer
American Home Products (Anacin, Kolynos, Bi-So-Dol), Sponsor
"The Case of the Lingering Death"

Keen and Clancy learn that Herbert Farrow is the beneficiary of his wife's insurance policy, and that he also inherited a large sum. Lila Farrow and her brother Jim were both poisoned.

CONTINUITY #241 [1201]
Thursday, August 26, 1948
8:30–9:00 p.m. EDST
CBS
Richard Leonard, Director
Lawrence M. Klee, Writer
Richard Leonard, Editor
Larry Elliott, Announcer
American Home Products (Anacin, Kolynos, Bi-So-Dol), Sponsor
"The Most Amazing Case of Murder"

Fred Rogers thought he had killed Dan Hillyard in self-defense. But the body was gone when Keen arrived at his hotel room. Is the "victim" possibly planning to blackmail Rogers?

CONTINUITY #242 [1202]
Thursday, September 2, 1948
8:30–9:00 p.m. EDST
CBS
Richard Leonard, Director
Lawrence M. Klee, Writer

Richard Leonard, Editor
Larry Elliott, Announcer
American Home Products (Anacin, Kolynos, Bi-So-Dol), Sponsor
"The Tomcat Murder Case"
    Henry Carleton is murdered. His Uncle Jeremiah left a fortune in his will to Bobby, his pet tomcat. The tracer and his partner call on the widow Irma at a modest suburban home.

CONTINUITY #243 [1203]
Thursday, September 9, 1948
8:30–9:00 p.m. EDST
CBS
Richard Leonard, Director
Lawrence M. Klee, Writer
Richard Leonard, Editor
Larry Elliott, Announcer
American Home Products (Anacin, Kolynos, Bi-So-Dol), Sponsor
"The Signet Ring Murder Case"
    Two days after the murder of Robert Hicks, the gumshoes are deeply involved. They await the arrival of George Gale at the office. Gale's wife initially brought the case to them.

CONTINUITY #244 [1204]
Thursday, September 16, 1948
8:30–9:00 p.m. EDST
CBS
Richard Leonard, Director
Lawrence M. Klee, Writer
Richard Leonard, Editor
Larry Elliott, Announcer
American Home Products (Anacin, Kolynos, Bi-So-Dol), Sponsor
"The Case of Murder on a Moonlight Night"
    Keen and Clancy scrutinize the murder of wealthy Philip Wharton, which occurred at a replica of a feudal castle he had built in Canada. The body was found inside a suit of black armor.

CONTINUITY #245 [1205]
Thursday, September 23, 1948
8:30–9:00 p.m. EDST
CBS
Richard Leonard, Director
Lawrence M. Klee, Writer
Richard Leonard, Editor
Larry Elliott, Announcer
American Home Products (Anacin, Kolynos, Bi-So-Dol), Sponsor

"The Case of the Strange Death of Stuart Blair"
    Investigating the death of Stuart Blair, who was poisoned, Keen and Clancy encounter another attempted poisoning—of attractive Lenore Barclay, publisher Alfred Carter's aide.
    This same story line was reprised for the broadcast of August 17, 1951, under a different case title but using the same characters' names.

CONTINUITY #246 [1206]
Thursday, September 30, 1948
8:30–9:00 p.m. EST
CBS
Richard Leonard, Director
Lawrence M. Klee, Writer
Richard Leonard, Editor
Larry Elliott, Announcer
American Home Products (Anacin, Kolynos, Bi-So-Dol), Sponsor
"The Black Slipper Murder Case"
    Well-heeled Flo Hemley is murdered, and a bloodstain is found on a gown owned by her sister Janet. Janet feigns innocence, as Flo's spouse Rod and seamstress Katy Barker react in horror.

CONTINUITY #247 [1207]
Thursday, October 7, 1948
8:30–9:00 p.m. EST
CBS
Richard Leonard, Director
Lawrence M. Klee, Writer
Richard Leonard, Editor
Larry Elliott, Announcer
American Home Products (Anacin, Kolynos, Heet), Sponsor
"The Case of Murder at Sixty Miles an Hour"
    Jerry Haines, suspected of killing prosperous Tom Middleton, accuses a girl named Adele, who turned down Haines' marriage proposal. Tom's brother Frank stares in utter amazement.

CONTINUITY #248 [1208]
Thursday, October 14, 1948
8:30–9:00 p.m. EST
CBS
Richard Leonard, Director
Lawrence M. Klee, Writer
Richard Leonard, Editor
Larry Elliott, Announcer
American Home Products (Anacin, Kolynos, Bi-So-Dol), Sponsor

"The Brocade Chair Murder Case"
An elderly woman's body is found in a chest in an antique furniture shop. Mr. Keen locates the victim's sister, Edna Bentley, who informs him that her life is in danger, too.

CONTINUITY #249 [1209]
Thursday, October 21, 1948
8:30–9:00 p.m. EST
CBS
Richard Leonard, Director
Lawrence M. Klee, Writer
Richard Leonard, Editor
Larry Elliott, Announcer
American Home Products (Anacin, Kolynos, Heet), Sponsor
"The Case of Murder in the Air"
Jonas Allen, en route from Cleveland to New York City, is poisoned on a plane. Edgar Black, a black-bearded man on that same aircraft who is possibly an escaped homicidal maniac, vanishes.

CONTINUITY #250 [1210]
Thursday, October 28, 1948
8:30–9:00 p.m. EST
CBS
Richard Leonard, Director
Lawrence M. Klee, Writer
Richard Leonard, Editor
Larry Elliott, Announcer
American Home Products (Anacin, Kolynos, Bi-So-Dol), Sponsor
"The Identical Twins Murder Case"
Howard Lathrop, a handsome, young man-about-town, is shot to death while dining in a downtown restaurant. Mike Clancy discovers a new and startling clue, which he reveals to Keen.
This story was repeated, under a different title, for the broadcast of January 10, 1952.

CONTINUITY #251 [1211]
Thursday, November 4, 1948
8:30–9:00 p.m. EST
CBS
Richard Leonard, Director
Lawrence M. Klee, Writer
Richard Leonard, Editor
Larry Elliott, Announcer
American Home Products (Anacin, Kolynos, Heet), Sponsor
"The Howling Dog Murder Case"
Margaret Elliot is so devoted to her brother Ralph that she thwarted a suitor proposing marriage so she could keep house for Ralph. Now Ralph has vanished.

CONTINUITY #252 [1212]
Thursday, November 11, 1948
8:30–9:00 p.m. EST
CBS
Richard Leonard, Director
Lawrence M. Klee, Writer
Richard Leonard, Editor
Larry Elliott, Announcer
American Home Products (Anacin, Kolynos, Bi-So-Dol), Sponsor
"The Fashion Show Murder Case"
Larry Adams appeals to Keen and Clancy to find the killer of the girl he had hoped to marry, Nancy Owen. She died during a fashion show, taking a bullet in her heart.

CONTINUITY #253 [1213]
Thursday, November 18, 1948
8:30–9:00 p.m. EST
CBS
Richard Leonard, Director
Lawrence M. Klee, Writer
Richard Leonard, Editor
Larry Elliott, Announcer
American Home Products (Anacin, Kolynos, Heet), Sponsor
"The Case of Murder Meets the Train"
Phil Wilson and his sister Elsie were so close that when she wed Chuck Farnum she insisted that Phil live with them. She has been pushed under a train, and Chuck doesn't seem to give a toot.

CONTINUITY #254 [1214]
Thursday, November 25, 1948
8:30–9:00 p.m. EST
CBS
Richard Leonard, Director
Lawrence M. Klee, Writer
Richard Leonard, Editor
Larry Elliott, Announcer
American Home Products (Anacin, Kolynos, Bi-So-Dol), Sponsor
"The Case of the Amazing Death of Cyrus Wake"
When Henry the valet and Martha the

housekeeper found Cyrus Wake, he was swinging from the chandelier. Literally. Dead. He had tied one on that night and was higher than a kite.

CONTINUITY #255 [1215]
Thursday, December 2, 1948
8:30–9:00 p.m. EST
CBS
Richard Leonard, Director
Lawrence M. Klee, Writer
Richard Leonard, Editor
Larry Elliott, Announcer
American Home Products (Anacin, Kolynos, Heet), Sponsor
"The Case of the Package of Death"
   Stockbroker Gary Thurston sent Laura Townsend, his sweetie, a gift that blew up in her face. The cops arrested him for murder, but he claims they've blown it all out of proportion.

CONTINUITY #256 [1216]
Thursday, December 9, 1948
8:30–9:00 p.m. EST
CBS
Richard Leonard, Director
Lawrence M. Klee, Writer
Richard Leonard, Editor
Larry Elliott, Announcer
American Home Products (Anacin, Kolynos, Bi-So-Dol), Sponsor
"The Case of the Invisible Murderer"
   Ed Rogers didn't plan to kill John Barrett as they struggled for the gun. He only wanted to scare him off from his wife because Barrett was seeing her so often. Mission accomplished.

CONTINUITY #257 [1217]
Thursday, December 16, 1948
8:30–9:00 p.m. EST
CBS
Richard Leonard, Director
Lawrence M. Klee, Writer
Richard Leonard, Editor
Larry Elliott, Announcer
American Home Products (Anacin, Kolynos, Heet), Sponsor
"The Case of the Arrow of Death"
   Eloise Burton says she only picked up an archery bow she found on the ground to return it to its set. The bow had just shot an arrow into the air, and it hit a body nearby.

CONTINUITY #258 [1218]
Thursday, December 23, 1948
8:30–9:00 p.m. EST
CBS
Richard Leonard, Director
Lawrence M. Klee, Writer
Richard Leonard, Editor
Larry Elliott, Announcer
American Home Products (Anacin, Kolynos, Bi-So-Dol), Sponsor
"The Case of Murder Evidence from the Dead"
   Laura Evans calls an airline to confirm her seat on the next plane when someone interrupts her. "What are you doing with that gun in your hand?" she asks. Cancel that ticket.

CONTINUITY #259 [1219]
Thursday, December 30, 1948
8:30–9:00 p.m. EST
CBS
Richard Leonard, Director
Lawrence M. Klee, Writer
Richard Leonard, Editor
Larry Elliott, Announcer
American Home Products (Anacin, Kolynos, Heet), Sponsor
"The Blue Dust Murder Case"
   Somebody at Frawley's department store didn't care much for the owner's son, Robert. He was found with a hunting knife protruding from his back. It's a unique way to cut staff.

CONTINUITY #260 [1220]
Thursday, January 6, 1949
8:30–9:00 p.m. EST
CBS
Richard Leonard, Director
Lawrence M. Klee, Writer
Richard Leonard, Editor
Larry Elliott, Announcer
American Home Products (Anacin, Kolynos, Bi-So-Dol), Sponsor
"The Case of the Raffle of Death"
   Poor Edna Harrington was pulled from the car she had won a day earlier as a raffle prize at a charity bazaar, now crushed and burned beyond recognition.

CONTINUITY #261 [1221]
Thursday, January 13, 1949
8:30–9:00 p.m. EST
CBS

Richard Leonard, Director
Lawrence M. Klee, Writer
Richard Leonard, Editor
Larry Elliott, Announcer
American Home Products (Anacin, Kolynos, Heet), Sponsor
"The Case of the Murdered Bridegroom"

Bob Tate and Eleanor Burton had a history. But she dropped him for her boss, Alfred Andrews. Alf died on his wedding night as she returned to Bob.

CONTINUITY #262 [1222]
Thursday, January 20, 1949
8:30–9:00 p.m. EST
CBS
Richard Leonard, Director
Lawrence M. Klee, Writer
Richard Leonard, Editor
Larry Elliott, Announcer
American Home Products (Anacin, Kolynos, Bi-So-Dol), Sponsor
"The Beautiful Showgirl Murder Case"

The aquarium intrigued Millicent Le Marr. "There's someone in there!" she yelled to the watchman. "It's my sister! It's Eve!" Eve may have had a little too much to drink.

This story was repeated for the broadcast of August 21, 1952, under a different title but using the same character names.

CONTINUITY #263 [1223]
Thursday, January 27, 1949
8:30–9:00 p.m. EST
CBS
Richard Leonard, Director
Lawrence M. Klee, Writer
Richard Leonard, Editor
Larry Elliott, Announcer
American Home Products (Anacin, Kolynos, Heet), Sponsor
"The Case of Murder on the High Seas"

Before leaving Europe, Ellen Dawes' father told her that someone was trying to steal his gems and kill him. En route home on a cruise ship, he falls overboard. There go the family jewels.

CONTINUITY #264 [1224]
Thursday, February 3, 1949
8:30–9:00 p.m. EST
CBS
Richard Leonard, Director
Lawrence M. Klee, Writer
Richard Leonard, Editor
Larry Elliott, Announcer
American Home Products (Anacin, Kolynos, Bi-So-Dol), Sponsor
"The Case of Murder on the Dance Floor"

Businessman Kenneth Kirby, estranged from his wife Laura, took Eloise Daniels to a nightspot, the Sapphire Club. Eloise is poisoned.

CONTINUITY #265 [1225]
Thursday, February 10, 1949
8:30–9:00 p.m. EST
CBS
Richard Leonard, Director
Lawrence M. Klee, Writer
Richard Leonard, Editor
Larry Elliott, Announcer
American Home Products (Anacin, Kolynos, Heet), Sponsor
"The Case of the Murder on Phantom Beach"

Claire Rogers wins a beauty contest in Florida. Her body is later washed ashore. She was struck on the head by a heavy object while swimming. Is Miss Congeniality only a façade?

CONTINUITY #266 [1226]
Thursday, February 17, 1949
8:30–9:00 p.m. EST
CBS
Richard Leonard, Director
Lawrence M. Klee, Writer
Richard Leonard, Editor
Larry Elliott, Announcer
American Home Products (Anacin, Kolynos, Bi-So-Dol), Sponsor
"The Case of Murder at Dawn"

Margaret Johnson awaits trial in jail for the murder of her spouse. Someone put a sedative in his coffee and poisoned his food.

CONTINUITY #267 [1227]
Thursday, February 24, 1949
8:30–9:00 p.m. EST
CBS
Richard Leonard, Director
Lawrence M. Klee, Writer
Richard Leonard, Editor
Larry Elliott, Announcer
American Home Products (Anacin, Kolynos, Heet), Sponsor

"The Case of the Murdered Heiress"

Society debutante Sandra Crawford inherited over $20 million when her parents died in an automobile accident a year ago. Now she has been shot to death at her Long Island estate.

CONTINUITY #268 [1228]
Thursday, March 3, 1949
8:30–9:00 p.m. EST
CBS
Richard Leonard, Director
Lawrence M. Klee, Writer
Richard Leonard, Editor
Larry Elliott, Announcer
American Home Products (Anacin, Kolynos, Bi-So-Dol), Sponsor
"The Case of Murder and the Strange Woman"

A handsome, talented, famous musician, Don Mason, who played countless benefits for the poor and the sick, and who himself was the idol of women throughout the country, is murdered.

Some parallels can be drawn between this story (including the title) and the episode that was later broadcast on June 20, 1951. At least a partial adaptation may have been made.

CONTINUITY #269 [1229]
Thursday, March 10, 1949
8:30–9:00 p.m. EST
CBS
Richard Leonard, Director
Lawrence M. Klee, Writer
Richard Leonard, Editor
Larry Elliott, Announcer
American Home Products (Anacin, Kolynos, Heet), Sponsor
"The Case of the Murder Calendar"

Lorna Caraway is murdered, leaving a calendar with two dates circled on it — one indicating the day she died, and the other a week hence, with the initials M. B. written on it. Martha Bragg, Lorna's sister, is petrified.

CONTINUITY #270 [1230]
Thursday, March 17, 1949
8:30–9:00 p.m. EST
CBS
Richard Leonard, Director
Lawrence M. Klee, Writer
Richard Leonard, Editor
Larry Elliott, Announcer
American Home Products (Anacin, Kolynos, Bi-So-Dol), Sponsor
"The Case of the Amazing Clue to Murder"

Doris Ralston, who lives with her aunt and uncle, was shot in the head at 3 a.m. while sleeping. The kinfolk were both conveniently out of the house at the time. Did one of them return?

CONTINUITY #271 [1231]
Thursday, March 24, 1949
8:30–9:00 p.m. EST
CBS
Richard Leonard, Director
Lawrence M. Klee, Writer
Richard Leonard, Editor
Larry Elliott, Announcer
American Home Products (Anacin, Kolynos, Heet), Sponsor
"The Case of Murder and the Suspicious Wife"

Jane Cromwell, a new bride, asks Mr. Keen to look into the strange behavior of her spouse, Robert, whom she suspects of being involved in a murder. Someone tries to poison Jane.

CONTINUITY #272 [1232]
Thursday, March 31, 1949
8:30–9:00 p.m. EST
CBS
Richard Leonard, Director
Lawrence M. Klee, Writer
Richard Leonard, Editor
Larry Elliott, Announcer
American Home Products (Anacin, Kolynos, Bi-So-Dol), Sponsor
"The Mirror Murder Case"

Everett Clark, the owner of a second-hand furniture shop, is murdered, and an antique gold mirror goes missing. Just before Everett died, Mrs. Lawrence Kelcy was there. Is she being framed?

CONTINUITY #273 [1233]
Thursday, April 7, 1949
8:30–9:00 p.m. EST
CBS
Richard Leonard, Director
Lawrence M. Klee, Writer
Richard Leonard, Editor
Larry Elliott, Announcer
American Home Products (Anacin, Kolynos, Heet), Sponsor

"The Ace of Spades Murder Case"
Probing the murder of Sandra Vickers, the gumshoes learn that the glamorous lady secretly ran gambling operations in her home. In her hand she held the Ace of Spades, a symbol of death.

CONTINUITY #274 [1234]
Thursday, April 14, 1949
8:30–9:00 p.m. EST
CBS
Richard Leonard, Director
Lawrence M. Klee, Writer
Richard Leonard, Editor
Larry Elliott, Announcer
American Home Products (Anacin, Kolynos, Bi-So-Dol), Sponsor
"The Poison Pen Murder Case"
While investigating the murder of pretty Doris Wayne, Mr. Keen and Mike Clancy learn that the body of Paul Wayne, her husband, has been found in the river. He was shot to death.

CONTINUITY #275 [1235]
Thursday, April 21, 1949
8:30–9:00 p.m. EST
CBS
Richard Leonard, Director
Lawrence M. Klee, Writer
Richard Leonard, Editor
Larry Elliott, Announcer
American Home Products (Anacin, Kolynos, Heet), Sponsor
"The Birthday Party Murder Case"
Keen and Clancy, trying to solve Larry Carr's murder, are stunned when his partner Philip Duncan barely escapes the same fate. Carr was poisoned, and a similar attempt is made on Duncan.

CONTINUITY #276 [1236]
Thursday, April 28, 1949
8:30–9:00 p.m. EST
CBS
Richard Leonard, Director
Lawrence M. Klee, Writer
Richard Leonard, Editor
Larry Elliott, Announcer
American Home Products (Anacin, Kolynos, Bi-So-Dol), Sponsor
"The Deserted House Murder Case"
Inside her country home, the sleuths find a fully clothed skeleton of stage star Victoria Cripps, who has been missing for eight years. Huge footprints outside lead to a clump of trees and vanish.
This story was reprised, under another title, for the broadcast of January 15, 1954.

CONTINUITY #277 [1237]
Thursday, May 5, 1949
8:30–9:00 p.m. EDST
CBS
Richard Leonard, Director
Lawrence M. Klee, Writer
Richard Leonard, Editor
Larry Elliott, Announcer
American Home Products (Anacin, Kolynos, Heet), Sponsor
"Murder Comes to Supper"
The tracer of lost persons and his partner explore the death of George Brandon, wealthy man-about-town. He was shot to death in his hotel apartment. His friends are interrogated.

CONTINUITY #278 [1238]
Thursday, May 12, 1949
8:30–9:00 p.m. EDST
CBS
Richard Leonard, Director
Lawrence M. Klee, Writer
Richard Leonard, Editor
Larry Elliott, Announcer
American Home Products (Anacin, Kolynos, Bi-So-Dol), Sponsor
"The Beauty Salon Murder Case"
When beautiful stage star Elaine Stevens is murdered at a beauty salon, Keen and Clancy think actor Philip Bixby may be guilty. Honestly, only her hairdresser knows for sure.

CONTINUITY #279 [1239]
Thursday, May 19, 1949
8:30–9:00 p.m. EDST
CBS
Richard Leonard, Director
Lawrence M. Klee, Writer
Richard Leonard, Editor
Larry Elliott, Announcer
American Home Products (Anacin, Kolynos, Bi-So-Dol), Sponsor
"The Case of the Murder on Edgewood Lake"
It's 3 a.m. and Keen calls the occupants of

the Waverly home to the library. He has just found the cook's body in the yard.

CONTINUITY #280 [1240]
Thursday, May 26, 1949
8:30–9:00 p.m. EDST
CBS
Richard Leonard, Director
Lawrence M. Klee, Writer
Richard Leonard, Editor
Larry Elliott, Announcer
American Home Products (Anacin, Kolynos, Bi-So-Dol), Sponsor
"The Green Stocking Murder Case"
The detectives try to solve the murder of glamorous Elinor Perry. The model was strangled in the studio apartment of photographer Robert Bradshaw, who is being held by police.

CONTINUITY #281 [1241]
Thursday, June 2, 1949
8:30–9:00 p.m. EDST
CBS
Richard Leonard, Director
Lawrence M. Klee, Writer
Richard Leonard, Editor
Larry Elliott, Announcer
American Home Products (Anacin, Kolynos, Bi-So-Dol), Sponsor
"The Case of the Wife Who Confessed Murder"
Wealthy young widow Barbara Forbes is shot to death. Nancy Woodring confesses, but Keen thinks she's the victim of a plot. And prowler Allen Craig carries a gun missing two bullets.
Actors in this episode include Robert Donley, Anne Seymour, Toni Darnay, Helen Claire, Ian Martin and Karl Weber. This story was reprised, under a different title and using different character names, for the broadcast of August 3, 1951.

CONTINUITY #282 [1242]
Thursday, June 9, 1949
8:30–9:00 p.m. EDST
CBS
Richard Leonard, Director
Lawrence M. Klee, Writer
Richard Leonard, Editor
Larry Elliott, Announcer
American Home Products (Anacin, Kolynos, Bi-So-Dol), Sponsor
"The Case of Murder and the Star of Death" (*Extant Episode*)
The murder of jewel merchant Mark Adams puts Keen and Clancy on the trail of a clever thief. Adams was killed for the Star of Death, a sapphire Keen thinks is still in Adams home.

CONTINUITY #283 [1243]
Thursday, June 16, 1949
8:30–9:00 p.m. EDST
CBS
Richard Leonard, Director
Lawrence M. Klee, Writer
Richard Leonard, Editor
Larry Elliott, Announcer
American Home Products (Anacin, Kolynos, Bi-So-Dol), Sponsor
"The African Blow Gun Murder Case"
Prominent scientist-explorer Roger Cameron is killed by a poison-tipped dart blown from a gun he acquired in Africa. A second murder attempt soon follows at his Long Island home.

CONTINUITY #284 [1244]
Thursday, June 23, 1949
8:30–9:00 p.m. EDST
CBS
Richard Leonard, Director
Lawrence M. Klee, Writer
Richard Leonard, Editor
Larry Elliott, Announcer
American Home Products (Anacin, Kolynos, Bi-So-Dol), Sponsor
"The Case of Murder and the Policeman's Wife"
The famous investigator and his partner are attempting to solve the mysterious killing of patrolman Danny Mulchan. The police are holding Mulchan's wife Bridget for murder.

CONTINUITY #285 [1245]
Thursday, June 30, 1949
8:30–9:00 p.m. EDST
CBS
Richard Leonard, Director
Lawrence M. Klee, Writer
Richard Leonard, Editor
Larry Elliott, Announcer
American Home Products (Anacin, Kolynos, Bi-So-Dol), Sponsor

"The Case of Murder on the Boardwalk"

The sleuths go to Silver Beach, where June Ainsley was shot to death on her honeymoon. Roy Farnum, who loved her before she wed Steven Ainsley, has a gun with three missing slugs.

CONTINUITY #286 [1246]
Thursday, July 7, 1949
8:30–9:00 p.m. EDST
CBS
Martha Atwell, Director
Lawrence M. Klee, Writer
Richard Leonard, Editor
Larry Elliott, Announcer
American Home Products (Anacin, Kolynos, Bi-So-Dol), Sponsor
"The Silver Locket Murder Case"

Aideen Ellsworth, a beautiful and talented artist, plans a trip to Europe. Shortly before her departure her body is found in a trunk.

CONTINUITY #287 [1247]
Thursday, July 14, 1949
8:30–9:00 p.m. EDST
CBS
Martha Atwell, Director
Lawrence M. Klee, Writer
Richard Leonard, Editor
Larry Elliott, Announcer
American Home Products (Anacin, Kolynos, Bi-So-Dol), Sponsor
"The Perfect Place for Murder"

Rich and socially prominent Robert Denham meets an unusual fate: his body is found among a group of wax figures in an amusement park concession known as the Chamber of Horrors.

CONTINUITY #288 [1248]
Thursday, July 21, 1949
8:30–9:00 p.m. EDST
CBS
Martha Atwell, Director
Lawrence M. Klee, Writer
Richard Leonard, Editor
Larry Elliott, Announcer
American Home Products (Anacin, Kolynos, Bi-So-Dol), Sponsor
"The Case of Murder and the Bolted Room"

The murder of wealthy book publisher and collector James Pomeroy is perplexing. The murder room has no windows, and its one door was bolted from the inside when its occupant was shot.

CONTINUITY #289 [1249]
Thursday, July 28, 1949
8:30–9:00 p.m. EDST
CBS
Martha Atwell, Director
Lawrence M. Klee, Writer
Richard Leonard, Editor
Larry Elliott, Announcer
American Home Products (Anacin, Kolynos, Bi-So-Dol), Sponsor
"The Society Murder Case"

Wealthy, socially prominent widow Elizabeth Perry dies in Keen's office of poisoning. While interrogating her friend Sheila Randolph, Keen notes that Sheila's parrot was poisoned, too.

CONTINUITY #290 [1250]
Thursday, August 4, 1949
8:30–9:00 p.m. EDST
CBS
Richard Leonard, Director
Lawrence M. Klee, Writer
Richard Leonard, Editor
Larry Elliott, Announcer
American Home Products (Anacin, Kolynos, Bi-So-Dol), Sponsor
"The Case of Murder and the Picnic in the Country"

Keen and Clancy want to know who put poisoned coffee in Fred Hammond's thermos bottle. Though his wife Doris is being held by the police, Keen thinks she may be innocent.

CONTINUITY #291 [1251]
Thursday, August 11, 1949
8:30–9:00 p.m. EDST
CBS
Richard Leonard, Director
Lawrence M. Klee, Writer
Richard Leonard, Editor
Larry Elliott, Announcer
American Home Products (Anacin, Kolynos, Bi-So-Dol), Sponsor
"The Yellow Rose Murder Case"

Talented Ann Gilmore, recently awarded a contract to sing on a major radio series, is murdered. Brothers Allen and Bob Walsh had competed fiercely for the victim's affections.

CONTINUITY #292 [1252]
Thursday, August 18, 1949
8:30–9:00 p.m. EDST
CBS
Richard Leonard, Director
Lawrence M. Klee, Writer
Richard Leonard, Editor
Dick Dunham, Announcer
American Home Products (Anacin, Kolynos, Bi-So-Dol), Sponsor
"The Sleep Walker Murder Case"
  Peggy Marsh is stabbed to death in her friend Alicia Boyd's summer cottage near New York. Alicia walked in her sleep that night, awakening to find her gown smeared with blood.
  This story was repeated, under a different case title and with different character names, for the broadcast of September 6, 1951.

CONTINUITY #293 [1253]
Thursday, August 25, 1949
8:30–9:00 p.m. EDST
CBS
Richard Leonard, Director
Priscilla Ames, Writer
Richard Leonard, Editor
Dick Dunham, Announcer
American Home Products (Anacin, Kolynos, Bi-So-Dol), Sponsor
"The Case of the Telephone That Would Not Stop Ringing"
  Mike Clancy finds the tracer of lost persons in the Marlowe library, his body swathed in bandages. Clancy looks down at his friend with a faint smile, speaking rather dryly to him.

CONTINUITY #294 [1254]
Thursday, September 1, 1949
8:30–9:00 p.m. EDST
CBS
Richard Leonard, Director
Lawrence M. Klee, Writer
Richard Leonard, Editor
Dick Dunham, Announcer
American Home Products (Anacin, Kolynos, Bi-So-Dol), Sponsor
"The Case of the Million Dollar Murder"
  It seems that—for $1 million in insurance money—prominent businessman David Mason was murdered. Gilbert Thayer traps Keen and Clancy in a midtown flat, holding them at gunpoint.

CONTINUITY #295 [1255]
Thursday, September 8, 1949
8:30–9:00 p.m. EDST
CBS
Richard Leonard, Director
Lawrence M. Klee, Writer
Richard Leonard, Editor
Dick Dunham, Announcer
American Home Products (Anacin, Kolynos, Bi-So-Dol), Sponsor
"The Case of the Unmarried Husband"
  Walter Burton is assistant sales manager of a radio supply parts firm. He's also married—or *was*. Nobody at work knew that, however, until his wife Ella was strangled to death.

CONTINUITY #296 [1256]
Thursday, September 15, 1949
8:30–9:00 p.m. EDST
CBS
Richard Leonard, Director
Lawrence M. Klee, Writer
Richard Leonard, Editor
Dick Dunham, Announcer
American Home Products (Anacin, Kolynos, Bi-So-Dol), Sponsor
"The Case of Murder and the Bloodstained Necklace" (*Extant Episode*)
  Grace Bradley recently lost her wealthy spouse to death by natural causes. Now she has been murdered in a hotel and found with a string of inexpensive cultured pearls clutched in her hand.

CONTINUITY #297 [1257]
Thursday, September 22, 1949
8:30–9:00 p.m. EDST
CBS
Richard Leonard, Director
Lawrence M. Klee, Writer
Richard Leonard, Editor
Dick Dunham, Announcer
American Home Products (Anacin, Kolynos, Bi-So-Dol), Sponsor
"The Yellow Talon Murder Case" (*Extant Episode*)
  The murder of Helen Carter takes the gumshoes to the Carter home 50 miles away. A giant bird apparently attacked Helen, as evidenced by a large broken talon, as sharp as a knife, found at the scene.

CONTINUITY #298 [1258]
Thursday, September 29, 1949
8:30–9:00 p.m. EST
CBS
Richard Leonard, Director
Lawrence M. Klee, Writer
Richard Leonard, Editor
Larry Elliott, Announcer
American Home Products (Anacin, Kolynos, Bi-So-Dol), Sponsor
"The Case of Murder with a Thousand Witnesses" (*Extant Episode*)
   William Brooks, a wealthy country squire, is poisoned while judging a baking contest at a county fair. Ann Brooks, his wife, hides in a nearby hotel under an assumed name.

CONTINUITY #299 [1259]
Thursday, October 6, 1949
8:30–9:00 p.m. EST
CBS
Richard Leonard, Director
Lawrence M. Klee, Writer
Richard Leonard, Editor
Larry Elliott, Announcer
American Home Products (Anacin, Kolynos, Heet), Sponsor
"The Case of the Man Who Invented Death" (*Extant Episode*)
   Eccentric inventor Amos Piper is electrocuted when his killer tampers with one of his inventions. Keen follows a woman to a home in an affluent suburb, entering through a rear door.
   This story was reprised, under another title but using the same character names, for the broadcast of August 27, 1954.

CONTINUITY #300 [1260]
Thursday, October 13, 1949
8:30–9:00 p.m. EST
CBS
Richard Leonard, Director
Lawrence M. Klee, Writer
Richard Leonard, Editor
Larry Elliott, Announcer
American Home Products (Anacin, Kolynos, Heet), Sponsor
"The Silver Dagger Murder Case" (*Extant Episode*)
   The murder of well-heeled Edna Coring takes Keen and Clancy to the scene, her residence. The victim secretly wed Anson Howe, though she had been close to playwright Allen Cody.

CONTINUITY #301 [1261]
Thursday, October 20, 1949
8:30–9:00 p.m. EST
CBS
Richard Leonard, Director
Lawrence M. Klee, Writer
Richard Leonard, Editor
Larry Elliott, Announcer
American Home Products (Anacin, Kolynos, Heet), Sponsor
"The Martin Street Murder Case"
   Nicky Slade, the ex-spouse of murdered showgirl Doris Milford, enters the flat she shared with Arlene Williams, another showgirl, brandishing a gun. Clancy disarms Slade.

CONTINUITY #302 [1262]
Thursday, October 27, 1949
8:30–9:00 p.m. EST
CBS
Richard Leonard, Director
Lawrence M. Klee, Writer
Richard Leonard, Editor
Larry Elliott, Announcer
American Home Products (Anacin, Kolynos, Bi-So-Dol), Sponsor
"The Case of the Ruthless Murders" (*Extant Episode*)
   Keen is ambushed when he keeps an appointment with Luke Homer, a suspect in the murder of businessman Neal Justin. Ron Marble and Tom Sopher are also suspects.

CONTINUITY #303 [1263]
Thursday, November 3, 1949
8:30–9:00 p.m. EST
CBS
Richard Leonard, Director
Lawrence M. Klee, Writer
Richard Leonard, Editor
Larry Elliott, Announcer
American Home Products (Anacin, Kolynos, Heet), Sponsor
"The Forgotten Cave Murder Case" (*Extant Episode*)
   Edward Johnson tells Keen his friend Jim Ramsey was murdered in an old cave on Long Island, but that the body is missing. Johnson himself is soon pushed off a cliff into the sea.

CONTINUITY #304 [1264]
Thursday, November 10, 1949
8:30–9:00 p.m. EST
CBS
Richard Leonard, Director
Lawrence M. Klee, Writer
Richard Leonard, Editor
Larry Elliott, Announcer
American Home Products (Anacin, Kolynos, Bi-So-Dol), Sponsor
"The Engaged Girl Murder Case" (*Extant Episode*)
Martha Langley is killed at her fabulous Connecticut estate. The housekeeper, Mrs. Wrightson, is Audrey Stafford's mother. Audrey plans to wed Herbert Langley, Martha's brother.

CONTINUITY #305 [1265]
Thursday, November 17, 1949
8:30–9:00 p.m. EST
CBS
Richard Leonard, Director
Lawrence M. Klee, Writer
Richard Leonard, Editor
Larry Elliott, Announcer
American Home Products (Anacin, Kolynos, Heet), Sponsor
"The Concrete Cellar Murder Case"
Keen and Clancy discover the body of Joyce Warren, a young bride who was murdered and buried in the cellar of her home. Following an autopsy, Keen calls Bill Warren, her husband.

CONTINUITY #306 [1266]
Thursday, November 24, 1949
8:30–9:00 p.m. EST
CBS
Richard Leonard, Director
Lawrence M. Klee, Writer
Richard Leonard, Editor
Larry Elliott, Announcer
American Home Products (Anacin, Kriptin, Bi-So-Dol), Sponsor
"The Crown of Doom Murder Case"
Gem importer Howard Somers dies for the Crown of Asia, a jeweled crown with a fatal curse. While Keen speaks with Ed and Charlotte Stuart, a man enters, wounds Edward and flees.

CONTINUITY #307 [1267]
Thursday, December 1, 1949
8:30–9:00 p.m. EST
CBS
Richard Leonard, Director
Lawrence M. Klee, Writer
Richard Leonard, Editor
Larry Elliott, Announcer
American Home Products (Anacin, Kriptin, Heet), Sponsor
"The Masquerade Ball Murder Case"
Dick Henshaw is stabbed to death with the sword he wore to a masquerade charity ball hosted by socialite Grace Stevenson. Charity donations vanish, as does Grace's niece, Vivian Lake.

CONTINUITY #308 [1268]
Thursday, December 8, 1949
8:30–9:00 p.m. EST
CBS
Richard Leonard, Director
Lawrence M. Klee, Writer
Richard Leonard, Editor
Larry Elliott, Announcer
American Home Products (Anacin, Kriptin, Bi-So-Dol), Sponsor
"The Case of the Sign of Death"
Frank Parish is murdered shortly after he argued with one of his daughter's beaus, Jack Prescott. Loretta Courtney, whom Parish tried to call when he was killed, is also a suspect.

CONTINUITY #309 [1269]
Thursday, December 15, 1949
8:30–9:00 p.m. EST
CBS
Richard Leonard, Director
Lawrence M. Klee, Writer
Richard Leonard, Editor
Larry Elliott, Announcer
American Home Products (Anacin, Kriptin, Heet), Sponsor
"The Chinchilla Coat Murder Case"
Mr. Keen and Mike Clancy investigate the murder of Joan Owens, a beautiful young actress shot to death after receiving a fabulously expensive coat made of rare chinchilla fur.

CONTINUITY #310 [1270]
Thursday, December 22, 1949
8:30–9:00 p.m. EST
CBS
Richard Leonard, Director

Lawrence M. Klee, Writer
Richard Leonard, Editor
Larry Elliott, Announcer
American Home Products (Anacin, Kriptin, Bi-So-Dol), Sponsor
"The Case of the Three Fingered Murderer"

There is evidence the murderer of elderly William Hollison — strangled in his study — has only three fingers on one hand. George, Hollison's chauffeur, is missing a couple of digits.

CONTINUITY #311 [1271]
Thursday, December 29, 1949
8:30–9:00 p.m. EST
CBS
Richard Leonard, Director
Lawrence M. Klee, Writer
Richard Leonard, Editor
Larry Elliott, Announcer
American Home Products (Anacin, Kolynos, Heet), Sponsor
"The Octopus Murder Case"

Motion picture executive Howard Creighton is struck on the head and pushed overboard on a fishing trip off the Florida coast. A later attempt is made on another passenger's life.

CONTINUITY #312 [1272]
Thursday, January 5, 1950
8:30–9:00 p.m. EST
CBS
Henry Howard, Director
Lawrence M. Klee, Writer
Richard Leonard, Editor
Larry Elliott, Announcer
American Home Products (Anacin, Kolynos, Bi-So-Dol), Sponsor
"The Case of the Rushville Murder" (*Extant Episode*)

The sleuths search the Prentiss estate for Nettie Craven, a mental hospital escapee. Laura Digby, daughter of Prentiss, was murdered. The insane Nettie is the principal suspect.

CONTINUITY #313 [1273]
Thursday, January 12, 1950
8:30–9:00 p.m. EST
CBS
Richard Leonard, Director
Lawrence M. Klee, Writer
Richard Leonard, Editor
Larry Elliott, Announcer
American Home Products (Anacin, Kriptin, Heet), Sponsor
"The Case of Murder on the Sightseeing Bus"

Aboard a sightseeing bus, Arthur Wilson is murdered with a poison-tipped pin. His stepdaughter, Margaret Wilson, is a suspect. Mr. Keen trails her to John Harvey's apartment.

CONTINUITY #314 [1274]
Thursday, January 19, 1950
8:30–9:00 p.m. EST
CBS
Richard Leonard, Director
Lawrence M. Klee, Writer
Richard Leonard, Editor
Larry Elliott, Announcer
American Home Products (Anacin, Kolynos, Bi-So-Dol), Sponsor
"The Bride and Groom Murder Case" (*Extant Episode*)

Olivia Farnum, a bride of less than a week, is pushed from the terrace of a fourteenth-floor restaurant. The groom's mother faints upon hearing that her son may be implicated in the murder.

CONTINUITY #315 [1275]
Thursday, January 26, 1950
8:30–9:00 p.m. EST
CBS
Richard Leonard, Director
Lawrence M. Klee, Writer
Richard Leonard, Editor
Larry Elliott, Announcer
American Home Products (Anacin, Kriptin, Heet), Sponsor
"The Telephone Book Murder Case" (*Extant Episode*)

Wealthy oilman Brad Andrews is about to marry beautiful divorcee Eve Lawford. But he is murdered. Lila Edwards, the wife of Andrews' valet, soon disappears into thin air.

CONTINUITY #316 [1276]
Thursday, February 2, 1950
8:30–9:00 p.m. EST
CBS
Richard Leonard, Director
Lawrence M. Klee, Writer
Richard Leonard, Editor
Larry Elliott, Announcer

American Home Products (Anacin, Kolynos, Bi-So-Dol), Sponsor
"The Weeping Willow Murder Case"

Ellen Sprague is shot to death under a weeping willow at the home she occupied with spouse Jonathan and stepdaughter Dot. Keen corners Bart Wilson after Wilson's wife had held Keen at gunpoint.

CONTINUITY #317 [1277]
Thursday, February 9, 1950
8:30–9:00 p.m. EST
CBS
Richard Leonard, Director
Lawrence M. Klee, Writer
Richard Leonard, Editor
Larry Elliott, Announcer
American Home Products (Anacin, Kriptin, Heet), Sponsor
"The Case of Murder and the Jewel Thief" (*Extant Episode*)

Carl Rollins, alias Kansas Carl, a jewel thief who preyed on the social register set, is murdered. The detectives rescue Grace Bentley from the clutches of gunman George Darcy.

CONTINUITY #318 [1278]
Thursday, February 16, 1950
8:30–9:00 p.m. EST
CBS
Richard Leonard, Director
Lawrence M. Klee, Writer
Richard Leonard, Editor
Larry Elliott, Announcer
American Home Products (Anacin, Kolynos, Bi-So-Dol), Sponsor
"The Case of the Two-Faced Murderer" (*Extant Episode*)

At Barbara Tate's insistence, her husband Jeffrey goes into hiding after the murder of Russel Owens. Owens was shot to death outside his suburban cottage. A clue points to Babs.

CONTINUITY #319 [1279]
Thursday, February 23, 1950
8:30–9:00 p.m. EST
CBS
Richard Leonard, Director
Lawrence M. Klee, Writer
Richard Leonard, Editor
Dick Dunham, Announcer
American Home Products (Anacin, Kriptin, Heet), Sponsor
"The Tea Leaf Murder Case" (*Extant Episode*)

Anita Holland is stabbed to death in her tearoom. Mr. Keen thinks she was forecasting the future by tea leaves when the killer struck. The killer added cloves to his cup, a clue.

CONTINUITY #320 [1280]
Thursday, March 2, 1950
8:30–9:00 p.m. EST
CBS
Richard Leonard, Director
Lawrence M. Klee, Writer
Richard Leonard, Editor
Larry Elliott, Announcer
American Home Products (Anacin, Kolynos, Bi-So-Dol), Sponsor
"The Haunted House Murder Case"

Believing he saw a ghost at his Catskill Mountain residence, Arnold Archer fired a gun in the dark at the apparition. When his brother's body is found on the floor, Arnold is arrested.

CONTINUITY #321 [1281]
Thursday, March 9, 1950
8:30–9:00 p.m. EST
CBS
Richard Leonard, Director
Lawrence M. Klee, Writer
Richard Leonard, Editor
Larry Elliott, Announcer
American Home Products (Anacin, Kriptin, Heet), Sponsor
"The Case of the Melody of Murder" (*Extant Episode*)

Imogene Harper, a young piano prodigy, is strangled to death in her apartment. A chief suspect is Professor John Graf, who was instructing Harper in preparation for her recital.

CONTINUITY #322 [1282]
Thursday, March 16, 1950
8:30–9:00 p.m. EST
CBS
Richard Leonard, Director
Lawrence M. Klee, Writer
Richard Leonard, Editor
Larry Elliott, Announcer
American Home Products (Anacin, Kolynos, Bi-So-Dol), Sponsor
"The Innocent Flirtation Murder Case" (*Extant Episode*)

Architect Kenneth Leighton is murdered. Contractor Arthur Wills, violently jealous of his wife Mary, falls under suspicion. Mary had flirted with Leighton, who had just jilted Dorothy Grafton.

CONTINUITY #323 [1283]
Thursday, March 23, 1950
8:30–9:00 p.m. EST
CBS
Richard Leonard, Director
Lawrence M. Klee, Writer
Richard Leonard, Editor
Larry Elliott, Announcer
American Home Products (Anacin, Kriptin, Heet), Sponsor
"The Yellow Parrot Murder Case"

Alice Ross, an elderly, wealthy widow, is strangled to death in her home. Her yellow parrot is found in a cage nearby, poisoned to death. Keen sees this as a clue.

CONTINUITY #324 [1284]
Thursday, March 30, 1950
8:30–9:00 p.m. EST
CBS
Richard Leonard, Director
Lawrence M. Klee, Writer
Richard Leonard, Editor
Larry Elliott, Announcer
American Home Products (Anacin, Kolynos, Bi-So-Dol), Sponsor
"The Fashion Model Murder Case"

Fashion magazine editor Ellen Wright receives a package that contains an alarm clock and a note threatening death after an employee, fashion model Julie Portland, is killed.

CONTINUITY #325 [1285]
Thursday, April 6, 1950
8:30–9:00 p.m. EST
CBS
Richard Leonard, Director
Lawrence M. Klee, Writer
Richard Leonard, Editor
Larry Elliott, Announcer
American Home Products (Anacin, Kolynos, Bi-So-Dol), Sponsor
"The Case of the Murdered Detective" (*Extant Episode*)

Det. Jim Ryan phones his friend Mr. Keen from a booth at the Hotel Metropol, telling him he's tracking Martin Cook, who runs a real estate concern. Ryan is stabbed in the back.

CONTINUITY #326 [1286]
Thursday, April 13, 1950
8:30–9:00 p.m. EST
CBS
Richard Leonard, Director
Lawrence M. Klee, Writer
Richard Leonard, Editor
Larry Elliott, Announcer
American Home Products (Anacin, Kolynos, Bi-So-Dol), Sponsor
"The Eccentric Millionaire Murder Case" (*Extant Episode*)

John Prague visits Mr. Keen after the death of his half-brother Otis in Pennsylvania Dutch country. Keen's name and phone number were on a slip of paper found near the body.

CONTINUITY #327 [1287]
Thursday, April 20, 1950
8:30–9:00 p.m. EST
CBS
Richard Leonard, Director
Lawrence M. Klee, Writer
Richard Leonard, Editor
Larry Elliott, Announcer
American Home Products (Anacin, Kolynos, Bi-So-Dol), Sponsor
"The Country Club Murder Case" (*Extant Episode*)

During a young people's dance at a Westchester country club, well-heeled socialite Arlene Graham is strangled to death. Her partner, Alan Rogers, who hoped to marry her, seeks help.

The same case title (but a different plot) was later used for the episode that aired October 4, 1951.

CONTINUITY #328 [1288]
Thursday, April 27, 1950
8:30–9:00 p.m. EST
CBS
Richard Leonard, Director
Lawrence M. Klee, Writer
Richard Leonard, Editor
Larry Elliott, Announcer
American Home Products (Anacin, Kolynos, Bi-So-Dol), Sponsor
"The Case of the Woman Who Married a Murderer" (*Extant Episode*)

Linda Roberts solicits Mr. Keen's help in solving the death of former lover Kenneth Ward, gunned down late at night in his apartment by an intruder who awaited his return.

CONTINUITY #329 [1289]
Thursday, May 4, 1950
8:30–9:00 p.m. EST
CBS
Richard Leonard, Director
Lawrence M. Klee, Writer
Richard Leonard, Editor
Larry Elliott, Announcer
American Home Products (Anacin, Kolynos, Bi-So-Dol), Sponsor
"The King Cobra Murder Case" (*Extant Episode*)
    Mr. Keen is enlisted by Alice Walker to find the murderer of her sister Doris, believing a former swain killed her. Doris died on a passenger ship entering New York Harbor.

CONTINUITY #330 [1290]
Thursday, May 11, 1950
8:30–9:00 p.m. EDST
CBS
Richard Leonard, Director
Lawrence M. Klee, Writer
Richard Leonard, Editor
Larry Elliott, Announcer
American Home Products (Anacin, Kolynos, Bi-So-Dol), Sponsor
"The Case of Murder and the Missing Car" (*Extant Episode*)
    The body of Bob Richards, a young bond salesman, is found in the trunk of a car owned by rich Thomas Fielding. Elizabeth Armstrong may have been with Richards when he met his fate.

CONTINUITY #331 [1291]
Thursday, May 18, 1950
8:30–9:00 p.m. EDST
CBS
Richard Leonard, Director
Lawrence M. Klee, Writer
Richard Leonard, Editor
Larry Elliott, Announcer
American Home Products (Anacin, Kolynos, Bi-So-Dol), Sponsor
"The Case of the Murdered Countess"
    Countess Victoria Dulong, an American widow of a European nobleman, is murdered after her return from abroad, her body found in a lonely wood. An intruder strikes Clancy down.

CONTINUITY #332 [1292]
Thursday, May 25, 1950
8:30–9:00 p.m. EDST
CBS
Richard Leonard, Director
Lawrence M. Klee, Writer
Richard Leonard, Editor
Larry Elliott, Announcer
American Home Products (Anacin, Kolynos, Bi-So-Dol), Sponsor
"The Broken Window Murder Case" (*Extant Episode*)
    Wealthy philanthropist John Franklyn is stabbed to death in his home. A broken windowpane stained with blood offers a vital clue. This puts George Haycraft high on the suspect list.

CONTINUITY #333 [1293]
Thursday, June 1, 1950
8:30–9:00 p.m. EDST
CBS
Richard Leonard, Director
Lawrence M. Klee, Writer
Richard Leonard, Editor
Larry Elliott, Announcer
American Home Products (Anacin, Kolynos, Bi-So-Dol), Sponsor
"The Quicksand Murder Case" (*Extant Episode*)
    Betsy Harlow asks Keen and Clancy to investigate her sister Edna's disappearance. They find her body in a closet in a house she had recently rented from Henry and Alice Wicker.

CONTINUITY #334 [1294]
Thursday, June 8, 1950
8:30–9:00 p.m. EDST
CBS
Richard Leonard, Director
Lawrence M. Klee, Writer
Richard Leonard, Editor
Larry Elliott, Announcer
American Home Products (Anacin, Kolynos, Bi-So-Dol), Sponsor
"The Amusement Park Murder Case"
    Allen Davis is killed in a shooting gallery at an amusement park that he visited with his

wife Rosalind. His mother-in-law is a prime suspect; she violently opposed the marriage.

CONTINUITY #335 [1295]
Thursday, June 15, 1950
8:30–9:00 p.m. EDST
CBS
Richard Leonard, Director
Lawrence M. Klee, Writer
Richard Leonard, Editor
Larry Elliott, Announcer
American Home Products (Anacin, Kolynos, Bi-So-Dol), Sponsor
"The Skull and Crossbones Murder Case" (*Extant Episode*)

Wealthy Lemuel Barker is poisoned to death. Early suspects are Barker's housekeeper, Emily Cross, currently sought by police, and Peter Hunt, a nephew, caught in Barker's Fifth Avenue home.

The broadcast date of this episode is misidentified on some extant copies in circulation. The title of this story was later used for the broadcast of November 14, 1952, but with an altogether different plot.

CONTINUITY #336 [1296]
Thursday, June 22, 1950
8:30–9:00 p.m. EDST
CBS
Richard Leonard, Director
Lawrence M. Klee, Writer
Richard Leonard, Editor
Larry Elliott, Announcer
American Home Products (Anacin, Kolynos, Bi-So-Dol), Sponsor
"The Diamond Mine Murder Case"

John Andrews is shot to death in a hotel room while in New York on business. Police hold Kenneth Harlan, who fell in love with John's wife Laura, on suspicion of murder.

CONTINUITY #337 [1297]
Thursday, June 29, 1950
8:30–9:00 p.m. EDST
CBS
Richard Leonard, Director
Lawrence M. Klee, Writer
Richard Leonard, Editor
Larry Elliott, Announcer
American Home Products (Anacin, Kolynos, Bi-So-Dol), Sponsor
"The Dance Hall Murder Case"

Doris Lee is murdered in a dance hall. Suspects include Jim Creighton, the son of a millionaire, who was in love with her; his fiancée, Imogene Lawrence; and Jim's brother Bob.

CONTINUITY #338 [1298]
Thursday, July 6, 1950
8:30–9:00 p.m. EDST
CBS
Richard Leonard, Director
Lawrence M. Klee, Writer
Richard Leonard, Editor
Larry Elliott, Announcer
American Home Products (Anacin, Kolynos, Bi-So-Dol), Sponsor
"The Case of Murder and the Missing Clue"

The chief suspect in the murder of wealthy Anita Chalmers is her chauffeur, Vincent, who smashes her limousine in a fit of rage. Passengers Keen and Clancy nearly become victims.

CONTINUITY #339 [1299]
Thursday, July 13, 1950
8:30–9:00 p.m. EDST
CBS
Richard Leonard, Director
Lawrence M. Klee, Writer
Richard Leonard, Editor
Larry Elliott, Announcer
American Home Products (Anacin, Kriptin, Bi-So-Dol), Sponsor
"The Ice Cube Murder Case"

Millionaire John Brandon is killed by means of poisoned ice cubes at his Cape Cod summer home. Mr. Keen interrogates Edson, Brandon's butler.

CONTINUITY #340 [1300]
Thursday, July 20, 1950
8:30–9:00 p.m. EDST
CBS
Richard Leonard, Director
Lawrence M. Klee, Writer
Richard Leonard, Editor
Larry Elliott, Announcer
American Home Products (Anacin, Kolynos, Bi-So-Dol), Sponsor
"The Case of Murder in the Old Curiosity Shop"

As Keen and Clancy probe the murder of curiosity shop owner Jonathan Petrie, they discover that someone planted a capsule of flammable liquid in a storeroom, which launched a blaze.

CONTINUITY #341 [1301]
Thursday, July 27, 1950
8:30–9:00 p.m. EDST
CBS
Richard Leonard, Director
Lawrence M. Klee, Writer
Richard Leonard, Editor
Larry Elliott, Announcer
American Home Products (Anacin, Kriptin, Bi-So-Dol), Sponsor
"The Case of Murder on a Foggy Night"
Businessman Frank Bradley is pushed from a high bridge over a river. He falls to his death in the water below. Helen Temple, gun in hand, forces her way into the Bradley home.

CONTINUITY #342 [1302]
Thursday, August 3, 1950
8:30–9:00 p.m. EDST
CBS
Richard Leonard, Director
Lawrence M. Klee, Writer
Richard Leonard, Editor
Larry Elliott, Announcer
American Home Products (Anacin, Kolynos, Bi-So-Dol), Sponsor
"The Silver Wedding Murder Case"
Mr. Keen calls for a reenactment of a crime. He asks the five people who were nearby when Elizabeth Sumner was murdered on her silver wedding anniversary to participate.

CONTINUITY #343 [1303]
Thursday, August 10, 1950
8:30–9:00 p.m. EDST
CBS
Richard Leonard, Director
Lawrence M. Klee, Writer
Richard Leonard, Editor
Larry Elliott, Announcer
American Home Products (Anacin, Kriptin, Bi-So-Dol), Sponsor
"The Case of the Model for Murder"
After Charles Gaynor's murder, his body disappears. Stymied by the lack of evidence (and body), Mr. Keen resorts to a startling strategy to break the case.

CONTINUITY #344 [1304]
Thursday, August 17, 1950
8:30–9:00 p.m. EDST
CBS
Edward Slattery, Director
Lawrence M. Klee, Writer
Richard Leonard, Editor
Larry Elliott, Announcer
American Home Products (Anacin, Kolynos, Bi-So-Dol), Sponsor
"The Emerald Necklace Murder Case"
Former stage star Sandra Worthing is murdered, an emerald necklace found around her neck. Yet a cheap imitation of a genuine emerald necklace was apparently stolen from the victim.

CONTINUITY #345 [1305]
Thursday, August 24, 1950
8:30–9:00 p.m. EDST
CBS
Edward Slattery, Director
Lawrence M. Klee, Writer
Richard Leonard, Editor
Larry Elliott, Announcer
American Home Products (Anacin, Kriptin, Bi-So-Dol), Sponsor
"The Case of Murder and the Howling Ghost"
The murder of newlywed Bob Sanders takes the gumshoes to an old mansion in the Catskills. Owners Paul and Mona Stover have just returned after two years, oblivious of the crime.

CONTINUITY #346 [1306]
Thursday, August 31, 1950
8:30–9:00 p.m. EDST
CBS
Richard Leonard, Director
Lawrence M. Klee, Writer
Richard Leonard, Editor
Larry Elliott, Announcer
American Home Products (Anacin, Kolynos, Bi-So-Dol), Sponsor
"The Case of Murder and the Sacred Tiger"
Novelist Madeline Lawrence bought a small jade replica of a tiger while visiting Asia. An unlucky superstition follows the tiger: it brings death to its owner. Sorry, Madeline.

CONTINUITY #347 [1307]
Thursday, September 7, 1950

8:30–9:00 p.m. EDST
CBS
Richard Leonard, Director
Lawrence M. Klee, Writer
Richard Leonard, Editor
Larry Elliott, Announcer
American Home Products (Anacin, Kriptin, Bi-So-Dol), Sponsor
"The Lighthouse Murder Case"

Keen and Clancy probe the murder of Amos Wells, keeper of a lighthouse on a rock ledge on the Long Island shore. Peter Duncan, estranged spouse of Wells' daughter, is suspect number one.

CONTINUITY #348 [1308]
Thursday, September 14, 1950
8:30–9:00 p.m. EDST
CBS
Richard Leonard, Director
Lawrence M. Klee, Writer
Richard Leonard, Editor
Larry Elliott, Announcer
American Home Products (Anacin, Kolynos, Bi-So-Dol), Sponsor
"The Silver Treasure Murder Case"

Well-heeled eccentric William Greeley is shot to death in his New Jersey home. His daughter-in-law Doris subsequently disappears, and Edna, Greeley's second wife, is attacked.

This story was later reprised for the broadcast of October 1, 1954, using the same title and character names.

CONTINUITY #349 [1309]
Thursday, September 21, 1950
8:30–9:00 p.m. EDST
CBS
Richard Leonard, Director
Lawrence M. Klee, Writer
Richard Leonard, Editor
Larry Elliott, Announcer
American Home Products (Anacin, Kriptin, Bi-So-Dol), Sponsor
"The Case of Murder in the Elevator"

Vocalist Angela Powers is killed in a self-service elevator at her apartment complex. Opera star Francine Morley locks Keen, Clancy and voice teacher Carlo Trask in her apartment.

CONTINUITY #350 [1310]
Thursday, September 28, 1950
8:30–9:00 p.m. EST
CBS
Richard Leonard, Director
Lawrence M. Klee, Writer
Richard Leonard, Editor
Larry Elliott, Announcer
American Home Products (Anacin, Kolynos, Bi-So-Dol), Sponsor
"The Swiss Clock Murder Case"

When retired jewel merchant Abner Walton is found murdered, he is clutching a small hand-carved piece of wood, perhaps a clue. Mike Clancy catches Allen Blakley prowling around Walton's home.

CONTINUITY #351 [1311]
Thursday, October 5, 1950
8:30–9:00 p.m. EST
CBS
Richard Leonard, Director
Lawrence M. Klee, Writer
Richard Leonard, Editor
Larry Elliott, Announcer
American Home Products (Anacin, Kriptin, Heet), Sponsor
"The Case of Murder and the Phantom Voice"

Julie Chalmers is murdered at her apartment. Though the police arrest Edna Waters, Keen is interested in the maid, Marie Carpenter, who tried to blackmail the victim.

CONTINUITY #352 [1312]
Thursday, October 12, 1950
8:30–9:00 p.m. EST
CBS
Richard Leonard, Director
Lawrence M. Klee, Writer
Richard Leonard, Editor
Larry Elliott, Announcer
American Home Products (Anacin, Kolynos, Bi-So-Dol), Sponsor
"The Hitchhiker Murder Case"

Don Westmore is shot while hitchhiking to New York. Eddie Grimes, who argued with him, is lured to the funeral parlor. Upon viewing the body, Grimes grows fearful and tries to run off.

CONTINUITY #353 [1313]
Thursday, October 19, 1950

8:30–9:00 p.m. EST
CBS
Richard Leonard, Director
Lawrence M. Klee, Writer
Richard Leonard, Editor
Larry Elliott, Announcer
American Home Products (Anacin, Kriptin, Heet), Sponsor
"The Beautiful Dancer Murder Case"

Beautiful young ballet dancer Yvonne Bengal is murdered. A major clue is a bill for two dozen roses charged to dancer John Chatham. Yvonne died from poisoned thorns on a bouquet.

CONTINUITY #354 [1314]

Thursday, October 26, 1950
8:30–9:00 p.m. EST
CBS
Richard Leonard, Director
Lawrence M. Klee, Writer
Richard Leonard, Editor
Larry Elliott, Announcer
American Home Products (Anacin, Kolynos, Bi-So-Dol), Sponsor
"The Case of the Man Who Wanted to Murder"

Alfred Stockton is shot to death in his home. Son-in-law Jack Wilmott earlier threatened to murder Stockton. A renter, Jason Ashley, casts suspicion on Jack's wife Margaret.

Although apparently unintended, this turned out to be the final broadcast featuring Bennett Kilpack as Mr. Keen.

CONTINUITY #355 [1315]

Thursday, November 2, 1950
8:30–9:00 p.m. EST
CBS
Richard Leonard, Director
Lawrence M. Klee, Writer
Richard Leonard, Editor
Larry Elliott, Announcer
American Home Products (Anacin, Kriptin, Heet), Sponsor
"The Lonely Acres Murder Case"

Summoned to a house in Lonely Acres, a wooded suburb, Keen and Clancy find the body of Helen Peabody, shot to death. Stephen, her second husband, tries to hide her in the attic.

Philip Clarke substitutes for Bennett Kilpack in the role of Mr. Keen, marking Clarke's initial appearance on the program.

CONTINUITY #356 [1316]

Thursday, November 9, 1950
8:30–9:00 p.m. EST
CBS
Richard Leonard, Director
Lawrence M. Klee, Writer
Richard Leonard, Editor
Larry Elliott, Announcer
American Home Products (Anacin, Kolynos, Bi-So-Dol), Sponsor
"The One-Legged Man Murder Case"

Frank Allison is shot to death in a hunting cabin he owned with John Wells. With a one-legged culprit's imprint found, attention focuses on guide Alf Grimes, who has a wooden leg.

Philip Clarke substitutes for Bennett Kilpack in the role of Mr. Keen.

CONTINUITY #357 [1317]

Thursday, November 16, 1950
8:30–9:00 p.m. EST
CBS
Richard Leonard, Director
Lawrence M. Klee, Writer
Richard Leonard, Editor
Larry Elliott, Announcer
American Home Products (Anacin, Kriptin, Heet), Sponsor
"The Gorilla Murder Case"

Zoo director Gilbert Anderson is strangled to death in the monkey house. Authorities blame an escaped gorilla. But Mr. Keen is convinced that a different species of primate is responsible.

Philip Clarke substitutes for Bennett Kilpack in the role of Mr. Keen.

CONTINUITY #358 [1318]

Thursday, November 23, 1950
8:30–9:00 p.m. EST
CBS
Richard Leonard, Director
Lawrence M. Klee, Writer
Richard Leonard, Editor
Larry Elliott, Announcer
American Home Products (Anacin, Kolynos, Bi-So-Dol), Sponsor
"The Music Box Murder Case"

Heiress Doris Payne dies on her wedding day when a bomb hidden in a music box she received as a wedding gift explodes.

Philip Clarke substitutes for Bennett Kilpack in the role of Mr. Keen.

CONTINUITY #359 [1319]
Thursday, November 30, 1950
8:30–9:00 p.m. EST
CBS
Richard Leonard, Director
Lawrence M. Klee, Writer
Richard Leonard, Editor
Larry Elliott, Announcer
American Home Products (Anacin, Kriptin, Heet), Sponsor
"The Eight Million Dollar Murder Case"
 Wealthy philanthropist John Ashton is strangled with a rope tied in an Asiatic knot, a Strangler's Noose. One suspect is John's granddaughter, who was about to be cut from his will.
 Philip Clarke substitutes for Bennett Kilpack in the role of Mr. Keen.

CONTINUITY #360 [1320]
Thursday, December 7, 1950
8:30–9:00 p.m. EST
CBS
Richard Leonard, Director
Lawrence M. Klee, Writer
Richard Leonard, Editor
Larry Elliott, Announcer
American Home Products (Anacin, Kolynos, Bi-So-Dol), Sponsor
"The Case of the Redheaded Murderer"
 Mr. Keen and Mike Clancy pursue the trail of a redheaded individual believed responsible for the murder of Hollywood columnist Barbara Tate. More than one suspect qualifies.
 Philip Clarke is named as the actor permanently playing the role of Mr. Keen.

CONTINUITY #361 [1321]
Thursday, December 14, 1950
8:30–9:00 p.m. EST
CBS
Richard Leonard, Director
Lawrence M. Klee, Writer
Richard Leonard, Editor
Larry Elliott, Announcer
American Home Products (Anacin, Kriptin, Heet), Sponsor
"The Powder Puff Murder Case"
 Arthur Jeffries, an importer of semi-precious jewels, is murdered. As Mr. Keen talks by phone with Laura Robins, who met the victim in Europe, an intruder suddenly cuts her off.

CONTINUITY #362 [1322]
Thursday, December 21, 1950
8:30–9:00 p.m. EST
CBS
Richard Leonard, Director
Lawrence M. Klee, Writer
Richard Leonard, Editor
Larry Elliott, Announcer
American Home Products (Anacin, Kolynos, Bi-So-Dol), Sponsor
"The Case of Murder and the Voodoo Doll"
 The discovery of a voodoo doll, sometimes used in witchcraft ceremonies in Haiti, adds a weird dimension to the puzzling case of Marlene Rockwell, who was shot to death in her apartment.

CONTINUITY #363 [1323]
Thursday, December 28, 1950
8:30–9:00 p.m. EST
CBS
Richard Leonard, Director
Lawrence M. Klee, Writer
Richard Leonard, Editor
Larry Elliott, Announcer
American Home Products (Anacin, Kriptin, Heet), Sponsor
"The Case of Murder and the Poisoned Towel"
 Affluent Franklin Powell is murdered when his barber, Ernest Martin, places a hot towel over his face following a shave. The towel has been treated with a deadly fuming poison.

CONTINUITY #364 [1324]
Thursday, January 4, 1951
8:30–9:00 p.m. EST
CBS
Richard Leonard, Director
Lawrence M. Klee, Writer
Richard Leonard, Editor
Larry Elliott, Announcer
American Home Products (Anacin, Kolynos, Bi-So-Dol), Sponsor
"The Homing Pigeon Murder Case"
 Mr. Keen and Mike Clancy find the body of respected scientist John Farrington, who was shot to death in a lonely Jersey shack after being abducted from New York City by a kidnapper.

CONTINUITY #365 [1325]
Thursday, January 11, 1951
8:30–9:00 p.m. EST
CBS
Richard Leonard, Director
Lawrence M. Klee, Writer
Richard Leonard, Editor
Larry Elliott, Announcer
American Home Products (Anacin, Kriptin, Heet), Sponsor
"The Case of Murder and the Thousand Dollar Bill"

After a quarrel with his wife over his brother-in-law, newly married Ralph Anders leaves home and takes a furnished room. He is found shot dead, with a thousand dollar bill nearby.

CONTINUITY #366 [1326]
Thursday, January 18, 1951
8:30–9:00 p.m. EST
CBS
Richard Leonard, Director
Lawrence M. Klee, Writer
Richard Leonard, Editor
Larry Elliott, Announcer
American Home Products (Anacin, Kolynos, Bi-So-Dol), Sponsor
"The Rich Sister-Poor Sister Murder Case"

The tracer of lost persons and his partner attempt to learn who murdered Lois Brooks, a beautiful and very wealthy young widow. She was shot to death in her penthouse apartment.

CONTINUITY #367 [1327]
Thursday, January 25, 1951
8:30–9:00 p.m. EST
CBS
Richard Leonard, Director
Lawrence M. Klee, Writer
Richard Leonard, Editor
Larry Elliott, Announcer
American Home Products (Anacin, Kriptin, Heet), Sponsor
"The Nylon Stocking Murder Case"

A nylon stocking is used to strangle James Carrington to death. Elsie, the victim's wife, is arrested for the crime, but Keen believes the real murderer may still be at large.

CONTINUITY #368 [1328]
Thursday, February 1, 1951
8:30–9:00 p.m. EST
CBS
Richard Leonard, Director
Lawrence M. Klee, Writer
Richard Leonard, Editor
Larry Elliott, Announcer
American Home Products (Anacin, Kolynos, Bi-So-Dol), Sponsor
"The Diamond Necklace Murder Case"

A fabulous diamond necklace worth a fortune is stolen from jewelry salesman Charles Haven, who is killed. Countess De Vere, who hoped to buy the choker, is subsequently murdered.

Actors in this episode include Florence Williams, Sylvia Leigh and Karl Weber.

CONTINUITY #369 [1329]
Thursday, February 8, 1951
8:30–9:00 p.m. EST
CBS
Richard Leonard, Director
Lawrence M. Klee, Writer
Richard Leonard, Editor
Larry Elliott, Announcer
American Home Products (Anacin, Kriptin, Heet), Sponsor
"The Grandmother's Warning Murder Case"

Wealthy Alice Bradford meets death via a poison-tipped needle placed inside a thimble. The victim was about to alert her grandson, Don Bradford, about something.

CONTINUITY #370 [1330]
Thursday, February 15, 1951
8:30–9:00 p.m. EST
CBS
Richard Leonard, Director
Lawrence M. Klee, Writer
Richard Leonard, Editor
Larry Elliott, Announcer
American Home Products (Anacin, Kolynos, Bi-So-Dol), Sponsor
"The Deep Well Murder Case"

Hope Norton is murdered, her bullet-ridden body stuffed in a deep well at Carleton Manor, her Westchester estate. Spouse Clark Norton had just retuned home after having vanished earlier.

CONTINUITY #371 [1331]
Thursday, February 22, 1951

8:30–9:00 p.m. EST
CBS
Richard Leonard, Director
Lawrence M. Klee and Frank Hummert, Writers
Editor's name omitted
Larry Elliott, Announcer
American Home Products (Anacin, Kriptin, Heet), Sponsor
"The Case of Murder and the Gypsy Palm Reader"

The sleuths pursue the murderer of George Graham. Madame Zuka, a fortune-teller, predicted the death, and claimed that a mysterious woman — to whom Graham had sent gifts — was his stepdaughter.

This episode was reprised, under another title and using altered character names, for the broadcast of May 15, 1952.

CONTINUITY #372 [1332]

Thursday, March 1, 1951
8:30–9:00 p.m. EST
CBS
Richard Leonard, Director
Lawrence M. Klee, Writer
Richard Leonard, Editor
Larry Elliott, Announcer
American Home Products (Anacin, Kolynos, Bi-So-Dol), Sponsor
"The Wristwatch Murder Case"

Wealthy businessman Victor Hubbard is stabbed to death in his car, parked outside his home. Later an unknown would-be assailant tries to run down the gumshoes.

CONTINUITY #373 [1333]

Thursday, March 8, 1951
8:30–9:00 p.m. EST
CBS
Edward Slattery, Director
Lawrence M. Klee, Writer
Richard Leonard, Editor
Larry Elliott, Announcer
American Home Products (Anacin, Kriptin, Heet), Sponsor
"The Yellow Monster Murder Case"

Grace Buchanan is stabbed to death with a sharpened stake. Giant webbed footprints are found, and a maid reports seeing something yellow glowing in the dark as the murderer escaped.

CONTINUITY #374 [1334]

Thursday, March 15, 1951
8:30–9:00 p.m. EST
CBS
Richard Leonard, Director
Lawrence M. Klee, Writer
Richard Leonard, Editor
Larry Elliott, Announcer
American Home Products (Anacin, Kolynos, Bi-So-Dol), Sponsor
"The Checkerboard Murder Case"

Well-heeled Alfred Blake dies while playing checkers with an unidentified opponent. Peter Winthrop threatens widow Janet Blake if she fails to run away with him as promised.

Actors in this episode include Henry Norell, Jan Miner, Ronald Long, Anne Burr and James Meighan.

CONTINUITY #375 [1335]

Thursday, March 22, 1951
8:30–9:00 p.m. EST
CBS
Richard Leonard, Director
Lawrence M. Klee, Writer
Richard Leonard, Editor
Larry Elliott, Announcer
American Home Products (Anacin, Kriptin, Heet), Sponsor
"The Airport Murder Case"

Walter Haskell, an exporter of costume jewelry, is stabbed to death in an airport phone booth. Half-brother Charlie Prentiss is nabbed in a railway depot trying to leave town.

CONTINUITY #376 [1336]

Thursday, March 29, 1951
8:30–9:00 p.m. EST
CBS
Richard Leonard, Director
Lawrence M. Klee, Writer
Richard Leonard, Editor
Larry Elliott, Announcer
American Home Products (Anacin, Kolynos, Bi-So-Dol), Sponsor
"The Case of Murder and the One-Eyed Man"

Newlywed Frank Manning is shot to death. At the same time, a man wearing a black patch over one eye was seen leaving the victim's home. Manning's partner, Earl Knox, wears a patch.

CONTINUITY #377 [1337]
Thursday, April 5, 1951
8:30–9:00 p.m. EST
CBS
Richard Leonard, Director
Lawrence M. Klee, Writer
Richard Leonard, Editor
Larry Elliott, Announcer
American Home Products (Anacin, Kolynos, Bi-So-Dol), Sponsor
"The Alarm Clock Murder Case"
George Decker touches a wired alarm clock and is electrocuted. Suspects include Eve Maxwell, whose ties to him remain unclear; landlord Ernest Black; and Hugo Porter, who argued with him.

CONTINUITY #378 [1338]
Thursday, April 12, 1951
8:30–9:00 p.m. EST
CBS
Richard Leonard, Director
Lawrence M. Klee, Writer
Richard Leonard, Editor
Larry Elliott, Announcer
American Home Products (Anacin, Kolynos, Bi-So-Dol), Sponsor
"The River Warehouse Murder Case"
Warehouse night watchman Jim Everett is murdered. Stepson Bill Everett, who tries to run away, is a prime suspect. Bill is believed to have robbed the warehouse several times.

CONTINUITY #379 [1339]
Thursday, April 19, 1951
8:30–9:00 p.m. EST
CBS
Richard Leonard, Director
Lawrence M. Klee, Writer
Richard Leonard, Editor
Larry Elliott, Announcer
American Home Products (Anacin, Kolynos, Bi-So-Dol), Sponsor
"The Matinee Idol Murder Case"
Actor–matinee idol Lawrence Creighton is shot to death in his dressing room following a show. Cynthia Mitchell, an actress who tried to lure him away from his wife, may be guilty.
Actors in this episode include Horace Braham, Sylvia Leigh, Elizabeth Morgan, Cathleen Cordell, Chuck Webster and James Meighan.

CONTINUITY #380 [1340]
Thursday, April 26, 1951
8:30–9:00 p.m. EST
CBS
Richard Leonard, Director
Lawrence M. Klee, Writer
Richard Leonard, Editor
Larry Elliott, Announcer
American Home Products (Anacin, Kolynos, Bi-So-Dol), Sponsor
"The Missing Wife Murder Case"
Ellen Digby's body was put into a cellar freezer. Judith Wayne convalesces in the Digby home from a broken ankle, while sister-in-law Clara Digby burns some bloodstained gloves.
Actors in this episode include Julie Stevens, Karl Weber, Helen Claire, Billy Quinn and Anne Seymour.

CONTINUITY #381 [1341]
Thursday, May 3, 1951
8:30–9:00 p.m. EDST
CBS
Richard Leonard, Director
Lawrence M. Klee, Writer
Richard Leonard, Editor
Larry Elliott, Announcer
American Home Products (Anacin, Kolynos, Bi-So-Dol), Sponsor
"The Duck Pond Murder Case"
The bullet-ridden body of a young insurance agent, Gerald Hewitt, is discovered in a shallow duck pond in a park. A prime suspect is the man who was given Gerald's job, Arthur Bligh.
Actors in this episode include Hal Studer, Gertrude Warner, Lauren Gilbert, Jan Miner and Ned Wever.

CONTINUITY #382 [1342]
Thursday, May 10, 1951
8:30–9:00 p.m. EDST
CBS
Richard Leonard, Director
Lawrence M. Klee, Writer
Richard Leonard, Editor
Larry Elliott, Announcer
American Home Products (Anacin, Kolynos, Bi-So-Dol), Sponsor
"The Typewriter Murder Case"
Private secretary Alice Bentley is stabbed to death at her typewriter in the architect's

office in which she works. Keen and Clancy find a typed note implicating employer Lester Archer.

Actors in this episode include Florence Williams, James Meighan, Richard Newton, Arline Blackburn and Joan Alexander. Typical notations on Richard Leonard's master copy of this script refer to a planned rehearsal on Wednesday evening, May 9, 1951, as follows: "FLORENCE WILLIAMS coming from 'Front Page Farrell.' Her stand-in until 6:10 p.m. will be Marion Carr. ARLINE BLACKBURN coming from 'Lorenzo Jones.' Her stand-in until 5:00 p.m. will be Barbara Bell Wright. RICHARD NEWTON coming from 'Just Plain Bill.' His stand-in until 6:00 p.m. will be Humphrey Davis."

CONTINUITY #383 [1343]
Thursday, May 17, 1951
8:30–9:00 p.m. EDST
CBS
Richard Leonard, Director
Lawrence M. Klee, Writer
Richard Leonard, Editor
Larry Elliott, Announcer
American Home Products (Anacin, Kolynos, Bi-So-Dol), Sponsor
"The Dance Hall Murder Case"

Nancy Slade, a beautiful young dance hall hostess, is poisoned to death. Keen and Clancy question Martha Blaine, a wealthy society matron who attempts to conceal a revolver.

CONTINUITY #384 [1344]
Thursday, May 24, 1951
8:30–9:00 p.m. EDST
CBS
Richard Leonard, Director
Lawrence M. Klee, Writer
Richard Leonard, Editor
Larry Elliott, Announcer
American Home Products (Anacin, Kolynos, Bi-So-Dol), Sponsor
"The Hotel Carling Murder Case"

Wealthy George Akron is stabbed to death in his suite at the fashionable Hotel Carling. Singer Natalie West, occupying an adjacent room, tries to prevent the sleuths' entry.

CONTINUITY #385 [1345]
Thursday, May 31, 1951
8:30–9:00 p.m. EDST
CBS
Richard Leonard, Director
Lawrence M. Klee, Writer
Richard Leonard, Editor
Larry Elliott, Announcer
American Home Products (Anacin, Kolynos, Bi-So-Dol), Sponsor
"The Bonfire Murder Case"

Keen and Clancy probe the murder of Mary Jennings, whose body was found after her home burned. Her cook, Kate Higgins, has suffered burns on her hand. She could be implicated.

Actors in this episode include Sarah Burton, Florence Freeman, James Meighan, Anne Elstner and John Stanley.

CONTINUITY #386 [1346]
Thursday, June 7, 1951
8:30–9:00 p.m. EDST
CBS
Richard Leonard, Director
Lawrence M. Klee, Writer
Richard Leonard, Editor
Larry Elliott, Announcer
American Home Products (Anacin, Kolynos, Bi-So-Dol), Sponsor
"The Locked Room Murder Case"

Keen and Clancy find the body of William Arnold buried in his home garden. Arnold was shot in the head. His divorced wife Gwen, who has remarried, is under suspicion.

Actors in this episode include Ian Martin, Lauren Gilbert, Florence Williams, Karl Weber and Mary Jane Higby.

CONTINUITY #387 [1347]
Thursday, June 14, 1951
8:30–9:00 p.m. EDST
CBS
Richard Leonard, Director
Lawrence M. Klee, Writer
Richard Leonard, Editor
Larry Elliott, Announcer
American Home Products (Anacin, Kolynos, Bi-So-Dol), Sponsor
"The Candid Camera Murder Case"

Rich Joan Harper is shot dead on the terrace of her home. Herbert Barrett, upset over his love affair with the victim, grabbed a bundle of letters in her home, and thus became a suspect.

Actors in this episode include Audrey Egan, Sidney Smith, Peggy Stanley, Richard Janaver and Horace Braham.

CONTINUITY #388 [1348]
Thursday, June 21, 1951
8:30–9:00 p.m. EDST
CBS
Richard Leonard, Director
Lawrence M. Klee, Writer
Richard Leonard, Editor
Larry Elliott, Announcer
American Home Products (Anacin, Kolynos, Bi-So-Dol), Sponsor
"The Hidden Body Murder Case"
John Clyde disappears. Keen and Clancy are sure he's the victim of murder. They question Clyde's brother, Henry, in the presence of Lorna Manning, the victim's sweetheart.

CONTINUITY #389 [1349]
Thursday, June 28, 1951
8:30–9:00 p.m. EDST
CBS
Richard Leonard, Director
Lawrence M. Klee, Writer
Richard Leonard, Editor
Larry Elliott, Announcer
American Home Products (Anacin, Kolynos, Bi-So-Dol), Sponsor
"The Swimming Pool Murder Case"
Young society girl Lois Trask drowns in the swimming pool on her Long Island estate. Her butler, William, tries to bury a large sum that may have come from the home's wall safe.
Actors in this episode include Horace Braham, Gertrude Warner, Ian Martin, Elizabeth Morgan and Richard Newton.

CONTINUITY #390 [1350]
Thursday, July 5, 1951
8:30–9:00 p.m. EDST
CBS
Richard Leonard, Director
Lawrence M. Klee, Writer
Richard Leonard, Editor
Larry Elliott, Announcer
American Home Products (Anacin, Kolynos, Bi-So-Dol), Sponsor
"The Dummy Key Murder Case"
Donald Rand, manager of an exclusive Fifth Avenue jewelry store, is shot to death during a $200,000 robbery. A doorman employed by the store has vanished.
Actors in this episode include Frank Chase, Anne Seymour, Sarah Burton, Lauren Gilbert and Staats Cotsworth.

CONTINUITY #391 [1351]
Thursday, July 12, 1951
8:30–9:00 p.m. EDST
CBS
Richard Leonard, Director
Lawrence M. Klee, Writer
Richard Leonard, Editor
Larry Elliott, Announcer
American Home Products (Anacin, Kolynos, Bi-So-Dol), Sponsor
"The Poison Pen Murder Case"
Affluent Betsy Paine is stabbed in her Connecticut home. Unsigned poison pen letters accuse her husband George of marrying her for her money and killing her to control it.
Actors in this episode include Elizabeth Morgan, Richard Janaver, Florence Freeman, Audrey Egan and Ian Martin. This is the last in the continuing series of CBS Radio broadcasts begun in 1942, though the program did eventually return to CBS at a later date.

CONTINUITY #392 [1352]
Friday, July 20, 1951
9:30–10:00 p.m. EDST
NBC
Richard Leonard, Director
Writer's name omitted (Lawrence M. Klee, original script)
Richard Leonard, Editor
Jack Costello, Announcer
Liggett & Myers Tobacco Co. (Chesterfield), American Home Products (Anacin), Radio Corp. of America (RCA Victor), Sponsors
"The Case of Murder and the Strange Woman"
(*Extant Episode*)
Immensely popular vocalist Don Taylor is shot to death in a rehearsal studio. Mildred Sellers, who attempted to steal some photographs of the murdered man, has managed to escape.
Actors in this episode include James Meighan, Mary Jane Higby, Mary Beth Hughes, John Stanley, Audrey Egan and Sarah Burton. This episode borrowed some elements, including the title, from an earlier story broadcast on March 3, 1949.

CONTINUITY #393 [1353]
Friday, July 27, 1951
9:30–10:00 p.m. EDST
NBC
Richard Leonard, Director
Jean Carroll, Writer
Richard Leonard, Editor
Jack Costello, Announcer
American Home Products (Anacin), Radio Corp. of America (RCA Victor), Liggett & Myers Tobacco Co. (Chesterfield), Sponsors
"The Photograph Album Murder Case" (*Extant Episode*)

Young actress June Reynolds is stabbed to death at the home of wealthy society matron Elsa Foster, who sponsored her career. A missing diamond necklace appears in June's room.

Actors in this episode include Sylvia Leigh, Abby Lewis, Richard Janaver, Frank Thomas Jr. and Florence Williams.

CONTINUITY #394 [1354]
Friday, August 3, 1951
9:30–10:00 p.m. EDST
NBC
Richard Leonard, Director
Writer's name omitted (Lawrence M. Klee, original script)
Richard Leonard, Editor
Jack Costello, Announcer
Radio Corp. of America (RCA Victor), Liggett & Myers Tobacco Co. (Chesterfield), American Home Products (Anacin), Sponsors
"The Strange Murder of Carrie Ellis" (*Extant Episode*)

Carrie Ellis, a wealthy, beautiful young widow, is murdered. Helen Taylor confessed, but strange circumstances lead Mr. Keen to believe she is the victim of a diabolical plot.

Actors in this episode include Bob Donley, Mary Jane Higby, Ned Wever, Gertrude Warner, Toni Darnay and Lauren Gilbert.

CONTINUITY #395 [1355]
Friday, August 10, 1951
9:30–10:00 p.m. EDST
NBC
Richard Leonard, Director
Jean Carroll, Writer
Richard Leonard, Editor
Jack Costello, Announcer
Liggett & Myers Tobacco Co. (Chesterfield), American Home Products (Anacin), Radio Corp. of America (RCA Victor), Sponsors
"The Abandoned Well Murder Case" (*Extant Episode*)

Henry Kellogg is shot to death, and his body dropped down a well on an abandoned farm next to his estate. Jasper Gibbs, an embittered old farmer, hides in the study at Kellogg's home.

Actors in this episode include Irene Hubbard, Cathleen Cordell, Horace Braham, Richard Newton and Arthur Maitland.

CONTINUITY #396 [1356]
Friday, August 17, 1951
9:30–10:00 p.m. EDST
NBC
Henry Howard, Director
Writer's name omitted (Lawrence M. Klee, original script)
Frank and Anne Hummert, Editors
Jack Costello, Announcer
American Home Products (Anacin), Radio Corp. of America (RCA Victor), Liggett & Myers Tobacco Co. (Chesterfield), Sponsors
"The Poisoned Sandwich Murder Case" (*Extant Episode*)

While investigating the death of young Stuart Blair, who was murdered when he ate a poisoned sandwich, Keen and Clancy happen upon another attempted poisoning, of Lenore Barclay.

This episode is a repeat of the story broadcast on September 23, 1948; it employs a different case title but uses the same character names.

CONTINUITY #397 [1357]
Friday, August 24, 1951
9:30–10:00 p.m. EDST
NBC
Henry Howard, Director
Jean Carroll, Writer
Richard Leonard, Editor
Jack Costello, Announcer
Radio Corp. of America (RCA Victor), Liggett & Myers Tobacco Co. (Chesterfield), American Home Products (Anacin), Sponsors
"The Fire Escape Murder Case"

A bronze paperweight is used to strike and kill prominent dress designer Hilda Cobb. Clancy stops an intruder trying to leave the victim's room by the fire escape.

CONTINUITY #398 [1358]
Friday, August 31, 1951
9:30–10:00 p.m. EDST
NBC
Henry Howard, Director
Helen Walpole, Writer
Frank Hummert, Editor
Jack Costello, Announcer
Liggett & Myers Tobacco Co. (Chesterfield), American Home Products (Anacin), Radio Corp. of America (RCA Victor), Sponsors
"The Rose Garden Murder Case"

Affluent Roger Dixon follows an evening ritual of watering the roses at his home. This time someone put deadly poison in the nozzle of the hose, which killed him instantly.

CONTINUITY #399 [1359]
Thursday, September 6, 1951
8:30–9:00 p.m. EDST
NBC
Richard Leonard, Director
Writer's name omitted (Lawrence M. Klee, original script)
Richard Leonard, Editor
Jack Costello, Announcer
American Home Products (Anacin), Radio Corp. of America (RCA Victor), Sponsors
"Murder and the Sleep Walker"

Lovely Julie Nash is stabbed to death in Dorothy Boyd's summer cottage. Dorothy walked in her sleep on the night of the murder, awakening to find her gown smeared with blood.

Actors in this episode include Cathleen Cordell, Florence Williams, Lauren Gilbert and Ned Wever. This episode is a repeat (employing a different case title and character names) of the story broadcast on August 18, 1949.

CONTINUITY #400 [1360]
Thursday, September 13, 1951
8:30–9:00 p.m. EDST
NBC
Richard Leonard, Director
Jean Carroll, Writer
Editor's name omitted
Jack Costello, Announcer
Radio Corp. of America (RCA Victor), American Home Products (Anacin), Sponsors
"The Surprise Motive Murder"

Is violinist Mark Russell, who loved well-heeled Stephanie Hardwick and was bitter over her marriage, to blame for her death? Strangled, she was thrown from a boat into a lake.

Actors in this episode include Vivian Smolen, James Meighan, Ann Seymour, Hal Studer and Alan MacAteer.

CONTINUITY #401 [1361]
Thursday, September 20, 1951
8:30–9:00 p.m. EDST
NBC
Richard Leonard, Director
Helen Walpole and Frank Hummert, Writers
Editor's name omitted
Jack Costello, Announcer
American Home Products (Anacin), Radio Corp. of America (RCA Victor), Sponsors
"The Guilty Conscience Murder Case"

Wealthy contractor Steve Clark is murdered, and $10,000 in cash is found nearby. Clark had a guilty conscience for letting his sister die in poverty. Now her daughter is a murder suspect.

Actors in this episode include John Stanley, Anne Elstner, Richard Newton, Toni Darnay, Henry Norell and Peggy Stanley.

CONTINUITY #402 [1362]
Thursday, September 27, 1951
8:30–9:00 p.m. EDST
NBC
Richard Leonard, Director
Frank Hummert, Writer
Editor's name omitted
Jack Costello, Announcer
American Home Products (Anacin), Liggett & Myers Tobacco Co. (Fatima), Radio Corp. of America (RCA Victor), Sponsors
"The Cat's Milk Murder Case"

Elsa Massey and her cat are killed by poisoned milk. When the sleuths arrive at the murder scene, the cat is there but Elsa's body is gone. She turns up in a bag in a laundry truck.

Actors in this episode include Helen Claire, Sarah Burton, Lauren Gilbert, Peggy Sanford and Bradley Barker.

CONTINUITY #403 [1363]
Thursday, October 4, 1951
8:30–9:00 p.m. EST
NBC
Richard Leonard, Director

Jean Carroll, Writer
Richard Leonard, Editor
Jack Costello, Announcer
Liggett & Myers Tobacco Co. (Chesterfield), American Home Products (Anacin), Sponsors
"The Country Club Murder Case"

Wealthy Bruce Gaynor is shot to death on the terrace of the fashionable Birchwood Country Club. Carl Fleming, who owed Gaynor a wad of dough, finds he's the most likely suspect.

Actors in this episode include Ivor Francis, James Meighan, Cathleen Cordell, Elizabeth Morgan, Berel Firestone and Margot Stevenson.

This same case title, but with a different plot, was first used for the episode aired April 20, 1950.

CONTINUITY #404 [1364]

Thursday, October 11, 1951
8:30–9:00 p.m. EST
NBC
Richard Leonard, Director
Frank Hummert, Writer
Editor's name omitted
Jack Costello, Announcer
American Home Products (Anacin), Liggett & Myers Tobacco Co. (Chesterfield), Sponsors
"The Fantastic Murder of Peter Nash"

Keen and Clancy investigate the murder of rich banker Peter Nash, whose second wife Marion pleads with Keen to prove her innocence. Keen was murdered in bed while she slept next to him.

Actors in this episode include Ned Wever, Anne Seymour, Charita Bauer, Ronald Long and Richard Janaver.

CONTINUITY #405 [1365]

Thursday, October 18, 1951
8:30–9:00 p.m. EST
NBC
Richard Leonard, Director
Jean Carroll, Writer
Richard Leonard, Editor
Jack Costello, Announcer
Liggett & Myers Tobacco Co. (Chesterfield), American Home Products (Anacin), Sponsors
"The Rich Young Widow Murder Case"

When handsome Larry Evans is murdered by a glass of poisoned brandy, Mr. Keen and Mike Clancy are called to investigate by Beverly Crail, a rich young widow who was Evans' fiancée.

Actors in this episode include Lauren Gilbert, Toni Darnay, Mary Orr, Ivor Francis and Ian Martin. Ed Latimer plays the role of Mike Clancy, substituting for James Kelly, "who was unable to appear" in this episode.

CONTINUITY #406 [1366]

Thursday, October 25, 1951
8:30–9:00 p.m. EST
NBC
Richard Leonard, Director
David Davidson, Writer
Richard Leonard, Editor
Jack Costello, Announcer
American Chicle Co. (Dentyne and Chiclets), Liggett & Myers Tobacco Co. (Chesterfield), American Home Products (Anacin), Sponsors
"The Case of Murder with Style"

Nancy Reed is strangled with a belt in her fashionable dress shop while serving socially prominent Mrs. Richard Prescott, a customer. Pierre Marcel fires a revolver at the gumshoes.

Actors in this episode include Helen Claire, Sidney Smith, Berel Firestone, Guy Sorel and Peggy Stanley. Ed Latimer plays the role of Mike Clancy, substituting for James Kelly, "who was unable to appear."

CONTINUITY #407 [1367]

Thursday, November 1, 1951
8:30–9:00 p.m. EST
NBC
Richard Leonard, Director
David Davidson and Frank Hummert, Writers
Editor's name omitted
Jack Costello, Announcer
Liggett & Myers Tobacco Co. (Chesterfield), American Home Products (Anacin), American Chicle Co. (Dentyne and Chiclets), Sponsors
"The Phone Call Murder Case"

Ralph Morley leaves his apartment after an 8:30 p.m. phone call and is shot dead in the lobby. Later, in Morley's office, cousin John Warren tries to abscond with a letter.

Actors in this episode include Tom Collins, Elizabeth Morgan, Harold Huber, Sylvia Leigh, Bill Quinn and James Meighan. Ed Latimer plays the role of Mike Clancy, substituting for James Kelly, "who was unable to appear."

CONTINUITY #408 [1368]

Thursday, November 8, 1951
8:30–9:00 p.m. EST
NBC
Richard Leonard, Director
Jean Carroll, Writer
Richard Leonard, Editor
Jack Costello, Announcer
American Home Products (Anacin), American Chicle Co. (Dentyne and Chiclets), Liggett & Myers Tobacco Co. (Chesterfield), Sponsors
"The Case of Murder on a Lonely Street"

Elsie Roberts, an attractive social secretary, is stabbed to death on a lonely street a block from her apartment complex. Roy Adams, who wed her secretly, asks Keen to investigate.

Actors in this episode include Audrey Egan, Bill Redfield, Peggy Stanley, Ann Seymour and Horace Braham. Ed Latimer plays the role of Mike Clancy, substituting for James Kelly, "who was unable to appear."

CONTINUITY #409 [1369]

Thursday, November 15, 1951
8:30–9:00 p.m. EST
NBC
Richard Leonard, Director
Frank Hummert, Writer
Editor's name omitted
Jack Costello, Announcer
American Chicle Co. (Dentyne and Chiclets), Liggett & Myers Tobacco Co. (Chesterfield), American Home Products (Anacin), Sponsors
"The Deceived Woman Murder Case"

Matron Mrs. Wynne is killed after the theft of her fortune. Her friend Martha Timpkins is anxious about her son Bill. He served time; Wynne gave him a second chance. He won't talk.

Actors in this episode include Ethel Wilson, Marjorie Maude, Margot Stevenson, Ian Martin and Bill Quinn. Ed Latimer plays the role of Mike Clancy, substituting for James Kelly, "who was unable to appear."

CONTINUITY #410 [1370]

Thursday, November 22, 1951
8:30–9:00 p.m. EST
NBC
Richard Leonard, Director
Frank Hummert, Writer
Frank Hummert, Editor
Jack Costello, Announcer
Liggett & Myers Tobacco Co. (Chesterfield), American Home Products (Anacin), American Chicle Co. (Dentyne and Chiclets), Sponsors
"The Strange Caller Murder Case"

This tale involves the Jones clan — Celia, Arlene, Agatha and Acton. Phoebe Phipps is attempting to keep up with them, as the famous old investigator takes from his files...

Actors in this episode include Mary Jane Higby, Mary Orr, Irene Hubbard, James Meighan and Helen Claire. Ed Latimer plays the role of Mike Clancy, substituting for James Kelly, "who was unable to appear."

CONTINUITY #411 [1371]

Thursday, November 22, 1951
8:30–9:00 p.m. EST
NBC
Richard Leonard, Director
Jean Carroll, Writer
Richard Leonard, Editor
Jack Costello, Announcer
American Home Products (Anacin), American Chicle Co. (Dentyne and Beemans Pepsin), Liggett & Myers Tobacco Co. (Chesterfield), Sponsors
"The House of Hate Murder Case"

Eccentric Jason Sharplee is shot dead in his Fifth Avenue mansion. The old man was highly suspicious of three people who shared his home — a nephew and his wife, and a single niece.

Actors in this episode include Arthur Maitland, Ivor Francis, Florence Freeman, Florence Williams, Mary Beth Hughes and Abby Lewis. Ed Latimer plays the role of Mike Clancy, substituting for James Kelly, "who was unable to appear."

CONTINUITY #412 [1372]

Thursday, December 6, 1951
8:30–9:00 p.m. EST
NBC
Richard Leonard, Director
Writer's name omitted
Frank Hummert, Editor

Jack Costello, Announcer
American Chicle Co. (Dentyne and Beemans Pepsin), Liggett & Myers Tobacco Co. (Chesterfield), American Home Products (Anacin), Sponsors
"The Case of Murder at a Mile a Minute" (*Extant Episode*)

Young Glen Larkin is suspected of murdering affluent Ted Masters. Larkin accuses a girl named Elinor, who turned down his proposal. Mr. Keen reveals an obvious fact.

Actors in this episode include John Stanley, Cathleen Cordell, Toni Darnay, Henry Norell and Richard Newton. Ed Latimer plays the role of Mike Clancy, substituting for James Kelly, "who was unable to appear."

CONTINUITY #413 [1373]

Thursday, December 13, 1951
8:30–9:00 p.m. EST
NBC
Richard Leonard, Director
Frank Hummert, Writer
Frank Hummert, Editor
Jack Costello, Announcer
Liggett & Myers Tobacco Co. (Chesterfield), American Home Products (Anacin), American Chicle Co. (Dentyne and Chiclets), Sponsors
"The Famous Actress Murder Case"

Maud Barrinton, Hollywood and Broadway star, is stabbed to death in her theater dressing room. She had predicted her own murder, naming two associates who wanted to kill her.

Actors in this episode include Helen Claire, Horace Braham, Berel Firestone, Mary Orr, Ronald Long and Elizabeth Morgan. It is uncertain who plays the role of Mike Clancy, as the designation was left blank on this script's list of cast members.

CONTINUITY #414 [1374]

Thursday, December 20, 1951
8:30–9:00 p.m. EST
NBC
Richard Leonard, Director
Jean Carroll, Writer
Richard Leonard, Editor
Jack Costello, Announcer
American Home Products (Anacin), American Chicle Co. (Dentyne and Beemans Pepsin), Liggett & Myers Tobacco Co. (Chesterfield), Sponsors
"The Footprints of Terror Murder Case"

Invalid Cecilia Faraday is stabbed to death in her bedroom. Keen discovers huge phosphorescent footprints on the velvet carpet. Son Don accuses his father of the crime.

Actors in this episode include Ann Seymour, Billy Redfield, Toni Darnay, Ray Johnson, Lucille Wall and Henry Norell. James Kelly returns to play Mike Clancy.

CONTINUITY #415 [1375]

Thursday, December 27, 1951
8:30–9:00 p.m. EST
NBC
Richard Leonard, Director
Jean Carroll, Writer
Richard Leonard, Editor
Jack Costello, Announcer
American Chicle Co. (Dentyne and Beemans Pepsin), Liggett & Myers Tobacco Co. (Chesterfield), American Home Products (Anacin), Sponsors
"The Case of Murder in the Snow"

Marcia Gordon is strangled in a snowstorm near a fountain on her palatial estate. She hoped to break her engagement to Douglas Crane, who had jilted Connee Richards, Keen learns.

Actors in this episode include Audrey Egan, Richard Janaver, Arthur Maitland, Mary Jane Higby and Hal Studer.

CONTINUITY #416 [1376]

Thursday, January 3, 1952
8:30–9:00 p.m. EST
NBC
Richard Leonard, Director
Jean Carroll, Writer
Richard Leonard, Editor
Jack Costello, Announcer
Liggett & Myers Tobacco Co. (Chesterfield), American Home Products (Anacin), American Chicle Co. (Dentyne and Beemans Pepsin), Sponsors
"The Open Window Murder Case"

Someone lurking in the garden outside the home of jewelry firm partner Peter Lewis shoots him. Housekeeper Agatha Stark is violently jealous of Myrna Lewis, Peter's wife.

Actors in this episode include Lauren

Gilbert, Florence Freeman, Helen Claire, Sidney Smith and Chuck Webster.

CONTINUITY #417 [1377]
Thursday, January 10, 1952
8:30–9:00 p.m. EST
NBC
Richard Leonard, Director
Writer's name omitted (Lawrence M. Klee, original script)
Richard Leonard, Editor
Jack Costello, Announcer
American Home Products (Anacin), American Chicle Co. (Dentyne and Beemans Pepsin), Liggett & Myers Tobacco Co. (Chesterfield), Sponsors
"The Beautiful Twins Murder Case"
Howard Lathrop, a handsome young man-about-town, is shot to death while dining in a downtown restaurant. Mike Clancy discovers a startling clue and hurries to report to Keen.
Actors in this episode include Ronald Long, Cathleen Cordell, Mary Orr, Toni Darnay, Florence Williams, Bob Donley and Ned Wever. This episode repeats the story broadcast on October 28, 1948, when it aired under a slightly different title.

CONTINUITY #418 [1378]
Thursday, January 17, 1952
8:30–9:00 p.m. EST
NBC
Richard Leonard, Director
Frank Hummert, Writer
Frank Hummert, Editor
Jack Costello, Announcer
American Chicle Co. (Dentyne and Beemans Pepsin), Liggett & Myers Tobacco Co. (Chesterfield), American Home Products (Anacin), Sponsors
"The Alcoholic Bride Murder Case"
Wealthy, middle-aged Bruno Forbes is shot to death at the wedding breakfast after his marriage to 23-year-old Anna Humphrey, when an intoxicated Anna announced she loved another man.
Actors in this episode include Horace Braham, Charita Bauer, Ed Jerome, Elizabeth Morgan, Richard Newton and Sandy Strouse.

CONTINUITY #419 [1379]
Thursday, January 24, 1952
8:30–9:00 p.m. EST
NBC
Richard Leonard, Director
Jean Carroll, Writer
Richard Leonard, Editor
Jack Costello, Announcer
Liggett & Myers Tobacco Co. (Chesterfield), American Home Products (Anacin), American Chicle Co. (Dentyne and Beemans Pepsin), Sponsors
"The Evil Husband Murder Case"
Rupert Drake is shot to death in his Park Avenue home. His ex, Ellen, claims he obtained a divorce and custody of their child through falsified evidence supplied by her sister, Rhoda Simms.
Actors in this episode include Ray Johnson, Helen Claire, Mary Jane Higby, James Meighan and Ronald Long.

CONTINUITY #420 [1380]
Thursday, January 31, 1952
8:30–9:00 p.m. EST
NBC
Richard Leonard, Director
David Davidson, Writer
Richard Leonard, Editor
Jack Costello, Announcer
American Home Products (Anacin), American Chicle Co. (Dentyne and Beemans Pepsin), Liggett & Myers Tobacco Co. (Chesterfield), Sponsors
"The Frightened Husband Murder Case"
Mrs. Doris Benton is stabbed to death in the lobby of her apartment complex. A man wielding a gun surprises Mr. Keen and Mike Clancy when they go to the Benton home.
Actors in this episode include Ned Wever, Cathleen Cordell, Elizabeth Morgan, Guy Sorel and Tom Collins.

CONTINUITY #421 [1381]
Thursday, February 7, 1952
8:30–9:00 p.m. EST
NBC
Richard Leonard, Director
Jean Carroll, Writer
Richard Leonard, Editor
Jack Costello, Announcer
American Chicle Co. (Dentyne and Beemans Pepsin), Liggett & Myers Tobacco Co. (Chesterfield), American Home Products (Anacin), Sponsors

"The Lake in the Park Murder Case"

Jennifer Larke is strangled to death near a lake in Central Park. She received expensive clothes from Howard Price, who turns out to be her father through a marriage he kept secret.

Actors in this episode include Audrey Egan, Hal Studer, Horace Braham, Ann Seymour, Mary Beth Hughes and Grace Valentine.

CONTINUITY #422 [1382]
Thursday, February 14, 1952
8:30–9:00 p.m. EST
NBC
Richard Leonard, Director
David Davidson, Writer
Richard Leonard, Editor
Jack Costello, Announcer
Liggett & Myers Tobacco Co. (Chesterfield), American Home Products (Anacin), American Chicle Co. (Dentyne and Beemans Pepsin), Sponsors
"The Happy Couple Murder Case"

Jerry Fulton is shot dead on the lawn of his suburban home. His wife Jane is suspicious of Martha Hoyt, a client of her spouse's investment firm. Keen and Clancy check it out.

Actors in this episode include Richard Janaver, Cora B. Smith, Mary Jane Higby, Karl Weber and Arthur Maitland.

CONTINUITY #423 [1383]
Thursday, February 21, 1952
8:30–9:00 p.m. EST
NBC
Richard Leonard, Director
Jean Carroll, Writer
Richard Leonard, Editor
Jack Costello, Announcer
American Home Products (Anacin), American Chicle Co. (Dentyne and Beemans Pepsin), Liggett & Myers Tobacco Co. (Chesterfield), Sponsors
"Murder and the Girl in the Mink Cape"

When model Roberta Storm is stabbed to death, another model, Gail Banning, begs for Keen's help, insisting it was *she* who was the killer's intended victim. The two resemble one another.

Actors in this episode include Gertrude Warner, Cathleen Cordell, Ivor Francis, Ronald Long, James Meighan and Bob Donley.

CONTINUITY #424 [1384]
Thursday, February 28, 1952
8:30–9:00 p.m. EST
NBC
Richard Leonard, Director
David Davidson, Writer
Editor's name omitted
Jack Costello, Announcer
American Chicle Co. (Dentyne and Beemans Pepsin), Liggett & Myers Tobacco Co. (Chesterfield), American Home Products (Anacin), Sponsors
"The Box Office Murder Case"

Helen Tyler, though from a wealthy clan, is hired to work in a movie theater box office and is killed. A cruel uncle threatened her, and she left her husband after only a brief marriage.

Actors in this episode include Florence Williams, Toni Darnay, Horace Braham, Peter Capell and Richard Janaver.

CONTINUITY #425 [1385]
Thursday, March 6, 1952
8:30–9:00 p.m. EST
NBC
Richard Leonard, Director
Jean Carroll, Writer
Richard Leonard, Editor
Jack Costello, Announcer
Liggett & Myers Tobacco Co. (Chesterfield), American Home Products (Anacin), American Chicle Co. (Dentyne and Beemans Pepsin), Sponsors
"The Honeymoon Cottage Murder Case"

When young architect Mark Richards is shot to death in the guest cottage on his employer's estate, where he was spending his honeymoon, Karen Grant — whom he jilted — is accused.

Actors in this episode include Bob Donley, Richard Newton, Sylvia Leigh, Audrey Egan, Arthur Maitland and Abby Lewis.

CONTINUITY #426 [1386]
Thursday, March 13, 1952
8:30–9:00 p.m. EST
NBC
Richard Leonard, Director
Jean Carroll, Writer
Richard Leonard, Editor
Jack Costello, Announcer
American Home Products (Anacin), American

Chicle Co. (Dentyne and Beemans Pepsin), Liggett & Myers Tobacco Co. (Chesterfield), Sponsors

"The Silver Candlestick Murder Case" (*Extant Episode*)

Handsome actor and artist's model Neil Denning vanishes. Keen and Clancy find his body in the cellar of a grim old Fifth Avenue mansion, whose occupants say they never heard of him.

Actors in this episode include Karl Weber, Mary Jane Higby, Cora B. Smith, Ronald Long, Irene Hubbard and Ned Wever.

CONTINUITY #427 [1387]

Thursday, March 20, 1952
8:30–9:00 p.m. EST
NBC
Richard Leonard, Director
Jean Carroll, Writer
Richard Leonard, Editor
Jack Costello, Announcer
American Chicle Co. (Dentyne and Beemans Pepsin), Liggett & Myers Tobacco Co. (Chesterfield), American Home Products (Anacin), Sponsors

"The House on the Cliff Murder Case"

Peter Bedford, owner of a New York dress shop, is stabbed to death at his home on a cliff near the sea. Someone tries to kill the sleuths by rolling a stone at them down the cliff.

Actors in this episode include Ian Martin, Toni Darnay, James Meighan, Florence Freeman and Lauren Gilbert.

CONTINUITY #428 [1388]

Thursday, March 27, 1952
8:30–9:00 p.m. EST
NBC
Richard Leonard, Director
Lawrence M. Klee, Writer
Richard Leonard, Editor
Jack Costello, Announcer
Liggett & Myers Tobacco Co. (Chesterfield), American Home Products (Anacin), American Chicle Co. (Dentyne and Beemans Pepsin), Sponsors

"The Case of the Murdered Bridegroom"

Wealthy Alfred Reed's body is found in the trunk of a car driven by Eleanor Hazlett, his fiancée. The tracer and his partner return to the office to pursue the case further.

Actors in this episode include Audrey Egan, Billy Redfield, Richard Newton, Arthur Hughes, Cathleen Cordell and Horace Braham.

CONTINUITY #429 [1389]

Thursday, April 3, 1952
8:30–9:00 p.m. EST
NBC
Richard Leonard, Director
Frank Hummert, Writer
Editor's name omitted
Jack Costello, Announcer
American Home Products (Anacin), American Chicle Co. (Dentyne and Beemans Pepsin), Liggett & Myers Tobacco Co. (Chesterfield), Sponsors

"The Rented Cottage Murder Case" (*Extant Episode*)

Salesman Tom Haynes, crippled and on crutches, is shot to death in a cottage he and wife Jennie rented for an incredible $25 per month. Another murder took place there a year earlier.

Actors in this episode include Lucille Wall, Sidney Smith, Harold Huber, Anne Seymour and Ed Jerome.

CONTINUITY #430 [1390]

Thursday, April 10, 1952
8:30–9:00 p.m. EST
NBC
Richard Leonard, Director
Frank Hummert, Writer
Editor's name omitted
Jack Costello, Announcer
American Chicle Co. (Dentyne and Beemans Pepsin), Liggett & Myers Tobacco Co. (Chesterfield), American Home Products (Anacin), Sponsors

"The Mother's Plea Murder Case" (*Extant Episode*)

Gilbert Grey asks wife Agnes for a divorce so he can marry his young secretary, Shirley Spears. Agnes goes to plead with Shirley, and Shirley is shot to death during their quarrel.

Actors in this episode include Ned Wever, Anne Elstner, Hal Studer, Berel Firestone, Richard Janaver, Cathleen Cordell and Bob Donley.

CONTINUITY #431 [1391]

Thursday, April 17, 1952

8:30–9:00 p.m. EST
NBC
Richard Leonard, Director
Jean Carroll, Writer
Richard Leonard, Editor
Jack Costello, Announcer
Liggett & Myers Tobacco Co. (Chesterfield), American Home Products (Anacin), American Chicle Co. (Dentyne and Beemans Pepsin), Sponsors
"The Apple Orchard Murder Case"

Nancy Dalton is shot to death in the apple orchard of her stepmother's estate. Stepmother Carol Dalton shows Keen a note that incriminates Andy Kealing, who loved Nancy.

Actors in this episode include Toni Darnay, Julie Stevens, Richard Newton, Ronald Long and Arthur Maitland.

CONTINUITY #432 [1392]

Thursday, April 24, 1952
8:30–9:00 p.m. EST
NBC
Richard Leonard, Director
Jean Carroll, Writer
Richard Leonard, Editor
Jack Costello, Announcer
American Home Products (Anacin), American Chicle Co. (Dentyne and Beemans Pepsin), Liggett & Myers Tobacco Co. (Chesterfield), Sponsors
"The Tunnel of Love Murder Case"

When beautiful Adele Redding is strangled to death while in a small boat gliding through the Tunnel of Love at an amusement park, fiancé Jeff Martin begs for Mr. Keen's help.

Actors in this episode include Gertrude Warner, Karl Weber, Toni Darnay, Guy Sorel and Horace Braham. This was the final episode of the series broadcast over NBC Radio; it subsequently returned to CBS.

CONTINUITY #433 [1393]

Thursday, May 1, 1952
9:30–10:00 p.m. EDST
CBS
Richard Leonard, Director
Jane Weldon, Writer
Richard Leonard, Editor
Harry Kramer, Announcer
Sustaining

"The Case of Murder and the Broadway Star"

Mr. Keen and Mike Clancy send out an alarm for the arrest of Philip Perry, a young actor suspected of having something to do with the murder of beautiful stage star Elaine Rogers.

Actors in this episode include Florence Robinson, Julie Stevens, Karl Weber, James Monks and Audrey Egan. The series returned to CBS Radio with this episode.

CONTINUITY #434 [1394]

Thursday, May 8, 1952
9:30–10:00 p.m. EDST
CBS
Richard Leonard, Director
Jean Carroll, Writer
Richard Leonard, Editor
Harry Kramer, Announcer
Sustaining
"The Lonesome Road Murder Case"

When Ralph Dixon is shot to death in his car on a deserted country road, his wife Charlotte, whose two previous husbands had been killed in accidents, asks Mr. Keen to investigate.

Actors in this episode include Sidney Smith, Mary Jane Higby, Arthur Hughes, Ivor Francis, Alan MacAteer, Kenneth Lynch and Joan Lorring.

CONTINUITY #435 [1395]

Thursday, May 15, 1952
9:30–10:00 p.m. EDST
CBS
Richard Leonard, Director
Jane Weldon and Frank Hummert, Writers (Lawrence M. Klee and Frank Hummert, original writers)
Editor's name omitted
Harry Kramer, Announcer
Sustaining
"The Fortune Teller Murder Case"

Fortuneteller Madame Luna predicts the murder of George Rowland. She's good at her trade: his body is found in an empty lot. He sent gifts anonymously to his stepdaughter.

Actors in this episode include Irene Hubbard, John Stanley, Lucille Wall, Cora B. Smith, Karl Weber and Sandy Strouse. This same story was previously broadcast on February 22, 1951, under another title and with different character names.

CONTINUITY #436 [1396]
Thursday, May 22, 1952
9:30–10:00 p.m. EDST
CBS
Richard Leonard, Director
Jean Carroll, Writer
Richard Leonard, Editor
Harry Kramer, Announcer
American Chicle Co. (Dentyne), Sponsor
"The Lost Letter Murder Case"

Rich, elderly Oliver Grant threatens his accountant Richard Niles with prison, presuming him guilty of theft. Then Grant is poisoned to death.

Actors in this episode include Ed Jerome, Julie Stevens, James Meighan, Hal Studer, Ethel Wilson and Florence Williams.

CONTINUITY #437 [1397]
Thursday, May 29, 1952
9:30–10:00 p.m. EDST
CBS
Richard Leonard, Director
Jean Carroll, Writer
Richard Leonard, Editor
Harry Kramer, Announcer
American Chicle Co. (Dentyne), Sponsor
"The Red Candle Murder Case"

Beautiful young Valerie Knight is found shot to death inside her burning house. Husband John, who managed the costume jewelry shop she owned, begs Keen to investigate.

CONTINUITY #438 [1398]
Thursday, June 5, 1952
8:00–8:30 p.m. EDST
CBS
Richard Leonard, Director
Jean Carroll, Writer
Richard Leonard, Editor
Harry Kramer, Announcer
American Chicle Co. (Dentyne), Sponsor
"The Swimming Pool Murder Case"

Cora Harper is stabbed to death in the pool of a luxurious Long Island estate. Spouse Charles, believing she died in a plane crash earlier, remarried two days ago and is arrested.

Actors in this episode include Gertrude Warner, Ronald Long, Mary Jane Higby, Richard Newton, Abby Lewis and Bob Donley.

CONTINUITY #439 [1399]
Thursday, June 12, 1952
8:00–8:30 p.m. EDST
CBS
Richard Leonard, Director
Jane Weldon, Writer
Richard Leonard, Editor
Harry Kramer, Announcer
American Chicle Co. (Dentyne), Sponsor
"The Wedding Anniversary Murder Case"

Addie, housemaid to George and Elizabeth Wharton, becomes a prime suspect in Elizabeth's murder and the theft of $5,000. Addie's bags are packed to go.

Actors in this episode include Florence Williams, Karl Weber, Grace Valentine, Julie Stevens and Ronald Long.

CONTINUITY #440 [1400]
Thursday, June 19, 1952
8:00–8:30 p.m. EDST
CBS
Richard Leonard, Director
Jane Weldon, Writer
Richard Leonard, Editor
Harry Kramer, Announcer
American Chicle Co. (Dentyne), Sponsor
"The Sleeping Woman Murder Case"

Mr. Keen and Mike Clancy attempt to clear Alice Jackson of the murder of her husband Alfred. She was with him in their apartment when he was poisoned to death, and the evidence against her is substantial.

Actors in this episode include Cathleen Cordell, Abby Lewis, Ethel Wilson, Horace Braham and James Meighan.

CONTINUITY #441 [1401]
Thursday, June 26, 1952
8:00–8:30 p.m. EDST
CBS
Richard Leonard, Director
Jane Weldon, Writer
Richard Leonard, Editor
Harry Kramer, Announcer
American Chicle Co. (Dentyne), Sponsor
"The Case of the Man Who Expected Murder"

The gumshoes send out an alarm for the capture of chauffeur George Bellows, a suspect in the murder of rich William Young. They escort Young's daughter, Lois, in love with Bellows, to her home.

Actors in this episode include Ed Jerome, Lucille Wall, Cora B. Smith, Mary Jane Higby and Bill Quinn.

CONTINUITY #442 [1402]
Thursday, July 3, 1952
8:00–8:30 p.m. EDST
CBS
Richard Leonard, Director
Lawrence M. Klee, Writer
Richard Leonard, Editor
Harry Kramer, Announcer
American Chicle Co. (Dentyne), Sponsor
"The Cliffside Murder Case"

Keen and Clancy go to Cliffside, a rural Long Island hamlet, to probe the murder of Martha Forbes, a retired fisherman's wife. On the beach they confront a mad woman, gun in hand.

Actors in this episode include Ethel Wilson, Arthur Maitland, Peggy Stanley, Ivor Francis, Elizabeth Morgan and Berel Firestone.

CONTINUITY #443 [1403]
Thursday, July 10, 1952
8:00–8:30 p.m. EDST
CBS
Richard Leonard, Director
Lawrence M. Klee, Writer
Richard Leonard, Editor
Harry Kramer, Announcer
American Chicle Co. (Dentyne), Sponsor
"The Howling Dog Murder Case"

Young invalid Ralph Elliot disappears. Mr. Keen believes he may have been the victim of foul play. His neighbor, Janet Thrasher, gives Mr. Keen a letter she received from Elliot.

Actors in this episode include James Meighan, Abby Lewis, Tom Collins, John Stanley and Vivian Smolen.

CONTINUITY #444 [1404]
Thursday, July 17, 1952
8:00–8:30 p.m. EDST
CBS
Richard Leonard, Director
Lawrence M. Klee, Writer
Richard Leonard, Editor
Harry Kramer, Announcer
American Chicle Co. (Dentyne), Sponsor
"The Snake Bite Murder Case"

Wealthy industrialist Fred Farnsworth is poisoned with cobra venom at his palatial suburban home. Brother-in-law George Norton is nearly bitten by a snake, which Mike Clancy kills.

Actors in this episode include Ned Wever, Helen Claire, Katherine Emmet, David Gothard and Henry Norell.

CONTINUITY #445 [1405]
Thursday, July 24, 1952
8:00–8:30 p.m. EDST
CBS
Richard Leonard, Director
Albert Sanders and Frank Hummert, Writers
Editor's name omitted
Harry Kramer, Announcer
American Chicle Co. (Dentyne), Sponsor
"The Case of Murder and the Man Who Loved Danger"

Walter Grant, daring explorer, was stabbed while talking into a dictating machine about a perceived danger he faced. Eric Bancroft attempts to steal a dictation recording.

CONTINUITY #446 [1406]
Thursday, July 31, 1952
8:00–8:30 p.m. EDST
CBS
Richard Leonard, Director
Lawrence M. Klee, Writer
Richard Leonard, Editor
Harry Kramer, Announcer
American Chicle Co. (Dentyne), Sponsor
"The Garden Party Murder Case"

Tom Carlton's fiancée, Lucille, is murdered in the garden of wealthy Mrs. Carlton's home during an engagement party. One of the guests has also apparently lost a diamond necklace.

Actors in this episode include Irene Hubbard, Hal Studer, Richard Newton, Peggy Stanley, Lauren Gilbert and Helen Claire. This story originally aired on August 12, 1948, under another title and using different character names.

CONTINUITY #447 [1407]
Thursday, August 7, 1952
8:00–8:30 p.m. EDST
CBS
Richard Leonard, Director
Albert Sanders, Writer
Richard Leonard, Editor

Harry Kramer, Announcer
American Chicle Co. (Dentyne), Sponsor
"The Night of Terror Murder Case"

Frank Gordon is accused of stabbing a nightclub chorus girl, Rachel Stone, for breaking their engagement. Middle-aged stockbroker Allen Fenway, who was charmed by Rachel, flees.

Actors in this episode include Audrey Egan, Harold Huber, Abby Lewis, Richard Janaver, Staats Cotsworth, Peggy Danford and Anne Seymour.

CONTINUITY #448 [1408]
Thursday, August 14, 1952
8:00–8:30 p.m. EDST
CBS
Edward Slattery, Director
Albert Sanders, Writer
Richard Leonard, Editor
Announcer's name omitted
American Chicle Co. (Dentyne), Sponsor
"The Dinner Guest Murder Case"

Oklahoma oil millionaire Ward Blackwell is shot dead in a New York hotel suite awaiting a dinner guest. The sleuths try to clear Mary Cole, who arrived to find him murdered.

Actors in this episode include Julie Stevens, Ray Johnson, Chuck Webster, Helen Claire, Karl Weber and Mary Jane Higby.

CONTINUITY #449 [1409]
Thursday, August 21, 1952
8:00–8:30 p.m. EDST
CBS
Edward Slattery, Director
Lawrence M. Klee, Writer
Richard Leonard, Editor
Harry Kramer, Announcer
American Chicle Co. (Dentyne), Sponsor
"The Beautiful Swimming Star Murder Case"

Glamorous showgirl Eve Le Marr dies at the city aquarium, and her body is put into a glass tank full of water. Accused is her manager, Paul Franklyn, who claims he can prove his innocence.

Actors in this episode include Audrey Egan, Ivor Francis, Arthur Maitland, Sarah Burton and Ronald Long. This episode utilizes the same story heard on the broadcast of January 20, 1949, but under a different title (though keeping the same character names).

CONTINUITY #450 [1410]
Thursday, August 28, 1952
8:00–8:30 p.m. EDST
CBS

The script for this sequence is missing from the permanent file.

CONTINUITY #451 [1411]
Thursday, September 4, 1952
8:00–8:30 p.m. EDST
CBS
Richard Leonard, Director
Harry Junkin, Writer
Richard Leonard, Editor
Harry Kramer, Announcer
American Chicle Co. (Dentyne), Sponsor
"The Famous Author Murder Case"

Keen and Clancy go to the luxurious Connecticut estate of playwright Howard Forrest, whose son Bob is being held by police for his father's murder, to which Bob confessed hysterically.

Actors in this episode include Teri Keane, Hal Studer, Anne Seymour, Julie Stevens, Peggy Sanford and Staats Cotsworth.

CONTINUITY #452 [1412]
Thursday, September 11, 1952
8:00–8:30 p.m. EDST
CBS
Richard Leonard, Director
Jean Carroll, Writer
Richard Leonard, Editor
Harry Kramer, Announcer
American Chicle Co. (Dentyne), Sponsor
"The Yellow Scarf Murder Case"

Jane Horning is strangled to death with a yellow silk scarf belonging to her sister, Rowena Dilling, in the garden of her home. Jane and Rowena had inherited an old mansion.

Actors in this episode include Sylvia Leigh, Audrey Egan, David Gothard, James Meighan and Peter Capell.

CONTINUITY #453 [1413]
Thursday, September 18, 1952
8:00–8:30 p.m. EDST
CBS
Richard Leonard, Director
Harry Junkin, Writer
Richard Leonard, Editor
Harry Kramer, Announcer

American Chicle Co. (Dentyne), Sponsor
"The Greek Vase Murder Case"

Wealthy art collector Eleanor Towers is poisoned to death in her apartment. Young art dealer John Scranton, fiancé of Towers' niece, has a valuable antique Greek vase she owned.

Actors in this episode include Ethel Wilson, Abby Lewis, Mary Jane Higby, David Gothard and Arthur Maitland.

CONTINUITY #454 [1414]
Thursday, September 25, 1952
8:00–8:30 p.m. EDST
CBS
Richard Leonard, Director
Albert Sanders and David Davidson, Writers
Richard Leonard, Editor
Harry Kramer, Announcer
American Chicle Co. (Dentyne), Sponsor
"The Top Hat Murder Case"

Carol Hat, a hatcheck girl in an upscale bistro, is killed as she returns a top hat to movie chain manager Robert Wilson, who flees. Wilson is also interested in another woman.

Actors in this episode include Ronald Long, Florence Freeman, Toni Darnay, Guy Sorel, Harold Huber and Cathleen Cordell.

CONTINUITY #455 [1415]
Friday, October 3, 1952
8:00–8:30 p.m. EST
CBS
Richard Leonard, Director
Lawrence M. Klee, Writer
Richard Leonard, Editor
Announcer's name omitted
American Chicle Co. (Dentyne), Sponsor
"The Case of Murder and the Emerald Snuffbox"

Jeffrey Page dies after inhaling a deadly poison contained in a valuable emerald snuffbox. Suspects include his wife Ellen and father-in-law James Badger.

CONTINUITY #456 [1416]
Friday, October 10, 1952
8:00–8:30 p.m. EST
CBS
Richard Leonard, Director
Lawrence M. Klee, Writer
Richard Leonard, Editor
Announcer's name omitted

American Chicle Co. (Dentyne), Sponsor
"The Case of the Voice of Murder"

Keen and Clancy visit an old mansion in the Catskills to probe the murder of Doris Haven, Elliot's bride. The focus is on a ghostly voice that threatened Doris and now menaces Keen.

Actors in this episode include James Meighan, Toni Darnay, Arthur Hughes, Cathleen Cordell and Sarah Burton.

CONTINUITY #457 [1417]
Friday, October 17, 1952
8:00–8:30 p.m. EST
CBS
Richard Leonard, Director
Lawrence M. Klee, Writer
Richard Leonard, Editor
Harry Kramer, Announcer
Liggett & Myers Tobacco Co. (Chesterfield), American Chicle Co. (Dentyne), Sponsors
"The Case of Murder and the Baldheaded Man"

Inventor John Woodley, working on a cure for baldness, is murdered. A prime suspect is a baldheaded man who tries to kill Keen. Mike Clancy overpowers the would-be assassin.

Actors in this episode include Arthur Maitland, Florence Williams, Frank Thomas Jr., Julie Stevens, Elizabeth Morgan and John Stanley.

CONTINUITY #458 [1418]
Friday, October 24, 1952
8:00–8:30 p.m. EST
CBS
Richard Leonard, Director
Lawrence M. Klee, Writer
Richard Leonard, Editor
Harry Kramer, Announcer
American Chicle Co. (Dentyne), Liggett & Myers Tobacco Co. (Chesterfield), Sponsors
"The Gossip Column Murder Case"

The tracer of lost persons, Mr. Keen, and his partner Mike Clancy interact with Terry and Helen Bradford, Allan Decker, Kent Claxon and Laura Gayle in a tale involving a gossip column.

Actors in this episode include Ian Martin, Staats Cotsworth, Ronald Long, Audrey Egan and Helen Claire.

CONTINUITY #459 [1419]
Friday, October 31, 1952

8:00–8:30 p.m. EST
CBS
Richard Leonard, Director
Lawrence M. Klee, Writer
Richard Leonard, Editor
Harry Kramer, Announcer
Liggett & Myers Tobacco Co. (Chesterfield), American Chicle Co. (Dentyne), Sponsors
"The Case of Murder and the Sealed Box Mystery"

Alice Stafford puts a note in a sealed box indicating that Elizabeth, her stepdaughter, hates her enough to kill her. Alice dies, and Elizabeth and her sweetheart, Jeffrey Tate, become prime suspects.

CONTINUITY #460 [1420]

Friday, November 7, 1952
8:00–8:30 p.m. EST
CBS
Richard Leonard, Director
Lawrence M. Klee, Writer
Richard Leonard, Editor
Harry Kramer, Announcer
American Chicle Co. (Dentyne), Liggett & Myers Tobacco Co. (Chesterfield), Sponsors
"The Case of Murder and the Prize-Winning Bull"

Wealthy animal breeder John Stevens and his $50,000 prize bull are both shot to death. Mr. Keen interrogates Stevens' half-sister Emma and two neighbors, Paul and Evelyn Kincaid.

Actors in this episode include Ned Wever, Anne Seymour, Karl Weber, Cathleen Cordell and Chuck Webster.

CONTINUITY #461 [1421]

Friday, November 14, 1952
8:00–8:30 p.m. EST
CBS
Richard Leonard, Director
Lawrence M. Klee, Writer
Richard Leonard, Editor
Harry Kramer, Announcer
American Chicle Co. (Dentyne), Sponsor
"The Skull and Crossbones Murder Case"

Joyce Mayling, known in the theater as "the woman who never grew old," won't. She was murdered. A skull and crossbones appeared on her door, and subsequently on Keen's office door.

Actors in this episode include Helen Claire, Lucille Wall, Horace Braham, James Meighan and Mary Jane Higby. This episode borrows the title from the broadcast of June 15, 1950, but offers an altogether different plot.

CONTINUITY #462 [1422]

Friday, November 21, 1952
8:00–8:30 p.m. EST
CBS
Richard Leonard, Director
Lawrence M. Klee, Writer
Richard Leonard, Editor
Harry Kramer, Announcer
American Chicle Co. (Dentyne), Sponsor
"The Case of Murder and the Magician"

Lovely Gloria Scott, magician John Merlin's assistant in a nightclub act, is poisoned to death during a performance. Merlin tries to leave town, but Keen orders his detainment.

Actors in this episode include Ivor Francis, Claire Niesen, Elizabeth Morgan, Staats Cotsworth and Charita Bauer.

CONTINUITY #463 [1423]

Friday, November 28, 1952
8:00–8:30 p.m. EST
CBS
Richard Leonard, Director
Lawrence M. Klee, Writer
Richard Leonard, Editor
Harry Kramer, Announcer
American Chicle Co. (Dentyne), Sponsor
"The Monkey Mask Murder Case"

Someone wearing a monkey mask shoots wealthy man-about-town Fredric Brace to death. Business partner David Eliot's wife, Margaret, is holding just such a monkey mask when Mr. Keen arrives.

Actors in this episode include Sidney Smith, Grace Valentine, Mary Orr, Abby Lewis and John Stanley.

CONTINUITY #464 [1424]

Friday, December 5, 1952
8:00–8:30 p.m. EST
CBS
Richard Leonard, Director
Lawrence M. Klee, Writer
Richard Leonard, Editor
Harry Kramer, Announcer
American Chicle Co. (Dentyne), Sponsor

"The Case of Murder and the Girl in a Trance"
Ellen Woodley is murdered. Attractive young Joyce Harper confesses. But Mr. Keen thinks Joyce is under the influence of drugs, or that a sinister personality has overtaken her.

Actors in this episode include Florence Williams, Helen Claire, Horace Braham, Ethel Wilson, Alan MacAteer and Danny Ocko.

CONTINUITY #465 [1425]
Friday, December 12, 1952
8:00–8:30 p.m. EST
CBS
Richard Leonard, Director
Lawrence M. Klee, Writer
Richard Leonard, Editor
Harry Kramer, Announcer
American Chicle Co. (Dentyne), Anahist Co., Inc. (Anahist), Sponsors
"The Sharpshooter Murder Case"
Rich Philip Carleton is killed by a sniper's bullet fired from a roof near his apartment window. A tuft of hair from the hide of a bear is one clue Mr. Keen uncovers.

Actors in this episode include Karl Weber, Lucille Wall, Ned Wever, Jay Jostyn and Peggy Stanley.

CONTINUITY #466 [1426]
Friday, December 19, 1952
8:00–8:30 p.m. EST
CBS
Richard Leonard, Director
Lawrence M. Klee, Writer
Richard Leonard, Editor
Harry Kramer, Announcer
American Chicle Co. (Dentyne), Anahist Co., Inc. (Anahist), Sponsors
"The Skating Rink Murder Case"
Attractive young Ellen Burton is stabbed to death while at a skating rink with her husband John. Mr. Keen interrogates John's brother, Bob, and his wife Rita in their apartment.

Actors in this episode include Vivian Smolen, Frank Thomas Jr., James Meighan, Elizabeth Morgan and Julie Stevens.

CONTINUITY #467 [1427]
Friday, December 26, 1952
8:00–8:30 p.m. EST
CBS
Richard Leonard, Director
Lawrence M. Klee, Writer
Richard Leonard, Editor
Harry Kramer, Announcer
American Chicle Co. (Dentyne), Anahist Co., Inc. (Anahist), Sponsors
"The Sister-in-Law Murder Case"
Wealthy widow Elizabeth Hastings, who has just returned from a European trip, is murdered. Among the suspects Mr. Keen interviews is the late woman's sister-in-law, Harriet Lang.

Actors in this episode include Toni Darnay, Helen Claire, Ronald Long, Henry Norell, Sarah Burton and Rosalind Green.

CONTINUITY #468 [1428]
Friday, January 2, 1953
8:00–8:30 p.m. EST
CBS
Richard Leonard, Director
Lawrence M. Klee, Writer
Richard Leonard, Editor
Harry Kramer, Announcer
Sustaining
"The Triple Warning Murder Case"
A double murder and forewarning of a third confronts Keen. Copper mining co-partners George Pelley and Frank Carlson are shot; regional manager William Sage is told he'll be number three.

Actors in this episode include Guy Sorel, Tom Collins, Lucille Wall, James Meighan and Anne Elstner.

CONTINUITY #469 [1429]
Friday, January 9, 1953
8:00–8:30 p.m. EST
CBS
Richard Leonard, Director
Lawrence M. Klee, Writer
Richard Leonard, Editor
Harry Kramer, Announcer
Eno-Scott and Bowne (Brylcreem), Procter & Gamble Co. (Lava), Sponsors
"The Footprint Murder Case"
Wealthy widow Emma Armstrong is bludgeoned to death in her suburban home. Outside the house, Mr. Keen finds imbedded in mud a smudged footprint — with only a single toe recognizable.

Actors in this episode include Ethel Wilson, Abby Lewis, Frank Thomas Jr., Chuck Webster and Peggy Stanley.

CONTINUITY #470 [1430]
Friday, January 16, 1953
8:00–8:30 p.m. EST
CBS
Richard Leonard, Director
Lawrence M. Klee, Writer
Richard Leonard, Editor
Harry Kramer, Announcer
Procter & Gamble Co. (Lava), Eno-Scott and Bowne (Brylcreem), Sponsors
"The Snowman Murder Case"

Furniture dealer George Carter is murdered. Mr. Keen finds a mystery woman heavily veiled and dressed in black near a snowman built in the yard behind the murder victim's store.

Actors in this episode include Henry Norell, Cathleen Cordell, Ned Wever, Karl Weber and Julie Stevens.

CONTINUITY #471 [1431]
Friday, January 23, 1953
8:00–8:30 p.m. EST
CBS
Richard Leonard, Director
Lawrence M. Klee, Writer
Richard Leonard, Editor
Harry Kramer, Announcer
Eno-Scott and Bowne (Brylcreem), Sponsor
"The Case of Murder and the Pretty Young Actress"

Lovely, talented actress Janet Pryor is struck with a heavy weapon and then thrown from a high bridge to her death. Helen Sears is caught with a blackjack in her possession.

Actors in this episode include Audrey Egan, Billy Redfield, Horace Braham, Irene Hubbard and Mary Jane Higby.

CONTINUITY #472 [1432]
Friday, January 30, 1953
8:00–8:30 p.m. EST
CBS
Richard Leonard, Director
Lawrence M. Klee, Writer
Richard Leonard, Editor
Harry Kramer, Announcer
Eno-Scott and Bowne (Brylcreem), Sponsor
"The South American Poison Murder Case"

Edna Calvin is stabbed to death with a sharp pointed pen dipped in a deadly South American poison. Keen discovers that nephew Peter Harrow spent some time in South America.

Actors in this episode include Lucille Wall, Ivor Francis, Helen Claire, Ronald Long and Cathleen Cordell.

CONTINUITY #473 [1433]
Friday, February 6, 1953
8:00–8:30 p.m. EST
CBS
Richard Leonard, Director
Lawrence M. Klee, Writer
Richard Leonard, Editor
Harry Kramer, Announcer
Eno-Scott and Bowne (Brylcreem), Procter & Gamble Co. (Lava), Sponsors
"The Case of Murder and the Clawing Hand"

Movie star Peter Ellsworth is shot to death, his handsome face clawed and disfigured as if by some gigantic hand. Later his brother-in-law, Henry Carr, becomes a second target.

Actors in this episode include Richard Newton, Florence Williams, Sarah Burton, Tom Collins and David Gothard.

CONTINUITY #474 [1434]
Friday, February 13, 1953
8:00–8:30 p.m. EST
CBS
Richard Leonard, Director
Lawrence M. Klee, Writer
Richard Leonard, Editor
Harry Kramer, Announcer
Procter & Gamble Co. (Lava), Eno-Scott and Bowne (Brylcreem), Sponsors
"The Hidden Fortune Murder Case"

Eccentric old Kate Webley is stabbed to death in her shabby hotel room on the Bowery. A thousand dollar bill is found under the carpet; it may be part of the victim's hidden fortune.

CONTINUITY #475 [1435]
Friday, February 20, 1953
8:00–8:30 p.m. EST
CBS
Richard Leonard, Director
Lawrence M. Klee, Writer
Richard Leonard, Editor
Harry Kramer, Announcer
Eno-Scott and Bowne (Brylcreem), Procter & Gamble Co. (Lava), Sponsors

"The S. O. S. Murder Case"

Young Jerry Mitchell, an amateur short wave radio operator, is shot to death at his radio while sending an S.O.S. call to a friend. He had inherited a large home and much money.

Actors in this episode include Frank Thomas Jr., Richard Janaver, Horace Braham, Charita Bauer, Toni Darnay and Chuck Webster.

CONTINUITY #476 [1436]
Friday, February 27, 1953
8:00–8:30 p.m. EST
CBS
Richard Leonard, Director
Lawrence M. Klee, Writer
Richard Leonard, Editor
Harry Kramer, Announcer
Procter & Gamble Co. (Lava), Eno-Scott and Bowne (Brylcreem), Sponsors
"The Case of Murder and the Haunted Farm"

Mary Otis, a widow, is shot to death in her Pennsylvania farmhouse, which neighbors say is haunted. Mr. Keen and Mike Clancy interview a host of suspects.

Actors in this episode include Elizabeth Morgan, Helen Claire, Bob Donley, Ned Wever and Cathleen Cordell.

CONTINUITY #477 [1437]
Friday, March 6, 1953
8:00–8:30 p.m. EST
CBS
Richard Leonard, Director
Lawrence M. Klee, Writer
Richard Leonard, Editor
Harry Kramer, Announcer
Eno-Scott and Bowne (Brylcreem), Procter & Gamble Co. (Lava), Sponsors
"The Jealous Father Murder Case"

John Hawley, a poor, retired railway engineer who is jealous of his daughter Ellen, is murdered. She was a virtual prisoner in their home. Philip Trask feigns being hit by an assailant.

Actors in this episode include John Stanley, Audrey Egan, Ronald Long, Ethel Wilson and Frank Thomas Jr.

CONTINUITY #478 [1438]
Friday, March 13, 1953
8:00–8:30 p.m. EST
CBS
Richard Leonard, Director
Lawrence M. Klee, Writer
Richard Leonard, Editor
Harry Kramer, Announcer
Procter & Gamble Co. (Lava), Eno-Scott and Bowne (Brylcreem), Sponsors
"The Platinum Blonde Murder Case"

Monica Worthing, a platinum blonde beauty who manages a large department store, is murdered. Suspects include owner Oliver Hadley and his wife Helen, who tries to shoot Oliver.

Actors in this episode include Sarah Burton, Ivor Francis, James Meighan, Horace Braham and Mary Jane Higby.

CONTINUITY #479 [1439]
Friday, March 20, 1953
8:00–8:30 p.m. EST
CBS
Richard Leonard, Director
Lawrence M. Klee, Writer
Richard Leonard, Editor
Harry Kramer, Announcer
Eno-Scott and Bowne (Brylcreem), Procter & Gamble Co. (Lava), Sponsors
"The Fish Market Murder Clue"

George Taggart, who made a fortune in the fish business, is stabbed to death in his Wall Street skyscraper headquarters. Bookkeeper and cook Martha Styles hides in Taggart's office.

Actors in this episode include Henry Norell, Helen Claire, Anne Elstner, Karl Weber and Chuck Webster.

CONTINUITY #480 [1440]
Friday, March 27, 1953
8:00–8:30 p.m. EST
CBS
Richard Leonard, Director
Lawrence M. Klee, Writer
Richard Leonard, Editor
Harry Kramer, Announcer
Procter & Gamble Co. (Lava), Eno-Scott and Bowne (Brylcreem), Sponsors
"The Case of Murder and the Girl at the Piano"

Emily Winters is strangled with a piece of piano wire while practicing on the piano for a concert debut. When her sister Joyce calls Mr. Keen, an intruder interrupts her.

Actors in this episode include Claire Niesen, Toni Darnay, Sidney Smith, Anne Seymour and Staats Cotsworth.

CONTINUITY #481 [1441]
Friday, April 3, 1953
8:00–8:30 p.m. EST
CBS
Richard Leonard, Director
Lawrence M. Klee, Writer
Richard Leonard, Editor
Harry Kramer, Announcer
Eno-Scott and Bowne (Brylcreem), Procter & Gamble Co. (Lava), Sponsors
"The Black Feather Murder Case"
Young, brilliant scientist Frank Sutter is murdered at home. Mr. Keen surprises the victim's wife, Joan, in the act of hiding someone unknown, who may have taken part in the crime.
Actors in this episode include David Gothard, Abby Lewis, Cathleen Cordell, James Meighan and Richard Janaver.

CONTINUITY #482 [1442]
Friday, April 10, 1953
8:00–8:30 p.m. EST
CBS
Richard Leonard, Director
Lawrence M. Klee, Writer
Richard Leonard, Editor
Harry Kramer, Announcer
The Nestle Co., Inc. (Nescafe), Eno-Scott and Bowne (Brylcreem), Procter & Gamble Co. (Lava), Sponsors
"The Gift Package Murder Case"
A time bomb in a package delivered to her Park Avenue home kills wealthy socialite Ellen Blakely. Jilted suitor Philip Wharton threatens Robert Blakely, Ellen's spouse.
Actors in this episode include Gertrude Warner, Ronald Long, Ned Wever, Florence Williams and Toni Darnay.

CONTINUITY #483 [1443]
Friday, April 17, 1953
8:00–8:30 p.m. EST
CBS
Richard Leonard, Director
Lawrence M. Klee, Writer
Richard Leonard, Editor
Harry Kramer, Announcer
Procter & Gamble Co. (Lava), The Nestle Co., Inc. (Nescafe), Eno-Scott and Bowne (Brylcreem), Sponsors
"The Wax Doll Murder Case"
Wealthy luggage manufacturer Charles Weston is shot to death in front of his suburban home. The police seek ex-cook and housekeeper Lorna Gates because she had threatened him when he dismissed her.
Actors in this episode include John Stanley, Frank Thomas Jr., Anne Seymour, Karl Weber and Peggy Stanley.

CONTINUITY #484 [1444]
Friday, April 24, 1953
8:00–8:30 p.m. EST
CBS
Richard Leonard, Director
Lawrence M. Klee, Writer
Richard Leonard, Editor
Harry Kramer, Announcer
Eno-Scott and Bowne (Brylcreem), Procter & Gamble Co. (Lava), The Nestle Co., Inc. (Nescafe), Sponsors
"The Case of Murder on the Fifteenth Floor"
Ellen Peters is shot in her apartment. Keen is baffled as to how the murderer entered: the door was bolted from the inside, and the only other way in was via a terrace 15 floors above the street.
Actors in this episode include Cathleen Cordell, Sydney Smith, Mary Jane Higby, Jan Miner and Horace Braham.

CONTINUITY #485 [1445]
Friday, May 1, 1953
8:00–8:30 p.m. EDST
CBS
Richard Leonard, Director
Lawrence M. Klee, Writer
Richard Leonard, Editor
Harry Kramer, Announcer
The Nestle Co., Inc. (Nescafe), Eno-Scott and Bowne (Brylcreem), Procter & Gamble Co. (Lava), Sponsors
"The Case of Murder and the Glittering Eye"
Beautiful young heiress Eloise Dunn is bludgeoned to death in her suburban home. Cook and housemaid Mary Sutter caught a glimpse of the killer—who she describes as monstrous, with one glittering eye!
Actors in this episode include Ann Lorring,

Naomi Campbell, Guy Sorel, Elizabeth Morgan and Ronald Long.

CONTINUITY #486 [1446]
Friday, May 8, 1953
8:00–8:30 p.m. EDST
CBS
Richard Leonard, Director
Lawrence M. Klee, Writer
Richard Leonard, Editor
Harry Kramer, Announcer
Procter & Gamble Co. (Lava), The Nestle Co., Inc. (Nescafe), Eno-Scott and Bowne (Brylcreem), Sponsors
"The Case of Murder and the Disappearing Dagger"

Wealthy George Maynard is stabbed to death in his home. Mr. Keen learns that Allen, the victim's son, found his father a few seconds before he died, but failed to relate this little detail to the police.

Actors in this episode include Staats Cotsworth, Vivian Smolen, Frank Thomas Jr., Abby Lewis and Henry Norrell.

CONTINUITY #487 [1447]
Friday, May 15, 1953
8:00–8:30 p.m. EDST
CBS
Richard Leonard, Director
Lawrence M. Klee, Writer
Richard Leonard, Editor
Harry Kramer, Announcer
Eno-Scott and Bowne (Brylcreem), Procter & Gamble Co. (Lava), The Nestle Co., Inc. (Nescafe), Sponsors
"The Green Ghost Murder Case"

Wealthy Ellen Young is strangled to death in her suburban home. Her husband Herbert accuses her half-sister, Martha Barrett, saying she's insane because Martha claims to see a green ghost.

Actors in this episode include Mary Jane Higby, James Meighan, Helen Claire, Peggy Stanley and Bill Quinn.

CONTINUITY #488 [1448]
Friday, May 22, 1953
8:00–8:30 p.m. EDST
CBS
Richard Leonard, Director
Lawrence M. Klee, Writer
Richard Leonard, Editor
Harry Kramer, Announcer
The Nestle Co., Inc. (Nescafe), Eno-Scott and Bowne (Brylcreem), Procter & Gamble Co. (Lava), Sponsors
"The Surprise Party Murder Case"

Lovely, young Elizabeth Lawton is stabbed to death as she is about to leave her apartment to attend a surprise party in honor of her engagement to wealthy socialite Paul Enfield.

Actors in this episode include Sylvia Leigh, Toni Darnay, Frank Thomas Jr., Anne Seymour and Harold Huber.

CONTINUITY #489 [1449]
Friday, May 29, 1953
8:00–8:30 p.m. EDST
CBS
Richard Leonard, Director
Lawrence M. Klee, Writer
Richard Leonard, Editor
Harry Kramer, Announcer
Procter & Gamble Co. (Lava), The Nestle Co., Inc. (Nescafe), Eno-Scott and Bowne (Brylcreem), Sponsors
"The Case of Murder and the Handsomest Man"

Jeffrey Hargate, who was selected as the country's handsomest man in a contest, and subsequently won a Hollywood movie contract, is shot to death upon leaving for California.

Actors in this episode include Karl Weber, Joy Hathaway, Guy Sorel, Cathleen Cordell and David Gothard.

CONTINUITY #490 [1450]
Friday, June 5, 1953
8:00–8:30 p.m. EDST
CBS
Richard Leonard, Director
Lawrence M. Klee, Writer
Richard Leonard, Editor
Harry Kramer, Announcer
Eno-Scott and Bowne (Brylcreem), Procter & Gamble Co. (Lava), The Nestle Co., Inc. (Nescafe), Sponsors
"The Case of Murder and the Jack-in-the-Box"

Diana Kendal dies from a deadly poison gas released by opening a jack-in-the-box that was mailed to her. John Stapleton, who loved her, often sent her toys as a joke.

Actors in this episode include Rosemary Prinz, Richard Newton, Toni Darnay, Helen Claire and Ivor Francis.

CONTINUITY #491 [1451]
Friday, June 12, 1953
8:00–8:30 p.m. EDST
CBS
Richard Leonard, Director
Lawrence M. Klee, Writer
Richard Leonard, Editor
Harry Kramer, Announcer
The Nestle Co., Inc. (Nescafe), Eno-Scott and Bowne (Brylcreem), Procter & Gamble Co. (Lava), Sponsors
"The Bow and Arrow Murder Case"
An arrow takes the life of brilliant young businessman Anthony Blake. Wealthy sportsman Horace Worthing, upon whose fabulous estate Blake met his end, becomes a prime suspect.
Actors in this episode include Richard Janaver, Vivian Smolen, Horace Braham, Abby Lewis and Staats Cotsworth.

CONTINUITY #492 [1452]
Friday, June 19, 1953
8:00–8:30 p.m. EDST
CBS
Richard Leonard, Director
Lawrence M. Klee, Writer
Richard Leonard, Editor
Harry Kramer, Announcer
Procter & Gamble Co. (Lava), The Nestle Co., Inc. (Nescafe), Eno-Scott and Bowne (Brylcreem), Sponsors
"The Borrowed Money Murder Case"
George Pawling is shot in his office. Edward Squire lent him money, which Pawling couldn't repay. Ralph Graves, suspected of theft, loves Pawling's foster daughter, Amy.
Actors in this episode include Raymond Johnson, Ivor Francis, Audrey Egan, Helene Dumas and Frank Thomas Jr.

CONTINUITY #493 [1453]
Friday, June 26, 1953
8:00–8:30 p.m. EDST
CBS
Richard Leonard, Director
Lawrence M. Klee, Writer
Richard Leonard, Editor
Harry Kramer, Announcer
Eno-Scott and Bowne (Brylcreem), Procter & Gamble Co. (Lava), The Nestle Co., Inc. (Nescafe), Sponsors
"The Case of Murder and the Bullfighter's Sword"
Beautiful, wealthy young Lorna Creighton is stabbed to death with a bullfighter's sword. Neighbors Otis and Grace Burnam imprison young Ellen Wayne in a closet at their mansion.
Actors in this episode include Gertrude Warner, Karl Weber, Guy Sorel, Elizabeth Morgan and Julie Stevens.

CONTINUITY #494 [1454]
Friday, July 3, 1953
8:00–8:30 p.m. EDST
CBS
Richard Leonard, Director
Lawrence M. Klee, Writer
Richard Leonard, Editor
Harry Kramer, Announcer
The Nestle Co., Inc. (Nescafe), Eno-Scott and Bowne (Brylcreem), Procter & Gamble Co. (Lilt), Sponsors
"The Piggy Bank Murder Case"
Widower Andrew Perkins is found dead at home near a broken piggy bank. Young, powerfully-built bully Ed Coates attacks John Baxter, the son-in-law.
Actors in this episode include Arthur Maitland, Mary Jane Higby, Tom Collins, Grace Valentine and William Lipton.

CONTINUITY #495 [1455]
Friday, July 10, 1953
8:00–8:30 p.m. EDST
CBS
Richard Leonard, Director
Lawrence M. Klee, Writer
Richard Leonard, Editor
Harry Kramer, Announcer
Procter & Gamble Co. (Lilt), The Nestle Co., Inc. (Nescafe), Eno-Scott and Bowne (Brylcreem), Sponsors
"The Case of Murder and the Giant Shadow"
Wealthy manufacturer William Danton is shot to death in the library of his home by a killer who is identified only by the fact his shadow appears as that of a towering giant.
Actors in this episode include Henry Norell,

Horace Braham, Helen Claire, Raymond Johnson and Sarah Burton.

CONTINUITY #496 [1456]
Friday, July 17, 1953
8:00–8:30 p.m. EDST
CBS
Richard Leonard, Director
Lawrence M. Klee, Writer
Richard Leonard, Editor
Harry Kramer, Announcer
Eno-Scott and Bowne (Brylcreem), The Nestle Co., Inc. (Nescafe), Sponsors
"The Case of Murder on Skeleton Beach"

Young Dick Rawlins is shot to death on a deserted beach. Charles Brewster, a young, successful acquaintance whose sister Sally was about to marry Rawlins, is a chief suspect.

Actors in this episode include Audrey Egan, Hal Studer, Arthur Hughes, Richard Newton and Charita Bauer.

CONTINUITY #497 [1457]
Friday, July 24, 1953
8:00–8:30 p.m. EDST
CBS
Richard Leonard, Director
Lawrence M. Klee, Writer
Richard Leonard, Editor
Harry Kramer, Announcer
The Nestle Co., Inc. (Nescafe), Eno-Scott and Bowne (Brylcreem), Sponsors
"The Ghost Wife Murder Case"

Lovely Mary Haynes is stabbed to death at her suburban home. Earlier she and her cook Elsie Bligh claimed they saw the ghost of Philip Haynes' first wife.

Actors in this episode include Naomi Campbell, Richard Janaver, Cathleen Cordell, James Monks and Ethel Wilson.

CONTINUITY #498 [1458]
Friday, July 31, 1953
8:00–8:30 p.m. EDST
CBS
Richard Leonard, Director
Lawrence M. Klee, Writer
Richard Leonard, Editor
Olin Tice, Announcer
The Nestle Co., Inc. (Nescafe), Eno-Scott and Bowne (Brylcreem), Sponsors
"The Hall of Mirrors Murder Case"

Howard Dale is shot to death on a visit to an amusement park concession called the Hall of Mirrors. Mary Bartlett, his stepson's fiancée, appears at the Dale house packing a pistol.

Actors in this episode include Ted Osborn, Abby Lewis, William Lipton, Sylvia Leigh and Harold Huber.

CONTINUITY #499 [1459]
Friday, August 7, 1953
8:00–8:30 p.m. EDST
CBS
Richard Leonard, Director
Lawrence M. Klee, Writer
Richard Leonard, Editor
Harry Kramer, Announcer
Eno-Scott and Bowne (Brylcreem), The Nestle Co., Inc. (Nescafe), Sponsors
"The Final Warning Murder Case"

John Kendall is shot to death. Though the police finger Edward McKay, Mr. Keen is convinced that an unseen murderer, who was able to hide from both the victim and the accused, really fired the fatal shot.

Actors in this episode include James Meighan, Ronald Long, Helen Claire, Cathleen Cordell and Karl Weber.

CONTINUITY #500 [1460]
Friday, August 14, 1953
8:00–8:30 p.m. EDST
CBS
Richard Leonard, Director
Lawrence M. Klee, Writer
Richard Leonard, Editor
Harry Kramer, Announcer
The Nestle Co., Inc. (Nescafe), Eno-Scott and Bowne (Brylcreem), Sponsors
"The Strange Clue Murder Case"

Attractive young Jean Colby, a successful writer of mystery stories, is murdered in her apartment. Mike Clancy disarms Elsie Rand, her literary agent's wife, who brandishes a gun.

Actors in this episode include Sarah Burton, Ned Wever, Ian Martin, Arline Blackburn and Florence Williams.

CONTINUITY #501 [1461]
Friday, August 21, 1953
8:00–8:30 p.m. EDST
CBS
Richard Leonard, Director

A. J. Russell, Writer
Richard Leonard, Editor
Harry Kramer, Announcer
The Nestle Co., Inc. (Nescafe), Eno-Scott and Bowne (Brylcreem), Sponsors
"The Case of Murder and the Capsule of Death"

Rich Howard Henderson is poisoned to death in the greenhouse on his estate. Frank Todman, the gardener, appears with gun in hand; Mr. Keen and Mike Clancy reach for the sky.

Actors in this episode include Toni Darnay, Mary Jane Higby, Sydney Smith, Arthur Hughes and Raymond Johnson.

CONTINUITY #502 [1462]

Friday, August 28, 1953
8:00–8:30 p.m. EDST
CBS
Richard Leonard, Director
Lawrence M. Klee, Writer
Richard Leonard, Editor
Harry Kramer, Announcer
Eno-Scott and Bowne (Brylcreem), Sponsor
"The Poison Pen Letter Murder Case"

Wealthy widow Alice Hadley is beaten to death in her home after receiving a poison pen letter. Brother-in-law Charles Hadley later staggers into her home and collapses.

Actors in this episode include Mildred Clinton, Rosemary Prinz, Frank Thomas Jr., Ivor Francis and Cathleen Cordell.

CONTINUITY #503 [1463]

Friday, September 4, 1953
8:00–8:30 p.m. EDST
CBS
Richard Leonard, Director
Lawrence M. Klee, Writer
Richard Leonard, Editor
Olin Tice, Announcer
Eno-Scott and Bowne (Brylcreem), Procter & Gamble Co. (Lava), Sponsors
"The Case of Murder and the Limping Man"

Wealthy art dealer James Atwood is beaten to death as he debarks from a transatlantic liner at the pier. A limping man leaves the empty pier just after the crime is committed.

Actors in this episode include Staats Cotsworth, Ronald Long, Sarah Burton, Julie Stevens and James Meighan.

CONTINUITY #504 [1464]

Friday, September 11, 1953
8:00–8:30 p.m. EDST
CBS
Richard Leonard, Director
Lawrence M. Klee, Writer
Richard Leonard, Editor
Harry Kramer, Announcer
Procter & Gamble Co. (Lava), Eno-Scott and Bowne (Brylcreem), Sponsors
"The Hatpin Murder Case"

Edna Dalton is stabbed to death with a hatpin in her home. The suspects include her brother, Herbert Turner, disparaged in her diary, and Phoebe Sayers, the likely owner of the hatpin.

Actors in this episode include Florence Williams, Richard Newton, Helen Claire, Ted Osborn and Mary Orr.

CONTINUITY #505 [1465]

Friday, September 18, 1953
8:00–8:30 p.m. EDST
CBS
Richard Leonard, Director
Lawrence M. Klee, Writer
Richard Leonard, Editor
Harry Kramer, Announcer
Eno-Scott and Bowne (Brylcreem), Procter & Gamble Co. (Lava), Sponsors
"The Case of Murder and the Haunted Room"

Ellen James, who lived with her husband Philip and father-in-law Arthur James, is murdered in an old mansion on the Hudson River. She found a haunted room inside the house.

Actors in this episode include Gertrude Warner, Karl Weber, Ed Jerome, Mary Jane Higby and Ethel Wilson.

CONTINUITY #506 [1466]

Friday, September 25, 1953
8:00–8:30 p.m. EDST
CBS
Richard Leonard, Director
Lawrence M. Klee, Writer
Richard Leonard, Editor
Harry Kramer, Announcer
Eno-Scott and Bowne (Brylcreem), Procter & Gamble Co. (Lava), Sponsors
"The Case of Murder and the Green-Eyed Monster"

Wealthy young banker Charles Richards is

shot to death in his home. Richards' valet, Andrews, tells Mr. Keen a weird story about a green-eyed monster he saw peering in a window.

Actors in this episode include Sydney Smith, Julie Stevens, Treva Frazee, Horace Braham and Richard Janaver.

CONTINUITY #507 [1467]
Friday, October 2, 1953
8:00–8:30 p.m. EST
CBS
Richard Leonard, Director
Lawrence M. Klee, Writer
Richard Leonard, Editor
Harry Kramer, Announcer
Procter & Gamble Co. (Lava), Eno-Scott and Bowne (Brylcreem), Sponsors
"The Unpaid Alimony Murder Case"

Divorcee Irene Pryor is murdered. Her ex, Jeff, is a prime suspect because he owed her several thousand dollars in unpaid alimony. She also ended his engagement to Constance Grey.

Actors in this episode include Elizabeth Morgan, Abby Lewis, David Gothard, Toni Darnay, Ronald Long and Florence Robinson.

CONTINUITY #508 [1468]
Friday, October 9, 1953
8:00–8:30 p.m. EST
CBS
Richard Leonard, Director
Lawrence M. Klee, Writer
Richard Leonard, Editor
Harry Kramer, Announcer
Eno-Scott and Bowne (Brylcreem), Procter & Gamble Co. (Lava), Sponsors
"The Beautiful Widow Murder Case"

Beautiful young Edna Wales is strangled a few days after the death of her spouse, John. An autopsy is performed on John's body to determine the true cause of his death.

Actors in this episode include Virginia Kaye, Anne Seymour, Ned Wever, Richard Newton, Cathleen Cordell and Guy Sorel.

CONTINUITY #509 [1469]
Friday, October 16, 1953
8:00–8:30 p.m. EST
CBS
Richard Leonard, Director
Lawrence M. Klee, Writer
Richard Leonard, Editor
Harry Kramer, Announcer
Eno-Scott and Bowne (Brylcreem), Procter & Gamble Co. (Lava), Sponsors
"The Scandal-Monger Murder Case"

Elsie Waltham is stabbed to death in front of her home. She had spread malicious rumors about Frank and Doris West, and claimed that Doris was seeing another man, Alfred Powers.

Actors in this episode include Helen Carewe, Helen Claire, Julie Stevens, John Stanley and James Meighan.

CONTINUITY #510 [1470]
Friday, October 23, 1953
8:00–8:30 p.m. EST
CBS
Richard Leonard, Director
Lawrence M. Klee, Writer
Richard Leonard, Editor
Harry Kramer, Announcer
Procter & Gamble Co. (Lava), Eno-Scott and Bowne (Brylcreem), Sponsors
"The Jealous Rival Murder Case"

Lovely Carmella Scott is shot to death in her apartment. Both Roy Addison and his brother Tom wanted to marry Carmella. Their mother suspects Margaret Woods, Carmella's friend.

Actors in this episode include Charita Bauer, Audrey Egan, Richard Janaver, David Gothard and Katherine Emmet.

CONTINUITY #511 [1471]
Friday, October 30, 1953
8:00–8:30 p.m. EST
CBS
Richard Leonard, Director
Lawrence M. Klee, Writer
Richard Leonard, Editor
Harry Kramer, Announcer
Eno-Scott and Bowne (Brylcreem), Procter & Gamble Co. (Lava), Sponsors
"The Case of Murder and the Girl Who Couldn't Talk"

John Douglas is shot to death in his hotel room. Mr. Keen learns that hotel bellhop Eddie Lake has the murdered man's wallet and ring. Keen interrogates Lake in the murdered man's room.

Actors in this episode include Sydney Smith, Cathleen Cordell, Berel Firestone, Vivian Smolen and Arthur Hughes.

CONTINUITY #512 [1472]
Friday, November 6, 1953
8:00–8:30 p.m. EST
CBS
Richard Leonard, Director
Lawrence M. Klee, Writer
Richard Leonard, Editor
Olin Tice, Announcer
Procter & Gamble Co. (Lava), Eno-Scott and Bowne (Brylcreem), Sponsors
"The Death Bargain Murder Case"
Widowed Laura Preston, once a well-known actress, is murdered. A $500,000 insurance policy names Diana Vane as beneficiary, while a note Laura left labels Paul Ainsley an enemy.
Actors in this episode include Mary Jane Higby, Anne Seymour, Peggy Stanley, Horace Braham and Karl Weber.

CONTINUITY #513 [1473]
Friday, November 13, 1953
8:00–8:30 p.m. EST
CBS
Richard Leonard, Director
Lawrence M. Klee, Writer
Richard Leonard, Editor
Harry Kramer, Announcer
Eno-Scott and Bowne (Brylcreem), Procter & Gamble Co. (Lava), The Murine Co., Inc. (Murine), Sponsors
"The Case of Murder and the Face at the Window"
George Barlow is beaten to death with a fire poker at home. Richard Grange, ex-husband of Barlow's wife Rita, had sworn to kill any man she wed. His face appears in a window at the Barlow house.
Actors in this episode include David Gothard, Helen Claire, Ronald Long, Staats Cotsworth and Toni Darnay.

CONTINUITY #514 [1474]
Friday, November 20, 1953
8:00–8:30 p.m. EST
CBS
Richard Leonard, Director
Lawrence M. Klee, Writer
Richard Leonard, Editor
Harry Kramer, Announcer
Procter & Gamble Co. (Lava), Eno-Scott and Bowne (Brylcreem), Sponsors
"The Fifty Thousand Dollar Reward Murder Case"
Joan Bailey's husband Fred offers a $50,000 reward for the capture of his wife's killer. Before her death, she may have fallen for another man, Lawrence Wilson. Several people hope to collect the dough.
Actors in this episode include Vivian Smolen, James Meighan, Elizabeth Morgan, Ronald Long and Anne Seymour.

CONTINUITY #515 [1475]
Friday, November 27, 1953
8:00–8:30 p.m. EST
CBS
Richard Leonard, Director
Lawrence M. Klee, Writer
Richard Leonard, Editor
Harry Kramer, Announcer
Eno-Scott and Bowne (Brylcreem), Procter & Gamble Co. (Lava), The Murine Co., Inc. (Murine), Sponsors
"The Jungle Knife Murder Case"
Airline pilot Brad Raymond is killed with a large jungle knife. Racketeer Eddie Monks accuses Brad's wife Joyce of murdering her spouse after marrying him solely for his money.
Actors in this episode include Richard Janaver, Wendy Drew, Julie Stevens, Berel Firestone and Tom Collins.

CONTINUITY #516 [1476]
Friday, December 4, 1953
8:00–8:30 p.m. EST
CBS
Richard Leonard, Director
Lawrence M. Klee, Writer
Richard Leonard, Editor
Harry Kramer, Announcer
Procter & Gamble Co. (Lava), Eno-Scott and Bowne (Brylcreem), Sponsors
"The Career Girl Murder Case"
The brilliant career of attractive and talented Constance Roberts, head of a magazine syndicate, is cut short when she is stabbed to death at a banquet in her honor.
Actors in this episode include Anita Anton, Horace Braham, Helen Claire, Karl Weber and Treva Frazee.

CONTINUITY #517 [1477]
Friday, December 11, 1953

8:00–8:30 p.m. EST
CBS
Richard Leonard, Director
Lawrence M. Klee, Writer
Richard Leonard, Editor
Harry Kramer, Announcer
Eno-Scott and Bowne (Brylcreem), Procter & Gamble Co. (Lava), Sponsors
"The Case of Murder and the Broken Promise"

Successful businessman John Elton is shot to death in his office. Richard Elton, the victim's twin brother, appears and announces that he has vital information about the murder.

Actors in this episode include Lauren Gilbert, Mary Jane Higby, Andy Donnelly, Doris Dalton, John Stanley and Ian Martin.

CONTINUITY #518 [1478]

Friday, December 18, 1953
8:00–8:30 p.m. EST
CBS
Richard Leonard, Director
Lawrence M. Klee, Writer
Richard Leonard, Editor
Harry Kramer, Announcer
Procter & Gamble Co. (Lava), Eno-Scott and Bowne (Brylcreem), Sponsors
"The Shoplifter Murder Case"

Incurable shoplifter Mary Walsh is shot to death. Suspects include an aunt and uncle, due to inherit stocks; a man who encouraged her shoplifting; and a woman very jealous of her.

Actors in this episode include Audrey Egan, Abby Lewis, Henry Norell, Ivor Francis and Toni Darnay.

CONTINUITY #519 [1479]

Friday, December 25, 1953
8:00–8:30 p.m. EST
CBS
Richard Leonard, Director
Lawrence M. Klee, Writer
Richard Leonard, Editor
Harry Kramer, Announcer
Eno-Scott and Bowne (Brylcreem), Procter & Gamble Co. (Lava), Sponsors
"The Case of the Missing Witness"

George Page's daughter Cathy hasn't seen him in more than a week. He was to testify at a divorce trial. Both parties—Philip and Alma Craig—claim that he was going to testify on their behalf.

Actors in this episode include Treva Frazee, Richard Keith, Florence Freeman, David Gothard, Chuck Webster and Mary Orr.

CONTINUITY #520 [1480]

Friday, January 1, 1954
8:00–8:30 p.m. EST
CBS
Richard Leonard, Director
Lawrence M. Klee, Writer
Richard Leonard, Editor
Harry Kramer, Announcer
Procter & Gamble Co. (Lava), Eno-Scott and Bowne (Brylcreem), Sponsors
"The Case of Murder and the Fabulous Gift"

Actress Joan Carling is shot to death in her apartment. One lead is an expensive sable coat, a gift from either her press agent Peter Grant or married millionaire Lester Thornton.

Actors in this episode include Virginia Kay, Cathleen Cordell, John Stanley, Florence Robinson and Karl Weber.

CONTINUITY #521 [1481]

Friday, January 8, 1954
8:00–8:30 p.m. EST
CBS
Richard Leonard, Director
Lawrence M. Klee, Writer
Richard Leonard, Editor
Harry Kramer, Announcer
Eno-Scott and Bowne (Brylcreem), Procter & Gamble Co. (Lava), Sponsors
"The Case of Murder and the Grieving Cat"

When elderly Emma Saunders is murdered, the only witness is her pet cat, which spends much time grieving for its dead mistress. Keen finds four likely suspects for the crime.

Actors in this episode include Katherine Emmet, Wendy Drew, Andy Donnelly, Ethel Wilson, Arthur Hughes and Donald Bain.

CONTINUITY #522 [1482]

Friday, January 15, 1954
8:00–8:30 p.m. EST
CBS
Richard Leonard, Director
Lawrence M. Klee, Writer
Richard Leonard, Editor
Harry Kramer, Announcer
Procter & Gamble Co. (Lava), Sponsor

"The Forbidding House Murder Case"

Actress Victoria Crayton, missing eight years, turns up dead, seated in a chair in her country home, a fully clothed skeleton. There are large footprints outside the house.

Actors in this episode include Horace Braham, Julie Stevens, Richard Janaver, Audrey Egan and Chuck Webster. This episode repeats the story (under another title) broadcast on April 28, 1949.

CONTINUITY #523 [1483]
Friday, January 22, 1954
8:00–8:30 p.m. EST
CBS
Richard Leonard, Director
Lawrence M. Klee, Writer
Richard Leonard, Editor
Harry Kramer, Announcer
Procter & Gamble Co. (Lava), Sponsor
"The Case of Murder and the Killer with Purple Hands"

Wealthy widow Edith Winters is shot to death at home. Keen thinks the killer opened a desk drawer to get something and spilled a bottle of purple ink. The maid has purple hands.

Actors in this episode include Sylvia Davis, Andree Wallace, Mary Jane Higby, Ronald Long and Ivor Francis.

CONTINUITY #524 [1484]
Friday, January 29, 1954
8:00–8:30 p.m. EST
CBS
Richard Leonard, Director
Lawrence M. Klee, Writer
Richard Leonard, Editor
Harry Kramer, Announcer
Procter & Gamble Co. (Lava), Sponsor
"The Wooden Tombstone Murder Case"

Bandleader Jerry Blaxton is shot to death at night on the street. Mr. Keen learns he received a portent of his impending doom in the form of a miniature wooden tombstone.

Actors in this episode include Peter Capell, Cathleen Cordell, Donald Buka, Toni Darnay and Ted Osborn.

CONTINUITY #525 [1485]
Friday, February 5, 1954
8:00–8:30 p.m. EST
CBS
Richard Leonard, Director
Lawrence M. Klee, Writer
Richard Leonard, Editor
Harry Kramer, Announcer
Procter & Gamble Co. (Lava), Sponsor
"The Firebug Murder Case"

Henry Bolton is shot to death in his warehouse just moments after discovering the place was on fire. Mike Clancy nabs an ape-faced prowler spotted at the scene of the crime.

Actors in this episode include David Gothard, Katherine Emmet, Helen Claire, Ned Wever and Guy Sorel.

CONTINUITY #526 [1486]
Friday, February 12, 1954
8:00–8:30 p.m. EST
CBS
Richard Leonard, Director
Lawrence M. Klee, Writer
Richard Leonard, Editor
Harry Kramer, Announcer
Procter & Gamble Co. (Lava), Sponsor
"The Case of Murder and the Runaway Suspect"

George Evans, co-owner of a large department store, is murdered. John Preston, who ran away right after the murder, is sought. Both men were in love with Cora French.

Actors in this episode include Horace Braham, Wendy Drew, Hal Studer, Peggy Allenby, Henry Norell, Sarah Burton and Chuck Webster.

CONTINUITY #527 [1487]
Friday, February 19, 1954
8:00–8:30 p.m. EST
CBS
Richard Leonard, Director
Lawrence M. Klee, Writer
Richard Leonard, Editor
Harry Kramer, Announcer
Procter & Gamble Co. (Lava), Sponsor
"The Case of Murder and the Handwriting on the Wall"

Prosecuting attorney Alfred Howell is stabbed to death. Keen and Clancy capture escaped con Pete Cagle, who was sent to prison by Howell. Rumors fly regarding Howell's wife Jean and Ralph Wells.

Actors in this episode include Staats Cotsworth, Julie Stevens, Danny Ocko, Frank Thomas Jr. and Peggy Stanley.

CONTINUITY #528 [1488]
Friday, February 26, 1954
8:00–8:30 p.m. EST
CBS
Richard Leonard, Director
Lawrence M. Klee, Writer
Richard Leonard, Editor
Harry Kramer, Announcer
Procter & Gamble Co. (Lava), The Murine Co., Inc. (Murine), Sponsors
"The Birthday Gift Murder Case"
    Alice Bassett dies after eating poisoned candy sent to her husband Fred as a birthday gift. Police search for Martha Norton, Fred's former sweetheart, who sent the candy.

CONTINUITY #529 [1489]
Friday, March 5, 1954
8:00–8:30 p.m. EST
CBS
Richard Leonard, Director
Lawrence M. Klee, Writer
Richard Leonard, Editor
Announcer's name omitted
Procter & Gamble Co. (Lava), The Murine Co., Inc. (Murine), Sponsors
"The Paris Model Murder Case"
    Mr. Keen, tracer of lost persons, and partner Mike Clancy interact with a series of characters, including Joan Woodley, Yvonne Leclair, Madame and Ted Drury, and Arthur Earnshaw.
    Actors in this episode include Toni Darnay, Peggy Sanford, Grace Valentine, Berel Firestone and Ted Osborne.

CONTINUITY #530 [1490]
Friday, March 12, 1954
8:00–8:30 p.m. EST
CBS
Richard Leonard, Director
Lawrence M. Klee, Writer
Richard Leonard, Editor
Harry Kramer, Announcer
Procter & Gamble Co. (Lava), Sponsor
"The Case of Murder by Moonlight"
    Paul Roberts has a hunch he'll meet death during a full moon. It happens when he is shot in his apartment. Palm reader Abdul was paid to scare Roberts, making him wary of the full moon.
    Actors in this episode include James Meighan, Florence Williams, Helen Claire, Guy Sorel and Peggy Stanley.

CONTINUITY #531 [1491]
Friday, March 19, 1954
8:00–8:30 p.m. EST
CBS
Richard Leonard, Director
Lawrence M. Klee, Writer
Richard Leonard, Editor
Harry Kramer, Announcer
Procter & Gamble Co. (Lava), Sponsor
"The Case of Murder and the Dead Man's Secret"
    William Heming is shot to death while attempting to reveal some kind of secret to the police. Luther Knox tries to blackmail Mrs. Heming on the telephone, demanding $10,000.
    Actors in this episode include Horace Braham, Anne Seymour, Andree Wallace, Richard Janaver and Chuck Webster.

CONTINUITY #532 [1492]
Friday, March 26, 1954
8:00–8:30 p.m. EST
CBS
Richard Leonard, Director
Lawrence M. Klee, Writer
Richard Leonard, Editor
Harry Kramer, Announcer
Procter & Gamble Co. (Lava), Sponsor
"The Case of Murder and the Woman with Tangled Hair"
    Broadway stage star Richard Waverly is shot to death as he leaves a theater. An elderly stage doorman says he saw an old woman with long, tangled hair leave the scene of the crime.
    Actors in this episode include Tom Collins, Claire Niesen, Arthur Hughes, Karl Swenson and Cathleen Cordell.

CONTINUITY #533 [1493]
Friday, April 2, 1954
8:00–8:30 p.m. EST
CBS
Richard Leonard, Director
Lawrence M. Klee, Writer
Richard Leonard, Editor
Harry Kramer, Announcer
Procter & Gamble Co. (Lava), Sponsor
"The Case of Murder on Horror Hill"
    Attractive young secretary Betsy Went-

worth is bludgeoned to death on a driveway known as Horror Hill. Two people in her office may have been involved in forgeries she discovered.

Actors in this episode include Joy Hathaway, Audrey Egan, Ronald Long, Tom Collins and Mary Jane Higby.

CONTINUITY #534 [1494]
Friday, April 9, 1954
8:00–8:30 p.m. EST
CBS
Richard Leonard, Director
Lawrence M. Klee, Writer
Richard Leonard, Editor
Harry Kramer, Announcer
The Murine Co., Inc. (Murine), Procter & Gamble Co. (Lava), Sponsors
"The Case of Murder and the Leopard That Changed His Spots"

Wealthy big game hunter William Anders is shot to death in his Gotham town house. Anders broke the engagement between professional hunter Victor Marlin and Joyce Anders, his sister.

Actors in this episode include Toni Darnay, Richard Janaver, Karl Weber, Sylvia Davis, Henry Norell and Sarah Burton.

CONTINUITY #535 [1495]
Friday, April 16, 1954
8:00–8:30 p.m. EST
CBS
Richard Leonard, Director
Lawrence M. Klee, Writer
Richard Leonard, Editor
Harry Kramer, Announcer
Procter & Gamble Co. (Lava), Sponsor
"The Black Cloak Murder Case"

Joan Stacy is shot to death late at night on a city street. Mary Hull insists the bullet was meant for her, since Joan was wearing her black cloak; the killer simply made a mistake.

Actors in this episode include Florence Williams, Julie Stevens, Ned Wever, Elizabeth Morgan and James Meighan.

CONTINUITY #536 [1496]
Friday, April 23, 1954
8:00–8:30 p.m. EST
CBS
Richard Leonard, Director
Lawrence M. Klee, Writer
Richard Leonard, Editor
Announcer's name omitted
Procter & Gamble Co. (Lava), Sponsor
"The Knife-Thrower Murder Case"

Amy Bristol dies when someone throws a knife at her in her home. A prime suspect is professional knife-thrower Steve Gates, who lives next door.

Actors in this episode include Doris Dalton, Helen Claire, David Gothard, Wendy Drew and Chuck Webster.

CONTINUITY #537 [1497]
Friday, April 30, 1954
8:00–8:30 p.m. EDST
CBS
Richard Leonard, Director
Lawrence M. Klee, Writer
Richard Leonard, Editor
Announcer's name omitted
Procter & Gamble Co. (Lava), Sponsor
"The Death Rattle Murder Case"

George Slade is shot to death after he and his mother receive menacing letters demanding money. Signed "the Rattler," their arrival is preceeded by a rattling sound outside their home.

Actors in this episode include Andy Donnelly, Abby Lewis, Richard Keith, Mary Orr and Frank Thomas Jr.

CONTINUITY #538 [1498]
Friday, May 7, 1954
8:00–8:25 p.m. EDST
CBS
Richard Leonard, Director
Lawrence M. Klee, Writer
Richard Leonard, Editor
Announcer's name omitted
Procter & Gamble Co. (Lava), Sponsor
"The Million Dollar Murder Case"

Alfred Blair is shot to death in an automobile storage plant where he worked as a mechanic. Mike Clancy finds a revolver in the pocket of Gerald Norwich, one of at least three suspects.

Actors in this episode include William Quinn, Audrey Egan, Henry Norell, Mary Jane Higby and Guy Sorel.

CONTINUITY #539 [1499]
Friday, May 14, 1954

8:00–8:25 p.m. EDST
CBS
Richard Leonard, Director
Lawrence M. Klee, Writer
Richard Leonard, Editor
Announcer's name omitted
Procter & Gamble Co. (Lava), Sponsor
"The Cannibal Plant Murder Case"

Elderly William Hoyt is killed when poison replaces a tonic that he took. The disappearance of a cannibal plant, part of the rare foliage in his flower shop, may be a clue.

Actors in this episode include Arthur Maitland, Elizabeth Morgan, Sarah Burton, Haskell Coffin and Jackie Grimes.

CONTINUITY #540 [1500]

Friday, May 21, 1954
8:00–8:30 p.m. EDST
CBS
Richard Leonard, Director
Lawrence M. Klee, Writer
Richard Leonard, Editor
Announcer's name omitted
Procter & Gamble Co. (Lava), Sponsor
"The Case of Murder by Remote Control"

A gun set up mechanically to shoot the first person entering Eloise Marsh's bedroom claims the life of Eloise herself. Yet it appears the murder may have been intended for someone else.

Actors in this episode include Audrey Egan, Wendy Drew, Doris Dalton, Karl Weber and Andy Donnelly.

CONTINUITY #541 [1501]

Friday, May 28, 1954
8:00–8:25 p.m. EDST
CBS
Richard Leonard, Director
Lawrence M. Klee, Writer
Richard Leonard, Editor
Announcer's name omitted
Procter & Gamble Co. (Lava), Sponsor
"The Case of Murder and the Tattooed Arm"

A killer with a tattooed arm strangles Helen Taylor. Son-in-law George Wilson, with tattoos on both arms, hides in the back room of a tattoo artist's shop.

Actors in this episode include Florence Williams, Mary Jane Higby, Mandel Kramer, Richard Keith and Grace Valentine.

CONTINUITY #542 [1502]

Friday, June 4, 1954
8:00–8:30 p.m. EDST
CBS
Richard Leonard, Director
Lawrence M. Klee, Writer
Richard Leonard, Editor
Harry Kramer, Announcer
Procter & Gamble Co. (Lava), Sponsor
"The Case of Murder and the Ivory Monkey"

Wealthy John Endicott is shot to death after receiving a small ivory monkey. Jerry Haines is about to wed the victim's ward, Marian, and share in the fortune that she inherits.

Actors in this episode include Vivian Smolen, Ivor Francis, Frank Thomas Jr., Raymond Johnson and Sarah Burton.

CONTINUITY #543 [1503]

Friday, June 11, 1954
8:00–8:30 p.m. EDST
CBS
Richard Leonard, Director
Lawrence M. Klee, Writer
Richard Leonard, Editor
Harry Kramer, Announcer
Procter & Gamble Co. (Lava), Sponsor
"The Theatrical Star Murder Case"

Stage star Anita Bradford is shot to death in the theater wings before a rehearsal. Mike Clancy stops Henry Bowling from escaping. Bowling had sent the victim a threatening note.

Actors in this episode include Cathleen Cordell, Helen Claire, James Meighan, Lucille Wall and Richard Janaver.

CONTINUITY #544 [1504]

Friday, June 18, 1954
8:00–8:30 p.m. EDST
CBS
Richard Leonard, Director
Lawrence M. Klee, Writer
Richard Leonard, Editor
Harry Kramer, Announcer
Procter & Gamble Co. (Lava), Sponsor
"The Case of Murder and the Sultan's Dagger"

Wealthy Roger Slade is stabbed to death by a jeweled dagger once owned by a mad sultan. Clancy wounds a bearded giant in Arabian attire, Abou, trying to open the Slade wall safe.

Actors in this episode include Ned Wever,

Donald Buka, Andree Wallace, Toni Darnay and Guy Sorel.

NOTE: *Weeknight serialized sequences begin at this point, some of which run simultaneously with the weekly complete-in-one-chapter episodes. The numbering system for the continuing plotlines restarts at number one.*

CONTINUITY #1 [1505]
Monday, June 21, 1954
10:00–10:15 p.m. EDST
CBS
Blair Walliser, Director
Lawrence M. Klee, Writer
Richard Leonard, Editor
Stuart Metz, Announcer
Sustaining
"The Shrieking Prisoner Murder Case" (*Extant Episode*)

When Donald Travers goes to visit his wife Jane's two eccentric aunts, having not heard from them in more than six months, he is shot dead in their old home in a quiet suburb.

This is the first, since late 1943, in a series of weeknight episodes broadcast in serialized form. There was no episode broadcast on Tuesday, June 22, 1954.

CONTINUITY #2 [1506]
Wednesday, June 23, 1954
10:00–10:15 p.m. EDST
CBS
Blair Walliser, Director
Lawrence M. Klee, Writer
Richard Leonard, Editor
Stuart Metz, Announcer
Sustaining
"The Shrieking Prisoner Murder Case" (*Extant Episode*)

Handyman Luther Prague is a fourth suspect. But was Donald Travers' murder motivated by robbery? Or is his death linked to the insane woman so closely guarded by her sister?

CONTINUITY #3 [1507]
Thursday, June 24, 1954
10:00–10:15 p.m. EDST
CBS
Blair Walliser, Director
Lawrence M. Klee, Writer
Richard Leonard, Editor
Stuart Metz, Announcer
Sustaining
"The Shrieking Prisoner Murder Case" (*Extant Episode*)

Is Mr. Keen, tracer of lost persons, walking upstairs into the arms of a homicidal maniac? Which of his suspects murdered Donald Travers—and why? He's nearing a solution.

CONTINUITY #545 [1508]
Friday, June 25, 1954
8:00–8:30 p.m. EDST
CBS
Richard Leonard, Director
Lawrence M. Klee, Writer
Richard Leonard, Editor
Harry Kramer, Announcer
Procter & Gamble Co. (Lava), Sponsor
"The Case of Murder on the Waterfront"

John Kelcey is killed near a waterfront rooming house where he lived. His sister Helen had a violent quarrel with him. His landlady, Kate Dixon, may be dealing in stolen goods.

Actors in this episode include Alan MacAteer, Elizabeth Morgan, Henry Norell, Anne Elstner and Ted Osborne.

CONTINUITY #4 [1509]
Friday, June 25, 1954
10:00–10:15 p.m. EDST
CBS
Blair Walliser, Director
Lawrence M. Klee, Writer
Richard Leonard, Editor
Stuart Metz, Announcer
Sustaining
"The Shrieking Prisoner Murder Case" (*Extant Episode*)

Keen finds an empty hiding place in the wall of the Carsons' cellar, and footprints leading upstairs. Keen and Clancy mount the stairs, knowing they could be heading towards a homicidal maniac.

CONTINUITY #5 [1510]
Monday, June 28, 1954
10:00–10:15 p.m. EDST
CBS
Edward Slattery, Director
Lawrence M. Klee, Writer
Richard Leonard, Editor
Stuart Metz, Announcer

Sustaining
"The Case of Murder and the One-Eyed Gypsy"
　　Gypsy dancer Marie Kopec and her fortuneteller partner Boris Zoltar are performing for Eloise West and her friends when Mrs. West is stabbed to death in her New York town house.

CONTINUITY #6 [1511]
Tuesday, June 29, 1954
10:00–10:15 p.m. EDST
CBS
Edward Slattery, Director
Lawrence M. Klee, Writer
Richard Leonard, Editor
Stuart Metz, Announcer
Sustaining
"The Case of Murder and the One-Eyed Gypsy"
　　Gypsy fortuneteller Boris Zoltar, with only one eye (thanks to a knife fight long ago), wears a black patch over the damaged orb. He's also engaged in deceptive practices, such as forgery.

CONTINUITY #7 [1512]
Wednesday, June 30, 1954
10:00–10:15 p.m. EDST
CBS
Edward Slattery, Director
Lawrence M. Klee, Writer
Richard Leonard, Editor
Stuart Metz, Announcer
Sustaining
"The Case of Murder and the One-Eyed Gypsy"
　　Suspects in the crime include Joan Franklin, the murdered woman's social secretary, and Charles West, the victim's spouse, who swallows poison placed in a wine bottle.

CONTINUITY #8 [1513]
Thursday, July 1, 1954
10:00–10:15 p.m. EDST
CBS
Edward Slattery, Director
Lawrence M. Klee, Writer
Richard Leonard, Editor
Stuart Metz, Announcer
Sustaining
"The Case of Murder and the One-Eyed Gypsy"
　　Mystic Boris Zolter, wearing a patch over a sightless eye, told the victim she was in mortal danger; someone — her husband — intended to kill her, for he was in love with her secretary.

CONTINUITY #546 [1514]
Friday, July 2, 1954
8:00–8:25 p.m. EDST
CBS
Richard Leonard, Director
Lawrence M. Klee, Writer
Richard Leonard, Editor
Harry Kramer, Announcer
Sustaining
"The Case of Murder and the Three Alarm Fire"
　　Neil Graham is stabbed to death upon entering his invalid uncle's home in response to a three-alarm fire. The uncle and aunt may have set the blaze to collect insurance funds.
　　Actors in this episode include Berel Firestone, Horace Braham, Audrey Egan, Cathleen Cordell and Karl Swenson.

CONTINUITY #9 [1515]
Friday, July 2, 1954
10:00–10:15 p.m. EDST
CBS
Edward Slattery, Director
Lawrence M. Klee, Writer
Richard Leonard, Editor
George Bryan, Announcer
Sustaining
"The Case of Murder and the One-Eyed Gypsy"
　　Keen and Clancy pursue Boris Zolter, who turns the tables on them, kidnapping and forcing them into a car at gunpoint. Freed, they return to the West home to see a shadowy figure.

CONTINUITY #10 [1516]
Monday, July 5, 1954
10:00–10:15 p.m. EDST
CBS
Edward Slattery, Director
Marie Baumer, Writer
Richard Leonard, Editor
Stuart Metz, Announcer
Sustaining
"The Ticking Clocks Murder Case"
　　Marcia Van Cleve has 30 clocks in her bedroom. She says, "It's easier to regulate a clock than to control human beings." Then someone enters and stabs her with scissors.

CONTINUITY #11 [1517]
Tuesday, July 6, 1954
10:00–10:15 p.m. EDST

CBS
Edward Slattery, Director
Marie Baumer, Writer
Richard Leonard, Editor
Stuart Metz, Announcer
Sustaining
"The Ticking Clocks Murder Case"

Keen and Clancy go to the murder scene only to find that the victim's attorney, Mark Adams, has bolted himself inside her room and won't open the door, claiming he has a right to be there.

CONTINUITY #12 [1518]
Wednesday, July 7, 1954
10:00–10:15 p.m. EDST
CBS
Edward Slattery, Director
Marie Baumer, Writer
Richard Leonard, Editor
Stuart Metz, Announcer
Sustaining
"The Ticking Clocks Murder Case"

Adams was fired as Marcia's attorney and executor of her estate shortly before she died. Also, she planned to disinherit her nephew Philip if he married Adams' daughter Carol.

CONTINUITY #13 [1519]
Thursday, July 8, 1954
10:00–10:15 p.m. EDST
CBS
Edward Slattery, Director
Marie Baumer, Writer
Richard Leonard, Editor
Stuart Metz, Announcer
Sustaining
"The Ticking Clocks Murder Case"

Clancy remarks to Keen that Philip Van Cleve and Carol Adams "look like a couple of scared kids." Keen observes, "For some reason, they're afraid of Carol's father, Mark Adams."

CONTINUITY #547 [1520]
Friday, July 9, 1954
8:00–8:25 p.m. EDST
CBS
Richard Leonard, Director
Lawrence M. Klee, Writer
Richard Leonard, Editor
Harry Kramer, Announcer
Sustaining

"The Case of Murder and the Secret Wife"

Fred Stevens receives a telegram about the same time his wife Abigail is murdered. The telegram was dispatched from Stamford, Connecticut. Keen traces those who could have sent it.

Actors in this episode include Arthur Maitland, Ruth Gates, Peggy Stanley, Chuck Webster, Florence Robinson, Andy Donnelly and Peggy Allenby.

CONTINUITY #14 [1521]
Friday, July 9, 1954
10:00–10:15 p.m. EDST
CBS
Edward Slattery, Director
Marie Baumer, Writer
Richard Leonard, Editor
George Bryan, Announcer
Sustaining
"The Ticking Clocks Murder Case"

Keen determines that four people have reasons to hate the tyrannical victim: her companion-housekeeper, her lawyer, the lawyer's daughter, and her nephew and sole heir, who badly needed his inheritance.

CONTINUITY #15 [1522]
Monday, July 12, 1954
10:00–10:15 p.m. EDST
CBS
Edward Slattery, Director
Marie Baumer, Writer
Richard Leonard, Editor
Stuart Metz, Announcer
Sustaining
"The Fountain of Youth Murder Case"

Glamorous Madame DuBois, aka Irene Foreman, operator of the famous Renee Beauty Salon, dies after inhaling fatal poison. Her plain-Jane sister Ruth says Irene was good to her.

CONTINUITY #16 [1523]
Tuesday, July 13, 1954
10:00–10:15 p.m. EDST
CBS
Edward Slattery, Director
Marie Baumer, Writer
Richard Leonard, Editor
Stuart Metz, Announcer
Sustaining

"The Fountain of Youth Murder Case"

Keen observes, "All this luxury — a swanky front for a hugely successful business. And what's behind it? A lot of unhappy people, one of whom wanted to see Madame Renee dead!"

CONTINUITY #17 [1524]
Wednesday, July 14, 1954
10:00–10:15 p.m. EDST
CBS
Edward Slattery, Director
Marie Baumer, Writer
Richard Leonard, Editor
Stuart Metz, Announcer
Sustaining
"The Fountain of Youth Murder Case"

Seeing James Lowery making love to chemist Flora Benson, Keen learns from Henri DuBois that his wife fell for Lowery and tried to convince him to marry her after she divorced Henri.

CONTINUITY #18 [1525]
Thursday, July 15, 1954
10:00–10:15 p.m. EDST
CBS
Edward Slattery, Director
Marie Baumer, Writer
Richard Leonard, Editor
Stuart Metz, Announcer
Sustaining
"The Fountain of Youth Murder Case"

Keen deduces that Madame Renee's husband, chemist, manager and sister all could have killed her, dragging her body into her office from a perfume preparation room, where she died.

CONTINUITY #548 [1526]
Friday, July 16, 1954
8:00–8:25 p.m. EDST
CBS
Richard Leonard, Director
Lawrence M. Klee, Writer
Richard Leonard, Editor
George Bryan, Announcer
Sustaining
"The Wealthy Cat Murder Case"

Andrew Fulton, whose Uncle Humphrey left a fortune in his will to Whiskers, his pet tomcat, is murdered. Keen and Clancy visit Fulton's widow Joan in a modest suburban home.

Actors in this episode include Doris Dalton, Teri Keane, Ed Jerome, Ned Wever and Frank Milano.

CONTINUITY #19 [1527]
Friday, July 16, 1954
10:00–10:15 p.m. EDST
CBS
Edward Slattery, Director
Marie Baumer, Writer
Richard Leonard, Editor
George Bryan, Announcer
Sustaining
"The Fountain of Youth Murder Case"

Lowery says he studied chemistry and took a job at the salon to take away part of Renee's business and kill her, avenging his mother's death. She had suffocated at the victim's hands.

CONTINUITY #20 [1528]
Monday, July 19, 1954
10:00–10:15 p.m. EDST
CBS
Edward Slattery, Director
Lawrence M. Klee, Writer
Richard Leonard, Editor
George Bryan, Announcer
Sustaining
"The Case of Murder and the Poison Fangs"

Charged by India's government to find an antidote for cobra poison, researcher Henry Barret did so and was murdered. He also had made a financial pact with an aide, Ralph Lindley.

CONTINUITY #21 [1529]
Tuesday, July 20, 1954
10:00–10:15 p.m. EDST
CBS
Edward Slattery, Director
Lawrence M. Klee, Writer
Richard Leonard, Editor
Stuart Metz, Announcer
Sustaining
"The Case of Murder and the Poison Fangs"

Mr. Keen and Mike Clancy soon learn that Ralph Lindley's wife Thelma was said to be in love with the victim, although she denies it. She claims that Alice Barret murdered Henry.

CONTINUITY #22 [1530]
Wednesday, July 21, 1954

10:00–10:15 p.m. EDST
CBS
Edward Slattery, Director
Lawrence M. Klee, Writer
Richard Leonard, Editor
Stuart Metz, Announcer
Sustaining
"The Case of Murder and the Poison Fangs"

Ralph Lindley locks Keen and Clancy in a snake lab, leaving one poisonous reptile out of its cage. The tension mounts as the deadly snake inches toward them — until Clancy shoots off its head.

CONTINUITY #23 [1531]
Thursday, July 22, 1954
10:00–10:15 p.m. EDST
CBS
Edward Slattery, Director
Lawrence M. Klee, Writer
Richard Leonard, Editor
Stuart Metz, Announcer
Sustaining
"The Case of Murder and the Poison Fangs"

The gumshoes decide to search the Barret house from top to bottom, hoping to turn up a copy of the financial agreement the victim made with his associate, Ralph Lindley.

CONTINUITY #549 [1532]
Friday, July 23, 1954
8:00–8:25 p.m. EDST
CBS
Richard Leonard, Director
Lawrence M. Klee, Writer
Richard Leonard, Editor
George Bryan, Announcer
Sustaining
"The Case of the Date for Murder"

Attractive Emily Pomeroy, a successful interior decorator, is brutally murdered. Looking for clues, Mr. Keen carefully examines the victim's current personal income tax statement.

Actors in this episode include Mary Jane Higby, Tom Collins, Peggy Allenby, Richard Janaver and Cathleen Cordell.

CONTINUITY #24 [1533]
Friday, July 23, 1954
10:00–10:15 p.m. EDST
CBS
Edward Slattery, Director
Lawrence M. Klee, Writer
Richard Leonard, Editor
George Bryan, Announcer
Sustaining
"The Case of Murder and the Poison Fangs"

Mr. Keen learns that Ed Traynor, Henry Barret's brother-in-law, received a life sentence in Mexico for murder, but he escaped. Henry found out too, and was about to turn him in.

CONTINUITY #25 [1534]
Monday, July 26, 1954
10:00–10:15 p.m. EDST
CBS
Edward Slattery, Director
Marie Baumer, Writer
Richard Leonard, Editor
Stuart Metz, Announcer
Sustaining
"The Ice Queen Murder Case"

Wingfoot Wilson, a trainer of professional ice skaters who developed several stars, is murdered, struck on the head by an unidentified instrument that left a gash in his temple.

CONTINUITY #26 [1535]
Tuesday, July 27, 1954
10:00–10:15 p.m. EDST
CBS
Edward Slattery, Director
Marie Baumer, Writer
Richard Leonard, Editor
Stuart Metz, Announcer
Sustaining
"The Ice Queen Murder Case"

The haughty Mrs. Lane runs an indoor ice rink. Rosalie Clark laments that Wingfoot Wilson intended to take her from friends — against her wishes — to train up in Canada.

CONTINUITY #27 [1536]
Wednesday, July 28, 1954
10:00–10:15 p.m. EDST
CBS
Edward Slattery, Director
Marie Baumer, Writer
Richard Leonard, Editor
Stuart Metz, Announcer
Sustaining
"The Ice Queen Murder Case"

Ice skating instructor Tom Mitchell is a topic of debate. Wilson took Clark from him, robbing him of a star pupil. Lane thinks he's grand; Clark says he's a pathetic has-been.

CONTINUITY #28 [1537]
Thursday, July 29, 1954
10:00–10:15 p.m. EDST
CBS
Edward Slattery, Director
Marie Baumer, Writer
Richard Leonard, Editor
Stuart Metz, Announcer
Sustaining
"The Ice Queen Murder Case"
Mr. Keen, tracer of lost persons, finally discovers the murder weapon: an ice skate. Did it belong to Rosalie, or Bob Lewis, or to someone else? The answer comes tomorrow.

CONTINUITY #550 [1538]
Friday, July 30, 1954
8:00–8:25 p.m. EDST
CBS
Richard Leonard, Director
Lawrence M. Klee, Writer
Richard Leonard, Editor
George Bryan, Announcer
Sustaining
"The Rowboat Murder Case"
Rich matron Ellen Porter is murdered in a rowboat on Forest Lake. Keen and Clancy find the body of family cook Lizzie, who quit her job after calling the place a murder house.
Actors in this episode include Ara Gerald, Andy Donnelly, Ann Thomas, James Meighan, Arline Blackburn and Grace Valentine.

CONTINUITY #29 [1539]
Friday, July 30, 1954
10:00–10:15 p.m. EDST
CBS
Edward Slattery, Director
Marie Baumer, Writer
Richard Leonard, Editor
George Bryan, Announcer
Sustaining
"The Ice Queen Murder Case"
It's Bob Lewis' ice skate, but he isn't the killer; it's Mrs. Lane, who snapped when she saw Wilson overworking Rosalie. Mrs. Lane's own father had done that to her and left her a cripple for life.

CONTINUITY #30 [1540]
Monday, August 2, 1954
10:00–10:15 p.m. EDST
CBS
Edward Slattery, Director
Marie Baumer, Writer
Richard Leonard, Editor
Stuart Metz, Announcer
Sustaining
"The Flirtatious Secretary Murder Case"
Ruth Marlow is found with the smoking gun in her hand standing over spouse Herbert's body. The killer shot him and tossed the gun beside him, she says; she picked it up.

CONTINUITY #31 [1541]
Tuesday, August 3, 1954
10:00–10:15 p.m. EDST
CBS
Edward Slattery, Director
Marie Baumer, Writer
Richard Leonard, Editor
Stuart Metz, Announcer
Sustaining
"The Flirtatious Secretary Murder Case"
The Marlows had quarreled shortly before Herbert's death. The middle-aged man demanded a divorce from his wife of 25 years so he could marry a flirtatious young secretary, Kitty Page.

CONTINUITY #32 [1542]
Wednesday, August 4, 1954
10:00–10:15 p.m. EDST
CBS
Edward Slattery, Director
Marie Baumer, Writer
Richard Leonard, Editor
Stuart Metz, Announcer
Sustaining
"The Flirtatious Secretary Murder Case"
A new development focuses attention on the flirtatious secretary herself. Mr. Keen finds a letter in the murdered man's safe that might contradict his supposed intention to leave his wife.

CONTINUITY #33 [1543]
Thursday, August 5, 1954
10:00–10:15 p.m. EDST
CBS
Edward Slattery, Director

Marie Baumer, Writer
Richard Leonard, Editor
Stuart Metz, Announcer
Sustaining
"The Flirtatious Secretary Murder Case"

Evidence piles up against Kitty Page, whose flirtatiousness spelled tragedy for so many. But Keen is interested in her alibi, and anxious to hear her ex, William Sanders, repeat it.

CONTINUITY #551 [1544]
Friday, August 6, 1954
8:00–8:25 p.m. EDST
CBS
Richard Leonard, Director
Lawrence M. Klee, Writer
Richard Leonard, Editor
George Bryan, Announcer
Sustaining
"The Case of Murder and the Accused Actress"

Well-known theatrical producer Cyril Brentwood is shot to death in the apartment shared by actresses Maude Waters and Audrey Nelson. Keen and Clancy inspect the murder site.

Actors in this episode include Audrey Egan, Richard Keith, Frank Thomas Jr. and Madeleine Sherwood.

CONTINUITY #34 [1545]
Friday, August 6, 1954
10:00–10:15 p.m. EDST
CBS
Edward Slattery, Director
Marie Baumer, Writer
Richard Leonard, Editor
George Bryan, Announcer
Sustaining
"The Flirtatious Secretary Murder Case"

William Sanders was obsessed with his ex-wife. He took her gun and killed Marlow to rid himself of his main rival, thinking she would pay for it. He forged the letter in the safe.

CONTINUITY #35 [1546]
Monday, August 9, 1954
10:00–10:15 p.m. EDST
CBS
Edward Slattery, Director
Marie Baumer, Writer
Richard Leonard, Editor
Stuart Metz, Announcer
Sustaining
"The Case of Murder and the Girl Who Lost Her Memory"

A girl who cannot even recall who she is goes to Mr. Keen asking for help. She is accused of murdering banker Charles Billings—she's told she is his daughter, but can't recall.

CONTINUITY #36 [1547]
Tuesday, August 10, 1954
10:00–10:15 p.m. EDST
CBS
Edward Slattery, Director
Marie Baumer, Writer
Richard Leonard, Editor
Stuart Metz, Announcer
Sustaining
"The Case of Murder and the Girl Who Lost Her Memory"

Anita Harwood says Jane is pulling a hoax regarding memory loss, and that she's her sister. Peter Randall claims he and Jane are in love. Jane is sure she never saw either of them before.

CONTINUITY #37 [1548]
Wednesday, August 11, 1954
10:00–10:15 p.m. EDST
CBS
Edward Slattery, Director
Marie Baumer, Writer
Richard Leonard, Editor
Stuart Metz, Announcer
Sustaining
"The Case of Murder and the Girl Who Lost Her Memory"

Jane Billings regains her memory at last. Are Forbes and Anita Harwood afraid of something she may reveal? What impact does all this have on solving the murder?

CONTINUITY #38 [1549]
Thursday, August 12, 1954
10:00–10:15 p.m. EDST
CBS
Edward Slattery, Director
Marie Baumer, Writer
Richard Leonard, Editor
Stuart Metz, Announcer
Sustaining
"The Case of Murder and the Girl Who Lost Her Memory"

Keen announces: "Jane Billings, everyone in this case seems to have been lying, including you.... I find you receive half the estate; that makes you a very rich woman."

CONTINUITY #552 [1550]
Friday, August 13, 1954
8:00–8:25 p.m. EDST
CBS
Richard Leonard, Director
A. J. Russell, Writer
Richard Leonard, Editor
Harry Kramer, Announcer
Sustaining
"The Hidden Corpse Murder Case"

Dr. Philip Coleman disappears. Keen and Clancy go to the Cruett estate, where he was last seen. Finding the doc's bag floating on a lake, they suspect foul play.

Actors in this episode include Julie Stevens, Donald Buka, Arthur Maitland, Elizabeth Morgan and Richard Janaver.

CONTINUITY #39 [1551]
Friday, August 13, 1954
10:00–10:15 p.m. EDST
CBS
Edward Slattery, Director
Marie Baumer, Writer
Richard Leonard, Editor
George Bryan, Announcer
Sustaining
"The Case of Murder and the Girl Who Lost Her Memory"

Forbes Harwood confesses. He killed his father-in-law to prevent Anita from losing her inheritance. Charles Billings was always reminding Forbes that Anita did not love him.

CONTINUITY #40 [1552]
Monday, August 16, 1954
10:00–10:15 p.m. EDST
CBS
Edward Slattery, Director
Marie Baumer, Writer
Richard Leonard, Editor
Stuart Metz, Announcer
Sustaining
"The Waterfront Murder Case"

Why would someone be willing to pay Mr. Keen a fortune to investigate the murder of a skid row derelict — one wearing rags and tatters on the outside, and fine silk underclothes?

CONTINUITY #41 [1553]
Tuesday, August 17, 1954
10:00–10:15 p.m. EDST
CBS
Edward Slattery, Director
Marie Baumer, Writer
Richard Leonard, Editor
Stuart Metz, Announcer
Sustaining
"The Waterfront Murder Case"

Mr. Keen learns that the tramp was brilliant scholar Joseph Randolph Weeks, whose respected family — including a debutante daughter and politician brother — disappeared a decade ago.

CONTINUITY #42 [1554]
Wednesday, August 18, 1954
10:00–10:15 p.m. EDST
CBS
Edward Slattery, Director
Marie Baumer, Writer
Richard Leonard, Editor
Stuart Metz, Announcer
Sustaining
"The Waterfront Murder Case"

Years ago Uncle Harvey Weeks became involved in a crooked deal. The murdered Uncle Joe blackmailed him. At the same time, he was blackmailing his own wife, his daughter Melissa confirms.

CONTINUITY #43 [1555]
Thursday, August 19, 1954
10:00–10:15 p.m. EDST
CBS
Edward Slattery, Director
Marie Baumer, Writer
Richard Leonard, Editor
Olin Tice, Announcer
Sustaining
"The Waterfront Murder Case"

The disguised voice on the phone asking Keen to investigate the murder now says it will double the money if he drops it. But Keen won't. He verifies he'll have it solved by tomorrow.

CONTINUITY #553 [1556]
Friday, August 20, 1954

8:00–8:25 p.m. EDST
CBS
Steve Price, Director
Lawrence M. Klee, Writer
Richard Leonard, Editor
Harry Kramer, Announcer
Sustaining
"The Case of the Amazing Clue to Murder"

Investigating the mysterious murder of pretty young Doris Ralston, Mr. Keen and Mike Clancy learn that someone also tried to take the life of her uncle and guardian, Abner Craven.

Actors in this episode include Wendy Drew, Horace Braham, Helen Claire, Frank Thomas Jr., Rosemary Prinz and Betty Garde.

CONTINUITY #44 [1557]
Friday, August 20, 1954
10:00–10:15 p.m. EDST
CBS
Edward Slattery, Director
Marie Baumer, Writer
Richard Leonard, Editor
Olin Tice, Announcer
Sustaining
"The Waterfront Murder Case"

Melissa lied to Keen when she claimed she hadn't seen her father in 10 years. Fiancé Henry Van Dorn is from a proper family. If they knew Joe was a beggar they would've vetoed the nuptials.

The series was preempted on Monday, August 23; yet no storyline continuity is missing, since no broadcast was planned for that date.

CONTINUITY #45 [1558]
Tuesday, August 24, 1954
10:00–10:15 p.m. EDST
CBS
Steve Price, Director
Marion Scott, Writer
Richard Leonard, Editor
Stuart Metz, Announcer
Sustaining
"The Star Ruby Murder Case"

Glamorous society widow Grace Thorndyke is stabbed to death, her fabulous Star Ruby clutched in her hand. Keen observes that she was prouder of the gem than of her grown daughter Linda.

CONTINUITY #46 [1559]
Wednesday, August 25, 1954
10:00–10:15 p.m. EDST
CBS
Steve Price, Director
Marion Scott, Writer
Richard Leonard, Editor
Stuart Metz, Announcer
Sustaining
"The Star Ruby Murder Case"

Keen finds a tangle of hostile lives spun like a web around the luxury-loving victim. For instance, Linda hated her mother because she planned to marry a younger Peter Bradford, whom Linda loved.

CONTINUITY #47 [1560]
Thursday, August 26, 1954
10:00–10:15 p.m. EDST
CBS
Steve Price, Director
Marion Scott, Writer
Richard Leonard, Editor
Stuart Metz, Announcer
Sustaining
"The Star Ruby Murder Case"

Keen finds a secret stairway to the murder room that let the killer travel without detection. Keen also discovers that the victim's sister-in-law was incensed over how she was spending the family fortune.

CONTINUITY #554 [1561]
Friday, August 27, 1954
8:00–8:25 p.m. EDST
CBS
Steve Price, Director
Lawrence M. Klee, Writer
Richard Leonard and George Nobbs, Editors
George Bryan, Announcer
Sustaining
"The Case of the Man Who Turned Lead Into Gold"

Eccentric Amos Piper is electrocuted when his killer tampers with one of his inventions. Following a strange woman to the suburbs, Keen enters her home through a rear entrance.

Actors in this episode include Grace Valentine, Ned Wever, Ivor Francis, Charita Bauer and Donald Buka. This episode repeats the story broadcast on October 6, 1949, changing the title but using the same character names.

CONTINUITY #48 [1562]
Friday, August 27, 1954
10:00–10:15 p.m. EDST
CBS
Steve Price, Director
Marion Scott, Writer
Richard Leonard, Editor
Olin Tice, Announcer
Sustaining
"The Star Ruby Murder Case"

Linda Thorndyke slips into unconsciousness. The murderer of Linda's mother has apparently struck again. Is it Peter Bradford, Florence Stokes or jewel expert Arthur Quimby?

CONTINUITY #49 [1563]
Monday, August 30, 1954
10:00–10:15 p.m. EDST
CBS
Steve Price, Director
Marion Scott, Writer
Richard Leonard, Editor
Stuart Metz, Announcer
Sustaining
"The Star Ruby Murder Case"

Quimby saw the Star Ruby as his chance of a lifetime. He made a near-perfect copy, but Grace found out and planned to expose him. He killed her, with Bradford working as his accomplice.

CONTINUITY #50 [1564]
Tuesday, August 31, 1954
10:00–10:15 p.m. EDST
CBS
Steve Price, Director
Marion Scott, Writer
Frank and Anne Hummert, Editors
Stuart Metz, Announcer
Sustaining
"The Case of Murder and the Haunted Tower"

Jane Brady and her roommate (and best friend) are on vacation at the Silver Tree Lodge when someone whacks Maureen Miller on the head and pushes her from the venerated Haunted Tower.

CONTINUITY #51 [1565]
Wednesday, September 1, 1954
10:00–10:15 p.m. EDST
CBS
Steve Price, Director
Marion Scott, Writer
Frank and Anne Hummert, Editors
Stuart Metz, Announcer
Sustaining
"The Case of Murder and the Haunted Tower"

Keen learns that young, flirtatious Maureen spent her life savings to go to the exclusive summer resort to meet a man. She climbed the tower hoping Mark Sloan would follow her — and propose.

CONTINUITY #52 [1566]
Thursday, September 2, 1954
10:00–10:15 p.m. EDST
CBS
Steve Price, Director
Marion Scott, Writer
Frank and Anne Hummert, Editors
Stuart Metz, Announcer
Sustaining
"The Case of Murder and the Haunted Tower"

Sloan's fiancée, Claire Longwood, says Maureen was a nuisance. "Mark is a fool about women — he'll chase them, flirt with them." She says Maureen was dead when Sloan reached the tower.

CONTINUITY #555 [1567]
Friday, September 3, 1954
8:00–8:25 p.m. EDST
CBS
Richard Leonard, Director
Lawrence M. Klee, Writer
Richard Leonard and George Nobbs, Editors
Harry Kramer, Announcer
Sustaining
"The Egyptian Mummy Murder Case"

Alfred Scott, renowned scientist and authority on Egyptian relics, is murdered. A mummy is stolen from him for a reason Keen thinks may have a strong bearing on the killing.

Actors in this episode include David Gothard, Irene Hubbard, Florence Williams, Joseph Curtin and Harold Bromley.

CONTINUITY #53 [1568]
Friday, September 3, 1954
10:00–10:15 p.m. EDST
CBS
Steve Price, Director
Marion Scott, Writer
Frank and Anne Hummert, Editors

Olin Tice, Announcer
Sustaining
"The Case of Murder and the Haunted Tower"
 Mark and Claire plan to leave the country after pushing Keen and Clancy off a cliff, making it look accidental. But the pair of gumshoes outwit the tricksters and foil their plan.

CONTINUITY #54 [1569]
Monday, September 6, 1954
10:00–10:15 p.m. EDST
CBS
Edward Slattery, Director
Marie Baumer, Writer
Richard Leonard, Editor
Stuart Metz, Announcer
Sustaining
"The Trapped Man Murder Case"
 After brokerage operator Lewis Barlow is murdered, Mr. Keen, Mike Clancy and the victim's widow, Marcia, find that someone has torn his office apart looking for something.

CONTINUITY #55 [1570]
Tuesday, September 7, 1954
10:00–10:15 p.m. EDST
CBS
Edward Slattery, Director
Marie Baumer, Writer
Richard Leonard, Editor
Stuart Metz, Announcer
Sustaining
"The Trapped Man Murder Case"
 The culprit who tore up the office sought love letters Lois Creegan had sent to Lewis Barlow, which stated that if he didn't return her love she wouldn't be to blame for what happened to him.

CONTINUITY #56 [1571]
Wednesday, September 8, 1954
10:00–10:15 p.m. EDST
CBS
Edward Slattery, Director
Marie Baumer, Writer
Richard Leonard, Editor
Stuart Metz, Announcer
Sustaining
"The Trapped Man Murder Case"
 Janet Creegan insists that Marcia Barlow hated being tied to an invalid spouse so much she used his chauffeur Mitchell Wayne as a companion. Now Keen and Clancy are locked in her room.

CONTINUITY #57 [1572]
Thursday, September 9, 1954
10:00–10:15 p.m. EDST
CBS
Edward Slattery, Director
Marie Baumer, Writer
Richard Leonard, Editor
Stuart Metz, Announcer
Sustaining
"The Trapped Man Murder Case"
 About Wayne, Keen observes: "A charming, cultured man with something strange beneath that veneer — one of those men who step out of nowhere with no roots. He's also a first class liar."

CONTINUITY #556 [1573]
Friday, September 10, 1954
8:00–8:25 p.m. EDST
CBS
Richard Leonard, Director
Lawrence M. Klee, Writer
Richard Leonard, Editor
Ed Fleming, Announcer
Sustaining
"The Case of Murder and the Headless Statue"
 Beautiful young model Doris Brooke is bludgeoned to death in the studio of sculptor John Terrence. Having been spurned by Brooke, Terrence tries to hide her body in a cedar chest.

CONTINUITY #58 [1574]
Friday, September 10, 1954
10:00–10:15 p.m. EDST
CBS
Edward Slattery, Director
Marie Baumer, Writer
Richard Leonard, Editor
George Bryan, Announcer
Sustaining
"The Trapped Man Murder Case"
 Marcia Barlow put stolen jewels in Mitchell Wayne's room. Craving luxuries her spouse could no longer provide, she robbed wealthy friends. Lewis learned the truth and she killed him.

CONTINUITY #59 [1575]
Monday, September 13, 1954

10:00–10:15 p.m. EDST
CBS
Edward Slattery, Director
Marie Baumer, Writer
Richard Leonard, Editor
Stuart Metz, Announcer
Sustaining
"The Case of Murder in the Small Hotel"

Siblings Lawrence and Ellen Warner ran an industrial empire in Chicago. He secretly visited New York, staying in shabby digs while keeping a posh suite next door, and was murdered.

CONTINUITY #60 [1576]
Tuesday, September 14, 1954
10:00–10:15 p.m. EDST
CBS
Edward Slattery, Director
Marie Baumer, Writer
Richard Leonard, Editor
Stuart Metz, Announcer
Sustaining
"The Case of Murder in the Small Hotel"

Bill Parks tells Mr. Keen that nightclub singer Rosalie at the Van Dyke Hotel next door, and her bandleader Carl Carlson, visited Warner at the shabby Blue Eagle just before he died.

CONTINUITY #61 [1577]
Wednesday, September 15, 1954
10:00–10:15 p.m. EDST
CBS
Edward Slattery, Director
Marie Baumer, Writer
Richard Leonard, Editor
Stuart Metz, Announcer
Sustaining
"The Case of Murder in the Small Hotel"

Ellen Warner seems annoyed that Mr. Keen isn't making better progress in finding her brother's killer. Keen wryly notes that finding a murderer is unlike running a big business.

CONTINUITY #62 [1578]
Thursday, September 16, 1954
10:00–10:15 p.m. EDST
CBS
Edward Slattery, Director
Marie Baumer, Writer
Richard Leonard, Editor
Stuart Metz, Announcer
Sustaining
"The Case of Murder in the Small Hotel"

Rosalie tells Mr. Keen that Ellen Warner threatened her and told her to keep her mouth shut. Ellen *knew* her brother was in New York and at the Blue Eagle—she telephoned him twice.

CONTINUITY #557 [1579]
Friday, September 17, 1954
8:00–8:25 p.m. EDST
CBS
Richard Leonard, Director
Lawrence M. Klee, Writer
Richard Leonard, Editor
George Bryan, Announcer
Sustaining
"The Hoot Owl Murder Case"

Nancy Peters is shot to death in an empty field just outside New York City. Shortly before she died, the victim told her roommate, Cora Kingsley, she had learned a terrible secret.

Actors in this episode include Toni Darnay, Vivian Smolen, Ned Wever, Bert Cowlan and Mary Jane Higby.

CONTINUITY #63 [1580]
Friday, September 17, 1954
10:00–10:15 p.m. EDST
CBS
Edward Slattery, Director
Marie Baumer, Writer
Richard Leonard, Editor
George Bryan, Announcer
Sustaining
"The Case of Murder in the Small Hotel"

Had Rosalie and Carl Carlson been blackmailing the victim? Mr. Keen is now convinced there were *two* people involved in the murder of Lawrence Warner.

CONTINUITY #64 [1581]
Monday, September 20, 1954
10:00–10:15 p.m. EDST
CBS
Edward Slattery, Director
Lawrence M. Klee, Writer
Richard Leonard, Editor
Stuart Metz, Announcer
Sustaining
"The Temporary Wife Murder Case"

Nora Craven hears a scream in the adjacent cemetery that sounds like a shriek of terror. Checking it out the next morning, she finds the body of a girl in a shallow grave.

CONTINUITY #65 [1582]
Tuesday, September 21, 1954
10:00–10:15 p.m. EDST
CBS
Edward Slattery, Director
Lawrence M. Klee, Writer
Richard Leonard, Editor
Stuart Metz, Announcer
Sustaining
"The Temporary Wife Murder Case"

The body is that of Elsie Marsh. Visiting a florist shop run by Steven and Helen Page, Mr. Keen and Mike Clancy find Steven all too eager to denounce his wife as the murderer.

CONTINUITY #66 [1583]
Wednesday, September 22, 1954
10:00–10:15 p.m. EDST
CBS
Edward Slattery, Director
Lawrence M. Klee, Writer
Richard Leonard, Editor
Stuart Metz, Announcer
Sustaining
"The Temporary Wife Murder Case"

Elsie worked at the flower shop, and Steven Page attempted to force his attentions on her — or so claims Roger Atkins. Helen was so jealous that she would gladly have killed Elsie.

CONTINUITY #67 [1584]
Thursday, September 23, 1954
10:00–10:15 p.m. EDST
CBS
Edward Slattery, Director
Lawrence M. Klee, Writer
Richard Leonard, Editor
Stuart Metz, Announcer
Sustaining
"The Temporary Wife Murder Case"

The tracer and his partner find a blood-stained pair of heavy shears in the pocket of Elsie Marsh's dress. They deduce that this was the weapon used to bludgeon her to death.

CONTINUITY #558 [1585]
Friday, September 24, 1954
8:00–8:25 p.m. EDST
CBS
Richard Leonard, Director
Lawrence M. Klee, Writer
Richard Leonard, Editor
George Bryan, Announcer
Sustaining
"The Music Box Murder Case"

A time bomb hidden inside a music box kills dancer Joyce Farrow. She left her spouse, Curt, after Herbert Marlon offered to help her win a starring role in a Broadway musical.

Actors in this episode include Janet de Gore, Audrey Egan, Claire Niesen, Richard Janaver and Tom Collins.

CONTINUITY #68 [1586]
Friday, September 24, 1954
10:00–10:15 p.m. EDST
CBS
Edward Slattery, Director
Lawrence M. Klee, Writer
Richard Leonard, Editor
George Bryan, Announcer
Sustaining
"The Temporary Wife Murder Case"

Roger Atkins, whose fingerprints are all over the murder weapon, admits to killing Elsie. She loved Steven Page. When he learned that Page planned to divorce Elsie, "I went haywire."

CONTINUITY #69 [1587]
Monday, September 27, 1954
10:00–10:15 p.m. EST
CBS
Edward Slattery, Director
Lawrence M. Klee, Writer
Richard Leonard, Editor
Stuart Metz, Announcer
Sustaining
"The Case of Murder and the Phantom Melody"

Rooming house operator Sarah Tucker relates how the stabbing death of piano virtuoso Eric Barton occurred in her house just as his piano teacher, Laureen de Kempra, arrived.

CONTINUITY #70 [1588]
Tuesday, September 28, 1954
10:00–10:15 p.m. EST
CBS

Edward Slattery, Director
Lawrence M. Klee, Writer
Richard Leonard, Editor
Stuart Metz, Announcer
Sustaining
"The Case of Murder and the Phantom Melody"

Someone plays the melody on the victim's piano that he was playing at the time of his murder. But when Keen and George Leighton go to the murder room to check it out, it stops.

CONTINUITY #71 [1589]
Wednesday, September 29, 1954
10:00–10:15 p.m. EST
CBS
Edward Slattery, Director
Lawrence M. Klee, Writer
Richard Leonard, Editor
Stuart Metz, Announcer
Sustaining
"The Case of Murder and the Phantom Melody"

"I'm aware now that more than one person in this rooming house can play the piano, and perhaps I'm about to discover exactly how that phantom melody was played and by whom."

CONTINUITY #72 [1590]
Thursday, September 30, 1954
10:00–10:15 p.m. EST
CBS
Edward Slattery, Director
Lawrence M. Klee, Writer
Richard Leonard, Editor
Stuart Metz, Announcer
Sustaining
"The Case of Murder and the Phantom Melody"

Before his death, Eric Barton hired movers to pick up his piano. Mr. Keen says the piano holds the secret to solving the case. Taking it away would remove the evidence he needs.

CONTINUITY #559 [1591]
Friday, October 1, 1954
8:00–8:25 p.m. EST
CBS
Richard Leonard, Director
Lawrence M. Klee, Writer
Richard Leonard, Editor
George Bryan, Announcer
Sustaining
"The Silver Treasure Murder Case"

Well-heeled eccentric William Greeley is shot to death in his home. Daughter-in-law Doris Greeley disappears, and an unknown assailant strikes at the victim's second wife, Doris.

Actors in this episode include John Stanley, Andy Donnelly, Sarah Burton, Teri Keane and Henry Norell. This episode repeats the story broadcast on September 14, 1950, using the same title and character names. This was the final airing of the weekly complete-story-line series, ending an unbroken string of performances that had continued for many years.

CONTINUITY #73 [1592]
Friday, October 1, 1954
10:00–10:15 p.m. EST
CBS
Edward Slattery, Director
Lawrence M. Klee, Writer
Richard Leonard, Editor
George Bryan, Announcer
Sustaining
"The Case of Murder and the Phantom Melody"

Laureen admits she murdered Eric. She advanced him money to buy his piano, and he promised to share his earnings when he became a success, but he reneged, so she exacted her revenge.

CONTINUITY #74 [1593]
Monday, October 4, 1954
10:00–10:15 p.m. EST
CBS
Edward Slattery, Director
Lawrence M. Klee, Writer
Richard Leonard, Editor
Stuart Metz, Announcer
Sustaining
"The Marriage Bargain Murder Case"

Investment millionaire Lionel Rand is killed after making a bargain with Walter Blair, who suffered business losses and received $250,000 from Rand for his daughter Betty in marriage.

CONTINUITY #75 [1594]
Tuesday, October 5, 1954
10:00–10:15 p.m. EST
CBS

Edward Slattery, Director
Lawrence M. Klee, Writer
Richard Leonard, Editor
Stuart Metz, Announcer
Sustaining
"The Marriage Bargain Murder Case"

Clara Poole thought of killing Lionel Rand until overhearing Betty Blair arguing with him. She said he'd never get away with ruining her father, and that she would not marry him.

CONTINUITY #76 [1595]
Wednesday, October 6, 1954
10:00–10:15 p.m. EST
CBS
Edward Slattery, Director
Lawrence M. Klee, Writer
Richard Leonard, Editor
Stuart Metz, Announcer
Sustaining
"The Marriage Bargain Murder Case"

Betty Blair had packed her suitcase before Lionel Rand was murdered. Now she warns Mr. Keen not to search the contents of her suitcase, telling him she's sorry he's investigating.

CONTINUITY #77 [1596]
Thursday, October 7, 1954
10:00–10:15 p.m. EST
CBS
Edward Slattery, Director
Lawrence M. Klee, Writer
Richard Leonard, Editor
Stuart Metz, Announcer
Sustaining
"The Marriage Bargain Murder Case"

Mr. Keen finds the reason Betty didn't want the suitcase opened. Inside is an inscribed photo of Peter Townsend, whom she loves. She didn't want him connected with the murder.

CONTINUITY #78 [1597]
Friday, October 8, 1954
10:00–10:15 p.m. EST
CBS
Edward Slattery, Director
Lawrence M. Klee, Writer
Richard Leonard, Editor
George Bryan, Announcer
Sustaining
"The Marriage Bargain Murder Case"

Walter Blair confesses that something snapped when he heard Lionel Rand tell a peer that once he took Blair's daughter he intended to take his business, too. Thus, he killed him.

CONTINUITY #79 [1598]
Monday, October 11, 1954
10:00–10:15 p.m. EST
CBS
Edward Slattery, Director
Lawrence M. Klee, Writer
Richard Leonard, Editor
Stuart Metz, Announcer
Sustaining
"The Case of Murder and the Girl with Six Months to Live"

Wealthy industrialist James Granger is shot to death in his home. His wife Louise appeals to Mr. Keen to apprehend his killer, whom she claims is her husband's niece, Brenda Carr.

CONTINUITY #80 [1599]
Tuesday, October 12, 1954
10:00–10:15 p.m. EST
CBS
Edward Slattery, Director
Lawrence M. Klee, Writer
Richard Leonard, Editor
Stuart Metz, Announcer
Sustaining
"The Case of Murder and the Girl with Six Months to Live"

Brenda has six months to live. Louise says she had violent spats with James over spending. Brenda accuses Charles Newton, the victim's brother-in-law, an incurable alcoholic.

CONTINUITY #81 [1600]
Wednesday, October 13, 1954
10:00–10:15 p.m. EST
CBS
Edward Slattery, Director
Lawrence M. Klee, Writer
Richard Leonard, Editor
Stuart Metz, Announcer
Sustaining
"The Case of Murder and the Girl with Six Months to Live"

Mr. Keen takes a small bottle from Louise Granger as Brenda Carr looks on in fear. What do the bottle's contents have to do with the apprehension gripping the Granger household?

CONTINUITY #82 [1601]
Thursday, October 14, 1954
10:00–10:15 p.m. EST
CBS
Edward Slattery, Director
Lawrence M. Klee, Writer
Richard Leonard, Editor
Stuart Metz, Announcer
Sustaining
"The Case of Murder and the Girl with Six Months to Live"

Mr. Keen and Mike Clancy carefully examine a picture album kept by the murdered man, containing pictures of his family. "This photograph album will give us the final clue," Keen states.

CONTINUITY #83 [1602]
Friday, October 15, 1954
10:00–10:15 p.m. EST
CBS
Edward Slattery, Director
Lawrence M. Klee, Writer
Richard Leonard, Editor
George Bryan, Announcer
Sustaining
"The Case of Murder and the Girl with Six Months to Live"

Charles Newton admits that during a heated moment something snapped and he murdered his brother-in-law, saying he should have taken the cure to overcome his alcoholism as James wanted him to.

CONTINUITY #84 [1603]
Monday, October 18, 1954
10:00–10:15 p.m. EST
CBS
Edward Slattery, Director
Lawrence M. Klee, Writer
Richard Leonard, Editor
Stuart Metz, Announcer
Sustaining
"The Rival Brothers Murder Case"

Will Stanton's father died months ago, leaving a large estate in the hands of Will, a year older than brother Ralph. People had more confidence in Will, and now he has been murdered.

CONTINUITY #85 [1604]
Tuesday, October 19, 1954
10:00–10:15 p.m. EST
CBS
Edward Slattery, Director
Lawrence M. Klee, Writer
Richard Leonard, Editor
Stuart Metz, Announcer
Sustaining
"The Rival Brothers Murder Case"

Mr. Keen wonders if Will was murdered because of his rivalry with his brother Ralph. Or is his death linked to Lorna Worth or Barbara Haines, both former objects of Will's affections?

CONTINUITY #86 [1605]
Wednesday, October 20, 1954
10:00–10:15 p.m. EST
CBS
Edward Slattery, Director
Lawrence M. Klee, Writer
Richard Leonard, Editor
Stuart Metz, Announcer
Sustaining
"The Rival Brothers Murder Case"

George Farnum divulged to Will that he (Will) was a foundling. Will paid Farnum blackmail money to keep him from telling his brother Ralph. But Keen also sees *Ralph* paying off Farnum.

CONTINUITY #87 [1606]
Thursday, October 21, 1954
10:00–10:15 p.m. EST
CBS
Edward Slattery, Director
Lawrence M. Klee, Writer
Richard Leonard, Editor
Stuart Metz, Announcer
Sustaining
"The Rival Brothers Murder Case"

Barbara Haines switched loyalties from one suitor to the other, from Will to Ralph. She saw Ralph as a pathetic figure that desperately needed the help that only she could give.

CONTINUITY #88 [1607]
Friday, October 22, 1954
10:00–10:15 p.m. EST
CBS
Edward Slattery, Director
Lawrence M. Klee, Writer
Richard Leonard, Editor

George Bryan, Announcer
Sustaining
"The Rival Brothers Murder Case"

Barbara murdered Will. Mr. Keen says she wanted personal revenge, and she knew that Ralph would take her back and that he'd come into possession of the estate.

CONTINUITY #89 [1608]
Monday, October 25, 1954
10:00–10:15 p.m. EST
CBS
Edward Slattery, Director
Lawrence M. Klee, Writer
Richard Leonard, Editor
Stuart Metz, Announcer
Sustaining
"The Case of Murder and the Man Who Led Two Lives"

Alice Winslow tells Keen her son Philip has been living a double life: one with wife Helen, just murdered; the other with scheming Cathy Slade, who tried to break up their home.

CONTINUITY #90 [1609]
Tuesday, October 26, 1954
10:00–10:15 p.m. EST
CBS
Edward Slattery, Director
Lawrence M. Klee, Writer
Richard Leonard, Editor
Stuart Metz, Announcer
Sustaining
"The Case of Murder and the Man Who Led Two Lives"

Cathy Slade claims she didn't know Philip was married until she heard of the murder. She accuses his mother of wanting to break up his marriage. Phil gives Keen some startling information.

CONTINUITY #91 [1610]
Wednesday, October 27, 1954
10:00–10:15 p.m. EST
CBS
Edward Slattery, Director
Lawrence M. Klee, Writer
Richard Leonard, Editor
Stuart Metz, Announcer
Sustaining
"The Case of Murder and the Man Who Led Two Lives"

Mike Clancy finds the murder weapon, a bloodstained knife, hidden behind the kitchen stove. When Mr. Keen questions Philip about the identity of the knife's owner, he turns pale and says he can't tell him.

CONTINUITY #92 [1611]
Thursday, October 28, 1954
10:00–10:15 p.m. EST
CBS
Edward Slattery, Director
Lawrence M. Klee, Writer
Richard Leonard, Editor
Stuart Metz, Announcer
Sustaining
"The Case of Murder and the Man Who Led Two Lives"

"Apparently the chickens have come home to roost," Mr. Keen tells Philip Winslow. "Sooner or later you and Cathy were bound to reach a point of mutual distrust."

CONTINUITY #93 [1612]
Friday, October 29, 1954
10:00–10:15 p.m. EST
CBS
Edward Slattery, Director
Lawrence M. Klee, Writer
Richard Leonard, Editor
George Bryan, Announcer
Sustaining
"The Case of Murder and the Man Who Led Two Lives"

Philip admits he killed Helen: "I stood for her nagging long enough, and I was sick of being bullied by a woman." Keen concludes that his main motive was the insurance money.

CONTINUITY #94 [1613]
Monday, November 1, 1954
10:00–10:15 p.m. EST
CBS
Edward Slattery, Director
Lawrence M. Klee, Writer
Richard Leonard, Editor
Stuart Metz, Announcer
Sustaining
"The Case of Murder and the Woman Who Wouldn't Grow Old"

The late wealthy widow Anita Wharton was a vain woman, very concerned about her looks and always surrounded by people who flattered her. One of them murdered her. Enemies surface.

At the close of this episode, narrator Stuart Metz advises: "Due to CBS Radio's intensive election night coverage, Mr. Keen will not be heard tomorrow night. Be sure to listen Wednesday at this same time for Mr. Keen in the next episode of 'The Case of Murder and the Woman Who Wouldn't Grow Old.'" As a result, while the broadcast originally scheduled for Tuesday night never aired, the continuity sequence continued as if it had been. The next script to be aired was #96, just as if there had been a performance of #95.

CONTINUITY #96 [1615]
Wednesday, November 3, 1954
10:00–10:15 p.m. EST
CBS
Edward Slattery, Director
Lawrence M. Klee, Writer
Richard Leonard, Editor
Stuart Metz, Announcer
Sustaining
"The Case of Murder and the Woman Who Wouldn't Grow Old"
   Keen informs the victim's nephew, Richard Lang, that because he wasn't present when she died, poison could point to him as the killer. Paul Eldridge tells wife Isabel that Keen suspects them.

CONTINUITY #97 [1616]
Thursday, November 4, 1954
10:00–10:15 p.m. EST
CBS
Edward Slattery, Director
Lawrence M. Klee, Writer
Richard Leonard, Editor
Stuart Metz, Announcer
Sustaining
"The Case of Murder and the Woman Who Wouldn't Grow Old"
   Mrs. Wharton's manicurist, Lucy Betts, runs away but is caught. Keen threatens to arrest her if she attempts to flee again. Isabel Eldridge bickers with Lucy, trying to cast further suspicion on her.

CONTINUITY #98 [1617]
Friday, November 5, 1954
10:00–10:15 p.m. EST
CBS
Edward Slattery, Director
Lawrence M. Klee, Writer
Richard Leonard, Editor
George Bryan, Announcer
Sustaining
"The Case of Murder and the Woman Who Wouldn't Grow Old"
   Isabel Eldridge was driven to murder because she imagined she couldn't hold spouse Paul any longer; Anita Wharton, she thought, was winning him away from her. Paul is surprised.

CONTINUITY #99 [1618]
Monday, November 8, 1954
10:00–10:15 p.m. EST
CBS
Edward Slattery, Director
Lawrence M. Klee, Writer
Richard Leonard, Editor
Stuart Metz, Announcer
Sustaining
"The Case of Murder and the House of Fear"
   Infirm Victor Hayes is murdered. Granddaughter Loretta casts suspicion on housekeeper-cook-companion-helper Julia Cotter, whom she claims didn't want grandpa's health to improve.

CONTINUITY #100 [1619]
Tuesday, November 9, 1954
10:00–10:15 p.m. EST
CBS
Edward Slattery, Director
Lawrence M. Klee, Writer
Richard Leonard, Editor
Stuart Metz, Announcer
Sustaining
"The Case of Murder and the House of Fear"
   Loretta Hayes leads Keen outside, where they find a message on the wall written in green chalk: "Anyone who remains in this house of fear will join the soldiers in their graves."

CONTINUITY #101 [1620]
Wednesday, November 10, 1954
10:00–10:15 p.m. EST
CBS
Edward Slattery, Director
Lawrence M. Klee, Writer
Richard Leonard, Editor

Stuart Metz, Announcer
Sustaining
"The Case of Murder and the House of Fear"

Keen and Clancy are spending the night in the murder house. In the very bed they occupy, a Revolutionary War army officer had been strangled to death. Julia refers to the mansion as a house of horror.

CONTINUITY #102 [1621]
Thursday, November 11, 1954
10:00–10:15 p.m. EST
CBS
Edward Slattery, Director
Lawrence M. Klee, Writer
Richard Leonard, Editor
Stuart Metz, Announcer
Sustaining
"The Case of Murder and the House of Fear"

During that awful night, Mr. Keen observes, "Mike, someone's trying to trap us with a deadly gas! John Burnley's murderer wants to add us to the list!"

CONTINUITY #103 [1622]
Friday, November 12, 1954
10:00–10:15 p.m. EST
CBS
Edward Slattery, Director
Lawrence M. Klee, Writer
Richard Leonard, Editor
George Bryan, Announcer
Sustaining
"The Case of Murder and the House of Fear"

Vic Hayes admits: "Yes, I killed John Burnley! I thought he would die months ago, but he recovered! The old fool was going to live to a ripe old age — I had to finish him off!"

CONTINUITY #104 [1623]
Monday, November 15, 1954
10:00–10:15 p.m. EST
CBS
Edward Slattery, Director
Lawrence M. Klee, Writer
Richard Leonard, Editor
Stuart Metz, Announcer
Sustaining
"The Case of Murder and the Poisoned Tongue"

Rumormonger Vivian Bassett is stabbed to death. She spread lies about people. Barbara Frawley, whose marriage the dead woman's tales ended, happily observes that someone finally put an end to her malicious gossip.

CONTINUITY #105 [1624]
Tuesday, November 16, 1954
10:00–10:15 p.m. EST
CBS
Edward Slattery, Director
Lawrence M. Klee, Writer
Richard Leonard, Editor
Stuart Metz, Announcer
Sustaining
"The Case of Murder and the Poisoned Tongue"

Cynthia Frawley maintains that Barbara, her sister-in-law, possesses a poisoned tongue, too. Barbara has claimed that Cynthia plotted against her life. Cynthia defends herself.

CONTINUITY #106 [1625]
Wednesday, November 17, 1954
10:00–10:15 p.m. EST
CBS
Edward Slattery, Director
Lawrence M. Klee, Writer
Richard Leonard, Editor
Stuart Metz, Announcer
Sustaining
"The Case of Murder and the Poisoned Tongue"

Mike Clancy finds a telegram that Barbara tried to conceal. Mr. Keen thinks it's "very interesting." Cynthia Frawley telephones Mr. Keen — she's in danger, and a shot rings out.

CONTINUITY #107 [1626]
Thursday, November 18, 1954
10:00–10:15 p.m. EST
CBS
Edward Slattery, Director
Lawrence M. Klee, Writer
Richard Leonard, Editor
Stuart Metz, Announcer
Sustaining
"The Case of Murder and the Poisoned Tongue"

Ernest Frawley challenges George Addison to a fistfight after finding him making love to Barbara Frawley in a car. Mr. Keen assures him that a fight would not help either man.

CONTINUITY #108 [1627]
Friday, November 19, 1954
10:00–10:15 p.m. EST
CBS
Edward Slattery, Director
Lawrence M. Klee, Writer
Richard Leonard, Editor
George Bryan, Announcer
Sustaining
"The Case of Murder and the Poisoned Tongue"
Keen says: "You were the woman with the poisoned tongue, Cynthia! To break up your brother's marriage you put Vivian up to spreading rumors. But she found out they were lies."

CONTINUITY #109 [1628]
Monday, November 22, 1954
10:00–10:15 p.m. EST
CBS
Edward Slattery, Director
Lawrence M. Klee, Writer
Richard Leonard, Editor
Stuart Metz, Announcer
Sustaining
"The Wishing Well Murder Case"
Wealthy mining executive and prominent socialite Steven Wade is murdered. Joan Spencer begs Mr. Keen to help. Wade broke her engagement to stepson Howard, and she fears being accused.

CONTINUITY #110 [1629]
Tuesday, November 23, 1954
10:00–10:15 p.m. EST
CBS
Edward Slattery, Director
Lawrence M. Klee, Writer
Richard Leonard, Editor
Stuart Metz, Announcer
Sustaining
"The Wishing Well Murder Case"
Joan Spencer attempts to conceal something from Mr. Keen inside the home of the murdered Steven Wade. Will the clues point to Alice Spencer, daughter Joan or perhaps Howard Wade?

CONTINUITY #111 [1630]
Wednesday, November 24, 1954
10:00–10:15 p.m. EST
CBS
Edward Slattery, Director
Lawrence M. Klee, Writer
Richard Leonard, Editor
Stuart Metz, Announcer
Sustaining
"The Wishing Well Murder Case"
What is the clue that Mr. Keen has discovered? And what will the reenactment of the murder reveal? Howard Wade is now asking himself why Keen chose *him* for such a dramatic reenactment.

CONTINUITY #112 [1631]
Thursday, November 25, 1954
10:00–10:15 p.m. EST
CBS
Edward Slattery, Director
Lawrence M. Klee, Writer
Richard Leonard, Editor
Stuart Metz, Announcer
Sustaining
"The Wishing Well Murder Case"
Mr. Keen observes that, for the second time, Howard Wade has been able to "prove" who murdered his stepfather. Wade just accused Joan Spencer of "repeating the act with me!"

CONTINUITY #113 [1632]
Friday, November 26, 1954
10:00–10:15 p.m. EST
CBS
Edward Slattery, Director
Lawrence M. Klee, Writer
Richard Leonard, Editor
George Bryan, Announcer
Sustaining
"The Wishing Well Murder Case"
Keen confirms that Alice Spencer hadn't a penny but lived well: "When you met wealthy people you used your acquaintanceship as a means of charging expensive items to them."

There was no episode aired on Monday, November 29, 1954.

CONTINUITY #114 [1633]
Tuesday, November 30, 1954
10:00–10:15 p.m. EST
CBS
Edward Slattery, Director
Lawrence M. Klee, Writer

Richard Leonard, Editor
Stuart Metz, Announcer
Sustaining
"The Case of Murder and the Black Pearl Necklace"

The elder Herbert Page is murdered at home, and a black pearl necklace goes missing. Keen wonders if someone inside the family is guilty. The widow Diana claims her husband's niece is that individual.

CONTINUITY #115 [1634]
Wednesday, December 1, 1954
10:00–10:15 p.m. EST
CBS
Edward Slattery, Director
Lawrence M. Klee, Writer
Richard Leonard, Editor
Stuart Metz, Announcer
Sustaining
"The Case of Murder and the Black Pearl Necklace"

Alfred Browning once offered to buy the black pearl necklace from Herbert Page, to help him out financially. He also hoped to take Herbert's wife Diana from the murdered man.

CONTINUITY #116 [1635]
Thursday, December 2, 1954
10:00–10:15 p.m. EST
CBS
Edward Slattery, Director
Lawrence M. Klee, Writer
Richard Leonard, Editor
Stuart Metz, Announcer
Sustaining
"The Case of Murder and the Black Pearl Necklace"

Herbert tells Diana: "Your father is a habitual criminal. Your mother died of a broken heart because of his escapades. And now he's trying to drive you and me into our graves!"

CONTINUITY #117 [1636]
Friday, December 3, 1954
10:00–10:15 p.m. EST
CBS
Edward Slattery, Director
Lawrence M. Klee, Writer
Richard Leonard, Editor
George Bryan, Announcer
Sustaining
"The Case of Murder and the Black Pearl Necklace"

When Diana produces the missing black pearl necklace from her jewel box, Keen examines it closely. He tells her the necklace is an imitation, made of simulated black pearls.

CONTINUITY #118 [1637]
Monday, December 6, 1954
10:00–10:15 p.m. EST
CBS
Edward Slattery, Director
Lawrence M. Klee, Writer
Richard Leonard, Editor
Stuart Metz, Announcer
Sustaining
"The Case of Murder and the Black Pearl Necklace"

Alfred Browning admits he murdered Herbert Page. The black pearl necklace was worth a fortune, and he couldn't resist. Page caught him just after he took it from his wall safe.

At the conclusion of this episode the announcer advises: "Mr. Keen *will not be heard during the rest of this week. But be sure to listen to Mr. Keen next Monday at this same time when the kindly old tracer turns to 'The Case of Murder and the Face in the Fog.'"*

CONTINUITY #119 [1638]
Monday, December 13, 1954
10:00–10:15 p.m. EST
CBS
Edward Slattery, Director
Lawrence M. Klee, Writer
Richard Leonard, Editor
Stuart Metz, Announcer
Sustaining
"The Case of Murder and the Face in the Fog"

Alicia Farrow, on the verge of hysterics, appeals to Keen to solve the murder of Don Preston, co-owner of the Star Dramatic School. She's a pupil. He was shot to death on the street.

CONTINUITY #120 [1639]
Tuesday, December 14, 1954
10:00–10:15 p.m. EST
CBS
Edward Slattery, Director
Lawrence M. Klee, Writer

Richard Leonard, Editor
Stuart Metz, Announcer
Sustaining
"The Case of Murder and the Face in the Fog"
What will Mr. Keen find inside Gloria Farrow's makeup box? As he follows her into the dressing room, he takes note of her nervousness and wonders what she is hiding.

CONTINUITY #121 [1640]
Wednesday, December 15, 1954
10:00–10:15 p.m. EST
CBS
Edward Slattery, Director
Lawrence M. Klee, Writer
Richard Leonard, Editor
Stuart Metz, Announcer
Sustaining
"The Case of Murder and the Face in the Fog"
Keen tells Steve Gates he'll arrest him if he objects to having his pockets searched. "You're not putting me under arrest," Gates responds. "If you try it, I'll beat you within an inch of your life!"

CONTINUITY #122 [1641]
Thursday, December 16, 1954
10:00–10:15 p.m. EST
CBS
Edward Slattery, Director
Lawrence M. Klee, Writer
Richard Leonard, Editor
Stuart Metz, Announcer
Sustaining
"The Case of Murder and the Face in the Fog"
Henry Burgess discovers Alicia Farrow lying unconscious on the floor, having been struck by a heavy object. He summons Mr. Keen and Mike Clancy, who immediately call for a doctor.

CONTINUITY #123 [1642]
Friday, December 17, 1954
10:00–10:15 p.m. EST
CBS
Edward Slattery, Director
Lawrence M. Klee, Writer
Richard Leonard, Editor
George Bryan, Announcer
Sustaining
"The Case of Murder and the Face in the Fog"
Burgess planted bullets from the murder gun in Gloria's makeup box. He ran the school as a front for drug peddling. Preston threatened to expose him for it, so he killed him.

CONTINUITY #124 [1643]
Monday, December 20, 1954
10:00–10:15 p.m. EST
CBS
Edward Slattery, Director
Lawrence M. Klee, Writer
Richard Leonard, Editor
Stuart Metz, Announcer
Sustaining
"The Case of Murder and the Queen of Fashion"
Someone slashes the dresses of couturier Joyce Endicott and murdered her at her fashionable dress shop. Yvonne DeChamp, another designer, is sure Endicott was stealing her designs.

CONTINUITY #125 [1644]
Tuesday, December 21, 1954
10:00–10:15 p.m. EST
CBS
Edward Slattery, Director
Lawrence M. Klee, Writer
Richard Leonard, Editor
Stuart Metz, Announcer
Sustaining
"The Case of Murder and the Queen of Fashion"
Fred Baxter is with Yvonne DeChamp when Mr. Keen phones her. She tells him she has been threatened. "Someone is here who [*choking*]— no! Stop choking me! Help me, Mr. Keen!"

CONTINUITY #126 [1645]
Wednesday, December 22, 1954
10:00–10:15 p.m. EST
CBS
Edward Slattery, Director
Lawrence M. Klee, Writer
Richard Leonard, Editor
Stuart Metz, Announcer
Sustaining
"The Case of Murder and the Queen of Fashion"
Baxter tells Keen he's an honest businessman, not a racketeer. Joyce and he were in love but broke it off, deciding they had nothing in common. But he continued selling her textiles.

CONTINUITY #127 [1646]
Thursday, December 23, 1954
10:00–10:15 p.m. EST
CBS
Edward Slattery, Director
Lawrence M. Klee, Writer
Richard Leonard, Editor
Stuart Metz, Announcer
Sustaining
"The Case of Murder and the Queen of Fashion"

Emma Parsons is arrested for the murder after Keen learns she worked part time for Yvonne DeChamp. Emma stole Yvonne's designs and gave them to Joyce, saying they were her own.

Though the broadcast intended for Friday, December 24, was preempted, no break in continuity occurred.

CONTINUITY #128 [1647]
Monday, December 27, 1954
10:00–10:15 p.m. EST
CBS
Edward Slattery, Director
Lawrence M. Klee, Writer
Richard Leonard, Editor
Stuart Metz, Announcer
Sustaining
"The Case of Murder and the Woman Who Hid from the World"

Grace Larson hid from the world. In six months she never left her rented Regis Park home. In Philadelphia she had wed William Sage, then learned he was a bigamist. She has been murdered.

CONTINUITY #129 [1648]
Tuesday, December 28, 1954
10:00–10:15 p.m. EST
CBS
Edward Slattery, Director
Lawrence M. Klee, Writer
Richard Leonard, Editor
Stuart Metz, Announcer
Sustaining
"The Case of Murder and the Woman Who Hid from the World"

Sage is accused of murdering Grace. He protests: "I'm not a bigamist. I was never married before I married Grace." He says he was engaged to Helen Rand, but left her for Grace.

CONTINUITY #130 [1649]
Wednesday, December 29, 1954
10:00–10:15 p.m. EST
CBS
Edward Slattery, Director
Lawrence M. Klee, Writer
Richard Leonard, Editor
Stuart Metz, Announcer
Sustaining
"The Case of Murder and the Woman Who Hid from the World"

Sage menaces Keen: "Do you know what will happen if I push you out this window head first? Before you arrest me for bigamy I'll see you dead. You're going out of this window now!"

CONTINUITY #131 [1650]
Thursday, December 30, 1954
10:00–10:15 p.m. EST
CBS
Edward Slattery, Director
Lawrence M. Klee, Writer
Richard Leonard, Editor
Stuart Metz, Announcer
Sustaining
"The Case of Murder and the Woman Who Hid from the World"

The house apparently holds hidden money. John Durham claims that an agent offered $1,000 rent monthly on behalf of a client, and accuses Eloise. Mr. Keen points out that his refusal means that Durham hoped to find the loot.

CONTINUITY #132 [1651]
Friday, December 31, 1954
10:00–10:15 p.m. EST
CBS
Edward Slattery, Director
Lawrence M. Klee, Writer
Richard Leonard, Editor
George Bryan, Announcer
Sustaining
"The Case of Murder and the Woman Who Hid from the World"

Helen Rand is named as the killer. She told Grace Larson she was penniless and begged for money. Grace gave her money, and this convinced Helen that a hoard of cash was hidden in the house.

CONTINUITY #133–142 [1652–1661]
Monday, January 3, 1955–January 14, 1955
10:00–10:15 p.m. EST
CBS
Sustaining

No scripts have survived in the permanent file for the final fortnight of the serialized episodic run. Published reports document that the weeknight series continued through January 14, 1955, then left the air. While the title of the final case in the sequence is unknown, the next-to-last case for the week of January 3–7, 1955, is "The Scorpion Murder Case."

CONTINUITY #560 [1662]
Tuesday, February 22, 1955
8:30–9:00 p.m. EST
CBS
Richard Leonard, Director
Lawrence M. Klee, Writer
Richard Leonard, Editor
Harry Kramer, Announcer
Sustaining
"The Case of Murder and the Revengeful Ghost" (*Extant Episode*)

Widower Ivor Stacy, about to marry for the second time, is murdered. First wife Theresa swore before her death that if he remarried she would return from the grave for revenge.

Actors in this episode include Ivor Francis, Cathleen Cordell, James Meighan, Ronald Long and Helen Claire.

CONTINUITY #561 [1663]
Tuesday, March 1, 1955
8:30–9:00 p.m. EST
CBS
Richard Leonard, Director
Lawrence M. Klee, Writer
Richard Leonard, Editor
Harry Kramer, Announcer
Sustaining
"The Case of Murder and the Omen of Death"

Wealthy Anita Hayden feared she would be murdered after she saw a black hearse in front of her home several times. Mr. Keen finds her body inside a hearse parked in her garage.

Actors in this episode include Florence Freeman, Frank Thomas Jr., Charles Penman, Sarah Burton and Charita Bauer.

CONTINUITY #562 [1664]
Tuesday, March 8, 1955
8:30–9:00 p.m. EST
CBS
Richard Leonard, Director
Lawrence M. Klee, Writer
Richard Leonard, Editor
Harry Kramer, Announcer
Sustaining
"The Case of Murder and the Man Without a Conscience"

Philip Meeker, known as "the man without a conscience" due to ruthless business practices, is murdered. Suspect Franz Bulow answers Mr. Keen's queries with a volley of bullets.

Actors in this episode include John Stanley, Wendy Drew, Richard Janaver, Irene Hubbard and Peter Capell.

CONTINUITY #563 [1665]
Tuesday, March 15, 1955
8:30–9:00 p.m. EST
CBS
Richard Leonard, Director
Lawrence M. Klee, Writer
Richard Leonard, Editor
Harry Kramer, Announcer
Sustaining
"The Case of Murder and the Finger of Guilt"

Evelyn Mason, an attractive young woman, is shot to death in the home of wealthy Frank Chandler. Chandler's wife Dolores and foster brother Bruce Chandler are having an affair.

Actors in this episode include Ann Seymour, Arline Blackburn, Ned Wever, Andree Wallace and David Gothard.

CONTINUITY #564 [1666]
Tuesday, March 22, 1955
8:30–9:00 p.m. EST
CBS
Richard Leonard, Director
Lawrence M. Klee, Writer
Richard Leonard, Editor
Harry Kramer, Announcer
Sustaining
"The Full Moon Murder Case"

Landlady Edna Stockton is stabbed to death after discovering someone trying to set fire to her rooming house. The police seek a firebug who works during the time of the full moon.

CONTINUITY #565 [1667]
Tuesday, March 29, 1955
8:30–9:00 p.m. EST
CBS
Richard Leonard, Director
Lawrence M. Klee, Writer
Richard Leonard, Editor
Harry Kramer, Announcer
Sustaining
"The Case of Murder and the Woman with the Iron Will"
   Cornelia Hodge, "the woman with the iron will" who dominates the members of her household, is murdered. Keen and Clancy narrowly escape death when a boulder rolls toward them.

CONTINUITY #566 [1668]
Tuesday, April 5, 1955
8:30–9:00 p.m. EST
CBS
Richard Leonard, Director
Lawrence M. Klee, Writer
Richard Leonard, Editor
Harry Kramer, Announcer
Sustaining
"The Case of Murder and the Evil Eye"
   Night watchman John Wood is shot to death at a jewelry firm when a fabulous emerald known as the Evil Eye is heisted. An international jewel thief, William Roane, is in hiding.

CONTINUITY #567 [1669]
Tuesday, April 12, 1955
8:30–9:00 p.m. EST
CBS
Richard Leonard, Director
Lawrence M. Klee, Writer
Richard Leonard, Editor
Harry Kramer, Announcer
Sustaining
"The Case of Murder and the House of Horror"
   Edith Taylor is found beaten to death on a lonely road. Her roommate tells Mr. Keen that the victim was terrified of a nearby House of Horror, once owned by her late father.

CONTINUITY #568 [1670]
Tuesday, April 19, 1955
8:30–9:00 p.m. EST
CBS
Richard Leonard, Director
Lawrence M. Klee, Writer
Richard Leonard, Editor
Harry Kramer, Announcer
Sustaining
"The Case of Murder and the Woman Scorned"
   English nobleman Lord Edward Farnley is shot in his Gotham townhouse. Evelyn Worthing and daughter Betty, rivals for his affections, both quarreled with him and also threatened him.

CONTINUITY #569 [1671]
Monday, April 25, 1955
8:00–8:25 p.m. EDST
CBS
Richard Leonard, Director
Lawrence M. Klee, Writer
Richard Leonard, Editor
Harry Kramer, Announcer
Sustaining
"The Money Box Murder Case"
   Mr. Keen and Mike Clancy investigate the murder of Walter Stanfield, a miserly eccentric known to keep a fortune in cash in a money box hidden somewhere on his suburban estate.
   Douglas Edwards with the News *now airs in the five minutes immediately following* Mr. Keen, Tracer of Lost Persons. *Later, Charles Collingwood replaced Edwards.*

CONTINUITY #570 [1672]
Monday, May 2, 1955
8:00–8:25 p.m. EDST
CBS
Richard Leonard, Director
Lawrence M. Klee, Writer
Richard Leonard, Editor
Harry Kramer, Announcer
Sustaining
"The Cover Girl Murder Case"
   Beautiful young magazine cover girl Lois Dixon is stabbed to death in her apartment. Edgar Adams, who fell violently in love with her and was driven to theft, is a leading suspect.

CONTINUITY #571 [1673]
Monday, May 9, 1955
8:00–8:25 p.m. EDST
CBS
Richard Leonard, Director
Lawrence M. Klee, Writer

Richard Leonard, Editor
Harry Kramer, Announcer
Sustaining
"The Case of Murder and the Final Warning"

Assistant district attorney Rod Bolton is murdered after receiving two warning notes. He had planned to elope with Lucy Cromwell — over the objections of her father.

CONTINUITY #572 [1674]
Monday, May 16, 1955
8:00–8:25 p.m. EDST
CBS
Richard Leonard, Director
Lawrence M. Klee, Writer
Richard Leonard, Editor
Harry Kramer, Announcer
Sustaining
"The Case of Murder and the Man Who Talked Too Much"

Inventor John Kelvin's boasting about the success of his inventions apparently led to his being beaten to death. Later his niece, Catherine Barrett, is also killed.

CONTINUITY #573 [1675]
Monday, May 23, 1955
8:00–8:25 p.m. EDST
CBS
Richard Leonard, Director
Lawrence M. Klee, Writer
Richard Leonard, Editor
Announcer's name omitted
Sustaining
"The Case of Murder and the Unwanted Wife"

The sleuths probe Helen Spencer's murder, Lawrence Spencer's first wife. He remarried seven years after she vanished, and neither he nor second wife Elizabeth wanted her to reappear.

CONTINUITY #574 [1676]
Monday, May 30, 1955
8:00–8:25 p.m. EDST
CBS
Richard Leonard, Director
Lawrence M. Klee, Writer
Richard Leonard, Editor
Harry Kramer, Announcer
Sustaining
"The Case of Murder and the Captive Bride"

James Foster is shot to death at his estate near New York City. He imprisoned his young sister, Laura Rowe, in her room to separate her from her newly married husband, Arnold.

CONTINUITY #575 [1677]
Monday, June 6, 1955
8:00–8:25 p.m. EDST
CBS
Richard Leonard, Director
Lawrence M. Klee, Writer
Richard Leonard, Editor
Harry Kramer, Announcer
Sustaining
"The Case of Murder and the Crystal Ball"

Fortuneteller Boris Sardar claims he can see the future and read the past by way of a crystal ball. But he won't be doing that any more, as he's met his own demise.

CONTINUITY #576 [1678]
Monday, June 13, 1955
8:00–8:25 p.m. EDST
CBS
Richard Leonard, Director
Lawrence M. Klee, Writer
Richard Leonard, Editor
Harry Kramer, Announcer
Sustaining
"The Case of Murder and the Woman Who Worshipped Gold"

Due to her intense love of gold jewelry, the late Constance Bentley was called "the woman who worshipped gold." She ended one engagement and married another man, then divorced; consequently, she was unpopular with *two* men.

CONTINUITY #577 [1679]
Monday, June 20, 1955
8:00–8:25 p.m. EDST
CBS
Richard Leonard, Director
Lawrence M. Klee, Writer
Richard Leonard, Editor
Harry Kramer, Announcer
Sustaining
"The Case of Murder and the Fatal Bargain"

The late Bruce Evans made a death pact with his two business partners, John Cobb and Charles Drake. Each took $100,000 out in life insurance, naming the others as beneficiaries.

CONTINUITY #578 [1680]
Monday, June 27, 1955
8:00–8:25 p.m. EDST
CBS
Richard Leonard, Director
Lawrence M. Klee, Writer
Richard Leonard, Editor
Harry Kramer, Announcer
Sustaining
"The Case of Murder and the Grinning Skull"
    Fredric Palmer is stabbed to death after receiving a small grinning skull carved from ivory as a portent. Soon Mr. Keen himself receives a similar grinning skull.

CONTINUITY #579 [1681]
Monday, July 4, 1955
8:00–8:25 p.m. EDST
CBS
Richard Leonard, Director
Lawrence M. Klee, Writer
Richard Leonard, Editor
Harry Kramer, Announcer
Sustaining
"The Case of Murder and the Deadly Rivals"
    Barbara Wade is shot to death on a lonely street. Two rivals for her hand, Karl Thayer and William Graves, are suspected, for one may have been a disappointed suitor.

CONTINUITY #580 [1682]
Monday, July 11, 1955
8:00–8:25 p.m. EDST
CBS
Richard Leonard, Director
Lawrence M. Klee, Writer
Richard Leonard, Editor
Harry Kramer, Announcer
Sustaining
"The Case of Murder and the Guilty Secret"
    Hairdresser Edna Gale made some violent enemies, due to the fact she uncovered some guilty secrets they were hiding. Was one of them so unnerved that he or she took Gale's life?

CONTINUITY #581 [1683]
Monday, July 18, 1955
8:00–8:25 p.m. EDST
CBS
Edward Slattery, Director
Lawrence M. Klee, Writer
Richard Leonard, Editor
Harry Kramer, Announcer
Sustaining
"The Case of Murder and the Extravagant Wife"
    Paul Ogden is poisoned to death in his large suburban home. Mr. Keen finds evidence that Anita Ogden, the victim's wife, and his friend Howard Reeves had strong motives for murder.

CONTINUITY #582 [1684]
Monday, July 25, 1955
8:00–8:25 p.m. EDST
CBS
Edward Slattery, Director
Lawrence M. Klee, Writer
Richard Leonard, Editor
Harry Kramer, Announcer
Sustaining
"The Case of Murder and the Jeweled Crown"
    Rare jewel collector and dealer Mark Sheldon is murdered, and an ornate jeweled crown taken. Keen and Clancy are held at gunpoint by Jerry Bates, a gambler involved with the victim.

CONTINUITY #583 [1685]
Monday, August 1, 1955
8:00–8:25 p.m. EDST
CBS
Richard Leonard, Director
Lawrence M. Klee, Writer
Richard Leonard, Editor
Harry Kramer, Announcer
Sustaining
"The Case of Murder and the Rich Reward"
    Steven Tyler is shot just before exposing a swindler wanted by the police, and for whom a reward of $15,000 was offered. Could his father-in-law, Henry Burr, be the swindler-killer?

CONTINUITY #584 [1686]
Monday, August 8, 1955
8:00–8:25 p.m. EDST
CBS
Richard Leonard, Director
Lawrence M. Klee, Writer
Richard Leonard, Editor
Harry Kramer, Announcer
Sustaining
"The Case of Murder and the Yellow Horror"

Stage star Victoria Talbot is stabbed to death at a beach home owned by her niece's husband, Peter Howe. A terrifying "yellow horror" figure was seen at the time of her murder.

CONTINUITY #585 [1687]
Monday, August 15, 1955
8:00–8:25 p.m. EDST
CBS
Richard Leonard, Director
Lawrence M. Klee, Writer
Richard Leonard, Editor
Harry Kramer, Announcer
Sustaining
"The Case of the Secret Murder"
Mr. Keen and Mike Clancy find an entry in Jeffrey Barker's diary that seems to hint that his mother Helen murdered his father Kenneth. They confront her with their suspicions.
With some slight variation of names, but using the same title, this episode is a repeat of the story broadcast on March 11, 1948.

CONTINUITY #586 [1688]
Monday, August 22, 1955
8:00–8:25 p.m. EDST
CBS
Richard Leonard, Director
Lawrence M. Klee, Writer
Richard Leonard, Editor
Harry Kramer, Announcer
Sustaining
"The Case of Murder and the Broken Mirror"
The protesting, terrified voice of Stephen Crawford, coupled with the sound of two shots, on his office Dictaphone machine convince the tracer that the man is probably a victim of foul play.
This episode, under a slightly modified title, is reprised from the broadcast of April 15, 1948.

CONTINUITY #587 [1689]
Monday, August 29, 1955
8:00–8:25 p.m. EDST
CBS
Richard Leonard, Director
Lawrence M. Klee, Writer
Richard Leonard, Editor
Bob Hall, Announcer
Sustaining
"The Marked Man Murder Case"

An exchange overheard by Keen and Clancy hints that either James Marshall or son Carl may be the culprit in the murder of Robert Selby, stabbed to death days after his marriage.

CONTINUITY #588 [1690]
Monday, September 5, 1955
8:00–8:25 p.m. EDST
CBS
Richard Leonard, Director
Lawrence M. Klee, Writer
Richard Leonard, Editor
Harry Kramer, Announcer
Sustaining
"The Case of Murder and the Accusing Eyes"
In Laura Tate's home, where she was shot to death, Keen and Clancy examine an oil painting hanging on the wall. Spouse Paul claims the portrait has accusing eyes that follow him.

CONTINUITY #589 [1691]
Monday, September 12, 1955
8:00–8:25 p.m. EDST
CBS
Richard Leonard, Director
Lawrence M. Klee, Writer
Richard Leonard, Editor
Harry Kramer, Announcer
Sustaining
"The Case of Murder and the Man Who Made a Million"
Lois Blake will give the tracer of lost persons and his partner some vital information that could help them solve the murder of John Sawyer, the man she was once engaged to.

CONTINUITY #590 [1692]
Monday, September 19, 1955
8:00–8:25 p.m. EDST
CBS
Richard Leonard, Director
Lawrence M. Klee, Writer
Richard Leonard, Editor
Harry Kramer, Announcer
Sustaining
"The Case of Murder and the Poisoned Mind"
On the trail of Eloise Fuller's murderer, Mr. Keen and Mike Clancy go to the apartment of Helen Gage, a suspect thought to have been in love with the victim's husband, Charles.

CONTINUITY #591 [1693]
Monday, September 26, 1955
8:00–8:25 p.m. EDST
CBS
Richard Leonard, Director
Lawrence M. Klee, Writer
Richard Leonard, Editor
Harry Kramer, Announcer
Sustaining
"The Case of Murder and the Broken Promise"

A bullet is fired at Arthur Lambert as he accuses Nina Dixon or son Frank of murdering George Rockwell. Clancy is dispatched to fetch Frank, who fired the shot.

At the conclusion of this sequence the narrator states: "Mr. Keen, Tracer of Lost Persons *is based on the novel* Mr. Keen. *The radio sequel is originated and produced by Frank and Anne Hummert. Dialogue by Lawrence Klee, directed by Richard Leonard. Philip Clarke plays Mr. Keen. This concludes our present Mr. Keen series. Your announcer is Harry Kramer." This was the final broadcast of the series.*

Notes

Chapter 1

1. MacDonald, J. Fred. *Don't Touch That Dial!: Radio Programming in American Life from 1920 to 1960.* Chicago: Nelson-Hall, 1991, p. 158.
2. *Ibid.*
3. *Ibid.*, p. 193.
4. Personal communication with the author, May 6, 2002. Used by permission.
5. Sterling, Christopher H., and John M. Kittross. *Stay Tuned: A Concise History of American Broadcasting.* Second Edition. Belmont, Calif.: Wadsworth, 1990, p. 121.
6. *Ibid.*
7. Cox, Jim. *Radio Crime Fighters.* Jefferson, N.C.: McFarland, 2002, p. 229.
8. *Ibid.*
9. DeAndrea, William L. *Encyclopedia Mysteriosa: A Comprehensive Guide to the Art of Detection in Print, Film, Radio, and Television.* New York: Prentice Hall, 1994, p. ix.
10. Conquest, John. *Trouble Is Their Business: Private Eyes in Fiction, Film and Television, 1927–1988.* New York: Garland, 1990, p. x.
11. Private communication with the author, April 27, 2002. Used by permission.
12. Sterling and Kittross, p. 121.
13. Nachman, Gerald. *Raised on Radio: In Quest of The Lone Ranger, Jack Benny, Amos 'n' Andy, The Shadow, Mary Noble, The Great Gildersleeve, Fibber McGee and Molly, Bill Stern, Our Miss Brooks, Henry Aldrich, The Quiz Kids, Mr. First Nighter, Fred Allen, Vic and Sade, The Cisco Kid, Jack Armstrong, Arthur Godfrey, Bob and Ray, The Barbour Family, Henry Morgan, Joe Friday and Other Lost Heroes from Radio's Heyday.* New York: Pantheon Books, 1998, p. 308.
14. Dunning, John. *On the Air: The Encyclopedia of Old-Time Radio.* New York: Oxford University Press, 1998, p. 607.
15. Nachman, p. 298.
16. Dunning, p. 14.
17. Cox, Jim. *Radio Crime Fighters.*
18. Cox, Jim. *Say Goodnight Gracie: The Last Years of Network Radio.* Jefferson, N.C.: McFarland, 2002, p. 40.
19. *Ibid.*
20. MacDonald, p. 156.
21. Wolfe, Charles Hull. *Modern Radio Advertising.* New York: Printers' Ink, 1949, pp. 284–296.
22. Crossen, Ken. "There's Murder in the Air." *The Art of the Mystery Story.* New York: Carroll and Graf, 1992.
23. MacDonald, pp. 158–159.
24. Haycraft, Howard, editor. *The Art of the Mystery Story.* New York: Carroll and Graf, 1992, pp. 7, 14.
25. Adapted from Geherin, David. *The American Private Eye: The Image in Fiction.* New York: Ungar, 1985.
26. Conquest, p. xiii.
27. MacDonald, p. 157.
28. *Ibid.*, p. 42.
29. *Ibid.*, p. 160.
30. *Ibid.*, p. 163.

31. *Ibid.*, p. 172.
32. *Ibid.*, p. 193.
33. *Ibid.*, p. 183.

Chapter 2

1. Lackmann, Ron. *Remember Radio.* New York: G. Putnam's Sons, 1970, p. 13.
2. MegaWeb Internet site, reference to *The King in Yellow* by Robert W. Chambers, December 24, 2001: http://search.megaweb.com/web/o.html$2098239304?the+king+in+yellow+by+robert+w.+chambers.
3. A biography of R. W. Chambers appearing on the Miskatonic University web site, December 24, 2001: http://www.miskatonic.net.
4. Chambers, Robert W. *The Tracer of Lost Persons.* New York: D. Appleton, 1906, p. 18.
5. *Ibid.*, p. 119.
6. *Ibid.*, p. 142.
7. *Ibid.*, p. 76.
8. *Ibid.*, pp. 80–81.
9. *Ibid.*, p. 82.
10. *Ibid.*, p. 15.
11. Andrews, Robert Hardy. *Legend of a Lady: The Story of Rita Martin.* New York: Coward-McCann, 1949.
12. Dunning, John. *Tune in Yesterday: The Ultimate Encyclopedia of Old-Time Radio, 1925–1976.* Englewood Cliffs, N.J.: Prentice-Hall, 1976, p. 419.
13. *Ibid.*, p. 422.
14. Ash-Tree Press web site book review for *Out of the Dark, Volume 2: Diversions,* collected December 24, 2001: http://www.ash-tree.bc.ca/ashtreecurrent.html.
15. *Ibid.*
16. *Ibid.*
17. Chaosium Publications web site home page, February 4, 2002: http://www.geocities.com/Area51/Corridor/5582/chambers.html.
18. Brooks, Tim, and Earle Marsh. *The Complete Directory to Prime Time Network TV Shows, 1946–Present.* New York: Ballantine Books, 1988, p. 263.
19. McNeil, Alex. *Total Television: The Comprehensive Guide to Programming from 1948 to the Present.* Fourth Edition. New York: Penguin Books, 1996, p. 285.

Chapter 3

1. Radio script for October 12, 1937.
2. Chambers, Robert W. *The Tracer of Lost Persons.* New York: D. Appleton, 1906.
3. Broadcast script of June 14, 1938.
4. Summers, Harrison B., editor. *History of Broadcasting — Radio to Television: A Thirty-Year History of Programs Carried on National Radio Networks in the United States, 1926–1956.* New York: Arno Press and The New York Times, 1971, pp. 126, 168.

Chapter 4

1. Abelson, Joan S. "Mother of the Soaps." Goucher (College) *Quarterly*, Vol. 63, No. 3, Spring 1985, p. 5.
2. Personal communications with the author, March 8 and March 30, 2003. Used by permission.

Chapter 5

1. Dunning, John. *Tune in Yesterday: The Ultimate Encyclopedia of Old-Time Radio, 1925–1976.* Englewood Cliffs, N.J.: Prentice-Hall, 1976, p. 422.
2. *Ibid.*, p. 419.
3. *Ibid.*, p. 423.
4. *Ibid.*
5. Personal communication from Neil Crowley to the author, December 31, 2001. Used by permission.

Chapter 6

1. Mott, Robert L. *Radio Sound Effects: Who Did It, and How, in the Era of Live Broadcasting.* Jefferson, N.C.: McFarland, 1993, p. 23.
2. Higby, Mary Jane. *Tune in Tomorrow: Or How I Found the Right to Happiness with Our Gal Sunday, Stella Dallas, John's Other Wife, and Other Sudsy Radio Serials.* New York: Cowles Education Corp., 1968, p. 181.
3. Ansbro, George. *I Have a Lady in the Balcony: Memoirs of a Broadcaster in Radio and*

Television. Jefferson, N.C.: McFarland, 2000, p. 189.

4. Higby, p. 181.

5. Obituary appearing in *The New York Times*, December 29, 1949, p. 46.

6. Ansbro, p. 109.

7. Material on Klee's financial arrangements is included in personal correspondence files in the Lawrence M. Klee Collection at the American Heritage Center, University of Wyoming.

8. Margaret Klee Lichtenberg's comments were communicated to the author on June 4, 2002, and are used by permission.

9. Paul Klee's comments were communicated to the author on June 11, 2002, and are used by permission.

10. Kilpack, Dorothy. "My Husband, Mr. Keen." *Radio and Television Mirror*, June 1949, p. 91.

11. *The New York Times*, March 26, 1925.

12. *Ibid.*, pp. 62–63, 91–93.

13. Some of this information is gleaned from Kilpack's obituary appearing in *The New York Times*, August 21, 1962, p. 33.

14. Much of the material on Arthur Hughes is adapted from *The Great Radio Soap Operas* by Jim Cox, published in Jefferson, N.C. by McFarland, 1999.

15. Patti Wever Knoll supplied the author with a videotape of a cable show filmed in Leisure World, California, in which Wever recalled this colossal tale of woe.

16. DeLong, Thomas A. *Radio Stars: An Illustrated Biographical Dictionary of 953 Performers, 1920–1960*. Jefferson, N.C.: McFarland, 1996, p. 88.

17. *Radio and Television Mirror*, July 1942, p. 62.

18. Mott, pp. 29–31.

Chapter 7

1. Most of this material is adapted from the *Encyclopedia of Consumer Brands*, Volume 2, Detroit: St. James Press, 1994, pp. 20–22. Other sources consulted: *Hoover's Handbook of American Business 2002*, Austin, Tex.: Hoover's Business Press, pp. 148–149; *Hoover's Masterlist of Major U.S. Companies 2002*, Austin, Tex.: Hoover's Business Press, p. 64; *International Directory of Company Histories*, Chicago: St. James Press, 1987, pp. 622–624; *Plunkett's Health Care Industry Almanac 1999–2000*, Dallas: Corporate Jobs Outlook, p. 272; and AHP's company website, *www.wyeth.com*.

Bibliography

Abelson, Joan S. "Mother of the Soaps." *Goucher (College) Quarterly*, vol. 63, no. 3, Spring 1985.

Andrews, Robert Hardy. *Legend of a Lady: The Story of Rita Martin*. New York: Coward-McCann, 1949.

Ansbro, George. *I Have a Lady in the Balcony: Memoirs of a Broadcaster in Radio and Television*. Jefferson, N.C.: McFarland, 2000.

Brooks, Tim, and Earle Marsh. *The Complete Directory to Prime Time Network TV Shows, 1946–Present*. New York: Ballantine Books, 1988.

Buxton, Frank, and Bill Owen. *The Big Broadcast, 1920–1950*. Lanham, Md.: Scarecrow Press, 1997.

Chambers, Robert W. *The Tracer of Lost Persons*. New York: D. Appleton, 1906.

Conquest, John. *Trouble Is Their Business: Private Eyes in Fiction, Film and Television, 1927–1988*. New York: Garland, 1990.

Cox, Jim. *Frank and Anne Hummert's Radio Factory: The Programs and Personalities of Broadcasting's Most Prolific Producers*. Jefferson, N.C.: McFarland, 2003.

_____. *The Great Radio Audience Participation Shows: Seventeen Programs from the 1940s and 1950s*. Jefferson, N.C.: McFarland, 2001.

_____. *The Great Radio Soap Operas*. Jefferson, N.C.: McFarland, 1999.

_____. *Radio Crime Fighters*. Jefferson, N.C.: McFarland, 2002.

_____. *Say Goodnight Gracie: The Last Years of Network Radio*. Jefferson, N.C.: McFarland, 2002.

Crossen, Ken. "There's Murder in the Air." *The Art of the Mystery Story*. New York: Carroll and Graf, 1992.

DeAndrea, William L. *Encyclopedia Mysteriosa: A Comprehensive Guide to the Art of Detection in Print, Film, Radio, and Television*. New York: Prentice Hall, 1994.

DeLong, Thomas A. *Radio Stars: An Illustrated Biographical Dictionary of 953 Performers, 1920–1960*. Jefferson, N.C.: McFarland, 1996.

Dunning, John. *On the Air: The Encyclopedia of Old-Time Radio*. New York: Oxford University Press, 1998.

_____. *Tune in Yesterday: The Ultimate Encyclopedia of Old-Time Radio, 1925–1976*. Englewood Cliffs, N.J.: Prentice-Hall, 1976.

Encyclopedia of Consumer Brands, Volume 2. Detroit: St. James Press, 1994.

Extant recordings of the *Mr. Keen, Tracer of Lost Persons* radio series.

Geherin, David. *The American Private Eye: The Image in Fiction*. New York: Ungar, 1985.

Haycraft, Howard, ed. *The Art of the Mystery Story*. New York: Carroll and Graf, 1992.

Hickerson, Jay. *The 2nd Revised Ultimate History of Network Radio Programming and Guide to ALL Circulating Shows*. Hamden, Conn.: Jay Hickerson, 2001.

Higby, Mary Jane. *Tune in Tomorrow: Or How I Found the Right to Happiness with Our Gal Sunday, Stella Dallas, John's Other Wife, and Other Sudsy Radio Serials*. New York: Cowles Education Corp., 1968.

Hoover's Handbook of American Business 2002. Austin, Tex.: Hoover's Business Press, 2002.

Hoover's Masterlist of Major U.S. Companies 2002. Austin, Tex.: Hoover's Business Press, 2002.

Hummert (Frank and Anne) Collection. American Heritage Center, University of Wyoming.

International Directory of Company Histories. Chicago: St. James Press, 1987.

Kilpack, Dorothy. "My Husband, Mr. Keen." *Radio and Television Mirror*, June 1949.

Klee (Lawrence M.) Collection. American Heritage Center, University of Wyoming.

Lackmann, Ron. *Remember Radio*. New York: G. P. Putnam's Sons, 1970.

MacDonald, J. Fred. *Don't Touch That Dial!: Radio Programming in American Life from 1920 to 1960*. Chicago: Nelson-Hall, 1991.

McNeil, Alex. *Total Television: The Comprehensive Guide to Programming from 1948 to the Present*. Fourth Edition. New York: Penguin Books, 1996.

Mott, Robert L. *Radio Sound Effects: Who Did It, and How, in the Era of Live Broadcasting*. Jefferson, N.C.: McFarland, 1993.

Nachman, Gerald. *Raised on Radio: In Quest of The Lone Ranger, Jack Benny, Amos 'n' Andy, The Shadow, Mary Noble, The Great Gildersleeve, Fibber McGee and Molly, Bill Stern, Our Miss Brooks, Henry Aldrich, The Quiz Kids, Mr. First Nighter, Fred Allen, Vic and Sade, The Cisco Kid, Jack Armstrong, Arthur Godfrey, Bob and Ray, The Barbour Family, Henry Morgan, Joe Friday and Other Lost Heroes from Radio's Heyday*. New York: Pantheon Books, 1998.

The New York Times, March 26, 1925; December 29, 1949; August 21, 1962.

Plunkett's Health Care Industry Almanac 1999–2000. Dallas: Corporate Jobs Outlook, 1999.

Radio and Television Mirror, July 1942.

Scripts of the *Mr. Keen, Tracer of Lost Persons* radio series.

Sies, Luther F. *Encyclopedia of American Radio, 1920–1960*. Jefferson, N.C.: McFarland, 2000.

Sterling, Christopher H., and John M. Kittross. *Stay Tuned: A Concise History of American Broadcasting*. Second Edition. Belmont, Calif.: Wadsworth Publishing Co., 1990.

Summers, Harrison B., ed. *History of Broadcasting—Radio to Television: A Thirty-Year History of Programs Carried on National Radio Networks in the United States, 1926–1956*. New York: Arno Press and The New York Times, 1971.

Swartz, Jon D., and Robert C. Reinehr. *Handbook of Old-Time Radio: A Comprehensive Guide to Golden Age Radio Listening and Collecting*. Metuchen, N.J.: Scarecrow Press, 1993.

Terrace, Vincent. *Radio Programs, 1924–1984: A Catalog of Over 1800 Shows*. Jefferson, N.C.: McFarland, 1999.

Wolfe, Charles Hull. *Modern Radio Advertising*. New York: Printers' Ink, 1949.

Index

"The Abandoned Well Murder Case" 286
The Abbott Mysteries 9
"The Ace of Spades Murder Case" 266
Adair, Deborah 20
The Adventures of Caleb Williams 7
The Adventures of Captain Diamond 68
The Adventures of Christopher Wells 59
The Adventures of Sam Spade 9
The Adventures of Sherlock Holmes 3
The Adventures of the Falcon 3
The Adventures of Thin Man 9
"The African Blow Gun Murder Case" 267
AFTRA [American Federation of Television and Radio Actors] 49
Against the Storm 67–68
Air Features Incorporated 15
"The Airport Murder Case" 282
The Alan Young Show 71
"The Alarm Clock Murder Case" 283
"The Alcoholic Bride Murder Case" 291
Alexander, Joan 284
Aley, Albert 253
Alias Jimmy Valentine 65
Allen, Fred 10
Allen, Vera 243
Allenby, Peggy 311, 317, 319
Amanda of Honeymoon Hill 68
"The Amazing Case of the Broadway Cloumnist" 235
The American Album of Familiar Music 74

The American Melody Hour 71, 74
Ames, Priscilla 269
Amrhein, Jack 71–72
"The Amusement Park Murder Case" 275
Anacin 74
Andrews, Robert Hardy 18, 58
Angel of Mercy 69
Ansboro, George 1, 58, 70, 97, 139–141, 148, 155–157, 178
Anton, Anita 309
"The Apple Orchard Murder Case" 294
Arthur, Eric 136–137
Atwell, Martha 5, 57–59, 72, 104–114, 115–216, 218–226, 268
"The Auction Sale Murder Case" 252
Aunt Jenny's Real Life Stories 59–60
"Aunt Penny's Sunlit Kitchen" 54
Authors Today and Yesterday 17

Backstage Wife 16, 42, 48, 55, 59–60, 63, 74
Bain, Donald 310
"The Ballet Murder Case" 237
Barker, Bradley 287
Barry Cameron 59, 71
Barrymore, Ethel 16
Baruch, Andre 95–96
Bates, Barbara 59
Bauer, Charita 69, 243, 250, 288, 291, 299, 302, 306, 308, 323, 338
Baumer, Marie 59, 228–233, 235–238, 241–243, 246–250, 252, 254, 257–258, 316–323, 325–326

Beat the Clock 69
The Beatrice Lillie Show 71
"The Beautiful Dancer Murder Case" 279
"The Beautiful Showgirl Murder Case" 264
"The Beautiful Swimming Star Murder Case" 297
"The Beautiful Twins Murder Case" 291
"The Beautiful Widow Murder Case" 308
"The Beauty Salon Murder Case" 266
Behrens, Frank 249
Believe It or Not 59, 65
Bell, Ralph 247
Bellamy, Ralph 60
Bennett, Belle 16
Benny, Jack 10
Bentley, Spencer 244, 255
Bernhardt, Frances Von 58
Betty and Bob 68
The Bing Crosby Show 10
"The Birthday Gift Murder Case" 312
"The Birthday Party Murder Case" 266
Bi-So-Dol 74
"The Black Cloak Murder Case" 313
"The Black Feather Murder Case" 303
"The Black Slipper Murder Case" 261
Blackburn, Arline 49, 253, 284, 306, 320, 338
Blaine, Martin 253
Bleiler, E.F. 19
Blondell, Joan 10
"The Blue Dust Murder Case" 263

The Bob Hawk Show 71
Bond, Ford 42
"The Bonfire Murder Case" 284
"The Borrowed Money Murder Case" 305
Boston Blackie 71
"The Bow and Arrow Murder Case" 305
"The Box Office Murder Case" 292
Brady, Ben 185–196
Braham, Horace 283, 285–286, 289–295, 299–303, 305–306, 308–309, 311–312, 316, 323
Break the Bank 69
Brewster, John 239, 253
"The Bride and Groom Murder Case" 38, 272
Briggs, Donald 239, 253, 255
Briney, Al 72
Brinkmeyer, Bill 72
Broadway Is My Beat 13
"The Brocade Chair Murder Case" 262
"The Broken Window Murder Case" 39, 275
Bromley, Harold 324
Brothers, Dr. Joyce 29
Brown, Bill 72
Bryan, George 6, 70, 316–322, 323, 325–337
Bryan, Warren 253, 255
Buka, Donald 311, 314, 322, 323
Burr, Anne 69, 250, 252, 282
Burton, Sarah 284–285, 287, 297–298, 300–302, 306, 307, 311, 313, 314, 328, 338
Buss, Carl A. 184
By Kathleen Norris 68

Campbell, Bill 72
Campbell, Flora 239, 241
Campbell, Naomi 304, 306
"The Candid Camera Murder Case" 284
"The Cannibal Plant Murder Case" 314
Capell, Peter 292, 297, 311, 338
"The Career Girl Murder Case" 309
Carewe, Helen 308
Carlon, Fran 251, 254
Carr, Marion 49, 284
Carroll, Jean 43, 259, 286–295, 297
"The Case in Studio Nine" 215
"The Case Mr. Keen Recorded as His Only Failure" 168
"The Case of a Fresh Flower Every Day" 209
"The Case of a Handful of Diamonds" 219
"The Case of a Mother's Place in the Life of Her Son" 144
"The Case of a Suggestion for Murder" 220–221
"The Case of Death and the Weird Music" 259
"The Case of Death in the Park" 241
"The Case of Doctor Bruce's Son" 139
"The Case of Eight Hours Leave" 207
"The Case of From the Halls of Montezuma" 217
"The Case of Grandfather Gilbert" 96
"The Case of Home-Run Henry" 221
"The Case of John Leroy's Best Friend" 101–102
"The Case of Lord Bountiful" 167
"The Case of Lucy Diare's Real Family" 103
"The Case of Miss Cinderella" 84
"The Case of Miss Ellis, Tracer of Mr. Keen" 116
"The Case of Miss Wicks and Her Daughter" 100
"The Case of Miss Willow of the Public Library" 119–120
"The Case of Mr. and Mrs. Blake's Golden Wedding" 83–84
"The Case of Mr. Keen Takes a Partner" 231
"The Case of Mr. Keen's Dilemma" 203
"The Case of Mr. Keen's Disguise" 197
"The Case of Mr. Keen's Holiday Cruise" 115
"The Case of Mr. Trevor's Secret" 227
"The Case of Mr. Tweed" 201
"The Case of Mrs. Granville's Real Family" 92
"The Case of Mrs. Lovelace of Greenway Hall" 107–108
"The Case of Murder and a Thousand Witnesses" 38
"The Case of Murder and the Accused Actress" 321
"The Case of Murder and the Accusing Eyes" 342
"The Case of Murder and the Baldheaded Man" 298
"The Case of Murder and the Black Pearl Necklace" 335
"The Case of Murder and the Bloodstained Necklace" 269
"The Case of Murder and the Bolted Room" 268
"The Case of Murder and the Broadway Star" 294
"The Case of Murder and the Broken Mirror" 342
"The Case of Murder and the Broken Promise" 310, 343
"The Case of Murder and the Bullfighter's Sword" 305
"The Case of Murder and the Capsule of Death" 307
"The Case of Murder and the Captive Bride" 340
"The Case of Murder and the Clawing Hand" 301
"The Case of Murder and the Crystal Ball" 340
"The Case of Murder and the Dead Man's Secret" 312
"The Case of Murder and the Deadly Rivals" 341
"The Case of Murder and the Disappearing Dagger" 304
"The Case of Murder and the Double Mystery" 246
"The Case of Murder and the Emerald Snuffbox" 298
"The Case of Murder and the Evil Eye" 339
"The Case of Murder and the Extravagant Wife" 341
"The Case of Murder and the Fabulous Gift" 310
"The Case of Murder and the Face at the Window" 309
"The Case of Murder and the Face in the Fog" 335, 336
"The Case of Murder and the Fatal Bargain" 340
"The Case of Murder and the Final Warning" 340
"The Case of Murder and the Finger of Guilt" 338
"The Case of Murder and the Giant Shadow" 305
"The Case of Murder and the Girl at the Piano" 302
"The Case of Murder and the Girl in a Trance" 300
"The Case of Murder and the Girl Who Couldn't Talk" 308
"The Case of Murder and the Girl Who Lost Her Memory" 321, 322
"The Case of Murder and the Girl with Six Months to Live" 329, 330

Index

"The Case of Murder and the Glittering Eye" 303
"The Case of Murder and the Green-Eyed Monster" 307
"The Case of Murder and the Grieving Cat" 310
"The Case of Murder and the Grinning Skull" 341
"The Case of Murder and the Guilty Secret" 341
"The Case of Murder and the Gypsy Palm Reader" 282
"The Case of Murder and the Handsomest Man" 304
"The Case of Murder and the Handwriting on the Wall" 311
"The Case of Murder and the Haunted Farm" 302
"The Case of Murder and the Haunted Room" 307
"The Case of Murder and the Haunted Tower" 324, 325
"The Case of Murder and the Headless Statue" 325
"The Case of Murder and the House of Fear" 332, 333
"The Case of Murder and the House of Horror" 339
"The Case of Murder and the Howling Ghost" 277
"The Case of Murder and the Ivory Monkey" 314
"The Case of Murder and the Jack-in-the-Box" 304
"The Case of Murder and the Jewel Thief" 273
"The Case of Murder and the Jeweled Crown" 341
"The Case of Murder and the Killer with Purple Hands" 311
"The Case of Murder and the Leopard That Changed His Spots" 313
"The Case of Murder and the Limping Man" 307
"The Case of Murder and the Magician" 299
"The Case of Murder and the Man Who Led Two Lives" 331
"The Case of Murder and the Man Who Loved Danger" 296
"The Case of Murder and the Man Who Made a Million" 342
"The Case of Murder and the Man Who Talked Too Much" 340
"The Case of Murder and the Man Without a Conscience" 338
"The Case of Murder and the Mental Marvel" 250
"The Case of Murder and the Missing Car" 275
"The Case of Murder and the Missing Clue" 276
"The Case of Murder and the Night Club Singer" 137
"The Case of Murder and the Omen of Death" 338
"The Case of Murder and the One-Eyed Gypsy" 316
"The Case of Murder and the One-Eyed Man" 282
"The Case of Murder and the Phantom Melody" 327, 328
"The Case of Murder and the Phantom Voice" 278
"The Case of Murder and the Picnic in the Country" 268
"The Case of Murder and the Poison Fangs" 318
"The Case of Murder and the Poisoned Mind" 342
"The Case of Murder and the Poisoned Tongue" 333, 334
"The Case of Murder and the Poisoned Towel" 280
"The Case of Murder and the Policeman's Wife" 267
"The Case of Murder and the Pretty Young Actress" 301
"The Case of Murder and the Prize-Winning Bull" 299
"The Case of Murder and the Queen of Fashion" 336, 337
"The Case of Murder and the Revengeful Ghost" 338
"The Case of Murder and the Rich Reward" 341
"The Case of Murder and the Runaway Suspect" 311
"The Case of Murder and the Sacred Tiger" 277
"The Case of Murder and the Sealed Box Mystery" 299
"The Case of Murder and the Secret Wife" 317
"The Case of Murder and the Star of Death" 267
"The Case of Murder and the Strange Woman" 265, 285
"The Case of Murder and the Sultan's Dagger" 314
"The Case of Murder and the Suspicious Wife" 265
"The Case of Murder and the Tatooed Arm" 314
"The Case of Murder and the Thousand Dollar Bill" 281
"The Case of Murder and the Three Alarm Fire" 316
"The Case of Murder and the Unwanted Wife" 340
"The Case of Murder and the Voodoo Doll" 280
"The Case of Murder and the Woman Scorned" 339
"The Case of Murder and the Woman Who Hid from the World" 337
"The Case of Murder and the Woman Who Worshipped Gold" 340
"The Case of Murder and the Woman Who Wouldn't Grow Old" 331, 332
"The Case of Murder and the Woman with Tangled Hair" 312
"The Case of Murder and the Woman with the Iron Will" 339
"The Case of Murder and the Yellow Horror" 341
"The Case of Murder at Dawn" 264
"The Case of Murder at Mile a Minute" 290
"The Case of Murder at Sixty Miles an Hour" 261
"The Case of Murder by Candlelight" 235
"The Case of Murder by Moonlight" 312
"The Case of Murder by Remote Control" 314
"The Case of Murder by the Clock" 206–207
"The Case of Murder Evidence from the Dead" 263
"The Case of Murder in Room Three Twenty Seven" 258
"The Case of Murder in the Air" 213–214, 227, 262
"The Case of Murder in the Elevator" 278
"The Case of Murder in the Old Curiosity Shop" 276
"The Case of Murder in the Small Hotel" 326
"The Case of Murder in the Snow" 290
"The Case of Murder Meets the Train" 262
"The Case of Murder on a Foggy Night" 277
"The Case of Murder on a Lonely Street" 289

"The Case of Murder on a May Afternoon" 258
"The Case of Murder on a Moonlight Night" 261
"The Case of Murder on Horror Hill" 312
"The Case of Murder on Skelton Beach" 306
"The Case of Murder on the Beach" 235
"The Case of Murder on the Boardwalk" 268
"The Case of Murder on the Dance Floor" 264
"The Case of Murder on the Fifteenth Floor" 303
"The Case of Murder on the High Seas" 264
"The Case of Murder on the Sightseeing Bus" 272
"The Case of Murder with a Thousand Witnesses" 270
"The Case of Murder with Style" 288
"The Case of Rings on Her Fingers" 210
"The Case of Room 501" 234
"The Case of Shore Leave" 216–217
"The Case of the a la Carte Menu" 121–122
"The Case of the Absent-Minded Professor" 233
"The Case of the Actor Who Lived His Part" 93–94
"The Case of the Amazing Clue to Murder" 265, 323
"The Case of the Amazing Death of Cyrus Wake" 262
"The Case of the Appointment with Death" 253
"The Case of the Army Aviation Cadet" 181
"The Case of the Arrow of Death" 263
"The Case of the Author Who Lost His Soul" 102–103
"The Case of the Barber Shop Quartet" 231
"The Case of the Bargain for Murder" 250
"The Case of the Beating Drums" 123–124
"The Case of the Beckoning Voices" 250
"The Case of the Black Sheep" 234
"The Case of the Blackstone Mansion" 240
"The Case of the Bloodstained Bookmark" 249
"The Case of the Bloodstained Calendar" 246
"The Case of the Bloodstained Nail File" 252
"The Case of the Bloodstained Piece of Tin" 233
"The Case of the Bottomless Lake" 191
"The Case of the Boy Who Dreamed" 79
"The Case of the Boy Who Used Big Words" 227
"The Case of the Boy Who Wanted Parents" 118–119
"The Case of the Boy Who Whistled" 201
"The Case of the Boyhood Hero" 163
"The Case of the Broken Glass" 255
"The Case of the Broken Mirror" 257
"The Case of the Broken Promise" 187–188, 224
"The Case of the Bulletproof Vest" 253
"The Case of the Candid Cameraman" 240
"The Case of the Captain Who Didn't Like Fog" 171
"The Case of the Christmas Toy" 152
"The Case of the Closed Keyboard" 159–160
"The Case of the Convict's Fortune" 146
"The Case of the Corpse Who Struck Back" 245
"The Case of the Corpse Who Talked" 232
"The Case of the Cowardice of Captain Hardy" 94–95
"The Case of the Creeping Death" 255
"The Case of the Cross-Eyed Cat" 232
"The Case of the Crowded Cemetery" 245
"The Case of the Daily Flowers" 195
"The Case of the Dangerous Wedding" 233
"The Case of the Daring Young Man on the Flying Trapeze" 237
"The Case of the Date for Murder" 319
"The Case of the Dead Man Who May Be Living" 79–80
"The Case of the Deadly Perfume" 257
"The Case of the Death on Coral Beach" 260
"The Case of the Death Train" 231, 257
"The Case of the Delightful Mrs. Raine" 99–100
"The Case of the Disappearance of Marcia Blair" 201–202
"The Case of the Disappearance of Mr. Waters" 105
"The Case of the Disappearing Corpses" 238
"The Case of the Doctor and the Mummy" 190–191
"The Case of the Door Marked Private" 177
"The Case of the Dragon Fly" 132
"The Case of the Dripping Candlestick" 256
"The Case of the Elephant Gun Murder" 258
"The Case of the Emerald of Death" 257
"The Case of the Evil Spirit" 232
"The Case of the Fabulous Necklace" 241
"The Case of the Faded Sapphire" 249
"The Case of the Faithful Heart" 159
"The Case of the Famous Wife" 175
"The Case of the Fatal Ruby" 243
"The Case of the Father Who Crept into Darkness" 78–79
"The Case of the Father Who Didn't Understand" 199–200
"The Case of the Figure of Death" 260
"The Case of the Five Kinsmen" 161–162
"The Case of the Flower of Death" 250
"The Case of the Forecast of Death" 238
"The Case of the Fortune of Titus Drake" 183
"The Case of the Frightened Child" 230
"The Case of the Frightened Stepmother" 156
"The Case of the Frozen Body Murder" 255
"The Case of the Gentle People" 197–198
"The Case of the Ghost of Anita Marlowe" 248
"The Case of the Ghost Which

Appeared at Midnight" 155–156
"The Case of the Girl and the Lost Violin" 230
"The Case of the Girl at the Switchboard" 233
"The Case of the Girl in Gingham" 209–210
"The Case of the Girl in Red" 214
"The Case of the Girl Who Couldn't Be Found" 24, 77–78
"The Case of the Girl Who Couldn't Remember" 211
"The Case of the Girl Who Didn't Believe in Love" 131
"The Case of the Girl Who Didn't Come to Her Own Wedding" 145
"The Case of the Girl Who Flirted" 176, 227
"The Case of the Girl Who Had Only Herself to Fear" 184
"The Case of the Girl Who Hated to Say Goodbye" 151–152
"The Case of the Girl Who Learned How to Live" 89–90
"The Case of the Girl Who Never Forgot" 193
"The Case of the Girl Who Sang About Yesterday" 120–121
"The Case of the Girl Who Sang Too Well" 226
"The Case of the Girl Who Screamed in the Dark" 167
"The Case of the Girl Who Wanted Glamour" 128–129
"The Case of the Girl Who Wanted to Disappear" 127
"The Case of the Girl Who Went to Hollywood" 96–97
"The Case of the Girl Whose Mother Didn't Care" 179–180
"The Case of the Girl with a Secret Fear" 186
"The Case of the Girl with Crutches" 136–137
"The Case of the Girl with Red Hair" 122–123
"The Case of the Girl with the Lonely Heart" 149
"The Case of the Girl with the Lovely Eyes" 85–86
"The Case of the Glamorous Widow" 241
"The Case of the Glass Slipper" 157
"The Case of the Goat Woman" 247
"The Case of the Golden Palm" 239
"The Case of the Golden Scorpion" 241
"The Case of the Great Montclair" 245
"The Case of the Grieving Cat" 194
"The Case of the Guilty Conscience" 231
"The Case of the Hatpin Murders" 251
"The Case of the Haunted Client" 174–175
"The Case of the Hidden Corpse" 248
"The Case of the Hidden Motive" 228
"The Case of the Hidden Room" 236
"The Case of the Hidden Voice" 232
"The Case of the Highest Calling" 194–195
"The Case of the House of Death" 242
"The Case of the House on Washington Square" 234
"The Case of the Husband Who Asked Himself, 'Why Did My Wife Marry Me?'" 143–144
"The Case of the Husband Who Didn't Believe His Wife Was Dead" 103–104
"The Case of the Inherited Fear" 192–193
"The Case of the Invisible Murderer" 263
"The Case of the Iron Lady" 251
"The Case of the Jealous Husband" 249
"The Case of the Jealous Sister" 236
"The Case of the Jeweled Hat Pin" 229
"The Case of the Killer Who Struck Again" 192
"The Case of the Ladies Sewing Circle" 88
"The Case of the Lady in the Pullman" 207–208
"The Case of the Lady Who Didn't Want to Be Found" 227
"The Case of the Landlocked Sailor" 229
"The Case of the Laughing Woman" 198
"The Case of the Lawyer Whose Conscience Hurt Him" 143
"The Case of the Lead-Lined Capsule" 246
"The Case of the Leaping Dog" 228
"The Case of the Leaping Shark" 244
"The Case of the Letter of Death" 258
"The Case of the Lie That Love Told" 185–186
"The Case of the Lincoln Letter" 80
"The Case of the Lingering Death" 260
"The Case of the Little Black Book" 228
"The Case of the Little Girl from England" 161
"The Case of the Little Girl Left Alone" 141–142
"The Case of the Little Girl Who Asked Mr. Keen to Find Her Mother for Christmas" 177–178
"The Case of the Little Girl Who Didn't Want Her Mother and Father to Be Divorced" 148
"The Case of the Living Dead" 250
"The Case of the Loaded Suitcase" 229
"The Case of the Lonely Road" 235, 238
"The Case of the Long Distance Telephone Call" 125–126
"The Case of the Lost Boy" 154
"The Case of the Lost Mother" 129
"The Case of the Lost Song" 87–88
"The Case of the Lost Sword" 132–133
"The Case of the Lost Violin" 149–150
"The Case of the Loved One Who Never Came Back" 101
"The Case of the Magician's Assistant" 203
"The Case of the Man in Search of Christmas" 126, 127
"The Case of the Man in Search of Himself" 80–81
"The Case of the Man in the Tower" 232
"The Case of the Man She Might Have Married" 164–165
"The Case of the Man They All Hated" 98–99
"The Case of the Man Who Changed" 222

"The Case of the Man Who Confessed" 238
"The Case of the Man Who Deserted a Dream" 86
"The Case of the Man Who Didn't Come Home" 226
"The Case of the Man Who Didn't Know He Was Lost" 140–141
"The Case of the Man Who Expected Murder" 295
"The Case of the Man Who Invented Death" 38, 270
"The Case of the Man Who Lived in the Clouds" 117–118
"The Case of the Man Who Lost His Faith" 178
"The Case of the Man Who Never Laughed" 176–177
"The Case of the Man Who Repented" 245
"The Case of the Man Who Sent Flowers" 229
"The Case of the Man Who Threw Away His Chance" 90–91
"The Case of the Man Who Traveled with Death" 251
"The Case of the Man Who Turned Lead Into Gold" 323
"The Case of the Man Who Wanted to Murder" 279
"The Case of the Man Who Was Buried" 255
"The Case of the Man Who Was Found Before He Disappeared" 91
"The Case of the Man Who Was Killed Twice" 250
"The Case of the Man Who Was Not" 78
"The Case of the Man Who Was Once a Hero" 108–109
"The Case of the Man Who Was Seen in Two Places at Once" 142
"The Case of the Man Who Went Out to Smoke Between Acts" 150–151
"The Case of the Man Whom the World Scorned" 86–87
"The Case of the Man Whose Life Was a Grand Adventure" 114
"The Case of the Man Whose Story Didn't Ring True" 94
"The Case of the Man with the Loving Wife" 165–166
"The Case of the Man with the Scar" 233
"The Case of the Man with the Twisted Mouth" 237
"The Case of the Mapleton Murder" 244
"The Case of the Marked Hand" 229
"The Case of the Master Mind" 125
"The Case of the Mayor of Libbyville" 218
"The Case of the Meanest Man" 222–223
"The Case of the Melody of Murder" 273
"The Case of the Message That Came in the Night" 178–179
"The Case of the Million Dollar Girl" 205–206
"The Case of the Million Dollar Murder" 269
"The Case of the Mind That Wanted to Slumber" 104–105
"The Case of the Missing Bridegroom" 237
"The Case of the Missing Clown" 127–128
"The Case of the Missing Cop" 130–131
"The Case of the Missing Doll" 136
"The Case of the Missing Motive" 229
"The Case of the Missing Parents" 135
"The Case of the Missing Pilot" 133
"The Case of the Missing Shoes" 234
"The Case of the Missing Spectacles" 235
"The Case of the Missing Teacup" 246
"The Case of the Missing Witness" 226, 310
"The Case of the Model for Murder" 277
"The Case of the Moonless Night" 226
"The Case of the Mother Who Couldn't Forget" 82–83
"The Case of the Mother Who Thought Her Son Would Never Make Good" 165
"The Case of the Motion Picture Murder" 258
"The Case of the Murder and the Sharp Scissors" 257
"The Case of the Murder Calendar" 265
"The Case of the Murder in the House of Horrors" 259
"The Case of the Murder in the Zoo" 259
"The Case of the Murder Mansion" 246
"The Case of the Murder Monster" 259
"The Case of the Murder, Old and New" 260
"The Case of the Murder on Edgewood Lake" 266
"The Case of the Murder on Phantom Beach" 264
"The Case of the Murdered Author" 254
"The Case of the Murdered Bride" 239
"The Case of the Murdered Bridegroom" 264, 293
"The Case of the Murdered Countess" 275
"The Case of the Murdered Detective" 274
"The Case of the Murdered Heiress" 265
"The Case of the Music Box That Wouldn't Stop Playing" 232
"The Case of the Mystery of My Cousin Maria" 173
"The Case of the Necktie Murders" 235
"The Case of the Neglected Parents" 174
"The Case of the New Citizen" 134–135
"The Case of the Omen of Death" 258
"The Case of the Package of Death" 263
"The Case of the Painted Horse" 229
"The Case of the Parents Who Gave Their Daughter Everything" 111–112
"The Case of the Park Drive Murders" 251
"The Case of the People Who Didn't Exist" 188
"The Case of the Perfect Alibi" 189–190
"The Case of the Perfect Crime" 217–218
"The Case of the Perfect Murder" 236
"The Case of the Perfumed Handkerchief" 170–171
"The Case of the Perpetual Widow" 252
"The Case of the Phantom Bugler" 247
"The Case of the Phantom Killer" 242
"The Case of the Phantom Who Lurked from the Deep" 45

"The Case of the Picture of Death" 256
"The Case of the Pinpoint Murder" 244
"The Case of the Player with Two Strikes on Him" 113–114
"The Case of the Poisoned Glass" 251
"The Case of the Poisoned Quill" 240
"The Case of the Poisoned Well" 253
"The Case of the Polka Dotted Mask" 213
"The Case of the Prelude to Death" 244
"The Case of the Prophecy of Death" 259
"The Case of the Raffle of Death" 263
"The Case of the Rainbow Butterfly" 231
"The Case of the Rainbow Pins" 163–164
"The Case of the Redheaded Murderer" 280
"The Case of the Red-Headed Runaway" 218
"The Case of the Rehearsal of Death" 257
"The Case of the Rich Young Man in an Ivory Tower" 158–159
"The Case of the Room That Vanished" 227
"The Case of the Runaway Boy" 130
"The Case of the Runaway Horse" 240
"The Case of the Rushville Murder" 272
"The Case of the Ruthless Murders" 270
"The Case of the Sacred Trust" 162–163
"The Case of the Scar-faced Stoker" 243
"The Case of the Scarboro Murders" 239
"The Case of the Schoolmarm Who Learned a Lesson" 124–125
"The Case of the Sea Cove Strangler" 241
"The Case of the Second Marriage" 196
"The Case of the Secret Murder" 256, 342
"The Case of the Secret of Professor Grove" 181–182

"The Case of the Seventh Juror" 157–158
"The Case of the Shrunken Head" 239
"The Case of the Sign of Death" 271
"The Case of the Silver Pencil in the Sky" 172
"The Case of the Sinister Room" 243
"The Case of the Sins of the Father" 84–85
"The Case of the Smiling Buckaroo" 210–211
"The Case of the Smiling Corpse" 236
"The Case of the Smiling Mourner" 225
"The Case of the Soldier and His Bride" 195–196
"The Case of the Soldier Who Didn't Return" 186–187
"The Case of the Soldier Who Wanted to Disappear" 212
"The Case of the Solitary Witness" 199
"The Case of the Spider Killer" 254
"The Case of the Spinster Who Put Her Pride in Her Pocket" 168–169
"The Case of the Stolen Airplane Plans" 32
"The Case of the Stolen Airplane Secrets" 32
"The Case of the Stone That Was Worth a Fortune" 230
"The Case of the Stonehaven Hall" 204
"The Case of the Story Book Romance" 112
"The Case of the Strange Death of Stuart Blair" 261
"The Case of the Strange Display" 227
"The Case of the Straw-Hat Murder" 243
"The Case of the Stuffed Kangaroo" 242
"The Case of the Suspicious Playboy" 185
"The Case of the Table for Two" 110–111
"The Case of the Talking Corpse" 252
"The Case of the Talking Mummy" 240
"The Case of the Telephone That Would Not Stop Ringing" 247, 269

"The Case of the Teletype Murder" 253
"The Case of the Terror Over the Telephone" 256
"The Case of the Third Sermon" 147–148
"The Case of the Three Fingered Murderer" 272
"The Case of the Three Sisters" 95
"The Case of the Tin Pan Alley Killing" 254
"The Case of the Tragedy of Malicious Gossip" 180–181
"The Case of the Twelfth Juror" 215
"The Case of the 20,000 Alibis" 234
"The Case of the Twin Sister Team" 117
"The Case of the Twisted Ring" 240
"The Case of the Two-Faced Murderer" 273
"The Case of the Two Mrs. Marvins" 88–89
"The Case of the Two Sisters" 202
"The Case of the Two Strange and Beautiful Sisters" 230
"The Case of the Unclaimed Bank Account" 152–153
"The Case of the Understanding Heart" 224
"The Case of the Unexpected Wedding" 200
"The Case of the Unfinished Picture" 154–155
"The Case of the Unfinished Portrait" 242
"The Case of the Unknown Correspondent" 212
"The Case of the Unmarried Husband" 269
"The Case of the Unsigned Letters" 208
"The Case of the Unwanted Career" 190
"The Case of the Vanishing Bride" 138
"The Case of the Vanishing Murderer" 256
"The Case of the Vanishing Stranglet" 245
"The Case of the Velvet Park Jewel Murder" 248
"The Case of the Vindictive Wife" 214–215
"The Case of the Voice" 223
"The Case of the Voice of Murder" 298

"The Case of the Voices from the Past" 228
"The Case of the Walking Death" 247
"The Case of the Wayward Brothers" 140
"The Case of the Wedding of Mary Blair" 170
"The Case of the Wheel That Rolled Downhill" 169–170
"The Case of the Whimpering Dog" 242
"The Case of the White Carnation Murder" 246
"The Case of the Wife Who Confessed Murder" 267
"The Case of the Wife Who Dreamed of Murder" 246
"The Case of the Wife Who Grew Tired of Waiting" 92–93
"The Case of the Wife Who Lacked Faith" 134
"The Case of the Wife Who Ran Off to Die" 98
"The Case of the Wife Who Refused to Support Her Husband and Ran Away" 145–146
"The Case of the Wife Who Suffered in Silence" 182
"The Case of the Wife Who Wagered Her Love" 121
"The Case of the Wife Who Was Jealous of Her Husband's Work" 183
"The Case of the Witness Who Wasn't Afraid" 97–98
"The Case of the Woman in Blue" 228
"The Case of the Woman Who Dreamed Strange Dreams" 106
"The Case of the Woman Who Lived in a Glass House" 112–113
"The Case of the Woman Who Married a Murderer" 38, 274
"The Case of the Woman Who Vanished Into Thin Air" 109–110
"The Case of the Woman Who Was Found Before She Disappeared" 106–107
"The Case of the Woman Who Wasn't Needed" 138
"The Case of the Woman Who Wouldn't Die" 205
"The Case of the Worst Boy in Town" 188–189

"The Case of the XPBA Plans" 32, 81–82
"The Case of the Yellow Envelope" 244
"The Case of the Yellow Parrot" 204
"The Case of the Young Couple Who Couldn't Get Married" 139–140
"The Case of the Young Draftee" 150
"The Case of the Young Husband Who Thought His Wife Failed Him" 160–161
"The Case of the Young Man Who Lost Himself Because He Lost His Courage" 180
"The Case of the Young Man Who Promised to Work All Night" 153–154
"The Case of the Young Marine" 225–226
"The Case of Two Men, a Girl and a Violin" 90
"The Case of Two Soldiers and a Girl" 219–220
"The Case of Woman, Single, Forty-Five, Unemployed, Unwanted" 147
"The Case That the Visiting Nurse Brought to Mr. Keen" 172–173
"The Cat's Milk Murder Case" 287
Cavalcade of America 69
Chambers, Robert William 16–21, 24–25, 45
Chandler, Jeff 10
Chaplain Jim U.S.A. 16, 58–60, 63
The Chase 60
Chase, Frank 285
"The Checkerboard Murder Case" 282
"The Chinchilla Coat Murder Case" 271
Choate, Helen 250
Chopin 31
Church, James 194–195
Claire, Helen 69, 239, 247, 249, 250, 253–254, 267, 283, 287–291, 296–302, 304, 305–309, 311–314, 323, 338
Clarke, Philip 5, 36, 46–47, 53, 64, 66–67, 72, 279–280, 343
"The Cliffside Murder Case" 296
Clinton, Mildred 307
The Clock 60
Close, Eric 20
Coffin, Haskell 314

Coles, Stedman 59, 229
The Collier Hour 8, 68
Collingwood, Charles 339
Collins, Tom 288, 291, 296, 300–301, 305, 309, 312–313, 319, 327
Collyer, Clayton (Bud) 69
Conan Doyle, Arthur 8
"The Concrete Cellar Murder Case" 271
Conquest, John 8, 12
Cordell, Cathleen 257, 283, 286–288, 290–293, 295, 298–299, 301–304, 306–308, 310–312, 314, 316, 319, 338
Costello, Jack 6, 70, 285–294
Cotsworth, Staats 285, 297–299, 303–305, 307, 309, 311
Counterspy 12
"The Country Club Murder Case" 37, 274, 288
"The Cover Girl Murder Case" 339
Coward, Noel 31
Cowlan, Bert 326
Crawford, Boyd 240
Cromer, Mable Alice 65
Crosby, Bing 11
"The Crossword Murder Case" 253
"The Crown of Doom Murder Case" 271
Curtin, Joseph 250–251, 259, 324

Dahm, Frank 234–235
Daigneau, Ken 253
Dalton, Doris 313, 314, 318
"The Dance Hall Murder Case" 276, 284
Dane, Frank 244, 255
Danford, Peggy 297
Darnay, Toni 69, 244, 259, 267, 286–288, 290–294, 298, 300, 302–305, 307–313, 315, 326
David Harum 16, 58, 65, 68
Davidson, David 59, 175–183, 228–229, 231–233, 288, 291–292, 298
Davis, Humphrey 49, 284
Davis, Sylvia 311, 313
DeAndrea, William 8
"The Death Bargain Murder Case" 309
"The Death Rattle Murder Case" 313
"The Deceived Woman Murder Case" 289
"The Deep Well Murder Case" 281

de Gore, Janet 327
DeSales, Francis 239, 254
"The Deserted House Murder Case" 266
"The Diamond Mine Murder Case" 276
"The Diamond Necklace Murder Case" 281
Diebold, Albert 74
"The Dinner Guest Murder Case" 297
Doc Barclay's Daughters 65
Donley, Robert 267, 286, 291–293, 295, 302
Donnelly, Andy 313, 314, 317, 320, 328
Donnelly, Bob 252
Donnelly, Doris 310
"The Double Death Murder Case" 255
Dowling, Jeannette 249
Dragnet 13
"Dramatic Flyleaf" 32
Drew, Wendy 309, 310, 311, 313, 314, 323, 338
"The Duck Pond Murder Case" 283
Dumas, Helene 305
"The Dummy Key Murder Case" 285
Dunham, Dick 70, 269
Dunning, John 9
Dwan, Jimmy 72

East of Cairo 68
"The Eccentric Millionaire Murder Case" 274
The Editor's Daughter 58
Edwards, Douglas 339
Egan, Audrey 239, 247, 250, 285, 289–290, 292–294, 297–298, 301–302, 306, 308, 310–311, 313–314, 316, 321, 327
"The Egyptian Mummy Murder Case" 324
"The Eight Million Dollar Murder Case" 280
Elizabeth the Queen 68
Elliot, Bob 54–55
Elliot, Larry 5, 37, 66, 70–72, 226–268, 270–285
Elstner, Anne 69, 250, 257, 259, 284, 287, 293, 300, 302, 315
"The Emerald Necklace Murder Case" 277
Emmet, Katherine 253, 296, 308, 310, 311
Empire Builders 7
"The Engaged Girl Murder Case" 270

"The Engagement Party Murder" 260
Eno Crime Club 12
"The Enoch Arden Murder Case" 248
"The Evil Husband Murder Case" 291

The Falcon 13
"The Famous Actress Murder Case" 290
"The Famous Author Murder Case" 297
Famous Jury Trials 59
"Fantasie Impromptu" 31
"The Fantastic Murder of Peter Nash" 288
Fantasy Island 20
"The Fashion Model Murder Case" 274
"The Fashion Show Murder Case" 262
The Fat Man 60
The FBI in Peace and War 12
Feather Your Nest 69
Fenton, Mildred 104–114, 115–163
Ferguson, Lee 20
"The Ferryboat Murder Case" 254
Fibber McGee & Molly 9
"The Fifty Thousand Dollar Reward Murder Case" 309
"The Final Warning Murder Case 306
Finder of Lost Loves 20
"The Fire Escape Murder Case" 286
"The Firebug Murder Case" 311
Firestone, Berel 288, 290, 293, 296, 308–309, 312, 316
"The Fish Market Murder Clue" 302
Fleming, Ed 209, 325
Fleming, James 5, 70, 126, 128–209
"The Flirtatious Secretary Murder Case" 320
Folies de Paris 71
Follow That Man 61
"The Footlight Murder Case" 234
"The Footprint Murder Case" 300
"The Footprints of Terror Murder Case" 290
"The Forbidding House Murder Case" 311
Ford, Glenn 10
"The Forgotten Cave Murder Case" 38, 270

"The Fountain of Youth Murder Case" 318
Franciosa, Tony 20
Francis, Ivor 288–289, 292, 294, 296–297, 299, 301–302, 305, 307, 310–311, 314, 323, 338
Frank and Anne Hummerts' Radio Factory 15, 46
Frazee, Treva 308, 309, 310
The Fred Allen Show 71–72
Freeman, Austin R. 11
Freeman, Florence 69, 72, 251, 255, 259, 284–285, 289, 291, 293, 298, 310, 338
"The Frightened Husband Murder Case" 291
Front Page Farrell 16, 49, 59–60, 63, 71, 73
Frost, Alice 250–251
Fu Manchu 8, 67
"The Full Moon Murder Case" 338

Gangbusters 12, 65, 69
Garde, Betty 239, 251–252, 254, 259, 323
"The Garden Party Murder Case" 296
Gates, Ruth 317
Gayer, Anne-Marie 255, 259
Geherin, David 11
Gerald, Ara 320
Gerson, Noel B. 254
"The Ghost Wife Murder Case" 306
"The Gift Package Murder Case" 303
Gilbert, Lauren 283–288, 290–291, 293, 296, 310
Gilford, Jack 60
"The Girl with the Beautiful Eyes" 33
"The Girl with the Lovely Eyes" 33
Godfrey, Arthur 54, 70, 71
Godwin, William 7
The Goldbergs 65
Golden Boy 68
"The Good Samaritan Murder Case" 247
"The Gorilla Murder Case" 279
"The Gossip Column Murder Case" 298
Gothard, David 241, 243, 296–298, 301, 303–304, 308–311, 313, 324, 338
Gould, Mitzi 244, 252
Goulding, Ray 54–55
Grand Central Station 65, 69
"The Grandmother's Warning Murder Case" 281

Grauer, Ben 5, 23, 27, 70, 77–78, 91–128
Gray, Justin 20
Great Plays 65, 68
Greaza, Walter 251
"The Greek Vase Murder Case" 298
Green, Rosalind 300
"The Green Ghost Murder Case" 304
"The Green Stocking Murder Case" 267
Greet, Philip Ben 65, 67
Grimes, Jackie 314
Gross, Stephen 216–217
"The Guilty Conscience Murder Case" 287

Haag, Robert 244
Haines, Larry 239, 252
Hall, Bob 342
Hall, Louis 244
"The Hall of Mirrors Murder Case" 306
Halman, Doris 141–174, 183–186
"The Happy Couple Murder Case" 292
Harris, Stanley 247
Hathaway, Joy 244, 251, 255, 259, 304, 313
"The Hatpin Murder Case" 307
"The Haunted House Murder Case" 273
Hayworth, Vinton 239, 250, 251, 258
Hearthstone of the Death Squad 16
Hearts in Harmony 58, 60
Heflin, Van 10
Her Honor Nancy James 69
"The Hidden Body Murder Case" 285
"The Hidden Corpse Murder Case" 322
"The Hidden Fortune Murder Case" 301
Higby, Mary Jane 58, 69, 239, 250–252, 257, 259, 284–286, 289–299, 301–305, 307, 309–311, 313–314, 319, 326
"The Hitchhiker Murder Case" 278
Hitz, Elsie 240
"The Homing Pigeon Murder Case" 280
"The Honeymoon Cottage Murder Case" 292
"The Hoot Owl Murder Case" 326
Hope, Bob 10

"The Hotel Carling Murder Case" 284
"The House of Hate Murder Case" 289
"The House on the Cliff Murder Case" 293
How Now Dow Jones? 68
Howard, Henry 272, 286–287
"The Howling Dog Murder Case" 262, 296
Hubbard, Irene 286, 289, 293–294, 296, 301, 324, 338
Huber, Harold 288, 293, 297–298, 304, 306
Hubin, Allen J. 7, 8
Hughes, Arthur 46, 64, 66–68, 242, 244, 252, 256–257, 293–294, 298, 306–308, 310, 312
Hughes, Geneva (Harrison) 68
Hughes, Mary Beth 285, 289, 292
Hummert, Anne Schumacher Ashenhurst 14–16, 18–19, 26–27, 31–33, 38, 42–43, 45–52, 55, 57–60, 62–65, 67–69, 71–75, 77, 228–235, 286, 324, 343
Hummert, Edward Frank 14–16, 18–19, 26–27, 31–33, 38, 42–43, 45–52, 55, 57–60, 62–65, 67–69, 71–75, 77, 286–291, 293–294, 296, 324, 343
Hunter, John 163–166

"I Can't Resist You" 70
I Love Linda Dale 67
"The Ice Cube Murder Case" 276
"The Ice Queen Murder Case" 319
"The Identical Twins Murder Case" 262
Idiot's Delight 68
"I'm Always Chasing Rainbows" 31
In Search of the Unknown 20
Inner Sanctum Mysteries 69, 72
"The Innocent Flirtation Murder Case" 273
International Directory of Company Histories 73

"Jack Armstrong, the All-American American" 54
The Jack Benny Program 10
Janaver, Richard 285–286, 288, 290, 292–293, 297, 302–303, 305–306, 308–309, 311–314, 319, 322, 327, 338
"The Jealous Father Murder Case" 302

"The Jealous Rival Murder Case" 308
Jean-Baptiste, Marianne 20
Jeffreys, Anne 20
Jenkins, Larry Flash 20
Jerome, Ed 291, 293, 295–296, 307, 318
Johnson, Bess 239
Johnson, Lamont 255
Johnson, Ray 290–291, 297
Johnson, Raymond 305, 306, 307, 314
Jones, Lorenzo 49
Joseph and His Brethren 67
Jostyn, Jay 300
Julian, Joe 244
Jungle Jim 67
"The Jungle Knife Murder Case" 309
Junkin, Harry 297
Jurist, Edward 231–232
Just Plain Bill 46, 48–49, 58–59, 67, 73

Kane, Frank 232, 234–235
Kantor, Richard 20
Kaye, Virginia 308, 310
Keane, Teri 257, 297, 318, 328
Keith, Richard 310, 313, 314, 321
Kelly, James 68, 288–290
Kelly, Jim 5, 24, 30, 36, 46, 53, 251
Kent, Elaine 239, 250
Kilpack, Bennett 5, 24, 30, 46–47, 64–67, 72, 76, 229–230, 234, 242, 244, 249, 251–252, 256–257, 279–280
Kilpack, Dorothy 66
Kilpack, John 66–67
"The King Cobra Murder Case" 275
"King Yukon of the Northwest" 54
Kismet 65
Kittross, John 8, 9
Klee, Lawrence M. 16, 42, 46, 59, 60–64, 71–72, 77, 196–226, 231–285, 287, 291, 293–294, 296–297, 299–304, 306–321, 323–330, 333–343
Klee, Mel 60
Klee, Paul 61, 63
"The Knife-Thrower Murder Case" 313
Knight, William M. 74
Kolynos 74
Kraft Theater 71
Kramer, Harry 6, 49, 70, 294–304, 306–314, 316–317, 322–324, 338–343

Kramer, Jack 6
Kramer, Mandel 252

"The Lake in the Park Murder Case" 292
Lamb, Hugh 19
Lapaglia, Anthony 20
Latimer, Ed 288–290
Lazer, Joan 250
Legend of a Lady 18, 58
Leigh, Sylvia 283, 286, 288, 292, 297, 304, 306
Leonard, Allan 126–137
Leonard, Richard 5, 6, 35, 42, 46–47, 49, 57, 59, 63, 72, 228–304, 306–343
Lewis, Abby 286, 289, 292, 295–300, 303–306, 308, 310, 313
Lichtenberg, Margaret Klee 61–62
Life 17
The Light of the World 67
"The Lighthouse Murder Case" 278
Linda's First Love 58
The Line-Up 13, 60
Lipton, Bill 247, 251, 253, 305, 306
"The Locked Room Murder Case" 284
The Lone Ranger 9, 59
"The Lonely Acres Murder Case" 279
"The Lonesome Road Murder Case" 294
Long, Ronald 282, 288, 290–295, 297–298, 300–304, 306–309, 311, 313, 338
Lora Lawton 48, 58, 69
Lorde, Athena 253
Lorenzo Jones 74
Lorring, Ann 303
Lorring, Joan 294
Love Boat 20
Lynch, Jimmy 72
Lynch, Ken 239, 258, 294

Ma Perkins 59
MacAteer, Alan 287, 294, 300, 315
MacDonald, Fred 11, 12, 13
Maitland, Arthur 253, 286, 289–290, 292, 294, 296–298, 305, 314, 317, 322
Major Bowes' Shower of Stars 71
Malone, Florence 30, 68, 72
Man Against Crime 60–61
Manhattan Merry-Go-Round 74
Manhattan Mother 69

"The Marked Man Murder Case" 342
Maron, Mary 259
"The Marriage Bargain Murder Case" 328, 329
Martin, Ian 267, 284–285, 288–289, 293, 298, 306, 310
Martin, John 186, 191, 195
"The Martin Street Murder Case" 270
"Mary Backstage, Noble Wife" 54
"The Masquerade Ball Murder Case" 271
"The Matinee Idol Murder Case" 283
Maude, Marjorie 289
McCloskey, John 72
McDonald, John 72
McDonnell, Craig 253
McGrath, Paul 241, 249
Meighan, James 42, 48–49, 69, 250, 254–255, 282–285, 287–289, 291–293, 295–300, 302–304, 306–309, 312–314, 320, 338
Metz, Stuart 6, 70, 315, 316, 317, 318, 319, 320, 321, 322, 323, 324, 325, 326, 327, 328, 329, 330, 331, 332, 333, 334, 335, 336, 337
Milano, Frank 318
"The Million Dollar Murder Case" 313
Miner, Jan 69, 282–283, 303
"The Mirror Murder Case" 265
"The Missing Wife Murder Case" 283
Mr. and Mrs. North 9, 60
Mr. Chameleon 16, 19, 59, 72, 74
Mr. District Attorney 12, 59
Mr. Keen (novel) 343
Mr. Nobbs 243
"Mister Science" 54
"The Money Box Murder Case" 339
"The Monkey Mask Murder Case" 299
Monks, James 254, 259, 294, 306
Montgomery, Poppy 20
Moore, Nancy 63
Morgan, Elizabeth 283, 285, 288, 290–291, 296, 298–300, 302, 304–305, 308–309, 313–315, 322
Morse, Lloydv 72
Morwood, William 242
"The Most Amazing Case Murder" 260

"The Mother's Plea Murder Case" 293
Mourning Becomes Elektra 68
"Mrs. Granville's Real Family" 22
Mrs. Wiggs of the Cabbage Patch 58, 65
Murciano, Enrique 20
"Murder and the Absent-Minded Professor" 38
"Murder and the Girl in the Mink Cape" 292
"Murder and the Sleep Walker" 287
"Murder at a Mile a Minute" 38
"Murder Comes to Supper" 266
"The Music Box Murder Case" 279, 327
The Music of Andre Kostelanetz 71
Myrt and Marge 71
The Mysterious Traveler 72
Mystery Theater 58, 60

Nachman, Gerald 9
Native Son 67
Neeley, Henry 250
Newton, Richard 49, 284–287, 290–296, 301, 305–308
Nick Carter, Master Detective 3
Niesen, Claire 299, 303, 312, 327
"The Night of Terror Murder Case" 297
"The Nightmare Murder Case" 230
Nobbs, George 323, 324
Nona from Nowhere 68
Norell, Henry 282, 287, 290, 296, 300–302, 304–305, 310–311, 313, 315, 328
Norman Sweetser 118–119
"The Nylon Stocking Murder Case" 281

O'Brien, Edmund 10
Ocko, Danny 300, 311
"The Octopus Murder Case" 272
O'Keefe, Winston 240
On Whitman Avenue 67
"One Fella's Family" 54
"The One-Legged Man Murder Case" 279
"The Open Window Murder Case" 290
The Orange Lantern 67
Orr, Mary 288–291, 299, 307, 310, 313
Osborne, Ted 250, 306–307, 311–312, 315

Othello 65
"Our Fella Thursday" 54
Our Gal Sunday 16, 43, 48, 73
Out of the Dark, Volume 2: Diversions 19
Ovens, Latham 234
"The Overdose of Very Fatal Poison Murder Clue" 55

Parent, Gail 20
"The Paris Model Murder Case" 312
"The Peg Leg Man Murder Clue" 55
Penman, Charles 338
"The Perfect Place for Murder" 268
Perry Mason 69
The Philip Morris Playhouse 72
Philo Vance 59
"The Phone Call Murder Case" 288
"The Photograph Album Murder Case" 38, 286
"The Piggy Bank Murder Case" 305
"The Platinum Blonde Murder Case" 302
Podmore, William 250
Poe, Edgar Allan 7
"The Poison Pen Letter Murder Case" 64, 307
"The Poison Pen Murder Case" 266, 285
"The Poisoned Sandwich Murder Case" 286
Potter, Paul 239, 250, 254
"The Powder Puff Murder Case" 280
Powell, Dick 10
Pretty Kitty Kelly 68
Price, Steve 323, 324
Prinz, Rosemary 305, 307, 323
Prouty, Olive Higgins 16
Prud'homme, Cameron 250

"The Quicksand Murder Case" 38, 275
Quinn, Billy 283, 288–289, 296, 304, 313

Raby, John 251, 253–254
Radio and Television Mirror 26
Rathbone, Basil 10
Readick, Frank 252
Real Stories of Real Life 16
"The Red Candle Murder Case" 295
Reddick, Bob 239
Redfield, Bill 289–290, 293, 301

"The Rented Cottage Murder Case" 293
"The Rich Sister-Poor Sister Murder Case" 281
"The Rich Young Widow Murder Case" 288
Richards, Frank 244
Richards, Grant 244
Rickey, Al 71
"The Rival Brothers Murder Case" 330, 331
"The River Warehouse Murder Case" 283
The Robert Q. Lewis Show 72
Roberts, Ken 5, 70, 209–226
Robinson, Bartlett 243, 251, 253–254, 259
Robinson, Florence 294, 308, 310, 317
Robinson, Frances 239
Roger Kilgore — Public Defender 59
Rogers, Will 16
The Romance of Helen Trent 16, 59–60, 73
Roosevelt, Franklin D. 47, 60
The Roosevelt Story 60
Rose of My Dreams 71
Ross, Jerome D. 59, 104–115–126, 135, 188–189, 256
"The Rowboat Murder Case" 320
Rudy, Martin 241
Russell, A.J. 307, 322
Russell, Ruth 255

Sanders, Albert 296–298
Sands, Dorothy 250, 253
Sanford, Peggy 287, 312
Saturday Night Bandwagon 71
"The Scandal-Monger Murder Case" 308
Scheuer, Al 125
Schoen, Lillian 234
Scopp, Maurice (Mickey) 63
"The Scorpion Murder Case" 338
Scott, Marion 323, 324
Scourby, Alexander 253
The Sealed Book 67
"The Sedan Murder Case" 245
Seth Parker 65
Seymour, Anne 267, 283, 285, 287–290, 292–293, 297, 299, 303–304, 308–309, 312, 338
The Shadow 9, 13, 59
The Shadow of Fu Manchu 8
Shakespeare, William 65
"The Sharpshooter Murder Case" 300

Shaw, Bob 230
Shaw, Robert J. 59
Shenkin, Ernest R. 126, 129–130
Shepherd, Ann 240
Sherman, Eleanor 241, 244
Sherwood, Madeleine 321
"The Shoplifter Murder Case" 310
Shore, Dinah 11
"The Shrieking Prisoner Murder Case" 315
"The Signet Ring Murder Case" 261
"The Silver Candlestick Murder Case" 38, 293
"The Silver Dagger Murder Case" 270
"The Silver Locket Murder Case" 268
"The Silver Treasure Murder Case" 278, 328
"The Silver Wedding Murder Case" 277
Sinatra, Frank 10
The Singing Story Lady 68
"The Sinister Case of the Talking Bird" 238
"The Sinister Case of the Wandering Singer" 241
"The Sinister Case of the Yellow Roses" 252
"The Sister-in-Law Murder Case" 300
"The Skating Rink Murder Case" 300
Skelton, Red 11
Skinner, Cornelia Otis 65
"The Skull and Crossbones Murder Case" 276, 299
Slattery, Edward 6, 58–59, 72, 277, 282, 297, 316–323, 325–332, 334–337, 341
"The Sleep Walker Murder Case" 269
"The Sleeping Woman Murder Case" 295
Smith, Bill 251, 253
Smith, Cora B. 292–294, 296
Smith, Sydney 285, 288, 291, 293–294, 299, 303, 307–308
Smith, William J. 240, 243
Smolen, Vivian 69, 239–240, 247, 251, 253–254, 287, 296, 300, 304–305, 308–309, 314, 326
"The Snake Bite Murder Case" 296
"The Snowman Murder Case" 301
Society Girl 59
"The Society Murder Case" 268

The Soldier Who Came Home 59
"Someday I'll Find You" 31, 37, 54, 71
Sorel, Guy 69, 253, 288, 291, 294, 298, 300, 304–305, 308, 311–313, 315
"The S.O.S. Murder Case" 302
"The South American Poison Murder Case" 301
"Spellbound" 70
Spelling, Aaron 20
"The Spiny Ridge Murder Case" 252
Stanley, John 284–285, 287, 290, 294, 296, 298–299, 302–303, 308, 310–311, 328, 338
Stanley, Peggy 285, 287–289, 296, 300, 303–304, 309, 312, 317
Stanwyck, Barbara 16
"The Star Ruby Murder Case" 323, 324
Stehli, Edgar 249–250
Stella Dallas 16, 59–60, 67, 74
Sterling, Christopher 8, 9
Stevens, Julie 69, 239, 250, 253, 255, 257–258, 283, 294–295, 297–298, 300–301, 305, 307–309, 311, 313, 322
Stevens, Warren 257
Stevenson, Margot 288–289
The Story of Bess Johnson 68
"The Strange Caller Murder Case" 289
"The Strange Case of Anna Norton" 236
"The Strange Case of Charley Lorimer" 237
"The Strange Case of Nancy Rodgers" 239
"The Strange Case of the Baldheaded Man" 238
"The Strange Case of the Christmas Bells" 254
"The Strange Case of the Guilty Woman" 230
"The Strange Case of the Sound of Death" 238
"The Strange Clue Muder Case" 306
"The Strange Murder of Carrie Ellis" 286
The Strange Romance of Evelyn Winters 71
Strouse, Sandy 291, 294
Studer, Hal 283, 287, 290, 292–293, 295–297, 306, 311
Sunday 16
Superman 69

"The Surprise Motive Murder" 287
"The Surprise Party Murder Case" 304
Swenson, Karl 247, 254, 259, 312, 316
"The Swimming Pool Murder Case" 285, 295
"The Swiss Clock Murder Case" 278

"The Table for Two" 25
"The Tea Leaf Murder Case" 273
"The Telephone Book Murder Case" 272
"The Temporary Wife Murder Case" 326, 327
"The Terrifying Case of the Riderless Horse" 249
"The Terrifying Case of the Unhappy Bridegroom" 249
The Texaco Star Theater 71
"The Theatrical Star Murder Case" 314
Things as They Are 7
Thomas, Ann 320
Thomas, Frank 249, 254
Thomas, Frank, Jr. 286, 298, 300, 302–305, 307, 311, 313–314, 321, 323, 338
Thorn, Philip 166–226
Tice, Olin 306, 307, 309, 322, 323, 324, 325
"The Ticking Clocks Murder Case" 316
To Tell the Truth 69
Tom Shirley 118–119
"The Tomcat Murder Case" 261
Tompkins, Joan 251
"The Top Hat Murder Case" 298
Toscanini, Arturo 59
The Tracer of Lost Persons 17, 24
"The Tragic Case of the Chiming Watch" 242
"The Trapped Man Murder Case" 325
Treasury Star Parade 71
"The Triple Warning Murder Case" 300
"Trouble in Paradise" 70
"Trust in Me" 70
Truth 17
"The Tunnel of Love Murder Case" 294
Twenty-First Precinct 13
Two on a Clue 69
"The Typewriter Murder Case" 283

"The Unpaid Alimony Murder Case" 308

Valentine, Grace 292, 295, 299, 305, 312, 314, 320, 323
Valiant Lady 16, 60, 69
Van Dyk, James 239, 255
Variety 10
Vaughn, Walter 255
Vogue 17

Waldron, Ingrid Meighan 48–49
Wall, Lucille 69, 290, 293–294, 296, 299–301, 314
Wallace, Andree 311, 312, 315, 338
Walliser, Blair 315
Walpole, Helen 287
Waltz Time 74
Warner, Gertrude 69, 283, 285–286, 292–293, 295, 303, 305, 307
Warwick, Dionne 20
"The Waterfront Murder Case" 322, 323
"The Wax Doll Murder Case" 303
Wayside Inn 65
We the People 69
"The Wealthy Cat Murder Case" 318
Weber, Karl 69, 241, 257, 267, 283–284, 292–295, 297, 299–304, 305, 307, 309–310, 313–314
Webster, Chuck 239, 247, 250, 257, 259, 283, 291, 297, 299–300, 302, 310–313, 317
"The Wedding Anniversary Murder Case" 295
Weeks, Barbara 253
"The Weeping Willow Murder Case" 273
"The Weird Case of Death and the Shoplifter" 255
"The Weird Case of the Girl Named Ethel" 236
"The Weird Case of the Glass-Topped Coffin" 248
"The Weird Case of the Gulf Stream Horror" 248
"The Weird Case of the Roaring Lion" 243
"The Weird Case of the Tolling Bell" 237
"The Weird Case of William Hunter" 249
Weldon, Jane 61, 294–295
Wever, Ned 69–70, 72, 244, 250, 252, 255, 257, 283,

286–288, 291, 293, 296, 299–303, 306, 308, 311, 313–314, 318, 323, 326, 338
Wheatena Playhouse 68
Wheel, Patricia 253
When a Girl Marries 71
White, Bobby 250
Whitehall Pharmacal 74
Wiener, Willard 136–138
"The Wife Who Grew Tired of Waiting" 25
"The Wife Who Ran Away" 33
"The Wife Who Ran Off to Die" 33
Williams, Florence 49, 250, 252–253, 257, 284, 286–287, 289, 291–292, 295, 298, 300–301, 303, 306–307, 312–314, 324
Williams, Kenneth 258
Williams, Roger 17
Wilson, Ethel 289, 295–296, 298, 300, 302, 306–307, 310
Wingett, Byron 72
Winikus, Francis 139
Winters, John 71–72
"The Wishing Well Murder Case" 334
Without a Trace 20
Witter, Jimmy 1
Wolfe, Charles Hull 10
"Woman, Single, Forty-Five, Unemployed, Unwanted" 26
"The Wooden Tombstone Murder Case" 311
Wright, Barbara Bell 49, 284
"The Wristwatch Murder Case" 282

X-Minus One 68

"The Yellow Monster Murder Case" 282
"The Yellow Parrot Murder Case" 274
"The Yellow Rose Murder Case" 268
"The Yellow Scarf Murder Case" 297
The Yellow Sign and Other Tales 20
"The Yellow Talon Murder Case" 269
Yorke, Ruth 258
Young, John M. 138–141
Young Doctor Malone 71
Young Widder Brown 1, 16, 58–60, 65, 68–70, 71, 72, 74
[*Yours Truly*] *Johnny Dollar* 9

Zerbe, Lawson 255, 258–259
Zuckert, William 239, 251, 254

www.ingramcontent.com/pod-product-compliance
Lightning Source LLC
Chambersburg PA
CBHW081535300426
44116CB00015B/2641